The Use of Force in International Law

The International Law of Peace and Security
Series Editor: Nigel D. White

The Use of Force in International Law

Edited by

Tarcisio Gazzini

VU University, Amsterdam

Nicholas Tsagourias

University of Glasgow, UK

ASHGATE

Published by
Ashgate Publishing Limited
Wey Court East
Union Road
Farnham
Surrey GU9 7PT
England

Ashgate Publishing Company
Suite 420
101 Cherry Street
Burlington
VT 05401-4405
USA

www.ashgate.com

British Library Cataloguing in Publication Data
The use of force in international law. – (The
   international law of peace and security)
   1. War (International law) 2. Aggression (International
   law) 3. Just war doctrine.
   I. Series II. Gazzini, Tarcisio. III. Tsagourias, Nicholas K.
   341.6–dc22

Library of Congress Control Number: 2011930003

ISBN 9780754629481

Printed and bound in Great Britain by
TJ International Ltd, Padstow, Cornwall.

Contents

PART IV TERRORISM, WEAPONS OF MASS DESTRUCTION AND INFORMATION WARFARE

PART V HUMANITARIAN INTERVENTION AND THE RESPONSIBILITY TO PROTECT

Acknowledgements

The editors and publishers wish to thank the following for permission to use copyright material.

Brill N.V. for the essays: Jean Combacau (1986), 'The Exception of Self-Defence in U.N. Practice', in A. Cassese (ed.), *The Current Legal Regulation of the Use of Force*, Boston, MA: M. Nijhoff, pp. 9–38; Roberto Barsotti (1986), 'Armed Reprisals', in A. Cassese (ed.), *The Current Legal Regulation of the Use of Force*, Boston, MA: M. Nijhoff, pp. 79–110.

California Western Law Review for the essay: Jean-Pierre L. Fonteyne (1973–74), 'The Customary International Law Doctrine of Humanitarian Intervention: Its Current Validity under the U.N. Charter', *California Western International Law Journal*, **4**, pp. 203–70.

Cambridge Law Journal for the essay: J.L. Brierly (1930–32), 'International Law and Resort to Armed Force', *Cambridge Law Journal*, **4**, pp. 308–19.

Chatham House for the essay: Arnold D. McNair (1936), 'Collective Security', *British Yearbook of International Law*, **17**, pp. 150–64.

Copyright Clearance Center for the essays: Joachim von Elbe (1939), 'The Evolution of the Concept of the Just War in International Law', *American Journal of International Law*, **33**, pp. 665–88. Copyright © 1939 American Society of International Law; Hans Kelsen (1948), 'Collective Security and Collective Self-Defense under the Charter of the United Nations', *American Journal of International Law*, **42**, pp. 783–96. Copyright © 1948 American Society of International Law; Josef L. Kunz (1951), 'Bellum Justum and Bellum Legale', *American Journal of International Law*, **45**, pp. 528–34. Copyright © 1951 American Society of International Law; Thomas M. Franck (1970), 'Who Killed Art. 2(4)? Or: Changing Norms Governing the Use of Force by States', *American Journal of International Law*, **64**, pp. 809–37. Copyright © 1970 American Society of International Law; Louis Henkin (1971), 'The Reports of the Death of Article 2(4) Are Greatly Exaggerated', *American Journal of International Law*, **65**, pp. 544–48. Copyright © 1971 American Society of International Law; Derek Bowett (1972), 'Reprisals Involving Recourse to Armed Force', *American Journal of International Law*, **66**, pp. 1–36. Copyright © 1972 American Society of International Law; Oscar Schachter (1986), 'In Defense of International Rules on the Use of Force', *University of Chicago Law Review*, **53**, pp. 113–46. Copyright © 1986 University of Chicago Law School; Michael N. Schmitt (1998–99), 'Computer Network Attack and the Use of Force in International Law: Thoughts on a Normative Framework', *Columbia Journal of Transnational Law*, **37**, pp. 885–937. Copyright © 1998–99 Columbia Journal of Transnational Law.

Oxford University Press for the essays: Abraham D. Sofaer (2003), 'On the Necessity of Pre-emption', *European Journal of International Law*, **14**, pp. 209–26; Carlo Focarelli (2008),

'The Responsibility to Protect Doctrine and Humanitarian Intervention: Too Many Ambiguities for a Working Doctrine', *Journal of Conflict and Security Law*, **13**, pp. 191–213; Christian J. Tams (2009), 'The Use of Force against Terrorists', *European Journal of International Law*, **20**, pp. 359–97; Christopher C. Joyner and Catherine Lotrionte (2001), 'Information Warfare as International Coercion: Elements of a Legal framework', *European Journal of International Law*, **12**, pp. 825–65; Terry D. Gill (2004), 'Humanitarian Intervention: Legality, Justice and Legitimacy', *Global Community*, **4**, pp. 51–75.

Princeton University Press for the essay: Bassam Tibi (1996), 'War and Peace in Islam', in T. Nardin (ed.), *The Ethics of War and Peace*, New Jersey: Princeton University Press, pp. 128–45. Copyright © 1996 Princeton University Press, 1998 paperback edition Reprinted by permission of Princeton University Press.

Taylor & Franics for the essay: Spencer Zifcak (2009), 'The Responsibility to Protect', in *United Nations Reform: Heading North or South?*, London: Routledge, pp. 105–27, 200.

University of San Diego, School of Law for the essay: Christopher Greenwood (2003), 'International Law and the Pre-emptive Use of Force: Afghanistan, Al-Qaida, and Iraq', *San Diego International Law Journal*, **4**, pp. 7–37.

John Wiley & Sons Ltd for the essay: Victor Alonso (2007), 'War, Peace, and International Law in Ancient Greece', in K.A. Raaflaub (ed.), *War and Peace in the Ancient World*, New York: John Wiley & Sons, pp. 206–25.

Every effort has been made to trace all the copyright holders, but if any have been inadvertently overlooked the publishers will be pleased to make the necessary arrangement at the first opportunity.

Series Preface

The essays collected in the four volumes of this reprint series, The International Law of Peace and Security, focus on a number of facets of international law concerned with peace and security. Clearly there are existing volumes in the Library of Essays on International Law (series editor Robert McCorquodale) that are essential reading for anyone interested in this area of international law, primarily *Collective Security Law*, edited by Nigel White, and *International Peacekeeping*, edited by Boris Kondoch. However, the aim of this series is not simply to develop and deepen the reader's understanding of international law in the area of peace and security, but to introduce new areas and concepts, namely the international laws that purport to govern and regulate arms control, counter-terrorism, the use of force, and peace-building. The focus will be on peace and security rather than on conflict, as the law of armed conflict has already been covered in the aforementioned series, in *Humanitarian Law* edited by Judith Gardam.

The international laws in the area of peace and security are essentially different from those that apply in conflicts – basically, the difference is between the law of peace and the law of war. Simply put, the law of war is concerned with regulating warfare – its means, methods, and issues of targeting and protecting persons – thereby upholding principles of humanity while recognizing the dictates of military necessity. The law of peace and security is about preventing conflicts and wars, and is increasingly concerned with rebuilding a situation of peace and security on the other side of the conflict following a ceasefire and peace agreement. Of course, it is not always possible to maintain a clear line between the *jus ad bellum*, *jus in bello* and *jus post bellum* – an issue raised by the controversial 'war on terror', but coming through more practically in specific instances such as the application of international humanitarian law to peacekeepers. In addition, the series only considers issues of international criminal justice when analysing the rebuilding of a post-conflict state or as an element of counter-terrorism, thus giving rise to little overlap with the collection in the aforementioned series, *The International Criminal Court* edited by Olympia Bekou and Robert Cryer.

The focus of these four volumes is essentially on the law of peace, more specifically those laws and legal regimes that underpin peace by means of controlling the spread of dangerous weapons and by limiting the occasions when states can use force on the international stage, or restoring it when that peace has been broken. In times of peace the main fear is of sudden attacks, possibly by the use of WMD or by terrorists, signifying that arms control law, the law regulating the use of force and anti-terrorist laws are all potentially applicable. In post-conflict situations, peace is being restored usually with the involvement of international actors, which raises a whole host of legal issues, including the applicability of human rights law within the unstable post-conflict state and the principles governing international intervention and involvement. The presence of the UN Security Council, as principal international guarantor and guardian of peace and security, in each of the four volumes is not only illustrative of the unifying theme of peace and security, but also raises concerns and issues about the central role of this most political of bodies in this area of law.

In considering the four volumes in this series individually, it can be seen that the volume edited by Dan Joyner – *Arms Control Law* – is a pretty unique collection of secondary sources collected from both legal and non-legal areas. The essays in this collection review and analyse the major arms control treaties and institutions including the Security Council. The contribution of arms control law to international peace and security is a key theme.

In *The Use of Force in International Law*, Tarcisio Gazzini and Nicholas Tsagourias have carefully selected essays from a vast range of literature to reflect the debates and controversies of this most fundamental, but much contested, area. The rules on when states and organizations can use or authorize the use of force is not only confined to the primary international treaty governing peace and security – the UN Charter – but also includes different viewpoints on controversial (customary) exceptions such as humanitarian intervention, as well as the more recent debates on the responsibility to protect. All this again requires attention to be given to the Security Council.

In *Counter-Terrorism and International Law*, Katja Samuel and Nigel White consider the problem of international terrorism (embodied in the struggle to define it) and the range of responses crafted by states and international organizations in order to try to respond to it, ranging from declaring 'war' to consensual cooperative criminal justice-type measures. The role of the Security Council in developing the legal regimes here, by use for example of targeted sanctions, is considered against the backdrop of existing conventions and practices. The contribution of these measures to the goals of peace and security embodied in the UN Charter is central to this collection.

Finally, *Post-Conflict Rebuilding and International Law*, edited by Ray Murphy, comprises an interesting collection of essays illustrating the phenomenon of rebuilding peace within different regions, followed by a consideration of the general normative framework including the arguments for and against recognizing (the need for) a *jus post bellum*. The essays review and analyse various types, stages and institutions involved in post-conflict peace-building from an international law perspective. They include discussion of rebuilding and peace operations (a much wider concept than peacekeeping operations), electoral support, humanitarian assistance and rule-of-law capacity-building. Post-conflict accountability mechanisms (amnesties, truth commissions, criminal tribunals) and their contribution to peace-building, as well as the wider restoration of peace and security, are also covered. Because this area is new and still developing there will be a need to identify the applicable principles of international law (for example, human rights including economic, social and cultural rights and the right of self-determination, but also the right to security), and the possible development of a *jus post bellum*, but Ray Murphy identifies a number of other challenges to this most difficult of tasks – rebuilding peace.

Each volume of collected essays is of immense value in itself, but each is also supplemented by an introduction by the volume editors and a selected bibliography, both of which add considerably to the usefulness of the collections to the reader.

NIGEL D. WHITE
Series Editor
University of Nottingham

Introduction

War and the use of force have been constant features of human societies with morality, politics or law providing justifications for their use or reasons for their restriction, even abolition. This volume of essays will follow the development of moral, political and legal thinking regarding the use of force in international relations, examine the content of specific rules and project on the future of the law on the use of force.

Ancient-Medieval

Even if ancient Greek literature seems to glorify wars as for example in Homer's *Iliad*, Victor Alonso in the opening essay in this volume, 'War, Peace, and International Law in Ancient Greece' (Chapter 1), observes that Greek cities maintained three types of external relationships: (i) no relationship; (ii) war; and (iii) friendship. War meant 'total war' involving not only the military but also the population of the warring parties. However, both the initiation and the conduct of war were subject to certain conditions. There was public proclamation of war, previous consultation with the city authorities or demos was sought, truces were agreed during hostilities and wars were terminated with treaties of friendship whose aim was to bring peace. The reasons for going to war were also defined, including most prominently defence against aggression. As noted by Alonso (Chapter 1), 'the concept of open war served concrete purposes and had a teleological explanation' (p. 15). The existence of certain procedural as well as substantive requirements made war an institution of statecraft and distinguished it from other forms of violence such as private violence.

This tradition continued in the Roman world where priests (*fetiales*) certified whether the conditions for going to war had been satisfied in a particular instance. Such 'just causes' were for example violations of the Roman borders or breaches of treaties (Draper, 1992, p. 178). It was Christianity though that gave material content to the *just war* theory when religious and state authority converged with the conversion of the Roman Empire to Christianity. The question facing Christian theologians was how to reconcile Christian pacific teaching with the need to take up arms to protect the Empire. As Joachim von Elbe observes in 'The Evolution of the Concept of the Just War in International Law' (Chapter 2) 'the Christian concept of the just war furnishes rules for limiting and guarding it in accordance with the precepts of the new religion' (p. 25).

The just war theory as formulated by Thomas Aquinas contained three principles: (i) right authority; (ii) just cause; and (iii) right intention. The Pope being the superior authority within the *Respublica Christiana* and superior to the Emperor was the right authority to proclaim on the justness of war. Just cause referred to the reason justifying recourse to war: war should redress a wrong provided that some fault on the part of the wrongdoer also existed. Right intention referred to the purpose of the war which was to do good rather than evil.

Islamic conceptions of war and peace developed around the same time were premised on the division of the world into the house of war consisting of the unbelievers and the house of peace consisting of Muslims, with peace prevailing when the whole of mankind converts to Islam (Bassam Tibi, 'War and Peace in Islam' (Chapter 3), p. 48). The call to attain worldwide peace invited *jihad* which could take a military but also a non-military form. Its non-military aspect refers to the personal struggle to realize the faith whereas the military aspect includes war against those that oppose the call of Islam (pp. 49–52). It thus transpires that, unlike the Christian just war doctrine, *jihad* is not case specific as it invokes, at least in its traditional version, a state of perpetual war between the home of peace and the home of war until peace finally prevails (p. 50). What is central to Islam in its universalizing peace mission is the Muslim community, the *ummah*, not the state as a sovereign and territorially demarcated entity (pp. 53–60). As Tibi observes, a central problem with Islamic concepts of war and peace is that they are still 'scriptural and premodern' (p. 60).

This brings us to a central point of the whole debate, namely the role of the state in the way war and the use of force have been conceptualized and treated in international law. With the emergence of sovereign states and the collapse of ideological unity, the place of just war theory was 'taken by the law' (von Elbe, Chapter 2, p. 28).

This has been a lengthy process which reaped its benefits mainly in the twentieth century. In the meantime, war continued to have a place in international affairs. For Grotius, there needed to exist a just cause for waging a war such as defence, recovery of property or punishment but, because among sovereign states both sides may claim such a cause, what is just is determined by objective justice (von Elbe, Chapter 2, p. 37). In the same vein, Vattel employs the distinction between the 'necessary' and the 'voluntary' law of nations, with the former inquiring into the substantive justice of wars whereas the latter declaring its inability to make such judgements among equal states (von Elbe, Chapter 2, p. 41). When the grip of the law of nature on international law faded away and positive law as the law emanating from the sovereign authority of states became the new creed, war was accepted as a sovereign right and as a manifestation of state sovereignty. As Hall (1924, p. 82) put it, 'international law [had] no alternative but to accept war, independently of the justice of its origin as a relation which the parties to it may set up if they choose'. Until the beginning of the twentieth century, virtually all international lawyers recognized that given the horizontal structure of the international legal order, international law was incapable of distinguishing between legal and illegal uses of force. The role of international law was confined to regulating and mitigating the effects of hostilities. As pointed out by J.L. Brierly in 'International Law and the Resort to Armed Force' (Chapter 4), this approach had the merit of bringing the theory of law into accord with reality.

Yet, as much as war is a sovereign right, it is also a threat to sovereignty because it can lead to the demise of states. Thus, attempts to regulate the outbreak of war in addition to regulating its conduct did not die away, with sovereign states turning their focus to reaching negotiated agreements on the rules and procedures according to which war or armed force could be employed in their international relations.

League of Nations Era

It was only at the beginning of the twentieth century that states agreed for the first time to restrict the use of military force. By ratifying the second Hague Convention of 1907 they renounced the use of force to recover contractual debt, unless the concerned state had refused to settle the dispute through arbitration or failed to comply with an arbitral award.

After the First World War, time was ripe for a more comprehensive approach to issues of war and peace, leading to the creation of the League of Nations (1919) which established a collective security system and introduced rules, primarily procedural ones, on the use of force. The Covenant of the League of Nations did not abolish war as such but instead made its legality hinge on whether the Covenant's procedural rules have been satisfied, most importantly the obligation to submit the dispute to arbitration, judicial settlement or to inquiry by the Council or the Assembly.[1] As a result, a state could not legally wage war against a state that complied with the judicial decision or the arbitral award, or with the Council's report provided that it was adopted unanimously.

The Covenant suffered from several shortcomings. In the first place, it was completely oblivious to uses of force below the threshold of war. Since the definition of war has always been a fraught issue, states could use force of different intensity and for varied reasons by claiming that it does not amount to 'war'. Moreover, the failure by the Council or Assembly to adopt a binding report could not preclude the use of force, but subject states to a cooling-off period only. Finally, the assessment of whether a state has indeed complied with the decision, award or report was left to the assessment of the concerned state.

As a result, views about the contribution of the League of Nations to war prevention are divided. Arnold D. McNair, in 'Collective Security' (Chapter 5), placed emphasis on the process through which the use of force was 'collectivized [and] denationalized' (p. 90), whereas Brierly (Chapter 4) expressed serious doubts about the organization's capacity to provide an 'effective alternative way of securing the redress even of a legitimate grievance' (p. 77).

That notwithstanding, it is important to note the change of perspective concerning the permissibility of war. As McNair (Chapter 5) pointed out, the lawfulness of war became dependent on the Covenant's rules rather than on the intrinsic justice of its cause. Thus, the notion of *bellum legale* replaced that of *bellum justum* (p. 83).

In order to overcome the Covenant's shortcomings, states took a number of initiatives and negotiated a number of instruments such as the Geneva Protocol of 1924, which, however, never entered into force. The Protocol, which may be considered as the predecessor to the so called authorization practice which emerged in the 1990s, tried to enhance the collective control over the use of force by requiring a prior decision by the Council or the Assembly of the League of Nations (1924 Geneva Protocol, 1925, p. 9).

The diplomatic efforts to regulate the use of force culminated in the adoption of the *General Treaty for the Renunciation of War* in 1928 (Kellogg–Briand Pact or Pact of Paris). In Article 1, the contracting parties solemnly condemned recourse to war for the solution of international disputes and renounced it as an instrument of national policy in their relations with one another. The innovative character of such prohibition was commented upon by

---

[1]   Articles 11–15 Covenant of the League of Nations 1919.

McNair (Chapter 5) who argued that its breach would amount to a legal wrong not only against the state directly concerned but also against all other parties to the treaty (obligations *erga omnes contractantes*) (p. 86). Indeed, the Pact of Paris, which is still in force, was pivotal in securing prosecutions for the crime of aggression at the Nuremberg Trials. Yet, it suffers from a number of shortcomings. As with the Covenant, by prohibiting 'war' it seems to permit uses of force below the threshold of war. Moreover, war was prohibited as an instrument of national policy which implies, *a contrario*, that war has not been prohibited as an instrument of international policy.

United Nations Era

The United Nations was created in 1945 from the ashes of the League of Nations. Its primary objective is to maintain and restore international peace and security. Its constitutive instrument, the UN Charter, developed further the *bellum legale* notion (Josef L. Kunz, 'Bellum Justum and Bellum Legale' (Chapter 7)), and introduced a more sophisticated collective security system than that of the League of Nations.

The Charter law on the use of force is built upon two pillars. On the one hand, the threat or use of unilateral force is prohibited (Article 2(4)) except in self-defence (Article 51). On the other hand, the Security Council was granted the power to take military action in order to maintain or restore international peace and security through armed forces provided for by member states or, alternatively, by authorizing regional organizations to take such action.[2]

The first pillar, Article 2(4), is the culmination of a historical process to restrict the use of unilateral force. The view that Article 2(4) contains a comprehensive prohibition of the use of force is shared by the majority of authors and is supported by the jurisprudence of the International Court of Justice since the *Corfu Channel* case.[3] In the *Nicaragua* case, the ICJ also opined that the content of the customary and UN Charter law on the non-use of force are essentially identical.[4]

However, this interpretation of Article 2(4) has been challenged. Some authors rely on a literal interpretation of this provision and confine its application to cases where force is used against the territorial integrity or the political independence of states or it is against the UN's purposes (for example, Bowett, 1958, pp. 150–52).

Be that as it may, the Charter recognizes one instance where unilateral force can be used. According to Article 51 of the UN Charter and customary international law, states can use force by way of self-defence if an armed attack occurs. No definition of 'armed attack' is provided in the Charter but the International Court of Justice in a number of decisions defined an armed attack by its 'scale and effects'.[5] Nothing is also said about the author of the attack

---

[2]   Chapter VII and VIII of the UN Charter.

[3]   *Corfu Channel* case, ICJ Rep. (1949), 3, at 35.

[4]   *Case Concerning Military and Paramilitary Activities in and against Nicaragua*, ICJ. Rep. (1986), p. 14, para. 188 (hereinafter referred to as *Nicaragua* case).

[5]   *Nicaragua* case, paras 195, 210; *Case Concerning Oil Platforms (Islamic Republic of Iran* v. *United States of America)*, ICJ Rep. (2003), p. 161, paras 51, 64, 77 (hereinafter referred to as *Oil Platforms* case); *Legal Consequences of the Construction of a Wall in the Occupied Palestinian Territory Advisory Opinion of 9 July 2004*, I.C.J. Rep. (2004), 200, para. 139 (hereinafter referred to as Palestinian

although the International Court has insisted that it should be carried out by another state.[6] In addition to these conditions, the principles of proportionality and necessity, 'inherent in the very concept of self-defence' also need to be met.[7] Finally, according to the UN Charter, self-defence is temporally limited. It must be terminated once the Security Council has taken measures necessary to restore peace and security. Indeed, 'the right of self-defence is not a right which is left altogether outside the collective system for maintaining peace' (Waldock, 1952, p. 451, at p. 495; Brownlie, 1963, p. 273).

The second pillar of the UN system concerning the use of force is its collective security system according to which military force is placed under the control of the Security Council and is used only for the common interest. The legal issues pertaining to the UN collective security system have been dealt with in N.D. White's (2006) volume on Collective Security Law. For the purposes of this volume, there will be a succinct description of the UN collective security system in order to assess its impact on the rules prohibiting the use of unilateral force.

According to the UN collective security system, the Security Council (SC) has the power to determine whether a threat to the peace, a breach of the peace or an act of aggression exists,[8] and adopt provisional measures according to Article 40, non-military enforcement measures according to Article 41, or military measures according to Article 42, in order to maintain or restore international peace and security. In sum, the UN system provides for centralized and institutional decision-making processes and action in the area of peace and security and is premised on co-operation and agreement among Security Council members particularly the permanent ones.

However, the intervening Cold War and the antagonism between the two superpowers impacted on the operation of the collective security system which either underperformed or was simply paralysed. The implications of such a state of affairs were noted by Hans Kelsen in 'Collective Security and Collective Self-Defense under the Charter of the United Nations' (Chapter 6), p. 99. According to him, with an effective collective security system, the use of force in self-defence is an exceptional and provisional interlude between an act of illegal use of force and collective enforcement action. Without such a system, self-defence becomes an act of unilateral and uncontrolled self-help.

It is not only the right of self-defence that might be affected by the malfunctioning of the collective security system. The validity of the general prohibition on the use of force might also be questioned. The paralysis of the Security Council as well as other related developments – such as the rise of wars of national liberation, the proliferation of weapons of mass destruction and the aggressive role of regional organizations – prompted a few authors to question the existence of such a prohibition on two different grounds (Thomas M. Franck, 'Who Killed Article 2(4)?' (Chapter 8), p. 119). First, it has been claimed that there exists an 'organic dependence' between the renunciation of individual force and the effectiveness of the

---

Wall Advisory Opinion), para. 139; *Case Concerning Armed Activities on the Territory of the Congo (Democratic Republic of Congo v. Uganda)* ICJ Rep. (2005), para. 147 (hereinafter referred to as *Congo v. Uganda*).

[6]   *Palestinian Wall Advisory Opinion, supra,* para. 139; *contra* Sep. Op. Higgins *ibid.,* paras 33–34; Sep. Op. Kooijmans, *ibid.,* paras 35–36 and Decl. Burgenthal, *ibid.,* para. 6. Also *Congo* v. *Uganda,* para. 146. *Contra* Diss Op. Kateka, *ibid.,* para. 34 and Dis. Op. Koijmans, *ibid.,* para. 28.

[7]   *Nuclear Weapons Advisory Opinion,* at 40–41; *Oil Platforms* case, at 76, 77.

[8]   Article 39 UN Charter.

collective security system, so that states regain their pre-Charter rights concerning individual uses of force when the collective security system malfunctions. The disparity between the law and state practice has been highlighted by Jean Combacau ('The Exception of Self-Defence in U.N. Practice' (Chapter 11)) who commented that UN members are still bound by the rules on the use force but they collectively behave as if these rules did not exist. Second, it has also been argued that the repeated and serious violations of the rule on the non-use of force have inexorably compromised its legal force; as a result, it has been progressively eroded and eventually the rule has fallen into desuetude (Franck, Chapter 8, p. 119; Glennon, 2004, p. 939).

In the *Nicaragua* case, however, the International Court of Justice rejected both arguments. It held that the content of the customary and UN Charter law on the non-use of force are essentially identical. This implies that the customary prohibition is entirely independent from the provisions relating to the collective security system envisaged by the UN Charter, their implementation or their effective functioning.[9] The Court also affirmed the continuing validity of the general prohibition on the use of force by relying on states' declarations of compliance with the relevant rule. Rather controversially it also held that violations of a rule could strengthen rather than weaken it, provided that the concerned states invoked exceptions or justifications contained in the rule itself.[10] The view that State practice had not affected the general prohibition on the use of and threat to use force had been maintained in literature both before and after the Nicaragua Case, see respectively Henkin L., 'The Reports of the Death of Article 2 (4) Are Greatly Exaggerated', 65 AJIL (1971), p. 547 (Chapter 9) and Schachter O., 'In Defense of International Rules on the Use of Force', 53 UCLR (1986), p. 113 (Chapter 10).

The debate over the scope of the prohibition contained in Article 2(4) as well as its relationship with the collective security system affected the question of the legality of armed reprisals. Whereas according to a formalistic argument states sacrificed their traditional right to resort to armed reprisals by becoming members of the UN (Roberto Barsotti, 'Armed Reprisals' (Chapter 13)); according to another line of reasoning, it would be unrealistic to expect states to refrain from ensuring their rights by way of reasonable armed reprisals when other remedies are unavailable or ineffective. According to Derek Bowett ('Reprisals Involving Recourse to Armed Force' (Chapter 12)), the practice of states has shown that reasonable and proportional reprisals are *de facto* accepted although prohibited *de jure*.

In light of the above, it is submitted here that as any other rule of international law, the rules pertaining to the use of force evolve and possibly die through a process of claims and counterclaims, actions and reactions. Violations or alleged violations of the existing rules have always occurred and will continue to occur. The crux of the matter is to assess the impact of all such behaviours on the normative value of the rule in point. This implies that a threshold of deviating behaviour needs to be established before changing or relinquishing a rule. In practice, however, determining if and when such a threshold has been reached may be particularly arduous and legal incertitude may follow, which is probably the current situation concerning the rules on the use of force.

---

[9]   *Nicaragua* case, para. 189.
[10]   *Nicaragua* case, para. 186.

Terrorism, Weapons of Mass Destruction and Information Warfare

Events such as the war on Afghanistan (2001) and Iraq (2003) have tested the effectiveness of the rules on the use of force when applied to the threats that terrorism and weapons of mass destruction (WMD) represent. With regard to terrorism, it has been claimed that the existing rules are adequate to deal with this threat although they may need some adaptation. From this perspective, (a) a terrorist attack can qualify as an armed attack for Article 51 purposes and, (b) it can trigger the use of force by way of self-defence if the armed attack is attributed to state according to criteria found in the law of state responsibility[11] (Christopher Greenwood, 'International Law and the Pre-Emptive Use of Force' (Chapter 15); Christian J. Tams, 'The Use of Force against Terrorists' (Chapter 16)). More specifically, it is claimed that terrorist attacks – such as those perpetrated on 11 September 2001 – can be treated as armed attacks if they cause casualties and damage comparable to military attacks whereas the fact that no traditional weapons have been used is immaterial. Such an armed attack can trigger self-defence action during its deployment or, afterwards, if it is part of a larger plan of armed attacks. Secondly, it is also claimed that the attack can be attributed to a state when the attack is committed by any organ integrated in the state's official structure (*de jure* organs)[12] but also by individuals or groups acting on the state's instructions or under its direction or control (*de facto* organs).[13] With regard to the latter case, the International Court of Justice has affirmed the 'effective control'[14] criterion and rejected the looser 'overall control'[15] criterion. In all of the above cases, that state becomes the target of the self-defence action. It is finally claimed that a state will be targeted in self-defence if it acknowledges, endorses or adopts the terrorist attacks as its own.[16]

The threat that terrorism as well as WMD represent also give rise to questions as to whether self-defence can be exercised prior to an attack. It is now widely accepted that a state can use force by way of self-defence against an imminent threat of armed attack (Abraham Sofaer, 'On the Necessity of Pre-emption' (Chapter 14)) (see UN, 2004, paras 188 and 189–92; UN, 2005a, para. 124). Although better classified under the rubric of necessity, the *Caroline* incident of 1837 is often relied upon to provide the conditions according to which pre-emptive self-defence can be exercised (see Jennings, 1938, p. 82). Accordingly, there needs to be a 'necessity of self-defence, instant, overwhelming, leaving no choice of means and no moment of deliberation'.[17]

A more difficult case is that of preventive self-defence which can be defined as a military action against a potential adversary in advance of a suspected attack (United Kingdom, 2002–03, para. 48). It differs from pre-emptive self-defence in that it is deliberately future

---

[11] Articles 4–11, International Law Commissions' Articles on Responsibility of States for Internationally Wrongful Acts, 2001 (hereinafter 'ILC Articles 2001').

[12] Article 4, ILC Articles 2001.

[13] Article 8, ILC Articles 2001.

[14] *Nicaragua* case, para. 115; *Palestinian Wall Advisory Opinion*, para. 139; *Congo* v. *Uganda*, paras 146, 160; *Case concerning the Application of the Convention on the Prevention and Punishment of the Crime of Genocide (Bosnia and Herzegovina* v. *Serbia)*, ICJ Rep. (2007), paras 384, 391, 400, 401.

[15] *Prosecutor* v. *Dusko Tadic*, Case No. IT-94-1-A, Judgment of Appeal Chamber, 15 July 1999, paras 118–141.

[16] Article 11, ILC Articles 2001.

[17] 30 British and Foreign State P,apers 196–8.

oriented and goes well beyond military action against imminent and concrete threats. Such a claim was put forward by the United States in relation to the 2003 action against Iraq,[18] but it was met with the firm opposition of governments, international organizations and found rather limited and often conditional support in legal literature (UN, 2004, paras 189–92; UN, 2005a, para. 125).[19]

Another area where the application of the current rules on the use of force is tested is with regard to information warfare (IW). The information revolution created opportunities but also dangers. The use of information technology tools for 'offensive' or 'defensive' purposes is a reality and certain states, among them the USA, France, Israel and the UK, are developing counterpart doctrines. The first question is whether IW attacks fall within Article 2(4). At first glance, IW tools do not resemble armed weapons; instead among its 'weaponry' are 'sniffers', 'Trojan horses', 'trap doors', 'logic bombs', 'video morphing', 'denial of service attack', 'computer worms', 'infoblockable', 'spamming' and 'IP spoofing' (Christopher C. Joyner and Catherine Lotrionte, 'Information Warfare as International Coercion' (Chapter 18), pp. 444–6). According to Michael N. Schmitt ('Computer Network Attack and the Use of Force in International Law' (Chapter 17), pp. 394–417), nonetheless, what is critical are the consequences of the use or threat of using these tools. Thus, IW attacks that cause physical damage comparable to traditional military attacks can fall within the definition of Article 2(4) (Joyner and Lotrionte, Chapter 18, pp. 457–8). Concerning IW attacks that do not cause physical damage or at least, not directly, certain criteria such as those of severity, immediacy, directness, invasiveness and measurability can be used in determining whether the attack is similar to one producing physical destruction.

The next question concerns the available responses to such an attack. In the first place, the Security Council can adopt coercive or non-coercive measures under the collective security system (Schmitt, Chapter 17, pp. 418–22). Secondly, IW attacks can give rise to self-defence action since an armed attack for self-defence purposes is not determined by the type of weapons used but by its 'scale and effects' (Joyner and Lotrionte, Chapter 18, pp. 458–65). What is crucial in this case is to identify the target of such defensive action. As with terrorism, international law's response boils down to issues of attribution. A state can thus become the target of self-defence action if it is the author of the IW attack, exerts effective control over those that perpetuated such an attack or adopts the attack as its own. There are a number of other issues that are worth considering. One such issue is whether IW can give rise to pre-emptive self-defence. The possibility of pre-emptive self-defence does not practically arise due to the nature of information technology, which makes the attack almost instantaneous but issues of preventive self-defence may very well arise, albeit current international law seems to take a rather negative view on this right. Another issue relates to the temporal proximity of the self-defence action to the attack. Concerning IW attacks there may be a temporal hiatus between the attack and its detection but contemporary interpretations of self-defence allow for such a hiatus as was the case with the Falklands War of 1982 or the first Gulf War of 1990–91. Another issue is whether, due to the interconnectivity of the worldwide web and the fact that the attack can be transported through many states, states can exercise their right of collective

---

[18]   *National Security Strategy of the United States* (2002), at: www.whitehouse.gov/nsc/nss.html.

[19]   This is also the position of the Dutch government (2008, p. 132; see also United Kingdom, 2002–03, para. 154).

self-defence. Collective self-defence is not the sum of rights to individual self-defence; thus another state can come to the defence of the attacked state if they are bound by a treaty or it feels that the attack is also an attack on itself. Otherwise each state that has been attacked can exercise its right of individual self-defence separately. Related to the above is the question of whether the state through which the attack passes will bear any responsibility for aiding such attack or for failing in its duty of due diligence? Whether such responsibility can arise depends on whether that state is able to act although it should be stated that IW attacks often defy a particular state's capabilities.

Humanitarian Intervention and the Responsibility to Protect

Humanitarian intervention refers to the use of force by a state or a collectivity of states in order to put an end to egregious violations of human rights in another state. Its legality, a question not entirely divorced from morality and politics, remains rather controversial.

There are mainly three lines of reasoning regarding the lawfulness of humanitarian intervention. According to the first, humanitarian intervention is prohibited being contrary to Article 2(4) interpreted as protecting state sovereignty (Terry D. Gill, 'Humanitarian Intervention' (Chapter 20), pp. 551–2).[20] A number of policy considerations are also added to support such a view. It is claimed for example that an absolute prohibition on the use of force prevents power politics and minimizes the risk of abuse.[21]

According to the second line of reasoning, humanitarian intervention is lawful under existing customary international law. More specifically, state practice developed in the nineteenth century points to the emergence of a customary rule allowing intervention on humanitarian grounds. As Sir Hartley Shawcross said at the Nuremberg trials 'the right of humanitarian intervention … has been recognised long ago as an integral part of the Law of Nations' (Jean-Pierre L. Fonteyne, 'The Customary International Law Doctrine of Humanitarian Intervention' (Chapter 19), p. 500). From this perspective, such a right has been reaffirmed in the post-Charter period by practice such as the intervention in Bangladesh, Uganda or Kosovo, although the humanitarian argument was not always explicit. Moreover, it is maintained that Article 2(4), literally interpreted, is not prohibiting humanitarian intervention because such uses of force do not affect the territorial integrity or political independence of states and, besides, promote the UN's purpose of justice (Gill, Chapter 20, pp. 550–51). This argument was put forward by Belgium in the *Legality of the Use of Force* case concerning NATO's action in Kosovo.[22]

According to a third line of reasoning, humanitarian intervention is in principle illegal but may be justified if certain conditions are satisfied, for example if the scale of human rights deprivations is large, the intervening power is relatively disinterested, all peaceful means have been exhausted, the Security Council has failed to take action and the action is preferably collective (Fonteyne, Chapter 19, pp. 532–42; Gill, Chapter 20, pp. 564–5; see also ILA,

---

[20]   See also Article 2(1) UN Charter; *Corfu Channel* case, ICJ Rep. (1949), 3 at 35 and Diss. Op. Krylov *ibid.*, at 77.

[21]   *Corfu Channel* case, at 35; *Nicaragua* case, para. 268.

[22]   *Legality of Use of Force (Yugoslavia v. Belgium)*, Oral Pleadings, Verbatim Record, 10 May 1999, CR 99/15.

1974, p. 217; UK Paper on Humanitarian Intervention, 2001, p. 695). The role of these criteria is more or less to mitigate the wrongfulness of the use of force without declaring it legal in the abstract (Gill, Chapter 20, pp. 560–68). Concerning the collective character of the action, a point is in order here. Often such collective action is equated with UN authorized action. In this case, the action is not humanitarian intervention defined here as unilateral and unauthorized intervention but a collective security action according to Chapter VII or Chapter VIII of the UN Charter (Gill, Chapter 20, pp. 548–9). In contrast, humanitarian actions without Security Council authorization as, for example, those provided for in the African Union's Constitutive Act[23] are such collective humanitarian interventions.

The current legal framework as presented above being rather indeterminate led to the invocation of legitimacy to support humanitarian interventions. As the International Independent Commission on Kosovo reported, whereas NATO's action may have been illegal *stricto sensu*, it was however legitimate in view of the values it upheld (Independent International Commission on Kosovo, 2000). The distinction between legality and legitimacy is to some extent reminiscent of Vattel's distinction between the necessary and the voluntary law of nations whereby the use of force is assessed simultaneously by legal as well as axiological standards. That said, the Kosovo case acted as a catalyst in the way state sovereignty is approached in international law. It was realized that an undifferentiated approach to state sovereignty often leaves international law helpless in the face of heinous crimes, reveals its inherent contradictions and compromises its validity.

It is for this reason that the International Commission on Intervention and State Sovereignty, which was established in 2001, elaborated the doctrine of the Responsibility to Protect (R2P). The R2P has been embraced by the *World Summit Outcome Document* (UN, 2005b, paras 138–39) and reaffirmed since then by the Security Council[24] and by the AU.[25] It has also been mentioned in resolutions dealing with specific crises such as in Security Council resolutions on Darfur,[26] and a Special Adviser on R2P has been appointed.

The R2P doctrine is premised on two main ideas: (i) that sovereignty implies responsibility towards a state's own people but also towards the international community; and (ii) that there is a residual responsibility of the international community to protect such people when their own state is unwilling or unable to do so. That residual responsibility includes three specific responsibilities: the responsibility to prevent in the sense of addressing the root causes of the crisis; the responsibility to react in the sense of responding to humanitarian crisis; and the responsibility to rebuild in the form of follow-up assistance for reconstruction.

As far as the responsibility to react is concerned, it can justify the use of force if certain conditions are satisfied. First, there must be a just cause which refers to gross attacks on human life with or without genocidal intent as well as ethnic cleansing. Second, there must be a right intention which means that the primary purpose of the intervention must be to halt

---

[23]   Article 4(h) AU Constitutive Act. Article 4(j) and (k), 16–17 of the Protocol relating to the Establishment of the Peace and Security Council of the African Union (2002). Also see Article 52 of ECOWAS protocol relating to the Mechanism for Conflict Prevention, Management, Resolution, Peacekeeping and Security (1999).

[24]   SC Res 1674 (2006); SC Res 1894 (2009).

[25]   The common African Position on the proposed reform of the UN: 'the Ezulwini Consensus' 7th Extraordinary Session of the AU Executive Council, Addis Ababa, Ethiopia, 7–8 March 2005.

[26]   SC Res 1706 (2006); SC Res 1755 (2007).

or avert human suffering. Third, such use of force should be authorized by the right authority preferably the Security Council, but the General Assembly or regional organizations can play a role within their limits (International Commission on Intervention and State Sovereignty, 2001, pp. 49–55). It should be noted at this juncture that these criteria are reminiscent of the just war theory. In addition to the above, some prudential conditions have also been included, for example the use of force should be a measure of last resort when all other measures have been exhausted, it must be proportional and there must be reasonable perspectives of success. Still, as Spencer Zifcak ('The Responsibility to Protect' (Chapter 21), pp. 578–84) explains, many states were concerned about the extent to which state sovereignty can be undermined by this doctrine,[27] whereas certain among them did not lose sight of the fact that this doctrine is similar to the doctrine of humanitarian intervention.

Regarding the content of the R2P further clarifications are needed (Zifcak, Chapter 31, pp. 589–93; see also UN, 2009), whereas with regard to its legal status, according to Carlo Focarelli ('The Responsibility to Protect Doctrine and Humanitarian Intervention' (Chapter 22), p. 614), the R2P belongs to the dynamic and norm generating process of international law and to political communication, rather than to a norm established in international law. What particularly concerns the author is that the R2P as an umbrella doctrine lacks specific rules that have been accepted by states.

Be that as it may, even if the R2P cannot at present be said to constitute a legal norm, it is a political principle that might in due time bring about normative changes. Still, the different reactions to this doctrine reveal the indeterminacy of the rules on the use of force caught between competing principles – the principle of humanity on the one hand and state sovereignty on the other – as well as the dilemmas of international lawyers of having to choose one or other argument (Tsagourias, 2000a, p. 11).

Conclusions

As was said at the beginning, the aim of this book is to present the development of moral, political and legal thinking concerning war and the use of force in international affairs. This journey has shown that the society of states remains rather mystified when faced with the use of force. On the one hand, it acknowledges that armed force and its consequences are abhorrent and as a consequence it tries to excommunicate force morally, politically or legally. On the other hand, it accepts that the use of force seems to provide a means of achieving certain worthy ends which cannot otherwise be achieved. It thus tries to accommodate certain uses of force, even to provide legal grounding for them.

The safest prediction that can be made is that the use of force will not be eradicated from international society but will extend to new areas in line with technological or other developments. Concerning the law on the use of force, the tension between abstract legal norms and the context within which they operate will continue unabated. Law will endeavour to accommodate new phenomena, for example IW, terrorism, WMD and so on, by looking to the past for useful analogies and by making the necessary adaptations, but will always be overtaken by events. As a result, the rules on the use of force will never become too

---

[27] Article 2 paras (1), (4), (7) UN Charter.

prescriptive or too proscriptive but will continue to tread precariously between formalism, facts and ideals.

Selected Bibliography

Protocol for the Pacific Settlement of Disputes (Geneva Protocol, 1924) (1925) *American Journal of International Law Suppl*, **19**, pp. 9–17.

Arend, A.C. and Beck, R.J. (1993), *International Law and the Use of Force*, London: Routledge.

Bowett, D.W. (1958), *Self-Defence in International Law*, Manchester: Manchester University Press.

Brownlie, I. (1963), *International Law and the Use of Force by States*, Oxford: Clarendon Press.

Chesterman, S. (2001), *Just War or Just Peace? Humanitarian Intervention and International Law*, New York: Oxford University Press.

Corten, O. (2010), *The Law against War: The Prohibition on the Use of Force in Contemporary International Law*, Oxford and Portland, OR: Hart Publishing.

Dinstein, Y. (2011), *War, Aggression and Self-Defence* (5th edn), New York: Cambridge University Press.

Draper, G.I.A. (1992), 'Grotius' Place in the Development of Ideas about War', in H. Bull, B. Kingsbury and A. Roberts (eds), *Hugo Grotius and International Relations*, Oxford: Oxford University Press, pp. 177–208.

Franck, T.M. (2002), *Recourse to Force: State Action against Threats and Armed Attacks*, New York: Cambridge University Press.

Gazzini, T. (2005), *The Changing Rules on the Use of Force in International Law*, Manchester: Manchester University Press.

Glennon, M. (2004-2005), 'How International Rules Die', *Georgetown Law Journal*, **93**, p. 939–91.

Gray, C. (2008), *International Law and the Use of Force* (3rd edn), New York: Oxford University Press.

Hall, W.E. (1924), *A Treatise on International Law* (8th edn), ed. A.P. Higgins, Oxford: Clarendon Press.

Independent International Commission on Kosovo (2000), *Kosovo Report: Conflict, International Response, Lessons Learned.*, Oxford: Oxford University Press.

International Commission on Intervention and State Sovereignty (2001), *The Responsibility to Protect*, http://responsibilitytoprotect.org/ICISS%20Report.pdf.

Jennings, R.Y. (1938), 'The Caroline and McLeod Cases', *American Journal of International Law*, **32**, pp. 82–99.

McCoubrey, H. and White, N.D. (1992), *International Law and Armed Conflict*, Aldershot: Dartmouth.

Netherlands State Practice: Limitations and Abolition of the Right to War (2008), *Netherlands Yearbook of International Law*, **39**, pp. 300-317.

Thakur, R. (2010), *The Responsibility to Protect: Norms, Laws and the Use of Force in International Politics*, London: Routledge.

Tsagourias, N. (2000a), 'Humanitarian Intervention after Kosovo and Legal Discourse: Self-Deception or Self-Consciousness', *Leiden Journal of International Law*, **13**, pp. 11–32.

Tsagourias, N. (2000b), *Jurisprudence of International Law: The Humanitarian Dimension*, Manchester: Manchester University Press.

United Kingdom Materials on International Law 2001: Use of Force – Prohibition of the Use of Force (2001), *British Yearbook of International Law*, pp. 674–99.

UN (2004), *A More Secure World: Our Shared Responsibility*, UN Doc. A/59/565.

UN (2005a), *In Larger Freedom: Towards Development, Security and Human Rights for All*, UN Doc. A/59/2005.

UN (2005b), *World Summit Outcome Document*, UN Doc. A/RES/60/1.

UN (2009), *Implementing the Responsibility to Protect*, UN Doc. A/63/677.

Foreign Affairs Committee, Session 2002–03, *Second Report*.

Waldock, C.H.M. (1952), 'The Regulation of the Use of Force by Individual States in International Law', *Recueil des Cours*, **81**, pp. 451–517.

White, N.D. (ed.) (2006), *Collective Security Law*, Aldershot: Ashgate.

Part I
Ancient-Medieval

[1]

War, Peace, and International Law in Ancient Greece

Victor Alonso

Greek Civilization begins with a great poem celebrating war, the *Iliad*. This work's strength and beauty emanate largely from the fact that Homer does not hide the terrible face of the conflict between Achaeans and Trojans. Heroes fight and die on the battlefront before the walls of Ilium, the city which will one day be taken amidst a bath of blood. But all is not tragedy and pain in this hermeneutically inexhaustible story. The bard reserves the poem's final song to relate an act of reconciliation that belongs among the most moving and inspiring in world literature. Under the cover of night, King Priam, a desolate and unarmed old man, approaches Achilles' tent as a suppliant, with the consent of the gods, to reclaim, for appropriate burial and funerary rites, the body of his son Hector, whom Achilles still keeps as testimony of his victory and vengeance. Overcoming his legendary wrath, Achilles concedes to Priam's supplication with a display of recognition and pity. The work thus concludes with a funeral celebrating the fallen hero, the greatest of the Trojans, and according him a measure of poetic justice that cannot but bring us a sense of relief.

George Steiner (1984: 242–43) says that

> The more one experiences ancient Greek literature and civilization, the more insistent the suggestion that Hellas is rooted in the twenty-fourth Book of the *Iliad*. There are not many primary aspects of Greek moral, political, rhetorical practice which are not incipient in and, indeed, given unsurpassed imaginative formulation by, the night encounter of Priam and Achilles and the restoration of Hector's body. Much of what Greek sensibility knew and felt about life and death, about acceptance of tragic fate and the claims of mercy, about the equivocations of intent and of mutual recognition which inhabit all speech between mortals, is set out in this climactic, most perfect part of the epic.

There is, of course, an essential harmony between this song and Sophocles' *Antigone*, that pinnacle of Hellenic tragedy in the Classical Period. But three centuries before Sophocles, the singers of tales already understood that all military confrontations must obey a set of limits and rules, for as Antigone puts it, men are obliged to respect the unwritten and unfailing statutes of divine law (*Ant.* 454–55). And they are also compelled to search for reconciliation, provisional or definitive, beyond the imperatives of war.

Interestingly, the *Iliad*'s conclusion contains, along with Achilles' return to civilized order (to *humanitas*, as a reader of Cicero would have said), a complete retraction of his earlier position, when, at the culminating moment of his duel with Hector, he had rejected any accord with his opponent. The proposal the Trojan leader had offered conformed to a fundamental principle of the Greek code of war:

> But come here, let us call the gods to witness, for they will be the best witnesses and guardians of our covenants: I will do you no violent maltreatment if Zeus grants me strength to endure and I take your life; but when I have stripped from you your glorious armor, Achilles, I will give your dead body back to the Achaeans; and so too do you (*Il.* 22.254–59).

Achilles' immediate response had been a vow to fight to the bitter end:

> Hector, talk not to me, curse you, of covenants. As between lions and men there are no oaths of faith, nor do wolves and lambs have hearts of concord but plan evils continually one against the other, so is it not possible for you and me to be friends, nor will there be oaths between us till one or the other has fallen, and glutted with his blood Ares (22.261–67).

In other words, Achilles had announced that his personal conflict with this enemy, the killer of Patroclus, was situated at the margins of culture, in a natural state of brute force and simplicity, unmediated by cultural norms, and dominated by blind formlessness and moral chaos. The emblem of this chaos within the *Iliad*, as James Redfield has indicated (1975: 183), is the anti-funeral: the dead are stripped and left to the scavengers, "a prey to dogs and a feast for birds" (*Il.* 1.4–5).

Both the *Iliad* and the *Odyssey* conclude with scenes of reconciliation fostered by the gods who for their part have had to make an effort to overcome their own differences about the fates of the mortals. In the first poem, the private compromise between the two leaders has no political or military consequences, as it is limited to the retrieval of Hector's body, and does not end the hostilities (although it does serve symbolically to reaffirm the civilized condition of Achilles – that almost superhuman, ambiguous son of a god and a mortal). In the case of Odysseus, as we shall see shortly, the avenger's pact with the dead suitors' relatives will once again bring peace (*eirene*) and prosperity to Ithaca or, if we prefer, the end of civil discord (*stasis*) and the deactivation of the logic of *vendetta* (which is further complicated in this case by its international ramifications). Both episodes might be read as metaphors of Greek political history in its totality. In effect, the dynamics of war – with its multiple ways of suspending and overcoming conflict – along with the precariousness of peace, in the framework of intra-communal and inter-Hellenic dissensions, constituted the great argument of this history, from the Homeric epic to the Hellenistic period.[1]

The Institutionalization of International Relations: Friendship, War, and Reconciliation

War represented a structural component of the Greco-Roman world, as much or more than slavery or agriculture; from Herodotus to Xenophon and from Thucydides to Polybius, Greek historiography is above all political-military history. Any college graduate with a degree in Classical Studies understands this fact, and there are even surveys that elucidate for us the chain of conflicts to the end of the Hellenistic Period.[2] It is important, however, not to oversimplify the complexity of international relations by generalizing on the basis of its most dynamic actors, that is, precisely those the extant historical sources inform us about. Hellenic communities found themselves involved in armed conflicts in a variety of ways, a crucial fact which unfortunately remains insufficiently emphasized in the most recent studies on Greek political history. There were many *poleis* and federal states (*koina*) that found a way to keep themselves out of the great confrontations, pursuing a policy of neutrality (Alonso 1987, 2001), or concluding compromises with Greek superpowers (as did the Aegean cities of the Delian League, who freed themselves from military service in exchange for a monetary contribution), or even waging an indirect war. Argos and Corcyra offer well-known examples of abstinence from war during most of the fifth century, as do Megara in the fourth or Rhodes and Athens in some periods of the Hellenistic era (Habicht 1997: 173ff.). Prior to the prominent role it would play in the second half of the third century, the Achaean Confederacy presented an enviable case of splendid isolation. There were entire regions, like Aetolia, Epirus, or Crete, that refused to participate in the great conflagrations of the classical age, anchored as they were in policies of neutrality and non-alignment which do not lack certain present-day analogues. The same could be said for the colonial world occupied by Greek cities – Libya, the Black Sea region, Magna Graecia. Certainly, many of these areas experienced periods of hostilities of a more or less local character, but the fact is that these cannot have been important enough for our historical sources to pay them much attention.

We should therefore remain critical toward generalizations and occasional phrases on the phenomenon of war that we read in the works of some Greek philosophers (Phillipson 1911: 167–68, 173). They thought that war should be considered a natural and inevitable state inherent in both human and animal life on earth. Heraclitus called war the father of all things, in the sense that it is the fundamental principle causing all change and development (22 B53 in Diels and Kranz 1961). And so Cleinias, at the beginning of Plato's *Laws* (626a), addressing the Athenians on the subject of Cretan institutions and assuming that strife is inevitable for attaining political exclusiveness and national self-realization, says: "In reality every city is in a natural state of war with every other, not indeed proclaimed by heralds, but perpetual." In the "Melian Dialogue," the Athenian ambassadors, not without sophistry, say that the rule of the strongest, operative in nature, always prevails over law in governing relations between peoples. That well-known discussion between Melians and Athenians (Thucydides 5.84–116) might induce us to conclude that the Law of the Jungle defined interstate relations in Hellas. Yet not even those most convinced of the prevalence of a naturalist ideology of war among the Greeks (like Momigliano 1960) would be willing to subscribe to this conclusion. The problem with such sharp and doctrinary pronouncements, typical of Greek theoretical thinking (although less of historiography), is that they have contributed to confusing modern authors.[3]

Here it is necessary to mention Bruno Keil (1916: 5ff.). In a celebrated study, he defended the idea that during the first centuries of Greek history peace was nothing but a contractual interruption of the normal state of war between the *poleis*, little more than a respite, and that after the expiration of an international treaty the parties returned automatically to their natural situation of "war of all against all" (*bellum omnium contra omnes*). A decisive point for Keil was the fact that the word *eirene* did not emerge as a legal term in diplomatic language until the fourth century, with the "common peace" of 386, the first *koine eirene*. In effect, to label the legal instrument designated to stop an armed conflict between cities, international law still employed in the fifth century the noun *spondai*, "libations," in combination with the terms *synthekai* and *horkoi*, "stipulations" and "oaths."[4] The lack of a concept of "peace treaty" corresponded precisely with the establishment of a period of time for the *spondai* negotiated at the close of a conflict (50, 30, 10, 5 years of guaranteed non-aggression). This model of negotiation definitively reveals a negative conception of *eirene* as "not-war" or, if we prefer, as the provisional suspension of general belligerency between states.

Recent research has thus confirmed the validity of Keil's philological analysis in its essential points, but it has at the same time convincingly refuted the historical and legal premises he deduced from his analysis.[5] Our current understanding suggests that, far from being rooted in a naive belligerent state of everyone-against-everyone, early Greek communities maintained at least three types of external relationships: none at all, war, or friendship.[6]

1. A lack of relationship between parties (*ameixia*) is typically the starting point in the history of international law. This state of non-relationship corresponds with the absence of ties and contacts that Thucydides (1.2.2, 3.4) postulates for many early Greek communities that were closed off from each other in their autarky and too distant to maintain external relations, given the conditions of navigation and the difficulties of land travel. As Achilles recalls, he and his Myrmidons found themselves before the walls of Troy solely because of their commitment to Agamemnon:

> I did not come here to fight because of the spearmen of Troy, since they are in no way at fault toward me. Never did they drive off my cattle or my horses, nor ever in deep-soiled Phthia ... did they lay waste the grain, for many things lie between us – shadowy mountains and sounding sea (*Il.* 1.152–57).

Legal uncertainty – rather than lawlessness (*anomia*) – essentially characterizes any contacts with the exterior (*epimeixia*). These contacts usually assume the form of peaceful commerce (the Hesiodic *ergon*, the plebeian *emporie*), of piracy or banditry (*lesteia*), or of both simultaneously (the elite *prexis*).[7] It is in this context that we should interpret the first mythological frictions between Asia and Europe, in the form of the abduction of women, as narrated by Herodotus (1.1–5). Corresponding to the doubts that invariably beset the sailor upon arriving in a strange land, "whether its people are cruel, and wild, and unjust, or whether they are kind to strangers and fear the gods in their thoughts" (*Od.* 9.175–76), there appears the typical formula of salutation to the unknown visitor: "Whence do you sail over the watery ways? Is it on some business, or do you wander at random over the sea, as pirates do, who wander hazarding their lives and bringing evil to men of other lands?" (*Od.* 3.72–74).

The mute exchange practiced by the Carthaginians in some regions of Africa, as described by Herodotus (4.196), might be considered one degree above this state of incommunication. This minimal, but conventional (in the strict sense of the word) form of *epimeixia* illustrates the difficulties that divergent referential systems, beginning with language and religion, pose for human groups. The source of the Cyclopses' savage conduct is precisely their lack of understanding of the *themis* common to civilized societies (*Od.* 9.106), where *themis* refers to a customary rule of divine origin consecrating norms of behavior, such as hospitality, under the protection of Zeus Xenios (*Od.* 9.270). Hence the confrontation between man-eating Polyphemus and his unsuspecting guests in Book 9 of the *Odyssey*, or the impossibility of the Cyclopses' cohabitation with the Phaeacians, who are forced to emigrate to Scheria, a sort of promised land (ibid. 6.2–8). It is not by chance that in the Homeric world the utopian image *par excellence* is this Scheria, an island that barely "mixes" with the exterior (*Od.* 6.205, 279), although Nausicaa, perhaps overcome by *ennui*, will fall in love with a foreign shipwreck. Naturally, as is the case with Rokovoko, the isle of Queequeg, Phaeacia did not appear on maps.

2. For a negative relationship marked by a state of war (*polemos*) between communities, the struggle of the Achaeans against the Trojans might serve as a paradigm. In the Homeric poems, war already constitutes a well-defined legal situation, in which the fury of Ares appears counterbalanced by the rational calculation of Athena. Given that any confrontation potentially endangers the entire population and implies the mobilization of all or most of the military force, the decision to initiate hostilities is made public before the corresponding governing bodies (kings, counselors, and the assembly of the people). Before it comes to war, the offended party can request or receive a conciliatory proposal on the basis of satisfaction (*poine*). If armed conflict proves inevitable, the combatants have at their disposal a series of institutions and customary rules to limit and avoid its devastating effects: the proclamation of the conflict, the inviolability of heralds (*kerykes*), the possibility of diplomatic negotiations through ambassadors (*angeloi*), the recourse to single combat (*monomachia*) with the intention of sparing widespread bloodshed, the use of truces for the recovery of bodies, the condition of suppliant (*hiketes*), the inviolability of sanctuaries and sacred persons (*asylia* of priests like Chryses in *Iliad* 1), the contractual status of ally (*epikouros*), the regulated distribution of booty, including the honorary share of the leader (*geras*), and, of course, the figure of the primary combatant or head of the coalition (Agamemnon, Priam).[8]

Precisely because armed conflicts have causes and a beginning, and because they do not represent the natural state of relations between peoples, it is also recognized that they can be ended by means of a binding treaty. This is *philotes*, a pact of reconciliation and friendship which originates in the sphere of penal law and early on comes to be applied at the international level.[9]

Paris hopes that differences will cease altogether after his single combat with Menelaus:

> And whoever wins, and proves himself the better man, let him duly take all the wealth and the woman, and take them home. But you others, swearing friendship and solemn oaths (*philoteta kai horkia pista*), may you all live in deep-soiled Troyland, ... , and let the others return to Argos, ... and Achaea (*Il.* 3.71–75).

Philoteta kai horkia pista: this formulaic expression is repeated by both sides as many as three times (*Il.* 3.94, 256, 323), announcing the solemn accord that establishes first the celebration of a decisive duel (*monomachia*) and afterwards a new bond of friendship (*philotes*) between the contracting parties.[10] Agamemnon and Priam, the supreme leaders, grant their consent to the proposal and execute the oaths, the sacrifices, the pouring of libations (*spondai*), and the shaking of hands that sanction the pact, taking the gods as their witnesses and guarantors.[11] The process, however, will be suspended by the intervention of Aphrodite, who carries Paris away from the battlefield in the very moment of his defeat. It seems important to underline that, at this point, because none of the contracting parties is involved in the goddess' ploy,[12] the agreement has not yet been invalidated irreversibly. Zeus knows this and therefore continues to seek the possibility of a solution: "But surely victory rests with Menelaus, dear to Ares" – a thoroughly just ruling.

> Let us therefore take thought how these things are to be; whether we shall again rouse evil war (*polemon*) and the dread din of battle, or place friendship (*philoteta*) between armies. If this should in any way be welcome and sweet to all, then might the city of king Priam still be inhabited, and Menelaus might take back Argive Helen.[13]

A wise judge, the father of the gods makes a legally impeccable analysis of the situation: either leave things as they were, continuing with the hostilities, or conclude the accord in favor of the Achaeans (but with the unforeseen survival of the loser in the duel). The latter is Zeus' preferred option, because it leaves Troy safe, while at the same time preventing either of the two provokers of this absurd war from getting away completely with their own designs: Menelaus recovers Helen, but fails to avenge himself by killing Paris (a perfect *kadi* justice, as Max Weber would say). Nevertheless, the agreed-upon *philotes* will not be realized because Hera resists adamantly, sways her husband, and sends Athena to convince Pandarus to shoot his arrow at Menelaus, thus making the Trojans "the first in defiance of their oaths."[14]

The *Odyssey* concludes with a successful negotiation of a pact of reconciliation and friendship (*philotes*) to bring definitive resolution to an armed conflict. Odysseus returns to Ithaca and butchers without mercy all of Penelope's suitors who have defiled his house and squandered his possessions. In exacting vengeance, the hero has been

assisted by Athena, who is nevertheless the first in attempting to restore peace to
the community of Ithaca and to root out the insurrection of the dead suitors' relatives
against the king and his house. The danger for Odysseus is all the more serious as the
conflict exceeds the borders of his homeland and, since some of the fallen hail from
"other *poleis*" (24.418), acquires an international character. Athena now proposes to
Zeus the alternative that he himself had considered at Troy: "Will you still further bring
to pass evil war and the dread din of battle, or will you establish friendship (*philoteta*)
between the two sides?" (*Od.* 24.475–6). Zeus' answer confirms the judicial wisdom
of the king of the gods:

> Do as you will, but I will tell you what is fitting. Now that noble Odysseus has taken
> vengeance on the suitors, let them swear a solemn oath, and let him be king all his
> days, and let us on our part bring about a forgetting of the killing of their sons and
> brothers; and let them love one another as before, and let wealth and peace (*eirene*)
> abound (24.481–86).

Athena judiciously follows Zeus' counsel: after a mock attack that causes the death
of Eupeithes – the inconsolable father of one of the leaders of the suitors and head of
the uprising – the goddess imposes on both sides the exchange of oaths validating the
accord of reconciliation.

The vocabulary employed in this episode speaks eloquently to one of the fundamental principles of Greek international law in the archaic and classical periods. For
the agreement as such, Zeus uses the technical term *horkia pista*,[15] while the resulting legal relationship is defined as *philotes*, friendship in a positive and institutional
sense. The immediate and basic consequence of this solemn covenant is the return
of *eirene* to Ithaca, but technically this word neither designates the new relationship
between the parties nor the legal instrument itself. Typologically, the pact reached is
not an agreement of peace, but rather of friendship, from which the reality of *eirene*
derives logically, with all its benefits (beginning with *ploutos*, wealth, its inseparable
companion).[16] The idea of peace, therefore, does not figure in the legal culture of
early Greece as an institutional category *per se*, as an independent legal concept, but
rather as a state produced by a conventional relationship of *philotes* (or, later, *philia*).
Not only is Greek thought incapable of conceiving of peace as a natural and universal
right of all peoples (barbarians and Hellenes); as yet it cannot even conceive of peace
as a legal relationship in and of itself. Peace must be enveloped and supported by a
stronger bond with a bilateral character: friendship (which in this period can entail
mutual assistance in warfare).[17]

3. A completely positive and conventional relationship with a foreign community can
in principle be reached by means of two institutions: exogamic matrimony (*gamos*) and
guest friendship (*xenia*). Both of these ties create friendship and eventually military alliance between two kings or Homeric nobles from different communities (Finley 1977:
98ff.). If the wife who is handed over may be considered in a certain sense a token of
the *philotes* between father-in-law and son-in-law, the figure of the guest friend (*xenos*)
is intimately associated in Homeric language with the notion of *philos* and the emotional and legal values of friendship (Benveniste 1969: I, 341, 345). For this reason,

the verb *philein* expresses the conduct required of an individual who welcomes the *xenos* into his home and treats him according to ancestral customs (perfectly expressed in *Il.* 3.207). Moreover, it is not uncommon to seal a *xenia* (or a *philotes*) with matrimony, reinforcing the friendship between sides (*FGrHist* 26 F1; *Il.* 9.285–90). The classic scene illustrating the early *xenia*'s great potential is found in the *Iliad*, when Glaucus of Lycia and Diomedes of Argos shake hands upon recognizing one another as *xenoi* before the walls of Troy. Although one is an ally of Priam and the other of Agamemnon, they refuse to fight as enemies and instead exchange gifts in the middle of battle with the aim of renewing the guest friendship they inherited from their parents (*Il.* 6.119–231). It was precisely Paris' violation of the law of hospitality, with his abduction of Helen, that unleashed the Trojan War (Hdt. 2.115). Myth and legend offer other instances of similar transgressions, while also illuminating the great capacity of *xenia* for diplomatic mediation. For example, Antenor, the Trojan noble hosting Menelaus and Odysseus in his home when they arrive as ambassadors to negotiate a deal and avoid the war (*Il.* 3.207), will later be the first to argue before Priam and the assembly for the return of Helen and for reconciliation (7.347–53). His actions cannot but remind us of the functions of the *proxenos*, a sort of "consul," representing in one Greek city the interests of another, who later on the public level will replace the old *xenos* (Gschnitzer 1973: 632).

The institutions of international law that develop in the seventh and sixth centuries are directly derived from these experiments and achievements of early Greece that are reflected in the epics. In the Homeric world, the contracting subjects are always individuals, the kings, whose words bind the community as a whole: it is not the Cretans who conclude the alliance with the Argives, but rather Idomeneus who joins the king of Mycenae to fight against Troy; nor is it the Trojans or the Achaeans who ratify Paris' proposal, but Priam and Agamemnon. Which is not to say that their peers – those nobles who are also called *basileis* – and the people (*demos*) are marginalized in decisions concerning war and peace (Carlier 1991). In matters that are vital to them all, the members of the council are consulted by the king (Gschnitzer 2001: 199–211), and the men in the assembly make their voices heard through their shouts of consent or disagreement (Raaflaub 1997). These are the origins of war as an institution, that is, organized interstate violence, subjected to legal and political norms and differentiated from banditry and piracy (Ilari 1980: 41; Nowag 1983: 94ff.).

That the actors in inter-state relations were individuals and not the entire citizen body remained typical until the Hellenistic period of states and cities that were less developed politically or ruled by monarchs. Thus the tyrants in the archaic epoch were recognized as contracting parties by the other states: Thrasybulus of Miletus, for example, reached an agreement of reconciliation (*diallage*) with his enemy, the Lydian king Alyattes, in which "they agreed to be guest friends (*xeinous*) and allies (*symmachous*) of one another" (*StV* 105); Polycrates of Samos formed bonds of *xenia* with pharaoh Amasis of Egypt (*StV* 117); Peisistratus of Athens made an alliance with the Thessalians (*StV* 108). However, with the triumph of the idea of the *polis* and the transfer of sovereignty to the citizen body – both in oligarchies and democracies – a general change took place. As international relations were in this way "politicized," treaties were fixed in writing and publicly exhibited on monuments of stone and other materials; moreover, such displays were not confined to the cities involved but, for enhanced effect and publicity, also extended to the large panhellenic sanctuaries. Along with oral and customary traditions – that are historically the first source of international law – an ever more flexible and technical written law began developing as an expression of an ever more diversified and autonomous will to conclude contractual agreements.[18] Corresponding phenomena within the *polis* obviously were the codification of internal law and the appearance of great legislators (van Effenterre and Ruzé 1994; Hölkeskamp 1999), and in this sense every diplomatic instrument could also be considered a legal instrument. The sixth century represented a turning point in this process, as demonstrated in extant documents.

Toward the middle of that century King Croesus of Lydia entered into diplomatic relations with Sparta, the leading power in Greece, negotiating a pact of *xenia* and *symmachía* that was in line with the traditional uses of guest friendship. Nonetheless there were two differences: this pact incorporated a diplomatically more modern concept of military alliance, and it designated as the contracting party no longer the two Spartan kings, but rather the Lacedaemonians in their function as a sovereign political entity (*StV* 113). The old terminology is maintained on a bronze plate that the Sybarites and the Serdaioi deposited at Olympia prior to 510, establishing *philotes* "forever" (*StV* 120), that is to say, a pact of friendship that, I believe, put an end to hostilities between the Achaean colony and its Italic neighbors. This was surely the case with Cyrene and Amasis, who concluded a treaty of *philotes* and *symmachía* around 565, following upon the previous pharaoh's invasion of the territory of the Greek city.[19] We know from another bronze plate that the priests of Olympia intervened actively to facilitate a settlement of *philia* of 50 years' duration between two Elean communities, the Anaitoi and the Metapioi (*StV* 111); the covenant surely signaled the end of a period of confrontation between the contracting parties and established an arbitration procedure to resolve future differences between them (Gschnitzer 1973: 636–37). Significantly, interpersonal *xenia* became an increasingly antiquated way of designating and articulating relations between two civic collectivities; it was replaced by the more abstract and neutral terms *philotes* or *philia*.[20]

In all these interstate treaties we find a confirmation of the general principles governing the laws of peace and war in Greece since the Dark Age: from a non-existent relationship groups could arrive at a state of friendship (with the rather attractive possibility of an alliance) or they could go to war, after which they could also achieve definitive reconciliation, again by means of a friendship treaty. This fundamental distinction was maintained to the end of the Hellenistic age. In the most critical moment of diplomatic contacts between Antiochus III of Syria and Rome, which began at the no-relationship level, the Seleucid king's ambassadors proposed to the Roman senate a treaty of alliance and friendship (*philia kai symmachia*).[21] The agreement failed and war broke out, but the peace treaty concluded after the decisive victory of the Romans at Apamea (188) consecrated a new relationship precisely of *philia* "forever" between the two parties.[22]

Steps on the Way to Open War (*phaneros polemos*)

War, then, did not represent the primary and normal state of affairs between Greeks, but was just one of several normal and legitimate ways of relating to one another.[23] War represented an institutionalized procedure for settling differences and imposing decisions and sanctions at the international level; from the Homeric period, it coexisted with diplomacy and was increasingly subject to a series of rules and limitations. In general, the outbreak of hostilities was preceded by diplomacy in order to avoid, if possible, a military confrontation (which almost always proved very costly in human and economic terms). The essential functions of such diplomacy were prevention, dissuasion, and arbitration; the diplomatic agents working towards these ends often continued to operate once an armed conflict had begun. They included primarily the consul (*proxenos*), the arbiter (*diallaktes*), and the ambassador (*presbys*). At least in theory, Greek international law sought to limit the use of force in two respects: concerning the right to resort to war (*ius ad bellum*), and the laws of war (*ius in bello*). The institutionalization of war required that lines were drawn separating it from the state of peace and from other forms of violence (legitimate or not), and, in particular, that the condition of open war (*phaneros polemos*) was clearly defined.

A characteristic feature of Greek international law, at least until the third century, resided precisely in its definition of the state of open war, distinct from that of indirect war. *Phaneros polemos* between cities or federal states was considered an irreversible fact when one side had invaded another's territory (*chora*). The crossing of borders, that is to say, direct aggression against a community, constituted the reason for war and alliance (*casus belli* and *casus foederis*) par *excellence* among the Greeks. We have already heard Achilles express this idea very clearly: between his people and Troy there existed no cause for enmity, no Trojans had invaded his land to destroy crops or steal livestock. Conversely, King Cleomenes III of Sparta became the open enemy of the Achaeans when he used military force to occupy a place in the territory of Megalopolis (Pol. 2.46.6–7), thus causing the Cleomenic War (229/8-222). Such direct aggression is the only sort prohibited by post-war non-aggression treaties (long-term *spondai*) and treaties of friendship and alliance. For example, the *symmachia* of 367 between Athens and Dionysius I of Syracuse reads, "It shall not be permitted for an attack to be made by Dionysius or his descendants against the territory of the Athenians with hostile intent, either by land or by sea."[24] These legal instruments also regulated the conditions of alliance (*casus foederis*), which in any case were met by an outside attack against the allied territory: "If anyone comes against the land of the Athenians for the purpose of making war either by land or by sea, assistance shall be given by Dionysius and his descendants."[25] Shortly before the so-called "War of the Allies" (220–217) broke out, the *casus foederis* alleged by the Achaeans before the Hellenic coalition presided over by Philip V (*StV* 507) was that the Aetolians had invaded the confederation's territory (Pol. 4.15.1–2). Furthermore, nothing prevented two allied cities from fighting one another in the territory of a third party, in fulfillment of another contractual obligation: after the victory at Leuctra (371), the Athenians concluded a *symmachia* with the Spartans in 369 (*StV* 274) to put an end to Thebes' dominance, but in 366 they negotiated another alliance treaty with the Arcadians (*StV* 284), who for their part were in open war with Sparta because of their participation in the invasion of Laconia by Epaminondas. The Athenian assembly approved this second treaty because of the diplomatic benefit it brought (Xen. *Hell.* 7.4.2), and Sparta did not cancel its pact with the Athenians.[26]

Relations between Athens and Sparta during the (so-called) Peace of Nicias (*StV* 188), concluded in 421 after the first phase of the Peloponnesian War, are even more illuminating. The fact that the two cities had also forged an alliance between themselves (*StV* 189) proved no obstacle when, three years later in the battle of Mantinea, the Athenians and Lacedaemonians fought one another alongside their respective *symmachoi* (Thuc. 5.66ff.); nor was this an impediment for the Athenian deployment of Messenians and helots at Pylos with orders to ravage Spartan territory (5.56.3) – not to mention repeated violations of the stipulated terms of their agreement that were mutually tolerated (5.48.1; 56.3). For this reason Thucydides says:

> For six years and ten months the two powers abstained from invading each other's territory; in other regions, however, there was only an unstable cessation of arms and they kept on doing each other the greatest possible damage. But at last they were forced to break the treaty which had been concluded after the first ten years, and again engaged in open war (*polemon phaneron*, 5.25.3).

The breaking of *spondai* and the eruption of the Decelean War were results of an offensive action which was relatively unimportant from a military point of view but decisive from a legal standpoint: a raid against some Laconian communities perpetrated by the Athenian fleet in the summer of 414 (6.105.1). It was these thirty ships that "in the most clear way" (*phanerotata*) broke the state of peace: "For before this," comments Thucydides (6.105.2),

> the Athenians waged the war in cooperation with the Argives and Mantineans by predatory excursions from Pylos and by making landings round the rest of the Peloponnesus rather than in Laconia; and although the Argives frequently urged them only to make a landing with arms on Laconian territory, devastate in concert with them even the least part, and then go away, they refused.[27]

Things were simpler when military aid was lent to an ally fighting against a third state with whom peaceful relations were maintained by means of a post-war non-aggression treaty (long-term *spondai*), or against a state with whom there was no relationship at all. Let us take the well-known example of the events leading to the Peloponnesian War (431–404). Athens was able to ally itself with Corcyra (*StV* 161) in 433 and defend Corcyra against Corinth's attacks in the battle of Sybota despite the fact that the 30 Years' Peace of 446 between the Delian and Peloponnesian Leagues was still in force (*StV* 156). In order to avoid breaking this treaty, which included Corinth as an ally of Sparta, a specific type of alliance (called *epimachia*) was concluded between Athenians and Coryraeans, in which the contracting parties committed themselves to the defense of their respective territories and allies (Thuc. 1.44.1), while excluding their participation in offensive military campaigns (1.45.3). Accordingly, during the naval clash at Sybota the Athenian triremes limited themselves to repelling attacks against the Corcyraean fleet, but did not threaten the territory of Corinth or its allies (1.48–54). Hence the state of peace between Athens and the Peloponnesians was formally preserved (1.55.2, 66), even though henceforth Athens' relations with Corinth were strained and as a result also those with Sparta. When in the spring of 431 the Thebans decided on their own to attack Plataea, *eirene* was still intact on the Athenian side between the Peloponnesian and Delian Leagues (2.2.3).

The Corinthian War (395–386) offers an equally, or perhaps even more, eloquent testimony of this sort of situation. To my knowledge, scholars have generally supposed that Athens (and Argos) entered into war with Sparta and its allies in 395, without ever pausing first to consider in what type of conflict they were getting involved (Alonso 1999). The Athenians (as well as the Argives) entered a treaty of *symmachia* with the Boeotians in 395 (*StV* 223) and, not long thereafter, with the Corinthians (*StV* 224, l. 2), and they did, in effect, come to blows with the Peloponnesians at Coronea (in 394) in defense of Boeotia, and at Nemea (in 394) in defense of Corinth (*casus foederis par excellence*). But the direct war against Attica began only after 389, as a consequence of the failure of negotiations in 392–391, and, above all, of the Athenians' initiation of *phaneros polemos* at sea, as specified by Xenophon (*Hell.* 5.1.1), who reaches here Thucydidean quality. The Spartans were true masters in the art of economizing their forces, exposing themselves to a minimum of risk while achieving a maximum of results; indirect war afforded them a certain amount of relations (*epimeixia*) with third parties and, most importantly, allowed them to avoid the terrible danger of enemy counter-attacks in Laconian or Messenian territory (which Athens could very well have done from the sea, and why it did not do so is indeed a crucial question).[28]

What, then, were the established procedures for initiating *phaneros polemos*? In modern international law a simple diplomatic act is sufficient to establish a new legal relationship between two states: "A declaration of war is made by means of a unilateral notification to the other (…). The notification takes effect upon receipt. Thereupon a state of war comes into existence, without the need for subsequent military action."[29] Hence, the commencement of war in the legal sense does not need to coincide with the actual commencement of hostilities. However, things were neither so simple nor so profane in the ancient world, where wars were frequently initiated by ritual ceremonies. The Romans, for example, had an elaborate mechanism for maintaining a just cause in commencing war (the traditional rites of the *ius fetiale*, Livy 1.32). The Greeks could have agreed with us that war in the legal sense begins at the time when a legally recognized state of war comes into existence, that is to say, when the laws of war – the *nomoi tou polemou* of Polybius 5.11.3 – replace the law of peace in relations between the parties. But this definition certainly would have seemed insufficient to them, because it ultimately corresponds to the current state of our culture that conceives of law, like economy and the market, as an autonomous sphere, while antiquity did not produce anything approximating a "pure theory of law" or "principles of economics." Rather, representative thinkers like Herodotus, Xenophon, or Plutarch would have added that the transition from *eirene* to *polemos* also constituted a religious act, as it implicated certain changes in the war parties' relations with the gods – beginning with the divinities protecting the places that were to be attacked or crossed by the army. Hence the declaration of a war, a practice considered mandatory among the Greeks,[30] assumed a character *sui generis* or, to put it differently, was inserted in and conditioned by a group of rites of passage (or crossing) that could be more or less strict according to the religious customs of each *polis*.

Fourth century Sparta still mounted a veritable sacred and political spectacle when hostilities were to begin – in this sense King Agesilaus best embodied the ideal Spartan citizen (Spartiate). Following the failure of diplomatic negotiations with the other party and the assembly's approval of the armed conflict (which was not equivalent to a declaration of war nor did it necessarily imply breaking *epimeixia*), came the order, forwarded by the ephors to one of the king-priests, to mobilize the army. Mobilization was possible as long as the Spartans had not accepted a sacred truce for the Olympian, Isthmian, Pythian, or Nemean games and there was no conflict with the Karneia and Hyakinthia, two religious festivals of the Dorian-Spartan calendar which imposed an interruption of hostilities.[31] The king, who commanded the army, performed border-crossing sacrifices (*diabateria*) upon leaving Laconia; he also paid close attention to signs and portents (e.g. an earthquake) that might necessitate the campaign's interruption. During the campaign he received all embassies arriving from the adversary and transmitted ultimatums through such embassies, hoping (sometimes successfully) that the other side would yield at the last moment. Before entering enemy territory and thereby making the *phaneros polemos* manifest, the king appealed to the gods and heroes of the other country (*epitheiasmos*).[32]

In Greece, as in Rome, the passage of time and the expansion and increasing complexity of the international stage in the Hellenistic period led to the simplification of the formalities that preceded the start of hostilities and determined how a campaign was conducted. Polybius (13.3) laments the disappearance of the old customs of honest and noble war, above all censuring the Aetolians and their "politics of plunder" (Scholten 2000). This complaint echoes the nostalgia of Demosthenes (9.47–51), who was infuriated by the new methods employed by Philip II. Of course, there is a certain irony to the fact that the Athenians, of all people, reproached the Macedonian monarch for dehumanizing war, when it had been Athenian imperialism in the fifth century that had completely revolutionized traditional warfare (Meier 1990: 583; Hanson 2001). In reality, as we know all too well, criticism against violations of international law, whether in the form of undeclared war (*anepangeltos polemos*) or mistreatment of the conquered (Ducrey 1968) or any other sort, continue to the present day. Nostalgia for gentlemanly forms of battle has a long history, from at least as early as Xenophon to Katsumoto, most quixotic of all. Still in the first century AD, Onasander in a treatise about the good general insisted "that he should call heaven to witness that he is entering upon a war without offence" (*Strat.* 4.3).

All of this definitely contradicts the supposition that it was simple and easy for the Greeks to unleash *phaneros polemos*. The concept of open war served concrete purposes and had a teleological explanation. As already noted by Bickerman (1950: 125ff.), within an extremely fragmented political map, comprised mostly of dwarf states beset by endemic contentiousness and engaged in multiple sets of alliances, the limiting of *casus belli* and *casus foederis* helped preserve the state of peace between cities whose territories had not been attacked by armies.[33] The "philosophy" behind all this might be summarized as follows: if war is indeed frequently inevitable, let us limit it in space, delay its outbreak for as long as possible, leave a wide margin for diplomacy, and, once it begins, establish generally accepted formal procedures (such as truces, capitulations, and the protection of heralds) that will allow us to maintain relations between belligerent parties. In fact, *phaneros polemos* represented an extreme in a wide spectrum of legitimate uses of force in international relations. Excepting piracy, considered by most an illegal activity, the scale of tensions might be summarized as follows:

1   Diverse forms of private extralegal violence (self-help) were tolerated by Greek international custom in cases in which there were no agreements of legal assistance between two cities (*symbola*), that is to say, conventions offering non-violent, judicial means of settling claims between their respective citizens. Self-help meant in some cases the right to engage in reprisals (*sylan*, *rhysiazein*) against every fellow citizen of the debtor.[34] These were actions between individuals, and as such clearly distinguished from war, as specified by Polybius (22.4.15).

2   The right to raiding on land and sea conceded by public authority to private individuals under its jurisdiction against the citizens and territory of another state (*to laphyron epikeryttein*) was a kind of paramilitary action that was normally proclaimed either as a preliminary measure just before a war (Pol. 4.26.7, 4.53.2) or at the start of one (Pol. 4.36.6; Xen. *Hell.* 5.1.1). This proclamation did not necessarily produce open war between the parties (Thuc. 5.115.2), did not involve the mobilization of the citizen army, and cannot be considered an official declaration of war.[35]

3   Indirect war in the territory of a third party, as we have seen, did not cause a state of war between all parties engaged in such fighting. Obviously, indirect war did not require that war be declared or justified through diplomatic channels to the ally's enemy.

4   For open war (*phaneros polemos*) an announcement or declaration of war was required.

Long-term *spondai* and Peace Treaties (*koine eirene*)

Pataikos, a character in Menander's early Hellenistic comedy *Perikeiromene* ("Rape of the Locks"), says at the end of the work: "I greatly like your 'I'll make it up'. Accepting a fair settlement when you've been lucky – that's a mark of Greek behavior!" This does not differ much from Phoenix's advice to Achilles to make peace with Agamemnon in exchange for compensation for the offenses committed against his honor (*Il.* 9.496–605). Achilles' problem, in terms of modern sociology, is that he was completely unadapted, an absolutely heroic character who in some sense lived in conflict with the very idea of social contract. Hence his accord with Priam took place at the margins of the coalition, as a strictly private act, almost an act of natural law. Now,

Achilles obviously was an exceptional case. The distance between him and Pataikos is greater than that separating Roland from any bourgeois in the comedies of Molière. Ultimately, internal tensions within each *polis* needed to be controlled by some sort of arrangement; the same is true of corresponding tensions on the international level in the wide spectrum of conflicts just enumerated.

What is characteristic of the Hellenic experience, as already suggested, is that in order to discover the idea of peace as an autonomous legal category, international law had to take a roundabout route. Agreements in the form of *spondai*, which guaranteed *eirene* only for a specified period, were probably the diplomatic procedure adopted by Sparta in its relations with some cities that joined the Peloponnesian League after a military confrontation. In the fifth century, as demonstrated above all by the period of the so-called Peace of Nicias (421–414), the formula *spondai* or *spondai* + *symmachia* became the standard diplomatic model.

Before the Persian Wars in the early fifth century, Greece presented a panorama of local, seasonal, and quantitatively limited warfare. Scholars have often stressed the ritual, agonistic, and symbolic (although no less bloody) character of archaic land warfare.[36] Changes occurred, however, as a consequence of the challenges of the confrontation with Persia in 480–79, which represents the first globalization of the phenomenon of war in Greek history. Xerxes' invasion had a positive effect insofar as a great diplomatic effort was required to reconcile rivaling cities and unite forces in a great coalition under the hegemony of Sparta: the "Hellenic League" (*StV* 130; Brunt 1993: 47–83). In response to the globalization of war by the Achaemenid empire, the Greeks made a first attempt at globalizing the state of peace among themselves (Hdt. 7.145.1; Plut. *Them.* 6.3). Athens and Aegina, for example, had to settle their long-standing differences under Sparta's mediation, while the coalition's ambassadors opened negotiations to induce Argos to join the alliance, although the Argives preferred neutrality (Alonso 2001). We know that Argos then proposed to Sparta to agree on *spondai* for 30 years to terminate the old confrontation over Cynuria (Hdt. 7.148.4–149.2). I suggest that the Argive proposal copied an accord reached toward the middle of the sixth century between Tegea and Sparta (*StV* 112), the starting point of the "Peloponnesian League." Just as this league became the nucleus of the Hellenic League (Baltrusch 1994: 34–35), so must the Argives have been inspired by the Tegean model of relations with Sparta: post-war *spondai* as the basis of their *symmachia*, with both *spondai* and *symmachia* forming a single diplomatic instrument.

With the victory over Persia and the birth of the "Delian League" in 478–77 under the hegemony of Athens (*StV* 132), a dynamic interplay of power blocs emerged in Greek history. Sparta and the Peloponnesians observed a prudent moderation in their dealings with Athens until 461, when a regional conflict erupted in the Saronic Gulf that dragged the two superpowers into open war (beginning in 457). In a first attempt to resolve this conflict, in 451 the two sides agreed upon *spondai* for just five years (*StV* 143), essentially keeping swords drawn and ready. Taking advantage of this diplomatic opportunity, Pericles announced the convocation of a great Panhellenic Congress to ensure free navigation and peace among all parties (Plut. *Per.* 17, with comments by Stadter 1989: 201ff.). Perhaps this ambitious idea, which was crushed by the Peloponnesians' mistrust, was the first attempt to achieve something akin to a "general peace" (*koine eirene*) between the Hellenes. In any case, the Spartans and their allies invaded Attica when the pact of 451 expired, which left the dispute unresolved and eventually necessitated the negotiation of a balanced and realistic accord. The treaty of the "Thirty Years' Peace" of 446/5 recognized the Athenian empire, while at the same time confirming the Spartan coalition's dominance on the Greek mainland (*StV* 156). This excellent diplomatic instrument acknowledged the right to neutrality and prescribed arbitration for the resolution of differences between the contracting parties, but still failed to stabilize the Greek political map. Only 15 years later, in 431, the Peloponnesian War (431–404) broke out. It is worthwhile to read Thucydides' first book and draw our own conclusions about whether or not this "Great War" was inescapable (see also Tritle, this vol.). The so-called Peace of Nicias (421) was technically based on *spondai* for 50 years and a subsequent *symmachia* between Athens and Sparta. Rather than resolving conflicts, it only succeeded in further muddling international relations, until Sparta finally achieved victory.

It was only after the Corinthian War that Greek diplomacy managed to create a new institution of international law that overcame the provisional nature of treaties in the form of *spondai*. This was the *koine eirene*. In 386 the "King's Peace" (*StV* 242) inaugurated a series of common peace treaties, ranging over 50 years, leading to the "League of Corinth" in 337 (*StV* 403), and even inspiring the foundation of the Hellenic League under Antigonus and Demetrius in 303/2 (*StV* 446). Successively adapted and refined, these general peace treaties contain fundamental changes: the diplomatic instrument is designated as *eirene* and is now formally and properly a peace treaty; as in the modern law of nations, the peace treaty is concluded for an unlimited duration and therefore politically and legally terminates war. It is therefore not restricted to simply containing the conflict while leaving open the possibility of an eventual renewal of hostilities after the accord's expiration (as usually occurred with long-term *spondai*);[37] the pact ceases to be bilateral, restricted to two parties, and becomes genuinely multilateral, extending to all Greek states (whether adherent to the pact or not); it consecrates as universal the principle of *polis* autonomy; and beginning with the common peace concluded at Athens in 371, the contracting parties also swear to a guarantee-clause which obliges all parties to ward off with arms any assault against these agreements of peace and independence.[38] Politically and legally, this was, without doubt, the first great diplomatic movement in the history of Greece to organize peace on a general level.[39]

Notes

1 Martin 1940: 7ff. offers a good introduction to the general conditions of Greek international life. For *stasis*, see Gehrke 1985. Translations of Greek authors are taken from the Loeb Classical Library (A. T. Murray for Homer, C. F. Smith for Thucydides).

2 See, for example, Adcock and Mosley 1975: 14ff.; Ilari 1980: 373ff., and, masterfully, Will 1979–82.

3 "Trop souvent on commet l'erreur qui consiste à identifier l'histoire du droit international et l'histoire des idées sur ce droit" (Schwarzenberger), cited by Bierzanek 1960: 121; cf. Martin 1940: 493, 585ff.

4 The pouring of libations (to the gods) served to seal an agreement between belligerents; by extension it referred to the diplomatic instrument solemnized by the libation: Baltrusch 1994: 92ff.

5 See Santi 1985 for the vocabulary. For an accurate account, see Heuss 1946: 56 n.18; Fernández 1975: I, 94 n.3; Bravo 1980: 977ff. Ilari 1980: 38ff. Baltrusch 1994: 94 n.2.

6 Schmitt 1983: 33; Baltrusch 1994: 94. See also Paradisi 1974: 312 (with a quotation of Rousseau); Nowag 1983: 99–100.

7 Mele's masterful book (1979) is indispensable on this subject.

8 On these customs and institutions, see Bierzanek 1960; Wéry 1967; Ducrey 1968; Fernández 1975: II, nos. 1–7, 14–16; Nowag 1983: 98–99, 107ff.; Baltrusch 1994: 97 n.30, 104ff.; and, especially, Karavites 1992.

9 Glotz 1904: 135ff., 151–52; Trümpy 1950: 183–84. See also Benveniste 1969: I, 342–44, and Karavites 1992: 18ff.

10 As noted, correctly, by Baltrusch 1994: 105, 112.

11 *Il.* 4.245ff., 267ff.; 4.158–59. In the Achaean assembly Agamemnon had already mentioned the possibility of agreeing to *horkia pista* with the Trojans: *Il.* 2.123–4.

12 After all, the gods cannot violate a pact of which they themselves are named guarantors. Cf. also Karavites 1992: 69 n.45.

13 *Il.* 4.14–19. Meanwhile, the combatants have realized that Paris' disappearance is Zeus' doing and that his fate will determine whether the war is to go on or peace to be restored (4.82–84).

14 *Il.* 4.67, 72; 7.351–2: cf. Fernández 1975: II, 14; Karavites 1992: 78, 176.

15 "The religious ritual of the *horkia* ceremony prepared the contracting parties to enter into the type of binding political friendship which imposed reciprocal obligations and duties upon the parties ... *Horkia*, on the other hand, could denote pledges accompanied by oaths, pledges accompanied by sacrifice in confirmation of the pledges, the sacred items employed in confirmation of the newly established relationship, and, by extension, the agreement consecrated by the ceremonial procedure" (Karavites 1992: 65, 76).

16 As in Aristophanes' *Peace* and in the statue of Eirene carrying Ploutos by Kephisodotos: Keil 1916: 48; Pritchett 1979: 161.

17 See also Baltrusch 1994: 95 n.13, 124 n.188, 148, 204; Grewe 1997 for the concept of a peace treaty.

18 For the normative structure and sources of Greek international law, see Alonso 2003a.

19 Hdt. 2.181.1 (and Hdt. 2.161.4; 4.159.5), not included in Bengtson 1975. As in the case of Achaeans and Trojans, the *philotes* agreement closes a period of direct war.

20 This last institution, in reality, socialized the values of guest-friendship: the correspondence between *philos* and *xenos* (Benveniste) can be seen, for example, in Hdt. 1.69–70.1 and 2.182.2; 3.39.2 (Diod. Sic. 1.95.3).

21 Diod. Sic. 28.15.2; App., *Syr.* 6: see Will 1982: II, 197–98.

22 Pol. 21.43.1; App., *Syr.* 38: see Will 1982: II, 221ff.

23 The stance adopted by Polybius (4.31.3) is probably representative of the prevailing enlightened circles: "That war is a terrible thing I agree, but it is not so terrible that we should submit to anything in order to avoid it."

24 *StV* 280, l. 23–26 (tr. Harding 1985). See also ibid. nos. 188, 193, 201–02, among others.

25 *StV* 280, l. 12 15 (tr. Harding 1985).

26 See Mosley 1974: 49, and the comment by Bengtson 1975: 242. If we take this practice of Greek diplomacy into account, Polybius' criticism (4.15.8–11) of the resolution of the Aetolian *koinon* is more understandable.

27 See also Thuc. 7.18.2–3, and Busolt 1904: III 2, 1355; Alonso 1987: 38ff.

28 The same question should be asked, conversely, about the reasons for Sparta's inactivity (against Attika) after its victory over Athens at Tanagra in Boeotia in 457.

29 Meng 2000: 1339. The latter was the case in the war between the Latin American states and the German Reich in World War II.

30 See Alonso 1995, and Klose 1972: 148ff.

31 For Spartan delays in the Persian Wars because of the Hyakinthia and other religious scruples, see Hdt. 7.107, 120; 9.7–11.

32 See Popp 1957; Pritchett 1971: 113ff., 116ff.; 1979: 296ff., 322f.; Lonis 1979: 95ff.; Hanson 1991: 202f.; Alonso 1995: 218ff.

33 Even if a direct attack on a state's territory automatically resulted in an immediate state of war between the parties, this would not necessarily preclude the existence of other reasons for going to war. But in such cases the *casus belli* was a subjective determination.

34 See Gauthier 1972: 209ff.; Bravo 1980, and Gauthier's reply 1982.

35 See Ducrey 1968: 4 n.2; Klose 1972: 152 n.659 (against Bengtson 1963: 102); Bravo 1980: 844ff., 858ff. (and Gauthier's comments, 1982: 558ff.); Pritchett 1991: 86ff., 137f. No consensus has been achieved.

36 See Lonis 1979: 25ff.; Connor 1988; Hanson 1989: 27ff., 222f. For a comparative perspective, see Raaflaub and Rosenstein 1999.

37 Unlike Baltrusch 1994: 92ff., 123–24, 187, 192, I do not believe that the expiration of the *spondai* automatically signaled a return to war between the parties; cf. Hampl 1938: 2. The fact that the reasons for the conflict had not disappeared (although they may have become less important with the passage of time), did not negate the obligation to resuscitate the war in accordance with established procedures (discussed earlier). The resulting situation, I think, was a mixture of legal uncertainty and a *de facto* persistence of *epimeixia*. This explains the behavior of Argos in 420, already *aspondos* but sending ambassadors, and not heralds, to Sparta (Thuc. 5.40–1), and treating war as a possible outcome, not an existing state (5.44.1). On the other hand, the Athenian *spondai* (5.47.1: *StV* 193) with the Argives and the Mantineans were not post-war treaties, though those with the Eleans were (Alonso 1987: 154ff., 175ff., 479), and there was by no means any suggestion that hostilities would be renewed between the parties once the 100 years had elapsed.

38 Ryder 1965: xvi; Jehne 1994: 26 n.91, 28; Alonso 2003b.

39 I would like to thank Kurt Raaflaub for his corrections and suggestions on the final draft of this chapter.

Abbreviations

FGrHist	Jacoby 1923-
RE	*Realencyclopädie der classischen Altertumswissenschaft*
StV	Bengtson 1975; Schmitt 1969

References

Adcock, F., and D. J. Mosley. 1975. *Diplomacy in Ancient Greece*. London.

Alonso, V. 1987. *Neutralidad y neutralismo en la guerra del Peloponeso (431–404 a.C.)*. Madrid.

——. 1995. "Ultimatum et déclaration de guerre dans la Grèce classique." In E. Frézouls and A. Jacquemin (eds.), *Les relations internationales*, 211–95. Strasbourg.

——. 1999. "395–390/89 a.C., Atenas contra Esparta: ¿ de qué guerra hablamos?" *Athenaeum* 87: 57–77.

Alonso, V. 2001. "Die neutralen Staaten in den Perserkriegen und das griechische Völkerrecht." In D. Papenfuss and V. M. Strocka (eds.), *Gab es das griechische Wunder?* 365–77. Mainz.

——. 2003a. "L'Institution de l'hégémonie: Entre la coutume et le droit écrit." In G. Thür and F. J. Fernández Nieto (eds.), *Symposion 1999*, 339–54. Cologne.

——. 2003b. "La KOINH EIPHNH del 371 y el sistema griego de alianzas." *Les Etudes Classiques* 71: 353–77.

Baltrusch, E. 1994. *Symmachie und Spondai*. Berlin.

Bengtson, H. 1963. "Bemerkungen zu einer Ehreninschrift der Stadt Apollonia am Pontos." *Historia* 12: 96–104.

—— (ed.). 1975. *Die Staatsverträge des Altertums*, II: *Die Verträge der griechisch-römischen Welt von 700–338 v. Chr.* 2nd ed. Munich.

Benveniste, E. 1969. *Le Vocabulaire des institutions Indo-Européennes*. Paris.

Bickerman, E. 1950. "Remarques sur le droit des gens dans la Grèce classique." *Revue historique de droit français et étranger* 4: 99–127.

Bierzanek, P. 1960. "Sur les Origines du Droit de la Guerre et la Paix." Revue historique de droit français et étranger 38: 83–123.

Bravo, B. 1980. "Sylân." *Annali della Scuola Normale Superiore di Pisa* 10: 675–987.

Brunt, P. A. 1993. *Studies in Greek History and Thought*. Oxford.

Buraselis, K. 1982. *Das hellenistische Makedonien und die Ägäis*. Munich.

Busolt, G. 1904. *Griechische Geschichte bis zur Schlacht bei Chaeroneia*, III. 2. Gotha.

Carlier, P. 1991. "La procédure de décision politique du monde mycénien à l'époque archaïque." In D. Musti (ed.), *La transizione dal miceneo all'alto arcaismo*, 85–95. Rome.

Connor, W. R. 1988. "Early Greek Land Warfare as Symbolic Expression." *Past & Present* 119: 3–29.

Diels, H., and Kranz, W. 1961. *Die Fragmente der Vorsokratiker*, I. 10th ed. Berlin.

Ducrey, P. 1968. *Le Traitement des prisonniers de guerre dans la Grèce antique*. Paris.

Effenterre, H. van, and Ruzé, F. 1994. *Nomima: Recueil d'inscriptions politiques et juridiques de l'archaïsme grec*. 2 vols. Rome.

Fernández Nieto, F. J. 1975. *Los acuerdos bélicos en la antigua Grecia*. Santiago de Compostela.

Finley, M. I. 1977. *The World of Odysseus*. 2nd edn. London.

Gauthier, P. 1972. *Symbola*. Nancy.

——. 1982. "Les saisies licites aux dépens des étrangers dans les cités grecques." *Revue historique de droit français et étranger* 60: 553–75.

Gehrke, Hans-Joachim. 1985. *Stasis. Untersuchungen zu den inneren Kriegen in den griechischen Staaten des 5. und 4. Jh. v. Chr.* Munich.

Glotz, G. 1904. *La solidarité de la famille dans le droit criminel en Grèce*. Paris.

Grewe, W. G. 1997. "Peace Treaties." In Macalister-Smith 2000: 938–46.

Gschnitzer, F. 1973. "Proxenos." *RE* Suppl. XIII: 629–730.

——. 2001. *Kleine Schriften zum griechischen und römischen Altertum*, I. Stuttgart.

Habicht, C. 1997. *Athens from Alexander to Antony*. Cambridge, MA.

Hampl, F. 1938. *Die griechischen Staatsverträge des 4. Jahrhunderts v. Chr.* Leipzig.

Hanson, V. D. 1989. *The Western Way of War: Infantry Battle in Classical Greece*. New York.

——. 1991. *Hoplites: The Classical Greek Battle Experience*. London and New York.

——. 2001. "Democratic Warfare, Ancient and Modern." In D. R. McCann and B. S. Strauss (eds.), *War and Democracy: A Comparative Study of the Korean War and the Peloponnesian War*, 3–33. Armonk.

Harding, P. 1985. *From the End of the Peloponnesian War to the Battle of Ipsus*. Translated Documents of Greece and Rome 2. Cambridge.

Heuss, A. 1946. "Die archaische Zeit Griechenlands als geschichtliche Epoche." *Antike & Abendland* 2: 26–62.

Hölkeskamp, K.-J. 1999. *Schiedsrichter, Gesetzgeber und Gesetzgebung im archaischen Griechenland*. Stuttgart.

Ilari, V. 1980. *Guerra e diritto nel mondo antico.* Milano.

Jacoby, F. 1923–. *Die Fragmente der griechischen Historiker.* Multiple vols. Berlin, then Leiden.

Jehne, M. 1994. *Koine Eirene.* Stuttgart.

Karavites, P. 1982. *Capitulations and Greek Interstate Relations: The Reflection of Humanistic Ideals in Political Events.* Göttingen.

——. 1992. *Promise-Giving and Treaty-Making: Homer and the Near East.* Leiden.

Keil, B. 1916. *EIPHNH: Eine philologisch-antiquarische Untersuchung.* Leipzig.

Klose, P. 1972. *Die völkerrechtliche Ordnung der hellenistischen Staatenwelt in der Zeit von 280–168 v. Chr.* Munich.

Loenen, D. 1953. *Polemos: Een Studie over Oorlog in de Griekse Óudheid.* Amsterdam.

Lonis, R. 1979. *Guerre et religion en Grèce à l'époque classique.* Paris.

Macalister-Smith, P. (ed.). 2000. *Encyclopedia of Public International Law,* III. Amsterdam.

Martin, V. 1940. *La vie internationale dans la Grèce des cités (VIe–IVe s. av. J.-C.).* Paris.

Meier, C. 1990. "Die Rolle des Krieges im klassischen Athen." *Historische Zeitschrift* 251: 555–605.

Mele, A. 1979. *Il commercio greco arcaico: prexis ed emporie.* Naples.

Meng, W. 2000. "War." In Macalister-Smith 2000: 1334–42.

Momigliano, A. 1960. "Some Observations on the Causes of War in Ancient Historiography." In A. Momigliano, *Secondo Contributo alla Storia degli Studi Classici,* 13–27. Rome.

Mosley, D. J. 1974. "On Greek Enemies Becoming Allies." *Ancient Society* 5: 43–50.

Nowag, W. 1983. *Raub und Beute in der archaischen Zeit der Griechen.* Frankfurt.

Paradisi, B. 1974. *Civitas Maxima: Studi di storia del diritto internazionale.* Florence.

Phillipson, C. 1911. *The International Law and Custom of Ancient Greece and Rome.* London.

Popp, H. 1957. *Die Einwirkung von Vorzeichen, Opfern und Festen auf die Kriegführung der Griechen im 5. und 4. Jahrhundert v. Chr.* Erlangen.

Pritchett, K. 1971, 1979, 1991. *The Greek State at War,* I, III, V. Berkeley.

Raaflaub, K. 1997. "Politics and Interstate Relations in the World of Early Greek *Poleis*: Homer and Beyond." *Antichthon* 31: 1–27.

Raaflaub, K., and Rosenstein, N. (eds.). 1999. *War and Society in the Ancient and Medieval Worlds. Asia, the Mediterranean, Europe, and Mesoamerica.* Cambridge, MA.

Redfield, J. M. 1975. *Nature and Culture in the Iliad: The Tragedy of Hector.* Chicago.

Ryder, T. T. B. 1965. *Koine Eirene.* Oxford.

Santi Amantini, L. 1985. "Semántica storica dei termini Greci relativi alla pace nelle epigrafi anteriori al 387/6 a.C." In M. Sordi (ed.), *La pace nel mondo antico,* 45–68. Milano.

Schmitt, H. H. 1969. *Die Staatsverträge des Altertums,* III: *Die Verträge der griechisch-römischen Welt von 338 bis 200 v. Chr.* Munich.

——. 1983. "Friedenssicherung im griechischen Völkerrecht." In H. Kreutzer (ed.), *Wendepunkte, Acta Ising 1982,* 31–44. Munich.

Scholten, J. B. 2000. *The Politics of Plunder: Aitolians and their Koinon in the Early Hellenistic Era, 279–217 BC.* Berkeley.

Stadter, Philip A. 1989. *A Commentary on Plutarch's Pericles.* Chapel Hill.

Steiner, G. 1984. *Antigones.* New York.

Trümpy, H. 1950. *Kriegerische Fachausdrücke im griechischen Epos.* Basel.

Wéry, M. 1967. "Le Fonctionnement de la diplomatie à l'époque homérique." *Revue internationale du droit de l'antiquité* 14: 169–215.

Will, E. 1979–1982. *Histoire politique du monde hellénistique (323–30 av. J.-C.).* 2 vols. Nancy.

[2]

THE EVOLUTION OF THE CONCEPT OF THE JUST WAR IN INTERNATIONAL LAW

By Joachim von Elbe

Yale University Law School

War, as a social phenomenon, has been defined as "a fight between human societies, in primitive conditions between savage tribes, in the civilized world between states."[1] Ever since history has recorded the activities of organized groups, war has been one of its principal topics.[2] Since it appears to be a fundamental element in their life, its explanation has been sought in the basic conditions of their existence.[3] Thus, it is said, the law of growth and expansion, innate as a natural tendency in the individual being as well as in organized societies,[4] compels them with irresistible force to assert their rights and to seek "security"[5] by combating others. War, it seems, is ordained by nature and is an inevitable result of competition.

The civilization of antiquity is to be credited with serious attempts to overcome the natural state of war by institutionalizing it as part of religious and philosophical systems, and even to subject it to the rule of legal principles.[6] Thucydides calls it a "most lawful act when men take vengeance

---

[1] Encyclopedia Britannica, 14th ed., Vol. 23, article "War," p. 321; see also A. Johnson, in 15 Encyclopedia of the Social Sciences, p. 331. The term war is generally applied to "armed conflict between population groups conceived of as organic unities." Dickinson, G. L., Causes of International War (London, 1920), p. 7.

[2] Davie, The Evolution of War (New Haven, 1929), pp. 5, 9 ff.

[3] A systematic examination of the causes of war may be found in Barnes, The Genesis of the World War (New York, 1927), pp. 1–33. From the vast literature dealing with this subject may be quoted Bakeless, The Economic Causes of Modern War (New York, 1921); Crosby, International War, Its Causes and Its Cure (London, 1919); Reports of the Conference on the Cause and Cure of War, 1925–1933; Eagleton, Analysis of the Problem of War (New York, 1937), p. 541; Rogge, *Nationale Friedenspolitik* (Berlin, 1934), p. 21 ff.

[4] See the significant statement by Baron Reijiro Wakatsuki on "The Aims of Japan" (13 Foreign Affairs, 585): "When you know this historical background and understand this overflowing vitality of our race you will see the impossibility of compelling us to stay still within the confines of our little island home. We are destined to grow and expand overseas."

[5] "Security! The term signifies more indeed than the maintenance of a people's homeland, or even of their territories beyond the seas. It also means the maintenance of the world's respect for them, the maintenance of their economic interests, everything, in a word, which goes to make up the grandeur, the life itself, of the nation." Jules Cambon, The Permanent Bases of Foreign Policy (Council on Foreign Relations, New York, 1931), p. 25.

[6] Phillipson, The International Law and Custom of Ancient Greece and Rome, Vol. II (London, 1911), p. 167; Wegner, *Geschichte des Völkerrechts* (Stuttgart, 1936), p. 35: "We notice everywhere in the sources of Antiquity that the ancients conceived war and its extent as instituted by Divine command. In this conception, war is raised above the stage of blind passion; it has become a legal institution"; Holland, Lectures on International Law (London, 1933), p. 244 ff.; Leist, *Graeco-Italische Rechtsgeschichte* (Jena, 1884), p. 431;

666   THE AMERICAN JOURNAL OF INTERNATIONAL LAW

upon an enemy and an aggressor."[7] Aristotle speaks of the "art of war" which ought to be practised "against men who, though intended by nature to be governed, will not submit; for war of such kind is naturally just."[8] The object of war must be the establishment of peace.[9] As to the causes of war, Plato finds "at the root of all wars" the necessity to enlarge our borders. "The original healthy state is no longer sufficient. . . . The country which was enough to support the original inhabitants will be too small now."[10] While Greek thought on the problem of war produced but a loosely-stated set of political and philosophical ideas, the Romans, in their *ius belli ac pacis* and the writings of historians and philosophers, evolved a body of rules that were destined deeply to influence the growth of the European concept of war. A distinction is made between the institution of war as an element of the *ratio naturalis* or natural world order, and individual wars.[11] The former is accepted as part of the unwritten laws of nature which men may not alter; recourse to arms in a given case, however, may be had only for an injury suffered and after the refusal of the wrongdoer to atone for it.[12] Before hostilities are commenced, a collegium of priests, the fetials, determines whether the required conditions for going to war exist. The fetial procedure originated in the belief—common to all peoples of antiquity and even traceable to modern times—that battles are decided by providential interference and that victory is a gift of the gods who thereby legitimatize the conquests made in war.[13] Hence scrupulous precautions were taken to assure beyond doubt that a war was agreeable to the deity. A war commenced in accordance with the rules of the fetial proceedings was "justum," which means legally correct,[14] and at the same time "pium," *viz.*, sanc-

---

Ballis, The Legal Position of War: Changes in its Practice and Theory from Plato to Vattel (The Hague, 1937), p. 19.

[7] Alcibiades, VII, 68, 1, 2. Tr. by FitzGerald, A., Peace and War in Antiquity (London, 1931), pp. 11, 75 ff.   [8] Politics, I, 3, 8. Tr. by FitzGerald, *op. cit.*, pp. 29, 94.

[9] Nicomachean Ethics, Book X, Ch. VI, XVII, 6; Politics, VII, 14.

[10] Republic, II, 373 b; FitzGerald, *op. cit.*, pp. 14, 79. For further references to Greek authors, see Ballis, *op. cit.*, p. 17 ff.   [11] Leist, *op. cit.*, p. 456 ff.

[12] Seckel, *Über Krieg und Recht in Rom* (Berlin, 1915), pp. 9, 13; Leist, *op. cit.*, p. 439.

[13] Leist, *op. cit.*, pp. 432 ff., 435, 438, 440, 447, 452 ff.; Bender, *Antikes Völkerrecht* (Bonn, 1901), p. 13.

[14] Writers disagree as to the true significance of the fetial procedure. While a minority maintains that the fetials had to pass upon the equity or intrinsic justice of the cause (for instance, Müller-Jochum, *Die Geschichte des Völkerrechts im Altertum* [Leipzig, 1848], p. 155; Strisower, *Der Krieg und die Völkerrechtsordnung* [Wien, 1919], p. 42; Vanderpol, *La doctrine scolastique du Droit de guerre* [Paris, 1919], p. 44; Frank, The Import of the Fetial Institution [Classical Philology, VII], pp. 335, 339 ff.; Ballis, *op. cit.*, p. 30), a majority of writers holds that the fetial procedure was merely designed to invest a war with the character of a formally correct action. See Phillimore, Commentaries upon International Law, Vol. III (London, 1879), p. 79; Salvioli, *Le concept de la guerre juste* (Paris, 1918), p. 13 ff.; Wegner, *op. cit.*, p. 58; Phillipson, *op. cit.*, pp. 180, 193, 327 ff.: "The fetials determined whether a war was 'iustum'—'bellum nullum nisi iustum'—that is whether the preliminary proceedings were conducted in a legal manner, whether they fulfilled the requirements of

tioned by religion and, consequently, could be expected to receive divine blessings.[15]

It remained to Christianity to give material content to the formal concept of the *justum bellum* of the Romans. It is true, the institution of war is at first challenged by the early Church; its adherents boldly predict that the conversion of the world will lead to the establishment of perpetual peace. War is held to be a consequence of original sin; no Christian may, therefore, enlist as a soldier.[16] However, when, after Constantine's conversion, state and army ceased to be instruments of persecution against the Christian subjects of the Roman Empire, the stigma which the originally pacific spirit of the Church had attached to war gradually disappeared.[17] War, under certain conditions, was recognized as a necessity; the Christian concept of the just war furnishes rules for limiting and guarding it in accordance with the precepts of the new religion.

One is bound to misapprehend the significance of that doctrine if one loses sight of the political and intellectual conditions under which the Christian idea of the just war was born. Augustine is credited with having first

---

the prescribed law"; Seckel, *op. cit.*, p. 13; Buret, *Le Droit de la guerre chez les Romains* (Paris, 1888), p. 16: "Les Fétiaux étaient juges de la justice de la guerre, mais seulement dans le sens formel, et non dans le sens d'équité"; Le Fur, "*Guerre juste et juste paix*," 26 *Rev. Gén. Dr. Int. Pub.*, p. 9 ff.; Kosters, *Eenige geschiedkundige mededeelingen omtrent het begrip "justum bellum"* (Amsterdam, 1930), quoted by van der Molen, *Alberico Gentili* (Amsterdam, 1937), p. 93: "The standard for the legality of war was merely formal. The fact whether the grievances and demands, declared as just by Rome, were really well founded, did not play a part." Roman historians, however, extensively discuss the sufficiency or insufficiency of motives for war. A whole set of valid grounds for war can be gleaned from their writings. See Phillipson, *op. cit.*, p. 182 ff.; Bender, *op. cit.*, p. 15 ff.; Leist, *op. cit.*, p. 442 ff.; Lecky, History of European Morals, Vol. II (New York, 1893), p. 258. Thus Livius (Hist., IX, 1) lets the Samnite C. Pontius explain the reasons for going to war in the famous terms: "Justum est bellum quibus necessarium et pia arma quibus nulla nisi in armis relinquitur spes."

[15] Cicero's remarks with respect to *bellum justum* closely relate to the fetial procedure. In De Officiis (I, 12, 38; FitzGerald, *op. cit.*, pp. 40, 103 ff.) he declares that "when a war is fought out for supremacy and alien glory is the object of war, it must still not fail to start from the same motives which I said a moment ago were the only righteous grounds for going to war." As to those grounds, he had said (De Officiis, I, 11, 34–36; FitzGerald, *op. cit.*, pp. 43 ff., 106): "The only excuse . . . for going to war is that we may live in peace unharmed. As for war, human laws touching it are drawn up in the fetial code of the Roman people under all guaranties of religion; and from this it may be gathered that no war is just, unless it is entered upon after an official demand for satisfaction has been submitted, or warning has been given and a formal declaration made."

[16] Wünsch, *Evangelische Ethik des Politischen* (Tübingen, 1936), p. 585; Erdmann, *Die Entstehung des Kreuzzugsgedankens* (Stuttgart, 1936), p. 3; Lecky, *op. cit.*, Vol. II, p. 248; Salvioli, *op. cit.*, p. 19; Wright, R. F., Medieval Internationalism (London, 1930), p. 135 ff.; van der Molen, *op. cit.*, p. 95 ff.; Beaufort, *La guerre comme instrument de secours ou de punition* (La Haye, 1933), p. 3 ff.; Nys, *Les origines du droit international* (Haarlem, 1894), p. 44 ff.; Strisower, *op. cit.*, p. 44.

[17] Ballis, *op. cit.*, pp. 35, 37, 41; Erdmann, *op. cit.*, p. 3 ff.; Wünsch, *op. cit.*, p. 585; Lecky, *op. cit.*, pp. 247 ff., 250 ff., 260; Beaufort, *op. cit.*, p. 8 ff.

molded it into the form of a scientific system.[18] At the time he entered his ecclesiastic career the Christian character of the Empire was of very recent date and the deep impression created among the early Christians by that change was still unabated.[19] The Empire, after its Christianization, seemed to represent the *civitas dei* on earth, where state and Church are under the same head, thus symbolizing the political and spiritual unity of Christendom.[20] In such a unitary system, which is essentially a system of peace, war takes a strictly regulated place.[21] Theologically, the institution of war is explained as a means of punishment which God inflicts upon the sinful world; it appears as a sort of "police action taken by the Sovereign Judge to restore order and to lead the people back to the obedience of the law."[22] However, wars that must be suffered because they are ordained by Providence are to be distinguished from those which, lacking that character, are to be avoided. By what criterion can it be determined that a war falls within the permissible ones? The answer is that a war must be "just" in the substantive sense of the term. Just are those *"quae ulciscuntur injurias,"* i.e., which are waged to redress a wrong suffered. Thus, wars must always be preceded by an injury;[23] those waged for personal motives, like territorial aggrandizement, as practised by the Romans for many centuries, are *"grande latrocinium."*[24] The injury may consist either in the neglect of a state to suppress crimes committed by its subjects, or in attacks upon the rights of others. Consequently, the just war, as a procedure for the repression of wrongs, is either a punitive action or in the nature of a civil suit for

[18] In *De Civitate Dei, Contra Faustum* and *Epistula ad Bonifacium*. The relevant Latin texts are quoted by Beaufort, *op. cit.*, p. 14 ff. See also Scott, The Spanish Origin of International Law, Pt. I, Francisco de Vitoria and His Law of Nations (Carnegie Endowment for International Peace, 1934), p. 183 ff.; a survey of Augustinian texts dealing with the right of war, given by de la Brière, in 44 *Rev. Gén. Dr. Int. Pub.* (1937), p. 139.

[19] Troeltsch, E., *Augustin, die christliche Antike und das Mittelalter* (München, 1915), pp. 7, 51.

[20] Hearnshaw, Some Great Political Idealists of the Christian Era (London, 1937), p. 10 ff.: "The Church and the Empire were reconciled. Three centuries of dualism were brought to an end. A Respublica Christiana was, in theory at least, set up—a Christian State in which the Emperor as pontifex maximus became episcopus episcoporum."

[21] Beaufort, *op. cit.*, p. 28; de la Brière, *loc. cit.*, p. 144.

[22] Combès, *La doctrine politique de Saint Augustin* (Paris, 1927), p. 269 ff.; Beaufort, *op. cit.*, p. 20: "There exists no uncertainty any more; war in itself is not contrary to the Christian concept of life"; Fuchs, *Augustin und der antike Friedensgedanke* (Berlin, 1926), p. 16; Bernheim, *Mittelalterliche Zeitanschauungen*, Vol. I (Tübingen, 1918), p. 29 ff.; Ter Meulen, *Der Gedanke der internationalen Organisation*, Vol. I (Haag, 1917), p. 35; Mausbach, *Die Ethik des hl. Augustin*, Vol. I (Freiburg, 1909), pp. 313, 337, 426 ff.

[23] Beaufort, *op. cit.*, p. 21 ff.: "It is the crime of others which constitutes the justifying reason for war . . . this central and predominant idea that war can be justified only by the injustice of another"; Erdmann, *op. cit.*, p. 5 ff.: "Thus, Augustine was the originator of the idea of the war guilt which he introduced into history and which through him became the decisive element in the European concept of war"; Regout, *La doctrine de la guerre juste de Saint Augustin à nos jours* (Paris, 1934), p. 42.

[24] Strisower, *op. cit.*, p. 44, n. 14; Scott, *op. cit.*, p. 181; Beaufort, *op. cit.*, p. 23 ff.

CONCEPT OF JUST WAR IN INTERNATIONAL LAW 669

damages.[25] Punishment and measure of damages are determined by the purpose of the just war; its aim is not primarily victory, but the establishment of peace, *viz.*, a state of *"tranquillitas ordinis"* or ordered harmony where all things have their allotted place.[26] Thus, the concept of the just peace is from the outset closely associated with the idea of the just war.[27] No specific rules, however, are as yet laid down with respect to the content of the peace; it must, in general, restore the injured rights and lead to a well-ordered concord among men.

The scholastic doctrine of the just war as expounded by the greatest moralist of the Middle Ages, Thomas Aquinas,[28] is built upon the principles of Augustine whose teachings are reduced to three fundamental rules: A war, in order to be just, must (1) be waged under the authority of a prince as the responsible leader of a nation, not by a private individual; the latter may apply to a tribunal for the defense of his rights.[29] (2) It must have a just cause, and (3) the belligerents must be animated by the right intention, namely, to advance the good or to avoid the evil.[30] While to Augustine the injury itself provides the just cause for war, Thomas Aquinas demands some fault on the part of the wrongdoer: his culpability which deserves punishment is the justifying reason for going to war.[31] The just war is primarily in the nature of a punitive action against the wrongdoer for his subjective guilt rather than his objectively wrongful act.[32] Again, its aim must be peace in the Augustinian sense of the term, *viz.*, the maintenance of justice in the interest of the common good.[33]

The chief contribution of the numerous scholastics and canonists who,

[25] "A just war is wont to be described as one that avenges wrongs, when a nation or a state has to be punished for refusing to make amends for the wrongs inflicted by its subjects, or to restore what has been seized unjustly." See Scott, *op. cit.*, p. 192; Regout, *op. cit.*, p. 43; van der Molen, *op. cit.*, p. 97; Beaufort, *op. cit.*, pp. 20, 29.

[26] "Pax omnium rerum tranquillitatis ordinis. Ordo est parium dispariumque rerum, sua cuique loca tribuens, dispositio." *De Civitate Dei*, XIX, 13; Scott, *op. cit.*, pp. 185 ff., 189, 193 (*Ep. ad Bonif.*): "We do not seek peace in order to be at war, but we go to war that we may have peace"; Regout, *op. cit.*, p. 40; Beaufort, *op. cit.*, p. 28; de la Brière, *"Les étapes de la tradition théologique concernant le droit de juste guerre,"* loc. cit., p. 141 ff.

[27] de la Brière, *"Les droits de la juste victoire selon la tradition des théologiens catholiques,"* 32 *Rev. Gén. Dr. Int. Pub.* (1925), pp. 366 ff., 375, 382; Le Fur, *"Guerre juste et juste paix,"* loc. cit., p. 349 ff.; Regout, *op. cit.*, p. 40 ff.; Beaufort, *op. cit.*, p. 16.

[28] *Summa theologica. Secunda Secundae, Quaestio XL.* French translation of the relevant passages by Vanderpol, *op. cit.*, p. 308 ff.; see also Scott, *op. cit.*, p. 188 ff.; van der Molen, *op. cit.*, p. 101 ff.

[29] Scott, *op. cit.*, p. 192; Regout, *op. cit.*, p. 81; Nys, *Le Droit international*, Vol. I (Paris, 1912), p. 227 ff.; Beaufort, *op. cit.*, p. 56 ff.; Vanderpol, *op. cit.*, p. 309 ff.

[30] Scott, *op. cit.*, p. 192; Schilling, *Die christlichen Soziallehren* (Köln, 1926), p. 180; van der Molen, *op. cit.*, p. 102.

[31] "Ut scl. illi qui impugnantur propter aliquam culpam impugnationem mereantur." Regout, *op. cit.*, pp. 81, 83 ff., 91 ff., 141; Scott, *op. cit.*, p. 192; Beaufort, *op. cit.*, p. 62; Vanderpol, *op. cit.*, p. 251; de la Brière, loc. cit., Vol. 44, p. 148.

[32] Regout, *op. cit.*, pp. 83 ff., 92 ff.   [33] Regout, *op. cit.*, p. 84; Scott, *op. cit.*, p. 193.

after Aquinas, further elaborated the doctrine of the just war consists in detailed distinctions and subdivisions with regard to the just cause.[34]   On the whole, their teachings are closely in line with the principles laid down by the great Fathers of the Church, especially in their emphasis that the purpose of a war and one of the principal conditions of its justice is the restoration of the status of peace.[35]

The idea of the *Respublica Christiana* had ceased to be effective as a political reality when most of the scholastic treatises on the war problem were written.   The general trend of medieval society was towards the disintegration of unity and the establishment of independent political entities rather than the development of a unitary system.[36]   The anarchical situation which the breaking-up of the Christian world into sovereign states had created became particularly serious in Italy where the disappearance of the imperial authority had given rise to the coming into existence of innumerable small communities that were torn asunder by internecine strife and were in continual conflict with each other.[37]   To limit their interminable wars, a new principle for the regulation of their mutual relations had to be found. "When the Emperor was no longer recognized as superior, his place was taken by the Law."[38]   The *ius commune* of the Empire continued to exercise a "supra-national power" for the maintenance of justice and peace in the world. The limitation and regulation of wars between the members of the Empire thus becomes a matter of positive law; it is treated by

[34] Regout, *op. cit.*, pp. 94 ff., 142; Vanderpol, *op. cit.*, *passim;* Nys, *Les origines du droit international* (1894), p. 105 ff.; Strisower, *op. cit.*, p. 45; Beaufort, *op. cit.*, p. 63 ff.; Finke, *Der Gedanke des heiligen und gerechten Krieges*, p. 18 ff.

[35] The Reformation did not alter the fundamental idea that war must have a just cause if it is to be in harmony with the Christian faith. See Troeltsch, E., *Die Soziallehren der christlichen Kirchen und Gruppen* (Tübingen, 1912), pp. 549, 563 ff.; Ballis, *op. cit.*, p. 66 ff. To Luther, war is a necessary element of the world order; it is a consequence of original sin. The prince, however, is in duty bound to limit its occurrence. See Maine, International Law (New York, 1888), p. 209.   War is justified only if it is necessary to protect the peace and well-being of the subjects against external attacks. Wars of aggression are unjust. Troeltsch, *op. cit.*, p. 563.   The Augsburg Confession of 1530, Art. XVI, expressly recognizes the right of the Christian ruler to wage "just wars" (*rechte Kriege*), without, however, defining the term. As to the Calvinist conception of war, see Wünsch, *op. cit.*, p. 587, and Troeltsch, *op. cit.*, p. 725 ff.

[36] van Vollenhoven, The Law of Peace (London, 1936), p. 6 ff.; Carlyle, History of Mediæval Political Theory, Vol. VI (New York, 1922), pp. 111, 127; von Eicken, *Geschichte und System der Mittelalterlichen Weltanschauungen* (Stuttgart, 1887), pp. 213, 216, 222, 235, 279, 302.   [37] Carlyle, *op. cit.*, pp. 11, 123.

[38] Woolf, C. N. S., Bartolus of Sassoferrato, His Position in the History of Medieval Political Thought (Cambridge, 1913), pp. 198, 201, 208 ff.; see also Nys, *Le Droit international*, Vol. I (1912), p. 229: ". . . l'ancienne idée de l'unité romaine ne disparaît point; elle est invoquée pour justifier une théorie nouvelle: celle de l'empire du droit romain dans les relations internationales"; Oppenheim-Lauterpacht, International Law (5th ed.), Vol. I, p. 73; Verdross, *Völkerrecht* (Berlin, 1937), p. 6; van Vollenhoven, *op. cit.*, pp. 35 ff., 82.

secular lawyers of the Middle Ages in the familiar terms of the *Corpus Iuris*.[39]

Among the first to deal with war in that fashion is the great Italian Postglossator, Bartolus (1314–1357). The principal question as to whether the independent communities within the Roman Empire may engage among each other in so-called public wars, *viz.*, those regularly waged between the Romans and a foreign people or between the Emperor and his rebellious subjects and which confer upon the belligerents the specific rights of *captivitatis et postliminii*, is answered in the affirmative.[40] No mention is made of a justifying reason.[41] The just cause appears, however, in connection with reprisals, which Bartolus treats as identical with war.[42] This remedy, although originally designed as a means for settling private claims, was frequently resorted to by independent princes and communities to vindicate their injured rights after the paramount power of the Emperor had *de facto* vanished.[43] The legality of reprisals [44] is conditioned upon two requirements: the authority of a superior and a just cause,[45] the latter being given if "*dominus, gens, vel populus requisitus justitiam facere neglexit.*"[46] Since

[39] Woolf, *op. cit.*, pp. 202, 207: ". . . the medieval Italian lawyer, who lived in conditions where Roman law was actually a common law above the conflicting statutes of the Italian cities, naturally went to that common law for rules to guide international relations . . . seeing that the superiority of the Emperor was de facto gone, he did actually turn to the Law Books and the Canons in order to find rules which might regulate the relations of the cities"; van Vollenhoven, *op. cit.*, pp. 35 ff., 56.

[40] *Commentary on Digestum Novum*, Pt. II (ad lib. XLIX Dig. [Bâle ed., 1589, Vol. VI]), *De captivis et postliminii reversiis*, L. XXIV: "Bellum indicitur inter civitatem et civitatem, et in eo locum habeat ius postliminii." See also Woolf, *op. cit.*, p. 199 ff.

[41] A passage in *Commentary on Codex*, Pt. I (Bâle ed., Vol. VII, p. 84), where Bartolus declares it a "bona lex" that the Church makes war upon the Saracens "quia detinent terram nostram" and upon the Turks "quia non possumus aliter ire ad Saracenos," has been interpreted as showing that Bartolus felt the need for a legal ground of war. See Woolf, *op. cit.*, p. 202, n. 3. The passage, however, refers expressly to the Church, which does not wage public wars in the legal sense of the term.

[42] *Tractatus Represaliarum* (Bâle ed., Vol. X), p. 331: "Concedere represalias est indicere bellum." See also Woolf, *op. cit.*, p. 204; Spiegel, "Origin and Development of Denial of Justice," this JOURNAL, Vol. 32 (1938), p. 70; Vanderpol, *op. cit.*, p. 73 ff.; Verdross, *op. cit.*, p. 7.

[43] "Represaliarum materia nec frequens nec quotidiana erat tempore quo in statu debito Romanum vigebat Imperium . . . Postea vero peccata nostra meruerunt quod Romanum Imperium prostratum jaceret per multa tempora, et reges et principes ac etiam civitates, maxime in Italia, saltem de facto in temporalibus dominum non agnoscerent, propter quod de injustitiis ad superiorem non potest haberi regressus, coeperunt represalias frequentari . . ." Bartolus, *Tractatus Represaliarum* (Bâle ed., Vol. X), p. 327.

[44] Bartolus clearly distinguishes between the permissibility of reprisals "de foro conscientiae" and "de foro civili." *Ibid.* He quotes Augustine's definition of the just war as authority for the moral justification of reprisals: "non licet in foro conscientiae facere id quod repugnat naturali rationi; in contrariam quod sint licitae, videtur auctoritas Augustini in libro Quaestionum: Justa bella solent definiri quae ulciscuntur iniurias."

[45] Bartolus, *op. cit.*, p. 327; Woolf, *op. cit.*, p. 205.   [46] Bartolus, *op. cit.*, p. 327.

672   THE AMERICAN JOURNAL OF INTERNATIONAL LAW

a superior judge above the individual communities is wanting, each has to decide for itself whether a legitimate cause for resorting to war or reprisals exists.[47]

The *Treatise on War, Reprisals and Duels*, by Johannes de Legnano,[48] contemporary and compatriot of the great Postglossator, represents the first attempt to deal with the law of war, or, generally, with the legality of the use of force in civil as well as public matters, as a separate whole.[49]   Though identical in approach with Bartolus' treatment, it sharply contrasts with the latter's clear distinction between the legal and ethical aspects of the problem by that peculiar blending of theology, ethics and the Code of Justinian which was to become the main characteristic of the medieval concept of the right of war.[50]   Legnano, like Bartolus, treats war (1) as an institution of the general law of the Empire; (2) in connection with reprisals as an extraordinary remedy.   War originally rests upon Divine law; for its end is peace and tranquillity, and everything that tends to the good proceeds positively from God.[51]   In fact, war is a natural element of the creation; it is a remedy or medicament by which diseases of the world are exterminated.[52] This salutary effect, however, is attributable only to "lawful" wars, *viz.*, those instituted by the law, which allows no wars unless they are declared by an authority which has no superior; for otherwise, redress may be had through appeal to the latter.[53]   The Pope, being the "only Lord of the Earth" may wage war against the infidels, since he has jurisdiction to punish them for sins against the law of nature, and may recover the Holy Land;[54] the Emperor, who is independent in secular matters, conducts "public wars" as defined by the Roman law against peoples outside the Empire, against the Kings of France, Spain and England, and against rebellious Italian cities;[55] not, however, against the Pope, who is the Emperor's superior.[56]   Thus, the standard for the legality of a war within the realm of

[47] Bartolus, *op. cit.*, p. 329: "quis debeat requirere dominum, populum, seu gentem ut faciat justitiam? Respondeo, potestas eius qui concedet represalias, succedit in loco superioris deficientis."

[48] *Tractatus de Bello, de Represaliis et de Duello* (1360), edited by Sir Erskine Holland, in The Classics of International Law, edited by James Brown Scott, No. 8, Oxford, 1917 (Latin text and English translation).   [49] Holland, *loc. cit.*, p. XXXII.

[50] Holland, *loc. cit.*, p. IX; Nys, *Le Droit international*, Vol. I, p. 227 ff.

[51] Legnano, *op. cit.*, pp. 86, 228: "Bella iure divino inducta originaliter."

[52] Legnano, *op. cit.*, pp. 218, 224, 225, 227: "Sometimes the disease has advanced so far that a poisonous medicament is needed, extirpating the matter of disease entirely and such medicament is war to eradicate and exterminate the bad . . . God, as the most high doctor and preserver of the Universe, ordains wars in order that offense may be rooted out . . . God is the governor of the world, and the doctor who eradicates its vices, for the sake of the salvation and conservation of the world."

[53] If, however, the superior should act unlawfully, resistance may be offered. *Ibid.*, p. 289.   [54] Legnano, *op. cit.*, p. 231 ff.

[55] Legnano, *op. cit.*, p. 233.   See also Bartolus, *Tractatus Represaliarum*, p. 331: "Bellum justum non potest indicere nisi ille qui superiorem non habet."   [56] Legnano, *op. cit.*, p. 234.

the Roman law is merely formal; it depends upon the authority that declares it, not the underlying cause. A just cause, however, is required to legalize the recourse to force among those princes and peoples "who do not recognise a superior in fact."[57] Again, the institution of reprisals furnishes the legal rules for wars among the independent communities.[58] Since it is a sort of self-help, it is lawful "to take arms in defense of one's own body."[59]

The concept of reprisals had furnished the early jurists with rules governing the use of force among the "*communitates superiores non recognoscentes*";[60] their fundamental idea of subjecting the exercise of the right of war to the requirement of a just cause remained operative even after the latter had attained the status of full sovereignty.[61] Belli's *Treatise on Military Matters and Warfare*[62] which was written at a time when the Emperor's supremacy had long ceased to exist in reality, demonstrates the close correlation between the legal position of war in a world of sovereign states and the early thesis that force, if employed as a protective means in the absence of a superior authority, musu serve a just cause, namely, the defense or restoration of injured rights. It is true, "nature teaches us to oppose force with force, and arms with arms";[63] thus, "every ruler who is fully independent" may declare war.[64] However, "all good men agree that wars are to be undertaken only for reasons that are at once serious and cogent and just."[65] For "in war there is no other objective than peace, and there is no peace apart from justice."[66] A war is just that is undertaken for the defense or the en-

---

[57] Legnano, *op. cit.*, p. 234.

[58] Legnano, *op. cit.*, p. 307 ff.: "When the Empire began gradually to be exhausted, so that now there are some who in fact recognize no superior and by them justice is neglected, the need arose for a subsidiary remedy when the ordinary remedies fail . . . it has been necessary to resort to this device of a declaration of war lest justice should perish." This "extraordinary remedy" which originates in the law of nations is a form of "lawful war." *Ibid.* See also Bartolus, *op. cit.*, p. 327. It may not be used for "slight cause." Legnano, *op. cit.*, p. 323.

[59] Legnano, *op. cit.*, p. 308 ff.: ". . . it is the right, granted on the ground of necessity, to take the law into one's own hand."

[60] de la Brière, "*Évolution de la doctrine et de la pratique en matière des représailles*," 22 *Rec. des Cours de l'Acad. de Droit Int.* (1928, II), p. 256; Kappus, *Der völkerrechtliche Kriegsbegriff* (Breslau, 1936), p. 11 ff.; Bulmerinq, "*Staatenstreitigkeiten*," in *Handbuch des Völkerrechts*, Vol. IV (Hamburg, 1889), pp. 72 ff., 80; in particular with respect to the connection between war and reprisals in early theory, see Spiegel, *loc. cit.*, pp. 75, 78.

[61] Casulli, *La sovranità degli stati e la Società delle Nazioni* (Rome, 1934), p. 5.

[62] *De Re Militari et Bello Tractatus* (1536), in The Classics of International Law, No. 18, Oxford, 1936. Introduction by Arigo Cavaglieri and English translation by Herbert C. Nutting (Vol. II of the edition). [63] Belli, *op. cit.*, p. 61.

[64] Belli, *op. cit.*, pp. 6 ff., 10; see also Cavaglieri's introduction (Vol. II, p. 14a). Belli refers to "Innocent and Panormitanus who find illustrations in the case of the Pope and Emperor, and the Kings of Spain and France; and there is added a supplementary note assigning this same right to the Duke of Milan, since in his position the last named fills the room of supreme ruler, and has full powers like the Emperor." [65] Belli, *op. cit.*, p. 59.

[66] *Ibid.*; see also p. 279: "peace is nothing else than duly established concord."

forcement of one's rights;[67] even if declared on just grounds, a war may become unlawful if it is subsequently waged in a spirit of vengeance or for immoderate gains.[68] A foreshadowing of a modern attempt at defining the legal consequences of an unlawful war may be seen in the author's suggestion that things, cities or others, which are captured in an unjust war "do not become the property of the captors, but must be restored."[69]

A climax in the evolution of the medieval doctrine of the just war is reached by Franciscus de Victoria, whose teachings on the international law of war [70] combine a comprehensive exposition of the achievements of the past millennium with a clear foresight into its future problems.[71] He undertook to examine the right of war for the practical purpose of protecting the "Indians recently discovered" against the cruel treatment inflicted upon them by his Spanish fellow-countrymen; he was furthermore actuated by the desire to denounce as vain pretexts the various "just causes" for which Charles V pursued his policy of conquest and oppression throughout the world. Being a Spaniard, *i.e.*, the subject of a country where the claim of the Emperor to world supremacy had always met with strong opposition,[72] he makes the sovereign state the central point of his legal system. Each state, *viz.*, a community "which is complete in itself,"[73] has the right to declare war; it is an essential element of its sovereignty.[74] It may, however, be exercised only in cases where an adequate cause justifies forcible actions with their accompanying horrors and devastations. The answer as to what constitutes such cause is first stated in negative terms: Neither the difference of religion, nor the expansion of empire or the promotion of the personal glory of the ruler may justify resort to war.[75] The positive concept adopts Augustinian ideas. "There is a single and only cause for commencing a war, namely, a wrong received."[76] The definition refers to moral culpability

---

[67] Belli, *op. cit.*, pp. 8, 61, 78.   [68] *Ibid.*, p. 60.   [69] *Ibid.*

[70] *De Indis et de Iure Belli Relectiones* (1532), edited by E. Nys, in The Classics of International Law, Washington, 1917. Latin text and English translation; further, Scott, The Spanish Origin of International Law, Part I, Francisco de Vitoria and His Law of Nations (Carnegie Endowment for International Peace, 1934); *idem*, The Catholic Conception of International Law (Washington, 1934).

[71] Wegner, *op. cit.*, p. 139; Hentschel, "*Franciscus de Victoria und seine Stellung zum Völkerrecht*," 17 *Zeitschr. f. öffentliches Recht*, p. 388; de la Brière, in 44 *Rev. Gén. Dr. Int. Pub.*, p. 149; Scheuner, in XXII *Zeitschr. f. Völkerrecht* (1938), p. 453 ff.; Nys (ed.), Victoria, *De Iure Belli*, p. 95.

[72] Westlake, Introduction to Ayala, *De Iure et Officiis Belli*, in The Classics of International Law, Vol. I, p. XII; van der Molen, *op. cit.*, pp. 6 ff., 107.

[73] Victoria, *op. cit.*, p. 169: "A perfect State or community . . . is one which is complete in itself, that is, which is not a part of another community, but has its own laws, and its own council and its own magistrates."

[74] *Ibid.*: ". . . kings who are subordinate to the Emperor can make war on one another without waiting for the Emperor's authorization, for . . . a State ought to be self-sufficient, and this it would not be, if it had not the faculty in question." See also de la Brière, *loc. cit.*, p. 149 ff.   [75] Victoria, *op. cit.*, p. 170.

[76] *Ibid.*; see also von der Heydte, "*Franciscus de Victoria und sein Völkerrecht*," 13 *Zeitschr.*

as well as legal responsibility;[77] its practical application requires a system of law under which right and wrong may be distinguished, and a judgment as basis for the warlike action. The standards for evaluating the conduct of states are furnished by natural law, which medieval doctrine considered as above the states.[73] Thus, an injury to its honor entitles the state to punish the wrongdoer.[79] In the absence of a superior authority, each prince is plaintiff, prosecutor and judge at once.[80] "It is essential for a just war that an exceedingly careful examination be made of the justice and causes of the war and that the reasons of those who on grounds of equity oppose it be listened to."[81] As the prince is liable to make mistakes, war "ought not be made on the sole judgment of the King, nor, indeed, on the judgment of a few, but on that of many, and they wise and upright men."[82] Such procedure, however, does not exclude the possibility that both sides may believe in the justice of their respective causes. Can a war be just on both sides? The answer to this crucial question distinguishes between "true" or objective justice and subjective innocence. The case in which both parties have an objectively just cause "clearly cannot occur, for if the right and justice of each side be certain, it is unlawful to fight against it, either in offense or in defense."[83] However, "invincible ignorance" on the part of those who wage objectively unjust wars in good faith is "a complete excuse."[84] The prince engaged in a just war is entitled, after victory, to de-

f. öffentliches Recht, p. 264 ff.; Scott, The Catholic Conception of International Law, p. 38; *idem*, The Spanish Origin of International Law, p. 227; Nys (ed.), *loc. cit.*, p. 87; van der Molen, *op. cit.*, p. 109; de la Brière, *loc. cit.*, p. 151.   [77] de la Brière, *ibid.*

[78] Gierke, Political Theories of the Middle Ages, tr. by Maitland (Cambridge, 1900), p. 75 ff.; von der Heydte, *loc. cit.*, p. 248 ff.; Scott, The Catholic Conception of International Law, p. 491; Hentschel, *loc. cit.*, p. 371.

[79] Victoria, *op. cit.*, p. 173: ". . . among the things which a prince is bound to defend and preserve for his State are its honor and authority."

[80] *Ibid.*, p. 175: ". . . princes are judges in their own cases, inasmuch as they have no superior"; p. 171: ". . . if there were any competent judge over the two belligerents, he would have to condemn the unjust aggressors and authors of wrong . . . But a prince who is carrying on a just war is as it were his own judge in matters touching the war . . ."; and see Scott, The Spanish Origin of International Law, p. 210 ff.; von der Heydte, *loc. cit.*, p. 262; Beaufort, *op. cit.*, p. 123.   [81] Victoria, *op. cit.*, p. 173.   [82] *Ibid.*, p. 174.

[83] *Ibid.*, p. 177; Ballis, *op. cit.*, p. 86. Suarez, the other great founder of the Spanish school of international law, calls "entirely absurd" the assumption that war may be just on both sides; for "two rights contrary to each other cannot both be just." See Scott, The Catholic Conception of International Law, p. 449; Barcia Trelles, *"Francisco Suarez, Les Théologiens espagnols du XVIᵉ siècle,"* 43 Rec. des Cours de l'Acad. de Droit Int., p. 293 ff.; Ballis, *op. cit.*, p. 92.

[84] Victoria, *op. cit.*, p. 177: ". . . it may be that on the side where true justice is the war is just of itself while on the other side the war is just in the sense of being excused from sin by reason of good faith, because invincible ignorance is a complete excuse"; p. 186: ". . . princes . . . who in reality have no just cause of war, may nevertheless be waging war in good faith, with such good faith, I say, as to free them from fault; as, for instance, if the war is made after a careful examination and in accordance with the opinion of learned and upright men." See also von der Heydte, *loc. cit.*, p. 265; de la Brière, 44 Rev. Gén. Dr. Int. Pub., p. 152; van der Molen, *op. cit.*, p. 118; Regout, *op. cit.*, p. 267.

mand damages, restoration and guaranties, and to inflict punishment which, however, may "not exceed degree and nature of the offense."[85] What goes beyond those limits is unjust.

According to Ayala, another of the Spanish writers whom Grotius mentions among his chief predecessors, the justice of the cause, though still considered as a necessary prerequisite for going to war in accordance with the prevailing doctrine,[86] has no legal effect whatever upon the conduct of the war; it relates to politics and equity rather than to law.[87] "Nothing more is needed, then, so far as concerns the legal effects which are produced and the bringing into operation of the laws of war, than that the war should be waged by parties who are within the definition of 'enemies'[88] and who have the right to wage war."[89] Such wars that are begun and prosecuted in a regular manner are lawful in the Roman sense of the term [90] and, therefore, just on both sides.[91]

While Victoria and Ayala acknowledge an objective justice only on one side, though they admit that, either subjectively or with respect to its formal regularity, a war may be just on both sides, Gentilis thinks it possible that even objectively both belligerents may have a just cause. A war "may be just on one side, but on the other is still more just."[92] It is true, there exists that "purest and truest form of justice which cannot conceive of both parties

[85] de la Brière, *loc. cit.*, Vol. XXXII, p. 373 ff.; Scott, Spanish Origin of International Law, p. 210 ff.; Victoria, *op. cit.*, p. 184 ff. See also p. 187: ". . . the victor ought not to make seizures or exactions in temporal matters beyond the limits of just satisfaction, seeing that anything beyond these limits could only be justified as a punishment, such as could not be visited on the innocent."

[86] *De Iure et Officiis Bellicis et Disciplina Militari Libri III* (1582), in The Classics of International Law, ed. by Westlake, Latin text and English translation. Washington, 1912. See Chapter II: On the just war and just causes of war, such causes are principally the defense of one's own self and of one's friends and allies, the recovery of what has been unjustly taken away by violence and the vindication of injuries received.

[87] Ayala, *op. cit.*, p. 22: ". . . our remarks so far about the just causes of war deal rather with considerations of fairness and goodness and propriety, and not with the character of the legal result which is produced." Westlake, in his introduction to Ayala's treatise, *op. cit.*, Vol. I, p. VII, remarks with regard to this sudden flash of the light of legal thought in the otherwise impenetrable darkness of scholastic concepts: "Here then at last Ayala is alive to the difference between the provinces of the legist and the moralist in what concerns war."

[88] *I.e.*, not rebels, pirates, brigands.   [89] Ayala, *op. cit.*, p. 23.

[90] *Supra*, note 14; see also Westlake, *loc. cit.*, p. VIII.

[91] Ayala, *op. cit.*, p. 22; he immediately adds, however, that "if it be just cause of war that is adverted to . . . one and the same cause cannot be just for this side and that." *Ibid.*

[92] *De Iure Belli Libri Tres* (Hanau, 1593), in The Classics of International Law, Oxford, 1933. Latin text and English translation. Introduction by Coleman Phillipson. Vol. II, pp. 31, 32; van der Molen, *op. cit.*, p. 119; Westlake, Chapters on the Principles of International Law (Cambridge, 1894), p. 35. The term "just" is used by Gentilis in his definition of war. "War is a just and public contest of arms." *De Iure Belli*, p. 12. As Phillipson (Introduction, Vol. II, p. 33a) points out, the word "just" here signifies "not a question-begging epithet in regard to the justice of the cause," but rather a distinction of "warfare that is regular (*i.e.*, begun and prosecuted according to the rules by the sovereign authority) from the acts of marauders, pirates, etc., and insurgents."

to a dispute being in the right."[93] But "owing to the weakness of our human nature" we are "for the most part unacquainted with that truth"; and "from man's standpoint" it is "the nature of wars for both sides to maintain that they are supporting a just cause. In general, it may be true in nearly every kind of dispute that neither of the two disputants is unjust."[94] If it is doubtful on which side justice is, and if each side aims at justice, neither can be called unjust. In fact, both belligerents are in the position of parties to a lawsuit "who contend in the litigation of the Forum justly, that is to say, on a plausible ground, either as defendants or plaintiffs"; if they lose their case "they are not judged guilty of injustice."[95] Consequently, the rights of war are granted to both contestants "just as in the contests of the Forum the law is impartial towards each litigant."[96] The result of a war is no standard for a judgment as to the respective merits of the case; it is by no means certain that the just cause will win. "If the unjust man gain the victory, neither in a contention in arms nor in the strife carried on in the garb of peace is there any help for it."[97] There may be consolation in the thought that no sin is without retribution; but a war offers no such certainty. The victor's power to punish and destroy the vanquished is, however, limited by the concept of the just peace. The victor may not exact war indemnity and tributes or demand territorial cessions to such an extent as to endanger the establishment of a lasting peace. "That victor will be unjust who offers a peace which is no peace."[98]

Gentilis differs from his predecessors by a keen sense of realism which derives inspiration from human nature and concrete facts rather than abstract principles and metaphysical assumptions; he is the first to draw a clear line of demarcation between the legal aspects of the war problem on the one hand, theology and ethics on the other.[99] This approach reflects the

---

[93] *De Iure Belli*, p. 31.   [94] *Ibid.*

[95] The comparison of war to legal proceedings for the assertion of even doubtful rights has its theological counterpart in the so-called Probabilist Theory of the Spanish theologians Molina (1536–1600) and Gregorius de Valentia (1551–1603), who maintain that a prince may justly go to war if, according to his probable opinion, though not *realiter*, the right is on his side. See Valentia, *Commentaria Theologica*, quoted by Regout, *op. cit.*, at p. 248, n. 2: ". . . ille etiam qui re vera non haberet causam justam pugnaret juste per accidens propter opinionem probabilem. Sicut is etiam per accidens contendit juste in judicio, qui sequitur opinionem probabilem, quamvis falsam." See further, van der Molen, *op. cit.*, p. 119; Ballis, *op. cit.*, p. 129; Barcia Trelles, *loc. cit.*, p. 285; Vanderpol, *op. cit.*, p. 254 ff.

[96] *De Iure Belli*, Vol. II, p. 33: "Although it may sometimes happen . . . that injustice is clearly evident on one of the two sides, nevertheless this ought not to affect the general principles and prevent the laws of war from applying to both parties."   [97] *Ibid.*

[98] *De Iure Belli*, Vol. II, Bk. III, Chs. IV–VI, XIII, p. 353. Gentilis quotes here from Augustine: "by punishing past offenses we glut our anger; by being compassionate we ensure the future." See also Phillipson, in XII Jour. Comp. Leg. (1911), p. 76.

[99] Phillipson, Introduction, *loc. cit.*, Vol. II, pp. 18a, 33a; *idem*, in XII Jour. Comp. Leg. (1911), pp. 70, 80; van der Molen, *op. cit.*, pp. 210, 240 ff.; Ballis, *op. cit.*, p. 94; Holland, Studies in International Law (Oxford, 1898), p. 58; Holdsworth, A History of English Law (2d ed.), Vol. V, p. 53.

678   THE AMERICAN JOURNAL OF INTERNATIONAL LAW

larger movement of the sixteenth century "which witnessed a transformation of society . . . , the decline of theocracy, and the rise of the modern state."[100] International law is dissociated from the Roman *ius civile* and becomes a law regulating the mutual intercourse between sovereign states; its application is entrusted to the individual prince who is judge in his own case and from whose decisions there is no appeal.[101] It is true, the prince is still considered as bound to examine the justice of his cause before he engages in war;[102] but whatever the result of his decision may be, it never affects the legality of his action, since war is nothing more than a procedural device that may be resorted to even for the redress of a probable wrong without exposing either party to the blame of injustice.[103]

The demise of the concept of the just war to which the idea of the *bellum justum ex utraque parte* seemed to lead was averted by Grotius who made of it an issue of modern international law. Grotius had witnessed the catastrophic lawlessness of the Wars of Religion. "Throughout the Christian world," he said, "I observed a lack of restraint in relation to war, such as even barbarous races should be ashamed of; I observed that men rush to arms for slight causes, or no causes at all."[104] His problem was to find a law according to which righteous wars could be distinguished from unrighteous;[105] the solution was afforded by the traditional doctrine of the just war which Grotius adopts more or less unchanged from his predecessors.[106] Thus, in the manner of the "theologians" and "doctors" he inquires into the justifiableness of war. Just causes are primarily defense, recovery of

. [100] Phillipson, Introduction, *loc. cit.*, Vol. II, p. 25a; van Vollenhoven, *op. cit.*, p. 67.

[101] Phillipson, *loc. cit.*, p. 26a ff.; van der Molen, *op. cit.*, pp. 114 ff., 240 ff. As to the influence of Bodin's concept of sovereignty on Gentilis, see van der Molen, *op. cit.*, p. 226 ff.

[102] The main body of Book I of *De Iure Belli* is devoted to an examination of the causes of war, which Gentilis divides into Divine, natural and human causes. Thus, the command of God legitimatizes a war under Divine law; self-defense is an instinct implanted in all living beings and, therefore, a "natural" reason for taking up arms, like utility and honor. Human causes for war appear when an offended state proceeds to exact reparation for violated positive rights. See van der Molen, *op. cit.*, pp. 126, 129.

[103] Regout, *op. cit.*, pp. 249 n. 2, 273; van der Molen, *op. cit.*, p. 120: "As long as it is accepted as self-evident, that the sovereign (state) may take the law into his own hand, either to avenge a real or a supposed wrong or to assert real or supposed rights, the door is opened wide to the grossest wrong, in spite of the finest theories."

[104] *De Iure Belli ac Pacis*, in The Classics of International Law, Oxford, 1925, Vol. II. Translation. Prolegomena 28, p. 20. See also van Vollenhoven, *op. cit.*, p. 70; Walker, History of the Law of Nations (Cambridge, 1899), p. 284; Wright, Medieval Internationalism (London, 1930), p. 16.   [105] Hearnshaw, *op. cit.*, p. 87.

[106] Regout, *op. cit.*, p. 276; Beaufort, *op. cit.*, p. 176; Nys, *Les origines du droit international*, p. 95 ff.; Phillipson, Introduction, *loc. cit.*, Vol. II, p. 10a, n. 13. When reading Grotius after a study of his predecessors one cannot but agree with Walker, who states: "Again and again the reader of the pages of Grotius, who shall have made the acquaintance of the lights of moral and legal learning of the sixteenth century, will catch the echo of their opinions and their very phrases." *Op. cit.*, p. 333.

CONCEPT OF JUST WAR IN INTERNATIONAL LAW 679

property, and punishment;[107] unjust causes, among others, are the desire for richer land, the desire for freedom on the part of a state in political subjection, or the wish to rule others against their will on the pretext that it is for their good.[108] Generally speaking, war is a procedure for the assertion of rights. "It is evident that the sources from which wars arise are as numerous as those from which lawsuits spring; for where judicial settlement fails, war begins. Actions, furthermore, lie either for wrongs not yet committed, or for wrongs already done."[109] The question whether both parties may be just is answered in accordance with the older doctrine: Objective justice can exist only on one side;[110] either party, however, "may justly, that is in good faith, plead his case."[111] The distinction between just and unjust causes has a definite legal effect with respect to those "who are on neither side in war"; they must refrain from lending assistance to the one who supports a wicked

---

[107] *De Iure Belli ac Pacis*, Bk. II, Ch. I, sec. II, 2. As to the punitive war, see Bk. II, Ch. XX, sec. 40 ff.: "There is a just cause of war as against those who are without reverence for parents . . . who practice piracy . . ." . Van Vollenhoven, in "Grotius and Geneva" (*Bibliotheca Visseriana*, Vol. VI, 1926), maintains (p. 22) that "the topic of war against crime, of punitive warfare, overshadowed the other topics to the effect that the author often overlooked other kinds of justifiable warfare: those intended to recover property, to recover debts, to obtain reparation for losses and damages . . . All the author's real interest was centered on state crimes and on their punishments." It must, however, be noted that Grotius, like his theological predecessors, considers as a decisive test for the justness of a war "a wrong received" (Bk. II, Ch. I, sec. I, 4), regardless of its legal nature as civil wrong or crime. See Beaufort, *op. cit.*, p. 165 ff.; p. 175: "La guerre juste (bellum justum) telle que la conçoit Grotius est dans l'acceptation générale du terme, une guerre punitive en ce sens qu'elle combat l'injustice et venge l'injure faite au droit." See also Wehberg, in 20 *Die Friedenswarte* (1918), p. 270: "The war in Grotius' concept is a war of execution and punishment"; Wolzendorff, *Die Lüge des Völkerrechts, Der Krieg als Rechts-Institution* (Leipzig, 1920), p. 29 ff. [108] *De Iure Belli ac Pacis*, Bk. II, Ch. XXII, secs. VIII–XII.

[109] *Ibid.*, Bk. II, Ch. I, sec. II, 1.

[110] *Ibid.*, Bk. II, Ch. XXIII, sec. XIII: "In the particular sense and with reference to the thing itself, a war cannot be just on both sides, just as a legal claim cannot."

[111] *Ibid.* See also Holland, Lectures on International Law, p. 246: "Grotius distinguishes justice with reference to cause from justice with reference to effect: only quoad effectus quosdam iuris can a war be said to be 'just' on both sides (*i.e.*, the formal sense)." Zouche, Grotius' English follower, defines this principle in his *Iuris et Iudicii Fecialis, Sive Iuris Inter Gentes, et Quaestionum de Eodem Explicatio*, 1650 (The Classics of International Law, Washington, 1911), in the following terms which, incidentally, contain an express rejection of the Probabilist Theory (*supra*, note 95): "A thing is called just either in respect of the act or in respect of the person acting. In respect of the act a war cannot be just on both sides. But it may well be that neither of the belligerents acts unjustly. For none acts unjustly save he who knows that he is acting unjustly. Thus, two persons may go to the law justly, that is in good faith, on each side. But in embarking upon a war, the gravity of the matter is such that, not content with probable reasons, it demands reasons of the greatest clearness." *Op. cit.*, Vol. II, p. 112. To Zouche war is, in accordance with the teachings of Grotius, "but a means, whereby, in the last resort, the rights which Nations enjoy in time of peace may be vindicated." Holland, Introduction to Zouche, *Iuris et Iudicii, ibid.*, Vol. I, p. XIII.

cause and from placing obstacles in the way of the party which wages a just war.[112] The determination, however, where in a given case true justice lies is left to their own judgment, a conclusion which almost nullifies the practical value of the rule.[113]

Pufendorf, one of the most important among Grotius' immediate followers, while in general accepting the fundamental propositions of the master with respect to the just war,[114] makes a few significant additions which are worth mentioning in this connection. The crux of the matter, as was shown above, lay in the illimited freedom on the part of the prince in appraising weightiness and merits of the grievance for which redress was sought in war. Grotius had urged the prince not to undertake a war, even for an undoubtedly just cause, unless there was "supreme necessity" for it or no hope that the conflict could be settled "by inspiring fear and on the strength of reputation with little or no risk." [115] Pufendorf, while warning the prince to consider carefully these observations of Grotius, declares it a duty incumbent upon the states not "rashly to advance any vague claim" nor "fly at once at arms," but to try "one of three courses in order to prevent the affair from breaking out into open war, to wit, either a conference between the parties concerned or their representatives; or an appeal to arbitrators, or finally, the use of the lot." [116] His advice to neutrals assures better than Grotius' rule an attitude of impartiality. Neutrals should deny the belligerents passage through their territory and even oppose it; for any other course would involve a determination as to the justice of the war. Thrusting oneself, however, as a judge between two armed Powers would "make oneself a party to so great a quarrel." [117]

The same view that neutral behavior is an absolute duty unconnected with the justice of the war is held by Bynkershoek, the last in the line of the great international jurists who, following Grotius, carried the notion of the just war

---

[112] *De Iure Belli ac Pacis*, Bk. III, Ch. XVII; Oppenheim-Lauterpacht, International Law (5th ed.), Vol. II, p. 493.

[113] See Meinecke, *Die Idee der Staatsräson* (München, 1924), p. 262: "The old illusion to which Grotius still clung, namely, that in each case a 'just' war may be distinguished from an 'unjust' war was likely to confuse things and to increase existing possibilities for wars and conflicts rather than to reduce their occurrence. He declared it to be the duty of neutrals to do nothing whereby the party who supports a wicked cause would be rendered more powerful or whereby the movements of him who wages a just war would be hampered. In point of fact, that meant nothing more than urging the neutral to take sides on the basis of a value judgment which, in reality, is always dictated by reasons of state and by national interests."

[114] His emphasis, however, lies on the civil nature of the wrong which may justify resort to war. He reduces the just causes to three heads: (1) We may defend ourselves and our possessions against the attacks of others; (2) we may obtain by force the settlement of rightful claims that the debtor refuses to meet; (3) we may obtain reparations for losses which we have suffered by injuries and demand security for the future. *De Iure Naturae et Gentium Libri Octo* (1672), in The Classics of International Law, Oxford, 1934.

[115] *De Iure Belli ac Pacis*, Bk. II, Ch. XXIV, sec. IX.

[116] Pufendorf, *De Iure Naturae et Gentium*, Vol. II, p. 1295.   [117] *Ibid.*, p. 356.

from the Middle Ages into modern times. His definition of war as a "contest between independent persons carried on by force or fraud for the sake of asserting their rights" [118] implies the just cause, or, in Bynkershoek's words, the rule that "the only correct ground for war is the defense or recovery of one's own." [119] However, the question as to what party is carrying on a just war does not concern the neutral; "it is not his duty to sit in judgment between his friends . . . and to grant and deny anything to either belligerent through considerations of the relative degree of justice." [120] The case seems different with allies. If two nations with which a third state is allied are waging war with each other, the latter is obliged to side with the party that was unjustly attacked.[121] Whether the ally here actually "deviates from his solid standpoint of not judging a quarrel not his own nor submitted to him" [122] is, however, doubtful; what he does is to determine whether, according to the terms of the treaty of alliance, the *casus foederis* has arisen. The justice of the cause may or may not enter as an element into such interpretation.

Bynkershoek's contemporary, Heineccius, whose *Treatise on the Elements of the Law of Nature and the Law of Nations* [123] appeared one year after the former's *Quaestiones*, is the first to raise serious objections against at least part of the traditional doctrine. It is true, war is still considered a legal remedy for the assertion of rights [124] and hence presupposes a just cause which consists in a wrong received.[125] However, the idea that a punitive war in the Grotian sense may be just, *viz.*, a war to punish a nation for crimes which do not directly injure the punishing state, is rejected on the ground that the right to inflict punishment exists only as between a superior and his subjects and therefore not among nations, since they are equals.[126]

A similar position with respect to the legality of punitive wars is taken by Christian Wolff. "Punitive war is not legal except for one who has received irreparable injury. . . . For no one has a right of war except one to whom a

---

[118] *Quaestiones Iuris Publici Libri Duo* (1737), in The Classics of International Law, Oxford, 1930, Vol. II, p. 15.

[119] *Ibid.*, p. 15.   [120] *Ibid.*, p. 61.   [121] *Ibid.*, p. 62 ff.

[122] De Louter, Introduction to Bynkershoek, *ibid.*, Vol. II, p. XVIII.

[123] *Elementa Iuris Naturae et Gentium* (Halle, 1738).

[124] "Per bellum vero intellegimus statum liberarum gentium vel hominum, in statu naturali viventium, iuris sui persequendi caussa vi dolove concertantium, propositumve concertandi retinentium." *Ibid.*, Lib. II, Sec. 191. See also Secs. 195, 196.

[125] "Quemadmodum vero iuris tantum perfecti denegatio iustam belli caussam praebet . . . denegatio omnino in laesionem incidit, ac proinde bello defensivo caussam suppeditat iustissimam." *Ibid.*, Sec. 196.

[126] ". . . tertia caussa, quam commentus est Grotius de iure belli ac pacis II, 1, 2, 1, punitio nimirum scelerum, eo minus videatur admittenda, quo magis constat, parem a pari, adeoque gentem a gente puniri non posse." *Ibid.*, Sec. 195. Hobbes already had expressed the view that even if state crimes were possible, states would not be authorized to punish the offender because they have no jurisdiction over each other. See van Vollenhoven, *op. cit.*, p. 22; Beaufort, *op. cit.*, p. 166.

wrong has been done." [127]   His advance beyond the prevailing doctrine,
however, goes further than mere criticism of this Grotian concept.   By drawing a line of demarcation between natural law which governs nations in their
capacity as beings living in a state of nature,[128] and the voluntary law which
is based upon conscious acts of states for the purpose of ending their difficulties resulting from the natural state,[129] he is the first to recognize that the
question of the justice of wars falls outside the pale of positive law.   It is
natural law which imposes a duty on nations not to resort to war except for a
just cause, which is generally identical with a wrong done or likely to be
done.[130]   While following Grotius' lead in the question as to whether both
sides can be just,[131] Wolff adopts Pufendorf's and Bynkershoek's views as to
the absolute character of neutrality.   "It is plainly not in the power of the
neutral to give aid even to one carrying on a just war." [132]   Victory is no
indication of the justice of a war; it is "improperly put on an equality with
the decision of a judge."[133]   To decide the question, one must know "what
are the perfect rights of nations and how they can be violated." [134]   The
whole of the natural law has to be applied to the facts of the case.   However,
"as long as the facts are not yet definitely determined a decision as to the
justice of the war will be suspended." [135]   By the voluntary law of nations,
war is to be considered as just on either side, since no nation can assume the
functions of a judge and consequently cannot pronounce upon the justice of
the war.[136]   It follows that the laws of war apply to both belligerents alike.
"What is rightly allowable for one belligerent is also allowable for the other
without any consideration of the justice of the war." [137]

The positivist doctrine received its final and comprehensive exposition by
Wolff's disciple, Vattel, who adopts the fundamental distinction between the
"necessary law of nature" and the "voluntary law of nations."   The former
addresses itself to "the conscience of sovereigns"; the latter is the law which
nations apply in their intercourse with each other.[138]   It is only with respect

---

[127] *Ius Gentium Methodo Scientifico Pertractatum* (1749), in The Classics of International
Law, Oxford, 1934, Vol. II, p. 325.

[128] "Nations, in their relations to each other, are regarded as individual free persons living
in a state of nature." *Ibid.*, Vol. II, p. 313.   [129] *Ibid.*, Vol. II, p. 453 ff.

[130] *Ibid.*, Vol. II, pp. 314, 325; mere utility is no justifying reason, Vol. II, pp. 316, 331.
Wolff incidentally rejects here the theory of Machiavelli who, quoting approvingly Livius'
saying (*supra*, note 14), maintained that those wars are just which are necessary, *viz.*, dictated by reasons of state.   See Gilbert, Allen H., Machiavelli's *Prince* and its Forerunners
(1938), pp. 166, 224 ff.

[131] *Ius Gentium*, Vol. II, p. 324: "War cannot be just on each side.   For there is no just
cause of war save a wrong done or likely to be done"; p. 325: "The injustice of a war cannot
be imputed to one who, because of ignorance or irrefutable error, thinks that he has a just
cause of war when he has not."   [132] *Ibid.*, p. 347.

[133] *Ibid.*, p. 324.   See also p. 455: "War is not a suitable method for deciding the controversies of nations."   [134] *Ibid.*, p. 315.   [135] *Ibid.*

[136] *Ibid.*, p. 454.   [137] *Ibid.*, p. 455.

[138] Vattel, The Law of Nations (1758) [Tr. by Chitty. Philadelphia, 1872], p. 380 ff.

to the former that the question of the justice of a war may be raised; [139] the voluntary law of nations, or, as it is now called, positive international law, does not inquire into the intrinsic justice of wars. The reasons therefor are threefold: (1) There is no judge above nations who could authoritatively settle this question; [140] (2) warfare which would be illegal on one side and therefore outside the law would create chaotic conditions; [141] (3) there would never be peace, since the results of a war could always be challenged as illegally obtained and therefore not binding upon the other belligerent or third parties.[142]

[139] Vattel, The Law of Nations, p. 301: "Humanity revolts against a sovereign, who, without necessity or without very powerful reasons, lavishes the blood of his most faithful subjects. . . . He is responsible to God, and accountable to human nature, for every individual that is killed."

[140] *Ibid.*, p. 305 ff.: "Since nations are equal and independent and cannot claim a right of judgment over each other, it follows that in every case susceptible of doubt, the arms of the two parties at war are to be accounted equally lawful."

[141] *Ibid.*, p. 382: "The first rule . . . is, that regular war, as to its effects, is to be accounted just on both sides. This is absolutely necessary . . . if people wish to introduce any order, any regularity, into so violent an operation as that of arms . . ."

[142] *Ibid.*, pp. 382, 386: ". . . the rights founded on the state of war, the lawfulness of its effects, the validity of the acquisitions made by arms, do not, externally and between mankind, depend on the justice of the cause, but on the legality of the means in themselves. . . . There would be no stability in the affairs of mankind, no safety in trading with nations engaged in war, if we were allowed to draw a distinction between a just and an unjust war, so as to attribute lawful effects to the one which we denied to the other."

Similar arguments are set forth by Johann Jacob Moser in his *Versuch des neuesten europäischen Völkerrechts in Friedens- und Kriegszeiten* (1777). He declares (Sec. 52): "To the question as to whether it is possible to determine, under international law, what causes may justify war, we reply that it must of necessity be answered in the negative because (1) it is always doubtful what were the true causes for the resort to war; (2) the opponent will never recognize the justice or sufficiency of the alleged cause; (3) there is no judge who may decide the issue." Moser's approach was historical; he deduced his conclusions from the actual practice of states. See Verdross, "*J. J. Moser's Programm einer Völkerrechtswissenschaft der Erfahrung*," 3 Zeitschr. f. öffentliches Recht, p. 96 ff.; Rettich, *Zur Theorie und Geschichte des Rechts zum Kriege* (Stuttgart, 1888), p. 38 ff.

An interesting attempt to preserve the notion of an "unjust enemy" within the positivist system of law was made by Immanuel Kant in his Philosophy of Law (1796) [Tr. by Hastie, Edinburgh, 1887]. He rejects the concept of a punitive war. "No war of independent States against each other can rightly be a war of punishment (bellum punitivum). For punishment is only in place under the relation of a Superior (imperantis) to a Subject (subditum); and this is not the relation of the States to one another" (p. 219). This has an important consequence with respect to the "Right after the War." "The conqueror may not demand restitution of the cost of the war, because he would then have to declare the war of his opponent to be unjust or . . . to be punitive, and he would thus in turn inflict an injury" (p. 221; see also *Metaphysik der Sitten*, Sec. 58). However, the right of an injured state against its enemy in asserting what is its own has no limits because such war is waged against an unjust enemy. But "what is an unjust enemy according to the conceptions of the Right of Nations, when, as holds generally of the State of Nature, every State is judge in its own cause?" The answer is that an unjust enemy is "one whose publicly expressed will, whether in word or deed, betrays a maxim which, if it were taken as a universal rule, would make a

The majority of writers during the nineteenth and at the beginning of the twentieth century [143] who, following the positivistic school, rejected the distinction between just and unjust wars, considered war as an act entirely within the uncontrolled sovereignty of the individual state.[144] By applying armed force as the *ultima ratio* in international politics, a state creates a factual situation where the rules governing the peaceful intercourse among nations are replaced by the law of war.[145] As to the origin and the merits of the act, international law remains silent.[146] It is true, a state, by resorting to war, may act contrary to specific obligations incumbent upon it under general or particular international law—for instance, if a neutralized state declares war, or if a state employs force for the recovery of contractual debts in disregard of the Hague Convention of 1907,[147] or if states fail to announce their intention to open hostilities by a formal declaration issued in accordance with Convention III of the Hague Conference of 1907.[148] But once a state of war has arisen, its legal consequences with regard to the belligerents and third parties are the same irrespective of the fact that its outbreak involved the violation of a specific international legal duty.

Another group of writers conceive war as an institution of international law. Thus it is said that "in the absence of an international organ for enforcing the law, war is a means of self-help, an arm of the law," a remedy against a legal wrong; [149] it is in international law "the mode of giving effect

state of Peace among the nations impossible. . . . Such for instance is the violation of public Treaties" (p. 223). A similar idea is stated in Pitt Cobbett's Cases on International Law (5th ed. by W. L. Walker, 1937), Vol. II, p. 8: "The primary test of the justness or otherwise of war might, perhaps, well be found in the answer to the question, is the State at war bona fide endeavouring to restrain the use of physical force by another or is it endeavouring to make use of force to impose its will on others . . . ?" See further Ebbinghaus, *Kant's Lehre vom Ewigen Frieden und die Kriegsschuldfrage* (Tübingen, 1929), p. 34 ff.

[143] A comprehensive survey of the literature is given by Göhler, *Freies Kriegsführungsrecht und Kriegsschuld* (Leipzig, 1931).

[144] Oppenheim-Lauterpacht, International Law (5th ed.), Vol. II, p. 148.

[145] Balladore Pallieri, *"Il problema della guerra lecita nel diritto internazionale commune e nell' ordinamento della Società delle Nazioni,"* IX *Rivista di Diritto Internazionale*, 512; Funck-Brentano and Sorel, *Précis du droit des gens* (1900), p. 497; Lawrence, Principles of International Law (1928), p. 311; De Louter, *Le droit international positif* (1920), Vol. II, p. 213; Hold-Ferneck, *Lehrbuch des Völkerrechts* (2d pt., Leipzig, 1932), p. 238 ff.; Lueder, *"Krieg und Kriegsrecht im Allgemeinen,"* in *Handbuch des Völkerrechts*, Vol. IV, Hamburg, 1889, pp. 176, 221 ff.

[146] Quincy Wright, in this JOURNAL, Vol. 18 (1924), p. 758: "The question of when war exists is one of fact unrelated to the nature of the controversy beginning it"; von Waldkirch, *Völkerrecht* (1926), p. 338; Salvioli, *op. cit.*, p. 124; Strupp, *Grundzüge des Völkerrechts* (1928), p. 211; Heilborn, *System des Völkerrechts* (1896), pp. 330, 333, 364 ff.; *idem*, in *Handbuch des Völkerrechts*, Vol. I, p. 22 ff.; Ullmann, *Völkerrecht* (Tübingen, 1908), p. 465.

[147] Convention on the Limitation of the Employment of Force for the Recovery of Contractual Debts. Scott's Hague Peace Conferences, Vol. II, pp. 357–361.

[148] Convention (III) Relative to the Opening of Hostilities. Scott, The Hague Conventions and Declarations of 1899 and 1907 (New York, 1918), p. 96 ff.

[149] Oppenheim-Lauterpacht, *op. cit.*, p. 147 ff.; Lammasch, *Völkermord oder Völkerbund?* (1920), p. 39; Phillimore, Commentaries, *op. cit.*, p. 77; Holtzendorf, *Principien der Politik*

to its decisions." [150] War is the exercise of "the international right of action," [151] the highest trial of right in the sense of Bacon's famous saying.

According to Anzilotti, war is altogether outside the pale of the international legal system: It is a means of creating new law through the use of force; its counterpart in the internal sphere is revolution.[152] Thus, war is neither in contradiction with international law, nor is it specifically authorized under it.[153] "International law did not institute war, which it found already existing." [154] Its function is, in the absence of methods of peaceful change, "to bring positive law into conformity with fact." [155]

It must, however, be noted that regardless of profound changes in legal theory, the states in their practice, that remained constant over a period of several centuries up to recent times, always attempted to justify their wars with cogent reasons of law or equity,[156] in obvious response to a deep-seated spiritual need of human nature to base political actions on just and equitable grounds.[157] Thus, England declares war against France in 1689 because

(1869), p. 90; Lomonaco, *Trattato di diritto internazionale* (1905), p. 576; Hautefeuille, *Des droits et des devoirs des nations neutres* (Paris, 1848), Vol. I, titre III, Ch. 1.

[150] Hall, A Treatise on International Law (8th ed.), p. 81.

[151] Phillimore, Commentaries, *op. cit.*, p. 77.

[152] Anzilotti, *Corso di diritto internazionale* (1914–15), Vol. III, p. 183; see also Kunz, in this JOURNAL, Vol. 33 (1939), p. 33.　　　　[153] Balladore Pallieri, *loc. cit.*, p. 355.

[154] Westlake, International Law, Vol. II (2d ed. Cambridge, 1913), p. 3; Balladore Pallieri, *loc. cit.*, p. 522.

[155] Lorimer, The Institutes of the Law of Nations (London, 1884), Vol. II, p. 26; Lauterpacht, in Manning, Peaceful Change (New York, 1937), p. 163 ff.

[156] Lauterpacht, The Function of Law in the International Community (Oxford, 1933), p. 363 ff.; Strisower, *op. cit.*, p. 21 ff.; Bilfinger, *"Betrachtungen über politisches Recht,"* I *Zeitschrift für ausländisches öffentliches Recht und Völkerrecht*, 1, p. 66.

[157] Hedemann, *"Gedanken über Gerechtigkeit,"* 10 *Archiv für Rechtsphilosophie* (1916–17), p. 161 ff.; Kunz, in this JOURNAL, Vol. 33 (1939), p. 45. States, in their declarations of war, are wont to express the hope that the justice of their cause will procure Divine assistance. Thus, the Duke of Milan declares that he takes up arms against the Duke of Savoy "confident in the Divine mercy which always favors the just cause." Declaration of Sept. 4, 1427 (Du Mont, *Corps Universel Diplomatique du Droit des Gens*, Vol. II, 2, p. 193); King Charles II of England's declaration of war against The Netherlands in 1672 ends on the same note of "confidence which we have in God that he will assist us in our just enterprise" (Du Mont, Vol. VII, 1, p. 163); the King of England enters the War of 1812 against the United States "under the favour of Providence, relying on the justice of his Cause" (Br. and For. State Papers, Vol. I, 2, p. 1508); the same is true with regard to the Emperor of Russia in his wars against Turkey of 1828, 1853 and 1877 (Manifesto of the Emperor of Russia, 14–26 April, 1828, Br. and For. State Papers, Vol. 15, p. 655; Russian Declaration of War of Oct. 20–Nov. 1, 1853, *ibid.*, Vol. 61, p. 1056: "The Most High . . . may be pleased to bless our arms in the holy and just cause"; Manifesto of the Emperor of Russia, April 24, 1877, *ibid.*, Vol. 68, p. 845: "Profoundly convinced of the justice of our cause . . ."). Sometimes the cause itself is called "holy" or "sacred." See the Italian Manifesto of War with Austria, June 18, 1866 (*ibid.*, Vol. 63, p. 585): "You may rely more firmly upon the sacredness of your rights"; Proclamation of War by Serbia against Bulgaria, Nov. 2–14, 1885 (*ibid.*, Vol. 76, p. 1291): "The just cause of Serbia . . . the sacred cause of Serbia . . ."; Proclamation of the Prince of Bulgaria, Nov. 2–14, 1885 (*ibid.*, Vol. 76, p. 1295); Proclamation of the King of Prussia against France, March 17, 1813 (*ibid.*, Vol. I, 2, p. 1042); Circular addressed to

English subjects had been persecuted in France "contrary to the Law of Nations because of their religion." [158]   Russia's aim in the war against Turkey in 1828 is "the protection of her rights in the Levant" and the maintenance of respect for treaties.[159]   Uruguay speaks of "injured rights" in her war against Buenos Ayres.[160]   The President of the United States issues a proclamation to the American people at the beginning of the Mexican War "as they feel the wrongs which have forced on them the last resort of injured nations . . . , that they exert themselves in preserving order." [161]   The occupation, on the part of Russia, of the Danubian Principalities in 1853, is considered by Turkey as "a violation of treaties and consequently, a casus belli." [162]   The Emperor of Austria speaks of the "indisputable rights of my crown . . . and the integrity of the realm placed by God under my care" which both are threatened by Sardinia's inimical acts in 1859.[163]   In none of these cases is emphasis laid on the legal questions alone.   The bulk of the reasons advanced in declarations of war and accompanying diplomatic acts centers around national interests.   States defend their "rights and interests"; [164] others proceed to war because "their honor" or "dignity" has been violated or because "the glory of the state" is at stake.[165]   The defense of

Austrian Representatives at Foreign Courts, April 29, 1859 (*ibid.*, Vol. 57, p. 230); Declaration of War by Chile against Peru, April 5, 1879 (*ibid.*, Vol. 70, p. 184).

[158] British Declaration of War against France, May 17, 1689 (Du Mont, Vol. VII, 2, p. 230).

[159] Russian Declaration of War against Turkey, April 14–26, 1828 (Br. and For. State Papers, Vol. 15, p. 656); see also the Russian Declaration of War against Turkey of Oct. 20–Nov. 1, 1853 (*ibid.*, Vol. 61, p. 1056).   [160] *Ibid.*, Vol. 27, p. 1214.

[161] Proclamation of the President of the United States of War against Mexico, May 13, 1846 (*ibid.*, Vol. 34, p. 1137).

[162] Turkish Declaration of War against Russia, Oct. 4, 1853 (Br. and For. State Papers, Vol. 42, p. 1321); see also the note of the Brazilian Minister for Foreign Affairs of Sept. 1, 1864 (Makarov and Schmitz, Digest of the Diplomatic Correspondence of the European States, 1856–1871, No. 951): "The Imperial Government . . . recurs to coercive measures which the right of nations at last authorizes to carry out that which cannot be obtained by persuasive means, thus, so that justice may be done to its claims." The United States declare in 1861 that they do not contest the right of Spain, France and England "de déclarer la guerre au Mexique, afin d'obtenir satisfaction des injures qui leur ont été faites." Mr. Seward to Mr. Schurtz (Makarov and Schmitz, *op. cit.*, No. 895).

[163] Manifesto of the Emperor of Austria declaring War against Sardinia, April 28, 1859 (Br. and For. State Papers, Vol. 57, p. 228).

[164] See, for instance, *Déclaration de Guerre de la France contre les Hollandais*, Nov. 16, 1688 (Du Mont, Vol. VII, 2, p. 212); *Déclaration de Guerre de l'Empereur contre la France*, May 15, 1702 (*ibid.*, Vol. VIII, 1, p. 115); Message of the President of the United States, June 1, 1812 (Br. and For. State Papers, Vol. I, 2, p. 1316); Proclamation of the Emperor of Japan declaring war against China, Aug. 1, 1894 (*ibid.*, Vol. 86, p. 303): "Such conduct on the part of China is . . . a direct injury to the rights and interests of this Empire"; see also Tambaro, "*Das Recht Krieg zu führen*," XXXI Niemeyer's *Zeitschrift für internationales Recht*, pp. 44, 66; Italian Declaration of War against Austria-Hungary, May 23, 1915 (Br. and For. State Papers, Vol. 109, p. 963): "The Government of the King are firmly decided to assure the defense of Italian rights and interests."

[165] *Déclaration de Guerre des Provinces Unies contre la France*, March 9, 1688 (Du Mont, Vol. VII, 2, p. 213); *Déclaration de Guerre du Roi d'Espagne contre la France*, May 3, 1689 (*ibid.*, p. 226); *Déclaration de Guerre de la Grande Bretagne contre la France et l'Espagne*,

commercial interests is advanced as a motivating reason for war.[166]   During the seventeenth and eighteenth centuries, the political principle of the maintenance of the European balance of power frequently furnished a just cause for war.[167]

The conviction, as evidenced in the practice of states, that wars are fought for just causes, was strong enough to raise at the end of the World War once more the question as to the guilty party.   The Treaty of Versailles recognized the war guilt in its twofold form as entailing the civil liability of the vanquished for damages and his punishment for international crimes committed,[168] although international law, as generally accepted in 1914, did not support the idea that a state, by resorting to war, commits an international delinquency involving such liability.   Its revival by the Versailles Treaty became the starting-point for a movement once more to distinguish between just and unjust wars.[169]   The practical results hitherto achieved tend towards the establishment of a test as to the formal legality of a war rather than the setting up of standards for evaluating its intrinsic justice,[170] al-

---

May 4, 1702 (*ibid.*, Vol. VIII, 1, p. 115); *Déclaration du Roi d'Espagne contre Portugal*, April 30, 1704 (*ibid.*, 1, p. 154); *Déclaration de Guerre de Grande Bretagne contre l'Espagne*, Dec. 27, 1718 (*ibid.*, p. 555); *Manifesto de la Cour de Rio de Janeiro*, Dec. 10, 1825 (Br. and For. State Papers, Vol. 15, p. 655); Circular addressed to the Austrian Representatives at Foreign Courts, April 29, 1859 (*ibid.*, Vol. 57, p. 230): "The Emperor . . . has drawn the sword because guilty hands have attacked the dignity and honor of his Crown"; Special Message to the Legislative Chambers of the Argentine Republic, May 4, 1865 (*ibid.*, Vol. 66, p. 1274); Italian Manifesto of War with Austria, June 19, 1866 (*ibid.*, Vol. 63, p. 585): "I took up the sword to defend . . . the liberty of my people, the honor of the Italian name"; Declaration of War by Paraguay against Argentina, March 18, 1865 (*ibid.*, Vol. 66, p. 1272); French Declaration of War, July 19, 1870 (*ibid.*, Vol. 60, p. 907).

[166] See the *Déclaration de Guerre du Roi de France contre les Genois*, May 15, 1684 (Du Mont, Vol. VII, 2, p. 79): "Sa Majesté voulant empêcher la Continuation du commerce que les Genois font"; Russian Declaration of April 14–26, 1828 (Br. and For. State Papers, Vol. 15, p. 656): "Amenée par le besoin impérieux de guarantir au commerce de la Mer Noire . . . une liberté . . . inviolable."

[167] Dock, *Der Souveränitätsbegriff* (Strassburg, Diss. 1897), p. 87; this writer's article on the Congress of Vienna and the European Balance of Power, in 4 *Zeitschrift für ausländisches öffentliches Recht und Völkerrecht*, p. 228 ff.; ter Meulen, *Der Gedanke der Internationalen Organisation*, Vol. I, p. 38 ff.; see also *Déclaration de Guerre de la Grande Bretagne contre la France et l'Espagne*, May 4, 1702 (Du Mont, Vol. VIII, 1, p. 115); Austria's Declaration of War against France, Aug. 12, 1813 (Br. and For. State Papers, Vol. I, 1, p. 810).

[168] As to origin and significance of Art. 231 and the penal clauses of the Treaty of Versailles, see Holborn, *Kriegsschuld und Reparationen auf der Pariser Friedenskonferenz von 1919* (Berlin, 1932); exhaustive on the legal points: Kunz, *Die Revision der Pariser Friedensverträge* (Wien, 1932), pp. 166 ff., 172 (with further references); Göhler, *op. cit.*, p. 58 ff.; Beheim Schwarzbach, *Der Kriegsschuldartikel* (Berlin, 1934); Le Fur, *loc. cit.*, p. 368 ff.

[169] Verdross, *op. cit.*, p. 192; Oppenheim-Lauterpacht, Vol. II, p. 184 ff.; Göhler, *op. cit.*, p. 50 ff.; Bibo, "*Le dogme du bellum justum*," *Revue Internationale de la Théorie du Droit*, 1936, pp. 14–27; de la Brière, 44 *Rev. Gén. Dr. Int. Pub.*, p. 159; Wehberg, "*Das Kriegsproblem in der neueren Entwicklung des Völkerrechts*," 38 *Die Friedenswarte* (1938), pp. 129, 133 ff.; Campagnolo, "*La Paix, la Guerre et le Droit*," 45 *Rev. Gén. Dr. Int. Pub.*, p. 449 ff.

[170] See for instance the Report of the Special Committee set up to Study the Application of the Principles of the Covenant.   Adopted by the Committee on Feb. 2, 1938.   League

though the characterization of aggressive wars as crimes frequently recurs in official and semi-official pronouncements.[171] However, human thought, whose organic evolution Goethe conceives as ascending in the shape of a spiral reaching in its progress equal points on ever higher levels, has again entered the phase where the problem of war presents itself as a search for inherent restrictions on the use of force in international politics.[172] Recent events have shown "neither unquestioning acceptance of nor stumbling into war, but universal resistance, unprecedented objection." [173] A profound change in the general attitude towards war has occurred; the law must follow it.

---

of Nations Publications, VII. Political, 1938, VII, 1 (Doc. A. 7. 1938. VII), p. 51; Fischer Williams, Chapters on Current International Law (New York, 1929), p. 72: "We have thus an automatic test of, at any rate, one kind of 'unjust' war—war to which a State Member of the League resorts in violation of the League Covenant, or which is resorted to by a non-member of the League under similar conditions, is an unjust war."

[171] See Oppenheim-Lauterpacht, *op. cit.*, Vol. II, p. 151, for references to the various international declarations and instruments; further, Barandon, *Le système juridique de la Société des Nations pour la prévention de la guerre* (Paris, 1933), p. 280 ff.; Gretschaninov, *Politische Verträge* (Berlin, 1936), Vol. II, 1, pp. 323, 399, 486.

[172] See Scott, The Spanish Origin of International Law, p. 191; de la Brière, *Le droit de juste guerre: Tradition théologique, Adaptations contemporaines* (Paris, 1938), p. 186 ff.; Regout, *op. cit.*, p. 309 ff.

[173] E. Jackh, in IV New Commonwealth Quarterly, p. 313.

[3]

War and Peace in Islam

Bassam Tibi

ISLAM IS A SYSTEM of moral obligations derived from divine revelation and based on the belief that human knowledge can never be adequate. It follows that believers must act on the basis of Allah's knowledge, which is the exclusive source of truth for Muslims. Ethics in Islam, though concerned with man's actions, always relates these actions to the word of God as revealed to the Prophet, Muhammad, and as collected in the Qur'an. This understanding of ethics is shared by all Muslims, Sunni or Shi'i, Arab or non-Arab.[1]

In this chapter, I first identify the Qur'anic conceptions of war and peace that are based on this ethical foundation. I then consider several Islamic traditions pertaining to the grounds for war, the conduct of war, and the proper relation of Islam to the modern international system. I conclude that the Islamic worldview is resistant to change and that there are many obstacles to the development of an ethic of war and peace compatible with the circumstances of the modern age.

The basic scriptures of Islam, the Qur'an and the Hadith, are written in Arabic. My effort here to understand Islamic thinking on war and peace focuses on the Qur'an and on interpretations of Islamic tradition in contemporary Sunni Islam. Because the most important trends in Sunni Islam have been occurring in the Arab world (all Sunni Muslims are, for example, bound by the *fatwas* of the Islamic al-Azhar university in Cairo), my references to the Arabic Qur'an, to the teachings of al-Azhar, and to authoritative sources for Islamic fundamentalism reflect not Arab centrism but the realities of Islam.

CONCEPTIONS OF WAR AND PEACE

The Qur'an chronicles the establishment of Islam in Arabia between the years 610 and 632 A.D. In early Meccan Islam, before the founding of the first Islamic state at Medina, in a Bedouin culture hostile to state structures, one fails to find Qur'anic precepts related to war and peace. Most Meccan verses focus on spiritual issues. Following their exodus (*hijra*) from Mecca in 622, the Prophet and his supporters established in Medina the first Islamic political community (*umma*). All Qur'anic verses revealed between

622 and the death of the Prophet in 632 relate to the establishment of Islam at Medina through violent struggle against the hostile tribes surrounding the city-state.

Most debate among Muslims about the Islamic ethics of war and peace is based on literal readings of the Qur'anic verses pertaining to early Medina. Muslims believe in the absolutely eternal validity of the Qur'an and the Hadith (the sayings and deeds of the Prophet). Muslims believe that human beings must scrupulously obey the precepts of the Qur'an. In addition, Muslims are generally reluctant to take a historical view of their religion and culture. Quotations from the Qur'an serve as the point of departure for discussions of war and peace.[2]

Qur'anic traditions of war are based on verses related to particular events. At times, they contradict one another. It is not possible, therefore, to reconstruct from these verses a single Islamic ethic of war and peace.[3] Instead, there are a number of different traditions, each of which draws selectively on the Qur'an to establish legitimacy for its view of war and peace.

The common foundation for all Islamic concepts of war and peace is a worldview based on the distinction between the abode of Islam (*dar al-Islam*), the "home of peace" (*dar al-Salam*) (Qur'an, Jon. 10:25), and the non-Muslim world, the "house of war" (*dar al-harb*).[4] This distinction was the hallmark of the Islamic system before the globalization of European society and the rise of the modern international system.[5] In fact, however, the division of the world in early Islam into the abode of peace and the world of unbelievers clashed with reality long before the intrusion of Europe into the Muslim world. Bernard Lewis, for example, argues that by the Middle Ages, the dar al-Islam was dismembered into a "multiplicity of separate, often warring sovereignties." Lewis also holds that "in international . . . matters, a widening gap appeared between legal doctrine and political fact, which politicians ignored and jurists did their best to conceal."[6] As we shall see, this refusal to come to terms with reality remains a hallmark of Islamic thought today.

The establishment of the new Islamic polity at Medina and the spread of the new religion were accomplished by waging war. The sword became the symbolic image of Islam in the West.[7] In this formative period as well as during the period of classical Islam, Islamic militancy was reinforced by the superiority of Muslims over their enemies. Islamic jurists never dealt with relations with non-Muslims under conditions other than those of "the house of war," except for the temporary cessation of hostilities under a limited truce.

The military revolution that took place between the years 1500 and 1800 signaled the start of modern times and, ultimately, the rise of the West and the concomitant decline of the world of Islam. Since the beginning of the seventeenth century, Muslims have tried to establish armies on the European model to offset the increasing weakness of the "abode of Islam."[8] The rise of the West as a superior military power ultimately led to the globalization of the European model of the modern state. The changed historical balance presented Muslims with a major challenge, for the dichotomy between dar al-Islam and dar al-harb is incompatible with the reality of the world of nation-states. Each of these changes created pressure for Muslims to rethink their holistic worldview and their traditional ethics of war and peace. But despite its incompatibility with the current international system, there has yet to be an authoritative revision of this worldview.

At its core, Islam is a religious mission to all humanity. Muslims are religiously obliged to disseminate the Islamic faith throughout the world: "We have sent you forth to all mankind" (Saba' 34:28). If non-Muslims submit to conversion or subjugation, this call (*da'wa*) can be pursued peacefully. If they do not, Muslims are obliged to wage war against them. In Islam, peace requires that non-Muslims submit to the call of Islam, either by converting or by accepting the status of a religious minority (*dhimmi*) and paying the imposed poll tax, *jizya*. World peace, the final stage of the da'wa, is reached only with the conversion or submission of all mankind to Islam.

It is important to note that the expression "dar al-harb" (house of war) is not Qur'anic; it was coined in the age of Islamic military expansion. It is, however, in line with the Qur'anic revelation dividing the world into a peaceful part (the Islamic community) and a hostile part (unbelievers who are expected to convert to Islam, if not freely then through the instrument of war). In this sense, Muslims believe that expansion through war is not aggression but a fulfillment of the Qur'anic command to spread Islam as a way to peace. The resort to force to disseminate Islam is not war (*harb*), a word that is used only to describe the use of force by non-Muslims. Islamic wars are not *hurub* (the plural of *harb*) but rather *futuhat*, acts of "opening" the world to Islam and expressing Islamic *jihad*.

Relations between dar al-Islam, the home of peace, and dar al-harb, the world of unbelievers, nevertheless take place in a state of war, according to the Qur'an and to the authoritative commentaries of Islamic jurists. Unbelievers who stand in the way, creating obstacles for the da'wa, are blamed for this state of war, for the da'wa can be pursued peacefully if others submit to it. In other words, those who resist Islam cause wars and are responsible for them. Only when Muslim power is weak is "temporary peace" (*hudna*) allowed (Islamic jurists differ on the definition of "temporary"). The notion of temporary peace introduces a third realm: territories under temporary treaties with Muslim powers (*dar al-sulh* or, at times, *dar al-'ahd*).[9]

The attitude of Muslims toward war and nonviolence can be summed up briefly: there is no Islamic tradition of nonviolence and no presumption against war. But war is never glorified and is viewed simply as the last resort in responding to the da'wa to disseminate Islam, made necessary by the refusal of unbelievers to submit to Islamic rule. In other words, there is no such thing as Islamic pacifism.

THE GROUNDS FOR WAR

The Western distinction between just and unjust wars linked to specific grounds for war is unknown in Islam. Any war against unbelievers, whatever its immediate ground, is morally justified. Only in this sense can one distinguish just and unjust wars in Islamic tradition. When Muslims wage war for the dissemination of Islam, it is a just war (futuhat, literally "opening," in the sense of opening the world, through the use of force, to the call to Islam); when non-Muslims attack Muslims, it is an unjust war ('idwan).

The usual Western interpretation of jihad as a "just war" in the Western sense is, therefore, a misreading of this Islamic concept. I disagree, for example, with Khadduri's interpretation of the jihad as *bellum iustum*. As Khadduri himself observes:

> The universality of Islam provided a unifying element for all believers, within the world of Islam, and its defensive-offensive character produced a state of warfare permanently declared against the outside world, the world of war. Thus *jihad* may be regarded as Islam's instrument for carrying out its ultimate objective by turning all people into believers.[10]

According to the Western just war concept, just wars are limited to a single issue; they are not universal and permanent wars grounded on a religious worldview.

The classical religious doctrine of Islam understands war in two ways. The first is literal war, fighting or battle (*qital*), which in Islam is understood to be a last resort in following the Qur'anic precept to guarantee the spread of Islam, usually when non-Muslims hinder the effort to do so. The other understanding is metaphorical: war as a permanent condition between Muslims and nonbelievers. The Qur'an makes a distinction between fighting (qital) and aggression ('idwan) and asks Muslims not to be aggressors: "Fight for the sake of Allah against those who fight against you but do not be violent because Allah does not love aggressors" (al-Baqara 2:190). The same Qur'anic passage continues: "Kill them wherever you find them. Drive them out of places from which they drove you. . . . Fight against them until idolatry is no more and Allah's religion reigns supreme" (al-Baqara 2:190–92). The Qur'anic term for fighting is here *qital*, not *jihad.* The Qur'an prescribes fighting for the spread of Islam: "Fighting is obligatory for you, much as you dislike it" (al-Baqara 2:216). The qital of Muslims against unbelievers is a religious obligation: "Fight for the cause of Allah . . . how could you not fight for the cause of Allah? . . . True believers fight for the cause of Allah, but the infidels fight for idols" (al-Nisa' 4:74–76).

As noted above, Muslims tend to quote the Qur'an selectively to support their own ethical views. This practice has caused a loss of specificity in the meaning of jihad, as Saddam Hussein's use of the term during the Gulf War illustrates.[11] The current dissension about the concept of jihad dates from the rise of political Islam and the eruption of sectarian religious strife. Present-day Islamic fundamentalist groups—groups whose programs are based on the revival of Islamic values—often invoke the idea of jihad to legitimize their political agendas. The reason for this misuse of the concept is simple: most fundamentalists are lay people who lack intimate knowledge of Islamic sources and who politicize Islam to justify their activities. Before the Gulf War, for example, this occurred in Egypt, during the Lebanon War, and in the civil war in Sudan.[12] Through such overuse and misuse, the concept of jihad has become confused with the related Islamic concept of "armed fighting" (qital). Therefore, there is a great need for a historical analysis of the place of scripture in Islamic tradition. Although Islamic ethics of peace and war are indeed mostly scriptural, scriptural references can be adequately interpreted only in a historical context.

As we have seen, Islam understands itself as a mission of peace for all humanity, although this call (da'wa) can sometimes be pursued by war. In this sense, the da'wa is an invitation to jihad, which means fundamentally "to exert one's self" and can involve either military or nonmilitary effort.[13] Jihad can become a war (qital) against those who oppose Islam, either by failing to submit to it peacefully or by creating obstacles to its spread. Although Islam glorifies neither war nor violence, those Muslims who fight and die for the da'wa are considered blessed by Allah.

During the very beginnings of Islam (that is, before the establishment of the city-state at Medina in 622), the revealed text was essentially spiritual and contained no reference to war. In the Meccan chapter al-Kafirun ("the unbelievers"), the Qur'an asks supporters of the new religion to respond to advocates for other faiths in this manner: "You have your religion and I have mine" (al-Kafirun 109:6). In another Meccan chapter, the Qur'an simply asks believers not to obey unbelievers. Qur'anic verses from this period use the term *jihad* to describe efforts to convert unbelievers, but not in connection with military action. There is no mention of qital in the Meccan Qur'an. The Muslims then were, in fact, a tiny minority and could not fight. The verse "Do not yield to the unbelievers and use the Qur'an for your jihad [effort] to carry through against them" (al-Furqan

25:52) clearly illustrates this persuasive rather than military use of the word *jihad*: in Mecca, the only undertaking the Qur'an could ask of believers was the argument.

After the establishment of the Islamic state at Medina, however, the Qur'an comes gradually to offer precepts in which jihad can take the form of qital (fighting). Although the Qur'an teaches the protection of life as given by God and prohibits killing, this norm has an exception: "You shall not kill—for that is forbidden—except for a just cause" (al-An'am 6:151). But it is misleading to interpret this verse as a Qur'anic expression of just war because, as noted above, the distinction between just and unjust war is alien to Islam. Instead, the verse tells Muslims to remain faithful to morality during the qital.

THE CONDUCT OF WAR

When it comes to the conduct of war, one finds only small differences between Islam and other monotheistic religions or the international laws of war. Islam recognizes moral constraints on military conduct, even in wars against non-Muslims. As in other traditions, two categories of restrictions can be distinguished: restrictions on weapons and methods of war, and restrictions on permissible targets. And, just as other traditions sometimes permit these constraints to be set aside in extreme situations, in Islamic law (*shari'a*) we find the precept "Necessity overrides the forbidden" (*al-darura tubih al-mahzurat*). This precept allows moral constraints to be overridden in emergencies, though the criteria for determining whether an emergency exists are vague.

Islamic doctrine regarding the conduct of war developed in an age in which the destructive weapons of industrial warfare were not yet available. The Qur'anic doctrine on the conduct of war is also shaped by pre-Islamic tribal notions of honor. The Qur'an asks believers to honor their promises and agreements: "Keep faith with Allah, when you make a covenant. . . . Do not break your oaths" (al-Nahl 16:19). And: "Those who keep faith with Allah do not break their pledge" (al-Ra'd 13:19). It also prescribes that the enemy be notified before an attack.

Regarding permissible targets of war, Qur'anic doctrine is in line with the pre-Islamic norm of "man's boldness" (*shahama*) in strictly prohibiting the targeting of children, women, and the elderly. Consistent with this prohibition, as well as with the pre-Islamic tribal belief that it is not a sign of honor for a man to demonstrate his power to someone who is weaker, is the precept that prisoners be fairly treated (al-Insan 76:8–9). And because the goal of war against unbelievers is to force them to submit to Islam, not to destroy them, the rules of war forbid plundering and destruction.

134 · Bassam Tibi

Islam in the Age of the Territorial State

Like any text, Islamic scripture permits divergent readings or interpretations (*ta'wil*). I wish to turn now to a discussion of three divergent patterns of Islamic thinking about war and peace, each characteristic of a different period in Islamic history: the conformism of the Islamic scholar Ahmed Ben Khalid al-Nasiri; the more recent conformism of the al-Azhar; and finally, the contemporary fundamentalist reinterpretation of the concepts of jihad and qital. Conformism seeks to perpetuate, in an altered world, the traditional ethics and the religious doctrine on which it rests, whereas fundamentalism insists on the absolute truth of the religious doctrine.

The pattern of conformism is illustrated in Moroccan thought. Unlike most Islamic states, Morocco has been independent for more than three centuries. Moroccan dynastic history is state history, and is thus a good example of Islamic conformism. Morocco was the only Arab country the Turks failed to subordinate. Political rule in Morocco was legitimized by Sunni Islam in the Sultanate (*Makhzan*), just as Ottoman rule was legitimized by Sunni Islam in the Caliphate. Though nineteenth-century Muslim thinkers in general were confused by the changing global balance of power, those Muslim *'ulama* who stood in the service of the Moroccan sultan were in a better position to face the new reality. Ahmed Ben Khalid al-Nasiri (1835–97) was the first Muslim *'alim* (man of learning) of his age to acknowledge the lack of unity in the Islamic community (umma), as well as Islam's weakness in the face of its enemies.

Al-Nasiri provided the legitimizing device for the politics of his Moroccan sultan Hassan I, even though he was reluctant to legitimize the quasi-sovereign Moroccan state and to repudiate the duty of waging war against unbelievers. Conformism like that of al-Nasiri remains the typical pattern among Muslim statesmen and their advisors, many of whom do not even know of al-Nasiri. This pattern is characterized by submission to international standards of law and conduct and acceptance of peaceful relations with non-Islamic countries. But it retains the traditional Islamic belief in the superiority of Islam and the division of the world into Islamic and non-Islamic realms.[14] Al-Nasiri continually refers to the "abode of Islam" (dar al-Islam), even though he has only his own country, Morocco, in mind.

Al-Nasiri based his case on two arguments, one scriptural and one expediential. He selectively and repeatedly refers to the Qur'anic verse "If they incline to peace then make peace with them" (al-Anfal 8:61), which becomes the normative basis for the peace established between Morocco and Europe. Al-Nasiri's expediential argument pertains to the conditions of the Islamic community (umma):

> No one today can overlook the power and the superiority of Christians. Muslims
> . . . are in a condition of weakness and disintegration. . . . Given these circum-
> stances, how can we maintain the opinion and the politics that the weak should
> confront the strong? How could the unarmed fight against the heavily armed
> power?[15]

Despite these insights, al-Nasiri maintains that Islam is equally a "shari'a of
war" and a "shari'a of peace." He argues that the Qur'anic verse "If they
incline to peace then make peace with them" rests on the notion of "Islamic
interest" (*al-maslaha*). Under contemporary conditions, in al-Nasiri's view,
the interest of Islam forbids Muslims to wage war against unbelievers:

> The matter depends on the Imam who is in a position to see the interest of Islam
> and its people in regard to war and peace. There is no determination that they
> must fight forever or accept peace forever. . . . The authority that cannot be
> contested is the opinion of the Imam [Sultan Hassan I]. . . . Allah has assigned
> him to fix our destiny and authorized him to decide for us.[16]

The neo-Islamic notion of maslaha is strongly reminiscent of the Western
idea of the "national interest" of the modern state.

This pragmatic but submissive fatwa by a leading 'alim is reflected in the
position of most contemporary 'ulama regarding war and peace. Their
ethic of peace is implicitly determined by their view that non-Muslims are
enemies with whom Muslims can, at best, negotiate an armistice (*mu-
hadana*). The belief that true peace is only possible among Muslims persists, even though it runs counter to the idea of a pluralist, secular international society.

Today there are two contrary positions on the ethics of war and peace in
Islam. The Sunni Islamic establishment, as reflected in the scholarship
produced at the al-Azhar university, continues the tradition of Islamic conformism, reinterpreting the Islamic notion of jihad to discourage the use of
force. In contrast to this peaceful interpretation of Islamic ethics, contemporary Islamic fundamentalists have emphasized the warlike aspect of
jihad, while also emphasizing the dichotomy between the dar al-Islam and
the dar al-harb.

The authoritative textbooks of al-Azhar contain an ethic of war and
peace characterized both by selective use of the sacred text and by free
interpretation. Al-Azhar does not offer either a redefinition or a rethinking
of the traditional ethics of war and peace in Islam; it simply offers one
variety of Islamic conformism.

In the most authoritative textbook of this school, Sheikh Mahmud
Schaltut asserts that Islam is a religion for all mankind, but acknowledges
that it is open to pluralism.[17] Schaltut quotes the Qur'anic verse "We have

created you as peoples and tribes to make you know one another" (al-Hujrat 49:13) to support the legitimacy of interpreting scripture at the service of pluralism. He also rejects the notion that Islam must resort to war to spread its beliefs, again quoting the Qur'an: "Had Allah wanted, all people of the earth would have believed in Him, would you then dare force faith upon them?" (Jon. 10:99). War, he argues, is not a proper instrument for pursuing the call to Islam (da'wa). Because "war is an immoral situation," Muslims must live in peace with non-Muslims. Schaltut takes pride in the fact that centuries ago Islam laid the foundations for a peaceful order of relations among nations, whereas

> the states of the present [that is, Western] civilization deceive the people with the so-called public international law. . . . Look at the human massacres which those people commit all over the world while they talk about peace and human rights!

Peaceful coexistence should be sanctioned by treaties that "do not impinge on the essential laws of Islam."[18]

A two-volume textbook edited by the present sheikh of al-Azhar, Jad al-Haqq 'Ali Jad al-Haqq, continues the effort to establish the centrality of peace in Islamic ethics and offers a significant reinterpretation of the concept of jihad.[19] But, in line with Islamic tradition, there is no mention of states: at issue is the Islamic community (umma) as a whole on the one hand, and the rest of the world on the other.

In a chapter on jihad in the first volume of his textbook, Jad al-Haqq emphasizes that jihad in itself does not mean war. If we want to talk about war, he argues, we must say "armed jihad" (*al-musallah*), to distinguish between this jihad and the everyday "*jihad* against ignorance, *jihad* against poverty, *jihad* against illness and disease. . . . The search for knowledge is the highest level of *jihad*." Having made this distinction, the Azhar textbook downgrades the importance of armed jihad, since the da'wa can be pursued without fighting:

> In earlier ages the sword was necessary for securing the path of the *da'wa*. In our age, however, the sword has lost its importance, although the resort to it is still important for the case of defense against those who wish to do evil to Islam and its people. However, for the dissemination of the *da'wa* there are now a variety of ways. . . . Those who focus on arms in our times are preoccupied with weak instruments.[20]

Jad al-Haqq also avoids interpreting the da'wa as requiring the imposition of Islam on others: "The *da'wa* is an offer to join in, not an imposition. . . . Belief is not for imposition with force." Earlier Meccan verses are quoted again and again in an effort to separate the da'wa from any notion of qital or armed jihad. "Islam was not disseminated with the power of the sword.

The *qital* (fighting) was an exception only for securing and also for the defense of the *da'wa* (call) to Islam." Despite this substantial reinterpretation, however, the textbook insists on the traditional view of Islam as a mission for all of humanity, quoting the Qur'an: "We have sent you forth as a blessing to mankind" (al-Anbiya' 21:107).[21]

The Azhar believes that in the modern age, communication networks offer a much better medium than armed conflict for the pursuit of the da'wa. Jad al-Haqq does not work out the details, however. He does not resolve the question of treaties between Muslims and non-Muslims, nor does he mention territorial states. Jad al-Haqq quotes the classical al-Qurtubi commentary of the Qur'an.[22] According to this commentary, treaties creating an armistice (hudna) between Muslims and non-Muslims can be valid for a period of no more than ten years. The model here is the treaty of Hudaybiya, negotiated by the Prophet with the Quraysh in a state of war: it was a limited truce. If the Muslims are powerful, they may not hold an armistice for more than one year; if they are militarily inferior, an armistice of ten years is allowed. There is no discussion of what occurs after that time, which implies that it is seen as heretical to revise classical doctrine and that there is no desire to review this doctrine in the light of changed international circumstances. The result is conformity or acquiescence to the new international system, but no effort to alter the classic categories.

Unlike the al-Azhar conformists, who seek to read scripture in the light of present realities, Islamic fundamentalists are inclined to reverse the procedure: a true Muslim has to view reality in the light of the text. Islamic fundamentalism as a mass movement dates back to the 1970s, though its intellectual and organizational roots can be traced to 1928, when the Muslim Brotherhood (*al-Ikhwan al-Muslimun*) was created in Egypt.[23] The leading authorities on the political thought of Islamic fundamentalism are Hasan al-Banna, the founder of this movement, and Sayyid Qutb, its foremost ideologue. But they speak only for fundamentalism, which, because it is a recent trend within Islam, cannot be seen as representative of Islam as a whole—a mistake often made in the Western media.

In his treatise on jihad, Hasan al-Banna makes literal use of the Qur'an and Hadith to support conclusions opposed to those of the Islamic conformists quoted above. According to al-Banna, the jihad is an "obligation of every Muslim" (*farida*).[24] *Jihad* and *qital* are used interchangeably to mean "the use of force," whether in the pursuit of resistance against existing regimes or in waging war against unbelievers. Fundamentalists follow the Islamic tradition of not considering states in the context of war and peace; the term "war" is used here to mean fighting among loose parties of believers and unbelievers, no matter how they are organized politically. And in contrast to traditionalists, who distinguish between the use of force to further Islam and wars of aggression ('idwan), fundamentalists apply the word *jihad* indiscriminately to any use of force, whether against unbelievers or against fellow believers whom they suspect of being merely nominal Muslims.

Al-Banna begins his treatise by quoting the al-Baqara verse referred to above: "Fighting is obligatory for you, much as you dislike it" (2:216). He continues with another quotation from the Qur'an: "If you should die or be slain in the cause of Allah, his mercy will surely be better than all the riches you amass" ('Imran 3:158). And, "We shall richly reward them whether they die or conquer" (al-Nisa' 4:74). These and similar quotations serve as the basis for al-Banna's glorification of fighting and death in "the cause of Allah."

But al-Banna does not cite the tolerant Qur'anic verse from al-Kafirun, "You have your religion and I have mine," preferring instead to extend the obligation of the qital even against the "people of the book" (*ahl al-kitab*)— Christians and Jews—with the verse "Fight against those who neither believe in Allah nor in the Last Day . . . until they pay tribute out of hand and are utterly subdued" (al-Tauba 9:29). Allah, he concludes, "has obliged Muslims to fight . . . to secure the pursuit of *al-da'wa* and thus of peace, while disseminating the great mission which God entrusted to them."[25]

With a few exceptions, the al-Azhar textbook does not treat the armed jihad (*jihad al-musallah*) as a duty for Muslims in the modern age. It downgrades the status of fighting (qital) while it upgrades the nonmilitary jihad against such evils as ignorance, poverty, and disease. In contrast, al-Banna draws a distinction between "low jihad" (*al-jihad al-asghar*) and "high jihad" (*al-jihad al-akbar*), ridiculing those Muslims who consider the qital to be a "low jihad." He considers this denigration of qital to be a misunderstanding of qital as the true essence of jihad: "The great reward for Muslims who fight is to kill or be killed for the sake of Allah." Al-Banna's treatise is in fact permeated with rhetoric glorifying death, which seems to legitimize the suicidal terrorist acts often committed by Islamic fundamentalists:

> Allah rewards the *umma* which masters the art of death and which acknowledges the necessity of death in dignity. . . . Be sure, death is inevitable. . . . If you do this for the path of Allah, you will be rewarded.[26]

It is clear that for al-Banna, peace is possible only under the banner of Islam. Non-Muslims should be permitted to live only as members of protected minorities under Islamic rule. In all other cases, war against unbelievers is a religious duty of Muslims.

The other leading fundamentalist authority, Sayyid Qutb, has revived the dichotomous Islamic division of the world into "the house of peace" (dar al-Islam) and "the house of war" (dar al-harb). He employs this dichotomy to establish that war against "unbelievers" is a religious duty for

Muslims. Giving the old dichotomy a new twist, he coins the expressions "the world of believers" and "the world of *neo-jahiliyya*" (*jahiliyya* is the Islamic term for the pre-Islamic age of ignorance). For Qutb, modernity is nothing more than a new form of jahiliyya. Qutb claims that "the battle lying ahead is one between the believers and their enemies. . . . Its substance is the question *kufr aw iman?* (unbelief or belief?), *jahiliyya aw Islam?* (ignorance or Islam?)."[27] The confrontation, then, is "between Islam and the international society of ignorance"[28]—a confrontation in which victory is reserved for Islam.[29]

The large number of pamphlets industriously produced by Islamic fundamentalists during the past two decades seldom go beyond quoting passages from al-Banna and Qutb. Contemporary fundamentalists often cite passages like this from Qutb:

> The dynamic spread of Islam assumes the form of *jihad* by the sword . . . not as a defensive movement, as those Muslim defeatists imagine, who subjugate to the offensive pressure of Western orientalists. . . . Islam is meant for the entire globe.[30]

Qutb's repudiation of the mainstream conformist view that Islam resorts to war only for the defense of Muslim lands is central to fundamentalist thinking.

Qutb's influence is illustrated in Muhammad Na'im Yasin's 1990 book on jihad. The book develops an understanding of war between believers and unbelievers as a gradual process in which, in the last stage, "regardless of an attack of the Muslim lands by unbelievers, . . . fighting of Muslims against them ought to take place." Yasin then quotes the Qur'anic verse "Fight against the unbelievers in their entirety as they fight against you in your entirety" (al-Tauba 9:36), commenting on the verse as follows: "The duty of *jihad* in Islam results in the necessity of *qital* against everyone who neither agrees to convert to Islam nor to submit himself to Islamic rule." He concludes that the ultimate "return to Allah cannot be pursued through wishful thinking but only through the means of *jihad*."[31] According to Colonel Ahmad al-Mu'mini, an officer in the Jordanian army, this offensive view of jihad must determine the military policies of all Islamic states.[32] Al-Mu'mini's views have been widely circulated.

As we have seen, some Muslims have made the effort to adapt Islamic doctrine to the modern international system, but many go only so far as to make pragmatic adjustments to the doctrine that mankind must either accept Islam or submit to Muslim rule. It is true that Islamic states subordinate themselves to international law by virtue of their membership in the United Nations. But although international law prohibits war, Islamic law (the shari'a) prescribes war against unbelievers.[33] Does the recognition of international law by Islamic states really indicate a revision of Islamic ethics

140 · Bassam Tibi

regarding war and peace? Or does this recognition indicate no more than outward conformity of the Muslim world to international society?

Most Western authors on war and peace in Islam overlook the fact that there is no concept of the territorial state in Islam.[34] Therefore, Islamic thinkers view war as a struggle, not between states, but between Muslims as a community (umma) and the rest of the world inhabited by unbelievers (dar al-harb). In contrast, the classic treatise on Islamic "international law" by the Muslim legal scholar Najib Armanazi acknowledges that the international order established by the treaty of Westphalia—in which relations among states are organized on the basis of the mutual recognition of each other's sovereignty—is contradicted by the intention of the Arab conquerors to impose their rule everywhere. But despite this contradiction, Armanazi argues, Muslims do in practice recognize the sovereignty of states with whom they conduct relations on the basis of "the *aman*, customary law or the rule of honoring agreements (*'ahd, 'uhud*)." Nevertheless, "for Muslims war is the basic rule and peace is understood only as a temporary armistice. . . . Only if Muslims are weak [are their adversaries] entitled to reconciliation." And, he continues, "for Muslim jurists peace only matters when it is in line with the *maslaha* (interest) of Muslims."[35] Between Muslim and non-Muslim, peace is only a temporary armistice and war remains the rule.

In short, Muslim states adhere to public international law but make no effort to accommodate the outmoded Islamic ethics of war and peace to the current international order. Thus, their conduct is based on outward conformity, not on a deeper "cultural accommodation"—that is, a rethinking of Islamic tradition that would make it possible for them to accept a more universal law regulating war and peace in place of Islamic doctrine. Such a "cultural accommodation" of the religious doctrine to the changed social and historical realities would mean a reform of the role of the religious doctrine itself as the cultural underpinning of Islamic ethics of war and peace.[36] If this is correct, then Mayer's conclusion that "Islamic and international legal traditions, long separated by different perspectives, are now starting to converge in areas of common concern"[37] is far too optimistic. The convergence is limited to practical matters and does not reach to basic conceptions of war and peace.[38]

On the contrary, what we have seen, instead of convergence with Western ideas, is a revival of the classical doctrine of the dichotomy between dar al-Islam and dar al-harb. Muslim writers today commonly describe all the wars involving Muslim lands since 1798 (when Napoleon invaded Egypt) down to the Arab-Israeli wars and the Gulf War as "unjust wars" undertaken by the "crusaders" against the world of Islam.[39]

For Muslims, the modern age is marked by a deep tension between Islam and the territorial state.[40] In fact, there is no generally accepted concept of the state in Islam; the "community of believers" (umma), not the state, has always been the focus of Islamic doctrine. With a few exceptions, Islamic jurists do not deal with the notion of the state (*dawla*). As the Moroccan scholar 'Abdullatif Husni writes in his study of Islam and international relations, recent defenders of the classical Islamic division of the world

> confine themselves to quoting classical Islamic jurists. In their writings we do not even find the term "state." This deliberate disregard indicates their intention to ignore the character of the modern system of international relations. They refuse to acknowledge the multiplicity of states which are sovereign and equal in maintaining the notions of *dar al-Islam* and *dar al-harb*.[41]

Though the Islamic world has made many adjustments to the modern international system,[42] there has been no cultural accommodation, no rigorously critical rethinking of Islamic tradition.[43]

CONCLUSION

In discussing the basic concepts of the Islamic tradition of war and peace, and their understanding by Muslims at the present, my focus has been on Muslim attitudes toward war. The ground for war is always the dissemination of Islam throughout the world. And in conducting war, Muslims are to avoid destruction and to deal fairly with the weak. Muslims do not view the use of force to propagate Islam as an act of war, given their understanding of the da'wa as an effort to abolish war by bringing the entire world into the "house of Islam," which is the house of peace. For this reason, as we have seen, Islamic conquests are described by Islamic historians not as wars (hurub) but as "openings" (futuhat) of the world to Islam.

Despite the universal religious mission of Islam, the world of Islam was a regional, not a global, system.[44] The only global system in the history of mankind is our present international system, which is the result of the expansion of the European model. As we have seen, this modern international system has placed strain on the ethics of war and peace in Islam, generating the divergent responses of conformism and fundamentalism.

Islamic war/peace ethics is scriptural and premodern. It does not take into account the reality of our times, which is that international morality is based on relations among sovereign states, not on the religions of the people living therein. Though the Islamic states acknowledge the authority of international law regulating relations among states, Islamic doctrine governing war and peace continues to be based on a division of the world into dar al-Islam and dar al-harb. The divine law of Islam, which defines a partial community in international society, still ranks above the laws upon which modern international society rests.

142 · Bassam Tibi

The confrontation between Islam and the West will continue, and it will assume a most dramatic form.[45] Its outcome will depend on two factors: first, the ability of Muslims to undertake a "cultural accommodation" of Islamic religious concepts and their ethical underpinnings to the changed international environment; and second, their ability to accept equality and mutual respect between themselves and those who do not share their beliefs.

NOTES

1. George Makdisi, "Ethics in Islamic and Rationalist Doctrine," in Richard G. Hovannisian, ed., *Ethics in Islam* (Malibu, CA: Udena Publications, 1985), 47. On the concept of knowledge in Islam, see Bassam Tibi, *Islamischer Fundamentalismus, moderne Wissenschaft und Technologie* (Frankfurt am Main: Suhrkamp Verlag, 1992), 80–93; and Tibi, "Culture and Knowledge," *Theory, Culture, and Society* 12 (1995), 1–24.

2. Representative of this method, and equally authoritative, is a book by the former sheikh of al-Azhar, 'Abdulhalim Mahmud, *Al-jihad wa al-nasr* (Cairo: Dar al-Katib al-'Arabi, 1968). This work is the point of departure for the other books published in Arabic that are cited here.

3. On this point, I disagree with Muhammed Shadid, *Al-jihad fi al-Islam*, 7th ed. (Cairo: Dar al-tawzi' al-Islamiyya, 1989), the most widely known and authoritative study in Arabic on this topic, and with Majid Khadduri, *War and Peace in the Law of Islam* (Baltimore: The Johns Hopkins University Press, 1955). Both authors suggest, though from different points of view, that a consistent concept of jihad can be found in the Qur'an. My reading of the Qur'an does not support this contention.

4. Qur'anic references are to the Arabic text in the undated Tunis edition published by Mu'assasat 'Abdulkarim ben 'Abdullah. I have checked my translations against the standard German translation of Rudi Paret (Stuttgart: Kohlhammer Verlag, 1979), the new German translation by Adel Th. Khoury (Gütersloh: Gerd Mohn Verlag, 1987), and the often inadequate English translation by N. J. Dawood, 4th ed. (London and New York: Penguin, 1974).

5. See Bernard Lewis, "Politics and War," in Joseph Schacht and C. E. Bosworth, eds., *The Legacy of Islam*, 2d ed. (Oxford: Clarendon Press, 1974); Marshall G. S. Hodgson, *The Venture of Islam*, 3 vols. (Chicago: University of Chicago Press, 1974); Adam Watson, *The Evolution of International Society* (London: Routledge, 1992), 113ff.; and Hedley Bull, "The Revolt against the West," in Hedley Bull and Adam Watson, eds., *The Expansion of International Society* (Oxford: Clarendon Press, 1984), 217–28.

6. Lewis, "Politics and War," 173, 176.

7. See, for example, Beate Kuckertz, ed., *Das Grüne Schwert: Weltmacht Islam* (Munich: Heyne Verlag, 1992).

8. See David B. Ralston, *Importing the European Army: The Introduction of European Military Techniques and Institutions into the Extra-European World, 1600–1914* (Chicago: University of Chicago Press, 1990), esp. chs. 3 and 4.

9. See Sabir Tu'aymah, *Al-Shari'a al-Islamiyya fi 'asr al-'ilm* (Beirut: Dar al-Jil, 1979), 217, 223ff.

10. Khadduri, *War and Peace*, 63–64. Khadduri concludes, I think prematurely, that "at the present it is not possible to revive the traditional religious approach to foreign affairs. . . . The jihad has become an obsolete weapon" (p. 295). See the more recent survey by John Kelsay, *Islam and War: A Study in Comparative Ethics* (Louisville, KY: Westminster/John Knox Press, 1993).

11. See the Arabic text of the first call by Saddam Hussein to jihad in *Al-Muntada* (Amman) 5 (Sept. 1990), 21–22. The concept of jihad is considered by Kenneth L. Vaux, *Ethics and the Gulf War: Religion, Rhetoric, and Righteousness* (Boulder, CO: Westview Press, 1992), 63–86. See also James Piscatori, ed., *Islamic Fundamentalisms and the Gulf Crisis* (Chicago: American Academy of Arts and Sciences, 1991), esp. the entry for jihad in the index (p. 259). Earlier, Islamic jihad had been interpreted in Western terms as a war of liberation grounded in the right of self-determination against colonial rule. On this topic, see Rudolph Peters, *Islam and Colonialism: The Doctrine of Jihad in Modern History* (The Hague: Mouton, 1979); Bassam Tibi, "Politische Ideen in der 'Dritten Welt' während der Dekolonisation," in Iring Fetscher and Herfried Münkler, eds., *Pipers Handbuch der politischen Ideen*, vol. 5 (Munich: Pipers Handbuch, 1987), 363–402; and Jean-Paul Charney, *L'Islam et la guerre: De la guerre juste à la revolution sainte* (Paris: Fayard, 1986).

12. On Egypt, see Nabil 'Abdulfattah, *Al-mashaf wa al saif* (Cairo: Madbuli, 1984), and Nu'mat-Allah Janinah, *Tanzim al-jihad* (Cairo: Dar al-Huriyya, 1988); on Lebanon, see Martin Kramer, "Hizbullah: The Calculus of Jihad," in Martin Marty and Scott Appleby, eds., *Fundamentalisms and the State* (Chicago: University of Chicago Press, 1993); and on Sudan, see Bassam Tibi, *Die Verschwörung: Das Trauma arabischer Politik* (Hamburg: Hoffmann and Campe, 1993), 191–208.

13. See Shadid, *Al-jihad fi al-Islam*.

14. The work of al-Nasiri has been republished in nine volumes: Namudhaj Ahmed ben Khalid al-Nasiri, *Al-Istiqsa' fi akhbar al-Maghreb al-Aqsa* (Casablanca: Dar al-Kitab, 1955). I am relying on the comprehensive study by 'Abdullatif Husni, *Al-Islam wa al-'alaqat al-duwaliyya: Namudhaj Ahmed ben Khalid al-Nasiri* (Casablanca: Afriqya al-Sharq, 1991), which examines al-Nasiri's work in its entirety. See also Kenneth Brown, "Profile of a Nineteenth-Century Moroccan Scholar," in Nikki Keddie, ed., *Scholars, Saints, and Sufis: Muslim Religious Institutions in the Middle East since 1500* (Berkeley and Los Angeles: University of California Press, 1972), 127–48.

15. Quoted in Husni, *Al-Islam*, 141.

16. Quoted in Husni, *Al-Islam*, 149, 150.

17. Mahmud Schaltut, *Al-Islam 'aqida wa shari'a*, 10th ed. (Cairo: Dar al-Shuruq, 1980).

18. Schaltut, *Al-Islam*, 404, 409, 406.

19. Jad al-Haqq 'Ali Jad al-Haqq, for al-Azhar, *Bayan ila al-nas*, 2 vols. (Cairo: al-Azhar, 1984–88).

20. Jad al-Haqq, *Bayan ila al-nas*, 1: 277, 278–79.

21. Jad al-Haqq, *Bayan ila al-nas*, 1: 281; 2: 268; 1: 280.

22. Jad al-Haqq, *Bayan ila al-nas*, 2: 371.

144 · Bassam Tibi

23. See Richard Mitchell, *The Society of Muslim Brothers* (Oxford: Oxford University Press, 1969).

24. Hasan al-Banna, *Majmu'at Rasa'il al-Imam al-Shahid Hasan al-Banna*, new legal ed. (Cairo: Dar al-Da'wa, 1990), 275.

25. Al-Banna, *Majmu'at Rasa'il*, 275, 287.

26. Al-Banna, *Majmu'at Rasa'il*, 289, 291.

27. See Sayyid Qutb, *Ma'alim fi al-tariq*, 13th legal ed. (Cairo: Dar al-Shuruq, 1989); the quotation is from p. 201. For a commentary on Qutb's view, see Tibi, *Islamischer Fundamentalismus*.

28. Sayyid Qutb, *Al-Islam wa mushiklat al-hadarah*, 9th legal ed. (Cairo: Dar al-Shuruq, 1988), p. 195. See also his *Al-Salam al-'alami wa al-Islam*, 10th legal ed. (Cairo: Dar al-Shuruq, 1992).

29. Sayyid Qutb, *Al-Mustaqbal li hadha al-din* (Cairo: Dar al-Shuruq, 1981).

30. Sayyid Qutb, *Ma'alim fi al-tariq*, 72.

31. Muhammad N. Yasin, *Al-Jihad: Mayadinahu wa asalibahu* (Algiers: Dar al-Irschad, 1990), 76, 77, 81.

32. Colonel (al-Muqaddam) Ahmad al-Mu'mini, *Al-Ta'bi'a al-jihadiyya fi al-Islam* (Constantine, Algeria: Mu'asasat al-Isra', 1991).

33. For an interpretation of the shari'a, see Ann E. Mayer, "The Shari'a: A Methodology or a Body of Substantive Rules?" in Nicholas Heer, ed., *Islamic Law and Jurisprudence* (Seattle: University of Washington Press, 1990), 177–98; and Bassam Tibi, *Islam and the Cultural Accommodation of Social Change* (Boulder, CO: Westview Press, 1990), 59–75.

34. The concept of an "Islamic state" (*dawla islamiyya*) is not found in the classical sources; it is a new idea related to the concerns of Islamic fundamentalism. See, among others, Muhammad Hamidullah, *The Muslim Conduct of State* (Lahore: Sh. Muhammad Ashraf, 1977); Abdulrahman A. Kurdi, *The Islamic State* (London: Mansell Publishers, 1984); and Bassam Tibi, *Die fundamentalistische Herausforderung: Der Islam und die Weltpolitik* (Munich: C. H. Beck, 1992). A more detailed discussion of the confusion between the terms "community" (umma) and "nation" may be found in Tibi, "Islam and Arab Nationalism," in Barbara F. Stowasser, ed., *The Islamic Impulse* (Washington, DC: Center for Contemporary Arab Studies, 1987), 59–74.

35. Najib al-Armanazi, *Al-Shar' al-duwali fi al-Islam*, reprint of the 1930 edition (London: Riad El-Rayyes Books, 1990), 226, 157, 163.

36. See Tibi, *Islam and Cultural Accommodation*.

37. Ann E. Mayer, "War and Peace in the Islamic Tradition: International Law," mimeo, ref. no. 141 (Philadelphia: University of Pennsylvania, Wharton School, Department of Legal Studies, n.d.), 45.

38. Because the Islamic perception of non-Muslims either as *dhimmi* (Christians and Jews as protected minorities) or as *kafirun* (unbelievers) is untenable in the international system, there is an urgent need to revise the shari'a in the light of international law. See Abdullahi Ahmed an-Na'im, *Toward an Islamic Reformation: Civil Liberties, Human Rights and International Law* (Syracuse, NY: Syracuse University Press, 1990). This Islamic view of non-Muslims is incompatible with the idea of human rights, as an-Na'im clearly shows; on this point, see Ann E. Mayer, *Islam and Human Rights: Tradition and Politics* (Boulder, CO: Westview Press,

1991); and Bassam Tibi, "Universality of Human Rights and Authenticity of Non-Western Cultures: Islam and the Western Concept of Human Rights" (review article), *Harvard Human Rights Journal* 5 (1992), 221–26.

39. See Bassam Tibi, *Conflict and War in the Middle East* (New York: St. Martin's Press, 1993); and *Die Verschwörung*, 273–326.

40. For a different view, see James Piscatori, *Islam in a World of Nation-States* (Cambridge: Cambridge University Press, 1986), 40ff. I discuss this view in the introductory chapter of *Arab Nationalism: A Critical Inquiry*, 2d ed. (London: Macmillan Press, 1990).

41. 'Abdullatif Husni, *Al-Islam*, 59.

42. See the discussion above of the conformism of al-Nasiri and al-Azhar.

43. Bassam Tibi, *The Crisis of Modern Islam: A Preindustrial Culture in the Scientific-Technological Age* (Salt Lake City: University of Utah Press, 1988); Fazlur Rahman, *Islam and Modernity* (Chicago: University of Chicago Press, 1982); and W. Montgomery Watt, *Islamic Fundamentalism and Modernity* (London: Routledge, 1988).

44. Watson, *Evolution of International Society*, 112–19 and 214–18.

45. See Samuel P. Huntington, "The Clash of Civilizations?" *Foreign Affairs* 72 (1993), 22–49; and Bassam Tibi, *Der Krieg der Zivilisationen* (Hamburg: Hoffmann and Campe, 1995), esp. ch. 4.

Part II
League of Nations Era

[4]

INTERNATIONAL LAW AND RESORT TO ARMED FORCE.

J. L. BRIERLY.

I.

THE relation of war to the international system was stated by W. E. Hall in a well-known passage of his treatise in these words: 'International law has no alternative but to accept war, independently of the justice of its origin, as a relation which the parties to it may set up if they choose, and to busy itself only in regulating the effects of the relation.'[1] This view, which came to be more or less generally accepted by international lawyers in the course of the nineteenth century, marked the definite abandonment of the claim of the classical jurists to distinguish between *bellum iustum* and *bellum iniustum*, and it was in a sense an admission that international law had so far failed in the primary task of all legal systems, that of establishing and maintaining a distinction between the legal and the illegal use of force. But it had the great merit of candour, and it brought the theory of the law into accord with what had always been and still remained the facts of international practice.

War, however, is only the most extreme form that an appeal to force may take; and certain measures of coercion by violent means, but not amounting to war and regarded as consistent with the continuance of a state of peace between the parties, have also to be fitted into the international system. As regards these the attitude of the law has been hesitating. Westlake, indeed, says frankly that 'so far as any form of force in peace is recognized as an international institution, it is a weapon placed in the hands of States to be used, so far as law is concerned, in their discretion.'[2] Certainly when once we have admitted that the law must stand aside when States resort to war, there is a certain unreality in its undertaking to pronounce on the legality or otherwise of their conduct when they resort to a milder form of force, for an allegation of illegal action can easily be displaced

---

[1] International Law (8th ed.) p. 82.
[2] International Law, Part II, p. 19.

International Law and Resort to Armed Force. 309

by merely acknowledging the existence of a war. Thus in 1902 Germany, who, together with Great Britain, had instituted a blockade of Venezuelan ports, at first described her action as a *pacific* blockade, but on the United States protesting that a pacific blockade could not, as Germany proposed, be enforced against neutral ships, she accepted what appears to have already been the British view, and recognized that a state of war had come into existence [3] despite the fact that in most other respects the measures taken were nearer to a pacific blockade than to war as ordinarily waged.

On the other hand other writers have attempted to establish certain rather general conditions for the legal application of measures of force which do not amount to war. Hall says of reprisals that ' they are supposed to be used when an injury has been done, in the commission of which a State cannot be expected to acquiesce, for which it cannot get redress by purely amicable means, and which is scarcely of sufficient magnitude to be a motive of immediate war.' [4] ' To make reprisals either disproportioned to the provocation, or in excess of what is needed to obtain redress, is to commit a wrong.' Oppenheim's view is similar. ' Reprisals,' he says,[5] ' are admissible in the case of international delinquencies solely and exclusively.' They ' must be in proportion to the wrong done, and to the amount of compulsion necessary to get reparation.' They ' are admissible only after negotiations have been conducted in vain for the purpose of obtaining reparation from the delinquent State.' [6] Fauchille [7] insists in the same way on the rule of proportion to the offence and on the necessity for a previous demand for reparation having been made in vain. But it is noticeable that all these writers seem conscious of a certain unreality in the profession of the law to regulate reprisals. *Elles sont fréquemment*, says Fauchille, *un pur fait brutal, et non l'exercice régulier d'un droit.*

Apart from these rather uncertain limitations imposed by customary international law, the right to resort to armed force had been limited before the War in one case by convention. The second Hague Convention of 1907 provided in Art. I that: ' The contracting Powers agree not to have recourse to armed

---

[3] Cf. Moore, Digest, VII, 140.
[4] *Ibid.* p. 434.
[5] International Law (4th ed.), Vol. II, p. 84.
[6] These three conditions were applied judicially in an arbitration between Portugal and Germany arising out of damage caused in the Portuguese colonies by Germany during the war and justified by her as acts of reprisal. The award is reported in *Revue de droit international*, 1929, p. 255.
[7] *Traité de droit international public*, Tom. 1, 3me partie, p. 690.

force for the recovery of contract debts claimed from the Government of one country by the Government of another country as being due to its nationals. This undertaking is, however, not applicable when the debtor State refuses or neglects to reply to an offer of arbitration, or, after accepting the offer, prevents any *compromis* from being agreed on, or, after the arbitration, fails to submit to the award.'

II.

In the attempts that have been made since 1919 to organize the peaceful relations of the society of States, provisions limiting the right to resort to war hold a prominent place, and it is no longer true to say that international law accepts war 'as a relation which the parties to it may set up if they choose.' The most important limitations are those imposed by the Covenant of the League of Nations and by the Pact of Paris, which may be summarized as follows:

In the Covenant the member States have undertaken

(a) by Art. XII to submit 'any dispute likely to lead to a rupture' either to arbitration or judicial settlement or to inquiry by the Council, and 'in no case to resort to war until three months after the award by the arbitrators or the judicial decision, or the report by the Council.'

(b) by Art. XIII not to 'resort to war' against any member of the League that complies with an award or a decision.

(c) by Art. XV not to 'go to war' with any party to a dispute that complies with the recommendations of a report by the Council unanimously agreed to by the members thereof other than the parties to the dispute.

The general aim of these provisions is clear. They are intended to secure that a State shall not 'resort to war' without having first submitted its case either to international decision or at least to international consideration, or after such decision or consideration in defiance of its result. They leave open indeed certain cases (the so-called 'gaps' in the Covenant) in which resort to war is not in terms excluded, but by Art. XI the duty of the League to 'take any action that may be deemed wise and effectual to safeguard the peace of nations' in the event of 'any war or threat of war' remains applicable in such cases. They do not, as it is sometimes said, create any *right* to make war, and their practical importance is probably in any case not very great, for if another war should come, it is much more

International Law and Resort to Armed Force. 311

likely to come in breach of the Covenant rather than through one of the 'gaps.' Finally, 'should any member of the League "resort to war" in disregard of its covenants under Art. XII, XIII, or XV' the sanctions of Art. XV become applicable.

In the Pact of Paris the parties

(a) by Art. I 'condemn recourse to war for the solution of international controversies, and renounce it as an instrument of national policy in their relations with one another'; and

(b) by Art. II 'agree that the settlement or solution of all disputes or conflicts of whatever nature . . . shall never be sought except by pacific means.'

It will be noted that, with the exception of Art. II of the Pact, all these provisions contain prohibitions of or limitations on actual war. They do not, at any rate in terms, affect the right of a State to resort to armed force, unless the armed force takes the extreme form of war. Recent events have now revealed the great importance of this omission, and it is becoming clear that if this vital distinction between the lawful and the unlawful use of force in the international field is to be made effective, even to the extent that its effectiveness rests on a satisfactory state of the law, it is not enough to define the position of war in the international system. The law must have a clear policy also on the wider question of the use of armed force in general, and to that end I suggest that we shall have to be prepared with answers to three questions : —

(1) What is war in the legal sense?

(2) What limitations, if any, does the present law impose on resort to armed force which does not legally amount to war?

(3) What limitations on such measures are desirable and practicable for the future?

III.

As Dr. McNair [8] has pointed out in a valuable article on 'The Legal Meaning of War,' 'war is a state or condition of affairs, not a mere series of acts of force.' How does this state of affairs come into existence in law?

Some of the events which will give rise to the state of war are clear. It will come into existence (1) if a State expressly declares war to exist; (2) if without an express declaration a

---

[8] Grotius Society Transactions, Vol. 11, p. 29. A number of definitions by different writers are collected in the article.

State commits acts of force against another State and accompanies them by indications from which an *animus belligerendi* can be inferred, *e.g.* if it calls upon third States to observe the obligations of neutrality; (3) if a State commits acts of force without the *animus belligerendi*, but the State against which they are committed elects to treat such acts as having introduced a state of war.

So much seems to be clear. But what is not quite clear, is whether these three contingencies exhaust the possible ways in which war may begin.

In the present Sino-Japanese dispute it appears, so far as the facts are known, that none of these conditions has been satisfied. Are we therefore to conclude that there is no ' war ' in the Far East? The question is one of great difficulty, and probably before the present dispute had arisen most international lawyers would have said that it related to a contingency so improbable that it was unnecessary to consider it. Yet for about six months now hostilities on a considerable scale have been carried on which, for different reasons on each side, but for reasons which it is not difficult to guess at in the peculiar circumstances of the case, neither party is prepared to recognize as war.

The layman is apt to regard the lawyer's doubts in this matter with impatience. Would anyone but a lawyer hesitate to describe what has been happening as 'war,' and is it not certain that at least when that term was used in the Covenant and the Pact it was intended, or would have been intended if the case had been foreseen, to cover the situation which has now arisen? The layman's instinct may possibly be right even in law, but the issue is not a mere technicality as he is apt to think. It may seem absurd to say that peace has not been broken in the Far East, but on the other hand it is well to remind ourselves that what has been happening there, deplorable as it is, does differ in important respects from what probably would have happened if there had been an avowed state of war. It differs in particular in the limited objective of the hostile operations, in the continuance of diplomatic relations between the parties, and in the fact that, so far as is known, no claim to interfere with the normal rights of third States has been put forward on either side. These are not technical, but very practical differences.

In any case lawyers are bound to try to answer the question on legal grounds. Dr. McNair in the article already quoted, after mentioning certain authorities which I shall not repeat,

International Law and Resort to Armed Force. 313

concludes (1) that the State against which measures of force are taken has an option to treat them as war; (2) that the State which takes such measures does so at its peril—that is, at the peril of having initiated a war if the other State elects to regard them as war; (3) that that State may manifest its election in favour of war, *either by repelling force by force,*[9] or by a declaration that it regards the measures as war; (4) that if it elects for war, its election has a retroactive effect, and the state of war arises on the commission of the first act of force. There can be no doubt that these propositions correctly state the law, but they are not decisive of the actual point which has arisen in the Sino-Japanese dispute. China has ' repelled force by force,' but it appears that in doing so she did not intend to manifest an election in favour of treating the original force used by Japan as having initiated war, and I do not understand Dr. McNair to suggest that the act of ' repelling force by force ' raises more than a presumption of an intention to elect for war. In the present case it does not seem possible to attribute that intention to China. We are confronted then with this question : must we say that if acts of force are sufficiently serious and long con- tinued, then, even if both sides disclaim any *animus belligerendi* and refuse to admit that a state of war has arisen between them, there comes a point at which the law must say to the parties, ' you are refusing to recognize the facts; your actions are of a kind which it is the policy of the law to characterize as " war " ; and therefore, whatever you choose to say about it, you have in fact set up a state of things which in the eye of the law is a state of war ' ?

Whatever may be the true answer to that question—and I am inclined to think that the answer ought to be in the affirmative— it may be that for the proper interpretation of the term ' resort to war ' in the Covenant, the existence or non-existence of a legal ' state of war ' is not absolutely decisive. The main reason which has made it necessary for the law to distinguish very definitely between a state of war and a state of peace lies in the necessity for safeguarding the interests of third parties not engaged in the hostilities; if there is a state of war, but not otherwise, third parties are neutrals with the rights and duties created by the laws of neutrality. But when the authors of the Covenant used the term ' resort to war,' they were not concerned with the law of neutrality; they were concerned with the much more general problem of the establishment of peace

---

[9] The italics are mine.

between nations, and it may be therefore that a State 'resorts to war' within the meaning of the Covenant, if it resorts to acts which are intrinsically 'warlike' in character, even though a 'state of war' does not result from such acts owing to the refusal of the other State to treat them as having introduced it. 'To resort,' according to the Oxford English Dictionary, is 'to have recourse to something for assistance or furtherance of an object'; and when a State 'resorts to war,' it is to objective acts of a certain kind and not to the creation of a certain legal result that it looks 'for assistance or furtherance of its object.' It would not, I think, be straining the interpretation of the phrase 'resort to war' to say that it means 'resort to warlike acts' whether or not those acts lead as a legal consequence to a state of war.

IV.

Does the present law impose any limitations on resort to armed force which does not amount to war? I have already referred to the unsatisfactory state of the customary law on this matter and to the limitation imposed by the second Hague Convention, and I have suggested a doubt whether in the Covenant the term 'resort to war' ought not to be interpreted as extending to acts which are intrinsically acts of a warlike character.

Art. II of the Pact of Paris seems at first sight to be another clear limitation. Certainly the ordinary man would expect 'pacific means' to mean 'non-violent means,' and not merely 'means which do not amount legally to war'; and this view is perhaps supported by the following words in the preamble to the Pact, 'convinced that all changes in their relations with one another should be sought only by pacific means, and be the result of a peaceful and orderly process'; for even if we can bring ourselves to say that the use of armed force may be a 'peaceful,' it certainly is not an 'orderly process.' On the other hand we must remember that the law knows of no state intermediate between peace and war, and it may be argued that means which do not amount to war must necessarily in law be classed as 'pacific.' The word would then bear the same meaning as in the term 'pacific blockade,' where it obviously does not exclude the use of force. Further it is not very easy to believe that the parties, having in Art. I renounced 'war' but not apparently anything else, intended to go further and rule out other measures besides war in Art. II. The intention receives no elucidation from the diplomatic correspondence which

International Law and Resort to Armed Force. 315

preceded the Pact, nor, of course, has it received any authoritative interpretation since. Probably the fact that the term ' war ' does not cover *all* measures of violence was not present to the mind of any of the parties.

After the bombardment and occupation of Corfu in 1923 the Council of the League remitted certain questions to a commission of jurists for advice. The fourth question raised precisely the point under consideration here; it was: —

' Are measures of coercion which are not meant to constitute acts of war consistent with the terms of Arts. XII to XV of the Covenant when they are taken by one Member of the League of Nations against another Member of the League without prior recourse to the procedure laid down in these articles? '

The answer given by the commission to this question was: —

' Coercive measures which are not intended to constitute acts of war may or may not be consistent with the provisions of Arts. XII to XV of the Covenant, and it is for the Council, when the dispute has been submitted to it, to decide immediately, having due regard to all the circumstances of the case and to the nature of the measures adopted, whether it should recommend the maintenance or the withdrawal of such measures.'

This answer is unfortunately obscure, but one of the members of the commission of jurists, Prof. Ch. de Visscher, has told us in an interesting article [10] what he at least understood by it. He begins by pointing out that traditional international law has never had any solidly based theory of the use of measures of coercion. It has been influenced by political opportunism. Hitherto, however, such measures have found some juridical justification in two ways: (a) in the inadequate development of pacific methods of settling international differences; resort to force has, therefore, often been the only possible way in which a State could obtain satisfaction for an injury; and (b) in the fact that States in the past have had an absolute right to resort to war, and measures of force falling short of war were certainly preferable to war.

But neither of these justifications is now valid in the new juridical order instituted by the Covenant, for Art. XII has created an obligation to submit all differences to one or other of the procedures there mentioned, and it has taken away the old absolute right to make war. There is no weight in the objection that it may be impossible for a State to await the expiration of the stipulated period of delay before resorting to force, for this

---

[10] *L'interprétation du Pacte au lendemain du différend italo-grec.* Revue de dr. int. et de lég. comp. 1924, p. 377.

is to confuse reprisals with legitimate defence, which remains unaffected. Hence, he concludes, it is clear that armed reprisals are incompatible at least with the spirit of the Covenant. But are they actually incompatible with its terms? Prof. de Visscher thinks that they are for the following reasons. Art. XII, in imposing the obligation to resort to one or other of the pacific procedures there indicated, must by necessary inference impose at the same time a duty to abstain from any measure of which the natural effect would be either to provoke an immediate rupture, or to impede the course of the procedure laid down by the Article and thus to compromise the chances of its successful operation. Armed force would certainly have this effect; and we must take it therefore that the article, by implication but indisputably, enjoins abstention from acts of force until the award or decision or the report of the Council is rendered. This gives us the test of the legitimacy or otherwise of measures of coercion under the Covenant, which is implied but not made explicit in the answer of the jurists, for we must conclude that those which are calculated to lead to an immediate rupture or to impede the course of the pacific procedure prescribed are forbidden. The distinction must lie in the intrinsic character of the measures themselves, and armed reprisals must be condemned, whereas economic or financial measures may still be legitimate because they do not necessarily conflict with the operation of the article.

This argument is entitled to the most serious consideration, both because of its author's position as a member of the commission and also, if I may say so, because of its intrinsic reasonableness. It is independent of the question whether the prohibition of ' resort to war ' ought to be interpreted to cover all measures of resort to ' warlike ' acts, and rests on a theory of the implied incompatibility of such measures with the positive obligations imposed by Art. XII.

V.

This article has raised more questions than it has attempted to answer, for the truth is that events have revealed to us a lacuna in the law which had hardly been suspected, and it is perhaps more profitable to consider what the future law ought to aim at than to argue about the meaning of the present. *De iure condendo* therefore I make the following suggestions.

(1) We ought *not* to aim at the total abolition of measures

International Law and Resort to Armed Force. 317

of force falling short of war, for, as Dr. McNair has suggested, it may be desirable to give them an important place in the League's armoury of sanctions.

(2) Though Art. XII will certainly bear the construction that Prof. de Visscher desires to put on it, I hesitate to say that it is the only possible construction, and at present we have to face the regrettable fact that the commission of jurists of which Prof. de Visscher was a member has not adopted it in unequivocal terms. Their answer was ambiguous,[11] but having been adopted by the Council, it is at present our most, in fact apart from the article itself our only, authoritative text. I should like to see a resolution, either of the Council or of the Assembly, elucidating the answer of the jurists in the sense contended for by Prof. de Visscher. As long as it is even doubtful whether the Covenant requires States to abstain from armed force or only to abstain from actual war during the prescribed period of delay, so as to give its peaceful procedure a fair chance of success, there is a serious lacuna in our legal machinery for the protection of peace.

(3) The prohibition of the use of armed force as a means of applying pressure or obtaining redress cannot, however, extend to a prohibition of its use in legitimate defence. Nor is it practicable, I think, to aim at a definition of self-defence, nor even at the requirement of some form of prior League authorization before measures of defence are taken, for the occasions of such measures may arise suddenly and brook no delay. That consideration raises a question of great difficulty, for if on the one hand the right of self-defence is a door which we dare not close, it is on the other hand one which it is unfortunately very difficult to keep merely ajar. It expands very easily, as Sir Norman Angell once said, into 'the defence of a foreign policy which a nation thinks indispensable to its interests and the right to be the judge of those interests.' What, however, might be aimed at is the acceptance, whenever a State is impelled to resort to armed force in self-defence, of an obligation to communicate all the facts of the situation to the League. We cannot in the present state of international organization, or probably for a long time to come, demand the international *control* of a State's action in such a case, but it is not unreason-

---

[11] So ambiguous that Dr. McNair seems to interpret it in a sense exactly the opposite of that which Prof. de Visscher at least intended it to bear. He regards it as ' putting plainly on record ' that Art. XII is ' not necessarily violated by the use of coercive measures, even when—I think we may justifiably infer from the circumstances giving rise to the interpretation by the jurists—those coercive measures involve the application of force ': *loc. cit.* p. 43.

able to insist that what it does is 'a matter of concern to the whole League' which ought to be submitted to discussion in an international forum, and if necessary to criticism or to 'any action that may be deemed wise and effectual to safeguard the peace of nations.' This action was in fact taken by Great Britain in a communication addressed to the Secretary-General of the League on February 8, 1927, explaining the reasons which had led to the dispatch of the Shanghai Defence Force.[12] It is in sharp contrast with the attitude of Japan in the present dispute. Moreover, as the Sino-Japanese dispute has only too clearly shown, it is not only the original alleged justification for resorting to measures of defence, but the length to which those measures are subsequently carried, that calls for international supervision.

(4) The great difficulty of establishing any effective legal control over the resort to armed force in the past has been that international law offered no effective alternative way of securing the redress even of a legitimate grievance. This difficulty has been reduced by the new order introduced by the Covenant, but it has not been eliminated. The League does not yet offer an effective alternative either to war or to measures of force which do not amount to war. The full solution of this difficulty is not yet even in sight, but it is the fundamental difficulty which lies at the very heart of the whole problem of peace. We are too apt to think of war merely as an evil thing which can, though the task may be difficult, be excised from the international system. We overlook the fact that war has performed a necessary social function in the past, and that if we would eliminate it for the future we shall have to provide an alternative procedure for performing that function. War has been one of the means whereby from time to time States have revised the established international order. The analogy to war in the domestic sphere is neither the crimes nor the disputes of individuals; it is revolution, and our safeguard against revolution, such as it is, is our readiness to meet legitimate grievances by ordered change in the established order. For that our instrument is a legislature, and we shall not have solved the problem of peace until we have devised, not indeed any servile imitation of a national legislature in the international sphere, but some substitute for it, some ordered process whereby we can satisfy the demand for change which is the mark of any living human

---

[12] The letter is quoted by Toynbee, Survey of International Affairs, 1926, at p. 380.

International Law and Resort to Armed Force. 319

society.[13] The Covenant has recognized the problem in Art. XI, para. 2, which declares it to be 'the friendly right of each Member of the League to bring to the attention of the Assembly or the Council any circumstance whatever affecting international relations which threatens to disturb international peace or the good understanding between nations upon which peace depends,' and again in Art. XIX under which 'the Assembly may from time to time advise the reconsideration by Members of the League of treaties which have become inapplicable and the consideration of international conditions whose continuance might endanger the peace of the world.' But we are as yet far from having recognized all that these provisions ought to mean.

---

[13] I have attempted to discuss this question in an article on ' The Legislative Function in International Relations,' published in Problems of Peace, 5th series, pp. 205—229 (Oxford University Press).

[5]

COLLECTIVE SECURITY [1]

ARNOLD D. McNAIR, C.B.E., LL.D.,[*]

It would be a mistake to use this occasion for an attempt to say something which would be of interest only to my fellow international lawyers, and I prefer to try to answer some of the questions which are now stirring in the minds of many laymen upon the meaning of the term "Collective Security" and upon the true place of force in a system of international law. Two reasons impel me to do this. The first is that the Whewell Professor is particularly charged by the founder of his chair "to make it his aim in all parts of the subject to lay down such rules and to suggest such measures as may tend to diminish war and finally to extinguish war between nations". The second is that at present, unfortunately, we have in this University no chair of International Relations, so that the Whewell Professor may be forgiven if occasionally he strays a little across the frontier which divides law from politics, even when this can only be done at the cost of approaching the debatable zone of current controversy.

The Former Attitude Towards War

Let us put ourselves in the position of a student of international law in the first decade of this century who wanted to know what was the attitude of that system of law towards war. He would be told that three centuries ago Grotius, following some of his predecessors, had attempted to classify the causes of war (with particular reference to their bearing upon the attitude of third parties), and that, as Professor Brierly[2] has written, "at the heart of his system lay the attempt to distinguish between lawful and unlawful war", but that "this distinction never became part of actual international law" and "finally it disappeared even from theory". Our student would then turn to Hall's *International Law*, which was generally regarded as the most characteristically British exposition of the subject. There he would read that[3]

[*] Whewell Professor of International Law in the University of Cambridge; Fellow of Gonville and Caius College.

[1] An Inaugural Lecture delivered on January 23, 1936. (The Committee wish to acknowledge their indebtedness to the Cambridge University Press for permission to reprint this lecture. J.F.W.)

[2] *The Law of Nations*, 1st ed., pp. 25, 26.

[3] 5th ed. (1904), by J. B. Atlay, p. 60.

COLLECTIVE SECURITY 151

"As international law is destitute of any judicial or administrative machinery, it leaves States, which think themselves aggrieved, and which have exhausted all peaceable methods of satisfaction, to exact redress for themselves by force. It thus recognizes war as a permitted mode of giving effect to its decisions."

Hall then points out that theoretically international law, professing to be a comprehensive system, "ought to determine the causes for which war can be justly undertaken", but has tried and found it impossible to do so. He adds that

"it might also not unreasonably go on to discourage the commission of wrongs by investing a State seeking redress with special rights and by subjecting a wrong-doer to special disabilities",

but in his opinion

"it would be idle for it to affect to impart the character of a penalty to war, when it is powerless to enforce its decisions. . . . International law has consequently no alternative but to accept war, independently of the justice of its origin, as a relation which the parties to it may set up if they choose, and to busy itself only in regulating the effects of the relation. Hence both parties to every war are regarded as being in an identical legal position, and consequently as being possessed of equal rights."[1]

The Edwardian student would then turn to Westlake, of whom I like to remember that several of my colleagues were his colleagues, and there he would read that[2]

"International law did not institute war, which it found already existing, but regulates it with a view to its greater humanity. War is a piece of savage nature partially reclaimed, and fitted out for the purpose of such reclamation with legal effects, such as the abrogation or suspension of treaties, and legal restrictions, such as what are called the laws of war and neutrality."

Westlake then adds[3] that

"an attempt is sometimes made to determine in the name of international law the conditions on which a recourse may be had to arms . . . but these are not rules of law . . . and the legal character of a war is the same whether they have been observed or not."

To the same effect writes Oppenheim, our much loved colleague by adoption:[4]

"War is not inconsistent with, but a condition regulated by, international law. The latter at present cannot and does not object to States which are in conflict waging war upon each other instead of peaceably settling their difference."

Such were the opinions upon the relation of international law

[1] *Op. cit.*, p. 61.
[2] *International Law*, Vol. II, "War", 1st ed. 1907, 2nd ed. 1913, p. 3.
[3] *Ibid.* p. 4.
[4] *International Law*, Vol. II, "War and Neutrality", 1st ed. 1906, 2nd ed. 1912, § 53.

to war which I learned as a student. To regard as reactionaries the teachers whom I have quoted, would be absurd: they correctly described the contemporaneous attitude of international law towards war. Great efforts were made before and during that period, notably by the Conventions emanating from the two Hague Peace Conferences of 1899 and 1907, to introduce some order into the conduct of war, and those Conventions and the customary law underlying them had more success and effect than has been realized by laymen accustomed to see and hear more of their violation than of their normal operation. My immediate predecessor, Professor Pearce Higgins, made himself an acknowledged master of this branch of the law. His main inspiration, as I see it, was the desire to impress the public, and the generations of students here and naval officers at Greenwich who came under his influence, with a sense of the binding obligation of the rules which experience and humanity had evolved for placing some checks upon the licence and barbarity of war.

But there international law stopped. War itself was no illegality. Its outbreak might sometimes involve the breach of a treaty or some other international wrong, but it more frequently took rise in circumstances not falling within the sphere regulated by law. It was extra-legal rather than illegal. Whether or not the initiation of a war was a breach of law, the rules which regulated it, once it had broken out, were the same for both or all parties. And, what is more germane to my argument, the rules which governed the attitude of states not participating in a war towards the belligerents—the law of neutrality—were the same, regardless of the rights and wrongs of the war. A rigid impartiality in their conduct towards the belligerents was required by the law.

The Present Attitude

All this changed some years ago—at any rate for the greater part of the world. Most international lawyers have realized that change for some time and have been expounding it, but the majority of laymen had not grasped the change until quite recently, and many of them are reluctant to admit the change even now. Let me mention three facts before I attempt to trace the development which has culminated in this change. Firstly, on October 9, 1935, war having broken out between two states, Italy and Abyssinia, fifty governments, including our own, met in conference and put it on record that in their opinion Italy had

COLLECTIVE SECURITY 153

"resorted to war in disregard of its covenants under Article 12 of the Covenant of the League".

The second fact is that to-day fifty governments are engaged in a series of measures, directed to handicap one of two belligerents in its contest with its adversary and eventually to make it impossible for it to continue the contest. Examine those measures, which are four in number: (1) an embargo on the export, re-export, or transit to Italy and her possessions of arms, munitions, and implements of war, while leaving their supply to Abyssinia unrestricted; (2) the prohibition of the grant of loans and credits to the Italian Government and all persons and corporations in Italian territory, while leaving the supply of similar facilities to Abyssinia unrestricted; (3) the prohibition of imports (other than gold and silver bullion and coin) from Italy into the co-operating countries, while leaving imports from Abyssinia unrestricted; (4) the prohibition of the export or re-export or transit to Italy and her possessions of a long list of "key materials", particularly minerals and transport animals, while leaving supplies to Abyssinia unrestricted.

The third fact is that our government, which has always been foremost in pursuing a policy of strict impartiality in wars to which it is not a party, has recently passed a series of Orders in Council making it a penal offence for persons in the United Kingdom to carry on with one belligerent certain trades which in previous wars they have always been free to maintain with either or both belligerents so far as the law of this country is concerned.

Public opinion has been led up to these events so gradually and so patiently that their momentous character is obscured. I am not here concerned with British policy in regard to this dispute or with the questions whether sanctions might have been applied with greater determination and whether they ought to be increased. What I wish to emphasize is the legal character and the historical significance of what is now being done. The first feature is that it is an unheard of thing that fifty non-belligerents should meet and expressly concur in singling out one of two belligerents for condemnation as a treaty-breaker and an aggressor. The second is that most, if not all, of the measures now in force in the name of sanctions would twenty-five years ago have been serious breaches of the law of neutrality, affording to the victim of them good ground for reprisals or more serious action. There is no question but that these measures would have come as a

154   YEAR BOOK OF INTERNATIONAL LAW

surprise to Hall and Westlake[1] and above all to that exponent
of the law of neutrality, Sir William Harcourt, the first Whewell
Professor, had they not known of certain changes in the law
which have intervened; for it is impossible to reconcile these
measures with the duty of impartiality traditionally incumbent
upon neutral states.

What, then, are these changes in the law and to what cause
are they due? Let us deal with the second question first. The
Great War of 1914 to 1918, by reason of the area affected by it,
the destructive character of the instruments employed in it, and
the intensity of suffering on the part of combatants and non-
combatants alike, produced a revulsion of feeling against war
greater than that which usually follows the close of a war. Many
were driven to hold the view, held by an increasing number to-day,
that in no circumstances can the use of armed force as between
states be justified and in no circumstances should it be resisted.
Some base this view upon Christian or other principles of morality,
and there are others who base it upon historical and personal
experience, believing that no evil can be so great as the evils,
spiritual and material, which flow from taking up arms or from
resisting them, and that expressions such as "national self-
defence" are merely phrases used by governments to delude
their peoples. I have neither the skill nor the time to examine
this view from any of these aspects, nor is it essential to my
theme that I should do so; for this is not the view of force which
was adopted by the Peace Conference of 1919.

The Policy of Collective Security

The treaties emanating from that Conference embody a new
principle, commonly called the principle or policy of Collective
Security, to which at present fifty-eight governments (including
our own) stand pledged. Instead of the traditional legal indifference to the question of the responsibility for the outbreak of war
there is substituted machinery for determining the party responsible and for condemning as illegal a resort to war without previously exhausting the machinery of the Covenant of the League
for the settlement of disputes. In addition to the traditional
right and duty of individual self-defence there is created a collective obligation to apply economic pressure in order to restrain
an illegal resort to war, with an option to contribute armed force

---

[1] Westlake was fully alive to the moral necessity of the disappearance of the orthodox
attitude of strict indifference: see his *Collected Papers*, pp. 375 *et seq.*

COLLECTIVE SECURITY

if necessary. On the one hand, war in breach of the Covenant is made illegal; on the other, force which is collectivized and placed at the service of the international community is made legal.

This new policy of collective security has suffered, I think, in popular esteem by being treated too much as a great ethical ideal and too little as a sound business proposition. It seems to me to rest on three main reasons. In the first place, experience of the old system has shown that the claim of one state to be so strong as to feel secure against a rival state involves, as has been repeatedly pointed out, a denial of a similar claim to the latter, with the result that it sets to work to tip the balance in its favour either by increasing its armaments or by concerting precarious alliances and *ententes* which in turn provoke counter-alliances and counter-*ententes*. Secondly, it is felt that if a state can count upon a substantial and reasonably adjacent portion of the international community coming to its aid, and, if necessary, pooling forces to protect it from aggression, it and likewise other states will be content with a lower level of armaments than if it has to rely only upon itself and any allies it can pick up and feel sure of. The third reason is that force is less likely to be abused if for the purely national and subjective test of the justification of a war there is substituted a collective judgment by parties other than the states involved and a collective condemnation of any war found by that external test to be illegal. This view was only imperfectly carried out by the Covenant, but, as we shall see, the Kellogg-Briand Pact to some extent remedies this deficiency. In a sentence, if so much can be compressed in a single sentence, the principle underlying the Covenant, in relation to the preservation of peace, is the creation of machinery for the settlement of disputes and for stigmatizing certain wars as illegal and the concerting of collective action against a state initiating an illegal war.

The machinery for the settlement of disputes takes two forms, firstly, reference to the Permanent Court of International Justice or a tribunal of arbitration, and, secondly, reference to the Council of the League for an attempt at conciliation and, failing that, for a Report which when adopted unanimously (excluding the disputing parties) has certain definite legal consequences, as has been illustrated by the dispute between Italy and Abyssinia. The first of these methods is voluntary except in so far as the parties have already bound themselves in advance, as for instance

156 YEAR BOOK OF INTERNATIONAL LAW

by what is called the "Optional Clause" of the Statute of the Permanent Court, to refer disputes of certain categories to judicial or arbitral settlement. The second is, for members of the League, obligatory in default of arbitration or judicial settlement; it is also residuary in character in that it sweeps up and governs disputes not settled by the first kind of machinery. The Permanent Court has, since it opened its doors in 1922, rendered more than sixty Judgments and Advisory Opinions, and in no instance has any party to the litigation defied the authority of the Court by refusing to give effect to its decision. I cannot digress into a discussion of the judicial and arbitral settlement of disputes beyond saying that the output of international law from judicial and arbitral sources since the World War has been prodigious. Coupled with the increase in multipartite treaties laying down rules of law, this output is rapidly transforming international law from a body of general principles resting mainly on text-book authority into a system of rules for which authority can be quoted from judicial and conventional sources, much in the same way as a modern system of national law rests on judgments and legislation. Forty-nine years ago Sir Henry Maine in a course of twelve Whewell Lectures[1] found it necessary to cite only two national judgments, one English and the other American, and one international award, the *Alabama*. A glance at a modern text-book of international law shows what an enormous advance in the law-making process has been made in half a century.[2]

The Kellogg-Briand Pact

But the League machinery is limited in its scope. Only fifty-eight states and Dominions are bound by it and among the absentees are Germany, Japan, and the United States of America. Outside the League there is frequent resort to judicial and arbitral machinery for the settlement of disputes, but there is no effective provision for collective action against an act of aggression upon a state not a member of the League; though in theory, but at present only in theory, the League machinery of collective action could be applied as between non-members. Not only is membership of the League limited but the Covenant leaves outside its ban certain kinds of war, particularly war undertaken when the Council or the Assembly has announced its failure to

---

[1] *International Law*, published by John Murray in 1894.

[2] The volumes of the *Annual Digest of Public International Law Cases* give a more eloquent testimony.

COLLECTIVE SECURITY 157

reach a unanimous Report (excluding the disputing parties) and when three months have elapsed after that failure. Accordingly, in 1928 another change took place in the attitude of international society and international law towards war and is embodied in the Kellogg-Briand Pact, or Peace Pact of Paris as it is sometimes called. The articles of this simple document are two in number and are as follows:

Article 1

"The High Contracting Parties solemnly declare in the names of their respective peoples that they condemn recourse to war for the solution of international controversies, and renounce it as an instrument of national policy in their relations with one another.

Article 2

"The High Contracting Parties agree that the settlement or solution of all disputes or conflicts of whatever nature or of whatever origin they may be, which may arise among them, shall never be sought except by pacific means."

The distinctive characteristics of this Pact and its principal differences from the Covenant may be summarized as follows:

(*a*) the Pact has been accepted by sixty-two states and Dominions and is for all practical purposes universal in its territorial scope;

(*b*) the probable[1] effect of Article 2 is to make any resort to armed force for the settlement of an international dispute illegal and thus avoids the technical point, prominent under the Covenant in the Sino-Japanese dispute of 1931 to 1933, that not every resort to armed force amounts to "resort to war";

(*c*) it is a reasonable view, though I cannot assert it to be an established opinion, that a breach of the Pact is a legal wrong not merely against the victim of the resort to armed force but also against the other signatories of the Pact;

(*d*) it contains *within it* no provision for collective sanctions, thus avoiding one of the main obstacles preventing the ratification of the Covenant by the United States of America; but a breach of it can be met by its signatories, alone or collectively, by the measures[2] available for the prevention or redress of the breach of any other treaty, if they choose to take this course;

---

[1] I say "probable" because there is some controversy on the question whether the words "except by pacific means" permit a resort to armed force which does not technically amount to war: see Lauterpacht on Oppenheim, *International Law*, Vol. II (5th ed.), § 52 *l*.

[2] What these measures may be is a highly controversial matter: see Lauterpacht in *Transactions of Grotius Society*, Vol. XX (1935), pp. 178–202. It is worth noting that Mr. Eden (as Minister for League of Nations Affairs) speaking in the House of Commons

(e) most breaches of the Pact of 1928 will also be breaches of the Covenant, so that while the United States of America does not co-operate in the collective action under the Covenant the fact of their being a party to the Pact of 1928 tends to produce, between that country and the League, a coincidence in the condemnation of an aggressor, as happened in the recent Sino-Japanese dispute, and will, I hope, eventually happen in the case of the Italo-Abyssinian war.

Such, then, in the briefest outline, are the two main documents which express in legal form the changing attitude of international society towards force. They may be summed up in two propositions: resort to armed force for the settlement of an international dispute is an illegal act, and, I submit, that illegal act is the commission of an international wrong (breach of treaty) against every state in the world (with unimportant exceptions such as Thibet) and not merely upon the victim of the use of force. That is the big new factor added by the Kellogg-Briand Pact. It is that which might, and, I think, would, justify a signatory of the Pact in conducting itself towards an aggressor in a manner which before the Pact would have amounted to unneutral conduct.

Collective Revision of the " Status Quo "

I have touched on only one aspect of the collective system— the collectivization of force. Equally important is the collective and peaceful revision of treaties and other international conditions whose continuance is a reasonable cause of friction. This principle is embodied in Article 19 of the Covenant and in Article 2 of the Pact of Rome made on June 7, 1933, between France, Germany, Italy, and the United Kingdom, but in both cases only as a principle. There is urgent need of machinery to translate that principle into practice. It is also hinted at in Sir Samuel Hoare's speech to the League Assembly on September 11, 1935, when he referred to "fear of monopoly—of the withholding of essential colonial raw materials" and "the desire for a guarantee that the distribution of raw materials will not be unfairly impeded. . .". This is only a beginning. There are certain key commodities and key positions whose continuance in the sole control of a single Power or group of Powers produces a sense of unfair-

of a breach, not of the Kellogg-Briand Pact, but of the Covenant, said: "We do not consider that any Covenant-breaking State has any legal right to require the observance by other members of the League of any of the laws of neutrality." *Hansard* (Commons), Vol. 305, p. 218 (October 23, 1935).

COLLECTIVE SECURITY　　　　　159

ness and insecurity which will not be removed until that control (which is not the same as ownership) is vested in the hands of some international authority. I do not see how you can justify a situation in which one or a few Powers can hold others to ransom, if they choose to do so, because they happen to be in control of an international highway or a vital commodity.[1] If the control of such a highway were international, the exercise of that control in aid of collective security would be easier to justify and to effect than it is while the control resides in national hands. There has been a good deal of talk recently of transferring colonies to Powers who have few or none and of the possession of a colonial empire as essential to the *amour propre* of a powerful nation. My own view is that to do anything which would tend to stereotype the colonial system in any of its present stages would be unfortunate. I regard them as transitional. I should prefer to see the colonial Powers encouraging (as we are doing) certain of their colonies to become self-governing communities. As for those colonies and protectorates not likely to be suited in the comparatively near future for this development, I consider that more would be gained than lost if many of them, though not all, were administered under some kind of international guardianship like the mandate system for the benefit of their inhabitants and the world at large. I may mention as features of that system the prohibition of native military forces for other than police purposes and local defence, and the provision of the economic open door. All this lies outside the scope of this lecture. I merely remind my audience that a system which collectivizes the use of force and provides no machinery for the collective revision of the *status quo* is certain to fail, as has been cogently shown by Sir John Fischer Williams in his short book entitled *International Change and International Peace*. The direct and positive use of collective force for the revision of the *status quo* is in my opinion unthinkable. But it is worth considering whether as a first step consent to a revision may not be induced, indirectly and negatively, by making it clear that a state which obstinately declines to co-operate in a revision pronounced after due investigation to be essential to the general welfare cannot rely upon the use of collective force in support of an untenable claim.

---

[1] For a summary of the distribution of minerals and mineral products, including petroleum, and the manner in which the denial of them to an aggressor can be used as a collective sanction, see Sir Thomas H. Holland's most valuable book, *The Mineral Sanction* (1935).

The Role of the Individual

I have mentioned only two great international instruments, the Covenant of the League and the Kellogg-Briand Pact, and I mention them because they are in force between fifty-eight and sixty-two states and Dominions respectively. But I could point to many other treaties drafted during the past seventeen years, some not in force, others only sparsely ratified, but all of them indications of the new movement on foot for the organization of collective action for the preservation of peace; for instance, the Draft Treaty of Mutual Assistance of 1923, the "Geneva Protocol" of 1924, the "General Act of Arbitration" of 1928, the Convention on Financial Assistance of 1930, the Convention to Improve the Means of Preventing War of 1931, the Rio de Janeiro Pact of Non-Aggression and Conciliation of 1933, &c. In view of this persistent effort is it possible for any fair-minded man to dismiss this movement by saying that a zealous band of visionaries in 1919 stampeded the Allied Powers into the adoption of a crazy scheme? Is it not a more reasonable interpretation to regard these developments as evidence, in General Smuts's memorable phrase, that "mankind is on the march" and seeking for some new form of organization in which we can retain and develop our personal and national life and characteristics, without the constant fear and frequent happening of the collisions between national groups which throw back civilization and now threaten to overwhelm it? At any rate I submit to you the view that this is the correct interpretation of the years since the Armistice of November 1918. I also suggest that it is primarily to the individual citizen that we must look to supply the driving-force behind this movement and not to his government. It has been accepted as the business of governments to promote the interests of the nations whose professional champions they are. It is inevitable that governments should be reluctant to abate one iota of their clients' interests, and it is only when they can be absolutely convinced that in the long run the interests of the international community coincide with those entrusted to them that most of them will move a single step in an international direction. Some of them are very hard to convince. The application of collective security involves risks; but the success of flagrant aggression in breach of solemn treaties is a danger to avert which some risk is justified, and the risk will diminish as the precedents for successful collective action accumulate.

COLLECTIVE SECURITY 161

Most great movements in public affairs originate with individuals, not with governments. It was a popular movement in this country which, after securing the abolition of the slave-trade throughout the British Empire, compelled our representatives at Vienna in 1815 to insist upon annexing to the Congress Treaty a condemnation of the trade and later made the British Government the protagonist in the international suppression of that evil. It was the devotion of a single Swiss citizen, Dunant, which infected a group of his fellow-countrymen with his zeal and ultimately induced his government to convoke a conference and secure the adoption of the Geneva Red Cross Convention of 1864. The League of Nations originated in the parallel work of two groups of citizens, one in our country and the other in the United States of America. It is, I submit, only by the action of individuals in maintaining a constant pressure upon their governments that this new movement can be brought to fruition.

The League and Armed Force

What is happening now is not that force is being abolished. It is being collectivized, denationalized. The manner of its exercise remains national: the judgment which precedes and authorizes its exercise is collective.[1] When thus authorized, it acquires the character of a public sanction, while its actual exercise remains in private hands. Such, as I see it, is the essence of the system of collective security towards which the world, or at any rate Europe in the first place, is groping its way and which is at the moment on trial. Hitherto there has been a tendency to assume that it is the League whose duty it is to afford security, but we are now beginning to realize that it is upon the League's members that this duty rests. If we think that the principle of collective security can be established without incurring risk, we delude ourselves. To say, as some are now saying, that the

---

[1] There is at present a movement for the creation of an *international* force, that is, a force recruited by and responsible to a truly international organ. I do not propose to state here why I think that this proposal is not at present within the field of practical politics. I will merely point out that such a force is something quite different from *collective* force contributed by states in support of the policy of collective security. Among other differences there is the fact that in the case of collective force the responsibility for its use rests with governments, whereas the decision to use an international force would presumably rest with the individuals in control of the international organ. There are many who will prefer that a decision to employ armed force should only be taken by governments; for they are likely to realize that in so doing they are staking the future of their countries, and will probably act with a greater sense of responsibility than a group of individuals, though, it must be admitted, often with less promptitude.

Covenant does not contemplate the possible necessity of the use of armed force as part of that collective action is completely erroneous. It is only necessary to read Articles 10 and 16 of the Covenant and the British official "Commentary" on the Covenant published in 1919, while the memorandum addressed to the League Committee on Arbitration and Security in 1928 by the United Kingdom Government[1] and many other official declarations are to the same effect. Moreover, we have constantly been told that it is necessary to maintain our armaments at a level adequate to enable us to carry out our obligations under the Covenant, and as recently as December 21, 1935, the Chancellor of the Exchequer is reported in _The Times_ to have said that it would be "the duty of the Government in these coming years to restore our defence forces to a level at which we can feel that not only have we secured the safety of this country and those great trade routes between us and the other members of the British Empire upon which our existence depends, _but we are also in a position to back up our collective action at the League. . ."._[2] No member of the League is compelled to contribute armed force in defence of the Covenant, but in certain events the Covenant authorizes it to do so if in its discretion it should think fit. Moreover, a member of the League before co-operating in any sanction that is likely to provoke an attack by the aggressor affected by it must realize that in such an event it will be necessary to use force. It has therefore a right to receive in advance from a reasonably powerful section of its co-operators specific and satisfactory assurances of the mutual support stipulated for by paragraph three of Article 16.

United States of America

As for the United States of America, I will only say this. No reasonable person, in the present position of international affairs, can count upon that country contributing armed force for the repression of an aggressor in pursuance of a system of collective security. But is it too much to expect that, when there is a clear breach of the Kellogg-Briand Pact and in consequence a breach of a treaty with that country, the American Government, which with France was primarily responsible for the Pact, should reply to the breach of treaty by departing from the traditional law of neutrality and preventing its citizens from frustrating the efforts of its fellow signatories of that Pact by trading with a proclaimed

---

[1] _League of Nations Official Journal_, May 1928, p. 694.   [2] Italics mine.

COLLECTIVE SECURITY   163

aggressor ? In the present Italo-Abyssinian dispute the President has[1] "warned American citizens against transactions of any character with either of the belligerent nations except at their own risk". This warning does not in terms discriminate between the aggressor and the victim of the aggression. But if it means that the American Government would refrain from protecting American trade with the aggressor from interception by a group of states applying sanctions, then indirectly the new American policy would work in favour of collective security.

Conclusion

When I consider our own place in this movement, I sometimes think of Watts's picture entitled "For he had Great Possessions". We too have done pretty well out of the old system. Are we going to turn our back like the man in that picture on this new movement or are we going to shoulder our share of the responsibility and play our part with all the risks which the new policy entails ? It is difficult for us at home to realize how much other countries look to us to give the lead in this matter which our position entitles them to expect. I do not think I am guilty of national presumption when I say that our attitude towards the movement is one of outstanding and perhaps decisive importance. In the past two years the two periods during which our national prestige in the world has been at its highest have been those during which we have been taking a lead in the use of collective action in the interests of peace. The first period was when we proposed at Geneva that a collective force should be admitted to the Saar Territory and be responsible to the Governing Commission of that Territory for the maintenance of order during the dangerous time of the plebiscite and before the handing back of the Territory to Germany. That force was contributed by Italy, Holland, Sweden, and ourselves. The second was the period represented by Sir Samuel Hoare's great speech in the League Assembly on September 11, 1935, reaffirming his country's support of the League's obligations "for the collective maintenance of the Covenant in its entirety and particularly for steady, collective resistance to all acts of unprovoked aggression", and by our subsequent leadership in the policy of sanctions. During both these periods our international standing has been pre-eminent. During both our government has commanded a more united national support than democratic governments usually enjoy. But, as Sir

[1] *Bulletin of International News*, November 9, 1935, p. 60.

164   YEAR BOOK OF INTERNATIONAL LAW

Samuel Hoare said, "if the burden is to be borne it must be borne collectively". We cannot do more than our fair share. If through other nations failing to do their share the movement towards collective security receives a check, it must be no more than a check. We must make it clear that only those who are prepared to share the burden can expect to enjoy the benefit. *Qui sentit commodum sentire debet et onus.* Collective security will not be established in one year or in ten years. It will result from an accumulation of effective pieces of collective action. But if we are patient and hold firm to our declared policy (which comprises collective revision of the *status quo* as well as collective resistance to aggression), and if we insist that those are the terms on which we are prepared to co-operate in the preservation of peace, my belief is that eventually the principle of collective security will be established, that, though at first limited in territorial scope, it will spread, and that it will introduce a new and saner epoch in international relations, an achievement in which we shall be glad to have taken a leading part.

Part III
United Nations Era

[6]

COLLECTIVE SECURITY AND COLLECTIVE SELF-DEFENSE UNDER THE CHARTER OF THE UNITED NATIONS *

By Hans Kelsen

Professor of Political Science, University of California

Collective security is the main purpose of the United Nations, just as it was the main purpose of its predecessor, the League of Nations. What does collective security mean? Under general international law the principle of self-help prevails. The protection of the legal interests of the states against violations on the part of other states is left to the individual state whose right has been violated. General international law authorizes the state, *i.e.*, the individual member of the international community, to resort, in case of a violation of its rights, to reprisals or war against that state which is responsible for the violation. Reprisals and war are enforcement actions. Insofar as they are reactions against violations of the law, and authorized by it, they have the character of sanctions. We speak of collective security when the protection of the rights of the states, the reaction against the violation of the law, assumes the character of a collective enforcement action. The collective action may be carried out in different degrees. It may consist only in that the members of a particular international community, established for this purpose, are obliged by the constitution of the community to assist the member, whose right has been violated, in its reaction against certain or all violations of its rights, to resort to reprisals or war against the violator. The difference between such kind of collective security and the status of self-help is relatively small. It does not consist—as is sometimes assumed—in that, in case of collective security, the reaction against violations of the law is conferred upon an international community, whereas, in case of self-help, this reaction is an action of the individual state, not an action of the international community. Since the state, in exercising self-help by taking enforcement action against another state under definite conditions determined by international law, acts on authorization of general international law, it may be considered to act as an organ of the international community constituted by this law, so that its action may be interpreted as reaction of the international community against violations of law. It is through the individual state that the international community acts, although this reaction is completely decentralized. Even if decentralized,

* Address delivered at the regional meeting of the American Society of International Law held at Seattle, Washington, August 12, 1948.

this use of force may be conceived of as a monopoly of the community insofar as the legal order constituting the community precisely determines the conditions under which force is permitted to be used by one state against another, and as any other use of force is a violation of law. The difference between the most primitive type of collective security and the state of self-help consists only in that, in the case of collective security, states not directly violated in their rights are obliged to assist the violated state; whereas in the state of self-help under general international law, they are only allowed to do so.

A higher degree of collective security is reached if the collective enforcement actions provided for in the constitution of the international community are centralized, that is to say, if these actions are to be decided upon and directed by a central organ of the community. Such centralization of the use of force may be combined with the obligation imposed upon the individual members not to use force on their own initiative in their mutual relations, to abandon completely the principle of self-help —the use of force being reserved exclusively to the central organ of the community competent to take enforcement actions against members. In case of such centralization of the use of force, the force monopoly of the community is much more evident than in case of decentralization.

Collective security reaches the highest possible degree when the obligation of the members to refrain from the use of force is guaranteed by their disarmament, when the force monopoly of the community is constituted not only by the exclusive right of a central organ to take enforcement actions against members, but also by the fact that only a central organ of the international community has armed forces at its disposal to be employed against delinquent member states, whereas the single members of the community are allowed only to keep a police force for the maintenance of law and order among their subjects, that is to say, for enforcement actions against individuals. By such a high degree of centralization, the international community is about to be transformed into a national community, the union of states into a state.

However, the centralization of the use of force—be it in a state or in a true international organization—is possible only with an important limitation. This limitation refers to the case of self-defense. Self-defense is not identical with self-help; it is a special case of self-help. It is self-help against a specific violation of the law, against the illegal use of force, not against other violations of the law. Self-defense is the use of force by a person illegally attacked by another. The attack against which the use of force as an act of self-defense is permitted must have been made or must be intended to be made by force. Self-defense is that minimum of of self-help which, even within a system of collective security based on a centralized force monopoly of the community, must be permitted. As such it is recognized by national as well as by international law, within the state as well as within international organizations. For the system of collective security can absolutely prevent illegal attacks of one member by another neither in the one case nor in the others, and it is impossible to obligate the attacked person, in all cases of illegal use of force, to wait for the collective enforcement action to be taken by the central organ of the community. Between the moment the illegal attack starts and the moment the centralized machinery of collective security is put into action, there is, even in case of its perfectly prompt functioning, a space of time, an interval, which may be disastrous to the victim. Within a system of collective security organized on the basis of a complete centralization of the legitimate use of force, self-defense as a case of decentralized use of force is an exceptional and provisional interlude between an act of illegal use of force, an act of aggression, and the collective enforcement action which the community, through its central organ, is to take as a sanction against the illegal use of force. Totally different is the case when, within a community organized according to the principle of collective security, self-defense takes place because, for some reason or another, the collective security provided for does not work. Then self-defense is not an exceptional and provisional interlude between an illegal act of aggression, which has the character of a delict, and the collective reaction of the community as a sanction. It is not an inevitable measure taken within the framework of a working system of collective security, but is the replacement of this system, which is temporarily or definitely blocked, by the opposite principle of self-help.

In the Charter of the United Nations [1] the principle of collective security is placed ahead of all its provisions. Article 1, paragraph 1, states it to be a purpose of the United Nations "To maintain international peace and security, and to that end: to take effective collective measures for the prevention and removal of threats to the peace, and for the suppression of acts of aggression or other breaches of the peace. . . ." The force monopoly of the United Nations Organization is established by Article 2, paragraph 4, and Articles 24 and 39. Article 2, paragraph 4 provides that: "All Members shall refrain in their international relations from the threat or use of force against the territorial integrity or political independence of any state, or in any other manner inconsistent with the Purposes of the United Nations." The Charter forbids not only the use of force by one state against the other, but also any kind of threat of force. Use of force is reserved to a central organ of the organization: the Security Council, the only organ of the United Nations competent to use force against members as well as non-members. Article 24, paragraph 1, stipulates:

> In order to ensure prompt and effective action by the United Nations, its Members confer on the Security Council primary responsibility for

[1] Department of State, Conference Series 74 (Publication 2353).

the maintenance of international peace and security, and agree that in carrying out its duties under this responsibility the Security Council acts on their behalf.

That the Charter confers upon the Security Council only "primary" responsibility for the maintenance of peace and security seems to imply that other organs, as, for instance, the General Assembly, are not excluded from this responsibility; that they, too, but only secondarily, may be responsible for the maintenance of peace and security. If so, the responsibility of other organs certainly does not imply the duty or competence of "prompt and effective action by the United Nations." There cannot be the slightest doubt that the Charter confers upon no other central organ of the United Nations but the Security Council the power of using force. This use of force is called by the Charter taking enforcement action (Art. 5) or enforcement measures (Art. 50). With respect to regional arrangements which the members are allowed to enter into, Article 53 provides that the Security Council shall, where appropriate, utilize such regional arrangements or agencies for enforcement action under its authority. It is expressly stipulated that "no enforcement action shall be taken under regional arrangements or by regional agencies without the authorization of the Security Council. . . ." The Charter authorizes the Security Council, and only the Security Council, not the individual members or any other central organ of the United Nations, to ascertain the existence of the conditions under which the use of force within the system of collective security may take place. Article 39 provides:

> The Security Council shall determine the existence of any threat to the peace, breach of the peace, or act of aggression and shall make recommendations, or decide what measures shall be taken in accordance with Articles 41 and 42, to maintain or restore international peace and security.

Article 41 determines the enforcement action not involving the use of armed force; the measures concerned have the character of reprisals. Article 42 determines the enforcement action involving the use of armed force; the measures concerned have the character of war. Both enforcement actions are to be performed by the member states, in conformity with the decisions taken by the Security Council under Articles 39, 41, and 42. Article 48, paragraph 1 provides:

> The action required to carry out the decisions of the Security Council for the maintenance of international peace and security shall be taken by all the Members of the United Nations or by some of them, as the Security Council may determine.

Article 41 stipulates that measures not involving the use of armed force, such as complete or partial interruption of economic relations, of rail, sea, air, postal, telegraphic, radio and other means of communication, and the severance of diplomatic relations, shall be applied by the members on the "call" of the Security Council. Article 43 also stipulates that measures involving the use of armed force, such as blockade, operations by air, sea, or land forces, shall be applied by the members on the "call" of the Security Council. The armed forces by which the United Nations exercises its functions under Article 42 are composed of the contingents which the members are obliged to make available to the Council in accordance with special agreements. But these contingents are placed under the command of the Council, which has the power to dispose of them (Article 47). Both kinds of enforcement actions are centralized.

In this respect there exists an essential difference between the Charter of the United Nations and the Covenant of the League of Nations. The Covenant [2] did not impose upon the members of the League a duty to refrain from the threat of force and to refrain under all circumstances (except self-defense) from the use of force. The members were only obliged not to resort to war against a member which, in a dispute submitted to the Council, complied with the latter's unanimously adopted recommendations. In all other cases war was not forbidden, or at least not expressly so, by the Covenant. In these other cases the members were only bound not to resort to war until three months after the decision of an international tribunal or the recommendation of the Council, provided that the conflict had been submitted to one of these authorities. The Covenant did not establish a centralized force monopoly of the community, the principle of self-help was to a great extent maintained. Besides, collective security was restricted to the obligation of the members to take reprisals against the state which had resorted to war in violation of the Covenant. The members were not obliged to resort to war in such a case; and they were not obliged to assist a state in its reaction against a violation of its rights not constituted by an illegal resort to war. The collective enforcement actions provided by the Covenant were almost completely decentralized. It was for the members, and not for a central organ of the League to decide whether a violation of the Covenant by illegal resort to war had occurred, and to decide what enforcement action had to be taken. As to the enforcement action not involving the use of armed force, the so-called economic sanctions, no interference by a central organ of the League was provided for. As to enforcement action involving the use of armed force, so-called military sanctions, the Council had only the power to recommend to the several governments concerned what effective military, naval, or air force the members of the League should severally contribute for the purpose of protecting the covenants of the League (Article 16, paragraph 2). The members were not legally bound to comply

[2] U. S. Treaties, Conventions, International Acts, etc., Vol. III, p. 3336; Department of State, *Papers relating to the Foreign Relations of the United States, Paris Peace Conference, 1919*, Vol. XIII, p. 69.

with these recommendations. Consequently, the system of collective security as established by the Covenant was certainly much less effective than that established by the Charter, provided the latter can work at all.

The decentralized enforcement actions to be taken within the system of collective security established by the Covenant were true sanctions, that is to say, reactions against violations of the law. This, however, is doubtful with respect to the centralized enforcement actions to be taken within the system of collective security established by the Charter. Under the Covenant, enforcement action in conformity with Article 16 was admissible only in case of a specific violation of the Covenant, and only against the state responsible for this violation. The Charter authorizes the Security Council to take enforcement action if the latter determines the existence of a threat to the peace or a breach of the peace (including an act of aggression). Neither "threat to the peace" nor "breach of the peace" is necessarily constituted by a violation of the Charter. The members are obliged to refrain from the threat and use of force. Threat and use of force are not identical with threat to or breach of the peace. Since it is for the Security Council to interpret the terms "threat to the peace" and "breach of the peace," this organ may very well consider certain conduct of a state which is by no means a "threat of force," as a threat to the peace, and conduct which by no means is a "use of force," as a breach of the peace. That means that the Security Council has the power to take enforcement actions even in case no obligation expressly imposed on the members has been violated, provided that the Security Council considers such action necessary for the maintenance of international peace and security. It is especially important to note that the Charter does not bind the Security Council to direct the enforcement action only against the state responsible for a threat to or a breach of the peace; nor is the Council bound by the Charter to apply in its decision the existing law. Article 24, paragraph 2 provides only that the Security Council, in discharging its duties shall act in accordance with the principles and purposes of the United Nations; but Article 1 of the Charter, determining the purposes of the Organization, stipulates that the latter shall act in conformity with the principles of justice and international law. Since justice is not identical with international law, the Security Council has the choice between them. It may enforce justice, and that means what the Council considers to be justice, instead of the existing law. Besides, even this restriction—to act in conformity with law or justice —applies, according to the wording of Article 1, only to actions of the Organization which aim at the adjustment or settlement of international disputes or situations which might lead to a breach of the peace, and not to enforcement actions for the maintenance or restoration of international peace and security. When, for instance, the Security Council, in a territorial conflict between two members, considers it appropriate for the maintenance of peace to recommend to one party the cession of the disputed territory or part of it to the other party, the Council may enforce its recommendation even if it is not in conformity with existing international law. Hence it is doubtful whether the enforcement actions provided for in Articles 39, 41, and 42, have the character of legal sanctions, rather than that of mere political measures to be taken by the Security Council for the maintenance or restoration of international peace.[3] Since peace is not necessarily identical with law, the enforcement machinery established by the Charter is no guarantee for the maintenance or restoration of existing law; but it may create a new law.

If the principle of collective security is carried out by a complete centralization of the enforcement measures, if the use of force is reserved to a central organ of the international community and self-help of the members, except in the case of self-defense against aggression, is excluded, then the constitution of this community must provide a procedure guaranteeing the effective protection of the rights of the members against all possible violations. The rights of a state may be violated not only by an armed attack on the part of another state. If the individual member is not allowed to protect itself by its own action, it must be protected by an action to be taken by the central organ of the community. The obligation to submit conflicts for settlement to an international agency, even the establishment of compulsory adjudication of all conflicts by this agency, do not suffice. There must be provisions by which the enforcement of the decisions of this agency is secured.

The Charter is far from fulfilling these requirements. It does not establish compulsory adjudication of the conflicts which may arise among the members. The latter are not obliged to submit their conflicts, even their legal conflicts, to the International Court of Justice or to other international tribunals. They are obliged only to refer disputes not settled by means of their own choice to the Security Council. But the Council is not bound to settle all disputes brought before it and has only the power to make recommendations, legally not binding upon the parties. Besides, the peculiarity of the voting procedure in the Security Council may make such recommendations impossible, since the decision concerned refers to a non-procedural matter and is consequently subjected to the rule of unanimity of the five permanent members of the Council. Thus, the Charter does not at all exclude the possibility of unsettled disputes. An unsettled dispute means that a member whose right has been violated by another state, has neither the legal power to protect itself, nor is it protected by a centralized action of the community. Take, for instance, the case in which a state in violation of a treaty obligation refuses to withdraw its troops from the territory of the other contracting party, and the Security

---

[3] *Cf.* Hans Kelsen, "Sanctions in International Law under the Charter of the United Nations," Iowa Law Review, Vol. 31 (1946), pp. 499–543.

Council, before which the dispute has been brought, is not able to reach a decision; or the Council has recommended the withdrawal of the troops, but is not able to reach a decision concerning enforcement measures to be taken against the state which refuses to comply with the recommendations of the Council.

Totally different was the analogous situation under the League of Nations Covenant, where, in such a case, self-help, that is, reprisals or war on the part of the state violated in its right but not protected by a centralized action of the organization, was not excluded. Strange as it seems, the centralization of the legitimate use of force is a problematical achievement if not accompanied by the establishment of compulsory adjudication of all conflicts by decisions of a central organ, and the guarantee of prompt enforcement of these decisions through a centralized machinery.

Even if a dispute has been submitted by the parties to the International Court of Justice or another international tribunal and the Court or the tribunal has ascertained the violation of a right of one party by the other, enforcement of the judicial decision is by no means ensured by the Charter. First of all, Article 94 dealing with the execution of judicial decisions by the Council, applies only to decisions of the International Court of Justice, not to decisions of other tribunals to which the members are authorized to submit disputes. The corresponding Article 13, paragraph 4, of the Covenant, however, refers to decisions of the Permanent Court of International Justice as well as to those of all other international tribunals. The Charter imposes upon the members the obligation to comply with the decisions of the International Court of Justice. But the Charter, though depriving the members of the right of self-help against the state which in violation of its obligation does not comply with the decision of the Court, does not bind the organization to enforce the judicial decision against the recalcitrant party. The other party may, according to Article 94, paragraph 2, have recourse to the Security Council, and the Council may, if it deems necessary, make recommendations or decide upon measures to be taken to give effect to the decision of the Court. That means that the Security Council has the choice between two totally different means, a choice which is within its unlimited discretion. It may enforce the judicial decision; but it also may make recommendations concerning the settlement of the dispute, which has already been decided upon by the Court.

Thus, the Security Council may settle the dispute in a way different from the decision of the Court. That the Charter confers upon the Security Council this power, is certainly one of its most objectionable provisions. It places the Court, the "principal judicial organ of the United Nations," under the political control of the Council, a thoroughly political agency. Since, within the highly centralized system of collective security as established by the Charter, the party whose right has been confirmed by the decision of the Court is forbidden to enforce this right against the party which fails to perform its obligation, the former is compelled to have recourse to the Council.   But such recourse may have the effect of transforming the legal dispute, decided by the Court, into a political issue to Court.   For, by non-compliance it may bring the case decided by the Court is a permanent member of the Security Council, this party is practically exempted from the obligation to comply with the decision of the Court.   For, by non-compliance it may bring the case decided by the Court before the Council, and in the Council it has the power to prevent by its veto any settlement not acceptable to it, for it has the right to participate in the decision of the Council by which the settlement is to be made. The rule excluding members of the Security Council parties in a dispute from voting in decisions concerning the dispute does not apply to decisions taken under Article 94.

All this was impossible under the Covenant of the League of Nations due to the decentralization of the collective security system.   This decentralization is also the reason why the Covenant, in contradistinction to the Charter, did not contain an express provision concerning self-defense. The right of self-defense against acts of aggression was implied in the provision concerning the decentralized sanctions for illegal resort to war. The Charter, which establishes collective security by centralizing the legitimate use of force, must restrict this centralization expressly by authorizing the members to use force as self-defense.   This is the main purpose of Article 51, which reads as follows:

> Nothing in the present Charter shall impair the inherent right of individual or collective self-defense if an armed attack occurs against a Member of the United Nations, until the Security Council has taken the measures necessary to maintain international peace and security. Measures taken by Members in the exercise of this right of self-defense shall be immediately reported to the Security Council and shall not in any way affect the authority and responsibility of the Security Council under the present Charter to take at any time such action as it deems necessary in order to maintain or restore international peace and security.

This provision restricts the right of self-defense to the case of an "armed attack" actually made by one state against another.   It makes no difference whether the armed attack is made by a member or by a non-member state.   Only the attacked state must be a member of the United Nations. But what is the meaning of the term "armed attack"?   Who is competent to interpret this term and to ascertain that an armed attack exists in a concrete case?   According to Article 51, it is the states involved in the process of self-defense which are competent to interpret Article 51.   These states may or may not understand by "armed attack" not only the fact that a state has resorted to war against another state, using its own armed force. They may or may not understand by armed attack the fact also that a state has interfered in a civil war taking place within another state by arming or otherwise assisting the revolutionary group in its fight against the legitimate government. But this competence of the states involved exists only as long as the Security Council does not intervene. As soon as the Council takes the measures necessary to restore peace, the competence to interpret the term "armed attack" and to ascertain whether an armed attack exists in a concrete case, is transferred to the Council. The member states acting under Article 51 are, according to Article 25, obliged "to accept and carry out the decisions of the Security Council" in this respect.

Although, on the one hand, Article 51 restricts the right of self-defense, on the other hand it extends this right, insofar as it authorizes not only the attacked state, but any member of the United Nations to use force against a state guilty of an armed attack. This means that any member of the United Nations is authorized by the Charter to assist with its armed force the attacked state against an aggressor. This is implied in the provision recognizing not only the right of individual self-defense but also the right of collective self-defense. This terminology is rather problematical.[4] The term "self"-defense is correctly applied only to the state which is the victim of the armed attack. The other members of the United Nations which assist the attacked state, act in the defense of the latter, but not in self-defense. Such a collective defense may be organized by treaties previously concluded for this purpose, especially by so-called regional arrangements in accordance with Article 52, such as the Inter-American Treaty of Reciprocal Assistance, adopted by the Inter-American Conference of Continental Peace and Security at Rio de Janeiro on September 2, 1947;[5] the treaty signed by Belgium, France, Luxembourg, The Netherlands, and Great Britain at Brussels, on March 17, 1948;[6] or by a general protocol open to all members of the United Nations, as recently suggested.

The exercise of the right of self-defense and, consequently, also the action by which other states assist the attacked state, must stop as soon as the Security Council takes the measures necessary to restore peace. The wording is: "until the Security Council has taken the measures necessary to maintain international peace and security." This is not correct. In case of an armed attack, peace cannot be "maintained," but only restored. In order to enable the Security Council to take the necessary measures in time, the "measures taken by Members in the exercise of this right of self-defense shall be immediately reported to the Security

---

[4] *Cf.* Josef L. Kunz, "Individual and Collective Self-Defense in Article 51 of the Charter of the United Nations," this JOURNAL, Vol. 41 (1947), p. 872 ff.

[5] Department of State *Bulletin*, Sept. 21, 1947, p. 565; Pan American Union, Congress and Conf. Ser., No. 53.

[6] Department of State *Bulletin*, May 9, 1948, p. 600; Great Britain, Misc. Ser. No. 2 (1948), Cmd. 7367.

Council." Reported by whom? Probably by the states which have taken the measures. If this is the intended meaning of the sentence, it would have been correct to say: "The States which exercise the right of self-defense shall immediately report to the Security Council the measures taken by them," for it is obviously intended to establish an obligation of the members to report to the Council.

The obligation to stop the exercise of the right of self-defense is conditional upon the fact that the Security Council "has taken the measures necessary to maintain international peace and security." It is significant that Article 51 does not provide: "until the Security Council has taken enforcement action against the state guilty of an armed attack." The Security Council may take any "measures necessary" to restore peace. Among these measures are certainly the enforcement measures determined in Chapter VII of the Charter—the specific measures of collective security. This is not expressly stipulated but follows from the fact that Article 51 is placed in Chapter VII of the Charter. Self-defense must give way to collective security. Since the state guilty of an armed attack may not be a member of the United Nations, the enforcement action which the Security Council takes under Article 51 may be directed against a non-member state, although non-member states are not protected by the system of collective security established by the Charter.

Who is competent to decide the question whether the Security Council has taken the measures "necessary" to restore peace? The Security Council itself exclusively, or the member states involved in the process of self-defense? The Charter does not say in the first sentence of Article 51, as it does say in the last sentence: "measures which the Security Council deems necessary." Hence, there is not excluded an interpretation of the first sentence according to which a member state is not obliged to cease exercising its right of self-defense when it has reported to the Council and when the Council has taken measures which, in the opinion of that state, are not the measures "necessary to maintain international peace and security." It probably was not the intention of the legislator to confer upon the members involved in self-defense the power to decide whether the measures taken by the Council are adequate. The idea was probably that the exercise of the right of self-defense is allowed only until the Security Council has taken the measures which the Security Council deems necessary to restore peace. But this idea is not unambiguously expressed in Article 51.

So-called collective self-defense under Article 51 of the Charter of the United Nations is very similar to collective security under Article 16 of the Covenant of the League of Nations. Under the Covenant, collective security, because of its decentralization, was indeed nothing else but a kind of collective self-defense. "Should a Member of the League resort to war in disregard of its covenants," says Article 16, paragraph 1, "it

794   THE AMERICAN JOURNAL OF INTERNATIONAL LAW

shall *ipso facto* be deemed to have committed an act of war against all other Members of the League.'' Thus the sanction to be directed against the aggressor, and that means the working of the collective security, was presented as action of self-defense. The difference between self-defense under general international law and collective security under the Covenant consists only in that, in the first case, states not immediately attacked are entitled, not obliged; whereas, under the Covenant, they were obliged to assist the attacked state, provided that, in their opinion, a violation of the Covenant had been committed. The collective security established by the Charter is quite different from the so-called collective self-defense under Article 51. The measures of collective security taken under Chapter VII of the Charter are centralized actions of the Organization, whereas the process of collective self-defense is a completely decentralized reaction against armed attack. This reaction, it is true, takes place under the authorization of the Charter and, consequently, may be interpreted as an action of the Organization. The difference between collective self-defense under Article 51 and collective security under Chapter VII as a difference between two actions of the Organization, consists indeed only in that the one is decentralized, the other centralized. But this difference is essential. It manifests itself in the fact that the question as to whether there exists an act of aggression is to be decided in the case of collective security by a central organ of the United Nations, the Security Council; whereas in the case of collective self-defense, as long as the Security Council does not intervene, the question is to be decided by the individual states concerned. However, the states concerned are not only the member which considers itself to be attacked and the states which come to its assistance, but also the member against which this action is directed. This state has the same competence to interpret Article 51; and it is very probable that it will deny its guilt of an armed attack, especially by interpreting the term in another way than its opponent or opponents. Then, the member against which Article 51 is applied, might declare this action to be not legitimate self-defense, but an illegal attack, against which it considers itself to be entitled to exercise self-defense. Other members may come to its assistance, and justify this assistance as collective self-defense. In such case, the question as to which state exercises the right of self-defense and which state is guilty of an illegal attack remains undecided until the Security Council, the only organ of the United Nations competent to decide whether an armed attack occurred and who is responsible for it, intervenes. This state of uncertainty is a characteristic element of the status of collective self-defense as determined by Article 51 of the Charter. It does not exist within the system of collective security.

By a regional arrangement concluded for the purpose of collective self-defense the interpretation of Article 51 and the determination of the aggressor in a concrete case may, without prejudice to the competence of the Security Council to finally decide the questions involved in the application of Article 51, be conferred upon a central organ, a regional agency, established by the regional arrangement. Thus the state of uncertainty regarding the questions as to whether an armed attack within the meaning of Article 51 has actually occurred and which state is responsible for it, may be avoided. This is possible only in case the armed conflict takes place between two states, both parties to the regional arrangement, but not in that case for which such regional arrangements are concluded in the first place, namely, in case the armed conflict takes place between states which do not belong to the same regional organization. There may be even an armed conflict between two regional organizations, both established under Chapter VIII of the Charter, where both organizations claim to exercise collective self-defense under Article 51.

Finally, collective security differs from collective self-defense insofar as enforcement action taken by the Security Council under Chapter VII is the ordinary and (by the Charter) intended reaction against a breach of the peace committed through an act of aggression, whereas the use of force in the exercise of self-defense under Article 51 is intended by the Charter as a provisional and temporary measure, permitted only ''until'' the Security Council takes the necessary measures to restore peace, especially until collective security comes into action, and not as a substitute for it. However, it must be admitted that the wording of Article 51 does not exclude its application by both parties to the armed conflict in case the system of collective security is blocked because the Council is not able to fulfil its function with respect to an armed attack actually carried out against a member of the United Nations. The Security Council may be unable to fulfil its function, not only because its decision to take the measures necessary to restore the peace broken by an armed attack within the meaning of Article 51 is subjected to the veto power of the permanent members but also because, due to the veto right of the permanent members of the Security Council, until now it has been impossible to conclude the special agreements determining the contingents of armed forces to be made available by the members to the Council. As a matter of fact, the armed forces, which are the essential factor in the system of collective security, are not yet at the disposal of the Security Council. Enforcement measures not involving the use of armed force under Article 41 are inadequate in case of an armed attack. Hence, in such a case collective security has little chance to work. Then nothing else remains but collective self-defense. However, one should be aware of what that means. It means a war in which probably both parties will claim to apply Article 51, will claim to exercise their right of self-defense, just as under general international law, both belligerents may claim to wage a just war, since there is no objective authority to decide the question, who is the aggressor and who is the defender. The attempt to avoid this undesirable situation by having the General Assembly, instead of the paralyzed Security Council, decide the questions whether an armed attack has occurred and who is responsible for it—an attempt made by the Government of the United States in a draft resolution submitted on September 25, 1947, in the Greek case, to the Political and Security Committee of the General Assembly—is from a legal point of view rather problematical. The only organ competent to determine, in a way binding upon the members, the existence of an armed attack within the meaning of Article 51, is the Security Council, and not the General Assembly. It may become inevitable to substitute collective self-defense for collective security as established by the Charter, but such substitution would be the bankruptcy of that political and legal system for which the United Nations was created.

[7]

BELLUM JUSTUM AND BELLUM LEGALE

Josef L. Kunz

In 1914 and long before the right of every sovereign state to go to war was recognized by the practice of states and by the overwhelming majority of writers, war, the *"ultima ratio regum,"* served in the primitive international community a double purpose: a method of self-help to enforce a right, in the absence of international courts with compulsory jurisdiction, and a method of self-help to change the law, analogous to internal revolution, in the absence of an organ of international legislation in the true sense of this term.

In this century the old *bellum justum* doctrine, which played so great a rôle in the literature from the times of St. Augustine to Vattel, was, first, historically re-studied in great detail.[1] After the first World War, even attempts at the revival of this doctrine were made: it was asserted that this doctrine is a norm of positive international law, often coupled with the further assertion that recent developments in international organization constitute a return to this doctrine. These assertions, however, are not tenable in law, but are only political ideologies or the consequence of a theoretically incorrect analysis.

While Catholic international lawyers, such as Mausbach and Cathrein, retained the traditional concept of *bellum justum*, the revival was inspired by very different motives in other writers. Louis Le Fur,[2] an adherent of Catholic natural law, used the doctrine as a political instrument to prove the Treaty of Versailles to be a *justa pax* in the beginning struggle over the revision of this treaty. Leo Strisower[3] could in his book state with the utmost sincerity that he was not inspired by political motives. His approach was wholly ethical, a consequence of his basic philosophical conviction that law is a part of ethics. But exactly for this reason his argumentation is moral rather than legal. Hans Kelsen, the bitter antagonist of natural law, became the principal champion of the doctrine of *bellum justum*, which he felt compelled to defend for wholly logical reasons: If war cannot be interpreted either as a delict or as a sanction against a delict, then it is no longer possible to consider international law as law at all. But in his most recent treatment[4] he does not decide whether this doctrine is a norm of positive international law, and states forcefully the grave objections against the workability of this doctrine.

That this doctrine was not positive law in 1914 and long before, seems settled;[5] even in earlier times it was hardly ever a norm of positive interna-

---

[1] See, apart from monographs on St. Augustine, St. Thomas, Victoria, Suárez, Gentili, Grotius and others, the following works: A. Vanderpol, *Le droit de la guerre juste d'après les théologiens et les canonistes du Moyen-Âge* (1911); idem, *La doctrine scholastique du droit de la guerre* (1919); G. Salvioli, *Il concetto della guerra giusta negli scrittori anteriori a Grotius* (1915); P. Yves de la Brière, "*Les droits de la juste victoire selon la tradition des théologiens catholiques,*" *Revue Générale de Droit International Public*, Vol. XXXII (1925); idem, "*Les étapes de la tradition théologique concernant le droit de la guerre juste*, ibid., 1937, pp. 129 ff.; idem, *Le droit de juste guerre* (Paris, 1938); V. Beaufort, *La guerre comme instrument de secours ou de punition* (The Hague, 1933); Regout, *La doctrine de la guerre juste de St. Augustin à nos jours d'après les théologiens et canonistes catholiques* (1935); Kipp, *Moderne Probleme des Kriegsrechts in der Spätscholastik* (1935); J. von Elbe, "The Evolution of the Concept of Just War in International Law," this JOURNAL, Vol. 33 (1939), pp. 665–688.

[2] "*Guerre juste et juste paix,*" *Revue Générale de Droit International Public*, Vol. XXVI (1919), pp. 9–75, 268–309, 349–405.

[3] *Der Krieg und die Völkerrechtsordnung* (Vienna, 1919).

[4] H. Kelsen, General Theory of Law and State (1945), pp. 331–338. He is followed by P. Guggenheim, *Lehrbuch des Völkerrechts*, Vol. I, pp. 590–593.

[5] Naturally, an ethical and political critique of a concrete war has always existed; the ethical critique of the positive law, whether municipal or international, is socially indispensable. For, as the Romans said, *Non omne quod licet, honestum.*

tional law.[6] It is of Catholic origin, anchored in natural law, a theological, not a legal concept. That is proved by its content as well as by its historical origin. The early Church under the pagan Roman Empire took a strictly pacifist attitude, an attitude preserved even today by some Protestant sects. It was the anti-state attitude of the early Christians which led to their persecution. The Romans of the Empire had long ceased to believe in Roman mythology; many foreign cults were not only tolerated in imperial Rome, but some of them were extremely fashionable among the "élite." The Romans further failed entirely to understand the transcendental importance and future of Christianity; for them the Christians were no more than an insignificant Jewish sect. The persecutions were not directed against a religion, but against what would be called today a "subversive movement."

But when, with Constantine, Christianity became the official religion of the *orbis terrarum,* when Christian persecutions were followed by those of the pagans, the Church had naturally to revise its attitude toward the Empire. In this connection the purely theological problem arose: How can a Catholic participate in a war, without committing a sin? It was a theological, not a legal problem. To this theological problem St. Augustine gave the answer: He can do so, provided the war is just. Transforming the formal criterion of the ancient Roman *jus fetiale* into the substantive criterion of objective, intrinsic justice of the cause of war, he created this doctrine, which was later elaborated by other theologians, consolidated by St. Thomas of Aquinas, Victoria, Suarez and others, and secularized, divorced from its Catholic soil, by Gentili, Grotius and their successors.

In its purity the doctrine is wholly an ethical one. There must be an objectively just cause of war, waged by the authority of the prince, and he must be inspired by the *"recta intentio."* Even the prince who has a just cause of war, can make an unjust war, if he acts from wrong motives, such as territorial aggrandizement or elimination of the enemy as a competitor in the future. And, if all these are fulfilled, the war can still cease to be just, if the prince imposes an *"injusta pax."* Thus Victoria lays down that the victor in a just war can impose upon the vanquished only conditions proportionate to the wrong committed, must always act with moderation and Christian modesty, and never has the right to ruin the vanquished enemy as a nation.

Just war is, therefore, a reaction against a wrong,[7] a procedure either in tort (restitution, reparations, guarantees) or in criminal law (punishment, sanctions).[8]

---

6 See also A. Nussbaum, "Just War—a Legal Concept?" Michigan Law Review, Vol. 42 (1943–44), pp. 453–479.

7 Thus Victoria: *"Unica est et sola causa justa inferendi bellum injuria accepta";* Grotius: *"Causa justi belli suscipiendi nulla alia esse potest nisi injuria."*

8 Thus, *e.g.,* Cayetano: *"Habens justum bellum gerit personam judicis criminaliter procedentis."*

The *bellum justum* doctrine presupposes, therefore, the continuance of war and distinguishes between objectively just and unjust wars. If all the conditions of a just war are fulfilled, just war can be either a war of self-defense against the *"injustus aggressor"* or a war of execution to enforce one's right. In both cases it makes no difference whether the just war is, from a military point of view, waged defensively or offensively, nor is the factor who resorts to war first, decisive.

This doctrine in its purity, even if it might have been or were a norm of positive international law, would be practically valueless because of the grave objections against its workability. This very circumstance forced later writers to develop the doctrine in such a way as to deform it.

1. There are no objective criteria between ''just'' and ''unjust'' wars. If the just war is one of self-defense, it is just, if directed against a present or imminent unjust attack. When is an attack in a concrete case unjust? Gentili went so far as to call just wars even preventive wars, wars ''which anticipate dangers, not premeditated, but probable or possible.'' In a war of execution to enforce a right, the right and its violation need definition.

2. Who is to decide in an objective way, which belligerent has a just cause and who is the *"injustus aggressor"*? This decision must be left to each state itself, a consequence which, as Verdross states, deforms the *bellum justum* doctrine. Hence, even the classic doctrine distinguished between ''absolute'' and ''relative,'' [9] between ''objective'' and ''subjective'' justice. Therefore, war can be subjectively just on both sides, Gentili's *"bellum justum ex utraque parte"*; the same is proclaimed by Guggenheim today. Hence, practically every war is just, a doctrine identical with the traditional freedom of a state to resort to war. Sociological jurists therefore go so far as to see in this doctrine, which ''invites subjectivism and abuse by State practice,'' nothing but a ''degeneration into a mere ideology of power politics.'' [10]

Many other problems arise: [11] What of a belligerent who joins a war only in the last moment to participate in the advantages of victory? Or who changes sides during the course of the same war? Or who, with regard to partial wars constituting the same world war, has a just cause in one partial war, but is an *"injustus aggressor"* in others? The two world wars have given examples for all these hypotheses.

3. There is, further, the gravest objection that war is not an adequate means of enforcing the law: the *"injustus aggressor"* may be the victor. That is why Cayetano advises the prince not to go to war, even if he has a

---

[9] One belligerent can have a just cause, whereas the other has a ''still more just'' cause.

[10] Thus G. Schwarzenberger, ''Jus Pacis ac Belli,'' this JOURNAL, Vol. 37 (1943), pp. 460–477, at p. 465.

[11] See Antonio Truyol y Serra, *''Crímenes de guerra y derecho natural,''* *Revista Española de Derecho Internacional*, Vol. I, No. 1 (1948), pp. 45–73.

just cause, if he has not also the moral certainty of victory. Suárez' probabilism asks, at least, for the probability of victory. These statements show the radical deficiency, the "tragic confession of the negligible practical range of the classic bellum justum doctrine." [12]

Recent developments through the League of Nations, Kellogg Pact and United Nations, here mentioned as representative of the newer trend, do not constitute a return to the classic *bellum justum* doctrine.[13]

First, it must be emphasized that these treaties, as well as writers such as Strisower and Kelsen, are in a fundamental point different from the classic doctrine. They understand by the term "wrong" exclusively a violation of *positive* international law, whereas the classic doctrine means by "wrong" a violation both of positive and of *natural* law.[14] A just war can be waged to enforce not only a positive, but also a *natural* right, *e.g.*, the natural right of commerce. It is exactly by the enforcement of this *natural* right that Victoria ultimately justifies the conquest of America. Thus just war is given a *double* function: enforcement of *law* and enforcement of *justice;* law and justice need not be identical.

The League of Nations Covenant did not abolish war, but discriminated between different wars. The basis of distinction was *not*, as in the classic doctrine, between just and unjust wars, but between legal and illegal wars. The concept of *bellum legale* replaced the concept of *bellum justum*. The illegality of resort to war was not a function of the intrinsic injustice of the cause of war, but of the breach of a formal, procedural requirement. Hence, a legal war could have been waged even between Members of the League by a state which had no just cause of war, whereas a state which fully had a just cause of war could have been guilty of resorting to an illegal war. This is a very different thing from the *bellum justum* doctrine. The military *"action commune"* under Article XVI was a sanction in a truly legal sense, not against the *"injustus aggressor"* but against an *illegal* belligerent who had "resorted to war in disregard of his covenants under Articles XII, XIII or XV."

The Kellogg Pact, if taken at its surface value, could not constitute a return to the classic doctrine, as it did not distinguish between wars, but renounced war completely as an instrument of national policy. But the admitted legality of self-defense and the delegation to each state of the right to be the only judge to determine whether the conditions of self-defense exist, make this Pact practically only a restatement of general international law.

---

[12] *Ibid.*, at p. 60.

[13] See Verdross, *op. cit.;* Alf Ross, Constitution of the United Nations (New York, 1950), pp. 140–141; W. Schätzel, *"Friede und Gerechtigkeit,"* Die Friedenswarte, Vol. 50, No. 2 (1950), pp. 97–107.

[14] This essential distinction is pointed out in Josef L. Kunz, *Kriegsrecht und Neutralitätsrecht* (Vienna, 1935), p. 2, note 3, and in A. Verdross, *Völkerrecht* (Vienna, 1950), p. 339.

Compared with the classic doctrine, war is also renounced as a war of execution to enforce a right.

Experience had shown that the Covenant and the Kellogg Pact, because of the aura of uncertainty hovering around the legal concept of "war," made it possible to wage "wars in disguise." Hence, the United Nations Charter, in making great progress from the point of view of legal technique, replaced the concept of "war" by that of the "threat or use of force." The Charter, therefore, distinguishes between legal and illegal use of force; the distinction is again based on the legality, not on the intrinsic justice of the cause. Use of force is, generally speaking, forbidden; but under Article 51 force can legally be used against an "armed attack," "until the Security Council has taken the necessary measures." If the Security Council is paralyzed by the veto, we are back to general international law. On the other hand, the military measures which can be decided by the Security Council are, contrary to Article XVI of the Covenant, not necessarily sanctions in a juridical sense.[15]

Furthermore, these new developments have hardly been able to avoid the grave objections which have been stated above against the *bellum justum* doctrine.[16]

Roscoe Pound has stated that a primitive and weak law wants, first of all, to establish peace, *i.e.*, absence of violence, and to guarantee the *status quo*. It puts peace above justice, whereas the intrinsic justice of the cause was the heart of the classic doctrine. This emphasis on security, more than justice, can be seen in recent developments. The Kellogg Pact renounces war, the Charter forbids the use of force—except in self-defense—without giving the states as a substitute the compulsory peaceful settlement of international conflicts, without guaranteeing the enforcement of their rights, without creating a workable procedure of peaceful change, without a guarantee that United Nations force will be brought to bear not only against an illegal aggressor, but also against a state which, without using force, does not fulfill an international obligation, without guarantee that, if such force is exercised by the United Nations, its use will be reasonably assured of success.

Two world wars and the fear of more catastrophic wars have made the avoidance of war more important than the achievement of justice. The first aim in the preamble of the United Nations Charter is "to save succeeding generations from the scourge of war." The first purpose in Article 1 is not to achieve and maintain justice, but to "maintain international peace and security." Again, we are faced with the antinomy between the two juridical values of security and justice. Security is the lower, but

[15] H. Kelsen, The Law of the United Nations (London, 1950), pp. 732–739; Alf Ross, *op. cit.*, p. 141.

[16] See Robert W. Tucker, "The Interpretation of War," The International Law Quarterly (London), Vol. 4, No. 1 (1951), pp. 11–38.

most basic value. *"La sécurité d'abord,"* as the French thesis ran after the first World War; only then the intrinsic settlement of conflicts; here lies the difference between Chapters VI and VII of the Charter, between, within the Pan American orbit, the Rio Treaty and the Pact of Bogotá. First to establish security is the philosophy of recent developments, in the conviction that security is the indispensable pre-condition of later achieving justice. This philosophy may be wholly justified, but it is not the philosophy underlying the *bellum justum* doctrine.

[8]

WHO KILLED ARTICLE 2(4)?

OR:

CHANGING NORMS GOVERNING THE USE OF FORCE BY STATES

By Thomas M. Franck [*]

Twenty-five years ago, the Allied nations gathered at San Francisco in the warming glow of victory and signed a solemn treaty giving effect to their determination "to save succeeding generations from the scourge of war . . ." and "to ensure, by the acceptance of principles and the institution of methods, that armed force shall not be used, save in the common interest . . ." [1] Specifically, they undertook in Article 2(4) to "refrain in their international relations from the threat or use of force against the territorial integrity or political independence of any state . . ." They also committed themselves to "settle their international disputes by peaceful means . . ." [2]

Yet today the high-minded resolve of Article 2(4) mocks us from its grave. That the rules against the use of force should have had so short a life appears due to various factors. The rules, admirable in themselves, were seemingly predicated on a false assumption: that the wartime partnership of the Big Five would continue, providing the means for policing the peace under the aegis of the United Nations. They appeared to address themselves to preventing conventional military aggression at the very moment in history when new forms of attack were making obsolete all prior notions of war and peace strategy. And the Charter itself provided enough exceptions and ambiguities to open the rules to deadly erosion.

But if the rules prohibiting recourse to force were imperfect and, to some extent, already obsolescent by the time the Charter came into operation, this does not alone account for the demise of Article 2(4). Blame for this must be shared by powerful, and even some not-so-powerful, states which, from time to time over the past twenty-five years, have succumbed to the temptation to settle a score, to end a dispute or to pursue their national interest through the use of force.

The practice of these states has so severely shattered the mutual confidence which would have been the *sine qua non* of an operative rule of law embodying the precepts of Article 2(4) that, as with Ozymandias, only the words remain. Perhaps the nations, given the changed realities of the postwar quarter-century, could not realistically have been expected to live with Article 2(4). But its demise does raise a serious question for

[*] Center for International Studies, New York University.
[1] U.N. Charter, Preamble.
[2] U.N. Charter, Art. 2(3).

810   THE AMERICAN JOURNAL OF INTERNATIONAL LAW   [Vol. 64

the nations: Having violated it, ignored it, run roughshod over it, and explained it away, can they live without it?

I. FACTORS UNDERMINING ARTICLE 2(4)

The United Nations Charter today bears little more resemblance to the modern world than does a Magellan map. The real world is not necessarily nicer, but it is quite different. Chapter VII of the United Nations Charter, for example, makes extensive provision for collective action by the Organization "to maintain or restore international peace and security" when a threat to the peace or an act of aggression occurs. "Such action may include demonstrations, blockade and other operations by air, sea, or land forces of Members of the United Nations." In order to facilitate such collective enforcement actions, Chapter VII provides for a U.N. Military Staff Committee to command the international police forces. It also obligates Member States to "hold immediately available national air-force contingents for combined international enforcement action."

Unfortunately these ambitious projects were founded on an invalid premise: that the Security Council would be able to discharge its responsibility as the United Nations' principal organ for world peacekeeping. Under Chapter VII it is the Council which must decide whether, in any particular instance, a threat to the peace exists, or whether aggression has been committed and, if so, by whom, and, finally, what, if any, collective steps by the world organization would best remedy the situation. The Security Council, however, in all but procedural matters, can only act with the assent of nine members, including the affirmative vote or at least the benevolent abstention of each of the Big Five. Almost from the moment the San Francisco Charter was signed, this essential prerequisite for U.N. collective enforcement action—the unanimity of the great Powers—was seen to be an illusion. Consequently, with the exception of the U.N. action in defense of South Korea, it has never been possible to invoke these collective enforcement provisions. Even in that one instance, U.N. military action could not have occurred but for a fortuitous absence of the Soviet Union from the Security Council. As for the U.N. rôle in the Congo, it never technically became an enforcement action, since the enemies against which the action was directed were hunger, chaos, tribalism and freebootery, and not a transgressing state. Even at the beginning, when the Security Council authorized a U.N. presence to facilitate the withdrawal of Belgian paratroopers, no actual use of force for that purpose was contemplated. The initial purpose of stationing the U.N. contingent in the Congo was only to relieve the Belgian troops of their reason—or, as some saw it, their excuse—for remaining there, and to assist the Congolese authorities to maintain order.[3]

This paucity of actions under Chapter VII does not, unfortunately, denote a peaceful world community. In the twenty-five years since the San

---

[3] Security Council Res. 143, U.N. Security Council, 15th Year, Official Records, Resolutions and Decisions at 5, U.N. Doc. S/4387 (1960).

Francisco Conference, there have been some one hundred separate out-breaks of hostility between states. The fact that on only one of these occasions has the United Nations been able to mount a collective enforce-ment action—and that more by a fluke than by dint of organizational re-sponsiveness—indicates why, for security, nations have increasingly fallen back on their own resources and on military and regional alliances. And the Charter provided them with the necessary loopholes. As Chapter VII was seen to rust, increasing use began to be made of Articles 51, 52, and 53, which set out the rights of states themselves, under certain exceptional circumstances, to resort to various kinds of force outside the United Nations framework, until today, through practice, the exceptions have overwhelmed the rule and transformed the system.

Article 51 of the U.N. Charter permits the use of armed force by a state responding in self-defense to an armed attack. This right to respond can either be exercised individually by the state attacked or collectively by a group of states going to its rescue. At first glance, such an exception would appear to be both inevitable and modest. Although an instance of military aggression ought ordinarily to be met by the collective enforcement ma-chinery of the United Nations, it is only prudent that, in the event this machinery fails, an attacked state and its allies should be free to respond with force against the aggressor.

The simplicity of this is, however, misleading. In the first place, the failure of U.N. enforcement machinery has not been occasional but endemic, and so, concomitantly, has the resort to "self-defense." Equally important, since there is usually no way for the international system to establish con-clusively which state is the aggressor and which the aggrieved, wars con-tinue to occur, as they have since time immemorial, between parties both of which are using force allegedly in "self-defense." Thus the fighting between China and India, Pakistan and India, and even between North and South Korea began with both sides insisting that they were defending themselves against an armed attack by the other. India invaded Goa allegedly in self-defense. Presumably some or all parties to a dispute claim-ing to be acting in self-defense are lying: but which ones? And how is culpability to be made manifest? With no system for objective fact-finding, the concept of self-defense remains a convenient shield for self-serving and aggressive conduct. Even a highly probable proposition of fact, such as the allegation that the North rather than the South initiated the use of force in Korea, tends to be somewhat less persuasive when alleged by an interested party than when it is found by, for example, a commission of disinterested parties. Insofar as the facts about the initiation of a dispute have not been satisfactorily ascertainable, the operation of Article 51 is effectively and dangerously unlimited. The temptation remains what it was before Article 2(4) was conceived: to attack first and lie about it afterwards.

The outright lie about who attacked first is not, however, the only or, probably, the principal problem. The most significant factor in complicat-ing the "simple" right of self-defense accorded by Article 51, rather, has

812   THE AMERICAN JOURNAL OF INTERNATIONAL LAW   [Vol. 64

been the changing nature of warfare itself. The great wars of the past, up to the time of the San Francisco Conference, were generally initiated by organized incursions of large military formations of one state onto the territory of another, incursions usually preceded by mobilization and massing of troops and underscored by formal declarations of war. Because it was so familiar to them, it was to aggression of this kind that the drafters of Article 51 addressed themselves. Modern warfare, however, has inconveniently by-passed these Queensberry-like practices. It tends, instead, to proceed along two radically different lines, one too small and the other too large to be encompassed effectively by Article 51. These two categories are, first, wars of agitation, infiltration and subversion carried on by proxy through national liberation movements; and, second, nuclear wars involving the instantaneous use, in a first strike, of weapons of near-paralyzing destructiveness.

II. THE EFFECT OF SMALL-SCALE WARFARE ON ARTICLE 2(4)

Small-scale warfare takes the form of rural and urban hit-and-run operations by small bands of fighters, sometimes not in uniform and often lightly armed. During the wartime Nazi occupation of continental Europe, as well as in Japanese-occupied Asia, guerrilla tactics were perfected and demonstrated.[4] After the war, these tactics, utilizing indigenous partisan bands operating in the countryside, were employed in a number of states at the intersection of the Communist and non-Communist worlds. From Greece to Malaya and Indo-China a determined bid was made by the left to overthrow shaky or unpopular regimes. In these small-scale internal wars, the national Communist movements and their allies were able to plug themselves into an international power grid, and this gave the problem a new dimension.[5] Communist governments felt hardly constrained to respect national boundaries in helping fraternal socialists struggling for "national liberation." But the help they gave usually did not include the dispatch of armies. Instead, new kinds of assistance were developed along lines similar to those developed by the Allies for encouraging and aiding the guerrilla movements in occupied countries. These new kinds of assistance do not fit comfortably into conventional international legal concepts and categorizations. Insofar as one state merely encourages guerrilla movements within another, an "armed attack," at least in the conventional sense, cannot be said to have taken place. The more subtle and indirect the encouragement, the more tenuous becomes the analogy to an "armed attack." Article 51 does not, however, on its face, recognize the existence of these newer modes of aggression, or attempt to deal with the new problems of characterization which they create for international law.

The deficiency became clear early in the United Nations' history. When, in February, 1948, the Beneš-Masaryk Government of Czechoslovakia ap-

---

[4] *Cf.* Mao Tse-Tung, Selected Works, Vol. 1, pp. 153–175 (International Publishers Co., Inc., 1954).

[5] "All just wars should support each other and all unjust wars should be turned into just ones. . . ." *Ibid.* 174.

peared about to avail itself of Western economic assistance under the Marshall Plan, it was suddenly overthrown by the internal Communist minority.[6] According to Mr. Papanek, the Czechoslovak representative then at the United Nations, this group "was encouraged and given promise of help, if necessary, by the representatives of the Government of the Union of Soviet Socialist Republics who came to Prague for that purpose. . . ." He added that it was

> very clear that the coup by the Communist minority by force was effectuated successfully only because of official participation of representatives of the Union of Soviet Socialist Republics and because of the threat of the use of military force . . . in readiness on the north-west boundaries of Czechoslovakia. . . .[7]

But there was no invasion, no "armed attack" of the kind envisioned by Article 51. In the case of Greece, the support of indigenous Communist insurgents by neighboring Yugoslavia was far more tangible, as evidenced by the rapid fall-off in activity after the 1948 break between Tito and Stalin. Significant support has also been given indigenous Communist insurgent movements by China in Laos, Burma and South Viet-Nam and by Cuba in Venezuela, Bolivia and Colombia. The nature of such support ranges from military supplies and the training of recruits to money and radio propaganda. But since the Charter speaks only of a right to defend against an armed attack, the international community is left to ponder what principles govern the right to retort in instances of lesser trespass.

No doubt a line of continuity runs from invasions by tanks and divisions through training, arming, sheltering and infiltrating neighboring insurgents, all the way down to hostile radio propaganda calling for revolution in a foreign country. However, these acts, while generically related, are also significantly dissimilar, and the law, if there is to be one, cannot simply

[6] "On last Dec. 12, the Soviet Government newspaper *Izvestia* had warned that Czechoslovakia must not be a 'bridge' between west and east . . . The Russians want to prepare themselves and to take this initiative in Europe before the Marshall Plan can get started." The New York Times, Sec. IV, Feb. 29, 1948, p. 1. "The announcement of the Truman doctrine and the Marshall Plan gave a fresh impulse to the Czechoslovak reactionaries. They decided to pass to the offensive. Through their agents in government and parliament they tried to sabotage the program of the National Front government . . . This was crude work. The real character of the Marshall Plan is already pretty widely known in Europe." V. Medov, "The February Events in Czechoslovakia," New Times, No. 10, March 3, 1948, at pp. 4–5. "Upon orders from Wall Street and the city, the Czechoslovak reactionaries from the National Socialist Party, the Slovak Democratic Party, and others, attempted with all their might to sabotage and to disrupt the social and economic reforms in the country." Izvestia, Oct. 28, 1948, found in 4 Soviet Press Translations 15 at 17 (1949). *Cf.* B. Polevoy, "The Defeat of Reaction in Czechoslovakia," Pravda, March 16, 1948, found in 3 Soviet Press Translations 243 (1948), and E. Zhukov, "Marshall's Chicago Address," Pravda, Nov. 23, 1947, in 3 Soviet Press Translations 39 (1948).

[7] Letter dated March 10, 1948, from the Permanent Representative of Chile to the United Nations, addressed to the Secretary General, Security Council, 3rd Year, Official Records, Supp. for January, February and March, 1948, at 34, U.N. Doc. S/696 (1948).

814   THE AMERICAN JOURNAL OF INTERNATIONAL LAW   [Vol. 64

disregard the differences. Yet there is a strong temptation, in practice, to treat them all as analogous. This is illustrated by our own conduct during the Lebanon crisis of 1958, which is a particularly good illustration of two dilemmas inherent in Article 2(4): that of deciding the factual question of who attacked whom, and that of defining the level of foreign intervention which should suffice to permit counter-intervention by way of collective self-defense.

This particular Middle East crisis flared up in two stages, the first being the civil war which sought to overthrow the pro-Western regime of President Chamoun, whose constitutional status was in dispute. The second stage was the annihilation of the pro-Western monarchy of Iraq, which led to the prophylactic dispatch of U. S. troops to Lebanon and British forces to the Kingdom of Jordan.

Late in May, an embattled Lebanese Government lodged a complaint with the Security Council, alleging that a "situation" had arisen "the continuance of which" was "likely to endanger the maintenance of international peace and security" and that this situation of civil insurrection had arisen "from the intervention of the United Arab Republic in the internal affairs of Lebanon." [8] Specifically, Ambassador Malik of Lebanon complained to the Security Council that the United Arab Republic was guilty of "intervention" in the Lebanese civil war by the "supply of arms on a large scale . . . to subversives," by "training in subversion on the territory of the United Arab Republic of elements from Lebanon and the sending back of these elements to Lebanon to subvert their Government," and by the "participation of United Arab Republic civilian nationals residing in or passing into Lebanon in subversive and terrorist activities. . . ." None of these charges, however, amounted to an allegation of "armed attack." Ambassador Malik also singled out another kind of intervention: "The violent and utterly unprecedented press campaign . . ." and "radio campaign conducted by the United Arab Republic inciting the people of Lebanon to overthrow their Government." [9] This obviously constituted an even lower level of intervention. Yet one has only to have experienced a revolution in Africa or the Middle East to know that an effective, powerful radio transmitter may be worth more than its weight in grenades and pistols.

Significantly, Lebanon did not at this stage claim that these facts were sufficient to constitute an armed attack within the meaning of Article 51. It brought charges against the U.A.R. before the U.N. Security Council under Article 35 of the Charter, alleging only a "situation" likely to give rise to a breach of the peace and asking the Council to devise "appropriate . . . methods of adjustment" under Article 36(1). Responding on June 11, 1958, at the instance of the Swedish representative, the Council succeeded in establishing "an observation group to proceed to Lebanon so as to ensure that there is no illegal infiltration of personnel or supply of

---

[8] Letter dated May 22, 1958, from the representative of Lebanon to the President of the Security Council, Security Council, 13th Year, Official Records, Supp. for April, May and June, 1958, at 33, U.N. Doc. S/4007 (1958).

[9] U.N. Security Council, 13th Year, Official Records, 823rd meeting 4 (1958).

arms or other *matériel* across the Lebanese borders. . . ." [10] The United States supported this resolution, together with all other members of the Security Council except the Soviet Union, which abstained.

The U.N. group went into position and was able to report within a month that their "[p]ermanent stations have been moving progressively closer to the frontiers on all sides" [11] and that with "the increase in the Observer force and the addition of enlisted personnel, together with supporting equipment . . . direct and constant patrolling of the actual frontier will be possible." [12] The Group indicated confidence in its ability to keep the border situation under control: "We have not had anything from the Lebanese Government which would lead us to say there is massive infiltration." [13]

At precisely the same time as this report, however, the governments of Lebanon and the United States were acting on the opposite perceptions. U. S. troops were pouring onto the shores of Tripoli. Two principles justifying the marine landings were advanced, both of them relating to collective self-defense, the rationale of Article 51. The troops had been "asked . . . to preserve Lebanon's integrity and independence" [14] by the Chamoun Government, and they had also intervened in order to "afford security to the several thousand Americans who reside in that country." [15] In addition, Ambassador Lodge noted that the "territorial integrity of Lebanon is increasingly threatened by insurrection stimulated and assisted from outside" since "the overthrow in an exceptionally brutal and revolting manner of the legally established Government of Iraq." [16] This, the United States proclaimed, represents "a *ruthlessness of aggressive purposes* which tiny Lebanon cannot combat without support from friendly nations." [17]

The all-important shift had now taken place from the earlier allegation of a low-yield "intervention" of the kind warranting the dispatch of neutral observers to police the borders, to an "aggressive purpose" justifying the intervention of a super-Power with force by way of collective self-defense. Lest there be any misconception about this shift, the Jordanian delegate, whose country was concurrently receiving British troops, spoke of their dispatch in "generous response" to his government's request to a friendly Power "in accordance with the provisions of Article 51" of the Charter, while the U. S. representative also referred to the exercise by his country of the "inherent right" provided in the Charter—the language of Article 51. [18]

[10] U.N. Security Council, 13th Year, Official Records, 825th meeting 17; Security Council Res. 128, *ibid.*, Resolutions and Decisions at 5; U.N. Doc. S/4023 (1958).

[11] Second Interim Report of the U.N. Observation Group in Lebanon, U.N. Security Council, 13th Year, Official Records, Supp. for July, August and September, 1958, 34 at 36–37, U.N. Doc. S/4052 (1958).

[12] *Ibid.* at 37.

[13] U.N. Press Release LEB/15 of July 7, 1958.

[14] U.N. Security Council, 13th Year, Official Records, 827th meeting 6 (1958).

[15] *Ibid.* 7.

[16] *Ibid.* 6.

[17] *Ibid.* 8. Italics added.

[18] *Ibid.*, 831st meeting 5.

816   THE AMERICAN JOURNAL OF INTERNATIONAL LAW   [Vol. 64

The inherent right of individual and collective self-defense in Article 51 had thus been formally invoked in a non-conventional situation where no foreign army had moved across a border in an "armed attack." Significantly, it was not even alleged that the U.A.R. was massively infiltrating troops into Lebanon—the U.N. Observation Group had been positioned expressly to determine whether such was the case. The Lebanese representative, indeed, told the Security Council on July 15 that

> my Government has never claimed that there was massive infiltration into Lebanon. No representative of Lebanon . . . has used the term "massive infiltration." The expression we have used is "massive intervention in the internal affairs of Lebanon" . . . What we have in mind is the supply of arms, the training of personnel, radio propaganda, propaganda by the press, etc.[19]

It was against such "indirect aggression" that the United States invoked the collective self-defense exception to Article 2(4).

The Swedish Government, which had been instrumental in arranging the initial great-Power consensus or forbearance necessary to the establishment of the Observation Group, fought a rear-guard action against this interpretation of Article 51. "One of the conditions for Article 51 of the Charter to be applicable is that an armed attack has occurred against a Member State," its representative insisted.

> The Swedish Government does not consider that this condition has been fulfilled in the present case, nor does my Government consider that there is an international conflict in the terms of Article 51.[20]

The Lebanese crisis illustrates two problems inherent in applying Article 51. The first is procedural: How is the fact of an armed attack to be established? The Charter provides no answer, and, in its absence, Article 2(4) can be virtually nullified by self-serving allegations. The second problem is substantive: how to define "armed attack" in a way relevant to the modern conditions of indirect, limited warfare without broadening it to the point at which disproportionate armed force can be used under the guise of self-defense against imagined or slight provocation.

Obviously, a rule of law which permits a state to use force whenever it thinks it has been attacked is not much of a rule. If the use of force is to be permitted in self-defense by way of exception to the general prohibition of Article 2(4), there must be some machinery for determining whether that exception applies in particular instances. Although the Charter provides no mandatory machinery to determine when and at whose instigation an armed attack has occurred, some *ad hoc* machinery has been tried. As in Lebanon, so in Viet-Nam an international group had been constituted to police the critical borders against infiltrators.[21] But after

---

19 *Ibid.*, 828th meeting 10.

20 *Ibid.*, 830th meeting 9.

21 Agreement on the Cessation of Hostilities in Viet-Nam, July 20, 1954, Geneva Conference Doc. IC/42/Rev. 2; 60 A.J.I.L. 629 (1966); reprinted in Report on Indochina: Report of Senator Mike Mansfield on a Study Mission to Vietnam, Cambodia, Laos, Oct. 15, 1954, Senate Foreign Relations Committee, print, 83rd Cong., 2d Sess.,

the Saigon regime began to lose the ground war, it and United States policy-makers came to the conclusion, albeit one not wholly endorsed by their own principal information-gatherers,[22] that the operations in the South were less a civil war than a covert attack by North Viet-Nam. In March, 1965, Secretary Rusk announced:

> Without the control of these operations from the North, without the manpower, the trained manpower sent from the North into the South, without the supply of arms and other key items of equipment from North to South, the indigenous aspect of this problem, the genuinely indigenous aspect of this problem, would be quite a different matter. It was this external aspect of the matter which explains the presence of the American military personnel in that area, the rapid increase in American personnel since 1961. It was the escalation of that infiltration.[23]

Thus, as in Lebanon, the United States purported to answer a call to help a friendly government defend itself, in this instance by virtue of what the United States regarded as a commitment under the Manila Pact of February, 1955 (SEATO), and bilateral commitments to the Government in Saigon made by a succession of U. S. Presidents and endorsed by the August, 1964, joint resolution of Congress.[24] As with the Soviet invasion of Hungary in 1956, so in this case the decision to come to the aid of a friendly government under attack may have been permissible joint self-defense by allies within the meaning of Article 51, or it may have been aggression, the use of force in violation of Article 2(4). Which it was depends upon whether the supported regime really constituted the effective government, or was merely a fiction being propped up primarily for the purpose of legitimizing "help" from outside. In the absence of some universally credible fact-determination procedures, the effort to establish whether a use of force is illegal under Article 2(4) or legal under Article 51 is stymied by contradictory allegations of fact by the parties to the dispute and their allies. It is rather as if the law were to leave to the two drivers in a motor vehicle collision the sole responsibility for apportioning liability, helped only by the unruly crowd gathered around them at the scene of the accident.

---

pp. 16–26; and 1 Amer. For. Pol. 1950–1955 at 750 (1957); Final Declaration of the Geneva Conference on the Problem of Restoring Peace in Indo-China, July 21, 1954, Geneva Conference Doc. IC/43/Rev. 2; 60 A.J.I.L. 643 (1966); reprinted in Mansfield, above, at pp. 26–27; and Amer. For. Pol. 1950–1955, above, at p. 785; Statement by the Under Secretary of State at the Concluding Plenary Session of the Geneva Conference, July 21, 1954, Amer. For. Pol. 1950–1955, above, at p. 787; 31 Dept. of State Bulletin 162 (1954); 60 A.J.I.L. 645 (1966).

[22] Roger Hilsman, To Move a Nation 527–528 (Garden City, N. Y., Doubleday & Co., Inc., 1967).

[23] Secretary Rusk's News Conference of Feb. 25, 1965, 52 Dept. of State Bulletin 362 at 366 (1965).

[24] *Ibid.* at 362. See also "The Legality of United States Participation in the Defense of Viet-Nam," Memorandum of Law, Legal Adviser of the Department of State, March 4, 1966, 54 Dept. of State Bulletin 474 (1966), 60 A.J.I.L. 565 (1966); L. Meeker, "Viet-Nam and the International Law of Self-Defense," 56 Dept. of State Bulletin 54 (1967).

818   THE AMERICAN JOURNAL OF INTERNATIONAL LAW   [Vol. 64

Unfortunately, there is nothing in the U.N. Charter or in the machinery of the international system which limits the nation's right to determine for itself when an act of aggression has occurred, or whether the regime calling for help is, in fact, the legitimate government. The Security Council could, but in practice is virtually precluded by its voting rules from making such a determination. And the fact that the super-Powers have simply disregarded the findings of international peace-observation groups in the cases of both Lebanon and Viet-Nam puts in question the utility of such *ad hoc* fact-finding procedures as have been tried.[25] This is, therefore, another of the great vulnerabilities of the norm established by Articles 2(4) and 51: If the grievous threats to world peace are to appear hereafter in the guise of civil wars or wars involving partitioned states with rival regimes, then Article 51 by itself is likely to be of very little use in distinguishing individual or collective self-defense from aggression. The Charter is silent about the situation in which two great Powers, recognizing different regimes in the same country, exercise their right to come to the "collective self-defense" of the side each prefers. In the absence of an objective international system of recognition of governments and an international system for determining which party to a dispute is the aggressor and which the victim, Article 51 is a wide-open invitation to the great Powers to engage each other in limited wars fought vicariously on borrowed terrain and with others' lives.

There is, however, one substantial difference between the Lebanon and Viet-Nam operations. In the latter case, the United States thought itself entitled not merely to provide reinforcements to aid a friendly government in internal self-defense, but also to use direct force to attack an external enemy—North Viet-Nam—thought to be covertly fomenting and abetting the internal crisis.[26] In announcing its decision to carry bombing raids into the North, the United States insisted that "South Vietnam is being subjected to an aggression from the North, an aggression which is organized and directed and supplied with key equipment and personnel by Hanoi." [27] As in the case of the dispatch of troops to Lebanon, however, this U. S. decision was taken unilaterally on the basis of unilaterally determined facts, over the heads of the international control organ.[28]

Both at present and even in the past, a number of attempts have been made to draft rules taking into account these world-wide phenomena of

[25] Franck, "The Problem of Fact-Finding in International Disputes," 18 Western Reserve Law Rev. 1483 (1967).

[26] White House Statement, Feb. 7, 1965, "United States and South Vietnamese Forces Launch Retaliatory Attacks Against North Viet-Nam," 52 Dept. of State Bulletin 238 (1965).

[27] Secretary Rusk, "Some Fundamentals of American Policy," *ibid.* 398 at 401.

[28] For an analysis of the reports of the International Commission for Supervision and Control in Viet-Nam, *cf.* Younger, The Southeast Asia Crisis, The Eighth Hammarskjöld Forum of the Association of the Bar of the City of New York, pp. 116–118 (Dobbs Ferry, N. Y., Oceana, 1966). According to this study "both parties had immobilized the activities of the Commission's teams and hampered the Commission's proper discharge of its obligation to supervise the (Geneva) agreement." *Ibid.* 117–118.

indirect and vicarious aggression which have recently become endemic but which were not unknown in the past. The Inter-American Convention Concerning the Duties and Rights of States in the Event of Civil Strife of 1928 obliges the parties to

> use all means at their disposal to prevent the inhabitants of their territory, nationals or aliens, from participating in, gathering elements, crossing the boundary or sailing from their territory for the purpose of starting or promoting civil strife.[29]

The convention likewise forbids all traffic in arms and obliges the parties to disarm rebels who cross into their territory. In the same cause, the U.N. General Assembly on December 21, 1965, passed a Declaration on Inadmissibility of Intervention[30] which groups together "direct intervention, subversion and all forms of indirect aggression" as equally violating the U.N. Charter. The resolution holds that

> No State may use or encourage the use of economic, political or any other type of measures to coerce another State in order to obtain from it the subordination of the exercise of its sovereign rights or to secure from it advantages of any kind. Also, no State shall organize, assist, foment, finance, incite or tolerate subversive, terrorist or armed activities directed towards the violent overthrow of the régime of another State, or interfere in civil strife in another State.

But, of course, this resolution is not binding and it has not notably inhibited Member States' conduct.

Efforts to arrive at a formula that could be incorporated into a new treaty have also been fruitless. Several draft texts submitted to the Special Committee on Principles of International Law Concerning Friendly Relations and Co-operation Among States[31] contain prohibitions against such acts of a state as "organizing or encouraging the organization of irregular or volunteer forces or armed bands within its territory or any other territory for incursions into the territory of another State . . ."[32] as well as against "instigating" civil strife.[33] One definition of force, proposed by neutral states members of this committee, includes:

> All forms of pressure, including those of a political and economic character, which have the effect of threatening the territorial integrity or political independence of any State.[34]

But none of these efforts has produced agreement as to whether the abetting of civil strife or the exertion of overweaning political and economic

[29] Convention Concerning the Duties and Rights of States in the Event of Civil Strife, adopted by the Sixth International Conference of American States and signed at Habana, Feb. 20, 1928. 134 L. N. Treaty Series 47, No. 3082 (1932); 22 A.J.I.L. Supp. 159 (1928).

[30] Declaration on the Inadmissibility of Intervention in the Domestic Affairs of States and the Protection of their Independence and Sovereignty. General Assembly Res. 2131, U.N. Doc. A/6014 at 11 (1965); 60 A.J.I.L. 662 (1966).

[31] *Cf.* Draft Report of the 1968 Special Committee, U.N. Doc. A/AC.125/L.64/Add. 1 (1968).

[32] *Ibid.* 2.   [33] *Ibid.* 3.

[34] *Ibid.* 5.

820   THE AMERICAN JOURNAL OF INTERNATIONAL LAW   [Vol. 64

pressure should be analogized to an "armed attack" for the purpose of giving rise to a right of self-defense utilizing military force. Indeed, so muddied are these waters that the neutralist definition of the right of self-defense includes the right of insurgents, or states aiding insurgency, to attack with military force "in the exercise of their right to self-determination" in wars of national liberation. Such use of force, in the opinion of the neutralist draft proposal, constitutes "self-defence against colonial domination." [35] Naturally, there can be no broad agreement on such double-edged definitions.[36] One man's war of national liberation is another's aggression or subversion, and vice versa. Under the circumstances, there is little prospect that the new effort by the Special Committee on the Question of Defining Aggression, constituted by the Twenty-Second General Assembly, will be more successful.[37]

Failure is not necessarily the result of evil intentions. The small-scale and diffuse but significant and frequent new wars of insurgency have, by their nature, made clear-cut distinctions between aggression and self-defense, which are better adapted to conventional military warfare, exceedingly difficult. While it was not always possible even in classical combat to determine which army had started marching first, the scale, formations and strategy of conventional warfare did make the identification of aggression relatively easy. It stretched everyone's credulity to be told that Poland had attacked Germany or South Korea the North, when the armies of these self-proclaimed victims were, right at the very beginning, to be seen overrunning their opponents. Conventionally, an aggressor could almost be defined as the party winning the first round of a new war. With the hit-and-run tactics of wars of national liberation, on the other hand, it is often difficult even to establish convincingly, from a pattern of isolated, gradually cumulative events, when or where the first round began, let alone at whose instigation, or who won it.

III. THE EFFECT OF POTENTIAL NUCLEAR WARFARE ON ARTICLE 2(4)

If the growing fashion for mini-wars or quasi-wars has made the rules devised at San Francisco hard to apply, so, too, has the development of a capacity for warfare far more rapid and devastating than hitherto. Taken literally, Articles 2(4) and 51 together seem to require a state to await an actual nuclear strike against its territory before taking forceful countermeasures. If this is what the Charter requires, then, to paraphrase Mr. Bumble, the Charter is "a ass." No nation, it is safe to suppose, would willingly sit by while another prepares its doom. Article 51, however, permits the use of self-defense by nations only in the event of an armed attack.

[35] *Ibid.*, U.N. Doc. A/AC.125/L.64/Add 2 at 12–13.

[36] *Idem, passim.* See also Report of the Special Committee on the Question of Defining Aggression, U.N. General Assembly, 23rd Sess., Official Records, U.N. Doc. A/7185/Rev. 1 (1968).

[37] Report of the Special Committee on the Question of Defining Aggression, *ibid.* at 2–35. See also Hazard, "Why Try Again to Define Aggression?", 62 A.J.I.L. 701 (1968).

In construing the language of a treaty one ought not to assume that the drafters intended a patent absurdity.[38] But in correcting for a possible absurdity, it is also possible to over-correct. According to Professor Myres McDougal, Article 51 cannot be taken to read that a military response in self-defense is permitted if, and only if, an armed attack has actually occurred. It would be against reason and nature, particularly in the age of jets, rockets and nuclear weapons, to interpret Article 51 so literally as to preclude a victim from using force in self-defense until it has actually been attacked. From this he goes on to argue that the Article 51 rule should be interpreted to mean that a state may use military force when it "regards itself as intolerably threatened by the activities of another." [39] If customary international law, the doctrine of necessity, and human reason have always permitted pre-emptive strikes against an anticipated rather than only an actual attack, it follows in McDougal's argument that no nation can have intended, by adherence to Article 51, to have bound itself to sit still while another nation prepares to strike a first, and possibly lethal, blow. The problem is, however, that while a rule which permits a state to use force against another only after it has been attacked may not be satisfactory in the nuclear age, one which permits a pre-emptive strike whenever a nation regards itself as "intolerably threatened" is so subjective as to be no rule at all. Moreover, the McDougal reinterpretation of Article 51 permits a pre-emptive strike not only in cases of apprehended nuclear attack, but against any threatening "activities," including conventional military ones that do not raise the same threat of catastrophic destruction.

Tested against the perceptions of the reasonable man, most of the instances when states perceived themselves about to be attacked or in imminent danger are simply not credible. Perhaps only in the case of Israel's invasion of the Arab states in 1967 does it seem at all convincing, on the facts, that the use of force was truly pre-emptive in a strict sense, *i.e.* undertaken in reasonable anticipation of an imminent large-scale armed attack of which there was substantiated evidence. The territorial smallness of Israel, moreover, may make more plausible that country's case for striking first, lest a first blow even with conventional weapons by the other side be as decisive as a nuclear blow would be against a larger nation. Most other pre-emptive actions were launched in circumstances in which the imminence of a crippling attack by the other side was less persuasively demonstrable. It has been solemnly asserted that the United States believed itself imminently threatened by missiles stationed in Cuba, that the Portuguese in Goa really were about to invade India, that South Korea was about to attack the North and that Czechoslovakia was about to be

---

[38] "Nothing is better settled, as a canon of interpretation in all systems of law, than that a clause must be so interpreted as to give it a meaning rather than so as to deprive it of meaning." Cayuga Indians Claims case, 20 A.F. (1926) at p. 587; A.D. 1925-6, No. 271. See McNair, The Law of Treaties 383–385 (Oxford, Clarendon Press, 1961).

[39] 1963 Proceedings, American Society of International Law 164.

822   THE AMERICAN JOURNAL OF INTERNATIONAL LAW   [Vol. 64

snatched from the Socialist family. What is suggested by these and numerous other cases is that while Article 51, interpreted literally, appears to require an intended victim to sit still and do nothing until the enemy has had its first inning, an alternative, permitting each state to use military force in self-defense whenever it feels its territory or its interests threatened, is not a satisfactory alternative. All armed forces at the disposal of unfriendly states are a threat of sorts to their opponents, and the difference between an "offensive" and a "defensive" weapon, on which President Kennedy relied during the Cuba missile crisis, has yet to be defined.

IV. REGIONAL ENFORCEMENT AND ARTICLE 2(4)

Ambiguities and complexities thus lurk behind the misleadingly simple rule in Article 2(4) prohibiting the use of force in international relations and in the carefully delimited exceptions to that rule. Changing circumstances of international relations, of the way nations perceive their self-interest, of strategy and tactics, have combined to take advantage of these latent ambiguities, enlarging the exceptions to the point of virtually repealing the rule itself.

A particularly significant part in this development has been played by regional organizations. Articles 52 and 53 of the Charter have been interpreted to legitimate the use of force by regional organizations in their collective self-interest, and, specifically, the rôle and primacy of regional organizations in settling disputes between their members. These exceptions to Article 2(4) and their application in practice have played an important, perhaps the most important, rôle in the growth of international violence over these past twenty-five years. The regional organizations permitted by these articles have developed tight codes of loyalty and have not hesitated to enforce them against members suspected of deviation. Their activities have been effectively beyond the reach of the law of the larger community, especially if they happen to be led by one of the super-Powers. Intended to supplement the U.N. peacekeeping system, the regional organizations have too often instead become instruments of violence, eroding the Article 2(4) injunction. How this came about must be understood in the context of the historic negotiations leading to the insertion into the Charter of Articles 51, 52 and 53.

The Charter itself represents a compromise between universal and regional international systems: that is, between structured relations among states taking place in one loose, all-encompassing organization and, on the other hand, the norms applied in and between a number of tightly knit, relatively homogeneous groupings based frequently on contiguity, history and shared self-interest. This compromise was not easy to conceive nor has it been simple to apply, and the resultant balance has historically been an uneasy and shifting one.[40] The interests superficially predominant in the world organization, particularly in the General Assembly, are frequently not the same as the interests predominant in the regional grouping. Great-

---

[40] *Cf.* L. Miller, "Regional Organization and the Regulation of Internal Conflict," 19 World Politics 582 (July, 1967).

Power dominance has been, on the whole, more complete in certain regional organizations than in, for example, the U.N. General Assembly. The regional groupings are more amenable to *realpolitik* and secret diplomacy. Consequently, a dispute might be treated rather differently depending upon whether it is handled by the regional or the world body.

In the see-saw contest between regional and global forums, those who favored the paramountcy of the world organization were at their zenith just before and at the Dumbarton Oaks preparatory negotiations. Their cause was primarily championed at that time by Secretary of State Cordell Hull,[41] whose views on the idealized global system bore some resemblance to the morality of President Wilson. However, Hull was not the only force working to shape U. S. State Department strategy for a postwar world system. As Professor Inis Claude has pointed out, the

> triumph of universalist ideology was short-lived. "Regionalism Resurgent" was emblazoned on the banner hoisted at the Inter-American Conference on Problems of War and Peace in Mexico City, which culminated in the signing of the Act of Chapultepec on 3 March 1945. At this gathering, representatives of the Latin American states expressed their misgivings about the universalist bias of the Dumbarton Oaks Proposals, affirmed the value of the Inter-American system, proclaimed the intent to refurbish and strengthen that system, and insisted that the constitution of the new world organization should leave the way open for the functioning of a politically active and largely autonomous Inter-American agency.[42]

At San Francisco, these states, with the powerful support of Senator Arthur H. Vandenberg, were partially successful in their "campaign to make the United Nations Charter safe for regionalism." [43]

The first and preferred tactic of the regionalists was to establish a total exception within the Charter for regional organizations, removing them from the jurisdiction of United Nations organs, giving them primacy in peacekeeping, and a free choice of peaceful or military means of enforcement. To achieve this, it would have been necessary to go back on all the work done at Dumbarton Oaks, especially to secure the amendment of Article 53 in such a way as to exempt the inter-American system from the previously agreed requirement of Security Council approval prior to a regional enforcement action. Too many states saw such a total exclusion of regional military action from U.N. supervision as an abdication, and these head-on efforts failed at San Francisco. However, the inter-American regionalists did succeed in inserting what is now Article 51 of the Charter.[44] This article had not been in the Dumbarton Oaks draft. Significantly, it permits collective self-defense against an armed attack *unless* a Security Council resolution prohibits it, thus reversing, in situations of self-defense, the requirement for prior Security Council approval before armed force

---

[41] Inis L. Claude, Jr., "The OAS, the UN and the United States," International Conciliation, No. 547 (March, 1964), p. 5. See also Russell and Muther, A History of the United Nations Charter (Washington, D. C., Brookings, 1958).

[42] Claude, *loc. cit.*, p. 6.   [43] Claude, *loc. cit.*, p. 7.

[44] Doc. 576, III/4/9, XII U.N.C.I.O. Docs. 680 (1945).

is deployed. Under this new formulation, the veto thus operates to perpetuate rather than to prevent use of force as long as the action is technically taken under Article 51. The history of the article leaves little doubt as to the intended beneficiaries. Although Article 51, unlike the older Article 53, does not specifically mention regional organizations, the Colombian delegate read the following statement into the San Francisco record:

> The Latin American Countries understood, as Senator Vandenberg had said, that the origin of the term "collective self-defense" is identified with the necessity of preserving regional systems like the Inter-American one.[45]

It is poignantly noteworthy that this new provision was expressly welcomed at San Francisco by the Czechoslovak delegate, who "expressed his satisfaction that the text approved effectively reconciled the right of self-defense, individual and collective, with the maintenance of a central authority capable of dealing with the problems of security as they arose." [46] Thus, the regional organization was authorized, in the event of an armed attack, to use its collective force *without* the prior approval of the Security Council. At the time, of course, every delegation thought of these provisions primarily or exclusively in terms of regional defense by allied states freely combining to discourage or repel external aggressors such as Hitler and Mussolini and not as a way by which a "commonwealth" of states under the control of a super-Power would legitimize that super-Power's domination of its region.

Formally, the San Francisco compromise between regionalism and universalism is perfectly straightforward. A regional organization may act by means short of force to preserve the peace without having to await an outbreak of armed hostility (*Article 52*), but it may engage in enforcement action only after obtaining a fiat from the Security Council (*Article 53*). An individual state or group of states may use force defensively prior to Security Council approval, but only to respond to an armed attack (*Article 51*). However, between 1945 and 1969, the three articles have melded to produce an increasingly frequently asserted right of regional organizations to take the law into their own hands, to act militarily without Security Council approval even in the absence of an actual armed attack, and to exclude the United Nations from jurisdiction over disputes in which one member of a regional organization is being forcibly purged of ideological non-conformity by the rest.

The last-mentioned problem of regional self-policing has become particularly acute since the mid-1960's, after the days of abortive "détente" and "multipolarity" when small states in the regions of the super-Powers had briefly been encouraged to believe themselves to be on a rather long leash. Particularly significant, in this connection, were those compromises made at San Francisco that concern the balance of power between regional and world organization in pacific settlement, that area within which the regional

---

[45] *Ibid.* 680.   [46] *Ibid.* 681–682.

organization may wish to act to deter aggression by means less militant than an "enforcement action." Again, the issue was superficially simple: In the event of a dispute between two members of the same regional organization, who should have primary jurisdiction to bring about a peaceful settlement? Beneath the apparent issue, however, was a more subtle and profound one: To which international organization should the states of a geographic area be constrained to look for the regulation and legitimation of their conduct: the regional or the universal? Again at San Francisco the globalists were compelled to make concessions. The Dumbarton Oaks draft Chapter VIII, Section C, paragraph 1, was amended at San Francisco [47] by inserting what became Article 52 of the Charter. This provides that members of regional agencies "should make every effort to achieve peaceful settlement of local disputes through such agencies or arrangements before referring them to the Security Council." But even this confusingly non-obligatory prescription was made more ambiguous yet by the additional caveat that it "in no way impairs the application of Articles 34 and 35" of the Charter. These two provisions, in turn, state that the "Security Council may investigate any dispute . . ." and that any "Member of the United Nations may bring any dispute . . . to the attention of the Security Council or of the General Assembly." The Peruvian delegate, in trying unsuccessfully to get this caveat on a caveat deleted, correctly stated that it "set up a double jurisdiction." [48] To this the Colombian Chairman replied with the following masterful attempt at a compromise interpretation:

> If a dispute arises between two states which are members of a regional organization, such controversy should be settled by peaceful means established within the said organization. The obligation exists for all states which are members of a regional organization to make every effort to settle the controversy through this agency, and at the same time, the obligation exists for the Security Council to promote these regional peaceful settlements. But the Security Council has the right to investigate in order to determine whether the controversy may constitute a threat to international peace or security . . .[49]

This seems not, however, to have been the way the compromise was understood at the time by another delegate, John Foster Dulles. Showing a distinct preference for the new global organization, he interpreted the compromise to mean that the United Nations would be "given the first opportunity to maintain peace everywhere, using presumably regional organizations which it is invited to do but not absolutely compelled to do." [50] This statement visualizes a genuine superior-inferior relationship between the Security Council and the regional groups which has, in practice, almost been reversed.

This reversal is due largely to the subsequent policies pursued by the United States which became the active proponent of an interpretation

[47] Ibid. 684.   [48] Ibid. 685.
[49] Ibid. 686.
[50] Hearings before the Committee on Foreign Relations, U. S. Senate, 79th Cong., First Sess., on the Charter of the United Nations, p. 650 (Washington, D. C., GPO, 1945).

826   THE AMERICAN JOURNAL OF INTERNATIONAL LAW   [Vol. 64

much more favorable to the primacy of regional pacific settlement. More important, "peaceful settlement" has gradually been extended in U. S. practice to include such endeavors as the "peaceful" invasion of Guatemala covertly organized by the CIA,[51] the "peaceful" deployment of naval forces to blockade Cuba,[52] and the "peaceful" occupation of the Dominican Republic.[53] Such "peaceful" enterprises have had a major rôle in undermining Article 2(4). If the Cuban blockade was a peaceful quarantine, and the Dominican invasion a humanitarian intervention, what uses of force then remain prohibited by Article 2(4)?

Regionalism's potential as a legal loophole for avoiding the duty of Article 2(4) grew as more regional groupings came to see themselves as eligible. At the time of the San Francisco Conference, the fight to reassert the primacy of regional organization was still largely a project of the states of the Americas. A revival of hemispheric solidarity had been engendered by the war and was then incorporated by the Act of Chapultepec. But regionalism is not a sole prerogative of the Americas. Realizing this, there were some on the U. S. Delegation to the San Francisco Conference who would have preferred to have directed their efforts to securing amendments to the Dumbarton Oaks draft that would have applied specifically and exclusively to the new Organization of American States. This was not, of course, politically feasible. Even at the time, the delegate of Egypt served notice that the new text "should certainly extend to the League of Arab States." [54]

The decision, therefore, was to make provision for "regional organization" in general. But this created uneasiness. New Zealand, sensing the danger of a collision between the regionalism being endorsed by the San Francisco amendments to the Dumbarton Oaks formula, urged but failed to secure adoption of a requirement that all regional arrangements be submitted for the approval of the United Nations.[55] Its fears of proliferating, mutually hostile power blocs exempt from U.N. jurisdiction were substantiated by the ensuing declaration of France that bilateral treaties of mutual defense, such as the Franco-Soviet Pact, could also be understood as fitting into the category of regional arrangements.[56] Under the French formula, any states anywhere could bring themselves within the Charter's special dispensation for regional organizations simply by signing a treaty

[51] *Cf.* Ambassador Lodge (U.S.A.). U.N. Security Council, 9th Year, Official Records, 675th meeting 29 (1954).

[52] The blockade of Cuba was defined by Ambassador Stevenson as "anticipatory" self-defense, U.N. Security Council, 17th Year, Official Records, 1025th meeting 4 (1962), and by the State Department Legal Adviser as an action short of actual enforcement, *cf.* 1963 Proceedings, American Society of International Law 10 at 12.

[53] "Our goal, in keeping with the great principles of the inter-American system, is to help prevent another Communist state in this hemisphere. And we would like to do this without bloodshed or without large-scale fighting." President Johnson, Statement of May 2, 52 Dept. of State Bulletin 744 at 747 (1965).

[54] Doc. 576, III/4/9, XII U.N.C.I.O. Docs. 680, 682 (1945).

[55] *Ibid.* 688.

[56] Doc. 889, III/4/12, XII U.N.C.I.O. Docs. 689, 705 (1945).

of mutual assistance. In all, there emerged from San Francisco no generally accepted definition of a regional organization. There cannot, therefore, be any definitive enumeration of the regional organizations which are today entitled to those exemptions from Article 2(4) that were written into the Charter at San Francisco or which have since been grafted onto it by the practice of states. The discussions at the San Francisco Conference do, of course, clearly support the proposition that the regional groupings then in being regarded themselves, *ipso facto*, as beneficiaries of the new provisions in Article 51 which authorize their use of force in collective self-defense without prior United Nations approval. But does it follow, conversely, that any organization set up primarily to take advantage of the right to act in collective self-defense under Article 51, thereby also qualifies *ipso facto* as a regional organization entitled to maintain "peace and security" among its members under Articles 52 and 53? Except for the affirmative comment by the French delegate, the San Francisco record does little to answer this question.

The question is, however, of legal importance. The Charter's provisions for regional action in the field of pacific settlement—a field rapidly and alarmingly expanding in scope and practice—do not, at least on their face, apply to organizations for collective self-defense established under Article 51, but solely to regional organizations established under Article 52. When, therefore, a defense organization like the Warsaw Pact brings "peaceful" pressure to bear on one of its members or "settles" a regional dispute under Articles 52 or 53, is it entitled to assert, in the absence of any armed attack from outside, as was done in the case of the "peaceful settlements" in Hungary and Czechoslovakia,[57] that it is acting under the Charter as a regional organization? The United States, reacting with abhorrence after the Soviet "commonwealth" had "peacefully settled" the Czech question, took the position that the Warsaw Pact had not previously claimed to be a regional agency "and no such claim could at this late stage properly be put forward."[58]

In view of the fact that regional organizations are accorded such extensive powers in derogation of Article 2(4), and have garnered much greater powers in practice, it is important to have a clear view of which groupings of states are entitled to regard themselves as regional organizations. Many Americans tend to think that their grouping, the Organization of American States, is the sole beneficiary. If the inter-American system is to be regarded as setting a minimum standard for recognition as a regional organization, it is argued, no other multilateral treaty organization meets that standard. No other single grouping is as broadly extensive in its coverage of military *and* non-military matters.

[57] Ambassador Sobolev (U.S.S.R.), U.N. Security Council, 11th Year, Official Records, 754th meeting 10 (1956); also Mr. A. Gromyko, addressing the U.N. General Assembly, U.N. Doc. A/PV.1679, p. 26 at 30–31, Oct. 3, 1968.

[58] Legal Aspects of the Invasion and Occupation of Czechoslovakia. Statements made on Sept. 12 by U. S. Representative Herbert Reis in the U.N. Special Committee on Principles of International Law. 59 Dept. of State Bulletin 400 (1968); 63 A.J.I.L. 324, 331 (1969).

828   THE AMERICAN JOURNAL OF INTERNATIONAL LAW   [Vol. 64

It should first of all, however, be noted that the Organization of American States is based not on a single but on a double system of mutual obligations founded on different treaties and embodying different levels of integration. One of these deals primarily with mutual defense, while the second deals with other non-military aspects of co-operation. These two tiers of integration are quite separate, although the countries covered by them are the same. This is important in making comparisons to other regional systems of integration. Thus Western Europe and Eastern Europe, too, must each be regarded as a single integrative unit, although the defensive and economic aspects of their integration are established by separate treaties and within different treaty organizations, which are not entirely co-extensive in their membership.[59]

First, as to the collective use of force for self-defense, the Inter-American Treaty of Reciprocal Assistance,[60] known as the Rio Pact, sets a high standard of obligation. Under Article 3, "an armed attack by any State against an American State shall be considered as an attack against all the American States" and "each one of the said contracting parties undertakes to assist in meeting the attack." In the event of aggression, the Organ of Consultation, under Article 8, may choose among measures ranging from "recall of chiefs of diplomatic missions" to the "use of armed force." The decision to utilize one or more of these collective measures is taken under Article 17, "by a vote of two-thirds of the Signatory States which have ratified the Treaty," and those decisions which require the application of these measures are, by Article 20, made "binding upon all the Signatory States which have ratified this Treaty, with the sole exception that no State shall be required to use armed force without its consent." These provisions of the inter-American system may be applied not only against "outside" aggressors but also against member states. Significantly, "aggression" is stated in Article 6 to include acts against "the inviolability or the integrity of the territory or the sovereignty or political independence of any American State . . . or . . . any other fact or situation that might en-

---

[59] This comparison assumes, as it must, that a regional organization is to be found in a patchwork of treaties, establishing legal, administrative and informal working arrangements achieved by overlapping layers of functional integration among states in a geographically contiguous area. In this respect, the inter-American system is neater in that its two principal components, the Bogotá Charter and Rio Treaty, cover exactly the same constituents, while NATO is not so exactly coextensive with the European Communities. Nevertheless, since all members of the E.E.C. are also members of NATO, it would be unrealistic not to see their mutual collective defense obligations as complementary to their economic integration. NATO was, after all, formed first; and, since it establishes a defense relationship among all the members of the European Communities, it would have been redundant for them to set up a separate, parallel mutual defense arrangement unless the Western European Powers were prepared to develop a much closer military unity among themselves to the exclusion of the United States. The defeat of the European Defense Community proposal showed that this was not desired.

[60] Inter-American Treaty of Reciprocal Assistance, signed at Rio de Janeiro on Sept. 2, 1947. 21 U.N. Treaty Series 93 (1948); 43 A.J.I.L. Supp. 53 (1949). *Cf.* Arts. 3, 6, 17.

danger the peace of America," including an act "which is not an armed attack." By not making an "armed attack" prerequisite to collective self-defense, the Rio Pact seeks to authorize more than is permitted by Article 51 of the Charter.

The North Atlantic Treaty does not afford the same level of integration for Western Europe, the United States and Canada; nor does the Warsaw Pact for Eastern Europe. Neither system contains machinery for arriving by a majority vote at decisions regarding enforcement actions. In the case of NATO,[61] while there is agreement that an armed attack on one member "shall be considered an attack against them all," each state nevertheless retains unfettered discretion over the kind and scope of response "it deems necessary." So, too, with the Warsaw Pact,[62] which only obliges a party, in the event of an armed attack on another member, to consult, and to "afford . . . immediate assistance . . . by all the means it considers necessary . . ." The Warsaw Pact does establish a Unified Command,[63] as has NATO, and this may in practice be said to modify somewhat the prerogative of each member to determine for itself the extent of its participation in an act of collective self-defense. But France had no difficulty in pulling its forces out of this pooling arrangement, Albania has denounced the Warsaw Pact, and Rumanian troops played no part in the Czech invasion. Similarly, the members of SEATO, too, preserve full freedom of action to determine the extent of their own commitment.[64]

[61] North Atlantic Treaty, signed at Washington April 4, 1949. 34 U.N. Treaty Series 244 (1949), Art. 5; 43 A.J.I.L. Supp. 159 (1949).

[62] Treaty of Friendship, Co-operation and Mutual Assistance Between the People's Republic of Albania, the People's Republic of Bulgaria, the Hungarian People's Republic, the German Democratic Republic, the Polish People's Republic, the Romanian People's Republic, the Union of Soviet Socialist Republics and the Czechoslovak Republic, signed at Warsaw on May 14, 1955. 119 U.N. Treaty Series 24 (1955), Art. 4; 49 A.J.I.L. Supp. 194 (1955).

[63] Ibid., Art. 5.

[64] Southeast Asia Collective Defense Treaty, signed at Manila on Sept. 8, 1954. 209 U.N. Treaty Series 28 (1955), Art. 4; 60 A.J.I.L. 646 (1966). If these regions are not, at least in terms of legal obligation, as integrated for purposes of defense as the Americas, other regional arrangements are militarily even more tenuous. The Treaty establishing the Arab League, also by way of contrast, only prescribes that, in the event of aggression by a state against a member state, the Council of the League, on which all members are represented, "shall determine the necessary measures to repel" the aggressor, but that this "decision shall be taken unanimously." Pact of the League of Arab States, signed at Cairo March 22, 1945. 70 U.N. Treaty Series 248 (1950), Art. 6; 39 A.J.I.L. Supp. 266 (1945). In one dramatic case, that of the Lebanon intervention, the League did meet and take decisions, but the members were subsequently unable to agree on what these were. What actually was or was not voted at the meeting of the Council is in dispute, as is the veracity of the meeting's minutes. Cf. contradictory statements by Ambassadors Loutfi (U.A.R.) and Malik (Lebanon) in U.N. Security Council, 13th Year, Official Records, 824th meeting, June 10, 1958, pp. 9–19. Neither does the Charter of the Organization of African Unity bind the parties to defend each other. It merely states, in its preamble, a determination "to safeguard and consolidate the hard-won independence as well as the sovereignty and territorial integrity of our States." Charter of the Organization of African Unity, done at Addis Ababa on May 25, 1963. 479 U.N. Treaty Series 70 (1963); 58 A.J.I.L.

830   THE AMERICAN JOURNAL OF INTERNATIONAL LAW   [Vol. 64

Obligations to use force in the common cause are not, however, the sole standard by which a regional system can be measured and its legitimacy determined. Economic integration and the development of common judicial and administrative organs are perhaps even more important. In these other respects, the inter-American system is not pre-eminent. The Treaties of both the European Economic Communities [65] and COMECON [66] impose a substantially higher level of economic cohesion than does that other basis of the inter-American system, the Bogotá Treaty. As revised,[67] the O.A.S. Charter now contains an extensive new Chapter VII on "economic standards," Chapter VIII on "social standards," and Chapter IX on "educational, scientific and cultural standards." But these are couched primarily in terms of obligations which each member assumes and administers vis-à-vis itself. The General Assembly of the O.A.S., although it decides by simple or, in some cases, two-thirds majority, does not have power to implement the principles contained in the new chapters, nor to bind the members.[68] Both the Eastern and Western European continental systems have, in contrast, developed a notable degree of economic integration which includes the setting up of multinational administrative machinery and the partial elimination of *inter se* tariffs, and both have made more than a start at

873 (1964). While the O.A.U. Charter makes provision for decisions by two-thirds majority of the Assembly of Heads of State and Government (*ibid.*, Art. 10), and by simple majority of the Council Ministers (*ibid.*, Art. 14), it severely limits these principal organs' powers to discussion, co-ordination and harmonization (*ibid.*, Art. 8).

[65] Treaty establishing the European Coal and Steel Community, 261 U.N. Treaty Series 140 (1957), Arts. 13–16, 28; 46 A.J.I.L. Supp. 107 (1952); Treaty establishing the European Atomic Energy Community, 298 U.N. Treaty Series 249 (1958), Arts. 118, 119, 132; 51 A.J.I.L. Supp. 955 (1957); Treaty establishing the European Economic Community, 298 U.N. Treaty Series 11 (1958), Arts. 148–163; 51 A.J.I.L. 865 (1957).

[66] Charter of the Council for Mutual Economic Assistance (COMECON Treaty), signed at Sofia Dec. 14, 1959, 368 U.N. Treaty Series 264 (1960). Note, however, Art. 4(3) which states that "All recommendations and decisions of the Council shall be adopted only with the consent of the member countries concerned . . ."

[67] Revised Charter of the Organization of American States, Revised by the Protocol of Buenos Aires, Feb. 27, 1967. Pan American Union, Treaty Series, No. 1-B; O.A.S. Official Records, OEA/SER.A/2, Add. 2 (1967); T.I.A.S., No. 6847; printed below, p. 996. See also Charter of the Organization of American States, signed at Bogotá, April 30, 1948. 119 U.N. Treaty Series 48 (1952); 46 A.J.I.L. Supp. 43 (1952).

[68] Two Inter-American Councils subordinate to the General Assembly of the O.A.S., one for economic and social, the other for cultural, scientific and educational matters, have powers to recommend, promote, foster, study, co-ordinate and encourage, but not to implement or enforce. A sole exception is noteworthy: the Inter-American Council for Education, Science and Culture may "adopt . . . pertinent measures to give effect to the standards contained in Chapter IX . . ." Protocol of Buenos Aires, cited above, Art. 101(b). This largesse is, however, elsewhere vitiated by the provision that both Councils' powers are clearly limited to making "recommendations on matters within their authority," and that they may only "present . . . studies and proposals, drafts of international instruments, and proposals on the holding of specialized conferences, on the creation, modification, or elimination of specialized organizations and other Inter-American agencies, as well as the co-ordination of their activities . . ." *Ibid.*, Arts. 70, 71.

regional planning of integrated economic growth.[69] In addition, the European Communities have developed a regional court with wide powers to apply and interpret the basic instruments,[70] and the Communities' Council and Commission both have power to bind all members.[71] These considerable accomplishments have as yet no counterpart in the inter-American system.

A comparison of the various regional arrangements would therefore seem to indicate that in enforcement and collective defense the inter-American system may be somewhat ahead, at least in legal principle, if not in practice, of the level of integration so far achieved in Western Europe and Eastern Europe. On the other hand, both Eastern and Western Europe are far ahead of the inter-American system in economic and related integration. Thus, the inter-American, Western European and Eastern European systems are different in their distribution of strengths and weaknesses, but there is no basis for recognizing one as a "regional organization" while withholding legitimation from the others.

The Organization of African Unity, the Arab League and several other regional groupings do fall substantially behind the standards set by the Americas and Western and Eastern Europe in the degree of their integration. We have already noted the relatively low level of their members' commitment to collective defense and enforcement.[72] At the non-military level, the O.A.U. provides for the establishment of four commissions at the ministerial and expert levels [73] to deal with economic, social, educational, cultural, health, scientific and technical co-operation under the aegis of the Assembly of Heads of State. While this Assembly has virtually unlimited jurisdiction and may make decisions by two-thirds majority of the members,[74] in such matters as "political and diplomatic co-operation; economic co-operation," [75] et cetera, its decisions are not binding on the dissenting minority. Although there are starts at smaller customs unions within the O.A.U. (as also within parts of the inter-American system), there is no African common market or joint economic planning to compare with that of the European Communities of East and West. In the Arab League, too, specialized commissions are provided, and they, together with the Council of the League, are enjoined to work for the preparation and adoption of the treaties and agreements by which the cultural, social and economic purposes of the Organization may be advanced. As in the O.A.U., the process is essentially consensual.[76]

[69] E.E.C. Treaty, cited above, Arts. 145–154; COMECON Treaty, cited above, Arts. 1, 3, 4, 5. For a recent assessment of the COMECON (CMEA) cf. V. Shelepin, "Socialist Integration," New Times, No. 46, Nov. 19, 1969, p. 9.

[70] E.E.C. Treaty, loc. cit., Arts. 164–188.   [71] Ibid., Arts. 155–163, esp. 163.

[72] Note 64 above.   [73] O.A.U. Charter, ibid., Arts. 20, 21.

[74] Ibid., Art. 10.

[75] Ibid., Art. 2(2). Cf. Cervenka, The Organization of African Unity (Prague, Academia Nakladatelstvi Czeckoslovenske, 1968).

[76] Pact of the League of Arab States, note 64 above, Arts. 2, 4. See also Franck, East African Unity Through Law (New Haven, Yale University Press, 1965); Franck (ed.), Why Federations Fail, Ch. 1 (New York, New York University Press, 1968).

832   THE AMERICAN JOURNAL OF INTERNATIONAL LAW   [Vol. 64

We must thus conclude that, if the regional system of the Americas is the standard for qualifying as a regional organization within the meaning of Article 53 of the U.N. Charter, then both the regional systems of Western Europe and Eastern Europe also qualify. Even at that, the standard is probably set too high. The Organization of American States, as it is today, is a far more sophisticated system than it was at the time Article 53 was adopted at San Francisco, before the Bogotá Conference formally established the framework of the O.A.S. Moreover, the fact that the Organization of African Unity and the Arab League would not qualify under any test using the Organization of American States as the standard, suggests that the test cannot be set so high. The test, if it is to admit to regional status the O.A.S. on the one hand and the Arab League and O.A.U. on the other, cannot be much more exacting than this: A regional organization is any grouping of states in some defined geographic context with historic, ethnic, or socio-political ties, which habitually acts in concert through permanent institutions to foster unity in a wide range of common concerns.

In practice this unity has frequently been established by the use or threat of military force. Both the Soviet Union and the United States have done much to transform their respective regional organizations into instruments facilitating the threat or use of violence in advancing their regional interests. Under the guise of Articles 51, 52 and 53, both super-Powers have succeeded in establishing norms of conduct within their regional organizations which have effectively undermined Article 2(4). These norms have most recently been set out for the "Socialist Commonwealth" in the Brezhnev Doctrine and its corollaries:

1. A dispute within the Socialist "family" or "commonwealth" of Eastern Europe must be resolved within that grouping and not by or in the United Nations.[77]

2. A member of the family of Socialist states must limit its sovereignty to conform to the requirements of the grouping.[78]

3. The family of Socialist states may use force, even military force, by way of collective self-defense against any attempt to divert a member of the Socialist Commonwealth from orthodox conformity.[79]

[77] "The events taking place in Czechoslovakia are a matter for the Czechoslovak people and the States of the socialist community, linked together as they are by common responsibilities, and are a matter for them alone . . . they consider the matter as lying outside the purview of the Security Council." Mr. Malik, U.S.S.R., addressing the Security Council, U.N. Doc. S/PV.1441, Aug. 21, 1968, pp. 48–50.

[78] Czechoslovakia "is responsible not only to its own people, but also to all the socialist countries . . ." It cannot follow a sovereign policy "opposed to the interests of the world of socialism" because the "weakening of any of the links of the world system of socialism directly affects all the socialist countries which cannot look indifferently upon this." Pravda, reprinted in the translation of the Soviet Press Agency, The New York Times, Sept. 27, 1968, p. 3.

[79] When "a danger arises to socialism itself in a particular country . . ." an "encroachment on the foundations of socialism, on the principles of Marxism-Leninism," when "anti-socialist and revisionist elements . . . under the guise of 'democratization' . . . befog the minds of the masses, stealthily hatching a counter-revolutionary coup" and they are "not duly rebuffed inside the country," then the family of states may act

These are the principles on which the 1968 invasion of Czechoslovakia was justified by the nations of the Eastern European bloc, but the concepts are not new. Rather, they are the restatements by the Soviets of a law of super-Power regional paramountcy which the United States itself did much to formulate through the O.A.S. It is the United States which first insisted that a dispute within a regional grouping should be settled by that grouping to the exclusion of the United Nations. In June, 1954, during what *The New York Times* has described as the "CIA-engineered revolution against the Communist-oriented President of Guatemala," [80] we said at the United Nations that

> if the United Nations Security Council does not respect the right of the Organization of American States to achieve a pacific settlement of the dispute between Guatemala and its neighbors . . . the result will be a catastrophe of such dimensions as will gravely impair the future effectiveness both of the United Nations itself and of regional organizations such as the Organization of American States.[81]

When the Soviets tried to raise the matter in the United Nations, Ambassador Lodge warned: "I say to the representative of the Soviet Union, stay out of this hemisphere and do not try to start your plans and your conspiracies over here." [82] Later, the United States insisted on the same principle when Cuba tried to complain of hostile acts by the U. S. and the O.A.S. just prior to the Bay of Pigs invasion. This time Washington's representative stated that "recourse of the Cuban Government to the Security Council . . . is not in harmony with its treaty obligations under the Inter-American Treaty of Reciprocal Assistance . . . and the Charter of the Organization of American States. . . ." [83] Most recently, during the Dominican invasion, Ambassador Stevenson opposed any involvement by the Security Council because it "would tend to complicate the activities of the Organization of American States by encouraging concurrent and independent considerations and activities by this Council." It would be unwarranted and in violation of the Charter's provisions for regional settlement if the Security Council were to intervene "just when the regional organization seems to be dealing with the situation effectively." [84]

---

to restore normality and to defeat the forces of "world imperialism." Pravda, reprinted *ibid.* "The countries of the socialist commonwealth have . . . their own socialist principles of mutual relations based on fraternal assistance, solidarity and internationalism." Foreign Minister A. Gromyko, addressing the U.N. General Assembly, U.N. Doc. A/PC.1679, Oct. 3, 1968, p. 26 at 30–31. "This [socialist] commonwealth constitutes an inseparable entity cemented by unbreakable ties such as history has never known . . . The Soviet Union and other socialist countries have on many occasions warned those who are tempted to roll back the socialist commonwealth, to snatch at least one link from it, that we will neither tolerate nor allow that to happen." *Ibid.*

[80] The New York Times series on CIA Operations, April 28, 1966, p. 25, col. 8.

[81] Ambassador Lodge (U.S.A.). U.N. Security Council, 9th Year, Official Records, 676th meeting 28–29 (1954).

[82] *Ibid.*, 675th meeting 32.

[83] Ambassador Lodge (U.S.A.). U.N. Security Council, 15th Year, Official Records, 874th meeting 27 (1960).

[84] Ambassador Stevenson (U.S.A.). U.N. Security Council, 20th Year, Official Records, 1204th meeting 17 (1965).

834   THE AMERICAN JOURNAL OF INTERNATIONAL LAW   [Vol. 64

It is also the United States which advanced the idea that a state's sovereignty is subject to the overriding right of a region to demand conformity to regional standards. In pushing for a condemnation of the leftist Guzman regime at the Tenth Inter-American Conference in March, 1954, the self-proclaimed aim of the Department of State was to achieve regional "solidarity" and to have "a clear-cut and unmistakable policy determination against the intervention of international communism in the hemisphere. . . ." [85] What was here condemned was not intervention by foreign troops but of a "foreign" ideology. It was against this that the United States pushed the regional organization to commit itself to "take effective measures, individually and collectively. . . ." [86]

At the Punta del Este meeting of the Organ of Consultation, convoked at the U. S. initiative under Article 6 of the Rio Treaty, it was further agreed that

> adherence by any member of the Organization of American States to Marxism-Leninism is incompatible with the Inter-American system and . . . breaks the unity and solidarity of the hemisphere. [87]

Specifically, it was "decided" that the

> Government of Cuba, which has officially identified itself as a Marxist-Leninist government, is incompatible with the principles and objectives of the Inter-American system . . . [88]

In announcing the U. S. naval and air "quarantine" during the missile crisis, President Kennedy justified this limitation on a state's sovereignty by pointing out that Cuba was "in an area well known to have a special and historical relationship to the United States and the nations of the Western Hemisphere." [89]

It was during the Dominican crisis that the United States openly asserted the right of a regional grouping to use force to secure conformity—in "self-defense" against the "attack" of an alien ideology and foreign "inspiration." In the words of the Legal Adviser of the Department of State:

> Participation in the Inter-American system, to be meaningful, must take into account the modern day reality that an attempt by a conspiratorial group *inspired from outside* to seize control by force can be an assault upon the independence and integrity of a state. [90]

[85] Bowdler, "Report on the Tenth Inter-American Conference," 30 Dept. of State Bulletin 634 (1954).

[86] *Ibid.*

[87] Inter-American Treaty of Reciprocal Assistance, Applications, Vol. 1, 1948–59 (Washington, D. C., Pan American Union, General Secretariat), Part One, Resolution VI of the Eighth Meeting of Consultation, Punta del Este, Uruguay, January, 1962, p. 9; U.N. Security Council, 17th Year, Official Records, Supp. for January, February and March, 1962, at 63, U.N. Doc. S/5075 (1962); 56 A.J.I.L. 611 (1962).

[88] *Ibid.*

[89] "The Soviet Threat to the Americas," 47 Dept. of State Bulletin 715, 716 (1962).

[90] L. C. Meeker, "Legal Basis for the United States Actions in the Dominican Republic," in 2 Chayes, Ehrlich and Lowenfeld, International Legal Process: Materials for an Introductory Course 1179 at 1182 (New York, Little Brown and Co., 1969). Italics added.

And President Johnson spoke of the "international conspiracy from which the United States servicemen have rescued the people . . ."[91] and enunciated what has since become known as the Johnson Doctrine: "American nations cannot, must not, and will not permit the establishment of another Communist government in the Western Hemisphere."[92]

The United States and the Soviet Union have, in short, both asserted the right to establish regions of super-Power paramountcy to which Article 2(4) of the U.N. Charter does not apply. Nations within the regional grouping are subject not to the rights of sovereign equality but to a duty to conform. Violence may be used by the region in "self-defense" against a deviationist. And the United Nations' rôle in such a dispute is at most peripheral; the "family" acts as judge, plaintiff and executioner.

All this is a long way from the solemn obligation of Article 2(4). Perhaps the world of Article 2(4) never did and never could exist. But the world that has taken its place cannot long exist, either. As Secretary General U Thant has recently pointed out,

> It is, certainly, a frightening commentary on the ominous state of world affairs that one super-State or the other can become exercised to the point of resorting to military action because of a liberalization of a regime in a small country like Czechoslovakia or because of an internal upheaval in another small State such as the Dominican Republic. . . . It is . . . a dismal outlook for the small and militarily weak States of the world—as the overwhelming majority of States are—if they can hope to control their own affairs only in so far as they do nothing to displease a powerful neighbour. . . .
> In the final analysis there can be no solid foundation for peace in the world so long as the super-Powers insist on taking unilateral military action whenever they claim to see a threat to their security.[93]

V. THE WAY AHEAD

The prohibition against the use of force in relations between states has been eroded beyond recognition, principally by three factors: 1, the rise of wars of "national liberation"; 2, the rising threat of wars of total destruction; 3, the increasing authoritarianism of regional systems dominated by a super-Power. These three factors may, however, be traced back to a single circumstance: the lack of congruence between the international legal norm of Article 2(4) and the perceived national interest of states, especially the super-Powers.

There are, however, two kinds of worlds which may emerge from the ashes of Article 2(4), each incorporating certain new normative restraints on the use of force by states. The first of these is a world of peacefully co-existing, super-Power-dominated regional spheres. As the military pre-eminence of the super-Powers increases by quantum leaps, it is possible

---

[91] Statement by President Johnson, May 2, 52 Dept. of State Bulletin 744 at 745–746 (1965).

[92] *Ibid.* at 746.

[93] Introduction to the Annual Report of the Secretary General on the Work of the Organization covering the period 16 June 1967 to 15 June 1968. Sept. 24, 1968, 23rd Sess., Supp. No. 1A (U.N. Doc. A/7201/Add. 1 (1968)), at 21–22.

836   THE AMERICAN JOURNAL OF INTERNATIONAL LAW   [Vol. 64

that existing regional spheres will expand, largely eliminating the gray areas in which Russia and the United States have fought their surrogate wars. It is already a norm of U. S.-Soviet practice not to use force in the region of the other's primacy. If these areas of primacy expand and if China, at least in Asian terms, becomes a super-Power with its own regional system, then we may be entering a world in which the threat or use of violence by super-Powers within their own spheres will largely displace the threat or use of violence among super-Powers. This would, at least, reduce the risk of large-scale catastrophe, since hostilities between a super-Power and a smaller state within its region is unlikely to engender sustained high-level violence. The sort of world which this model visualizes, a world of super-Power-run ghettos, is not, however, one marked by much freedom for individuals, groups or even nations. It is not a world of much diversity except, perhaps, among spheres. It does, however, appear to be one of the two possible worlds that could succeed the normative U.N. system, satisfying the dictates both of power-oriented *realpolitik* and of the need for a minimum of world law and order.

The failure of the U.N. Charter's normative system is tantamount to the inability of any rule, such as that set out in Article 2(4), in itself to have much control over the behavior of states. National self-interest, particularly the national self-interest of the super-Powers, has usually won out over treaty obligations. This is particularly characteristic of this age of pragmatic power politics. It is as if international law, always something of a cultural myth, had been demythologized. It seems this is not an age when men act by principles simply because that is what gentlemen ought to do. But living by power alone, even in a world of relatively balanced regional spheres of predominance that mutually acknowledge each other's power parity, is a nerve-wracking and costly business. To do it, much must be surrendered by the citizen: individual freedom, a large part of his national budget, and the chance to live in that comparative tranquillity which comes of being liked by others and liking oneself. There are, increasingly, signs that the citizen will not indefinitely pay the price demanded by the conventional national interest, and that his rejection of the traditional values, the realities of old-fashioned power-oriented *realpolitik* may not be confined merely to one age group of one nation but may turn into a universal, skeptical reassessment of the classical definition of national interest. From such a reassessment could emerge a new set of criteria by which to determine the goals of foreign policy, a *realpolitik* which, for example, measures the national interest in terms of the ecological quality of territory already possessed rather than in new lands to be acquired; or which measures security in terms of the mental health, low level of tension and centeredness of one's own population rather than in control exercised over others. Today, a large and loyal part of the population of the United States actually perceives a defeat of Viet-Nam to be in the national interest, not because they believe we cannot, but because we should not, win. Consciously or not, the popular redefinition of national interest is already under way.

Any nation, to remain great, must sustain a self-image of its greatness. Historically, this has been done by the great Powers through territorial expansion, whether a *Drang Nach Osten,* dominion over palm and pine, or the opening of the West. Today, we appear on the verge of a new definition of expansion which is qualitative, rather than quantitative. Conceivably, this may turn out to be an inevitable historical trend which will make an impact on all states and on each super-Power in particular.

If such a redefinition of the national interest succeeds over a period of time and not only in one super-Power, then there may be an opportunity to return to an international legal system of norms such as that in Article 2(4). What killed Article 2(4) was the wide disparity between the norms it sought to establish and the practical goals the nations are pursuing in defense of their national interest. So long as there are nations—which is likely to be for a very long time—their pursuit of the national interest will continue; and where that interest habitually runs counter to a stated international legal norm, it is the latter which will bend and break. The other world that could arise from the ruins of Article 2(4) is one in which the redefined national interest is no longer calculated in integers amenable to military manipulation and in which, consequently, the national interest is perceived to be congruent with a renunciation of the use of military force in inter-state relations.

[9]

THE REPORTS OF THE DEATH OF ARTICLE 2(4) ARE GREATLY EXAGGERATED

LOUIS HENKIN

Dr. Thomas Franck, pathologist for the ills of the international body politic, has pronounced the death of the heart of the United Nations Charter, and proceeded to tell us who killed it.[1] In my view, the death certificate is premature and the indictment for legicide must be redrawn to charge lesser though aggravated degrees of assault. Article 2(4) lives and, while its condition is grave indeed, its maladies are not necessarily terminal. There is yet time to prescribe, transplant, salvage, to keep alive at all cost the principal norm of international law in our time.[2]

It is difficult to quarrel with Dr. Franck's diagnosis of the ills of the Charter, congenital, hereditary, acquired, and induced: the mistaken original assumption of Big-Power unanimity; the changing character of war; the loopholes for "self-defense" and "regional" action; the lack of impartial means to find and characterize facts; the disposition of nations to take law into their own hands and distort and mangle it to their own purpose. Distracted and distraught by these ills, one can indeed fall into the conclusion that Article 2(4) is virtually dead, but that, I believe, would mistake the lives and the ways of the law.

My principal difference with Dr. Franck's diagnosis is that it judges the vitality of the law by looking only at its failures. The purpose of Article 2(4) was to establish a norm of national behavior and to help deter violation of it. Despite common misimpressions, Article 2(4) has indeed been a norm of behavior and has deterred violations. In inter-state as in individual penology, deterrence often cannot be measured or even proved, but students of politics agree that traditional war between nations has become less frequent and less likely. The sense that war is not done has taken hold, and nations more readily find that their interests do not in fact require the use of force after all. Expectations of international violence no longer underlie every political calculation of every nation, and war plans lie buried deep in national files. Even where force is used, the fact that it is unlawful cannot be left out of account and limits the scope, the weapons, the duration, the purposes for which force is used. Of the "some one hundred separate outbreaks of hostilities" to which Dr. Franck refers, less than fingers-full became "war" or successful conquest, and hundreds of other instances of conflict of interest and tension have not produced even an international shot: cold war has remained cold, threats to the peace have remained threats, issues have remained only issues, for peaceful settlement or non-settlement (as in Cyprus, Kashmir, Berlin).

Many will refuse credit to Article 2(4), attributing the lack of traditional war to other factors—to nuclear weapons and the changing charac-

---

[1] "Who Killed Article 2(4)? Or Changing Norms Governing the Use of Force By States," 64 A.J.I.L. 809 (1970).

[2] With some of what I say here I deal at length in: How Nations Behave: Law and Foreign Policy (1968), especially in Chaps. X and XI.

ter of war, to greater territorial stability, to other changes in national interests reducing national temptation to use force. If it were so, Article
2(4) would not be the less a norm: law often reflects dispositions to behavior as much as it shapes them. Like others, Dr. Franck concludes
that, by the time the Charter came, "new forms of attack were making
obsolete all prior notions of war and peace strategy." If it were so, one
might yet conclude that that development reflected and supported Article
2(4) and made it viable. In fact, nothing, alas, has rendered war obsolete
—between India and Pakistan, India and China, Turkey and Greece, Honduras and El Salvador, Egypt and Israel. The occasions and the causes
of war remain. What has become obsolete is the notion that nations are
as free to indulge it as ever, and the death of that notion is accepted in
the Charter.

The supposed transforming impact of nuclear weapons is also miscon-
ceived. For a time the United States had a virtual monopoly and its
nuclear weapons might have induced rather than deterred aggressive ten-
dencies. For many years now, the United States and the U.S.S.R. have
had an effective duopoly: nuclear war between them is indeed happily
unlikely, but many believe that, in their balance of terror, nuclear weapons
cannot in fact be used and are effectively neutralized. The overwhelming
military superiority of either super-Power over any other nation might
encourage rather than deter war, and each has been amply tempted. The
nuclear weapons of the super-Powers surely do not deter war by lesser
Powers—as in the Middle East.

The fissures of the Charter are worrisome but they, too, are not as wide
in international life as they loom in academic imagination. Pre-emptive
war as "anticipatory self-defense" has been hypothesized by many professors but asserted by few governments: President Kennedy may have
talked about "offensive weapons" in the Cuban missile crisis but he did
not claim to be acting in self-defense under Article 51. A few nations
have falsely claimed self-defense against actual attack, but there are effective limits to unwarranted claims, in what nations dare assert and what
others will believe: no one accepted that North Korea acted in self-defense
in 1950, and she was not induced to attack by the expectation that she
would be believed. India violated the Charter at Goa but few accepted
her rationalizations, and neither act nor justification significantly modified
the norm. (Viet-Nam is a very different story, of course, and the applicable law depends on the characterization of the war or wars there in progress; unhappily, as Dr. Franck stresses, that characterization has not been
impartially made.) Troops were sent to Lebanon or Jordan upon invitation, not against the political independence and territorial integrity of the
host country; if Article 51 was at all relevant, it was invoked, not to justify
the use of force contrary to Article 2(4), but only to support collective,
defensive deployments by *bona fide* invitation, as in NATO. If some governments have theorized that abiding colonialism is a legitimate target
for armed attack from outside, there are few such targets left; and, in
fact, few have claimed the right of unilateral force against colonialism,

only of collective U.N. action (which has its own justifications and limitations). "Self-defense against colonial domination" invoked by those suffering that domination is rhetoric, not international law, and the law of the Charter, surely, does not forbid a people to liberate itself from colonial yoke.

The regional loophole, too, is not as wide as might seem, dangerous but not fatal. There have been few instances of groups claiming the right to do together what the Charter forbids them singly, and little reason to expect that it will happen frequently in future. Some will say that to suggest that the United States and the Soviet Union have "both asserted the right to establish regions of super-Power paramountcy to which Article 2(4) of the U.N. Charter does not apply," is to overlook differences of degree (if not of kind) on which all law—and all politics—depend. But even if one equates the O.A.S. with the Warsaw Pact, the Dominican Republic (or Cuba) with Czechoslovakia, surely donning the mantle of regionalism does not dispose of Article 2(4). Short of voluntary, recognized federation eliminating constituent identities and rendering all that goes on "internal," "regional organizations," to whatever degree integrated or dominated, acquire no license for all actions by all means for all purposes. Whatever a regional grouping can do in *bona fide* collective security against armed attack, whatever pressures short of military force it can impose on members that disturb regional peace or relations, no regional organization may collectively use force or take any other action not "consistent with the Purposes and Principles of the United Nations." (Article 52(1).) Whether or not the Warsaw Pact has as good a claim as the O.A.S. to be a regional organization, in 1968 in Czechoslovakia its members abetted the Soviet Union in an indisputable violation of the Charter. Nothing in Articles 52–53 remotely affords the Brezhnev Doctrine a scintilla of legitimacy, and its own proponents have not seriously pursued that construction. There is reason to hope that the Soviet Union will not lightly repeat Czechoslovakia (especially if the victim fights back), with or without a "regional" umbrella. And while I have no legal brief for U.S. actions in regard to Cuba, Guatemala, or the Dominican Republic, neither the United States nor the Organization of American States has claimed the right to invade Cuba or the Dominican Republic, and few believe that the O.A.S. or even the United States alone would use force against the political independence or territorial integrity of any country in the Hemisphere, even in the event of sharp local deviation, if it was not in fact abetted from the outside. (Compare Chile, 1970.)

As Dr. Franck tells us, however, war has not been eliminated but has been channeled into more or less blatant intervention in internal wars and affairs, often by more than one Power, often by major Powers. In various internal wars one group or side, and sometimes both (or all), have sought outside support. Old nations and new nations have seen their interest in inviting, responding to, or tolerating such intervention. The irregular triangle of big Powers—United States, Russia, China—has made competition in intervention a dominant political determinant. International society has no principle for choosing sides in internal wars and has not seen the same interest in excluding external intervention.

Assuming—as many do—that Article 2(4) intended to forbid these interventions, clearly it has not prevented, deterred, or terminated a number of them although, again, one cannot say confidently that it has not deterred many others. To me, if Article 2(4) signaled the effective end of conventional war though not of intervention, even, indeed, if it induced this alternative form of organized violence, it would signify a substantial advance in international order: the temptation to military intervention in internal affairs is largely an affliction of the few big Powers and even for them military intervention to promote or maintain internal wars is not always and everywhere possible; intervention by invitation on one side is not so great an aggression against sovereignty and independence; internal wars are generally limited in area and in scope of military operation and therefore less terrible in their destructiveness.

It makes other real differences: The United States cannot itself invade Cuba; it can connive with Cuban exiles at the Bay of Pigs, but it must do so without providing air cover. The United States could obtain a plausible invitation from someone in the Dominican Republic but not in Cuba. It can send Marines to the Dominican Republic, but only for limited times and purposes, and the political consequences make the next time less likely. If it finds justification in ratification by the Organization of American States, it can do so only for acts which will in fact receive that ratification, and subject to its conditions. It can do less, or nothing, in Chile or Peru. For its part, the Soviet Union, unable to arrange, even to fabricate, an invitation by Czechoslovakia, has to invade, not intervene, and bear even within its family the full onus of blatant violation. The occasional small-Power intervention is also limited and hampered: Syria can send masked tanks, but not its air force, to help Palestine guerrillas against Jordan.

Dr. Franck's dramatic title makes its point, and his cry of alarm is warranted and necessary. But one must not allow it to be seized by the "super-realists" to prove that the effort to control international violence by law has again failed and the Charter is now as irrelevant as the Kellogg-Briand Pact. For me, if Article 2(4) were indeed dead, I should have to conclude that it rules—not mocks—us from the grave.[3] In fact, despite common misimpressions (from which it suffers in common with other international law) Article 2(4) lives and can live. No government, no responsible official of government, has been prepared or has wished to pronounce it dead. Article 2(4) was written by practical men who knew all about national interest. They believed the norms they legislated to be in their nations' interest, and nothing that has happened in the past twenty-five years suggests that it is not. There is reason to pray and strive for the change in individual and national perceptions which Dr. Franck invokes, but the need is not to condemn Article 2(4) to death

[3] Compare 64 A.J.I.L. at 809 (1970).

and pray for its resurrection in the end of days when men and nations will not learn war any more. The need is for citizens, policy-makers, national societies, transnational and international bodies to be reminded that this law is indeed in the national interest of all nations; that a decision to initiate force always involves a preference for one national interest over another; that in the cost-accounting of national interest a decision to go to war grossly depreciates the tangible cost to the citizen—in life, in welfare, in aspiration—and usually prefers the immediate and short-sighted to the longer, deeper national interest.

[10]

In Defense of International Rules on the Use of Force

Oscar Schachter†

The Nuremberg principles that emerged at the end of World War II were hailed as a momentous advance toward an effective rule of law in international society. They affirmed in unmistakable terms that aggressive war is illegal and that persons responsible for such wars are guilty of an international crime. These principles were first expressed in the London agreement of 1945, by which the leading victorious allied states—the United States, the Soviet Union, Great Britain, and France—established the International Military Tribunal to try the leaders of Nazi Germany for their role in planning and waging the war.[1] An eleven-power agreement established a similar international tribunal in Tokyo to try Japanese officials and military leaders for their part in the Far Eastern war.[2] Both tribunals convicted a number of defendants and imposed sentences of death or long imprisonment.[3] The legal principles

† Hamilton Fish Professor Emeritus of International Law and Diplomacy, Columbia University; Member, Institut de Droit International.

This article has been written in honor of Professor Bernard Meltzer on his attainment of emeritus status at The University of Chicago. Professor Meltzer served on the staff of the Chief Prosecutor at the Nuremberg Trial of the Nazi war criminals. In an article on Nuremberg written for this *Review* in 1947, he reflected on the problem of outlawing war in a world where force had a dominating role. It seems fitting to take this as the theme of this article.

This also gives me a welcome opportunity to acknowledge my debt to Professor Meltzer for his guidance and stimulation when I served with him in the State Department in 1942-43. It was not only his intellectual energy and quickness of mind that impressed me then. I found his combination of sagacity, zest, and idealism to be admirable, especially in combating bureaucratic apathy and resistance. I was glad to see that a recent scholarly work, *The Abandonment of the Jews*, by David Wyman, has brought some of this to public light.

[1] Agreement for the Prosecution and Punishment of the Major War Criminals of the European Axis (The London Agreement), August 8, 1945, 59 Stat. 1544, 3 Bevans 1238, 82 U.N.T.S. 279, *rectified by* Protocol of October 6, 1945, 59 Stat. 1586, 3 Bevans 1286.

[2] U.S. DEP'T OF STATE, PUB. NO. 2675, THE CHARTER OF THE INTERNATIONAL MILITARY TRIBUNAL FOR THE FAR EAST (1946).

[3] *See Judgment of the International Military Tribunal at Nuremberg*, 1 TRIAL OF THE MAJOR WAR CRIMINALS BEFORE THE INTERNATIONAL MILITARY TRIBUNAL 365-66 (1947) [hereinafter cited as *Judgment*]; TELFORD TAYLOR, THE NUREMBERG WAR CRIMES TRIALS 241, 332 (Int'l Conciliation No. 450, 1949). Taylor's survey also includes an account of the 12 Nuremberg trials conducted by the U.S. military government in Germany under the authority of an Allied Control Council law. On the proceedings of the Tokyo trials, see SOLIS HORWITZ, THE TOKYO TRIAL 475, 572 (Int'l Conciliation No. 465, 1950).

they applied became known as the Nuremberg principles.

In a unanimous resolution adopted in 1946, the United Nations General Assembly affirmed the Nuremberg principles as existing in international law.[4] No government then or since has expressed dissent from these principles, and it is almost inconceivable today that any government would challenge them.

Yet the facts of international life seem to make a mockery of the Nuremberg principles. Wars and invasions occur with alarming frequency; armed force is used in many contexts—overthrowing governments, capturing territory, avenging old wrongs, or coercing favorable settlement of disputes. Veiled or open threats of violence provide undercurrents to all interactions between states. States spend huge sums on munitions; the looming threat of nuclear holocaust endangers all states. Our political and social systems are deeply influenced by the fear of war and a conviction that nothing can be done to oust armed force as the final arbiter in international conflicts.

These facts of life stand in striking contrast to the hopes implicit in the Nuremberg judgments. Not surprisingly, people generally are skeptical that legal rules can restrain violent acts. At the same time, awareness of the horrors of war and its threat to human survival compels us to seek ways of combating the near anarchy of international society.

This essay examines current efforts in that direction that are of particular interest for international lawyers and governments. The questions I discuss were raised or implied in the Nuremberg cases, but they remain important today in light of increasing government employment of armed force to achieve a multiplicity of goals.

The article is divided into the following four parts:

I.   Rules on Force and Rule-Skepticism
II. Implied Conditions and Changed Circumstances
III. Necessary Self-Defense
IV. Justification of Force for Higher Ends

I. Rules on Force and Rule-Skepticism

A. The Nuremberg Trials

A central issue in the Nuremberg trials was whether aggressive war had been illegal and criminal under international law prior to

---

[4] G.A. Res. 95, U.N. Doc. A/64, at 188 (1946).

1945.[5] Counsel for the defendants claimed that the principles laid down in the four-power London agreement had not previously been customary international law, and that to apply them would violate the basic juridical postulate prohibiting punishment of a crime in the absence of a pre-existing law. "Nullum crimen sine lege, nulla poena sine lege."[6]

The tribunal rejected defense counsel's contention, citing in particular the General Treaty for the Renunciation of War as an Instrument of National Policy (the Kellogg-Briand Pact) of 1928, which in 1939 had 63 parties including Germany.[7] That treaty condemned recourse to war for the solution of international disputes.[8] The tribunal also referred to other international declarations (including a resolution of the League of Nations, a declaration of a Pan-American Conference, a protocol on dispute settlement not yet in force, and a draft treaty on mutual assistance) to support the conclusion that aggressive war had long been branded as criminal by the international community.[9] These treaty commitments, the tribunal declared, necessarily postulated the illegality of aggressive war and the criminality of its promoters. In drawing this implication, the tribunal reasoned that wars of aggression were illegal under general customary international law and not simply a violation of the treaty in question.[10] The judgment discussed the role of state practices in developing international law and, particularly, noted how the Hague Conventions on the laws of war had grown out of and, in turn, become accepted as customary law.[11]

The tribunal considered it important to establish this proposition, which would move the issue beyond specific treaty terms and elevate the illegality of aggression to a universal rule.[12] It also seems plausible that the tribunal found it desirable to emphasize customary law to rebut defense counsel's contention that aggres-

---

[5] *See* Schachter, *The Right of States to Use Armed Force*, 82 MICH. L. REV. 1620, 1628-33 (1984).

[6] *Judgment, supra* note 3, at 219.

[7] *Id.*

[8] Kellogg-Briand Pact, August 27, 1928, 46 Stat. 2343, T.S. No. 796, 94 L.N.T.S. 57.

[9] *Judgment, supra* note 3, at 221-22.

[10] *Id.* at 220-21 ("The law of war is to be found not only in treaties, but in the customs and practices of states which gradually obtained universal recognition. . . . [I]n many cases treaties do no more than express and define for more accurate reference the principles of law already existing.").

[11] *Id.* at 253-54.

[12] The tribunal's emphasis on customary law is also underlined by its rather cursory consideration of the London agreement provision stating that crimes against peace included wars in violations of international agreements. *Id.* at 219. While it found this provision relevant to Germany's treaty violations, it did not make this the main ground of the judgment.

sion could not be a standard of criminal liability because it had not been defined in any international document.[13] By relying on customary law, the tribunal could draw an analogy to the historic development of the criminal law. Common crimes such as murder, robbery, and rape were punished by societies long before they were defined in general terms.[14]

In the same sense, the tribunal found it unnecessary to define aggression. It set forth the historical facts and deemed them proof enough that the defendants planned, initiated, and waged aggressive war under any conceivable definition of aggression.[15] Moreover, the absence of a definition did not mean that the accused had no idea they were doing wrong. The tribunal was convinced that the Nazi leaders were aware of the Kellogg-Briand Pact and of other agreements labeling aggressive war as illegal. On that premise it would have been unreasonable to conclude that the defendants were being prosecuted for an offense that was being applied retroactively against them, for the rule against retroactivity was intended to protect persons who could not have known of their guilt.

B.   The Gap Between Rules and State Practice

Of particular interest in the present context is that the tribunal did not find it necessary to examine any specific state conduct in order to establish customary practice: it considered the several declarations already noted to be evidence enough of customary law.[16] It did not ask whether those declarations accorded with the "constant and uniform practice" of states which international lawyers consider an essential constitutive element of customary law.[17] It did not compare practice and preaching. It took the declarations as the *opinio juris communis* of international society without trying to discover the "real" attitudes of states.

A perceptive observer such as Professor Meltzer was bound to be troubled by this. Writing in this law review[18] soon after the Nu-

---

[13] *Id.* at 219-22.

[14] In a statement to the U.N. General Assembly's Legal Committee, the Netherlands judge who sat in the Tokyo trial said that "as easily as [a judge] operates with the crime of 'murder' he might operate with the crime of 'aggression.' " Roling, *On Aggression, On International Criminal Law, On International Criminal Jurisdiction—I*, 2 NEDERLANDS TIJDSCHRIFT VOOR INTERNATIONAAL RECHT 167, 169 (1955).

[15] *Judgment, supra* note 3, at 186-216.

[16] *Id.* at 220-22.

[17] *See* Right of Passage over Indian Territory (Port. v. India), 1960 I.C.J. 4, 38; North Sea Continental Shelf (W. Ger. v. Den.), 1969 I.C.J. 4, 41-45 (especially paragraphs 74-77).

[18] Meltzer, *A Note on Some Aspects of the Nuremberg Debate*, 14 U. CHI. L. REV. 455

remberg judgment, he contrasted the declarations and realities. He commented that "[w]ar in Europe had been almost as natural a relation as peace," reflecting a "tradition of aggression and its moral acceptance."[19] This led him to ask whether condemning aggression as a violation of existing law meant positing "order and morality where only anarchy and amorality prevail."[20] Without referring to the international law requirement of uniform practice, he posed the underlying question of whether verbal declarations might not be mistaken for meaningful standards that governed actual conduct.[21] But after raising these issues, Meltzer concluded by supporting the tribunal's reliance on "the most solemn, widespread and unequivocal condemnations of aggression."[22] "When a standard of conduct has been embodied and repeatedly reaffirmed, in the most solemn and unequivocal international formulations, it would be a dangerous invitation to anarchy to disavow it on the basis of doubtful conjectures as to the 'real' state of international psychology."[23]

Professor Meltzer characteristically chose his words carefully. He is surely right to counsel against disavowing states' declarations against aggression because of "doubtful conjectures" about "international psychology." But this does not fully answer his own question about meaningful standards, nor does it meet the basic doctrinal point that practices rather than mere words become customary law rules. These issues still haunt us. They arise whenever states use armed force in circumstances inconsistent with the present law as set forth in the U.N. Charter and the authoritative definition of aggression adopted by consensus in the U.N. General Assembly of 1974.[24]

It is not difficult to think of recent cases in which the rule against the use of force was probably violated. Consider some of the recent hostilities in: Afghanistan, Angola, Cambodia, Chad, Falkland Islands, Grenada, Iraq-Iran, Lebanon, Mozambique, Nicaragua, Vietnam. In each of these places, foreign states employed

---

(1947).

  [19] *Id.* at 459.
  [20] *Id.*
  [21] *Id.*
  [22] *Id.*
  [23] *Id.* at 460.
  [24] G.A. Res. 3314, 29 U.N. GAOR Supp. (No. 31) at 142, U.N. Doc. A/9631 (1974) [hereinafter cited as Aggression Resolution], *reprinted in part in* L. HENKIN, R. PUGH, O. SCHACHTER & H. SMIT, INTERNATIONAL LAW: CASES AND MATERIALS 915-18 (2d ed. 1980) [hereinafter cited as CASEBOOK].

military force for one reason or another, generally claiming legal
justification in the language of the U.N. Charter.[25] The most frequent stated ground was self-defense, either individual or "collective" (i.e., on behalf of a state attacked by others). In some cases, a
government or head of state facing internal or external opposition
was said to have requested the military intervention.[26] The state
supplying aid maintained that the force was not used "against the
territorial integrity or political independence" of the requesting
state or in any other manner contrary to the principles of the U.N.
Charter.[27]

The quality of these justifications varies. The U.S. has tended
to provide fuller and more sophisticated legal justifications than
most other countries, probably because Congress and important
sectors of public opinion are concerned about the legitimacy of
American action.[28] For example, the U.S. State Department offered
three justifications for the U.S. invasion of Grenada on October 25,
1983: (1) the Governor-General of Grenada explicitly requested
U.S. military assistance; (2) the Organisation of Eastern Caribbean
States, composed of Grenada and its island neighbors, requested
U.S. help in abating what it perceived as a threat to its member
nations' security; and (3) a state has a right under customary international law to protect its nationals facing imminent danger of
death in other countries.[29]

Many countries, in contrast, have limited their claims to brief
and general phrases of Charter terminology and their own version
of the relevant facts. When the Soviet Union sent troops into
Czechoslovakia in 1968, for example, it asserted that this action
came in response to that government's "urgent" request for assistance.[30] After this justification had been repudiated repeatedly by
the Czechoslovak National Assembly, and was specifically dis-
avowed in a message from the Czechoslovak Foreign Ministry to

---

[25] U.N. CHARTER arts. 2(4), 51 & 42.

[26] *See infra* text accompanying notes 29-30.

[27] U.N. CHARTER art. 2, para. 4 reads as follows: "All Members shall refrain in their
international relations from the threat or use of force against the territorial integrity or
political independence of any state, or in any other manner inconsistent with the Purposes
of the United Nations."

[28] As one observer stated after the U.S. action in Grenada, "The American people will
not tolerate continuous illegal conduct." Remarks by Senator Nunn, University of Georgia
Law Day (April 14, 1984).

[29] Letter from Davis P. Robinson, Legal Adviser, U.S. Dep't of State, to Professor Edward Gordon (Feb. 10, 1984) (outlining U.S. legal position concerning Grenada), *reprinted
in* JOHN NORTON MOORE, LAW AND THE GRENADA MISSION 125-29 app. (1984).

[30] 7 I.L.M. 1283 (1968).

the Security Council,[31] the Soviet Union relied instead on a more general claim of self-defense under the U.N. Charter.[32] Not surprisingly, most outsiders view many of these legal contentions skeptically, primarily because states, in substantiating their claims, frequently seem to cite carefully chosen, if not fabricated, sets of facts. Thus, the legal justifications offered by states are often perceived as rationalizations contrived after the decision to intervene had been made.

C. The Paradox of Rules

It is a small step from these skeptical reactions to the conclusion that legal principles mean little in practice. At the least, the law in reality differs from the law on the books. The very fact that states can advance a legal argument for every use of force is a ground for skepticism. It brings to mind a well-known "paradox" of Wittgenstein (which I amend slightly): "No course of action can be determined by a rule because every course of action can be made out to conform with every rule."[33] This paradox seems especially pertinent in view of the absence of a compulsory system of adjudication. The ostensible freedom of states to define the rules for themselves, particularly where the rules are highly general and strong political motives govern behavior, builds into a strong case for rule-skepticism. Hence many are inclined to agree with Raymond Aron that international society is an "anarchical order of power" in which might makes right.[34]

1. *The Core Meaning of the Rules.* Strong as the case for rule-skepticism appears to be, it unduly simplifies the complex interactions between norms and state conduct. To begin with, it is an exaggeration to consider the Charter rules so indeterminate and malleable that governments can always make out a plausible case for the legality of their actions. Of course, like all general rules, they give rise to problems of interpretation in their application to concrete situations. They are not free of ambiguity and they may call for factual appraisals as to which reasonable persons can differ.

---

[31] 7 I.L.M. 1294, 1305, 1313 (1968); U.N. Doc. S/P.V.1441, ¶¶ 31, 34 (Provisional Record) (1968).

[32] U.N. Doc. S/P.V.1441, ¶¶ 90, 93 (Provisional Record). To justify its action, the Soviet Union also announced the "Brezhnev Doctrine," which proclaims that socialist states have a right to intervene in other socialist states where necessary to meet threats to socialism. 7 I.L.M. 1323 (1968). The doctrine has not been reasserted since that time.

[33] LUDWIG WITTGENSTEIN, PHILOSOPHICAL INVESTIGATIONS 201 (1953).

[34] Aron, *The Anarchical Order of Power*, in CONDITIONS OF WORLD ORDER 25 (S. Hoffman ed. 1968).

120   *The University of Chicago Law Review*   [53:113

One cannot expect them to be applied by computers. Nevertheless, the rules have a core meaning that governments and legal experts generally accept. Thus it is perfectly clear that states may not invade others for gain or domination, a principle affirmed in the judgments of the Nuremberg and Tokyo trials.

The present rules go beyond this: states may no longer take up arms to avenge past injustices or to vindicate legal rights.[35] This is widely agreed, even though some contemporary writers argue for broader rights to use force.[36] Of course, states have the unquestioned right to use armed force in response to an armed attack on them.[37] There is some disagreement whether the requirement of an armed attack has superseded the somewhat broader customary law right of defense against an imminent attack.[38] However, this difference is narrow if "imminent attack" is strictly construed.

Self-defense must not only be necessary but also proportional to the offense in its extent, manner, and goal. The criterion of proportionality leaves a broad margin of discretion to a defending state but it also imposes well-understood limits. Thus, it would undoubtedly be disproportionate to bomb cities in response to a frontier raid or to invade and occupy territory of a state because that state has illegally aided insurgents in a civil war.

The law also clearly allows collective self-defense, so that a state may aid a victim of actual aggression.[39] This right has been invoked by several countries as a legal basis for their armed interventions in civil wars where insurgents have been aided by an outside power.[40] A counter-intervention is permissible against a prior illegal intervention provided it is not disproportionate in manner and extent.[41] However, difficulties do arise in this context.

---

[35] *See* Schachter, *supra* note 5, at 1625-27; The Corfu Channel Case (U.K. v. Albania), 1949 I.C.J. 4, 35.

[36] *See, e.g.,* JULIUS STONE, AGGRESSION AND WORLD ORDER 92-134 (1958); A.V. THOMAS & A.J. THOMAS, JR., NON-INTERVENTION 208-10 (1956).

[37] U.N. CHARTER art. 51.

[38] *See infra* note 89 and accompanying text (discussing Israel-Iraq conflict).

[39] *See, e.g.,* U.N. CHARTER art. 51. There are, however, several possible interpretations of the scope of permissible collective self-defense. The NATO and Warsaw Pacts and the InterAmerican Rio Treaty are premised on the right of any party to the treaty to come to the aid of an attacked state whether or not the acting party faces a threat to its security. *See* Schwebel, *Aggression, Intervention and Self Defence in Modern International Law,* 136 RECUEIL DES COURS 411, 478-83 (1972).

[40] Two recent examples are the Soviet Union's claim in regard to its actions in Afghanistan and the United States' claim with respect to its activities in Nicaragua.

[41] *See* Resolution of Institut de Droit International on the Principle of Non-Intervention in Civil Wars, 56 ANN. INST. DR. INT'L 544, 549 (1975) [hereinafter cited as Resolution on Non-Intervention]. John Stuart Mill made the point in 1859: "Intervention to enforce

The facts are often disputed and sometimes the claim of a prior illegal intervention has lacked credible evidence.[42] In still other cases, the counter-intervention has been clearly disproportionate.[43] Yet the problems of weighing facts should not be exaggerated: they make it difficult to apply the agreed rules but they do not mean that the rules lack content.

In short, it is unwarranted to view the Charter rules as entirely "open-textured," allowing states unlimited latitude to interpret them. The general contours of the rules are clear.

2. *Third-Party Determinations.* A skeptic may respond that it hardly matters whether the rules have a core meaning in the absence of compulsory third-party adjudication of unilateral interpretations. As the Nuremberg tribunal declared in its judgment: "whether action taken under the claim of self-defense was in fact aggressive or defensive must ultimately be subject to investigation or adjudication if international law is ever to be enforced."[44] The point has often been made. It is incompatible with the concept of law that an entity subject to the law should have the final authority to determine whether a legal rule applies to it.

One answer to this line of argument is that third-party judgments are in fact made; self-serving unilateral justifications are not always accepted by the international community. Whenever a state has recourse to armed force outside of its territory, the legitimacy of that action is appraised by other states, organizations, non-governmental groups, and individuals. The more formal and prominent judgments issue from the international political organs that deal with issues of peace and security, notably the U.N. Security Council and General Assembly. These decisions generally command state attention. They are more likely to persuade where the facts are reasonably clear and critical resolutions receive substantial majority support, especially where the majority includes governments allied to or generally sympathetic to the impugned states.[45]

---

non-intervention is always rightful, always moral, if not always prudent." J.S. Mill, *A Few Words on Non-Intervention,* in 21 COLLECTED WORKS OF JOHN STUART MILL 109, 123 (J. Robson ed. 1984).

[42] *See, e.g., supra* notes 30-32 and accompanying text (discussing the Soviet invasion of Czechoslovakia).

[43] For example, invasions by Vietnam of Cambodia, by Syria of Lebanon, and by Libya of Chad.

[44] *Judgment, supra* note 3, at 208.

[45] *See* Schachter, *supra* note 5, at 1622-23; G.A. Res. 37/37, 37 U.N. GAOR Supp. (No. 51) at 25, U.N. Doc. A/37/P.V. 82 (1983) (condemnation of the Soviet Union for its invasion of Afghanistan); G.A. Res. 38, 38 U.N. GAOR Supp. (No. 47) at 19, U.N. Doc. A/38/P.V. 43

But decisions of the U.N. political bodies—or their failure to decide—should not be considered definitive in every case. These are political, not judicial bodies. Their members are free to pass on the issues of legality for whatever reasons they deem appropriate. Political pressures and "mechanical" bloc voting may detract from the persuasive authority of those decisions. Thus, the collective judgments may lack the respect and authority normally associated with judicial tribunals. Moreover, the judgments of U.N. political organs are not legally binding except in the rare instances where they form part of a mandatory decision of the Security Council.[46] Still, they remain an important means for the international community to express its collective opinion of state claims.

Criticism from non-governmental groups may be even more significant—not because these groups voice an amorphous world opinion but rather because their particular composition and concerns lend significance to their judgment. Recall, for example, the criticism by non-Soviet bloc communist parties of the Soviet uses of force in Czechoslovakia in 1968 and in Afghanistan in 1981.[47] The fact that these parties previously had consistently supported Soviet political positions gave more weight to their subsequent opposition.

Another important category of unofficial judgments is that of the international lawyers, especially their academic component. This is not mere professional conceit. Because of the paucity of case law and the politicized character of governmental positions, the expert opinions of legal scholars and their professional bodies command attention and respect. The views of these experts are persuasive when they are expressed in reasoned discourse supported by authority and principle. Moreover, since international lawyers come from many countries and have diverse approaches, their opinions have added weight when they coincide and reinforce each other.[48]

3. *The Political Costs to the Targets of International Censure.* The skeptic may concede these points but still persist in his

---

(1983) (condemnation of the U.S. for its invasion of Grenada). For a critical comment on the U.N. resolution and arguments for the U.S. position on Grenada, see J. MOORE, *supra* note 29. On the unanimous condemnation of Iran for its part in the seizure of American diplomatic personnel in Tehran, see Security Council Res. 457, U.N. Doc. S/INF/35 (1979).

    [46] *See* U.N. CHARTER arts. 12, 14.

    [47] *See, e.g.,* 7 I.L.M. 1285 (1968) (the Czechoslovak Communist Party condemns the Soviet Union).

    [48] *See* Schachter, *The Invisible College of International Lawyers,* 72 Nw. U.L. REV. 217 (1977); *see also* TERRY NARDIN, LAW, MORALITY AND THE RELATIONS OF STATES 173-77 (1983).

doubts. He can argue that without international enforcement, censure has no impact on state actions: it remains merely rhetorical condemnation without sanctions. Law must be more than aspiration or ideal. However, states do in fact strongly object to such condemnation and will make determined efforts to forestall censure by the U.N.[49] That they do so shows that a condemnation of illegality by an international organ, even if not binding, is regarded as detrimental, imposing political costs on the offender.[50] Such condemnations by large majorities have contributed to transforming the image of a great power from a champion of national independence to that of a threat to the sovereignty of weaker states. One cannot doubt that this transformation of image has negative political consequences for the state criticized.

Thus, we can plausibly infer that governments consider the possibility of such censure when they face a decision to use force. That this frequently happens is suggested by the fact that for virtually every use of force, the responsible state has sought to justify it under the accepted Charter rules. Though such legal justification may merely rationalize a decision made for reasons of interest or power, the felt need of governments to advance a legal argument is itself a fact of some consequence. The fact that their legal arguments may be rationalizations does not mean they are without influence. The claims, however hypocritical, have a political object; they must be believed to serve that purpose and to be credible they must appear to influence conduct. Hence governments have good reason to keep from doing what cannot be justified.

Of course these considerations do not add up to an iron law of rule-governed conduct. States may still decide to violate the law and face a loss of credibility and other negative consequences. In most cases, they need not fear that effective collective sanctions will be imposed by the U.N. or other groups of states. But they are nevertheless aware that the illicit use of force is not cost-free. Insofar as that perception exists, it has an impact on state conduct. The legal restraints thereby acquire a measure of efficacy; they are

[49] *See* THOMAS FRANCK, NATION AGAINST NATION chs. 10 & 11 (1985).

[50] "The ability of the United States to exert its influence in world affairs in furtherance of the humane and democratic values we most deeply believe in will be determined in the long run by the perceived legitimacy of our imposing national power, as well as by that power itself." Gordon, Bilder, Rovine & Wallace, *International Law and The United States Action in Grenada: A Report*, 18 INT'L LAW. 331, 332 (1984) [hereinafter cited as *Grenada Report*]; *see also* LOUIS HENKIN, HOW NATIONS BEHAVE 314-39 (2d ed. 1979); Christopher, *Introduction, to* AMERICAN HOSTAGES IN IRAN 10-13 (P. Kreisberg ed. 1985); Cutler, *The Right to Intervene*, 64 FOREIGN AFF. 96, 96-97 (1985).

not simply aspirations or paper rules.

4. *The Basic Need for Rules.* We are left then with the political scientists and journalists who remain cynical about attempts "to suppress the chaotic and dangerous aspirations of governments in the international field by the acceptance of some system of legal rules and restraints."[51] Their basic hypothesis is that states act out of national interest, constrained, in the last analysis, only by power. Not only apparent violations of rules but even compliance verifies their view, since compliance can also be motivated by the state's perceived national interest. In short, no matter what a state does, it must be acting for reasons of interest, not law.

This line of reasoning begs the questions of whether states consider law-observance generally in their interest and whether that perceived interest occasionally prevails over other interests. This is an empirical matter to which no final answer can be given. However, in considering the reality of rules on force we must not forget that the distinction between illicit and allowable uses of force is essential to every legal system. International society requires it no less than national communities. Charles De Visscher, a past President of the International Court of Justice, stated: "It is not possible at one and the same time to base international relations on the independent existence of States and to concede to each State the sovereign right to take up arms to attack or destroy that independence."[52] The logic of that proposition underlies the common interest in maintaining the restraints on force.

II. IMPLIED CONDITIONS AND CHANGED CIRCUMSTANCES

It is one thing to conclude that we need some restraints on force; it is another matter to determine their precise limits. The existing rules cannot be considered necessary in the philosophical sense. They have a contingent character in that they depend on human choices and on the myriad factors conditioning such choices. The rules may be defended as established law, but that does not foreclose demands for change, whether by way of reinterpretation or explicit revision.

Consideration of these demands for change is particularly timely: they are now advanced with increasing frequency and intensity. Proponents of change contend at bottom that recent devel-

---

    [51] *See* GEORGE KENNAN, AMERICAN DIPLOMACY 1900-1950, at 94 (1951).
    [52] CHARLES DE VISSCHER, THEORY AND REALITY IN PUBLIC INTERNATIONAL LAW 294 (Corbett trans. 2d ed. 1968).

opments in international relations have significantly altered the conditions on which the restrictive Charter rules were based. We now require new interpretations and new rules, it is argued, to secure minimal order and justice among states.[53] Significantly, no responsible person proposes abandoning all rules; everyone appears to recognize the need to limit each state's right to take up arms. Generally the revisionists seek to broaden the grounds for recourse to force by individual states without reverting to a Hobbesian state of nature.

A. Dependency of the Charter Rules on the Effectiveness of International Law

The case for revision rests on a mix of juridical and political arguments. First, the existing rules—of the Charter or general customary law—were premised on the effective functioning of a collective security system. As argued by Julius Stone, one of the earliest and most forceful revisionists, the Charter's renunciation of unilateral force was intended to be "organic[ally] dependen[t] . . . on the effective establishment of collective institutions and methods."[54] Since the U.N. collective security system has failed (as shown by the continued frequency of violent international acts), states should be released from their unilateral commitments to eschew force.[55] The critical policy question is then posed: Why should states abide by the law to their disadvantage when lawless states violate it with impunity?

Although the question is basically political, the legal arguments are relevant. The legislative history of article 2 of the Charter does not support the notion that effective enforcement of collective security was a prerequisite to renouncing the use of force.[56]

---

[53] [E]xisting legal norms governing the use of armed force reflect past needs and experiences more than current ones. To the extent . . . that reasonable efforts to counter insidious forms of aggression, protect human rights, restore civil order or achieve other legitimate ends do not square with the law[,] . . . perhaps the law needs amendment . . . .

Grenada Report, supra note 50, at 334.

[54] J. STONE, *supra* note 36, at 96.

[55] *See, e.g.,* A.V. THOMAS & A.J. THOMAS, JR., *supra* note 36, at 209 ("[I]f the collective organization, through a fault in its organizing instrument, leaves a gap where the use of force is necessary but the collective organization is impotent to act, then the legal right to use force must . . . revert back to the members."). *But see Grenada Report, supra* note 50, at 362 (rejecting this argument on the ground that "a state which has benefited from the Charter cannot belatedly interpose the failure of consideration as a ground for invalidating its consent to be bound by it").

[56] *See, e.g.,* DJURA NINCIĆ, THE PROBLEM OF SOVEREIGNTY IN THE CHARTER AND IN THE

True, the Charter's drafters must have hoped that the Security Council and other relevant U.N. organs would obviate individual recourse to force. But they were realistic enough to recognize that this might not be achieved; that is precisely why they preserved the right of self-defense to respond to armed attack.[57] Force could meet force but, unless authorized by the Security Council,[58] force could not answer a non-forcible deprivation of rights. It is hardly plausible to infer from these provisions that the failure to prevent illegal force now allows an individual state to use force freely. No evidence or logical reason supports the assumption that the drafters or the signatory governments intended this radical result. Rather, widespread affirmation of the rules on force as *jus cogens*, peremptory norms of customary law,[59] shows that states regard those rules as legally independent of the proper functioning of U.N. organs.

B. Necessity of Force to Safeguard Legal Rights

The political case for revision includes another argument: if individual force is limited to self-defense, states may have no adequate means of resisting violations of their legal rights.[60] States often cannot obtain satisfaction through international judicial or political processes, yet they are barred from resorting to force unless they are attacked (or facing imminent danger of attack).[61]

This does not leave states without remedies. Aggrieved states may employ economic and other non-military countermeasures[62] to

---

PRACTICE OF THE UNITED NATIONS 72, 76-77 (1970) (guarantees of territorial integrity in article 2(4) were not intended to limit the article's broad prohibition of self-help measures).

[57] U.N. CHARTER art. 51.

[58] *Id.* arts. 36, 39-42.

[59] *See infra* note 72.

[60] J. STONE, *supra* note 36, at 98-101.

[61] The Charter does, however, give the Security Council the power to authorize economic sanctions against errant states, including "complete or partial interruption of economic relations and of rail, sea, air, postal, telegraphic, radio, and other means of communication, and the severance of diplomatic relations." U.N. CHARTER art. 41. This power has been used only infrequently.

[62] *See* Schachter, *Self-Help in International Law*, 37 J. INT'L AFF. 231 (1984); *see also* ELIZABETH ZOLLER, PEACETIME UNILATERAL REMEDIES *passim* (1984).

It is worth noting that the line between self-help and self-defense has never been entirely clear in customary law. *See* HANS KELSEN, PRINCIPLES OF INTERNATIONAL LAW 15-17, 58-62 (1952). Prior to the adoption of the U.N. Charter, many writers and governments thought that the right of self-defense applied not only to an actual or threatened physical attack on the state or its instrumentalities but also to violations of legally protected interests. *See, e.g.,* D. NINCIĆ, *supra* note 56, at 53 (explaining rationale of the "war as a sanction" theory). Some writers have distinguished self-defense from the wider category of self-help by limiting self-defense to responses to violations of rights essential to the security and

respond to illegal action.[63] In many cases threats or actions to suspend treaty benefits, fishing rights, imports, immigration, or air transit have succeeded in bringing violations to an end.[64] Of course these measures do not always redress the wrong. Even powerful countries such as the U.S. have occasionally imposed economic sanctions without conspicuous success.[65]

---

independence of the state. *See* DEREK W. BOWETT, SELF-DEFENCE IN INTERNATIONAL LAW 270-71 (1958); Bowett, *International Law and Economic Coercion,* 16 VA. J. INT'L L. 245, 251 n.21 (1976). Even when so limited, self-defense would allow forcible responses to a wide range of unlawful and injurious acts by others. The argument of some political theorists that "aggression" must be understood as contrary to "peace-with-rights," *see* MICHAEL WALZER, JUST AND UNJUST WARS 51 (1977); T. NARDIN, *supra* note 48, at 284, and that therefore a state using force to defend its rights (even when not attacked) is upholding the common rules of the society of states, has the same flaws as the argument that article 51 of the Charter preserves the "inherent right" of self-defense, which is discussed *infra* at text accompanying notes 83-86. *See* WILLIAM VINCENT O'BRIEN, THE CONDUCT OF JUST AND LIMITED WAR 38-55, 67-70 (1981); WAR, MORALITY AND THE MILITARY PROFESSION 232-487 (M.M. Wakin ed. 1979). The theorists' position begs the question since the issue is whether the legal limits on force, including article 51, are part of the common rules. If they are, then one cannot override them in order to safeguard other legal rights.

[63] States occasionally also use or threaten non-military coercion for political ends such as overthrowing a state's regime or effecting massive changes in its policies. For example, Arab states continue to implement a coercive multi-level boycott designed to destroy the state of Israel. *See* Joyner, *The Transnational Boycott as Economic Coercion in International Law: Policy, Place and Practice,* 17 VAND. J. TRANSNAT'L L. 205, 216-20 (1984); Shihata, *Destination Embargo of Arab Oil: Its Legality Under International Law,* 68 AM. J. INT'L L. 591, 592-93 (1974). Non-military coercion for these purposes is arguably illegal because it is aimed at subordinating the target state's sovereign rights to the will of the coercing state. *See* Declaration on the Inadmissibility of Intervention in the Domestic Affairs of States, G.A. Res. 2131, 20 U.N. GAOR Annex 3 (Agenda Item 107) at 10, U.N. Doc. A/6220 (1965); CHARTER OF THE ORGANIZATION OF AMERICAN STATES arts. 15-16; *see also* Bowett, *supra* note 62, at 249 (drawing a distinction between allowable and illicit "economic coercion" based on whether the state's motive is economic or political: "once a State is allowed to coerce in the furtherance of its political goals, there is little point even in attempting legally to restrict economic coercion").

Some commentators have gone so far as to contend that economic action of such intensity and magnitude would justify forcible self-defense by the target state, and collective defense by its allies. *See* Farer, *Political and Economic Coercion in Contemporary International Law,* 79 AM. J. INT'L L. 405 (1985). I disagree. Even egregious economic aggression, whether or not illegal, does not constitute an armed attack or a use of force in the Charter sense. Allowing forcible reprisal to non-military coercion would broaden the grounds for use of force to an intolerable degree.

[64] *See, generally,* G. HUFBAUER & J. SCHOTT, ECONOMIC SANCTIONS RECONSIDERED (1985).

[65] When armed conflict broke out between the United Kingdom and Argentina over the Falkland (Malvinas) Islands in 1982, the U.S. first attempted to mediate the dispute. When this failed, it imposed several sanctions against Argentina: "(1) suspension of all military exports and security assistance to Argentina; (2) withholding of certification of Argentine eligibility for military sales; (3) suspension of new Export-Import Bank credits and guarantees; and (4) suspension of Commodity Credit Corporation guarantees." Acevedo, *The U.S. Measures Against Argentina Resulting from the Malvinas Conflict,* 78 AM. J. INT'L L. 323, 326 (1984). Despite the seriousness of the measures taken, they had no appreci-

Still, the failure of self-help and international institutions to provide adequate remedies for breaches of legal rights does not impugn the efficacy of the Charter's collective machinery. That machinery does not purport to safeguard legal rights: it was meant to ensure peace and security.[66] Optional judicial machinery is available for legal disputes, and a preamble in the Charter expresses the intent to establish conditions under which justice and respect for law could be maintained. But no language of the Charter supports the view that the failure to safeguard legal rights should nullify the renunciation of individual force. And the consequence of such a view—return to the near anarchy of pre-Charter international society—is too drastic to have been what states contemplated when the Charter was adopted.[67]

C. Theories of Changed Circumstances

Two other legal theories support the view that the rules on force have been abrogated by developments in international relations. One is the general requirement of reciprocity.[68] Widespread violations by states should, in law, release others from the duty to comply. This theory developed by analogy to the right of one treaty party to suspend the treaty between it and a violator for a violation especially affecting that party.[69] Thus it has been sug-

---

able effect on the course of the war.

[66] *See* HANS KELSEN, THE LAW OF THE UNITED NATIONS 15-16 (1950).

[67] The International Court of Justice had occasion to pass judgment on this issue when Britain used forcible self-help to vindicate its right of passage through the Corfu Channel. The court considered Britain's claim of right unacceptable, observing that a right to use armed force "in the cause of justice" would "be reserved for the most powerful states and might easily lead to perverting the administration of justice itself. . . . [A] policy of force such as [this] has in the past given rise to most serious abuses and . . . cannot, whatever be the defects in international organization, find a place in international law." The Corfu Channel Case (U.K. v. Albania), 1949 I.C.J. 4, 35.

[68] Ambassador Jeane Kirkpatrick declared in April, 1984: "The first principle of the law is the equal application of the law. Unilateral compliance with the Charter's principles of nonintervention and non-use of force may make sense in some specific isolated instances, but are hardly a sound basis for either United States policy or for international peace and stability." Address by Ambassador Kirkpatrick to the American Society of International Law 16 (Apr. 1984) (not yet published; copy on file with *The University of Chicago Law Review*); *see also* JULIUS STONE, VISIONS OF WORLD ORDER 54-55 (1984). For a forceful rebuttal of Kirkpatrick, see Gardner, *Sovereignty and Intervention: A Challenge of Law-Making for the Industrialized Democracies,* 35 TRIALOGUE 3 (1984).

An interesting discussion of the role of reciprocity in international law may be found in Gottlieb, *Relationism: Legal Theory for a Relational Society,* 50 U. CHI. L. REV. 567 (1983).

[69] *See* Vienna Convention on the Law of Treaties, *done on* May 23, 1969, art. 60, U.N. Doc. A/CONF. 39/27 (entered into force Jan. 27, 1980) [hereinafter cited as Vienna Convention]. Apart from the right of suspension, a party has the right to refuse to perform an

gested that serious violations of article 2(4) by the Soviet Union would entitle the United States, if it were especially affected, to suspend its obligations to the U.S.S.R.[70] An even broader contention is that Charter breaches have so radically changed the position of all states that any party may now invoke those violations as a ground for suspending its obligations.[71] Although these legal principles (contained in the Vienna Convention on the Law of Treaties) cannot be denied, their application to these issues is by no means clear. Significantly, no state has invoked another state's breach of article 2(4) as a legal reason to abrogate the Charter rules. And as we noted, article 2(4) is the exemplary case of a peremptory norm (*jus cogens*).[72] Moreover, the Charter stipulates that its obligations prevail over those of any other agreement.[73] Theoretically the parties to the Charter may bring it to an end but obviously no present disposition exists to do that.

The Charter provides for legal responses to a breach of article 2(4)—most importantly for the right of self-defense in case of an armed attack.[74] If self-defense is not permissible under the circum-

---

obligation corresponding to the obligation violated by the other party. The applicable customary law principle is known as *inadimplenti non est adimplendum. See* ZOLLER, *supra* note 62, at 14-27.

[70] *See* Kirkpatrick, *supra* note 68, at 17 ("We cannot permit . . . ourselves to be bound to unilateral renunciation of rights which do in fact exist under the Charter.").

For a political argument to the same effect, see NORMAN PODHORETZ, THE PRESENT DANGER 39-42, 96-101 (1980). Eugene Rostow concludes that in view of Soviet and other violations of article 2(4), it is impossible to determine whether that article "is an operative legal norm." Rostow, *The Legality of the International Use of Force by and from States,* 10 YALE J. INT'L L. 286, 290 (1985). For the contrary U.S. State Department position, see Memorandum of R.B. Owen, Legal Adviser of the State Department, *quoted in* Nash, *Contemporary Practice of the United States Relating to International Law,* 74 AM. J. INT'L L. 418, 418-20 (1980).

[71] *See* Vienna Convention, *supra* note 69, art. 60, para. 2(c). This provision in the Vienna Convention is a carefully circumscribed codification of the customary law doctrine of *rebus sic stantibus,* the principle that treaty obligations may "terminate when a change occurs in those circumstances which existed at the time of the conclusion of the treaty and whose continuance formed, according to the intention or wills of the parties, a condition of the continuing validity of the treaty." Hill, *The Doctrine of "Rebus Sic Stantibus" in International Law,* U. MO. STUD., July 1, 1934, at 8; *see also* L. HENKIN, *supra* note 50, at 137-38; *cf.* U.C.C. § 2-615 (1978) (codifying the common-law contract doctrine of frustration or commercial impracticability).

[72] The United States has taken the legal position that article 2(4) is a peremptory norm from which no derogation by treaty is permitted. *See* Memorandum of R.B. Owen, *supra* note 70, at 418-20.

[73] U.N. CHARTER art. 103.

[74] U.N. CHARTER art. 51 reads:

Nothing in the present Charter shall impair the inherent right of individual or collective self-defence if an armed attack occurs against a Member of the United Nations, until the Security Council has taken measures necessary to maintain international

stances, an injured state (or indeed any state) may bring the violation to the attention of the Security Council or the General Assembly.[75] Or, the International Court of Justice may be seized of the case if a jurisdictional basis is available under its statute. That these remedies may not effectively redress the violation evidences the system's weakness. But a legal system's failure to prevent or punish wrongs by some entities does not entitle all the others to violate a basic obligation.

In stating this conclusion, I must also note its limits. Persistent serious violations by one party may erode the minimum level of mutuality required to maintain observance by others. Particularly in adversary relations between the superpowers, reasonable reciprocity in the use of force is a political necessity. But this should not become a game of tit-for-tat, in which violation by one allows a reciprocal violation by the other. The rules on use of force allow for legitimate responses to aggression; they do not permit reciprocal law-breaking.

A related argument is based on state conduct. Some commentators contend that the widespread and consistent violations of article 2(4) constitute practice sufficient to supersede the Charter rules and their customary law counterpart.[76] This argument is no more convincing than the assertion that if a large number of rapes and murders are not punished, the criminal laws are supplanted and legal restraints disappear for everyone.

Although it is reasonably easy to determine when crimes such as murder have been committed, state conduct in the international field involves relatively few clear violations. Aggressive wars similar to the Nazi and Japanese invasions are rare. Most allegedly illegal uses of force arise out of armed interventions in situations involving charges and counter-charges of prior illegalities and aggressive intent. Certainly an impartial tribunal would find culpability in some of these cases. But we must remember that hundreds of political conflicts exist, and many if not most actions taken by states do not constitute illegal uses of force. Therefore, to conclude that some violations constitute "practice accepted as law" gives "prac-

---

peace and security. Measures taken by Members in the exercise of this right of self-defence shall be immediately reported to the Security Council and shall not in any way affect the authority and responsibility of the Security Council under the present Charter to take at any time such action as it deems necessary in order to maintain or restore international peace and security.

[75] U.N. CHARTER art. 35, para. 1.

[76] *See, e.g.,* Franck, *Who Killed Article 2(4)? or: Changing Norms Governing the Use of Force by States,* 64 AM. J. INT'L L. 809 (1970); Rostow, *supra* note 70, at 287-88.

tice" a peculiar meaning, quite different from "widespread and uniform" usage. Moreover, such violations as do occur are not "accepted as law." On the contrary, in virtually every case one state's use of force has been condemned by large numbers of states as violating existing fundamental law.[77]

This agreement on the rules' fundamental character takes us to the heart of the matter. When a principle is repeatedly and unanimously declared to be a basic legal rule from which no derogation is allowed, even numerous violations do not become state practice constitutive of a new rule. Contrary usage alone should not terminate a principle that states have strongly affirmed to be a condition necessary for order. Infringements of existing rules reflect expediency and political motives: it would make nonsense of customary law to treat them as repealing an accepted basic obligation.[78] No state has ever suggested that violations of article 2(4) have opened the door to free use of force. Nor have international lawyers (with a few ambiguous exceptions) supported so radical a conclusion.

It is not my purpose here to argue that the Charter rules, or their customary law counterparts, are immutable. We cannot exclude the possibility that new configurations of power and altered psychological attitudes will wreak a fundamental change in the state system. Some envisage a single world authority, others a hegemonial condominium, and still others a basic shift of authority to non-territorial entities. If such a change occurs in one form or another, the rules governing force will change correspondingly. But with the existing balance of power and strong nationalist loyalties, the basic Charter principles themselves are unlikely to change. However, pressures for loosening the restraints on the use of force in some situations are likely to increase. They call for analysis.

III. NECESSARY SELF-DEFENSE

A. Limits on Defense

When states resort to armed force these days, they most commonly claim self-defense, either individual or collective, as their legal justification. Under the U.N. Charter it is clear that self-defense is legitimate "if an armed attack occurs."[79] The necessity of

---

[77] *See* JOHN MURPHY, THE UNITED NATIONS AND THE CONTROL OF VIOLENCE 125-26 (1982); *see also* EDWIN HOYT, LAW AND FORCE IN AMERICAN FOREIGN POLICY 19 (1985).

[78] *See* C. DE VISSCHER, *supra* note 52, at 156-57.

[79] U.N. CHARTER art. 51, quoted in full *supra* at note 74.

defense in this situation is taken for granted.

The question becomes more complicated when the armed attack has succeeded in seizing territory and some time has elapsed. Has a state a continuing right to self-defense to recover territory unlawfully taken by armed force? Once the emergency of an armed attack has ended, a victim of aggression can reasonably be required to seek and exhaust all avenues of peaceful settlement. But if such avenues prove futile, is self-defense then "necessary"?

I suggest that the idea of self-defense contains a temporal element. It refers to a response made close in time to an attack or imminent threat. Without that limitation, self-defense would sanction armed attacks for countless prior acts of aggression and conquest. It would completely swallow up the basic rule against using force. The difficulty of defining a precise time limit—a statute of limitations, as it were—does not impugn the basic idea. In most cases irredentist demands for lost territory or claims for restoration of the status quo ante are based on attacks that occurred many years or even decades ago.[80] To extend self-defense to such cases is to stretch the notion of defense far beyond its basic meaning.[81]

An additional requirement of proportionality is linked to necessity: acts done in self-defense must not exceed in manner or aim the necessity provoking them. This definition leaves room for differences in particular cases but there is no mistaking its core meaning. Security Council decisions have condemned defensive action that greatly exceeded the provocation (as measured by scale of weaponry and relative casualties) as illegal reprisals rather than legitimate self-defense.[82] It seems reasonable, however, to allow an attack victim to retaliate with force beyond the immediate area of attack when it has good reason to expect further attacks from the same source. Such action would not be merely "anticipatory" since prior attacks took place; nor would it be a reprisal inasmuch as its prime motive is protective, not punitive.

B. Proposed Expansions

The most controversial question is whether self-defense may extend to situations not involving armed attack. It has been argued

---

[80] For example, see the Argentine statement on its use of force in the Malvinas (Falkland Islands), 37 U.N. GAOR (51st meeting) at 7, U.N. Doc. A/37/353 (1982).

[81] *See* Schachter, *supra* note 5, at 1627-28.

[82] *See* Bowett, *Reprisals Involving Recourse to Armed Force*, 66 AM. J. INT'L L. 1, 33-36 (1972).

that Charter article 51 does not say that an armed attack is always required. Some scholars infer from this that the drafters of article 51 did not intend to impair the customary law "inherent right" of defense.[83] Despite this ingenious argument, most commentators agree that article 51 defines and limits self-defense to cases of armed attack.[84] To treat that phrase as only a "hypothesis" or an example of one aspect of self-defense does not make much sense of the text or the intent to impose limits on force.

Whatever the intended meaning of article 51, most U.N. members tend to favor the more restrictive interpretation.[85] They fear that deletion of the armed attack requirement and reliance on an "inherent right" undefined in customary law would so expand self-defense as to eliminate virtually all restraints on force. "Armed attack" is a factual, objective condition; it can generally be verified.

In contrast, the "inherent right" is open to subjective interpretation. Customary law offers few firm guidelines—understandably, since war itself was not considered illegal for many centuries. History abounds with examples of self-defense claims serving as pretexts for aggressive acts. For example, Germany and Japan contended that their military actions leading to World War II were defensive responses to actions by others aimed at denying them their rightful territorial and economic claims.[86] The Nuremberg and Tokyo tribunals had no difficulty rejecting these arguments in light of the evidence on intent to dominate and expand. But the fact that self-defense could be claimed (and probably believed by many German and Japanese people) showed how important it was to limit and define the grounds for its exercise.

Accepting the need for limits on self-defense does not negate the contention that the armed attack requirement is too rigid. One may grant that the Charter restricts self-defense to cases of armed attack, yet conclude that a strict application of that requirement does not satisfy present perceptions of necessary defense. Several situations raise this issue:

---

[83] *See* D. BOWETT, *supra* note 62, at 187-93; M. McDOUGAL & F. FELICIANO, LAW AND MINIMUM WORLD PUBLIC ORDER 232-44 (1961). *But see* H. KELSEN, *supra* note 62, at 58-62; *see also* L. HENKIN, *supra* note 50, at 141-45 (discussing the importance that the drafters of article 51 attached to the phrase "if an armed attack occurs").

[84] The International Law Commission, after a survey of writers in many countries, concluded that the majority favor the restrictive view. *See* Report of the International Law Commission to the General Assembly, U.N. Doc. A/35/10 (1980), *reprinted in* [1980] 2 Y.B. INT'L L. COMM'N 52-53 & nn.174-75, U.N. Doc. A/CN.4/SER.A/1980/Add.1/pt.2.

[85] *See* ROSALYN HIGGINS, THE DEVELOPMENT OF INTERNATIONAL LAW THROUGH THE POLITICAL ORGANS OF THE UNITED NATIONS 167-230 (1963).

[86] *See Judgment, supra* note 3, at 191, 194, 206-15; S. HORWITZ, *supra* note 3.

1) Credible threats of force by hostile states;

2) "Indirect aggression"—instigating or aiding subversive and armed activities to overthrow the regime of another state;

3) Foreign state intervention in civil strife by providing arms and personnel to one side;

4) Terrorist activities against a state's nationals, especially seizure of hostages whom the territorial sovereign is unable or unwilling to protect.[87]

In each of these situations, the injured state may reasonably believe that non-forcible measures cannot provide adequate redress. Hence it will see armed force as necessary. Also, since the injured state may have insufficient military strength for self-defense, it probably will seek outside aid for collective self-defense. In this situation, states not themselves injured may also claim self-defense though no state suffered an actual armed attack.

To deal adequately with these situations would require far more space than this article allows. However, a brief summary of the considerations pertinent to each case may be of interest.

1. *Threats of Force and Anticipatory Defense.* The Nuremberg and Tokyo trials emphasized the significance of Germany's and Japan's planning and preparation for war. Many people today believe that the threatened powers and their allies could have prevented the war by defensive action. This line of reasoning suggests that anticipatory defense may be warranted against a state that credibly threatens war by stockpiling armaments and expressing hostile intent.

The Cuban missile crisis in 1962 presented a variant of this situation. The U.S. saw the installation of missiles in Cuba as a threat, and they responded with a blockade implicitly involving a use of force. Although the U.S. perceived its actions as a defensive response, it officially justified the blockade by pointing to an ex post facto "authorization" by the Organization of American States.[88] By not asserting a legal self-defense claim, the U.S. sought to avoid a reciprocal claim that U.S. missile bases near the Soviet Union were unlawful and justified Soviet armed response.

On the other hand, Israel asserted self-defense when it destroyed an Iraqi nuclear reactor, citing Iraq's declared state of war

---

[87] This list of situations to which commentators propose extending the self-defense exception is not exhaustive, but illustrative. *See* Schachter, *supra* note 5, at 1633-45.

[88] *See* 4 MARJORIE WHITEMAN, DIGEST OF INTERNATIONAL LAW 523-24 (1965); *see also* ABRAM CHAYES, THE CUBAN MISSILE CRISIS 41-68 (1974); L. HENKIN, *supra* note 50, at 227-31.

against Israel and the actual menace of a reactor capable of producing nuclear weapons.[89] In the U.N. debates on this action, most states rejected Israel's contention because the reactor in question was devoted to peaceful uses and they viewed the possibility of its conversion to military use as only a remote threat to Israel.[90] Interestingly, in the debates some delegates referred favorably to Daniel Webster's formulation in the *Caroline* case of a right to self-defense where an attack is imminent. In Webster's eloquent phrase, a state has a right to self-defense prior to an armed attack only when the "necessity of that self-defence is instant, overwhelming, and leaving no choice of means, and no moment for deliberation."[91]

Some hold that the *Caroline* principle still leaves too much latitude for a state to use force prior to an actual attack.[92] Others fear that it takes inadequate account of a build-up of arms—especially nuclear missiles—that could on first strike destroy a victim's defensive capability.[93] Both concerns are understandable. They reveal the inability of a general principle to capture the full dimensions of the problem of dangerous threats. We need specific legal regimes setting limits on force and providing means of verification. Some such regimes exist in treaties and by informal arrangements: these and future agreements may provide a blueprint for arms controls.[94]

---

[89] *See* D'Amato, *Israel's Air Strike upon the Iraqi Nuclear Reactor*, 77 Am. J. Int'l L. 584 (1983); Mallison & Mallison, *The Israeli Aerial Attack of June 7, 1981, Upon the Iraqi Nuclear Reactor: Aggression or Self-Defense?* 15 Vand. J. Transnat'l L. 417, 435-37 (1982).

[90] *See* 36 U.N. SCOR (2285-88th mtg.) *passim*; U.N. Docs. S/P.V.2285-89 (1981).

[91] 2 John Bassett Moore, A Digest of International Law 412 (1906); *see also* Casebook, *supra* note 24, at 890-91.

[92] *See, e.g.*, L. Henkin, *supra* note 50, at 141-45.

[93] *See, e.g.*, Wolfgang Friedmann, The Changing Structure of International Law 259-60 (1964); Schachter, *supra* note 5, at 1633-35; Singh, *The Right of Self-Defence in Relation to the Use of Nuclear Weapons*, 5 Indian Y.B. of Int'l Aff. 3 (1956).

[94] Existing treaties include those limiting areas in which nuclear weapons can be employed, *see, e.g.*, Treaty Banning Nuclear Weapon Tests in the Atmosphere, in Outer Space and Under Water, *opened for signature* Aug. 5, 1968, 14 U.S.T. 1313, T.I.A.S. 5433, 480 U.N.T.S. 43; Treaty on Principles Governing the Activities of States in the Exploration and Use of Outer Space, *opened for signature* Jan. 27, 1967, 18 U.S.T. 2410, T.I.A.S. 6347, 610 U.N.T.S. 205; those establishing regional nuclear-free zones, prohibiting proliferation, and limiting size and number of weapons, *see, e.g.*, Treaty on the Non-Proliferation of Nuclear Weapons, *opened for signature* July 1, 1968, 21 U.S.T. 483, T.I.A.S. 6839, 729 U.N.T.S. 161; Treaty on the Limitation of Anti-Ballistic Missile Systems, May 26, 1972, United States-U.S.S.R., 23 U.S.T. 3435, T.I.A.S. 7503; those providing for emergency communication and notification of dangerous situations (U.S.-U.S.S.R bilateral treaties); and those providing for international inspection of nuclear facilities (International Atomic Energy Agency). Future arrangements being considered in intergovernmental negotiations include exchanges of detailed military information, advance notification of military movements, reports on military expenditures, and measures for inspection and verification. Detailed proposals on these lines

On the level of principle, it makes sense to support a norm that opposes the preemptive resort to force but acknowledges its necessity when an attack is so immediate and massive as to make it absurd to demand that the target state await the actual attack before taking defensive action. Webster's statement in the *Caroline* case is probably the only acceptable formulation at the present time to meet this situation.

2. *Indirect Aggression.* States generally agree that it violates article 2(4) to support armed activities or subversive infiltration to overthrow a regime in another state. The regime attacked may of course take armed action in its territory. May it also use force against the state supporting the hostile activities, and may third states attack that state as part of a collective defense arrangement? Should a line be drawn between support of armed activities and an armed attack within the meaning of article 51?

The latter issue arose in the Nicaragua-U.S. dispute.[95] The U.S. contended that Nicaragua's provision of war matériel and technical aid to El Salvadoran insurgents constituted an armed attack on El Salvador, allowing that state and others to attack Nicaragua in collective self-defense.[96] Nicaragua maintained that such aid—whether legal or not—fell short of an armed attack and consequently did not justify armed defense.[97] More particularly, Nicaragua asserted that its aid did not legally warrant U.S. support through arms and training of the "contras" fighting against the Nicaraguan regime.[98]

Although the U.N. has condemned indirect aggression as illegal, most states have been reluctant to label it as "aggression" within the definition adopted by the General Assembly in 1974.[99] Extending the scope of "aggression," they fear, would expand the right of self-defense. Memories still remain of armed interventions

---

were made in 1985 by European governments and by the United States to the Conference on Confidence-Building and Disarmament established pursuant to the Helsinki Final Act of 1975. The draft Contadora agreement for Central America also includes provisions for limits and verification in regard to armaments.

[95] At the time of writing, the International Court of Justice has not decided the Nicaragua-U.S. case. The positions of the two governments on the merits were indicated in the Court's Order of May 10, 1984, and more fully in Judge Schwebel's dissenting opinion. *See* Military and Paramilitary Activities in and against Nicaragua (Nicaragua v. U.S.), 1984 I.C.J. 169, 191-99 (Schwebel, J., dissenting).

[96] *Id.* at 191-92.

[97] *Id.* at 190-91, 193.

[98] *Id.* at 170-72 (majority opinion); *id.* at 193 (Schwebel, J., dissenting).

[99] *See* Aggression Resolution, *supra* note 24.

on the pretext of combating alleged illegal acts.[100] On the other hand, when armed guerrillas are supported by an outside state, the aggrieved state may reasonably view that outside state as the source of an armed attack even if the latter's armed forces are not directly engaged. The aggrieved state's only effective defense may be collective military action against the indirect aggressor. It does not seem unreasonable to interpret "armed attack" to cover the indirect but substantial support of military action directed against a government.[101] Accordingly it would not only be illegal for a state to finance insurgent movements or to allow its territory to be used for organizing and training armed opposition movements, but such tactics would open that state to an armed defensive action by or on behalf of the victim of the indirect aggression.

3. *Intervention in Civil Strife.* It is well established that a state acts illegally by sending armed forces or matériel to support an insurgency. If its action falls within the definition of armed attack, both the attacked state and its allies may employ armed defense against the intervening state. In short, counter-intervention in civil strife may be an exercise of collective self-defense.

These rules are universally accepted where the illegal intervention occurs on the side of the insurgency. In addition, many legal scholars (and some U.N. resolutions, by implication) support the proposition that direct or indirect armed intervention on *either* side in a civil war is illegal.[102] Under article 2(4) intervention constitutes a use of force "against the political independence" of the state in question because it interferes with its people's right to determine their own political destiny. Consequently, collective self-defense could allow a state to give military aid in a civil war if another foreign power is already giving military aid to the opposite side.[103]

On its view of the facts, Nicaragua could argue that these principles justify its "counter-intervention" in El Salvador. The U.S., which takes the position that the Sandinista regime has illegally intervened in El Salvador, could claim a collective self-de-

---

[100] *See* E. Hoyt, *supra* note 77, at 19 (discussing various covert interventions by the United States and the Soviet Union since World War II).

[101] *See* Resolution on Non-Intervention, *supra* note 41; *see also* LAW AND CIVIL WAR IN THE MODERN WORLD (J. Moore ed. 1974) (especially the essays by Moore and Bowett and the comments by Falk, Farer, and Sohn) [hereinafter cited as CIVIL WAR].

[102] *See* Resolution on Non-Intervention, *supra* note 41; *see also* Moore, *Toward an Applied Theory for the Regulation of Intervention,* and Bowett, *The Interrelation of Theories of Intervention and Self-Defense,* in CIVIL WAR, *supra* note 101, at 26, 41-46.

[103] *See* Schachter, *supra* note 5, at 1641-42.

fense right to attack Nicaragua, directly or indirectly. This issue may be decided by the International Court of Justice in the case now before the court.

This position on defensive counter-intervention ignores the ideological stamp of the regime or insurgency involved in the conflict. The principle is neutral as between democratic and nondemocratic governments. However, one commentator argues that counter-intervention should only be permitted on the side of a party (whether government or insurgency) that supports self-determination and popular rule.[104] In other words, counter-intervention based on collective self-defense should be in accord with the basic principles of the U.N. Charter and the Universal Declaration of Human Rights.[105] Thus, collective self-defense would have a moral legitimacy beyond its role as a sanction against a prior illicit intervention.

Under this view, the initial intervention remains illegal but counter-intervention would be permissible against a party that violates principles of self-rule and human rights. However, such a rule would be very imprecise in application. Most governments facing popular revolt violate those principles, and the insurgents invariably assert their democratic aims. Thus, aid to insurgents, while illicit in theory, could be freely rendered since it could not be countered with aid to the repressive government. Conversely, insurgencies may be labeled "totalitarian" by unsympathetic observers. If that occurred, aid to insurgents could be attacked as illegal even if it would otherwise be justified as a counter-intervention.

Adopting a standard based on the ideological position of a particular government or faction would create serious difficulties. Even the democracies of Europe often differ with the U.S. about the political tendency of any particular group. This indicates how difficult it would be to reach consensus on the legality of a counter-intervention. The problematic nature of the inquiry should encourage us to pause before adopting such a test.

   4. *Terrorism and the Taking of Hostages.* May a state whose nationals have been seized by terrorists and held as hostages, or threatened with death, use armed force to rescue them? This issue has been raised with increasing frequency as seizure of hostages becomes ever more the favorite tactic of terrorist groups. Generally speaking, a state has no right to invade a foreign state to rescue or

---

[104] Cutler, *supra* note 50, at 106-09.
[105] G.A. Res. 217, U.N. Doc. A/777 (1948).

protect its nationals who are considered to be held unlawfully by that state or by private persons.[106] This proposition also holds where a state fails to protect a foreign national from criminal acts or injuries by private persons in that country. A government may strongly protest a national's arbitrary detention or inhumane treatment in prison, but it must have recourse to available diplomatic and possibly judicial procedures. The government may also impose non-military sanctions on the state that shirked its obligations under international law.

In some situations, however, such as the Israeli hostages held at Entebbe Airport or the American hostages held in Tehran, when lives are in imminent danger, a good case exists for an exercise of self-defense through a rescue attempt.[107] Such attempts must be limited to the rescue and must not serve as a basis for political pressure or reprisal.

A more controversial question concerns a state's use of force to apprehend alleged terrorists who are within another state's jurisdiction or control. This issue was raised dramatically in 1985. Four U.S. military planes intercepted an Egyptian aircraft flying over the Mediterranean Sea, compelling it to change course and land in

---

[106] RESTATEMENT OF THE FOREIGN RELATIONS LAW OF THE UNITED STATES (REVISED) §§ 431-432 (Tentative Draft 1985).

[107] In both the Entebbe and Iranian situations, the hostages were seized and held as part of a political action against the state of their nationality. The attack on the individuals was clearly meant as an attack on their government. The territorial state was unwilling to rescue them and in fact supported the seizure. The hostages were believed to be in imminent peril of death. On the Israeli mission to free the hostages at Entebbe, see Boyle, *The Entebbe Hostages Crisis*, 22 INDIAN J. INT'L L. 199 (1982), and Paust, *Entebbe and Self-Help: The Israeli Response to Terrorism*, 2 FLETCHER FORUM 86 (1978).

On these facts, the U.S. representative at the U.N. Security Council debate advanced a legal justification for the Entebbe rescue action. He conceded that the rescue action violated Uganda's territorial integrity and would normally be illegal. But he went on to say:

> [T]here is a well-established right to use limited force for the protection of one's own nationals from an imminent threat of injury or death in a situation where the state in whose territory they are located either is unwilling or unable to protect them. The right, flowing from the right of self-defense, is limited to such use of force as is necessary and appropriate to protect threatened nationals from injury.

Statement of Ambassador Scranton, 1976 DIGEST OF UNITED STATES PRACTICE IN INTERNATIONAL LAW 150-51.

This statement follows from Sir Humphrey Waldock's 1952 formulation of principles on the use of force. *See* Waldock, *The Regulation of the Use of Force by Individual States in International Law*, 81 RECUEIL DES COURS 451, 467 (1952). The stringent conditions for intervention are as follows: The action must be for rescue and protection, not punitive reprisal, and it must not intervene beyond its necessity; an action legal in its inception would become illegal if prolonged or used for political pressure. *See* Schachter, *International Law in the Hostage Crisis: Implications for Future Cases*, in AMERICAN HOSTAGES IN IRAN 325 (P. Kreisberg ed. 1985); *see also* Schachter, *supra* note 5, at 1631-32 (discussing the Grenada incident).

Italy, so that the accused persons on board would be prosecuted for seizing an Italian vessel, taking hostages, and murdering an American passenger. The U.S. considered the action necessary because the alleged terrorists were presumably being taken to a destination where their offense would go unpunished.

Neither the President nor any senior U.S. official offered an explicit legal ground for the interception of the Egyptian plane.[108] The implicit premise of the U.S. action appeared to be that any state (or at least any specially affected state) could use force to obtain custody of terrorists when the state having control of them was unwilling or unable to bring them before a court of justice. No one referred at the time to the possible relevance of either Charter article 2(4) or of rules in civil aviation treaties prohibiting interceptions of civilian aircraft over the high seas.[109] The overriding consideration expressed by the President was that "there must be no asylum for terrorists or terrorism."[110]

It might have been argued that Egypt had violated a new (or nascent) international obligation of all states to prosecute accused terrorists or takers of hostages or to extradite them to countries where they would be subject to prosecution. But even if that proposition were sustainable on the law and facts, it does not follow that another state may use or threaten force against a civilian plane outside that state's jurisdiction. That situation is clearly distinct from the seizure of a "pirate ship or aircraft" (or a ship seized by pirates and under their control). In the latter case, as long as the vessel or aircraft is on the high seas or anywhere else outside every state's jurisdiction, any state may take such action and arrest the wrongdoers on board.[111] However, the fact that a state's vessel or plane is carrying "pirates" (or terrorists) and intends to release them does not transform the vessel or plane into a "pirate" ship or aircraft.

Strong public revulsion against terrorism has spurred increased demands for concerned states to deny all sanctuary to terrorists. Proposals have been made that the United States (and pre-

---

[108] *See Terrorists Seize Cruise Ship in Mediterranean*, 85 DEP'T ST. BULL. 74-81 (Dec. 1985).

[109] *See* Hailbronner, *Freedom of the Air and the Convention on the Law of the Sea*, 77 AM. J. INT'L L., 490, 513-19 (1983).

[110] White House Statement of October 9, 1985, *reprinted in* 85 DEP'T ST. BULL. 74 (Dec. 1985).

[111] U.N. Convention on the Law of the Sea, art. 105, U.N. Doc. A/CONF.62/122 (1982), *reprinted in* 21 I.L.M. 1261, 1289 (1981). This article repeats article 19 of the 1958 Convention on the High Seas and is declaratory of customary law.

sumably any capable state) be permitted to seize accused terrorists from within states which fail to bring them to justice. Moreover, under these proposals every state could determine unilaterally its right to take action against a person it believes guilty. This of course represents a radical departure from the basic rule of territorial sovereignty. Thus one can safely predict that states generally will reject these proposals.

Such far-reaching revision of the rules may not even be necessary. The existing framework of law provides a remedy in the international conventions dealing with offenses related to terrorism. Each state party to those conventions undertakes to treat a terrorist offense as a serious crime, and either to prosecute the offenders itself or to extradite them to a state that will prosecute them.[112] Obviously, these conventions do not solve the problem of non-cooperative states, and expecting such states to become parties to the conventions may be excessively hopeful. However, if the great majority of states become parties (as has happened in the cases of the conventions on hijacking and aerial sabotage), the pressures on a few recalcitrant states may prove effective. Underlying that assumption is the hope that states generally will perceive their common interest in punishing criminal acts that threaten all of them.

If these conventions prove ineffective, some countermeasures against the countries of refuge may be necessary. Suspension of air flights, trade and financial embargoes, and curtailment of travel rights are among the nonforcible measures available against a state which by support of or complicity with terrorists violates its international obligation toward all states.[113]

Recapitulation. In short, under existing law an armed attack is a basic condition of legitimate self-defense. That requirement may be reasonably construed to include both an imminent attack (as defined earlier) and indirect attacks. Unlawful acts that involve these uses of force, as well as direct attacks, give rise to the right to take forcible defensive action.

By and large, states profess adherence to the restrictive view

---

[112] *See, e.g.,* Convention for the Suppression of Unlawful Seizure of Aircraft (Hijacking), *opened for signature* Dec. 16, 1970, 22 U.S.T. 1641, T.I.A.S. No. 7192; International Convention Against the Taking of Hostages, G.A. Res. 34/146, U.N. Doc. A/C.6/34/L.23 (1979), *reprinted in* 1979 U.N. JURIDICAL Y.B. 124; *see also* Convention to Prevent and Punish Acts of Terrorism, *opened for signature* Feb. 2, 1971, 27 U.S.T. 3949, T.I.A.S. No. 8413 (adopted by the United States and six Latin American states in 1976).

[113] For example, see the recent U.N. General Assembly resolution on measures to prevent international terrorism, G.A. Res. 40/61, (Dec. 1985), and Security Council Resolution 579 (Dec. 1985) on international terrorism.

of self-defense. They do not resort to force—or claim the right to such recourse—merely because a state has violated customary law or, for example, a treaty pertaining to treatment of nationals. Even when a state is labeled an "outlaw" for its gross or continuing breaches of clear rules of law, aggrieved states rarely assert a right to use force unilaterally, except in response to a prior use of force. Underlying this manifest reluctance of the community of states to legitimate forcible self-help is the conclusion, based on historical experience, that individual use of force is more likely in the end to jeopardize than to support the effort to obtain effective law.

IV. JUSTIFICATION OF FORCE FOR HIGHER ENDS

The comments just made apply also to suggestions that individual states should be permitted to use force to achieve major political or moral ends.[114] These suggestions fall within the conception of "just war" and resemble some of the classical efforts to place the legality of war on a moral plane.[115] There are several variants of this general attitude but one is of particular interest today. It would allow force to be used when necessary to achieve self-determination, whether that involves freedom from foreign domination or freedom from repressive and tyrannical government.[116] This position, it is interesting to observe, was once taken by spokesmen for newly independent and Third World states. They argued that wars of national liberation were not only legal under international law (a point generally conceded), but that other states had a right and even a duty to use force to assist the liberation effort.[117] Western states contested this argument as violating the basic norms of non-intervention and non-use of force.[118] More recently, U.S. writers who tend to be identified with conservative opinion have asserted that democratic states are entitled to use armed force to overthrow tyranny elsewhere and to bring about popular democratic rule.[119]

---

[114] *See* J. STONE, *supra* note 36.

[115] *See, e.g.,* W. O'BRIEN, *supra* note 62, at 13-35; WAR, MORALITY AND THE MILITARY PROFESSION, *supra* note 62, at 237-487.

[116] *See* Reisman, *Coercion and Self-Determination: Construing Charter Article 2(4),* 78 AM. J. INT'L L. 642 (1984).

[117] *See, e.g.,* Firmage, *The "War of National Liberation" and the Third World,* in CIVIL WAR, *supra* note 101, at 317-23 (discussing Soviet and Chinese statements to this effect); *see also* Cohen, *China and Intervention: Theory and Practice, id.* at 376; Butler, *Soviet Attitudes Toward Intervention, id.* at 380-98.

[118] *See, e.g.,* Schwebel, *supra* note 39, at 483-86.

[119] *See, e.g.,* Will, *The Perils of Legality,* NEWSWEEK, Feb. 27, 1984, at 84

One international law scholar has declared that article 2(4) of the Charter is only a "means," which must yield to the higher purpose of self-rule. Self-determination in his view is the "key postulate of political legitimacy in the 20th century."[120] A similar position has been articulated in the U.S. by commentators who supported the U.S. military action in Grenada. They assert that such action was legitimate because it was aimed at overthrowing a repressive government and bringing about democracy and freedom. Although this was not one of the stated legal justifications put forward by the U.S. government, many have considered it the real and better reason.[121] Similar contentions are being made in favor of taking military steps to overthrow the non-democratic regime in Nicaragua.

This argument clearly appeals to the widespread sentiment that repressive and tyrannical regimes should be overthrown and that in many cases this "higher end" warrants the use of force. Moral reasons, whether based on utilitarian-welfare premises or the inherent dignity of human persons, have been advanced in support of that sentiment.[122] From a legal standpoint, however, neither the U.N. Charter nor the extensive government commentary thereon supports an interpretation subordinating the basic prohibition against unilateral use of force to ends other than self-defense or U.N. enforcement action.

Significantly, except for some oratorical flourishes, the U.S. has never claimed a right to intervene forcibly to bring about democratic government. In regard to Vietnam and, currently, Nicaragua, the United States has justified its intervention as a necessary response to illegal use of force and therefore as justified under the collective defense provision of article 5.[123] In Grenada it presented other legal grounds but did not rely upon the right to introduce popular rule there or elsewhere.[124] Whatever the merits of these various grounds, it is noteworthy that the U.S. has not declared that Charter article 2(4) may be suspended or ignored in the inter-

---

("[I]nternational law . . . is an intramural code, useful among nations that share common values but not germane to dealings with totalitarian or gangster regimes."); *see also* Kristol, *International Law and International Lies*, Wall St. J., June 21, 1985, at 26, col. 4.

[120] Reisman, *supra* note 116, at 643.

[121] *See, e.g.*, Kristol, *supra* note 119, at 26, col. 4.

[122] *See* N. PODHORETZ, *supra* note 70, at 86-101.

[123] *See* Military and Paramilitary Activities in and Against Nicaragua (Nicar. v. U.S.), 1984 I.C.J. 169, 191-99 (Schwebel, J., dissenting) (presenting U.S. position on Nicaragua).

[124] For the list of justifications offered by the United States, see *supra* note 29 and accompanying text.

est of "higher" political goals. Nor for that matter has any other state.

The position of governments in this respect cannot be attributed to legalism or a desire to pay rhetorical deference to the Charter.[125] A more fundamental reason goes back to the point I stressed earlier—that it is incompatible with the concept of a pluralist society of independent states to allow states to attack each other in order to impose a particular form of government. It is no answer to this to maintain that force should be allowed only to bring about a goal, such as self-determination, which all states profess to accept. Nor is it an answer to say that the force used would be proportionate to the end. These justifications ignore the realities of a world deeply divided about the meaning of democracy and self-determination. Powerful states would be given a virtually unlimited right to overthrow governments alleged to be unresponsive to the "true" will of the people. One side's favored test of self-rule would not be acceptable to the other side. The weakness and politicization of collective institutions enhance the danger that ideological confrontation will turn into clashes of military force. Most responsible governments, I believe, recognize these dangers. They are not likely to "reinterpret" the Charter so as to increase those risks.

Conclusion

No one, it is safe to say, is satisfied with the present state of international law on the use of force. Only a raving optimist could expect a transformation in the foreseeable future to the system of enforceable law envisaged in the rhetoric of Nuremberg. We now realize that the bright line between aggression and defense, so clear in Nuremberg and Tokyo, can be blurred in conflicts over competing rights. Agreement on words, solemnly affirmed, has repeatedly dissolved under the pressure of divergent interests and perceptions. Neither governments nor their peoples are ready, by and large, to entrust their security and vital interest to foreign judges or international organs. The nation-state, whatever its deficiencies, represents for most peoples the primary source of identity and protection. The legacies of history and the long pre-civilized past have left a common "syndrome of parochialism"[126] in which distrust of

---

[125] *But see* D'Amato, *Nicaragua and International Law: The "Academic" and the "Real,"* 79 Am. J. Int'l L. 657, 662 (arguing that government justifications for interventions comport with academic versions of the law, even though their real reasons differ).

[126] Lasswell, *Introduction: Universality Versus Parochialism,* to M. McDougal & F.

strangers and expectations of violence contribute to a climate of mutual fear. In that climate armed defense, a felt necessity, carries with it the threat of offense. Clashes of interest or of ideology turn into covert or open tests of force. Rules of law are bound to appear fragile in the face of these realities.

Yet a stable society of sovereign states cannot exist if each is free to destroy the independence of another. Nor can we reasonably contemplate, in the present conditions of power, that either of the superpowers could impose its rule by coercion on the rest of the world or establish a condominium of shared authority over the globe. Their ruling elites are surely aware of the supreme risks to their survival in the event of a major clash of arms. The legal constraints on unilateral recourse to force reflect this reality. They are not solely the product of moral sentiment.

It is appropriate, of course, to point to the inadequacies of these constraints and the failures of the existing system. Perhaps it is time to "demand a miracle," as Richard Falk has suggested,[127] and call for a truly global community that transcends the state system. I do not minimize the value of a vision of world order that looks beyond the present reality. "In dreams begin responsibilities," and it is not too soon to undertake the responsibilities of moving toward the dream of a demilitarized cooperative world society. But it is dangerous to cite the inadequacies of the present system as reasons for abandoning the basic restraints on the use of force. Neither the failures of the U.N. nor the violations of its Charter can justify a "realpolitik" that would allow states once again to wage war freely. It is foolish and perilous to conclude that infringements by some have, under principles of reciprocity, freed all from a rule so fundamental and essential to a stable world order. "Tit for tat" responses may help sustain some international rules, but to apply this approach to the basic rule on force is a path to anarchy.

That basic rule, as I have sought to show, is not simply an abstraction viewed as an ideal. It has evolved into a reasonably coherent set of principles and precepts derived from the Charter and a network of agreements. Much still remains to be done, but when we look back to Nuremberg and San Francisco in 1945, it is striking how the abstract notions of that time have been made concrete to cope with situations barely envisaged then.

FELICIANO, *supra* note 83, at xxi.

[127] Falk, *The Quest for World Order: The Legacy of Optimism Re-Examined,* 9 DALHOUSIE L.J. 132, 148 (1984); *see also* RICHARD FALK, THE END OF WORLD ORDER 25-32 (1983).

This process has also helped to counteract states' self-serving unilateral interpretations of the rules. For along with more specific rules have come collective judgments made inside and outside of international institutions. The states that have recourse to force cannot escape these judgments. To be sure, a nonbinding condemnation or rebuke does not have the enforceability of a judicial decision in a national court. But that is not to say that such critical judgments are without effect. Censure carries with it political costs. Those costs are not trivial, as shown by the intense efforts of governments to avoid censure and to demonstrate the legitimacy of their conduct. At times unilateralism may be tempting, especially for powerful states. The International Court of Justice may be defied by non-appearance. The condemnation of the General Assembly may be passed off with a quip. But in the end such unilateralism is bound to exact a steep price, by making it impossible to maintain the rules of co-existence necessary to avoid catastrophe.

[11]

THE EXCEPTION OF SELF-DEFENCE IN U.N. PRACTICE

Jean Combacau

In the U.N. Charter, self-defence does not appear as the subject of an independent rule, formulated in Art. 51, but rather as an exception to another rule, that contained in Art. 2(4). Thus, before going on to examine the 'exception of self-defence' in U.N. practice, the fundamental characteristics of the system laid down by the Charter to regulate the use of force must be briefly recalled.

It had two sides to it. First, States renounce the right to use force in their mutual relations; this is Art. 2(4): 'all members shall refrain in their international relations from the threat or use of force against the territorial integrity or political independence of any State, or in any other manner inconsistent with the purposes of the U.N.' Under these circumstances the use of force becomes a delict, exactly as it is in national law. It is evident that this rule makes no sense unless, precisely as in national law, a centralized authority is given the exclusive right to use force in place of the individual against any of its subjects that infringe Art. 2(4). This is dealt with in Chapter VII of the Charter, especially Art. 42 and the following articles, which allow the S.C. to use force against unlawful force.

It is all very straightforward, then: on the one hand the individual State forfeits its right to use force and individual use of force becomes a delict, while on the other hand a collective power to use force in response to this delict is created and vested exclusively in the U.N. The U.N. might be expected to act in its own right as a body, that is, using forces of its own; since it has none, Art. 43 and the following articles provide for forces to be put at its disposal by the member States. In case of need these troops will act in the name of the Organization; any act of force they perform will be attributed to the U.N. alone and not to the individual States. The U.N. also has the possibility of using its members' forces in a less centralized manner: that is, it may simply set things in motion, leaving it to the member States to carry out military operations (under its control) against a State which has violated Art. 2(4). This is the meaning of Art. 53(1): 'The Security Council shall,

10

where appropriate, utilize such regional arrangements or agencies for enforcement action under its authority'; however, it immediately adds that 'no enforcement action shall be taken under regional arrangements or by regional authorities without the authorization of the Security Council'. The use of force here is slightly more decentralized than in the normal procedure, in that the U.N. authorizes States to use it, instead of doing so itself. Nevertheless, it still commands the use of force and this does not therefore constitute an exception to its monopoly. Whether under the terms of Chapter VII or of Art. 53, States take part in the execution of an act of force which is decided on by the S.C., and by it alone.

In this context, the space for self-defence can only be limited: in fact it has the same role as it has in systems of national law, where subjects maintain the right to resort to force in reply to force, only in so far as the authority which legally holds the monopoly of the use of force is unable to ensure respect for that monopoly, that is, to prevent the use of force by the attacker. This is exactly the meaning of Art. 51: 'Nothing in the present Charter shall impair the inherent right of individual or collective self-defence if an armed attack occurs against a Member of the United Nations, until the Security Council has taken measures necessary to maintain international peace and security.'

Thus all is clear, as the majority of authors who have dealt with this subject have stressed[1]: the use of force by a State is either a delict against which the U.N. must take action, or a lawful act, either because it is performed at the request (Art. 42 sq.) or at least with the authorization (Art. 53(1)) of the S.C., or because it is a reaction to a previous act of force and as such lawful until such a time as the S.C. decides on the question. The classification of different uses of force as lawful or unlawful is therefore central to the system of the Charter. The particular aim of the present article is to establish how, in the context of Art. 51 alone, U.N. practice has answered this question of classification, and if it has been able to specify the conditions necessary for the exception of self-defence to apply. To begin with I must say what is meant by U.N. practice: this research raises certain questions of method, which I shall now consider.

11

I. QUESTIONS OF METHOD

1. ANALYSIS OF U.N. PRACTICE: CONFLICTING APPROACHES

(a) Induction versus deduction

Art. 51 states a 'right', or, to be more exact, an exception to a legal obligation, and it is as the 'exception of self-defence' that we shall henceforward refer to this so-called right. Implicitly linked to the rule it derogates from, Art. 51 need say nothing about the content of the exception, which can be deduced without difficulty from the terms of Art. 2(4): it is evident that the use of force which the exception permits is the same as that which the rule forbids. The text only deals with the legal regulation of self-defence, that is the fundamental and procedural conditions necessary for the exception to be operative. The only procedural condition is clearly stated: the S.C. must be immediately notified of any measures taken. But the fundamental conditions, and this is where the problem lies, are not specified at all, only indirectly indicated in the first sentence of the article; a circumstance which gives rise to much theoretical speculation among commentators. The reference to self-defence being a 'natural' (in French) or 'inherent' (in English) right, raises the question of whether Art. 51 refers back to the state of international law before the Charter, or if it is to be read more narrowly in connection with the general ban laid down in Art. 2(4); the use of the words 'armed attack' leads to an association between the exception of self-defence and one of the situations contemplated by Art. 39 of the Charter and later clarified by Resolution A/3314 (XXIX) of 14th December 1974, and hence to the conclusion that the applicability of the exception is dependent on the existence of an aggression so defined; the references to the individual or collective nature of self-defence and to the action expected from the S.C. are also open to interpretations which seek to establish the legal conditions for the applicability of the exception. And in fact this is how a fair number of writers on self-defence in the system of the U.N. Charter proceed, even if they also deal with U.N. practice. As a method claiming to establish what U.N. practice is, this appears unsuitable, since it gives too much weight to the text of the Charter and too little to practice.

If one holds that the conditions necessary to bring the exception of self-defence into force are to be found in the Charter or, still more, in elements of law external to the Charter, subsequent U.N. practice loses all autonomy: it becomes impossible to evaluate it on its own merits in order to establish the logic behind it, if any, since, legally, individual acts applying a

12

rule must conform to that rule; they can, of course, make the rule clearer and more concrete, but they cannot go against it. Seen from this 'legalistic' point of view, the study of U.N. practice only serves to establish the conformity or otherwise of the day to day conduct of the U.N. with a model which is defined once and for all in a prior, superior rule. I have explained at length elsewere why I think this method inadequate and why it prevents one from appreciating legal practices as distinct objects[2]. Whenever the drafters of a legal rule choose to draft it without laying down guidelines for its application, delegating the task of applying and hence of interpreting it to political agents, they give these agents discretional power to decide what it means, and any *a priori* judgment on the part of juridical critics, who may have 'scientific' authority but are totally lacking in official legal competence, which aims to pinpoint an indeterminate notion, constitutes a usurpation of a political and legal function. All the theorists can do is take note of the successive interpretations of the rule made by those to whom this power was delegated, as revealed by their application of it, and induce the theory from this practice; that is, establish whether a general interpretation of a provision can be drawn from these individual cases, and if not, throw light on the different reasoning behind these decidedly incompatible applications of the rule. In short, they must proceed with applications of a prior law as they would with precedents, which they would try to put in some kind of order so as to establish the existence or otherwise of elements constituting a customary law.

This is how we must proceed with self-defence. Art. 51 delegates to the State which invokes the exception of self-defence on its own behalf, to the S.C. which judges whether the conditions are fulfilled or not, and to the other States affected by the question, the power, which is not exclusive or without appeal for any one of them, to qualify the factual circumstances and establish whether the requisite legal conditions exist to justify the use of force. Do the single decisions of these different agents make it possible to trace a coherent practice? This is the only question I shall ask here and I shall make no attempt – this, in my opinion, being outside the jurisdiction of legal criticism – to judge the conformity of this practice with a conventional or customary statement of these same conditions by a prior rule.

(b) Study of cases versus study of rules

Without abandoning the idea of a study centred on practice, could one not include, alongside the decisions made in response to specific cases, the general rules formulated since the Charter which are meant to clarify its provisions and which might contribute to a surer definition of the conditions for self-defence? There are two reasons against this.

13

The first, which is one of principle, is perhaps not conclusive in itself: in so far, as is generally said, as declaratory resolutions claim to be true interpretations of the Charter – a claim which is open to question, for reasons which cannot be gone into here – and hence to be incorporated into it and to assume the same legal value, they still only lay down potential rules to govern future conduct. Now that interests us here is not this law-making process, but the practical recognition by the U.N. and its members, of the existence, in real-life situations where force has actually been used, of the conditions laid down by the rules, whether that contained in Art. 51 or those which complete it. In the present research I am concerned with how the exception of self-defence is applied in practice and not with how it ought to be ideally, when enunciated by States drafting an *a priori* rule with the calm artificially ensured by its abstract formulation.

The second reason, although more contingent, is also more telling. It has to do with the content of the resolutions which are generally quoted to back up interpretations of Art. 51: principally Resolution A/3314 (XXIX), of 14th December 1974, already mentioned, which contains a definition of aggression, and Resolution A/2625 (XXV) of November 4th, 1970, on the principles of international law concerning friendly relations and cooperation between States, which is often referred to by writers on self-defence. But a distinction must be made at this point: if one examines the lengthy debates which preceded the adoption of these resolutions, certain interesting declarations are to be found, which perhaps reveal, even if in the abstract, the individual *opinio juris* of the States taking part[3]. But these were only preparatory debates, with no bearing on the position of the U.N. as such[4]. As regards the latter, it must be pointed out that the resolutions say nothing on the subject of self-defence; indeed they both avoid the subject. The first principle of the statement on friendly relations – the only one with any bearing on the present topic – merely restates Art. 2(4) in greater detail, and, as will be seen[5], the content of the ban it imposes does not permit a definition of the scope of the exception of self-defence, which the last paragraph of Resolution 2625 anyway expressly omits[6]. It would therefore be improper to infer from the list of actions forbidden by it anything about the situations in which Art. 51 gives the right to use armed force to the State against which these actions are directed. The same is true of the definition of aggression, which, as such an act is nowhere specified among the conditions for self-defence[7], is totally irrelevant to the establishment of these conditions; and this is what the resolution itself says[8].

Consequently, unlike some writers[9], I shall restrict this study of U.N. practice to the circumstances in which States or the U.N. have invoked the notion of self-defence in connection with events which have actually taken place, and not in general declarations of a normative nature, orientated towards future behaviour.

14

2. IDENTIFICATION OF RELEVANT PRACTICE

These choices dictate the method to be used to establish the *corpus* of practice which will be considered relevant: to determine whether a case is to be included, the only criterion must be that one of the parties involved has pleaded self-defence, however questionable this may seem from a theoretical point of view. Conversely, the commentator must not take the place of the legal agents by qualifying as an act of self-defence a use of force which seems to him to conform to the proper definition of such an act, but which none of the parties involved has qualified as such. Thus it is only by reference to their declarations that U.N. practice will be identified hereafter. But this research encounters two serious difficulties.

(a) Difficulties involved in identification

Infrequency of appeal to the exception of self-defence – The first arises from the fact that in many cases States using armed force have either given no legal justification for their infringement of Art. 2(4), or have based their actions on other exceptions than that of Art. 51. Rejecting the simple alternative according to which any use of force in international relations is either a delict or is legally justified because authorized by the S.C. or by Art. 51, they hold either that this text does not preclude the validity of other exceptions to the ban on the resort to force, or that developments since 1945 have rendered this original dichotomy null and void. Further mention will be made of this latter view, which to a large extent explains the obsolescence of self-defence (*infra,* III); what needs to be said at this stage is only that, because of the possibility of invoking other excuses when resorting to force, the body of precedent connected with self-defence leaves aside a large number of cases in which the question of the existence of a right to resort to force under the terms of Art. 51 could, and perhaps should, have been raised. It is here that the theorist tends to be tempted to requalify acts of force otherwise motivated (self-preservation, lawful reprisals, humanitarian intervention, etc.) in terms of self-defence. Nevertheless, apart from the fact that these are dealt with in other parts of the present volume, they cannot in any way constitute predecents, even negative ones, on the subject of self-defence; if self-defence is not invoked by the State using force, it is impossible to appreciate the significance of the U.N.'s reaction; whether it tolerates the action or condemns it, it is certainly contributing to practice regarding Art. 2(4), but not Art. 51. The initial invocation of the latter by the State which resorts to force is therefore an essential condition[10], without which a case will not be held to be a precedent in the present survey. But here we come up against the second difficulty, which is that the procedural condition laid down by Art. 51 is rarely respected.

Failure to respect the procedure of Art. 51 – By the terms of the Charter it is for the State which resorts to force, and initially only this State, to claim the right to do so on grounds of self-defence. This claim can of course be challenged by its adversary, by the U.N. or by some of its members; but at least as a first step, the State which uses force should declare unilaterally that it is doing so in the exercise of its right of self-defence, before a third party of a supposedly impartial kind, like the S.C., can pronounce on the case. This being so, one might imagine that every State which decided to use force would immediately try to legitimize this infringement of Art. 2(4) by appealing to the exception of Art. 51 and informing the S.C. of the measures it is taking; by doing so it would have little to lose, even if the S.C. had to reject its claim, since, whether the State notifies the Council of its action or not, the Council may on its own initiative set in motion the measures foreseen by Chapter VII against it. An examination of practice should therefore be straightforward: if all States which claim to be acting in self-defence go to the S.C., the records of the Council will give all the debates on this subject. It should therefore be sufficient to look through the eight volumes of the *Repertoire of Practice of the Security Council*, at least for the first thirty years (1945-74), to find all the occasions when the exception of self-defence was invoked, all the replies to these claims made by the State taking part in the debates, and all the decisions of the Council. From the latter, if consistent, one could infer by induction a rule on the conditions for the applicability of the exception of self-defence, as they result from U.N. practice.

The fact is, however, that when States claim to be acting in self-defence they only very rarely inform the S.C. of the measures they take, as Art. 51 says they should, and this failure affects the task of analysing U.N. practice on the subject. This appears when examining the two ways (both infrequently used) by which a State resorting to force might submit a plea of self-defence.

The procedure which Art. 51 most probably suggests is that the State should report the action undertaken to the Council in a special act referring to the exception of self-defence, presumably backed up by arguments aimed at establishing the existence of the requisite conditions. If this procedure were followed, the debate would be concerned principally with establishing whether these conditions existed in the case in point. The Council could either find that the conditions were present and on this legal footing undertake a collective action under the terms of Chapter VII, substituting itself for the individual State, whose action would now become superfluous; or else it could declare that the conditions were not present, in which case it would take action against the State which had used force under the cover of self-defence and violated Art. 2(4). Such a step has only been taken by Tunisia in the Sakiet-sidi-Youssef case in 1958[11], by the U.S. in the S.S. Maya-

16

guez case in 1975[12], in the Tabas raid case in 1980[13] and the air incident in
the Gulf of Sidra in 1981[14], and by the Chinese People's Republic at the time
of the South East Asia crisis in 1979[15].

But a second, less formal procedure would fit the rule equally well, without involving any special form of notification: the State which refers a complaint to the S.C. could submit its plea of self-defence either in its letter to
the President or during the course of the debate. Examples of this second
procedure are even rarer, however. Although Art. 51 intends the State
which claims to be acting in self-defence to refer the case to the S.C. so that
the latter may take collective action in place of its own individual action in
as short a time as possible, this State usually leaves the task of bringing the
situation to the notice of the Organization to its adversary or to friends of
the latter.

As a result, the question of self-defence is generally only raised at a later
stage, and then incidentally, and no longer as the central point at issue; accused of infringing the ban on force, the State pleads self-defence, but this
plea is only one of the elements in the debate and loses the central position
it should rightfully have. This makes it harder to appreciate to what extent
consideration of whether the conditions for the application of Art. 51 are
satisfied enters into the decision or absence of decision made by the S.C.
and the individual opinions given by its members.

(b) Overview of practices

With this reservation, we shall now carry out an overview of U.N. practice
as it emerges through application of Art. 51. Practice or practices? We must
in fact sort out the various occasions on which self-defence has been invoked
in one way or another, and divide them into two groups containing practices
of different types. In the first figure those where an organ of the U.N. has
pronounced on whether the action involving the use of force can be classed
as self-defence under Art. 51: the only precedents which can be attributed
to the U.N. are those cases where a resolution can be considered to confirm
or reject the exception of self-defence. The second group includes those
cases were no decision has been taken by the U.N., or no decision on this
particular point, but where during the debate, States have expressed their
opinions on the subject: the State which used force, the State against which
it was used, and the other member States taking part in the discussion.
These views are interesting and no doubt a useful contribution to a study of
the application of Art. 51, but they do not constitute U.N. practice. Whatever the political reasons behind its silence, and even if only the veto of one
of the permanent members has prevented the S.C. from pronouncing on the
subject, there is no decision of the Council vested with the authority which

such declarations have, both in themselves and as precedents contributing to the formation of customary rules of the Organization; the opinions expressed cannot be said to be anything more than *opiniones juris*, which by their nature are partial and mutually conflicting. The greater the majority in favour of them, the more political weight they will carry, but they will have no more legal weight than any other declaration made by the single members of a corporate body.

Practice attributable to the U.N.
The only cases then which can be taken as precedents constituting U.N. practice are those where the Council has been able to pass a resolution from which it emerges clearly, even if not explicitly, that the State invoking Art. 51 has acted lawfully or unlawfully. Up to now it has never pronounced a country invoking self-defence to be acting lawfully, and this is already a worrying indication of the difficulty of deriving a definition of lawful self-defence from U.N. practice. In a fairly small number of cases, which will now be run through, it has pronounced such an act to be unlawful.

In the first place, the Council has repeatedly though not consistently rejected pleas of self-defence made by Israel to justify incursions made either against military installations of neighbouring States, or against bases used by the Palestinian organizations to launch offensives against its territory or territory occupied by it: for instance, when it attacked Jordan in 1966[16] and 1969[17] and Lebanon in the same year[18], in 1970[19], 1972[20], 1973[21] and 1974[22]; another such case is that of the Israeli attack on Tamuz in Iraq in 1981 (destruction of the Osiraq nuclear reactor)[23]. These constitute a series of precedents which give some idea of the conditions in which self-defence may be exercised, although the issue is confused by the fact that on successive occasions, although Israel's arguments remained the same, its reaction was incomparably more severe, and yet the resolutions adopted[24] do not contain any express condemnation. Even if this makes them less interesting, this does not mean that these cases need be excluded from the body of precedent listed here.

In the second place, self-defence is or has sometimes been invoked in Africa by colonial States (Portugal) and perhaps by South Africa, in the attempt to justify acts of force against rebels based in the territory of their neighbours, and resolutions have been passed in sufficiently clear terms to be seen as rejections of the plea of self-defence. For example Portugal pleaded self-defence in reply to a complaint made by Senegal in 1969 and was nevertheless condemned by the S.C.[25]. But it is more usual here for States using force to justify their action by claiming the right to substitute their neighbour in view of the latter's incapacity to ensure respect for their rights in its territory. Of course Israel does the same, but if, unlike Israel, a State fails to back up its claim to a right of substitution with a plea of self-de-

18

fence, its action cannot be held to constitute a precedent which will contribute to a definition of the latter. This explains why one cannot for example
include the case of Portugal's incursion on Zambian territory in 1969, although essentially the same as the case just mentioned[26]. As regards South
Africa's frequent actions of this kind, which are regularly condemned by the,
S.C., these cannot be taken as precedents relevant to Art. 51 since they are
not expressly based on it. South Africa has sometimes denied that the attack
took place[27] and has sometimes claimed the right to protect itself without
linking this claim to the specific plea of self-defence[28]; most frequently, however, the S.C. has not even heard the South African point of view and its
condemnations are therefore strictly without relevance to the present research since they cannot bear witness to the rejection of a plea of self-defence which never had the chance to be heard.

Except in these two groups of cases, where the kind of State invoking
self-defence has made it possible, given the political balance inside the
U.N., for the S.C. to make clearcut decisions, at least in certain circumstances, the Council has only pronounced on a very small number of cases
and always negatively. Despite the allegations of the States concerned, neither the measures taken by Egypt in 1951 to prevent the passage through
the Canal of merchandise bound for Israel[29], nor the British attack on the
Yemen carried out in 1964 at the request of the Southern Arabian Federation[30] were considered lawful by reference to Art. 51. In addition, as an example of the G.A.'s very small contribution to U.N. practice on this subject,
one can list its explicit rejection of the plea of self-defence invoked by the
Soviet Union to justify its intervention in Afghanistan in 1980[31].

This is the entire extent of the practice attributable to the U.N.; we must
now turn to State practice to eke out, though not a great deal, the *corpus* of
precedents available.

State practice inside the U.N.
This second group of precedents, the more limited authority of which has already been mentioned, is composed of the declarations made by States invoking self-defence and the States against which they claim to be defending
themselves, as well as the views of other States on the subject, expressed either individually during the course of the S.C. debate, or collectively, by
support to a draft resolution on the question, not actually adopted by the
Council. This last point calls for a brief explanation.

Draft resolutions ruling on the lawfulness of resort to force the States
which have invoked the exception of self-defence are sometimes rejected
because they fail to obtain the majority required by Art. 27(3): as was the
case when the Warsaw pact countries moved into Czechoslovakia in the
name of collective self-defence in 1968[32]. Adoption of the draft resolution
presented by several Western States, para. 2 of which 'condemn(ed) the

armed intervention of the U.S.S.R. and other members of the Warsaw Pact [...]'[33], even if it did not touch directly on the justification put forward by the Soviet Union, could have been considered as a U.N. precedent establishing that an intervention of this kind did not constitute self-defence. However, only ten votes were cast in favour of the motion, with two against (one that of the Soviet Union itself) and three abstentions[34]. It was therefore rejected and cannot strictly speaking do any more than testify to an opinion, held it is true by a majority of States in the S.C., but attributable only to these States and not to the U.N. The same conclusion is reached if draft resolutions are presented to the S.C. which do not pronounce on the lawfulness of resort to force of the kind considered, as happened at the beginning of the 'Six Day War' in 1967[35]; or if the Council adjourns without a resolution being put to the vote, as in the Gulf of Tonkin case in 1964[36]; or finally of course if the question has never been discussed by the S.C., in spite of its being notified as required by Art. 51, as in the incidents already mentioned between the U.S. and Cambodia (Mayaguez affair, 1975[37]) and Lybia (Gulf of Sidra, 1981[38]).

Looking beyond the few cases where a S.C. resolution has pronounced on the validity of a plea of self-defence, one might expect to find a large number of other cases where appeals to Art. 51 have been made. Curiously enough, if we leave on one side a certain number of brief references, more verbal than otherwise, we find very little trace of it in S.C. practice. We have already mentioned the reference made to it at different stages in the Arab-Israeli conflict, especially in the last twenty years, with the escalation of Israeli incursions against Palestinian bases abroad[39]. Apart from these, the *Repertoire of Practice* between 1945 and 1958 contains no really significant plea of self-defence under Art. 51; which is surprising if one thinks of the number of times it could have been invoked and when, according to the Charter, it constituted the only possible justification for military action. But even since then, debates on this subject have been much less numerous than infringements of the rule laid down by Art. 2(4); they took place in the following cases, in chronological order: the Franco-Tunisian incident of 1958[40] and the Lebanese crisis of the same year[41]; the new dispute between France and Tunisia in 1961[42]; the above-mentioned Gulf of Tonkin case of 1964[43]; an episode in the war between India and Pakistan over Kashmir in 1965[44]; the intervention in Czechoslovakia of the Warsaw Pact countries in 1968[45]; the frontier conflicts between China and Vietnam in 1979[46]; and few incidents which came to nothing because not discussed by the S.C., in spite of their being reported to the Council by the U.S. (incidents involving Cambodia and Libya and the Tabas raid[47]); and finally the reciprocal accusations made by the U.K. and Argentina over the Malvinas (Falklands) dispute in 1982[48].

It is therefore to this twofold body of practice – that of the U.N. and that

20

of the States within it – that we must turn to establish the conditions under which States may use force lawfully in self-defence, as these can be seen from the application of Art. 51 by the U.N.

II. CONDITIONS FOR APPLICABILITY OF THE EXCEPTION OF SELF-DEFENCE

There is no essential difference between the means used by a State in self-defence and those deployed by the aggressor, such as to make it possible to characterize an operation of self-defence by its content; it is therefore necessary to look elsewhere for the criteria which distinguish an unlawful attack from lawful defence. They can be found in the grounds for the State's use of armed force and its aim: its grounds are the legal reasons it can put forward to justify its action; its aim, what it can lawfully hope to achieve when it resorts to force. U. N. practice does not help to clear up the uncertainties present in Art. 51 on either of these points.

1. LEGAL GROUNDS FOR SELF-DEFENCE

An action in self-defence is in fact a reaction, State B's response to State A's acts, and these are its legal justification; this will be the first point. I shall then proceed to enquire into the nature of these acts: what does Art. 51 mean by 'armed attack' and is this the only possible justification for an act of self-defence?

a) Self-defence as a response

If there is a common element in the arguments which States use to justify their military actions, it is that they have been driven to them by a prior action taken by the State against which they are now using force: nothing now appears less admissible than to be the first to use force, and they always point to some act on the part of the other State which has led them to take this extreme step. It would seem that nothing could be easier than to determine, when confronted with two acts of the same nature attributable to two States, which is lawful and which is not. All that need be done is to establish the facts of the case and state which came first and which second. In practice, however, things are not so simple, because it is often hard to decide what the first unlawful act was.

First, it is not unusual for each of the States in question to accuse the other of being the first to use force and to claim this as its motive for responding in kind, only lawfully in its case. Now it is not always easy, going back along the chain of successive provocations, to establish which State started the process. For example, when in 1951 Egypt claimed to be acting in self-defence to justify its closure of the Suez canal to merchandise bound for Israel, the objection was made that the claim did not tally with the facts. Despite the state of war between the two States, there had been no effective hostilities for two and a half years[49], and at that distance in time, Israel's previous acts had lost any justificatory force they might have had; hence the rejection of Egypt's claim by the S. C.[50]. This was a straightforward case, but there are some where hostile acts on one side and the other are much harder to qualify. In 1961 France launched an armed attack against the city of Bizerte, pointing as justification to previous acts of aggression on the part of Tunisia against the base where French troops were stationed under the terms of a convention between the two States. On this occasion both parties claimed the right of self-defence against the other's aggression, and the S. C. was unable – and apparently did not even try – to decide which was responsible for making the first and, under the terms of Art. 51, only unlawful move[51]. Similarly, at various stages of the Kashmir conflict between India and Pakistan, the antagonists exchanged accusations, each claiming that its actions were defensive operations in reply to the other's offensive, and the Council came to no conclusion as to which was responsible for the initial act of aggression[52]. In fact, unless, in an escalating series of acts going from the insignificant local action of a nervous NCO to a full-scale army offensive, we can pick out the one which oversteps the bounds of legality, it will almost always be possible for one State to see in the previous conduct of the other party an antecedent which justifies its own.

If, on the other hand, the Council does not follow the logic of the Charter and determine after the event the circumstances which justified the use of force as a response, this initial failure will have repercussions on all later developments. This is what happens in situations of longstanding hostilities, as distinct from individual acts of force, when there is an unceasing exchange of military operations. The exception of self-defence, which if accepted as valid, would legalize once and for all all the initiatives taken to repulse the adversary by the State making it, until such a time as the Council took over from it, is instead invoked to justify each single military operation coming within the scope of the general action. No doubt it is understandable, for example, that the United Arab Republic should have pleaded self-defence in October 1967 to justify the sinking of an Israeli ship which had itself attacked its ships[53]; in such cases the violation of a ceasefire makes the violator a new 'aggressor' under the terms of Art. 51. But how can we explain the repeated appeals made by the U.K. to Art. 51 in the different phases of the reconquest of the Malvinas/Falklands[54]? Either the operation was lawful in its entirety as a response to the Argentinian attack and therefore each op-

22

eration was a lawful use of force in so far as it furthered the overall aim of driving out the aggressor; or else it was not, in which case partial military operations such as an attack on an Argentinian ship could not be justified in the name of 'partial' self-defence.

(b) Justifications for reaction: 1. Armed attack

Having admitted that an act of self-defence must necessarily be a response to another act, it remains to determine what kind of act this will be. Art. 51 talks of 'armed attack', but does not define the notion in any way; does U. N. practice throw any light on it?

As these words do not figure elsewhere in the Charter, it was tempting to link them with two other notions: aggression, which Art. 39 deals with, and the use of force, which is the subject of Art. 2(4). These could be helpful references, since, unlike armed attack, both have been dealt with in more recent developments of the rules: Resolutions A/3314 and A/2625 respectively. Now if one admitted that armed attack as in Art. 51 was the same thing either as 'aggression' or 'use of force' as defined in these resolutions, this would mean a considerable extension of the grounds for self-defence, because they refer to forbidden uses of force not covered by the concept of armed attack. Aggression is defined to include not only armed attack carried out by one State on another, but also acts which involve the deployment of force but not necessarily its use (blockade), and conduct which is at times close to complicity: that is, when one State allows its territory to be used by third parties as a base for their aggressive operations[55]. In the same way Resolution 2625 prohibits among other things the use of force to 'violate international lines of demarcation' (and not only the frontiers of a State's own territory) and the organization, or even mere encouragement of forces which have the aim of making incursions on the territory of another State[56]. U. N. practice has not taken a clear stand on this broad interpretation; those who hold that it has expressly rejected it lay great emphasis on the debates which preceded the adoption of the two important resolutions just mentioned[57], but do not in fact quote anything but individual declarations of States, whose point of view is not directly reflected in the texts eventually approved, which did not anyway aim to define the terms of Art. 51, but those of Arts. 2(4) and 39.

It remains to be determined whether we can find an interpretation of the words 'armed attack', taken strictly within the context of Art. 51, in the application of the Charter. It will not be possible to establish what in U. N. practice constitutes an armed attack under the terms of this article, unless one can find resolutions pronouncing on the lawfulness of a reaction of alleged self-defence and basing this decision directly on the fact that the use of

23

force by the other State does or does not constitute 'armed attack'. Well, there are no such resolutions. Portugal, for example, was condemned by resolutions of the Council in 1969 for military actions carried out in Senegalese[58] and Zambian[59] territory, having on both occasions invoked Art. 51. This certainly signifies that the Council rejected Portugal's justification for its action, especially as it quoted Art. 2(4), but it did not directly say that the actions of which Portugal had complained (actions taken in Angola and Guinea-Bissau by rebels based in neighbouring States) did not constitute armed attack, and this reason was not put forward clearly in the debates either. This being the case, the reference to Art. 2(4) might have any number of meanings and it is not possible to state for sure that the grounds for Portugal's condemnation were that it had not been defending itself against an 'armed attack'. The same year, when the Council condemned the Israeli attacks on Jordan and Lebanon[60], it did so in spite of the fact that Israel claimed the right to defend itself against the Palestinian terrorists based in these two countries. Nothing in the debates, however, or in the text of the resolution, makes it possible to conclude that in the eyes of the Council or its members the acts against which Israel was reacting did not constitute armed attack. As in the case involving Portugal, one could just as logically infer that Israel's reaction was one of self-help, condemned as such by international law, but on different grounds, even if what it was responding to was in fact armed attack.

The infrequency of precedents, their heterogeneity and the fact, above all, that condemnations of States' reactions are dictated by a multitude of motives, among which a critical analysis of the debates and resolutions cannot permit the inclusion of what in the last resort is the only decisive one, make it impossible to find a definition of armed attack under the terms of Art. 51 either in U. N. practice or in that of its members. This notion remains as indeterminate legally as it was when the Charter was drawn up, and can be freely construed case by case by its authorized interpreters.

(c) Justifications for reaction: 2. Acts not involving the use of force

Another problem is to know whether circumstances other than armed attack (whatever this means) can justify a reaction of self-defence. The point at issue here is no longer, as in the previous section, the nature or degree of the use of force by A against B which legitimizes B's reaction, but the question of whether B may respond with force against conduct on the part of A which may be unlawful but which does not involve the use of force. This question has many sides to it: can force be used to protect collective interests (humanitarian intervention[63]) or the rights of the State which uses it (in particular the protection of nationals abroad[64]? We shall leave on one side the

24

topics which will be dealt with in their own right in other parts of this volume, and will only consider one of them: can a State resort to force in anticipation of an armed attack and be said to exercise a 'right of anticipatory self-defence'? In other words, can a State find justification for its present armed action in previous acts of the potential adversary, even if the latter has not used force? Here the use of force is no longer taken to constitute a qualitative change in the nature of the relationship between the two States; it simply constitutes a change in degree, one step more in the escalation of means employed by the opposing sides, the taking of which is motivated by the taking of the preceding step by the other party; the use of force ceases to be the first act of a kind and simply becomes one step in a uniform process. Nothing in Art. 51 seems to justify this claim from a legal point of view: 'if an armed attack occurs' it says, and, by definition, prevention consists precisely in not letting the thing occur. However, it has been argued, chiefly by those who see Art. 51 as the symmetrical counterpart of Art. 2(4), that a State cannot wait peacefully for its potential adversary to be ready to launch military operations, leaving it to prepare an offensive and benefit from the considerable military advantage represented by the choice of timing: the 'threat of force', so the argument goes, is forbidden by Art. 2(4) and consequently Art. 51 should be interpreted in such a way as to permit acts of self-defence in situations of this kind. The argument is chiefly resorted to in connection with nuclear war, in view of the vital importance in this type of warfare of striking the first blow, as will be seen later[65]. Leaving this specific use on one side for the moment, does U. N. practice confirm the above view?

Although limited, it is more explicit here than in the preceding cases, and perhaps authorizes a negative answer. Leaving aside the precedents which are sometimes referred to, the relevance and bearing of which are limited[66], we shall concentrate on two cases and see what conclusion these lead to. At the time of the Arab-Israeli war in 1967 Israel used the plea of self-defence, seeing in the closure of the Gulf of Aaba, the Egyptian decision to require the withdrawal of the U. N. E. F., and the deployment of Arab troops, sufficient evidence that an act of aggression was imminent to justify a preventive attack on its part[67]. Opposed by the U. A. R.[68], this view was not given a hearing by the S. C. and its members and we can therefore deduce nothing from this phase of the affair; repeated before the G. A.[69], it aroused few signs of interest, all of which were negative[70]. The recent case of the destruction of the nuclear reactor at Osiraq[71] by the Israeli air force appears to be more conclusive. The S. C.'s clear and unanimous condemnation of this military attack, accompanied as it was most unusually by a statement of Iraq's right to 'appropriate reparations'[72], can be interpreted, taking account of the debate that went before it, as a firm denial of the existence of a right of anticipatory self-defence. We must make a further clarification, however:

was the Council rejecting the notion of anticipatory self-defence as such, or was it – as seems more likely – condemning its use in circumstances in which conditions of imminent danger were not present – this is what the debate was largely concerned with – or even any threat at all[73]? It is possible to see the resolution, not so much as a global rejection of the notion of anticipatory self-defence, but as a casuistic contribution to the determination of the situations in which self-defence might be used pre-emptively. Certainly no legal régime of anticipatory self-defence can be inferred from such a limited and equivocal body of precedent.

This statement can be generalized: U. N. practice on Art. 51, composed as it is of scanty, vague and contradictory elements, says nothing, or at least nothing clear, about the grounds for self-defence. Perhaps it will be less disappointing on the subject of its aim.

2. LEGAL AIMS OF SELF-DEFENCE

Admitting that State B can justify the use of force against State A by a previous act on the part of State A involving the use of force, does international law place any limit on the aims it intends to achieve? If in particular self-defence cannot legally have any aim other than to repulse the assailant, this must be considered as the only criterion for judging the lawfulness of measures which claim to be performed in self-defence; and a use of force, even if correctly motivated, would be unlawful if its purpose were different, and especially if it appeared as a means of law enforcement. Can a State submit a plea of self-defence when it has resorted to arms either to restore its right which another State has violated by itself infringing the rule laid down by Art. 2(4), or else to force it to perform its obligation with its own means but under pressure of an act of coercion?

(a) Self-defence and self-help

A distinguished expert on this problem has brilliantly upheld the view that self-defence could cover certain uses of force in reply to acts which have harmed a State's rights; the State's aim would be to substitute the other State and restore these rights itself[74]. In the present study we do not intend to compare self-defence with self-help in general, because a large number of acts of self-help are reactions to conduct which is claimed to be unlawful, but which does not involve force, and would in any case be excluded from the category of acts of self-defence by application of the criterion of motive. The only type of case relevant here is that in which State B claims to be using force in self-defence to reestablish for itself a state of affairs to which it

26

had a right and which has been modified by an unlawful use of force on the part of State A. Two series of cases can be taken as illustrations of this sort of situation in U. N. practice.

In the first, a State complains of armed attacks on its territory coming from that of a neighbouring State, not carried out by the latter's army, but by members of a liberation movement based in that country, whether the State in question tolerates or even encourages these actions or is simply unable to prevent them. This is the kind of situation we have already examined[75], that has led Israel, Portugal and South Africa to carry out so many retaliatory actions in the territory of neighbouring States. It should not be confused with the reaction of a State complaining of infiltration in its territory of armed elements hostile to its government, working on behalf of another State which is trying to 'destabilize' it[76]; such a State generally appeals for the intervention of an ally, on its own territory in this case, in the name of 'collective self-defence': this case of 'indirect aggression' has been excluded from the present study[77]. On the other hand, in the former hypothesis, it is not impossible to describe as an act of self-defence an operation whereby the State which is the victim of external attack replies with a counter-attack in foreign territory on the bases from which the original attack was launched. At the same time this would also be self-help because the State would be taking the place of the other State which is failing in its obligation to prevent its territory being used for the preparation and execution of acts which are hostile to a foreign State.

Has the U. N. admitted that the exception of self-defence covers such actions of self-help? It is hard to say: the repeated condemnations of Israel and South Africa in the cases examined earlier would seem to lead to the conclusion that the answer is no, but these condemnations were due, above all, to the extent of the countermeasures, considered excessive, and their delay, which qualified them as reprisals and as such to be condemned (*infra,* b). Moreover, the initial attack in all these cases came from liberation movements, whose struggle is considered legitimate by its very nature, which according to the current state of ideology in the U. N., renders any retaliatory use of force unlawful. Lacking any less ambiguous precedent, it is not certain that an action which was truly proportionate and carried out immediately in reply to an attack would be considered incompatible with the conditions for exercise of self-defence; this would mean that force could be used in retaliation in the territory of another State, even in the absence of an armed attack attributable to that State.

The second possibility is fairly similar and is that of incursions made by B on A's territory, to liberate persons, nationals or otherwise, who are held there irregularly, either by the State or by groups of persons unconnected with it. Cases of this kind have been on the increase, and occur most frequently when planes are hijacked and stay for long periods of time in countries the government of which cannot or will not attempt to free the passengers being kept as hostages; the questions they raise are connected with the problem of the protection of nationals abroad, which will not be dealt with here[78]. U.N. practice on this subject is anyway very slight and inconclusive: on several occasions action to free the hostages has been requested or acquiesced in by the host State, which completely changes the perspectives. As for those cases which can be presented as uses of force coming regularly under the ban of Art. 2(4), it does not appear that the action to which they are a response can be called an 'armed attack' in the sense of Art. 51, since it is not directed against the territory or the forces of the State which retaliates, and is not attributable to the State against which the latter retaliates; consequently they do not appear to qualify as self-defence by the sole criterion of their legal grounds. Nevertheless, in both the Entebbe and Tabas incidents reference was made to Art. 51, either by the State which claimed to be acting within its context[79] or by other States rejecting this claim[80]: conflicting positions, then, which were not settled by a S.C. decision[81].

(b) Self-defence and coercive sanctions (reprisals)

Finally, by looking at their aims, we can distinguish self-defence from coercive pressure, the most common form of which are reprisals. Unlike in the case of self-help, the State which carries out reprisals does not tend to substitute itself for the other State which is failing in the execution of an obligation, but to dissuade it, by a 'punitive' action, either from persisting in this failure or from reverting to it in the future; the aim is therefore entirely foreign to that of self-defence. The S.C. has on more than one occasion had to do with cases of reprisals involving the use of armed force, which are justified by their perpetrators as acts of self-defence: in particular the U.K. action against the Yemen in 1964[82], the Gulf of Tonkin episode between the U.S. and Vietnam in the same year[83] and, of course, the many Israeli incursions into the territory of its neighbours[84]: Syria in 1964[85] and 1966[86], Jordan in 1966[87] and 1969[88], Lebanon in 1969[89] and 1970[90]. S.C. practice in these affairs can be seen on the whole to confirm the existence of a distinction between reprisals and self-defence, and to clearly condemn all retaliatory use of force which by its aim can be classified as a reprisal.

The first of these episodes is perhaps the most typical example: in 1964, the Southern Arabian Federation, which had military agreements with the U.K., complained of an armed attack by the Yemen consisting of a 'series of aggressions'; at its request the U.K. launched an air attack and destroyed a fort. The S.A.F. and the U.K. invoked collective self-defence, claiming that the British action was intervention solicited from an ally by a State without military means, under the terms of Art. 51[91]. The S.C. did not accept this

28

reasoning. It did not of course condemn the U.K. which, being a perma-
ment member, would have vetoed the adoption of a resolution along these
lines; but it declared that it 'condemn(ed) reprisals as incompatible with the
principles and purposes of the U.N.'[92]: an abstract proposition, certainly,
but which, taken along with the fact that the British military action was deplored, evidences the clear intention of labelling this action as a reprisal.
Consequently, the British plea of self-defence was rejected.

The reason for this came out clearly in the debate, and was twofold: the
disproportionate nature of the reaction and the long delay between the initial use of force and the response. An excessive reaction[93] is characteristic of
the will to punish; the theory of reprisals recognizes the need for proportionality but admits that the response may be stronger than the original attack because the adequacy of a penal sanction is not measured by the harm
suffered by the victim but by its capacity to deter potential offenders. In
self-defence, on the other hand, there is no question either of preventing future delicts or of punishing present offenders, but only of stopping them,
and the proportionality of the reaction is assessed with regard to this end:
are countermeasures, whether proportional to the initial attack or not, necessary to repulse it? This question leads on to the second criterion, that the
reaction must follow the original attack without delay. In the Yemen dispute, some members of the Council pointed out that the British reaction had
been given 'long consideration'[94], which gave it the character of a 'punitive
expedition'[95], more typical of reprisals (and incidentally of self-help, in so
far as it was a case of destroying a base which would otherwise be used for
future attacks) than of self-defence.

These two criteria (want of proportion[96] and delay[97]) have been associated
in U.N. practice each time that a use of armed force, presented as an act of
self-defence by the State concerned, has been labelled, either by the Council or by some of its members, as a reprisal; for example whenever Israel has
been condemned for acts which were self-defence in its opinion, but reprisals according to the majority of the Council. In the 1966 incident with Jordan[98], its reaction was described as a 'large-scale and carefully planned military action'; in those involving Jordan[99] and Lebanon[100] in 1969 as a
'premeditated attack', and when it intervened in Lebanon in 1970[101] as a
'premeditated military action'. The word 'premeditated' is the key to the
S.C.'s firmly held conviction: that when the victim of the original use of
force does not only retaliate while the adversary's attack is taking place, but
prepares a further retaliation to take place at a later stage after the withdrawal of the attacking force, he goes beyond the limits of self-defence and
takes on himself the function of repression which belongs to no one but the
U.N.

From this narrowly filtered practice only limited conclusions can be
drawn, which do not make the conditions for access to self-defence that Art.

51 left unspecified any clearer; it says almost nothing certain about how to define those acts to which a State may lawfully reply by force, and not a great deal on the manner in which it may do so, except to specify that it must try to repulse its adversary, not punish him. Some may attribute this relative failure to the method used – which could be judged excessively critical – to select the precedents which are taken as evidence of U.N. practice; but this method seemed to be essential for the assessment of what the member States as a whole really agree on in practice, as distinct from what they may say in abstract normative declarations, and what they are ready to do to obtain respect for the ban on the use of force. No doubt this answer is somewhat frustrating if compared to the claims of some authors who have made a more easy-going assessment of U.N. practice, which permits them to see in it their own ideal vision of an efficient regulation of the use of force instead of the true picture of how the use of force is actually regulated by the U.N.

III. SELF-DEFENCE IN THE U.N. SYSTEM:
THE COGS AND THE MACHINE

Already disappointing from this first point of view, the enquiry has so far only dealt with the conditions under which the exception of self-defence comes into operation, and has left on one side the modalities of its application (except in so far as these can be deduced from its aim). We have not commented on the part of Art. 51, essential as it is, which specifies that the individual action of the State may continue 'until the Security Council has taken measures necessary to maintain international peace and security' and speaks of the 'authority and responsibility' of the Council to take over from it. This is because the aim was not to study the written rules, but to examine U.N. practice, which is more or less non-existent on this point[102]. This silence is perfectly comprehensible if we recall that, with few exceptions, the S.C. has never had situations of this kind referred to it by the State using force and putting forward Art. 51 as its justification, but always by the State under attack (or by its allies), which are not interested in this question[103]. This being the case, the problem of the S.C. standing in for the State which has been unlawfully attacked, that is, of the Council taking back its exclusive right to use force which it had temporarily lost, has never arisen. If the Council acts, it does not do so in the place of the State which could have invoked Art. 51 (but did not do so), but always against the State which invokes it wrongfully: not having been applied at the time of the individual State's use of force, Art. 51 cannot then come into its own to put an end to it.

More generally, one cannot fail to be surprised by the small number of

30

cases in which the exception of self-defence has been invoked before the
U.N.: the practice found by authors who have studied the phenomenon is
exiguous if compared to the number of times force has been used in international relations since 1945. With exceptions, self-defence has not been put
forward as a justification, even informally, except in secondary incidents,
episodes in longstanding conflicts, which, when they started, did not give
rise to any real questioning with regard to Art. 51 (the Vietnam war, the
Arab-Israeli conflict, now the war between Iran and Iraq). It does not often
appear even in the course of episodes of a secondary nature, in which
States, however sure of being in the right, tend to prefer to qualify their actions as self-help, humanitarian intervention, protection of nationals
abroad, etc. How can this statement of fact be reconciled with the assertion
that self-defence is the only possible lawful use of force? Can it reasonably
be concluded from the existence of this whole world in which the question of
self-defence is not even raised and about which the U.N. is often not even
consulted, that none of these acts involving the use of force 'against the territorial integrity or political independence' of another State, is lawful in the
eyes of the international community as it really is, forty years after the
drawing up of the Charter?

There is another explanation which seems more convincing and which
would also account for what we said before: that is, that neither Art. 51 nor
Art. 2(4), to which it was the conventional exception, are any longer considered by the States members of the U.N. to be valid provisions, because
they are part of a system of law which was consistent but is now a dead letter; namely, that of the Charter. It is not claimed here that these rules are
no longer legally binding on the members of the U.N., which is another
problem again, but only that they all collectively behave as if they did not
exist.

A few words must be said to explain this impression. The disintegration of
the logic behind the Charter is plain to see; it was based on the link between
a rule and a guarantee[114]: the rule (to which self-defence was only a limited
exception): that States should give up their legal right to use force; the guarantee: that a mechanism of collective security, put in motion by the S.C., in
whose favour they gave up this right, would substitute the individual mechanism by which each State had until then been judge of the merits of its own
case. The rule and the guarantee went together, and the success of the latter
was a necessary condition for respect of the former.

The failure of the guarantee mechanism has made the rule senseless: how
(and why), if it is not assured of a collective guarantee and a response on the
part of the U.N. to any use of force, can a State be expected to renounce the
power to guarantee its own rights individually – that is, to use force for the
protection of interests, the lawfulness of which it must decide unilaterally if
it does not wish the other State to proceed unilaterally and in the last resort

decide for it? The frequency of unilateral resort to force, without appeal to the U.N., is to be explained first by this failure of collective security, and in this context the invocation of self-defence is no more than a residual justification, a bit mechanical, and almost always backed up anyway by other motives which are now considered more convincing, based on the legitimacy of the interests which the use of force aims to protect. The logic of self-help, whereby each State guarantees its own subjective rights individually, thus takes the place of that of the collective guarantee of non resort to force, which the exception of self-defence was a part of.

The twofold product of the failure of collective security, military alliances and the strategy of nuclear deterrence, follow rules of logic which are diametrically opposed to those which were the basis of collective security, and make Art. 51 still more inadequate, a cog which is expected to adapt itself to a new machine which is totally alien to it.

Regional military alliances no doubt pay lip service to the universal organization and the system of collective security they were created to enforce[105], but the 'collective self-defence' they claim to guarantee is in fact a cloak to operations of partial collective security, which are a far cry from the logic of universal collective security as intended by the Charter. To say that an attack from outside against one of the members of the alliance constitutes an attack on all its members and can be held to justify collective use of force, is not to reiterate the right of attacked States to apply simultaneously and jointly the exception of self-defence which is open to them individually, as the drawers up of the Charter no doubt intended[106]; it is to reproduce on a regional scale the mechanism of the Charter itself, which was however meant to be exclusive because it was universal. The same can be said of 'requested interventions', which occur so often in contemporary practice[107], even where no institutional alliance exists. In both cases, the allies which claim to be acting in the name of collective self-defence use force in response to a use of force which was not directed against them; that is to say in a situation where they could not invoke it individually, exactly as States taking part in a collective action under the terms of Chapter VII would have done; and in neither case is their action intended as a short-term resistance to the attack, while waiting for an intervention which they know from the outset will not take place because it is inconceivable.

On the subject of nuclear strategy suffice it to say one thing; whether the concept of deterrence is compatible with Art. 2(4) of the Charter or not, the carrying out of the nuclear threat belongs in any case to the logic of reprisals, which has already been described as incompatible with the logic of self-defence[108]; it would be difficult to seriously portray the reply to a nuclear attack, which States with nuclear armaments consider lawful in principle since they only condemn the first blow, as the emergency action which Art. 51 permitted them to take while waiting for the S.C. to take over.

32

To conclude: the international community no longer believes in the system of the Charter, because the collective guarantee, in exchange for which its members had renounced their individual right to resort to force, does not work, and no real substitute for it has been found. In any society a collective system of guarantee protects the interests, rightful or not, of the members; when the authority which has the sole legal power to make this system work fails to do so, States will take back their individual means of protecting their own interests because they are no longer receiving that for which they had exchanged their freedom of action; that is, they will take back these means *de facto*, while still paying limited and derisory lip service, traces of which are to be found in U.N. practice. But whatever the official pretence, and perhaps the legal situation, the international community is in fact back where it was before 1945: in the state of nature; and as is well-known[109], the notion of self-defence makes no sense there. To study self-defence forty years after the Charter was drawn up is to look at a cog turning and pretend not to see that the machine is broken. Can we be surprised in these circumstances if the examination of an illusory practice leaves us with a sense of unreality?

NOTES

1. The present study is based exclusively on practice and will not on principle (*infra*, I.1) make any use of theoretical definitions, as these are untrue to the reduced body of precedents which a critical analysis permit us to use. There will therefore be no reference to sources other than U.N. practice itself. This does not take away from great theoretical interest of the following works: Ago, Additive to the 8th Report on State Responsibility, A/C-N.4/318/Add.5/7, YILC (1980), II, I (on Art. 34 of the draft of the I.L.C.; with a very ample bibliography); Lamberti Zanardi, La legittima difesa nel diritto internazionale, Giuffré, Milan, 1972, (esp. pp. 191-299); Bowett, Self-defence in international law, Manchester, The University Press, 1958. I have also used, among others: Brownlie, International law and the use of force by States, Oxford, Clarendon Press, 1963 (esp. part 3, pp. 214-349); Waldock, 'The regulation of the use of force by individual States in international law', 81 *Hague Recueil* (1952), pp.451/515 (esp. Chapters IV and V); Schwebel, 'Aggression, intervention and self-defence in modern international law', 136 *Hague Recueil* (1972), pp.411-497; Higgins, The development of international law through the political organs of the United Nations, London, Oxford University Press, 1963 (part 4, esp. pp.167-222); the proceedings of the Institut de droit international (Wiesbaden session, 1975), 56 AIDI (1975), pp.1-79 (including Zourek report and questionnaire); those of the International Law Association (New York session, 1958), 48 ILAReport (1958), pp.507-628.

2. Combacau, Le pouvoir de sanction de l'O.N.U.: étude théorique de la coercition non militaire, Paris, Pedone, 1974, pp.48-61.

3. See for example Lamberti Zanardi, *op.cit*, p.240 f, for and survey of the debates on the definition of aggression.

4. On this distinction between State practice and U.N. practice, see *infra*, b.

5. *Infra*, II.1.

6. 'Nothing in the foregoing paragraphs shall be construed as enlarging or diminishing in any

way the scope of the provisions of the Charter concerning cases in which the use of force is lawful.'

7. *Infra*, II.1.

8. Para. 6, substantially the same as the abovementioned paragraph of Resolution 2625.

9. Notably Lamberti Zanardi, *op.cit.*, pp.220 f, 240 f, who makes a great deal of use, very clearly, of declaratory resolutions.

10. Hence the incorrectness of using as a precedent relevant to self-defence a case such as that of the U.S. action against Cuba in 1962 (Higgins, *op.cit.*, p.203) in which, as other authors have established (Lamberti Zanardi, *op.cit.*, pp.244-5), the former never invoked Art. 51 or self-defence.

11. Letter to the Chairman of the S.C., 13th Feb., 1958, S/3951 (SCOR, 13th year) 'under Art. 51 of the U.N. Charter to inform the Security Council of the measures taken by the Tunistian government in exercise of its right of self-defence following upon the French Act of aggression at Sakiet-sidi-Youssef'.

12. Letter of 14th May 1975, S/11689 (SCOR, 30th year) on the occassion of the recovery of an American ship, captured by the Grunk forces when allegedly in Cambodian waters.

13. Letter of 25th April 1980, S/13908 (SCOR, 35th year), after the failed attempt to liberate the American hostages held in Iran on the 24th and 25th April.

14. Letter of 19th Aug., 1981, S/14632 (SCOR, 36th year), on the air incident with Libya of the same day.

15. Letter of 17th Feb. 1979, S/13094 (SCOR, 34th year), on its action against Vietnam of the same day.

16. S./Res.228, 25 Nov. 1966, which 'censures Israel for this large-scale military action in violation of the U.N. Charter' and qualifies it as 'reprisal'; see the debates in mins. 1320th to 1328th mtgs. Nov. 1966, and especially the declarations made by Israel and, opposed to it, the U.S. (*ibid.*) and France mins. (1321 mtg.). Cf. *a contrario* the lack of significance as precedents of the debates on Israel's military action against Syria in July 1966, where the situation was very similar but where the draft resolution (S/7437, of 29th July 1966, SCOR, 21st year) which condemned it in spite of Israel's allegations of self-defence, was not adopted mins. (1295th mtg., 3rd Aug. 1966: 6 votes for and 9 abstentions); the same is true of the lengthy debates concerning Israel's actions against Syria, U.A.R. and Jordan in June 1967, Oct. 1967 and Aug. 1968 (see *Repertoire of the Practice of the Security Council*, 1966-68, *re:* Situation in the Middle East, I and II), all situations in which Israel, either alone or concurrently with its adversary, invoked self-defence, but where the Council's response does not permit any clearcut conclusion to be drawn on this point.

17. S./Res.265, lst April 1969 (unanimous), which 'condemns the recent premeditated air attacks launched by Israel' after Israel had invoked self-defence with great insistence in its letter of 27th March 1969, S/9114 (SCOR, 24th year) and in its intervention mins. (1466th mtg., 27th March 1969).

18. S./Res.270, 16th Aug. 1969 (unanimous) condemning in the same terms: Israeli letter of 12th Aug. 1969, S/9387 (SCOR, 24th year) and declaration of 13th Aug. 1969 mins. (1498th mtg.).

19. S./Res. 279, 12th May 1970 (unanimous) and S/Res.280, 19th May 1970 (adopted by 11 votes and 4 abstentions), following the invasion of southern Lebanon. Resolution 280 'condemns Israel for its premeditated military action in violation of its obligations under the Charter of the U.N.: Israel invokes self-defence, although less clearly than previously (letter of 10th May 1970, S/9790, SCOR, 25th year; intervention in mins. 1597th mtg. 12th May 1970; communication of 13th May 1970, S/9801, SCOR, *loc.cit.*: intervention in mins. 1540th mtg., 14th May 1970). See also the debates on S/Res. 285, 5th Sept. 1970, at a later stage.

20. S/Res.313, 28th Feb. 1972, and more distinctly, S/Res.316, 26th June 1972 (adopted by 13

34

votes and 2 abstensions), which 'condemns [...] the repeated attacks of Israeli forces' in spite of the invocation of self-defence, mins. (1648th mtg., 23rd June 1972); see also S/Res.317, 21st July 1972.

21. S/Res.332, 21st April 1973 (adopted by 11 votes and 4 abstentions): 'condemns' Israel's 're-peated military attacks' on Lebanon. S/Res.337 15th Aug. 1973 (unanimous): 'condemns Israel for violating the sovereignty and territorial integrity of Lebanon': in this case a civil aircraft had been intercepted in Lebanese air space and this action was expressly justified by Israel by its right of self-defence against terrorism, mins. 1736th mtg., 13th Aug. 1973; the military authorities believed several Palestinian leaders to be abroad the aircraft), to which Peru in particular referred, denying that the conditions for its use were present mins. 1739th mtg., 15th Aug. 1973).

22. S/Res.347, 24th April 1974 (adopted by 13 votes, two States not voting): 'condemns Israel's violation of Lebanon's territorial integrity and sovereignty' (attack on frontier villages): see Israel's intervention, mins. 1766th mtg., 15th April 1974.

23. S/Res.488, 19th June 1981 (unanimous). Israel was invoking self-defence, (mins. 2289th mtg., 19th June 1981). The Assembly also considered the question and also condemned the Israeli action (A/Res.36/27, 13th Nov. 1981, adopted by 109 votes to 2 with 34 abstentions): see Israel's declaration appealing to Art. 51 and its letter of 19th Oct. 1981, A/36/610, GAOR, XXXVIth session, Annexes, item 130, and the many declarations on the other side; this was one of the rare occasions when the Assembly was persuaded to pronounce on the conditions in which self-defence may be exercised.

24. S/Res.425, 19th March 1978, on the occasion of the massive invasion of southern Lebanon after the massacre of Israeli civilians by the P.L.O.: S/Res.508 and 509, 5th and 6th June 1982, on the occasion of the launching of operations against Lebanon on June 4th. In the two cases (see especially the detailed arguments used in the declaration of 17th March 1978 mins 2072nd mtg.), the armed action is presented as a response to terrorist operations origi-nating in Lebanese territory which, in view of the government's inability to prevent them, called for an act of self-defence on the part of Israel.

25. S/Res.273, 9th Dec. 1969 (adopted by 13 votes with 2 abstentions): 'strongly condemns the Portuguese authorities for the shelling': the preamble also quotes Art. 2(4); see Portugal's arguments in mins. 1516th mtg., 4th Dec. 1969, and above all, mins. 1520th mtg., 9th Dec.

26. S/Res.268, 28th July 1969, which 'strongly censures the Portuguese attacks'; but Portugal simply denies that the bombing took place, and while it requests Zambia to respect its obli-gation of prevention on its territory, does not, failing this, invoke the right of self-defence (mins. 1486th mtg., 18th July 1969): the only reference to Art. 51 is made by Zambia and concerns its own right (*ibid*).

27. Complaint by Zambia concerning the attack on the village of Sialola of 11th July 1976: dec-laration by South Africa in mins. 1944th mtg. 27th July 1976; herce the lack of bearing of the condemnation included in S/Res.393 of 30th July 1976.

28. Complaint by Kenia concerning the attack carried out in Angola in March 1976 to protect a hydro-electric complex built by South Africa; the allegations of the latter mins. 1906th mtg., make no reference to self-defence, and the 'condemnation' of the South African 'ag-gression' (S/Res.387, 31st March 1976) is therefore of no interest here.

29. Res. S/2322, 1st Sept. 1951 (adopted by 8 votes with 3 abstentions) 'it is impossible, in the present circumstances, to justify these practices by alleging that reasons of self-defence ren-der them indispensable'. On the invocation of Art. 51, see Egypt's declaration mins. 550th mtg., 1st Aug. 1951; *contra*: especially U.K. and Israel, *ibid.* and mins. 551st mtg., on the same day.

30. S/Res. 188, 9th April 1964 (adopted by 9 votes and 2 abstentions) which 'condemns repri-sals' (in general) 'as incompatible with the purposes and principles of the U.N.' and thus disqualifies the action which the U.K. claimed to be of self-defence, which the Council any-

35

way 'deplores'. See the declarations of the U.K., mins. 1106th mtg., 2nd April 1964, and 1109th mtg., 7th April, and on the other side, those of the Arab States, mins. 1106th to 1109th mtgs..

31. A/Res.Es. 6/2, 14th Jan. 1980 (adopted by 104 votes with 18 abstentions) deploring the armed intervention, for which the U.S.S.R. had invoked individual and collective self-defence, especially in the S.C., mins. 2185th mtg., 5th Jan. 1980); see also the declaration along the same lines of Afghanistan, mins., *ibid.*; *contra*: see esp. the declaration of the U.S.A., mins., *ibid.*.

32. U.S.S.R., mins. 1441st-1442nd mtgs., 21st-22nd Aug. 1968.

33. S/8761 and Add 1, in mins. 1442nd mtg., 30.

34. mins. 1443rd mtg., 22nd Aug. 1968.

35. Egypt invoked self-defence in the debate immediately following: mins. 1347th mtg., 5th June 1967, declaration of the President, and Egypt letter S/7926 of the same day (SCOR 22nd year). The Resolution S/233 of 6th June 1967, calling for a cease fire, does not pronounce on this allegation.

36. The Council received a complaint from the U.S. against North Vietnam (letter S/5839, 4th Aug. 1964), supported by the U.K. (*ibid.*). The allies of North Vietnam said it was unfounded and saw the American retaliation as a reprisal (Czechoslovakia, mins. 1141st mtg., same day: U.S.S.R., *ibid.*), and as such unlawful.

37. *Supra*, note 12.

38. *Supra*, note 14.

39. To the case mentioned *supra* must be added those on which the S.C. did not pronounce; several have been already dealt with, but it is worth mentioning the case of the Israeli raids against Syria in 1964 (for the discussion on the qualification of self-defence: Israel, mins. 1162nd mtg., 16th Nov. 1964; Syria, mins. 1164th mtg., 27th Nov. 1964, and the draft resolution presented by Marocco, S/6085/Rev.1, SCOR 19th year, rejected by the Council: mins. 1179th mtg., 11th Dec. 1964) and in 1966 Israel (mins. 1288th mtg., 25th July 1966; Syria, *ibid.*, and the draft resolution presented by Jordan and Mali, S/7437, SCOR, 21st year, rejected by the Council: mins. 1295th mtg., 3rd Aug. 1966).

40. After the attack on Sakiet-sidi-Youssef by France, Tunisia had forbidden the French troops whose presence in its territory it declared to be against its will, to perform certain acts, and had declared that if France disregarded this interdiction, it would consider itself entitled to exercise self-defence (letter of 13th Feb. 1958, S/3951, SCOR, 13th year). When this came about, Tunisia invoked Art. 51 (letter of 29th May 1958, S/4013, *ibid.*, and mins. 819th mtg., 2nd June 1958); France considered this claim unjustified, mins. (*ibid*).

41. United States intervention solicited by Lebanon under Art. 51: Lebanon mins. 827th and 833rd mtgs., 15th and 18th July; on the same side: U.S., *ibid.*; France, mins. 828th mtg.; China, mins. 831st mtg., 17th July; against the existence of the conditions for self-defence: U.S.S.R. mins. 827th mtg.; U.A.R., mins. 828th mtg.; Sweden, mins. 830th mtg., 16th July. The draft resolution of the U.S., S/4050/Rev. 1, in mins. 829th mtg., rejected by the Council, refers to self-defence. Jordan had over the same affair also solicited external intervention from the U.K. and the U.S., using the same arguments, mins. 831st mtg..

42. French armed attack on Bizerte. Both sides invoked self-defence; Tunisia (letter S/4862, 20th July 1961, SCOR, 16th year; mins. 961st mtg., 21st July 1961) and France (letter S/4864, 20th July 1961, SCOR, *loc.cit.*, and mins. 961st mtg.).

43. *Supra*, note 36.

44. Pakistan, mins. 1238th mtg., 6th Sept. 1965.

45. *Supra*, notes 32, 33, 34.

46. *Supra*, note 15.

47. *Supra*, note 13.

48. The U.K. based its military venture clearly on Art. 51, especially in its letters of 20th and

36

26th April 1982, S/14988 and 15002; Argentina replied in a letter dated 29th April, S/15014 (see the British replies, 30th April, S/15016 and 15017, the Argentinian response of the same day, S/15018, and the new reply by Britain of 4th May, S/15045). At a later stage the U.K. invoked self-defence to justify certain individual incidents in the reconquest operation: establishment of a forbidden zone round the Falklands (letter of 1st May 1982, S/15025), sinking of the cruiser Belgrano (letter of 3rd May, S/15031, and Argentinian reply of same day, S/15032). None of the resolutions passed by the Council (see esp. S/Res. 502 and 505, 3rd April and 26th May 1982) seem to be a clear statement of position on these allegations. I have not unfortunately been able to consult the minute of the S.C. debates, and have had to make do with the summaries, which have recently been much too brief, in the UNMC (1982), n. 5, 6, 7.

49. U.K., mins. 550th mtg., 1st Aug. 1951.

50. Res. S/2322, 1st Sept. 1951, *supra*, note 29.

51. References *supra*, note 42.

52. In 1948, Pakistani forces having occupied Jammu and Kashmir, considered by India to be part of its own territory, the latter invoked self-defence to justify its past and future actions against Pakistan (mins. 328th mtg., 25th Nov. 1948); but Pakistan also claimed the same right then, and continued to do so after the Indian action which it invoked as justification for its response (mins. 536th mtg., 9th March 1951). The Council made no pronouncement on which country was responsible for the initial act.

53. U.A.R., S/mins. 1369, 24th Oct. 1967; see Israel's reply in the same meeting.

54. *Supra*, note 48, with references.

55. Art. 3, *c* and *f* respectively.

56. 1st principle, respectively paras. 5 and 8.

57. Lamberti Zanardi, *op.cit.*, p.220 ff.

58. S/Res.273, 9th Dec. 1969; *supra*, note 25.

59. S/Res.268, 28th July 1969; *supra*, note 26.

60. S/Res.265 and 270, 1st April and 16th Aug. 1969; *supra*, notes 17 and 18.

61. *Infra*, article by Farer.

62. *Infra*, article by Lamberti Zanardi.

63. *Infra*, article by Francioni.

64. *Infra*, article by Bowett, and infra II.2, (a), on self-help.

65. *Infra*, III.

66. Lamberti Zanardi, *op.cit.*, p.233 ff, does not attach a great deal of importance to the 1950 Kashmir affair (p.236), or to the work of the S.C. Committee on the control of atomic energy (p.234-5), but he draws some arguments in favour of the negative view from the debates on the definition of aggression (p.240 ff) and Res. 2625 (p.242, note 142) which I have already said I do not find convincing, and why (*supra*, I.1); the same can be said (that it is normative and *a priori*) of the argument drawn form the fact that treaties of collective self-defence make the reponse dependent on an attack having taken place (*ibid.*, p.243). In the Cuba affair, where the action of the U.S. was potentially a fine case of preventive action, the 'quarantine' was not based on this idea (*supra*, note 10).

67. Mins. 1342nd and 1343rd mtgs, 27th and 29th May; and above all the declaration of the Chairman of the S.C. in mins. 1347th mtg., 5th June.

68. *Ibid.*

69. GAOR, 5th special session, 1526th mtg. especially.

70. See the references in Lamberti Zanardi, *op.cit.*, pp.239-240, and his analysis.

71. *Supra*, note 23.

72. *Ibid.*

73. There was much insistence during the debates and in the resolution on the fact that Iraq's nuclear programme was strictly non military, and above all that the I.A.E. guarantee sys-

tem, to which it was subject, made it certain that it would not be deflected towards military objectives.

74. Bowett, *op.cit.*. This view is apparent from a certain number of statements of principle, and especially this one (p.9): 'The essence of self-defence is a wrong done, a breach of a legal duty owed to the State acting in self-defence', and the title itself of the first part of his book, 'The substantive rights for which self-defence is a permissible means of protection'.

75. *Supra*, I.2, (b), on the practice attributable to the U.N.; see notes 16-22 and 24-28.

76. Appeal by Lebanon and Jordan for American and British aid against Egypt (*supra*, note 41); similarly Afghanistan's hypothetical appeal for aid from the U.S.S.R. in December 1979 and the Soviet intervention in Afghanistan in the name of collective self-defence will be justified by reference to the material and financial aid given by the 'imperialist' countries to the internal rebels (*supra*, note 31); similarly again, the French intervention on request from Shaba in 1978 (Kolwezi case, not referred to the U.N.).

77. See *infra*, article by Lamberti Zanardi.

78. See *infra*, article by Bowett, which very clearly classifies acts of self-help carried out in favour of nationals as a form of self-defence under Art. 51.

79. Israel, mins. 1939th mtg., 9th July 1976, in the Entebbe case U.S. S/13908, *re* the hostages in Teheran (*supra*, note 13).

80. Rumania, mins. 1942nd mtg., July 1976, but this point of view if based on the absence of armed attack (that is to say on the grounds for the action) and therefore has no bearing as regards its aim. Note also on this point, even if this does not constitute U.N. practice as it has been defined here, that Judge Morozov held, though in a dissenting opinion, that the U.S. had forfeited the right 'to expect the Court to uphold any claim for reparation', chiefly because of its attempted self-help (ICJReports (1980), p.53).

81. In the Entebbe case the draft resolution S/12139 condemning the Israeli action was not put to the vote; draft resolution S/12138, which did not obtain the requisite majority, did not pronounce on its lawfulness. In the Tabas case although the U.S. had reported its action to the S.C., it was not discussed.

82. Complaint by Yemen, S/5635 1st April 1964 (SCOR, 19th year). On the events and the U.N. reaction, see *infra*, text and notes 91-92.

83. Complaint by U.S., S/5849 4th Aug. 1964 (SCOR, 19th year): American air raids on North Vietnamese territory following an attack on American destroyers by Vietnamese patrol boats. Debates: mins. 1140th and 1141st mtgs., 5th and 7th Aug. 1964; no action on the part of the Council, no draft resolution.

84. It will be no surprise not to find here the debates concerning Israel's largest and most systematic invasions of Lebanon, in 1978 and 1982: in both cases the argument of self-help (the need, in view of the host State's failure to do so, to destroy the terrorist bases) is more important even in the Israeli declarations than that of lawful reprisals, that is to say, limited pursuit of the enemy into foreign territory. Also not mentioned here are the debates on the raids carried out by South Africa which, unlike Israel, does not usually invoked self-defence to justify its acts of reprisal.

85. Bombings of Syrian villages by Israel, Nov. 1964. Debates: mins. 1162nd mtg., 16th Nov. 1964; 1164th mtg., 27th Nov., 1169th mtg., 9th Dec.; 1179th mtg., 11th Dec.: 1182nd mtg., 21st Dec. One of the two draft resolutions (S/6085/Rev.1; SCOR, 21st year) condemned the attack; it was not adopted (mins. 1169th mtg.: 3 votes for and 9 abstentions).

86. Action of the same kind, July 1966. Debates: mins. 1288th mtg., 25th July 1966; mins. 1289th mtg., 26th July; mins. 1291st-1295th mtgs., 28th July – 3rd Aug. Draft resolution S/7437 (SCOR, 21st year), condemning, but as being based on insufficient grounds, the Israeli attack, was not adopted (mins. 1295th mtg.: 6 votes for, 9 abstentions).

87. *Idem*, Nov. 1966. Debates: mins. 1320th-1322nd mtgs., 16-17 Nov. 1966; mins. 1324th mtg., 21st Nov.; mins. 1327th-28th mtgs., 24th-25th Nov. Adoption of Resolution

38

S/Res.228 (mins.1328th mtg., 25th Nov. 1966: 14 votes for, one abstention), which 'censures Israel for this large-scale military action' and 'emphasizes to Israel that actions of military reprisals cannot be tolerated'.

88. *Idem*, March 1969. Debates: mins.1466th mtg., 27th March 1969; mins. 1472nd-73rd mtgs., 1st April. Adoption of a resolution S/Res.265 (mins. 1473rd mtg., 1st April 1969: 11 votes for, 4 abstentions), which 'condemns the recent premeditated air attacks launched by Israel'.

89. *Idem*, Aug. 1969. Debates: mins.1498th mtg., 13th Aug. 1969; mins.1504th mtg., 16th Aug. 1969. Adoption of a resolution S/Res.270 (mins. 1504th mtg., 16th Aug. 1969: unanimous), which 'condemns the premeditated air attack by Israel'.

90. More far-reaching action, May 1970. Debates: mins.1537th-42nd mtgs. (12th-19th May 1970). Adoption of a resolution S/Res.280 (mins.1542nd mtg., 19th May 1970: 11 votes for, 4 abstentions), which 'condemns Israel for its premeditated military action'.

91. U.K., mins.1106th mtg., 2nd April 1964, and above all 1109th mtg., 7th April; on the other side: Iraq, mins.1106th-7th mtgs., 3rd April; mins.1109th mtg., 7th April; see also Marocco, mins.1108th mtg., 6th April, and mins.1109th mtg.; Syria, mins.1109th mtg.

92. S/Res.188, 9th April 1964 (adopted by 9 votes, with 2 abstentions).

93. See declarations by Iraq, mins.1106th and 1109th mtgs.; Czechoslovakia, mins.1110th mtg., 8th April 1964.

94. Iraq, mins.1107th mtg., 3rd April 1964.

95. Marocco, mins.1108th mtg., 6th April 1964.

96. See especially Bulgaria, mins.1292nd mtg., 19th July 1966 (Israel v. Syria) U.K., mins.1320th mtg., 16th Nov. 1966; U.S., *ibid.*; France, mins.1321st mtg., same date; Argentina, mins.1322nd mtg., 17th Nov. (Israel v. Jordan).

97. See especially U.K., 1320th mtg., 16th Nov. 1966; New Zealand, 1322nd mtg., 17th Nov. (Israel v. Jordan).

98. S/Res.228, *supra*, note 87.

99. S/Res.265, *supra*, note 88.

100. S/Res.270, *supra*, note 89.

101. S/Res.280, *supra*, note 90.

102. See for example Lamberti Zanardi, *op.cit.*, pp.261-67.

103. *Supra*, I.2 (a), on non respect of the procedure laid down in Art. 51.

104. *Supra*, introduction.

105. See for example North Atlantic Treaty, Art. 5; Warsaw Pact, Art. 4.

106. Bowett, *op.cit.*, p.215, and p.216-7 (hypothesis no.2).

107. Some examples have been quoted above, camouflaged as 'collective self-defence': Lebanon (1958), Czechoslovakia (1968), Afghanistan (1979), etc.

108. *Supra*, II.2 (b).

109. Zourek, Rapport provisoire à l'Institut de Droit International, SG AIDI (1975), p.24.

[12]

REPRISALS INVOLVING RECOURSE TO ARMED FORCE [1]

By Derek Bowett [*]

Few propositions about international law have enjoyed more support than the proposition that, under the Charter of the United Nations, the use of force by way of reprisals is illegal. Although, indeed, the words "reprisals" and "retaliation" are not to be found in the Charter, this proposition was generally regarded by writers [2] and by the Security Council as the logical and necessary consequence of the prohibition of force in Article 2(4), the injunction to settle disputes peacefully in Article 2(3) and the limiting of permissible force by states to self-defense. The U.N. Declaration on Principles of International Law concerning Friendly Relations and Co-operation among States, adopted by General Assembly Resolution 2625 (XXV) on October 24, 1970, contains the following categorical statement: "States have a duty to refrain from acts of reprisal involving the use of force."

In recent years, and principally though not exclusively in the Middle East, this norm of international law has acquired its own "credibility gap" by reason of the divergence between the norm and the actual practice of states. So much is this so that Professor Falk, in a recent article entitled "The Beirut Raid and the International Law of Retaliation," [3] has sug-

---

[1] This essay was commissioned by the American Society of International law as the working paper of its study Panel on Reprisals and Retaliation in International Law. The author revised his paper to take account of the Panel's discussion as well as important developments since the original version was written. Because of its significance, the article was referred to this JOURNAL in its revised Panel form and is being run without attempting to update it further.

The paper focuses on the experience in the Middle East, both because of its richness and importance, and because of the extensive consideration given to that experience by the Security Council and other international organs.—ED.

[*] Cambridge University.

[2] The literature on this point, though not very penetrating on account of the assumed authority of the proposition, is very extensive; the following is no more than a sample: Goodrich and Hambro, Charter of the United Nations 95–96, 102 (London: Stevens and Sons, 1949); Brownlie, International Law and the Use of Force by States, Ch. XI (Oxford University Press, 1963); Higgins, The Development of International Law through the Political Organs of the United Nations 202–205, 217–218 (Oxford University Press, 1963). Both Brownlie and Higgins cite additional authorities: Waldock, 81 Hague Academy, Recueil des Cours 475–494 (1952, II); Sørensen, 101 ibid. 219 (1960, III); Skubiszewski, in Sørensen, Manual of Public International Law 754–755 (New York: St. Martin's Press, 1968). The authors maintaining a contrary view, i.e., accepting a continuing, permissible rôle for armed reprisals, are Colbert, Retaliation in International Law 203 (New York: King's Crown Press, 1948); and Stone, Aggression and World Order 43, 94–98 (1958).

[3] 63 A.J.I.L. 415–443 (1969). For a critical reply to this article see Blum, "The Beirut Raid and the International Double Standard. A Reply to Professor Richard A. Falk," 64 ibid. 73–105 (1970).

2   THE AMERICAN JOURNAL OF INTERNATIONAL LAW   [Vol. 66

gested a framework for claims to use force in retaliation against prior terroristic acts, thereby conceding the impossibility or unreality of any blanket, unqualified proscription of reprisals involving force.

It cannot be doubted that a total outlawry of armed reprisals, such as the drafters of the Charter intended, presupposed a degree of community cohesiveness and, with it, a capacity for collective action to suppress any resort to unlawful force which has simply not been achieved. Not surprisingly, as states have grown increasingly disillusioned about the capacity of the Security Council to afford them protection against what they would regard as illegal and highly injurious conduct directed against them, they have resorted to self-help in the form of reprisals and have acquired the confidence that, in so doing, they will not incur anything more than a formal censure from the Security Council. The law on reprisals is, because of its divorce from actual practice, rapidly degenerating to a stage where its normative character is in question.

To arrest this process of degeneration may require effective sanctioning by the Security Council of reprisals or, alternatively, a policy of restraint by states which will involve the renunciation of armed reprisals: academic studies are not likely to play any major rôle in this. However, there is room for a study which is an attempt at clarification of the nature of reprisals, as distinct from permissible self-defense; at an examination of state practice and Security Council practice which will elucidate those features of a claim to use reprisals which will either avoid or minimize condemnation by the Council; and at suggested procedures or assistance by the organs of the international community which might arrest the process of degeneration.

1. THE DISTINCTION BETWEEN REPRISALS AND SELF-DEFENSE

Clearly, if self-defense is a permissible use of force and reprisals are not, the distinction between the two is vital. To some, the distinction is elementary and obvious. The Soviet representative in the Security Council, Mr. Morozov, in the course of the debate on the Gulf of Tonkin incidents in August, 1964, said:

> The difference between the right of self-defense and the right of retaliation is quite obvious to any first year student at any law school or any institution of legal studies.
> In fact, contemporary international law categorically denies and rejects a right of retaliation. The recognition of the right of self-defence in Article 51 of the United Nations Charter *ipso iure* precludes the right of retaliation. . . .[4]

The very fact that Mr. Morozov did not explain the "obvious" distinction is sufficient to alert the first-year law student—and even maturer brethren —to the possibility of latent difficulty.

Reprisals and self-defense are forms of the same generic remedy, self-help. They have, in common, the preconditions that:

[4] U.N. Security Council, Official Records, 19th Year, 1141st Meeting, pars. 82–83.

(1) The target state must be guilty of a prior international delinquency against the claimant state.

(2) An attempt by the claimant state to obtain redress or protection by other means must be known to have been made, and failed, or to be inappropriate or impossible in the circumstances.[5]

(3) The claimant's use of force must be limited to the necessities of the case and proportionate to the wrong done by the target state.

The difference between the two forms of self-help lies essentially in their aim or purpose. Self-defense is permissible for the purpose of protecting the security of the state and the essential rights—in particular the rights of territorial integrity and political independence—upon which that security depends. In contrast, reprisals are punitive in character: they seek to impose reparation for the harm done, or to compel a satisfactory settlement of the dispute created by the initial illegal act, or to compel the delinquent state to abide by the law in the future. But, coming after the event and when the harm has already been inflicted, reprisals cannot be characterized as a means of protection. This distinction would fit neatly into the general theory that punishment is a matter for society as a whole, whereas self-defense must still be permitted to the individual member, as an interim measure of protection and subject to a subsequent evaluation of the correctness of the individual's judgment as to the necessity for self-defense by the organized community of states.

This seemingly simple distinction abounds with difficulties. Not only is the motive or purpose of a state notoriously difficult to elucidate but, even more important, the dividing line between protection and retribution becomes more and more obscure as one moves away from the particular incident and examines the whole context in which the two or more acts of violence have occurred. Indeed, within the whole context of a continuing state of antagonism between states, with recurring acts of violence, an act of reprisal may be regarded as being at the same time both a form of punishment and the best form of protection for the future, since it may act as a deterrent against future acts of violence by the other party. To take what is now perhaps the classic case, let us suppose that guerrilla activity from State A, directed against State B, eventually leads to a military action within State A's territory by which State B hopes to destroy the guerrilla bases from which the previous attacks have come and to discourage further attacks. Clearly, this military action cannot

---

[5] This condition is usually based on the Naulilaa arbitration (Germany-Portugal, July 31, 1928, 2 Int. Arb. Awards 1013), but the arbitrators give no authority for this and, indeed, in the earlier textbooks (and some later) there is little mention of this condition as a specific requirement: see Holland, Lectures on International Law 236–238 (1933); Westlake, International Law: Part II, 8–11 (1913); 2 Hyde, International Law 1660–1667 (1945). The emphasis was more upon the *necessity* for the act of reprisal in the sense that it had to have a lawful motive. As we shall see later in this article, there is little evidence that the Security Council today regards this condition as an essential prerequisite of reprisals, although it would scarcely pronounce on the issue since it is committed to the proposition that *all* reprisals involving the use of force are illegal.

4   THE AMERICAN JOURNAL OF INTERNATIONAL LAW   [Vol. 66

strictly be regarded as. self-defense in the context of the previous guerrilla activities: they are past, whatever damage has occurred as a result cannot now be prevented and no new military action by State B can really be regarded as a defense against attacks in the past. But if one broadens the context and looks at the whole situation between these two states, cannot it be said that the destruction of the guerrilla bases represents a proper, proportionate means of defense—for the security of the state *is* involved—against future and (given the whole context of past activities) certain attacks? The reply that this constitutes an argument of "anticipatory" self-defense which is no longer permitted under the Charter, since Article 51 requires an actual "armed attack," [6] is scarcely adequate. It was never the intention of the Charter to prohibit anticipatory self-defense and the traditional right certainly existed in relation to an "imminent" attack.[7] Moreover, the rejection of an anticipatory right is, in this day and age, totally unrealistic and inconsistent with general state practice.[8]

In fact, the records of the Security Council are replete with cases where states have invoked self-defense in this broader sense but where the majority of the Council have rejected this classification and regarded their action as unlawful reprisals. These cases are worth the study, for they illustrate the importance of this question: Is the legality of the action to be determined solely by reference to the prior illegal act which brought it about or by reference to the whole context of the relationship between the two states?

The many examples of reprisal actions in the Arab-Israel conflict have, as a relevant background, the Armistice Agreements of 1949 [9] and successive Security Council resolutions. The Armistice Agreements did not specifically forbid reprisals. However, it was the Mediator's firm recom-

---

[6] This is the thesis ably argued by Brownlie, *op. cit.*, Ch. XIII. It has many adherents, of all "persuasions," but it has also been a thesis consistently adopted by the Communist bloc.

[7] The author has developed this reasoning elsewhere: see Bowett, Self-Defence in International Law 187–193 (Manchester University Press, 1958). This reasoning also has many adherents.

[8] Pakistan justified the entry of her troops into Kashmir in 1948 on this basis before the Security Council, an argument opposed only by India. Israel's invasion of Sinai in October, 1956, and June, 1967, rested on the same argument. The O.A.S. has used the same argument in relation to the blockade of Cuba during the 1962 missile crisis. Several states have expressed the same argument in the Sixth Committee in connection with the definition of aggression and the U.N. itself invoked the principle of anticipatory self-defense to justify action by O.N.U.C. in Katanga in December, 1961, and December, 1963. Following the invasion of Czechoslovakia by the U.S.S.R. in 1968, it is permissible to assume that the U.S.S.R. now shares this view, for there certainly existed no "armed attack."

[9] Israel-Egypt, Feb. 24, 1949, 42 U.N.T.S. 251; Israel-Lebanon, March 23, 1949, *ibid.* 287; Israel-Jordan, April 3, 1949, *ibid.* 303; Israel-Syria, July 20, 1949, *ibid.* 327. It is the existence of these Armistice Agreements and successive cease-fire resolutions of the Security Council which preclude the argument (advanced by Blum, *loc. cit.* 76) that Israel's actions are justified by reference to the status of belligerency and are not appropriately judged by reference to peacetime reprisal doctrines. The short answer to Blum is that, except as permissible self-defense, neither Israel nor any other state possesses belligerent rights under the U.N. Charter.

mendation [10] that reprisals and retaliation should not be permitted, although, as Mr. Eban, the representative of Israel, was at pains to clarify,[11] this did not prohibit self-defense. This recommendation was accepted by the Security Council which formally resolved that: "No party is permitted to violate the Truce on the ground that it is undertaking reprisals or retaliation against the other party." [12] Although the intervening years saw a number of acts of reprisals,[13] the Secretary General was able to report in 1956 on the status of compliance with the Armistice Agreements, and following assurances he had received from all the parties, that "the reservation as to self-defense does not permit acts of retaliation which have been repeatedly condemned by the Security Council." [14] Given this crucial distinction between self-defense and reprisals, it might be assumed that the Council's practice would identify those features which deprived an action of its legitimate character as self-defense and characterized it as an illegal act of reprisal.

In the discussion of Israel's complaint of Egyptian restrictions on the passage of ships through the Suez Canal in 1951, the representative of Israel, Mr. Eban, countered the Egyptian plea of self-defense by the argument that self-defense presupposed two conditions: first, an armed attack and, second, the absence of assumption of responsibility by the Security Council.[15] No attempt was made by Egypt to justify the action as a reprisal, possibly because the argument was deemed to be bad in law, and the Security Council condemned the Egyptian action on the basis that the permanent character of the Armistice Agreements precluded any claim to belligerent rights or to a right of search and seizure of vessels in self-defense.[16]

After the Qibya raid in 1953, Israel was perforce obliged to shift away from this restrictive view of self-defense and, for the first time, argued that its action was justified in the whole context of repeated theft, pillaging, border raids, sabotage and injury to Israeli property and life.[17] This argument of an "accumulation of events" became a recurring theme in Israeli statements long before the June, 1967, hostilities: it figured in Security Council debates over the Gaza incidents in February and Sep-

[10] U.N. Security Council, Official Records, 3rd Year, 354th Meeting, p. 40; telegram from the Mediator.

[11] *Ibid.*, p. 43.　　　　　　　　　　[12] *Ibid.*, Res. S/983.

[13] Notably the Israeli attack on Qibya on Oct. 14–15, 1953, condemned by Security Council Res. S/3139 (*ibid.*, Official Records, 8th Year, 642nd Meeting, p. 21); the Gaza incident of Feb. 28, 1955, in which an Israeli force attacked an Egyptian military camp in Gaza, condemned by Res. S/3378 on March 29, 1955 (*ibid.*, 10th Year, 695th Meeting, p. 22); the Israeli attack on Syrian positions near Lake Tiberias on Dec. 11–12, 1955, condemned by Res. S/3538 on Jan. 19, 1956 (*ibid.*, 11th Year, 715th Meeting, p. 26).

[14] *Ibid.*, 11th Year, Supp. for April, May, June, 1956, Doc. S/3596, par. 46.

[15] *Ibid.*, Official Records, 6th Year, 551st Meeting, p. 10.

[16] Res. S/2322, *ibid.*, 558th Meeting.

[17] *Ibid.*, 8th Year, 637th Meeting, pp. 15–38, statement by Mr. Eban. Note that, in this incident, Israel did not concede that the attack on Qibya was by Israeli regular armed forces but maintained that it was by border villagers, driven beyond endurance by Arab guerrilla attacks.

6   THE AMERICAN JOURNAL OF INTERNATIONAL LAW   [Vol. 66

tember, 1955, the Lake Tiberias incident of December, 1955, the Sharafi
and Qalqilya incidents of September and October, 1956, the Suez invasions of October, 1956, the Lake Tiberias incident of March, 1962, and
the Samu incident of November, 1966. The following statement by Mr.
Eban, representing Israel in the debate on the Gaza incident of February
28, 1955, is a typical formulation of this argument:

> My delegation feels justified in seeking a condemnation by the Se-
> curity Council of the Egyptian incursions, murders, demolition and
> sabotage activities described in General Burns' report [S/3373] as a
> "main cause" of present tension, and in the Mixed Armistice Com-
> mission resolutions as "repeated aggressive acts by Egypt against
> Israel." [18]

It may be noted that this argument of "accumulation of events" served
not only as the basis for an argument for self-defense, but also as the
basis upon which Israel sought to counter allegations of a lack of proportionality between her reaction and the prior incidents [19] and even as
the rationale for Israel's effort to have the Security Council condemn the
other party.

Indeed, on many occasions Israeli spokesmen have gone further than
even the "accumulation of events" thesis and, starting from the premise
that Israel is engaged in a struggle for survival, have argued that Israel's
entire policy is based upon self-defense. After the increased tension of
October–November, 1966, when the Middle East situation was again before
the Security Council, Ambassador Comay, representing Israel, argued that:

> . . . whatever we do, whatever our Government decides to do, it is
> done in order to defend and protect our national independence and
> our national security—on the sole responsibility of our Government
> and not on behalf of anybody else or on behalf of any other considera-
> tions but our own.[20]

One finds this theme repeated by Mr. Tekoah, speaking in the Security
Council debate on the Es-Salt raid of March, 1969:

> Yesterday's Israeli action was an act of self-defence. Where there is
> aggression there is defence. Where there is attack there is counter-
> attack . . . Israel has been in a state of self-defence since 1948. It
> will so remain until the Arab Governments agree to end the war waged
> against Israel and conclude peace.[21]

Nor is this plea without effect on public opinion, for it is probably true
that many people sympathetic to Israel are not prepared to enquire into

[18] *Ibid.*, 10th Year, 694th Meeting, p. 18. General Burns was then Chief of Staff
of the U.N. Truce Supervision Organization.

[19] See Eban's answer on the 1955 Lake Tiberias incident: "Some members of the
Security Council have referred to an apparent disproportion between the effects of
the Israeli response and the dimensions of the simple incident preceding it. This,
however, is not the true and valid comparison. The dimensions of Israel's occasional
reactions are more than matched by the accumulated effect of repeated incidents, of
a constant state of tension, of hostility and of aggression" (10th Year, 713th Meeting,
p. 19).

[20] *Ibid.*, 21st Year, 1321st Meeting, U.N. Doc. S/PV. 1321, p. 17.

[21] U.N. Docs. S/PV. 1466, p. 48, S/PV. 1468, p. 21, March 27–April 1, 1969.

responsibility for particular incidents but look rather at the whole situation: from this they conclude that Israel is faced with the need to defend its existence and, therefore, that all its military actions are essentially in the nature of self-defense.

However this may be, the Security Council has never accepted this widening of the context in which it will assess responsibility. On occasion after occasion (Qibya, October, 1953; Gaza, February, 1955; Lake Tiberias, December, 1955, and March, 1962; Jordan, November, 1966; Samu, November, 1966), the Security Council formally condemned Israel for illegal reprisals and rejected this form of plea of self-defense. It cannot be said that the Security Council, or even its individual members, have ever been particularly specific in their reasons for characterizing the Israeli actions as reprisals rather than self-defense. Certainly, occasional references to the "punitive" character of the actions are to be found.[22] More frequently emphasis is laid upon their disproportionate character,[23] although strictly this is scarcely relevant if reprisals are illegal in any event, whether proportionate or disproportionate. In some cases the view is expressed that prior incidents directed against Israel are not sufficient "provocation" to justify the reprisal,[24] although here again this is strictly irrelevant if the principle is that *all* reprisals are illegal.[25] There is also to be found an occasional stress on the "premeditated" character of the reprisal,[26] as opposed to the spontaneous reaction of self-defense, possibly a more relevant criterion, although even here one can envisage carefully pre-planned reactions in self-defense which would not cease to be self-defense merely because military prudence had suggested detailed planning for various possible contingencies. Were this not so, the whole basis of military planning such as one finds in N.A.T.O. and other military pacts would be suspect. However, the general conclusion which emerges from a reading of these debates is that the Council will not look to the whole context of the action so as to derive from that and accept the plea of self-defense in the face of continuing and repeated threats which, unless countered, will recur.

[22] For example, China, *ibid.*, 24th Year, S/PV. 1470, p. 27 (Es-Salt, 1969); U.K., *ibid.*, 19th Year, 1109th Meeting, p. 4 (Yemen, 1964).

[23] For example, China, *ibid.*, 19th Year, 1166th Meeting, p. 6 (Kibbutz Dan, 1964); France, *ibid.*, 21st Year, 1321st Meeting, S/PV. 1321, p. 2 (Samu, 1966); New Zealand, *ibid.*, S/PV. 1322, p. 7; Netherlands, *ibid.*, S/PV. 1323, p. 6; U.S.A., *ibid.*, 23rd Year, S/PV. 1402, pp. 3–5 (Karameh, 1968); U.S.A., *ibid.*, 23rd Year, S/PV. 1460, pp. 28–30 (Beirut airport, 1968).

[24] See the U.K. view, *ibid.*, 10th Year, 710th Meeting, p. 5, and U.S.A., p. 12 (Lake Tiberias, 1955); France, *ibid.*, 23rd Year, S/PV. 1402, p. 22 (Karameh, 1968).

[25] For example, U.S.A., *ibid.*, 10th Year, 695th Meeting, p. 9 (Gaza, 1955); U.K., *ibid.*, 10th Year, 710th Meeting, par. 36 (Lake Tiberias, 1955); Australia, *ibid.*, 712th Meeting, par. 11; U.S.A., *ibid.*, 17th Year, 999th Meeting, pars. 100–101 (Lake Tiberias, 1962).

[26] For example, China, *ibid.*, 17th Year, 1003rd Meeting, p. 3 (Lake Tiberias, 1962); U.K., *ibid.*, 1003rd Meeting, p. 7; Pakistan, *ibid.*, 23rd Year, S/PV. 1402, pp. 18–20 (Karameh, 1968). And see Security Council Res. 262 (1968), 265 (1969), 280 (1970).

8   THE AMERICAN JOURNAL OF INTERNATIONAL LAW   [Vol. 66

Nor is this approach of the Security Council confined to incidents stemming from the Middle East crisis. In 1964 the Council discussed the British air attacks on Yemeni positions, which followed a series of Yemeni attacks on the territory of the South Arabian Federation. The United Kingdom Representative invoked the whole background of attacks and hostility from the Yemen and concluded:

> It will also be abundantly plain that, contrary to what a number of speakers have said and implied, this action was not a retaliation or reprisal. . . . There is, in existing law, a clear distinction to be drawn between the two forms of self-help: One, which is of a retributive or punitive nature is termed "retaliation" or "reprisals"; the other, which is expressly contemplated and authorized by the Charter, is self-defence against armed attack . . . it is clear that the use of armed force to repel or prevent an attack—i.e. legitimate action of a defensive nature—may sometimes have to take the form of a counter-attack.[27]

One delegate was quick to point out the discrepancy between this reasoning and that adopted by the United Kingdom during the debates on the Lake Tiberias incident of 1962.[28] The Council condemned reprisals and "deplored" the British military action,[29] thereby rejecting the British plea of self-defense and, by necessary implication, the British use of the thesis of "accumulation of events."

In the Security Council discussion of the Gulf of Tonkin incident,[30] though no formal resolution was adopted condemning or deploring the United States action, the Soviet[31] and Czechoslovak[32] representatives rejected the U.S. plea of self-defense, as did the communication from the Democratic Republic of Viet-Nam.[33] What is of interest is the fact that the United States relied on a series of past incidents, involving attacks on U.S. vessels, and frankly avowed the aim of securing its naval units against "further aggression."[34] Again, in condemning the Portuguese attacks on the village of Samine in Senegal in November and December of 1969, the Security Council rejected the Portuguese plea of self-defense based upon the allegation of a whole series of past incursions into Portuguese territory by armed bands coming from Senegal.[35]

The Security Council's policy of making an assessment on the basis of the action taken and its *immediate* cause, or, to put it in different terms, of isolating the incident in question from the general context of the rela-

[27] *Ibid.*, 19th Year, 1109th Meeting, p. 4.

[28] *Ibid.*, 1106th Meeting, p. 14, 1107th Meeting, p. 6: the delegate was Mr. Pachachi of Iraq.

[29] U.N. Doc. S/5649, adopted at the 1111th Meeting on April 9, 1964, by 9 votes to 0, with two abstentions (U.K. and U.S.A.).

[30] *Ibid.*, 19th Year, 1140th and 1141st Meetings, Aug. 5–7, 1964.

[31] *Ibid.*, 1140th Meeting, p. 9, and 1141st Meeting, p. 15.

[32] *Ibid.*, 1141st Meeting, p. 4.

[33] Letter from U.S.S.R. to Secretary General, transmitting the views of the D.R.V., U.N. Doc. S/5888, *ibid.*, Supp. for July, August and September, 1964, p. 170.

[34] *Ibid.*, 1140th Meeting, p. 7. And note that the U.K. fully supported the U.S. argument of self-defense: 1141st Meeting, p. 12.

[35] S/Res/273 (1969).

tions between the parties has certain advantages. In the first place, since it is a restrictive view of self-defense, it necessarily limits the situations of permissible force; and, if our premise is that the less permissible force the better, this may be regarded as an advantage. Its other advantage is that it permits the Council to make a relatively easy judgment on the limited facts before it. Indeed, the judgment can then be made almost as a military assessment of the need to act, based upon a limited area of facts. This avoids the need to enter into the wider questions of responsibility, often involving legal and political judgments. There is, for example, no need to go into the question whether guerrilla action against Israel is lawful or unlawful, or whether the U.S. military participation in Viet-Nam is lawful or unlawful. The Council's reluctance to become involved in these wider questions is understandable and such involvement would almost certainly follow if the Council ceased to isolate the particular incident and, instead, looked to the whole relationship between the parties.

The disadvantages of this policy are that it may arouse a feeling of unfairness in the state condemned by the Council, and this has certainly been so with Israel, which has repeatedly protested against the Council's refusal to look at the whole context of a situation. It may also place the state claiming self-defense in a very difficult position strategically. Especially in the face of continuing guerrilla harassment, it is notoriously difficult to maintain an adequate defensive system which relies upon meeting attacks incident by incident. This is so whether one confines the defense to one's own territory or, under a doctrine of "hot pursuit," [36] extends the defense to the territory affording bases to the guerrillas. Even more important, a series of small-scale defensive measures will not have the same deterrent capacity as a large-scale strike and may even be more costly to the defending state. It seems well-nigh axiomatic that, in this age, a guerrilla movement has an initial advantage—due to the whole mode of operations which involves stealth, concealment, strike and withdrawal—and the target state of guerrilla activities is placed at an even greater disadvantage if its military potential is limited by a narrow view of self-defense. The special difficulty of guerrilla activity is a matter to which we must later return.

Weighing the advantages against the disadvantages, however, it would seem that the approach of the Security Council in assessing whether a case for lawful self-defense has been made out has been somewhat unrealistic. To confine this assessment to the incident and its immediate "cause," without regard to the broader context of the past relations between the parties and events arising therefrom, is to ignore the difficulties in which states may be placed, especially in relation to guerrilla activities. The result is not only that the Council finds itself being accused of being "one-sided" but it may also be forced to characterize as reprisals (and therefore illegal) action which, on a broader view of self-defense,

---

[36] For Israeli reliance on this doctrine, see Le Monde, April 20, 1968, and New York Times, Aug. 7, 1968.

10   THE AMERICAN JOURNAL OF INTERNATIONAL LAW   [Vol. 66

might be regarded as legitimate. Or, even worse, the Council characterizes such action as an unlawful reprisal but, realizing the difficulties
faced by the "defendant" state, does not make any formal condemnation
and thus appears to be condoning action which it holds is illegal.

2. RECENT PRACTICE ON REPRISALS

Recent practice, particularly in the context of the Arab-Israel confrontation, suggests that not only have states like Israel, the United States and
the United Kingdom not abandoned their wider view of self-defense—
based upon the "accumulation of events" theory—despite the Security
Council's rejection of the theory, but, even more striking, Israel has relied
less and less on a self-defense argument [37] and has taken action which is
openly admitted to be a reprisal. The Beirut raid of December 28, 1968,
is the obvious example of an action not really defended on the basis of
self-defense at all. Indeed, even as a reprisal, the motivation for reprisals
seems to have shifted from that of punishment for previous acts to deterrence of future possible acts.[38] Moreover, the more recent raids appear to
have had as their main purpose the general discouragement of any Arab
plans for military action against Israel by demonstrating Arab "incompetence." [39] This really shifts the justification away from any argument
traditionally accepted as relevant to reprisals and takes on the character
of a justification for "preventive" war or acts of warfare. It cannot be
expected that the Security Council will ever accept this justification. But
there is clearly some evidence that certain reprisals will, even if not accepted as justified, at least avoid condemnation. This shift in argument
from self-defense to reprisals may in part be due to the realization that
the self-defense argument is unlikely to be accepted in any event. It
may in larger part be due to a growing feeling that not only do reprisals
offer a more effective means of checking military and strategic gains by
the other party but also that they will meet with no more than a formal
condemnation by the Council, and that effective sanctions under Chapter
VII are not to be feared. Obviously, if this trend continues, we shall

[37] Although, interestingly enough, in relation to the Israeli incursions into Lebanese
territory in May and September of 1970, Israel reverted to the specific claim of self-
defense, this was not accepted by the Security Council (S/Res/280 and S/Res/285
(1970)).

[38] The Israeli Chief of Staff, General Yetzhak Bar Lev, was reported to have stated
the purpose as being "to make clear to the other side that the price they must pay for
terrorist activities can be very high"; see New York Times, Jan. 5, 1969, Sec. 4,
p. 1. However, Ambassador Rosenne, in the Security Council, did raise the justification of self-defense (see Doc. S/PV. 1460, pp. 22–23). It is of interest to note that
the Israeli practice of placing security guards on El Al aircraft (one of whom killed
an Arab guerrilla in the Zurich incident) does not seem to have met with any protest
and can thus be regarded as legitimate self-defense. This practice highlights the difference between defense of the aircraft, which is clearly permissible, and the broader
concept of self-defense which the Council rejects.

[39] The large-scale raid across the Red Sea, into Egyptian territory, on Sept. 8–9,
1969, was reported to have been "to demonstrate again to the Egyptians and other
Arabs their military incompetence and the boomerang folly of trying a war of attri-
tion"; see The Times Newspaper, Sept. 11, 1969, p. 8.

achieve a position in which, while reprisals remain illegal *de jure,* they become accepted *de facto.* Indeed, it may be that the more relevant distinction today is not between self-defense and reprisals but between reprisals which are likely to be condemned and those which, because they satisfy some concept of "reasonableness," are not.

A number of actions capable of characterization as reprisals have not, in practice, been condemned. Many are not even referred to the Security Council, presumably indicating that the target state felt there was little chance of condemnation.[40] An analysis of those that have been referred may suggest features or attendant circumstances which commend themselves to the Security Council in the sense of producing a reluctance to condemn the action.

After the Nahhalin incident of March 28, 1954, neither the Mixed Armistice Commission nor the Council condemned Israel. Perhaps the most striking feature about the incident is the equation—or proportionality—of the damage: the guerrilla attack from Jordan on an Israeli bus in the Negev killed eleven, the Israeli attack on the Jordanian village killed 9 and wounded 14.[41] A somewhat similar incident, the Karameh incident of March, 1968, brought unanimous condemnation of Israel.' But there, after an Israeli bus struck a mine in the Negev, killing two adults and injuring several school children, the Israeli reprisal took the form of a large-scale attack on Karameh with tanks, helicopters and aircraft in support, followed by claims to have killed 150 "terrorists." The debate in the Council emphasized the disproportionate character of the reprisal.[42] Indeed, time and time again (Qibya, 1952; Lake Tiberias, 1955 and 1962; Jordanian complaint of November 13, 1966; Samu Incident, 1966; Es-Salt Raids, 1968 and 1969, Beirut Raid, 1968) condemnations of Israel have followed when the Council has stressed the disproportionate nature of the reprisal.

One suspects that a somewhat similar adherence to the test of proportionality lies concealed in the reasoning that no useful purpose is served by the Council striking a balance-sheet of responsibility. This reasoning has been used by the Council on several occasions (the Patish, Gaza and Nahal Oz incidents of March–April, 1955;[43] the Gaza incident of September, 1955[44]) and the debates leave the impression that the Council found little to choose between the two sides. Indeed, in the *Eilat* in-

---

[40] For example, there were air strikes by Israel against Jordan on Feb. 11, March 16, March 26, April 20–21, 1969: of these only the Es-Salt raid on March 26 was referred to the Council.

[41] *Ibid.,* 9th Year, 665th to 671st Meetings; there was no vote on the Lebanese draft resolution condemning Israel for "aggression" (U.N. Doc. S/3209) and no discussion of reprisals.

[42] *Ibid.,* 23rd Year, Docs. S/PV. 1401–1407, March 21–24, 1968.

[43] This was an Israeli complaint against Egypt: see letter dated April 4, 1955 (Doc. S/3385, Supp. for April, May and June, 1955, p. 1). The debates are in 10th Year, 697th and 698th Meetings.

[44] Egyptian complaint of Israeli attack on Khan Younis, killing 10 soldiers and 25 civilians (Doc. S/3431, Supp. for July, August, September, 1955, p. 14). The debates are in 10th Year, 700th Meeting.

12   THE AMERICAN JOURNAL OF INTERNATIONAL LAW   [Vol. 66

cident of October 21, 1967, the rather neutral resolution condemning "the violations of the cease-fire" (but without singling out either Israel or Egypt) tends to suggest that the Council was disinclined to differentiate between the destruction of the Israeli destroyer and the bombardment of the Egyptian oil refineries.[45]   Another form of rather evasive reasoning, which may also conceal an attachment to the concept of proportionality, is that used by the Council when it declines to condemn either party because it sees its task as one of conciliation rather than condemnation.   This reasoning was surely applicable even in those cases where condemnation was made.   Yet, in the Kibbutz Dan incident of November 13, 1964, this formed part of the reasoning leading to the Council's not adopting any resolution.[46]   Thus, one arrives at a tentative conclusion that, given a situation in which both sides engage in violence or in breaches of a cease-fire, and given that the Council will not accept the "accumulation of events theory" but will look to the immediate cause and effect, a proportionate reprisal will not incur condemnation.   There are exceptions to this "rule."   The Israeli invasion of Gaza and Sinai in October, 1956, the British action in the Yemen in 1964 and the Portuguese attacks on Zambia in July, 1969, and on Senegal in 1969, prompted Security Council reactions which are difficult to reconcile with it.   The first involved a disproportionate Israeli reaction which was not condemned, largely because of the Anglo-French involvement, which seemed far more blameworthy to the majority of Council members and which could not be condemned because of the power of veto.   The latter two instances probably invoked a good deal of the anti-colonialist sentiment which operated against Britain's position in Southern Arabia and the Portuguese position in Africa and therefore brought a condemnation for actions which were probably not strikingly disproportionate.[47]

If a proportionate response is likely to avoid condemnation, it is of equal interest to ascertain what features of a reprisal action, other than disproportionality, are likely to incur condemnation.

There is a good deal of evidence to suggest that reprisals against civilian populations are more likely to be condemned than reprisals against armed forces.   Certainly there have been condemnations of attacks on armed forces (*e.g.*, Gaza incident of February, 1955; Lake Tiberias incident of December, 1955) and, contrariwise, there have been attacks on civilian populations which have not been condemned (Nahhalin incident, March,

[45] Both Israeli (Docs. S/8203, S/8204 and S/8298) and Egyptian complaints (Docs. S/8205 and S/8207), Supp. for October, November and December, 1967, pp. 188, 190–192. The debates are in Docs. S/PV. 1369–1371, Nov. 24 and 25, 1967. The Arab guerrilla attack on Eilat and the Israeli reprisal against Aqaba suggest a "tit-for-tat," proportionate reaction which apparently Jordan felt not worth referring to the Council: see Keesing's Contemporary Archives, 1969, p. 23327.

[46] *Ibid.*, 19th Year, 1162nd, 1165th–1169th Meetings, especially the U.K. (1165th Meeting), France (1166th Meeting) and Norway (1166th Meeting). However, China (1166th Meeting) did find the Israeli reaction disproportionate.

[47] U.N. Docs. S/5649, adopted April 9, 1964, and S/Res/268/1969, adopted July 28, 1969; both Britain and Portugal retaliated against repeated armed incursions.

1954, Kibbutz Dan incident, November, 1964). But, inconclusive though the practice may be, the fact that civilians have been killed has been stressed on a sufficient number of occasions to justify the assertion that this is a factor likely to bring about condemnation.[48] The non-involvement of civilians in any reprisal action would accord with the general thesis, accepted in the Geneva Civilians Convention of 1949, that civilian populations are not to be made the object of reprisals.[49] However, this does raise a difficult question of principle in situations where civilian populations aid, abet and harbor guerrillas or indeed form guerrilla units; this is a question to which we must return.

It may also be surmised that the Council will be readier to condemn a reprisal against human life than a reprisal against property. Israeli air attacks on the Jordan River development scheme in Syria in July, 1966,[50] and in Jordan on August 10, 1969,[51] have gone uncensored. However, the Beirut Airport raid of December, 1968, in which Israel took special precautions to avoid any loss of life, was nevertheless condemned [52] so that it must certainly not be assumed that reprisals against property will inevitably fall within the area of condoned reprisals. The "balance" between life and property is probably more a part of the general notion of proportionality.

The Beirut raid also illustrates the Security Council's tendency to reject any notion of "collective guilt" which might justify a reprisal against an Arab state irrespective of the origin of the injury which is the immediate cause of the reprisal action. In the Beirut case, Israel failed to adduce any convincing evidence that Lebanon was responsible for the attack on the El Al Boeing 707 at Athens airport by the two Arabs who apparently belonged to the Popular Front for the Liberation of Palestine and who

---

[48] This is clear from the debate on the Qibya incident of October, 1953, the Lake Tiberias incident of 1955 and, following the Karameh incident of March, 1968, Security Council Res. 248 (1968) specifically recalled the government's obligation to "ensure the safety, welfare, and health of the inhabitants of the areas" as a preliminary to deploring the loss of life. After the Es-Salt raid of August, 1968, in the debates preceding the condemnation of Israel, China and Senegal emphasized the fact that the raid caused civilian deaths (U.N. Docs. S/PV. 1435, pp. 63–65, S/PV. 1437, p. 8). So also after the Es-Salt raid in March, 1969, did Spain (U.N. Doc. S/PV. 1469, p. 27). Note also the U.S. statement after the Pleiku incident in February, 1965, when, following a Viet Cong attack on a U.S. airfield near Pleiku, destroying aircraft and killing U.S. servicemen, the "appropriate reprisal action," involving an attack on targets around Dong Hoi (50 miles north of the 17th parallel), was declared to be "carefully limited to military areas which are supplying men and arms for attacks in South Viet-Nam"; Press Release dated Feb. 7, 1965, 52 Department of State Bulletin 238 (1965).   [49] Art. 33. T.I.A.S., No. 3365.

[50] 21st Year, 1288th to 1295th Meetings; draft resolution S/7437 condemning Israel was not adopted.

[51] The attack on the Ghor Canal is reported in the Times Newspaper, Aug. 11, 1969; the Israeli Army is reported to have claimed this to be a reprisal for guerrilla attacks emanating from Jordanian territory.

[52] Security Council Res. 262 (1968), adopted unanimously on Dec. 31, 1968. And note that, prior to its air strike against the Yemen in 1964, the British first dropped warning messages to minimize loss of life: the British action was nevertheless condemned.

14   THE AMERICAN JOURNAL OF INTERNATIONAL LAW   [Vol. 66

had flown to Athens from Beirut, but who had otherwise no obvious connection with the Lebanon.[53] The general allegation by Israel that the Lebanon was "assisting and abetting acts of warfare, violence, and terror by irregular forces and organizations"[54] was not accepted as establishing Lebanese responsibility for this incident.[55] Clearly, even under traditional law, the target of any reprisal had to be shown to have committed a prior delict so that, without proof of delictual conduct *by the Lebanon,* the Council was disinclined to accept Israel's plea of justification, quite apart from the issue of proportionality. It is possible that the condemnation of Israeli action in the Samu incident in November, 1966,[56] was due not only to its disproportionate character but also to the fact that Israel attacked Jordan rather than Syria, which had been the country alleged by Israel to be responsible for the increase of terrorist activities only a month previously.[57]

The Israeli air strike on February 24, 1969, against guerrilla camps near Damascus was, according to some unofficial speculations,[58] motivated by the attack on El Al aircraft at Zurich on February 18 and the bombing of a Jerusalem supermarket. The camps belonged to the Popular Front for the Liberation of Palestine and those two incidents were, according to their own claim, the work of Al Fatah, a rival "terrorist" organization. Thus, as Falk points out,

> To attack Al Fatah bases in retaliation for activities of its rival organization, the Popular Front, appears at first to be rather surprising . . . If Israel, however, regards itself as confronted at this point by an adversary relying primarily on a multi-faceted liberation strategy employing a variety of terrorist tactics, then responses would seem rational that weaken this over-all para-military capability or that emphasize the collective responsibility of all liberation groups for any acts-of-terror kinds of responses. . . .[59]

[53] For a full discussion of this incident see Falk, *loc. cit.* 415–420. A parallel is to be found in the Soviet argument in the Security Council after the Pleiku reprisal in February, 1965: ". . . who gave the U.S. the right to retaliate for the actions of the guerrillas in South Vietnam by bombing the territory of a third country—the Democratic Republic of Vietnam?" (U.N. Doc. S/6178, 20th Year, Supp. for January, February and March, 1965, p. 48).

The validity of the argument of course depends upon the proof of responsibility, and Schick, "Some Reflections on the Legal Controversies concerning America's Involvement in Vietnam," 17 Int. and Comp. Law Q. 953 at 981 (1968), says: "No evidence has been produced by the American Government that these attacks were committed by North Vietnamese regulars, or with the knowledge and the approval of the Government of North Vietnam."

[54] U.N. Doc. S/8946, letter dated Dec. 29, 1968, from Israel to the President of the Security Council.

[55] The U.S. delegate stated: "Nothing that we have heard has convinced us that the Government of the Lebanon is responsible for the occurrence in Athens . . ." (U.N. Doc. S/PV. 1460, pp. 28–30).   [56] Res. 228 (1966).

[57] See the Financial Times, Nov. 14, 1966. Prime Minister Eshkol's speech in the Knesset on Oct. 17, accusing Syria, is summarized in Keesing's Contemporary Archives, 21817A, Jan. 14–21, 1967.

[58] James Feron, "New Israel Strategy Seen in Raid Near Damascus," New York Times, Feb. 25, 1969, p. 3.   [59] *Loc. cit.* 420.

It may be doubted whether this notion of "collective responsibility" will commend itself to the Security Council so as to avoid condemnation.[60] Nor, indeed, is it clear why it should, unless and until Israel can demonstrate that the various "liberation movements" fall under common planning and control, and so far the evidence is very much to the contrary.[61] The same would be true of reprisals directed against an Arab state as such (rather than guerrilla camps): unless and until the Arab armies are integrated and fall under a unified command,[62] there is no reason to justify a reprisal against, say, Jordanian Army units for activities undertaken by, say, Egyptian Army units. The whole notion of responsibility which was central to the Security Council's concern over the Beirut raid (and which is fundamental to accepted notions of state responsibility) would argue against any reprisals policy which allows the selection of targets irrespective of the origin of the particular cause of the reprisal.

There is also a possibility that, in determining "reasonableness," the Security Council will look to the question of how far the state taking the reprisal action has, by its own conduct, provoked the attack against which it subsequently takes reprisal action. In the discussions following the sinking of the Israeli destroyer, *Eilat*, although there remained a dispute as to whether the destroyer was on the high seas or, as Egypt alleged, in Egyptian territorial waters, there is evidence of a bias against the Israeli case precisely because, whatever the actual position of the vessel, it was in such proximity to Port Said as to constitute a kind of provocation, or at least a foolish maneuver under prevailing conditions; hence, the somewhat neutral resolution which emerged.[63]

Again, while it was an attack on the U.S. destroyer *Maddox* which gave rise to the Gulf of Tonkin incidents in August, 1964, and while, again, it was disputed whether the *Maddox* was in international waters or in the territorial waters of North Viet-Nam,[64] the pertinent question posed by Senator Nelson was:

[60] Although, to the author's knowledge, no proposal was presented to the Security Council to condemn the Damascus raid.

[61] For a useful account of Arab guerrilla organizations, their interrelationships and positions vis-à-vis Arab governments, see The Observer (London), May 18, 1969. The Cairo meeting of the Palestine National Council in February, 1969, virtually gave Al Fatah control of the Palestine Liberation Organization and specifically rejected the Security Council resolution of Nov. 22, 1967: see Keesing's Contemporary Archives, 1969, 23328. However, the Popular Front for the Liberation of Palestine (PFLP) and the Palestine Liberation Army (PLA) boycotted that meeting, so that unified control is far from achieved. There are reports of joint operations by Al Fatah and the PLO: see Egyptian Gazette, May 26, and July 2, 1968.

[62] An Arab Eastern Military Command, ostensibly designed to control Jordanian, Syrian and Iraqui forces, had been set up in 1968 (see Keesing's Contemporary Archives, 1969, 23328), but there is as yet no concrete evidence that these forces are actually controlled by a unified command: the command has been described as "embryonic" (Daily Telegraph, Dec. 7, 1968).

[63] S/Res. 240 (1967), adopted unanimously Nov. 25, 1967: for the debates see U.N. Docs. S/PV. 1369–1371, Nov. 24 and 25, 1967.

[64] See the contention of Czechoslovakia (19th Year, 1141st Meeting, p. 4). In fact, while it was known that the North Vietnamese claimed a 12-mile territorial sea,

16   THE AMERICAN JOURNAL OF INTERNATIONAL LAW   [Vol. 66

What purpose in the promotion of our mission in South Viet-Nam is served by having our ships go within 11 miles of the North Viet-Nam coast? . . . no two situations are comparable but it would be mighty risky, if Cuban P.T. boats were firing on Florida, for Russian armed ships and destroyers to be patrolling between us and Cuba, 11 miles out. . . . So the question was whether the patrolling that close was really necessary to the accomplishment of our mission.[65]

A further factor which apparently affects the Security Council's conception of "reasonableness" is the timing of the reprisal action in relation to efforts at peaceful settlement, the argument being that conduct which jeopardizes the chances of a peaceful settlement is the more reprehensible. It is obvious enough that conciliation efforts will be hampered by a spate of reprisals between the parties and this has figured in various discussions within the Council, condemning reprisals.[66] However, while this may be true as a short-term view, it appears to be part of the current Israeli thinking that, in the longer term, the prospects of a peaceful settlement are enhanced by a policy which forces the other party to realize that it has nothing to gain by continued attacks. This thinking certainly runs counter to that of the Security Council, where the theme "violence breeds violence" is a recurring one.[67] Which is the more correct, at least in the Middle East situation, time alone will tell. However, some two years after the June, 1967, conflict, the evidence suggested that Israeli thinking was a less correct assessment of the situation (or of Arab mentality) than the Security Council's. The incidence of violence had so increased as to call in question the effectiveness of the cease-fire. Indeed the Secretary General had conceded that, in the Canal Zone at least, it was "almost totally ineffective" and had been replaced by a "virtual state of active war." Since then, the situation in the Canal Zone has been stabilized, and, although tenuous at best, remains relatively quiet.[68] The degenerating effect of reprisals is possibly the strongest argument against them. Had the Israeli reprisal policy in the Middle East succeeded in the sense that it discouraged recourse to violence against Israel in breach of the cease-fire, whether by states through their regular armed forces or by guerrilla organizations, it would have been difficult for the Security Council to condemn it. Indeed, whatever the *prima facie* illegality of reprisals,

---

the U.S. did not recognize a territorial sea beyond 3 miles and the U.S.S. *Maddox* was apparently patrolling 11 miles offshore: see Senator Fulbright in 110 Cong. Rec. (1964) 18407, Aug. 6, 1964.   [65] *Ibid.* 18408.

[66] See, after the Es-Salt raid of March, 1969, Spain (U.N. Doc. S/PV. 1469, p. 27), and after the earlier Es-Salt raid of August, 1968, Denmark (U.N. Doc. S/PV. 1436, p. 52).

[67] Lord Caradon (U.K.) after the Karameh incident of March, 1966, stated: "Violence solves nothing. Violence does not prevent violence. Violence breeds more violence" (U.N. Doc. S/PV. 1403, p. 3). To the same effect, at an earlier stage, see the Netherlands representative (U.N. Doc. S/PV. 1323, pp. 6–7).

[68] Special Report of the Secretary General on the critical situation in the Suez Canal Sector (Doc. S/9171), April 21, 1969, par. 2. See report by the Secretary General on the Activities of the Special Representative to the Middle East (Doc. S/10070, Jan. 4, 1971) and Further Report by the Secretary General on the Activities of the Special Representative to the Middle East (Doc. S/10070/Add. 2, March 5, 1971).

the fact that they actively assisted in maintaining the cease-fire would have been enormously persuasive. However, in the event that reprisals produce an escalation of tension and violence, a situation diametrically opposite to the policy objectives of the Security Council, the basic antipathy of the Council towards reprisals is understandable.

3. THE SPECIAL PROBLEM OF REPRISALS AGAINST GUERRILLA ACTIVITY

Reference has already been made to the special difficulties encountered by a state which is forced to adjust its defensive measures against guerrilla activity to a narrow concept of self-defense.[69] The Israeli policy had shifted quite clearly to one of reprisal, with the avowed object of deterrence or "teaching a lesson"[70] and, while this may be regarded by Israel as the best means of defense, it is clear that the Security Council will certainly not accept this policy as one of legitimate self-defense.

Even a policy of reprisal which might seek to avoid condemnation because of its "reasonableness" encounters the initial difficulty of demonstrating the illegality of the activities against which it is directed. This is amply illustrated by the Arab-Israeli situation. Apart from using emotive terms such as "terrorists," Israel has sought to have the guerrilla activities condemned as illegal and has done so on a variety of grounds. Initially the main ground was violation of the Armistice Agreements and, clearly, the transgression of the Armistice Demarcation Lines (ADL) or other violations of the truce were breaches of these agreements.[71] It may also be noted that these agreements expressly recognized the responsibility of the territorial state for "non-regular" forces. Article III(2) provided:

> No element of the land, sea or air, military or para-military forces of either Party, including non-regular forces, shall commit any warlike or hostile acts against the military or para-military forces of the other Party, or against civilians in territory under the control of that Party; or shall advance beyond or pass over for any purpose whatsoever the Armistice Demarcation Lines. . . .

The Security Council, by resolution of August 19, 1948,[72] formally decided that

> (a) Each party is responsible for the actions of both regular and irregular forces operating under its authority or in territory under its control;

[69] P. 9 above.

[70] The raid on Es-Salt was conceived as a "warning" to the Jordanian Government about the consequences of aiding saboteurs and infiltrators. New York Times, Aug. 6, 1968. Similarly, the Israeli attack on Irbid was regarded as a "reminder of Jordan's vulnerability." Financial Times, Sept. 18, 1968. The Beirut raid was also certainly designed to teach a message about the price of encouragement of guerrilla attacks on Israeli aircraft. Le Figaro, Dec. 30, 1968.

[71] Especially Arts. III(2) and (3) and IV(3). As early as the debate on the Qibya incident, Mr. Eban (Israel) emphasized the relevance of the agreements to this kind of activity and referred to Art. IV(3) as "the crux of the agreement. Without it Israel's coastal plain becomes an inferno of chaos and lawlessness." (8th Year, 637th Meeting, p. 17.)   [72] U.N. Doc. S/983.

18   THE AMERICAN JOURNAL OF INTERNATIONAL LAW   [Vol. 66

(b) Each party has the obligation to use all means at its disposal to prevent action violating the Truce by individuals or groups who are subject to its authority or who are in territory under its control.

Indeed, the Security Council, in condemning the Israeli action at Qibya,[73] expressly rejected the plea that the forces responsible were not Israeli armed forces but Israeli civilians taking the remedy into their own hands.

The situation since the June, 1967, war has changed in the sense that Israel (but not the Security Council) has now rejected the validity of all the 1948 Armistice Agreements. The case for arguing the illegality of the guerrilla attacks has shifted to the general principle of non-intervention [74] and the Security Council's cease-fire resolutions.

However, there is growing evidence that, while some members of the Security Council remain emphatic in the view that guerrilla activities *are* illegal by reason of their violation of the cease-fire resolutions,[75] if for no other reason, other members are now reluctant to accept this view. One can see an argument that the cease-fire resolution prohibited guerrilla activities on the assumption that the other parts of the resolution would be given effect; and that, since this has not happened, and, in particular, Israel remains in occupation of the Arab territories first occupied in June, 1967, the prohibition has ceased to have effect. However, this argument must produce the logical conclusion that the entire resolution has ceased to have effect (one can scarcely sever parts of it for the benefit of guerrilla activities). Such a conclusion would not be likely to commend itself to the Council so that, understandably, this argument does not appear to have been used in the Council. The argument which has been used is the much wider one that, faced with a military occupation of Arab lands, guerrilla activities are permissible despite the continuing validity of the cease-fire resolution. The argument was put, in somewhat extreme terms, by the U.S.S.R., after the Es-Salt raid in August, 1968:

[73] U.N. Doc. S/3139/Rev. 2, adopted at the 642nd Meeting.

[74] See statement by Ambassador Comay (Israel), U.N. Doc. S/PV. 1323, Nov. 18, 1966 (although, at that stage, the argument was used as one supplementary to, and not in substitution for, the argument based on the Armistice Agreements). He there cited General Assembly Res. 2131(XX): "No State shall organize, assist, foment, finance, incite or tolerate subversive, terrorist or armed activities directed towards the violent overthrow of . . . another State."

[75] Hence, in the debate on the Karameh incident of March 21, 1968, the U.S. (U.N. Doc. S/PV. 1402, pp. 3–5) and the U.K. (U.N. Doc. S/PV. 1403, p. 3) condemned *all* breaches of the cease-fire: in the debate after the Es-Salt raid of March 26, 1969, the U.S. and the U.K. in fact abstained on the vote condemning Israel for the reprisal, on the ground that the resolution failed to condemn the attacks by Arab guerrillas which had precipitated it (U.N. Docs. S/PV. 1472, pp. 21–22, 23; S/PV. 1473, p. 56). It may be noted that S/Res. 270 (1969) of Aug. 26, 1969, while condemning Israel for the reprisal by air attack, did in fact contain a paragraph "deploring all violent incidents in violation of the cease-fire," so there is some evidence that the U.K./U.S.A. viewpoint is gaining ground. The Israel Government has always taken the view that guerrilla activities *are* breaches of the cease-fire. See Mr. Eshkol's speech to the Knesset, reported in Egyptian Gazette, March 26, 1968.

Recognition of the fact that people have the right to wage a just struggle for their freedom and independence against imperialist aggressors and usurpers is a very signal and progressive achievement of the present day, and no one these days will be able to call this right of peoples in question, however much the forces of imperialism and aggression try to turn the wheel of history backwards. Those who attempt to deny this right are in fact striking a blow against the sacred right of all peoples that are determinedly fighting for the liquidation of racist and colonial regimes and are fighting against imperialist aggression.[76]

In various forms, certain members of the Council have expressed their concern over the continued military occupation of Arab lands [77] and it seems clear that they are not only reluctant to share Israel's characterization of the "terrorist" activities as illegal but also reject any plea by Israel of justified reprisals against these activities. It may thus emerge that Security Council condonation is more likely in respect of reprisals taken to protect territory by the state which is the accepted sovereign over that territory. This view is strengthened by the 1964 condemnation of the British action in the Yemen and the 1969 and 1970 condemnations of Portuguese action against Zambia and Senegal. The sentiment emerging in the Council was that guerrilla activities designed to oust a colonialist Power were not illegal since the colonialist Power's title to the territory or control over it was itself illegal.

However, in relation to Israel, the distinction between the territories occupied in June, 1967, and the territories previously held by Israel is not one on which the Arab guerrilla movements place any great emphasis: both territories are, in their view, "illegally" occupied. This is clearly not the view of the Security Council, and one can reasonably expect a far more sympathetic reaction to reprisals taken in "defense" of Israel proper. Contrariwise, one can expect a more sympathetic reaction to guerrilla activities aimed at challenging the Israeli hold on the newly-occupied territories (and confined to bases, police and army posts, etc., rather than civilian targets in those territories) than to guerrilla activities aimed at Israel proper.[78]

The question of the illegality of guerrilla activities (and, correspondingly, the reasonableness of reprisals against them) is inevitably linked

[76] U.N. Doc. S/PV. 1437, p. 22. And note that the latest Soviet proposal on the definition of aggression expressly excludes the use of force in the exercise of the right of self-determination (U.N. Doc. A/AC 134/L. 12 of Feb. 27, 1969).

[77] France has stated: "Nor can we agree that it is possible to speak of necessary measures for the security of the territory and population under the jurisdiction of Israel, because we cannot recognize jurisdiction established by occupation" (U.N. Doc. S/PV. 1402, p. 22). See also Pakistan (U.N. Docs. S/PV. 1435, p. 36 and S/PV. 1468, p. 21); Senegal (U.N. Doc. S/PV. 1436, pp. 63–65); Zambia (U.N. Doc. S/PV. 1469, p. 51).

[78] However, it cannot be said that the Security Council has reacted with great energy to Israel's complaint of guerrilla attacks and hijacking of Israeli aircraft. Possibly the matter is not regarded as one with which the Council can deal easily and certainly the Secretary General seems to have assumed ICAO was the more competent: see Eban-U Thant exchange of letters, Feb. 20 and 26, 1969 (U.N. Monthly Chronicle, March, 1969, pp. 12–14).

20   THE AMERICAN JOURNAL OF INTERNATIONAL LAW   [Vol. 66

to that of the responsibility of the state on whose territory these activities are organized. As we have seen, the Security Council initially had no doubts about the general principle of the responsibility of the territorial state. However, international law has not developed any notion of absolute liability in this field and the basic assumption has been that the territorial state assumed responsibility because it had the power to prevent these activities. This assumption must now be called in question. It is probably unrealistic in relation to Jordan and the Lebanon,[79] and partly so in relation to Syria and Egypt. The lack of realism about this assumption depends in part on factors such as the size of the territory and the limited military capacity of a state when compared with the magnitude of the guerrilla activities, and in larger part on purely political factors. No Arab Government, given the enormous popular support for the guerrilla activities amongst its own population, appeared able to risk an intensive campaign to stamp out these activities; the consequence was judged likely to be an internal insurrection and overthrow of the government. Not until 1970 did the Jordanian Government commit its forces to intensive fighting against the Palestinian guerrillas.

In these circumstances, the aim of "teaching a lesson" to these governments may be misplaced. Reprisals are not likely to affect the toleration shown by a government to guerrilla activities when a show of intolerance would bring the downfall of the government. For these reasons, within a context like the Middle East situation, it would seem that a test of "reasonableness" would require a differentiation between the targets of a reprisal action. Hence, a reprisal aimed at the guerrillas, destroying their camps or bases, might be regarded as reasonable, whereas a reprisal aimed at the government or at state installations, such as airports, dams, irrigation systems, ports, etc., is far less likely to avoid condemnation.

A further indication of "reasonableness" would be the extent to which the state taking reprisals had exhausted all practical measures for the defense of its territory *within its own territory*. The bias against military action which transgresses a frontier or cease-fire line is marked and, in general terms, right. It is common form for reprisals to involve such transgression and, inevitably, the question is posed: "Why could not the state have defended itself against these guerrilla activities by measures of de-

---

[79] For details of clashes between Lebanese forces and Syrian-backed guerrillas within the Lebanon in April and May, 1969, see Keesing's Contemporary Archives, 1969, 23520. King Hussein had rejected the suggestion that he is under any duty to halt guerrilla activities and had justified those activities (New York Times, March 24, 1968). In the debate on the Es-Salt raid of March 26, the Israeli representative, Mr. Tekoah, alleged complete complicity between the Jordan Government and the guerrilla organizations, citing an agreement between them of Nov. 16, 1968. In 1970 in the debates on the Israeli incursions into the Lebanon in May and September, Mr. Tekoah alleged that similar agreements had been made between the Lebanese Government and guerrilla organizations. This position in Jordan had changed quite radically by the summer of 1970. On July 19, 1970, the Jordanian Government announced that, at the culmination of a series of clashes between its forces and guerrilla forces, it had destroyed the Palestinian guerrilla organization on Jordanian territory and all its bases. The Times Newspaper, July 20, 1970.

fense adopted on its own territory?" [80] It may be noted that the 10-Power, non-aligned proposal on the definition of aggression combines a concession that a state is entitled to take "all reasonable and adequate steps" against "subversive and/or terrorist" acts with the restriction that these may not take place on another state's territory. [81]

It may well be that some of the lack of sympathy for the Israeli policy stems from the belief that, in her reprisals policy, Israel has chosen the easy way and has not yet tried possible measures of defense against infiltration within her own territory (or that now militarily occupied by Israel). Or, alternatively, if Israel has exhausted all reasonable and possible measures of defense, she has failed to demonstrate this to bodies like the Security Council so as to convince them of the necessity for reprisal actions within Arab territories.

4. The Relevance of Security Council Attitudes on Reprisals

It must be accepted that, in situations like Viet-Nam, a pronouncement by the Security Council on the legality of reprisal actions is unlikely; certainly none has yet been made and the United States will probably continue to feel strongly enough about the situation to veto any resolution directed against her. This is not to assume that no Permanent Member will ever find its reprisals policy censured: the United Kingdom abstention in the Yemen case in 1964 permitted this to happen. And, even apart from a formal resolution of censure, discussion in the Council will have relevance to the extent that it will afford to the Member State a guide to the likely reaction in world opinion.

It must be expected that in situations like the Middle East there will be found a sufficient degree of unanimity in the Council over the general aim of maintaining the cease-fire (or, previously, the Armistice Agreements) to enable the Council to formulate a firm policy on reprisals. Indeed, as we have seen, the Council has, on many occasions and very often unanimously, taken a clear position on reprisals. It is nevertheless true that the Security Council has never been able to stop the practice of reprisals and, as suggested above, may now be moving towards a partial acceptance of "reasonable" reprisals. The Security Council's practice must nevertheless be viewed with caution. The clear position is that the Council, as a matter of principle, condemns armed reprisals as illegal. The unclear position emerges from the Council's failure to condemn in

---

[80] This is not a question to which lawyers can give persuasive answers. However, there would be advantage in a strategic study of the effectiveness against guerrilla activities emanating from abroad of measures of self-defense confined to the target state's own territory. Possibly, variations in circumstances (terrain, size of respective forces, length of frontier, etc.) are such as to permit no generalizations. But obviously a comprehensive study which demonstrated that self-defense, narrowly construed, is in general ineffective against guerrilla activities would strengthen the case for reprisals considerably. Apparently Israel had seriously considered sealing off the 50-mile cease-fire line with Jordan by a defensive barrier, a technique once regarded as impractical (James Feron in the Herald Tribune, Dec. 20, 1967).

[81] U.N. Doc. A/AC. 134/L. 16 of March 24, 1969.

22   THE AMERICAN JOURNAL OF INTERNATIONAL LAW   [Vol. 66

certain circumstances. This is possibly due to a number of factors: a formal condemnation may not have been sought, or may have been avoided because of the lack of accurate factual knowledge, or because the action was regarded as self-defense, or because the Council regarded the action taken as a "reasonable" reprisal. It is only in the last eventuality that we face a conceptual problem, since we would then have an apparent conflict between the principle of the illegality of *all* armed reprisals and the Council's practice in not condemning a particular reprisal because it appeared "reasonable."

The Security Council's practice certainly reveals a problem of this kind: there is a discrepancy between the formal principle and the actual practice (a discrepancy which would be reduced if, as suggested earlier,[82] the Council took a broader view of self-defense). Yet it is possibly premature to suggest that the principle is now jeopardized. The principle, as part of the broader prohibition of the use of force, is *jus cogens*, and no spasmodic, inconsistent practice of one organ of the United Nations could change a norm of this character.[83] This is the more so because, as we have seen,[84] in the context of the General Assembly's adoption of the "Declaration on Principles of International Law," etc., in October, 1970, the reiteration of the formal principle of the illegality of armed reprisals was quite categorical.

If we return, however, to situations where the Council does make a formal condemnation, there still remains a question whether the pronouncements of the Council are of any real relevance or authority either in qualifying the action as unlawful or, even more important, in affecting the future conduct of the parties.

(a) *Is the Council's authority vitiated by bias?*

Although few would quarrel with the general characterization of a Security Council resolution as an "authoritative pronouncement"[85] on the legality of action taken by a Member State, and few would deny the state's general obligation to accord respect to such a pronouncement, Israel has in fact adduced special arguments which, it maintains, entitle Israel to ignore Security Council pronouncements on the Middle East situation. Mr. Tekoah's reaction to the Council's condemnation after the Beirut raid was:

> Let no one make the mistake of thinking that the people of Israel
> might be swayed by inequitable pronouncements . . . not Security

[82] Above, p. 7.

[83] The Vienna Convention on the Law of Treaties, Art. 53, requires the development of a new peremptory norm to change an earlier peremptory norm.

[84] Above, p. 1.

[85] Falk, *loc. cit.* 436. He is here discussing the resolution following the Beirut raid (S/Res/262 (1968)) and presupposes that it was technically a recommendation and not a "decision" binding by virtue of Art. 25 of the Charter. And he concedes (p. 463, note 60) that the distinction between decisions and recommendations is not very apt when one is really dealing with a formal resolution of censure; it would be more apt to par. 4 of the resolution in which the Council considered that Lebanon was entitled to compensation.

Council resolutions, but the attitude and actions of the Governments in the area will determine the destiny of the Middle East.[86]

The view that its pronouncements are "inequitable" stems from the Israeli belief that the Council is biased.[87]   Again, in Mr. Tekoah's words:

> The Council has failed us again and again.   For the past fifteen years this organ has found itself paralyzed whenever Israel has had re-course to it.   The veto was cast to avert a reaffirmation of Israel's right to free navigation.   It was cast to torpedo even the mildest of requests to Arab States to cease their warfare against Israel . . . . Five of the members of the Security Council have no diplomatic re-lations with Israel.   All five have identified themselves unreservedly with the position of the Arab States.   Two of them deny Israel's right to exist.   One has participated in the war against Israel and refuses to accept the cease-fire ordered by the Security Council.[88]

This argument is not wholly convincing.   It fails to take account of the many cases in which Member States like the United States, the United Kingdom, The Netherlands, New Zealand, France, Belgium, etc. (not, in the Arab view, "pro-Arab") have joined in the condemnation of the Israeli reprisals policy.   It also fails to account for a similar "bias" in the Mixed Armistice Commissions which have frequently held Israel respon-sible for breaches of the Armistice.[89]   One is forced to consider the pos-sibility that, whether or not some Members were biased, the Council as a whole has usually taken a view which would seem objectively to be right.

However, bias is not the only Israeli argument, for it appears that rejection of the Council's authority is also based upon the view that the Council is ineffective [90] and weakened, morally, by the conduct of its own members.[91]

[86] U.N. Doc. S/PV. 1462, p. 52.

[87] The U.K. could, of course, maintain that a similar "anti-colonialist" bias lay behind the Council's condemnation of her action in the Yemen reprisal in 1964; and the U.S. would certainly find a general bias against her on any Viet-Nam incident. So, too, would Portugal in respect of the Council's condemnation of the attacks on Zambia (S/Res/268 (1969)), on Senegal (S/Res/273 (1969)), and on Guinea (S/Res/290 (1970)).

[88] U.N. Doc. S/PV. 1401, p. 4: statement on March 21, 1968, in the course of the debate on the Karameh incident.

[89] Israel declined to participate in the Syrian-Israeli MAC after 1951 and gave as her reason that she could no longer rely on the impartiality of the Chairman.   Even if this was justified, the fact still remains that, on the whole, the MAC's tended to find Israel responsible more frequently than the other parties for breaches of the Armistice.

[90] See Prime Minister Eshkol's statement to the Israeli Cabinet on Nov. 27, 1966: "The majority in the Security Council ignored the causes of the tension that exists on Israel's borders and dealt unilaterally with the results of one incident alone. . . . So long as the Security Council has not adopted effective measures to stop the ag-gressor, it is the duty and the right of an attacked State to defend itself . . ." (Keesing's Contemporary Archives, 1967–8, 21819).   The allegation of "one-sided-ness" is to some extent supported by the abstentions of members like the U.S.A. and U.K. which have opposed the Council's refusal to condemn guerrilla activities lead-ing to Israeli reprisals (see above, note 75).

[91] Mr. Eban suggested that anti-Jewish discrimination could alone explain Israel's isolation: "I have no other explanation for the fact that the Soviet Union, which

24   THE AMERICAN JOURNAL OF INTERNATIONAL LAW   [Vol. 66

(b) *Is the Council ineffective?*

Any view on the Council's effectiveness is conditioned by the expectations with which one begins. If the expectation was that the Council would itself take action safeguarding Israel from all attack, then the Council has certainly been ineffective: but the expectation is unrealistic and, coming from Israel (which opposed the stationing of UNEF on Israeli soil and still opposes more than a minimal rôle for UNTSO), somewhat surprising. Moreover, ineffectiveness in this sense is somewhat irrelevant to the issue of reprisals: it is highly relevant to Israel's case for maintaining her right of self-defense, but hardly relevant to the question whether Israel should go beyond self-defense and engage in reprisals which are *prima facie* unlawful. Were this not so, the "ineffectiveness" of the Council—which in the sense used above is common ground in more situations than the Middle East—would justify any Member State in totally rejecting the Charter prohibitions on the use of force.

The more germane question is whether the Security Council pronouncements are effective in the sense of influencing the "decision-makers." Israel would appear to have adopted the view that it will not now be influenced by these pronouncements. This is probably not completely the case in practice, for no state lightly incurs the burden of defending itself in more than one international forum, in the press and before world opinion if this can be avoided. And it appears clear that world opinion *is* affected. The Council's condemnations reach the headlines throughout the world and, certainly in Western Europe, the era of reprisals and condemnation which has occurred since the June, 1967, war has seen a marked shift of sympathy away from Israel. It is doubtful whether, without Security Council condemnation, the Pope [92] would have seen fit to condemn the Israeli action in the Beirut raid. Thus, Israel is forced to make a choice between abandoning its reprisals policy and suffering increasing loss of public sympathy.[93]

The Arab states are probably only marginally affected; an assessment is difficult because, in practice, the majority of pronouncements have gone against Israel, not the Arab states. But the Egyptian stance over free passage through the Suez Canal (which was opposed by the Council but maintained in spite of it) [94] and the pre-June, 1967, support for the Palestine Liberation Organization and Army (despite the terms of the Armistice Agreements and Council resolutions) and post-June, 1967, encouragement

---

invaded Czechoslovakia, can condemn alleged Israeli 'aggression' at the U.N. without the public gallery bursting into laughter" (Time Magazine, Jan. 10, 1969, p. 28).

[92] Blum, *loc. cit.* 92, regards even the Pope as biased, taking the somewhat uncharitable view that the Pope was influenced by the large numbers of Roman Catholics in the Lebanon.

[93] This is the same kind of choice made by the U.S.S.R. over Hungary and Czechoslovakia, or by France and the U.K. over Suez, or by the U.S. over Viet-Nam: the loss of public sympathy is not dependent on Security Council condemnation, but it is surely aggravated by it.

[94] Security Council Res. 95 (1951) and 118 (1956).

of guerrilla activities would suggest that the Council's influence is not great. And it is surely true that, at the level of the guerrilla movements themselves, the impact of any Security Council pronouncement on the legality of their actions would be minimal.

Thus, it seems likely that, simply as pronouncements, the Security Council resolutions have little real effect other than as one additional factor in the many which tend to shape world opinion. This can scarcely be accepted as adequate to maintain respect for these pronouncements and, demonstrably, it has not been adequate to check the growing practice of reprisals in the Middle East.

There remains the possibility that the Council might seek to achieve effectiveness by resort to its own punitive measures under Chapter VII. One of the least impressive aspects of Security Council action has been the frequency with which it has, in condemning reprisals, conveyed a threat of sterner action [95]—presumably meaning the use of its preventive or enforcement powers under Chapter VII—but yet never seriously considered the possibility of enforcing respect for its authority. The threat has lost all conviction and is now apparently without any deterrent effect whatever. Of course, the difficulty is that, while the Council can produce sufficient unanimity to condemn a reprisal action, a proposal to take sanctions against either the Arab or the Israeli side would be far more difficult for the Permanent Members to support. However, if we reject military sanctions as patently impossible, there yet remains a variety of measures available to the Council.

Practice in relation to South Africa, Portugal and Rhodesia (none of them a more serious threat to world peace than the Middle East situation) has shown a range of "sanctions" extending from calls for the cessation of arms supplies and the suspension of economic aid to full economic sanctions. It would seem likely that the parties to the Middle East conflict are more susceptible to these sanctions than South Africa, Portugal and, possibly, even Rhodesia, so that arguments about the proved ineffectiveness of such sanctions are not necessarily convincing.[96] Sanctions in the form of an embargo or calculated restraint on arms supplies to the area ought to be perfectly possible. There is, in fact, something ludicrous about a situation in which the Council condemns reprisals, but individual Members continue to provide the arms with which those reprisals are executed (and even more ludicrous when the United Kingdom

[95] U.N. Doc. S/7498, adopted on Nov. 25, 1966, envisaged "more effective steps as envisaged in the Charter to ensure against the repetition of such acts." S/Res. 270 (1969), following the August, 1969, air attack on South Lebanon, referred specifically to the possibility of "further and more effective steps as envisaged in the Charter to ensure against repetition of such acts." Also S/Res. 268 (1969), condemning Portugal for the attack on the Zambian village of Lote, threatened "to consider further measures" if Portugal continued raids on Zambia. Successive threats of sanctions, never implemented, can do little to enhance the reputation of the Security Council and were best not uttered at all.

[96] Apparently the threat by the U.S. to cease economic aid to Israel was the means whereby the Israeli project for diverting the River Jordan in 1953 was stopped. Burns, *Between Arab and Israel* 11 (New York: Obolensky, 1963).

26   THE AMERICAN JOURNAL OF INTERNATIONAL LAW   [Vol. 66

supplies to Jordan the missiles necessary to destroy the aircraft which the United States has supplied to Israel).[97] This is, therefore, a perfectly possible choice for the Security Council: if, for domestic or other reasons, its Members are not prepared to make that choice in the face of growing contempt for the authority of the Council, then those Members must face the probability that the Council's pronouncements will soon become almost totally irrelevant.

There is, of course, a special difficulty in a policy of sanctions which is directed to the suppression of guerrilla activities, for guerrilla movements are notoriously more immune from sanctions than are governments. However, guerrilla movements are financed and supplied to a large extent from external sources, so that any sanctions policy with this aim would have to envisage the possible extension of economic pressure to the states which are the source of supply.[98] One final argument against sanctions in a situation like the Middle East is its inequity in the sense that states like the United Kingdom, the United States, and the U.S.S.R. have, arguably, perpetrated greater offenses against international peace than those which may be committed by the states of the Middle East, and sanctions against the former cannot be contemplated. The argument is unconvincing. Given that the essential aim of the Council is to maintain world peace, if, say, an attempt at sanctions against the U.S.S.R. is likely to make an even greater threat to world peace, while sanctions in the Middle East may promote world peace, "equity" has nothing to do with it. The selectiveness of the policy is justified by the primary aim in view.

5. The Criteria of the "Reasonableness" of Reprisals as a Guide to a Policy of Restraint

As indicated earlier,[99] there is evidence to suggest that reprisals satisfying certain criteria of reasonableness may avoid condemnation by the Security Council even though the Council will maintain the general proposition that *all* armed reprisals are illegal. Even an indifference to Security Council attitudes may still leave a state persuaded of the political wisdom of a policy of reasonableness. It may still be concerned about the attitudes of individual states (which may, incidentally, find it difficult to depart too far, in their individual capacity, from the stand

[97] For a summary of the arms race in the Middle East after June, 1967, see Hurewitz, Middle East Politics: The Military Dimension 484–488 (New York: Praeger, 1967). The lack of any coherent policy among Council members is evident from the U.S. sale of 50 F.4 Phantom jets to Israel and France's embargo on fighter aircraft and spares to Israel: see the New York Times, Dec. 28, 1968, Jan. 12, and July 11, 1969.

[98] This eventuality might also arise if, in due course, a peace settlement is agreed between the states of the region but is rejected by the guerrilla movements; it might be that these guerrilla movements would remain as the only recalcitrant elements in an otherwise agreed settlement and, therefore, that sanctions would have to be applied to them. The various guerrilla organizations appear to find common ground in their rejection of the Security Council resolution of Nov. 22, 1967.

[99] Pp. 8–14 above.

they have taken in the Council) or, more generally, about the state's image in world public opinion. It may even decide that restraint might be reciprocated and that a general lowering of tension is in its own interest.

Thus, there is utility and purpose in clarifying the kinds of criteria of reasonableness which practice presently suggests are relevant. These have been admirably summarized by Falk [100] in the form of a "framework" embodying "certain general policies" and merit citation in full:

> (1) That the burden of persuasion is upon the government that initiates an official use of force across international boundaries; [101]
> (2) That the governmental user of force will demonstrate its defensive character convincingly by connecting the use of force to the protection of territorial integrity, national security, or political independence;
> (3) That a genuine and substantial link exists between the prior commission of provocative acts and the resultant claim to be acting in retaliation; [102]
> (4) That a diligent effort be made to obtain satisfaction by persuasion and pacific means over a reasonable period of time, including recourse to international organizations; [103]
> (5) That the use of force is proportional to the provocation and calculated to avoid its repetition in the future, and that every precaution be taken to avoid excessive damage and unnecessary loss of life, especially with respect to innocent civilians; [104]
> (6) That the retaliatory force is directed primarily against military and para-military targets and against military personnel; [105]
> (7) That the user of force make a prompt and serious explanation of its conduct before the relevant organ(s) of community review and seek vindication therefrom of its course of action;
> (8) That the use of force amounts to a clear message of communication to the target government so that the contours of what constituted the unacceptable provocation are clearly conveyed;
> (9) That the user of force cannot achieve its retaliatory purposes by acting within its own territorial domain and thus cannot avoid interference with the sovereign prerogatives of a foreign state; [106]
> (10) That the user of force seek a pacific settlement to the underlying dispute on terms that appear to be just and sensitive to the interests of its adversary;
> (11) That the pattern of conduct of which the retaliatory use of force is an instance exhibits deference to considerations (1)–(10), and that a disposition to accord respect to the will of the international community be evident;
> (12) That the appraisal of the retaliatory use of force take account of the duration and quality of support, if any, that the target government has given to terroristic enterprises. [107]

Certain comments on these twelve heads seem appropriate. Head (2) is perhaps too demanding within the context of reprisals and, indeed, tends to blur any distinction between reprisals and self-defense. It would, in practice, be difficult to apply so rigorous a test to a reprisal for guerrilla activities within occupied territory (for how is this necessarily re-

---

[100] *Loc. cit.* 441–442.   [101] Pp. 20–21 above.
[102] Pp. 13–15 above.   [103] Pp. 16 above.
[104] Pp. 11–12 above.   [105] Pp. 12–13 above.
[106] Pp. 20–21 above.   [107] Pp. 19–20 above.

28   THE AMERICAN JOURNAL OF INTERNATIONAL LAW   [Vol. 66

lated to the claimant state's "territorial integrity, national security, or political independence"?) or even, for example, to reprisals for attacks on civil aircraft. This is not to deny that the claimant state may invoke self-defense of its military installations in occupied territory or its civil aircraft, or, if self-defense is demonstrably ineffective as a means of protection, may invoke reprisals. But it is perhaps too restrictive to insist that reprisals should be limited to situations involving a need to protect "territorial integrity", etc. Indeed, this introduces the broader concept of self-defense and becomes applicable only by use of the "accumulation of events" theory which the Security Council has generally rejected. Hence, given the scope of the other heads, this Head (2) is probably unnecessary in relation to reprisals.

On somewhat similar reasoning, Head (10) may broaden the issue overmuch. Obviously, public sympathy will be greater towards a party actively seeking settlement of the underlying dispute, but the Security Council practice has been to concentrate on the specific act of reprisal, and it may be excessive to demand not only that in the specific circumstances the reprisal be reasonable but also that the claimant state be acting reasonably in relation to the basic dispute underlying the tension.

The only other reservation this author would have is as to the use of the notion of prior *provocative* acts (Heads (3) and (8)) rather than prior *illegal* acts: the notion of "illegality" is not easy, but it is far less ambiguous and more in accord with established doctrine than that of "provocation." For the rest, the insistence upon burden of proof (Head (1)), substantial link (Heads (3) and (8)), efforts at pacific settlement (Head (4)), proportionality (Head (5)), confinement to military targets (Head (6)), community review (Head (7)), necessity to go beyond territorial self-defense (Head (9)), respect for the will of the community (Head (11)) and responsibility for guerrilla activities (Head (12)) seems not only right but also in accord with the prevailing trends as revealed in Security Council debates. One might usefully add that the burden of proof should extend to the question why the claimant state found legitimate self-defense impossibly restrictive and found it necessary to resort to reprisals at all.

Whatever the intrinsic merits of these criteria or this "framework," to use Falk's expression, and however desirable it may be for the decision-makers of states undertaking reprisals (or of other states reviewing their conduct) to accept these guides to restraint, in final analysis one must face the question: What if they do not? This question is unavoidable for, on the past record, there is no strong indication that the Falk framework, or any appeal to reasonableness and restraint, is likely to stay the deteriorating pattern of behavior.

As suggested above, one possibility is that the Security Council might consider the desirability of limited sanctions designed to reinforce its authority and deter unreasonable reprisals. The other possibility, somewhat separate from this, is to consider institutional devices which may assist states in pursuing a policy of restraint. It is to this that we must now turn.

6. INSTITUTIONAL DEVICES FOR FACT-FINDING

The retention of a system of "community review" of any reprisal action is fundamental to any policy of restraint and, normally,[108] the Security Council will be the organ of review. Such review is, of course, essential if sanctions are in contemplation and, even apart from this, the possibility of review constitutes an important psychological deterrent to those contemplating reprisals. However, no system of review can operate satisfactorily without facilities for independent fact-finding: it is rarely satisfactory to rely entirely on the evidence adduced by the parties. Moreover, in situations where mutual distrust arises from the holding of different views about the facts, the production of evidence independently of both parties may help to allay that mistrust.

The Security Council, in dealing with incidents arising out of the Middle East conflict, has been assisted both by UNTSO and UNEF[109] to a considerable degree. Both organs have transmitted reports which have assisted the Council in assessing the responsibility for specific incidents, although on various occasions the Council has obviously been hampered by inadequate factual information.[110] In considering the complaint by Guinea of invasion by Portuguese forces on November 22–23, 1970, the Council established a fact-finding commission.[111] Other situations, such as the sinking of the Israeli destroyer *Eilat* or the attack on the U.S.S. *Maddox* (leading to the Gulf of Tonkin reprisals), which involved disputes about the location of the vessels, have arisen in which the Security Council had no U.N. observer machinery capable of assisting in verifying the facts. Moreover, along the Jordan River and the Israeli-Lebanon border there is no UNTSO observer activity, so that two areas vital to the control of reprisals in the Middle East are devoid of U.N. fact-finding machinery.[112]

[108] One cannot exclude the possibility that organs of regional arrangements will afford other organs of review in situations arising between members. The El Salvador-Honduras conflict of July, 1969, the "football war," would provide a possible situation of this kind and, in fact, O.A.S. mediation was accepted.

[109] A useful description of the observer functions of these two organs can be found in Wainhouse, International Peace Observation (Baltimore: The Johns Hopkins Press, 1966), and in Burns, Between Arab and Israeli (New York: Obolensky, 1963). For a brief description of these and other U.N. fact-finding bodies see Report of the Secretary General on methods of fact-finding, U.N. Doc. A/5694, May 1, 1964.

[110] The "neutral" resolution proposed by the U.S. and U.K. after the Kibbutz Dan incident in November, 1964 (U.N. Doc. S/6113, 19th Year, Supp for Oct., Nov. and Dec., 1964, p. 318), was largely because of inadequate facts (see U.K., 1165th Meeting, p. 13) and, in the event, no resolution at all was adopted. Similarly, after the fighting in the Lake Tiberias area in March, 1962, and in face of an inconclusive report from the UNTSO Chief-of-Staff Von Horn (U.N. Doc. S/5102 and Add. 1), the U.K. representative spoke of "the miserable paucity of hard facts on which to base a complete and just assessment of where the balance of right and wrong lies . . . This, of course, is absolutely no fault of the Truce Supervision Organisation, which has been severely handicapped in the exercise of its functions . . ." (17th Year, 1003rd Meeting, p. 6).

[111] Res. 289 (1970), U.N. Doc. S/10009 and Add. 1.

[112] For the Secretary General's proposal for observers on the Lebanon border, see an exchange of letters dated Aug. 16, 1969, Aug. 18 (Lebanon), and Aug. 25 (Israel): Israel rejected the proposal because it was made on the basis of the 1949 Armistice

The desirability of accurate reporting of the facts seems so obvious as to need no stress.[113] In practice, however, even the fairly sophisticated machinery of UNTSO has proved inadequate. Experience would suggest that specific improvements to any fact-finding machinery likely to be concerned with reprisals would be the following:

(1) The terms of reference of the fact-finding bodies should stem from the Security Council (or other review organ) and not be dependent upon the agreements of the parties.[114]

(2) Decisions on the interpretation and application of those terms of reference to specific cases should rest with the review organ and *not* the parties.[115]

(3) The fact-finding process should ideally be a continuing one, *i.e.* involving a continuing scrutiny of the compliance with any armistice, truce or cease-fire or inviolability of a border and *not* limited to investigating a complaint after the event.[116]

(4) Observers should have power of investigation of witnesses, though without power of compelling evidence to be given.[117]

Agreement. The U.S. abstained from voting on S/Res. 285 calling for the withdrawal of Israeli forces from Lebanese territory on the ground that, because UNTSO did not operate on that border, the Security Council lacked an objective report of the facts.

[113] For the view that fact-finding cannot be objective and is not necessary to prevent recurrence (and that the allocation of blame is undesirable), see Franck and Gold, "The Limits of Perceptual Objectivity in International Peace Observation," in The Middle-East Crisis: Test of International Law, 33 Law and Contemporary Problems 183–193 (1965). This argument appears to rely on the neuro-chemistry of visual perception and, as there stated, is totally unconvincing to this author. No lawyer would claim complete accuracy for any technique of adducing evidence. Indeed, legal systems involve rules of evidence and techniques of proof and cross-examination which assume unreliability of witnesses, etc., but which equally assume that, by these rules and techniques, it is possible to weigh evidence and arrive at a *reasonably* accurate version of the facts. This author does not accept that neuro-chemistry has demonstrated the falsity of that assumption and even less that the conclusion that it is unproductive to assess blame is justified in situations like the Middle East.

[114] For detailed argument on this point, demonstrating how, with terms of reference dependent solely on the agreement of the parties, it becomes possible for the parties to frustrate the supervision machinery, see Wainhouse, *op. cit.* 268–269, 272. This is not to suggest that, as a peacekeeping organ, an observer mission may not need the consent of the host state. The contention advanced above is that, once consent is given and agreement secured to terms of reference, these terms of reference should be contained in a Security Council resolution, and be interpreted by the Security Council.

[115] Many disputes of this character arose out of the Arab-Israeli Armistice Agreements. For a useful summary of the dispute over the Israeli project to drain Lake Huleh, which also involved a dispute on the competence of the MAC, see Higgins, United Nations Peacekeeping 1946–1967: Documents and Commentary 86–99 (London: Oxford University Press, 1969).

[116] This was the case with the Arab-Israeli MAC's: see Wainhouse, *op. cit.* 272.

[117] Thus, observers should be accorded the right to question civilians, army officers, government officials, etc. Refusal to testify or to allow such testimony to be taken would be made a matter for report to the review organ which would be free to draw its own conclusions. This extensive power of investigation would also suggest that military officers, such as the UNTSO observers, might usefully be supplemented by civilian international officials with police or legal training.

(5) The observers should be accorded freedom of movement on *both* sides of any frontier, ADL or cease-fire line.[118]

It may well be that one party will either refuse to accord these optimum conditions for fact-finding or, having initially accorded them, frustrate them in practice; such conduct will inevitably, and rightly, affect the review organ's judgment on questions of responsibility for reprisals and, if this be regarded as "bias" or judgment contrary to the facts, the aggrieved party will have no one but itself to blame. Thus, obstruction of optimum fact-finding will create a presumption against the reasonableness of a party's case.

The purely fact-finding or observer function may not, of course, be sufficient in situations when frequent violations of frontiers or cease-fire lines are occurring: and it is this situation which is most likely to give rise to reprisal action. In this situation, while fact-finding remains essential, there are basically two devices which can help: first, the "interposition" force (like UNEF) with power to prevent infiltrations; [119] second, the establishment of a buffer zone or "no man's land" which may reduce the risk of infiltration and facilitate its detection. Obstruction of these expedients by a party could also provide a presumption against the reasonableness of its case on reprisals.

It may also be the case that, with frequent but small-scale violations or even small-scale reprisals, the Security Council is not an appropriate review organ and a local, lower-powered forum is desirable. This, essentially, was the idea behind the Mixed Armistice Commissions established pursuant to the four Arab-Israeli Armistice Agreements.[120] A possible variant would be a body independent of the parties, but charged with fact-finding and conciliation and empowered to render reports [121] which could ultimately be reviewed by the higher review organ such as the Security Council. The Israeli criticism of the MAC's was that: "All the Commissions could do was to establish guilt and censure the guilty. They could not take preventive or even deterrent action." [122]

---

[118] By a note of Oct. 5, 1956, Israel informed the Chief-of-Staff of UNTSO that observers had no permission to investigate incidents occurring within Israel: see Burns, *op. cit.* 172. Obviously, this restriction is crippling if it is to be applied to guerrilla activities. For Security Council insistence on full freedom of movement, see Res. S/3575 and S/3605.

[119] For UNEF's limited power to apprehend infiltrators in a zone 500 meters from the ADL (and only on the Egyptian side) and, after interrogation, to hand them over to local police, see UNEF: Summary Study of the Experience derived from the establishment and operation of the Force, Report of the Secretary General, U.N. Doc. A/3943, Oct. 9, 1958.   [120] P. 4 above.

[121] The Commission on Human Rights, operating under the European Convention on Human Rights, is such a body which, although not concerned with reprisals, might offer a useful model: its reports are reviewable by the European Court of Human Rights if appeal is made to that body, and, ultimately, by the political organ, the Council of Ministers.

[122] Eytan, The First Ten Years 99–100 (London: Wiedenfeld and Nicholson, 1958). Mr. Eytan was the Director General of the Israeli Foreign Ministry.

This, with respect, seems a somewhat misplaced criticism. It could scarcely be a function of the MAC's to prevent or deter: that function might have been entrusted to a body like UNTSO or UNEF, capable of physical deterrence, but the Israeli Government was never, in fact, in favor of enlarged functions for either of these organs. The criticism has, however, some validity if applied to the absence of any enforcement by the Security Council of its injunctions against both violations of the armistice agreements and reprisals.

Indeed, the Middle East experience rather suggests that the various forms of machinery for observation, fact-finding, limited deterrence and even intermediate review of responsibility operate adequately only in a situation where both parties have an overriding interest in maintaining local peace. They all, therefore, have a vital rôle to play in reducing the risks of reprisals.

But, at the stage where one or both parties decide that their interest lies in an aggravation of the situation, either by initiating activities likely to cause reprisals or by taking reprisals, none of these devices will operate effectively unless they are backed by the authority of the Security Council and a determination by that body to bring real pressure to bear. Thus, in the final analysis, any approach to the problem of restraining resort to reprisals must involve three elements: (1) the serious consideration of guides to moderation by decision-makers (e.g., the Falk "framework") so as to contain reprisals within limits of reasonableness; (2) the establishment of appropriate and effective machinery for fact-finding and intermediate review by impartial agencies, with authority derived from competent international organs rather than the parties; (3) the application of constraint, in the form of sanctions, by the competent organs of final review such as the Security Council or, exceptionally, an appropriate regional body, designed to ensure compliance with authoritative censure of any policy of reprisals or illegal activities likely to give rise to reprisals.

Even if this optimum, three-angled, effort to restrain reprisals is attempted—an ambitious enough undertaking—a final caveat is necessary. In a situation so serious as to merit consideration of forceful reprisals by the parties, a policy of restraint remains a temporizing device: it seeks to contain a highly dangerous situation rather than solve it. Thus, so long as the international community can offer no prospect of settlement of the fundamental issues, the policy of restraint will be in jeopardy and the spiral of threat and counter-threat, of attack and reprisal, will remain a distinct possibility.

This approach obviously contains a judgment about policy which may be highly debatable. But the judgment is that reprisals have proved to be productive of greater violence rather than a deterrent to violence. From this flows an insistence upon minimizing reprisals and an argument for establishing presumptions against the reasonableness of the conduct of whichever party frustrates the techniques of fact-finding, interposition, review, etc., which are conceived as aids to restraint.

ANNEX

SYNOPSIS OF SELECTED REPRISAL INCIDENTS

Incident	Nature	Arguments in justification	Security Council Action	Basis
Qibya 14/15 Oct. 1953	500 Israelis, claimed not to be regular forces, attacked Jordanian village, killing 42 civilians. Also bombarded 2 villages in retaliation for Jordanian counter-attack.	Background of border raids, pillaging, wounding and killing of Israeli settlers by infiltrators from Jordan.	Condemned as a reprisal S/3139.	Reprisals illegal; lack of proportionality; fact that forces not regulars not a defense.
Nahhalin 28 March 1954	Israeli armed forces attacked Jordanian village, killing 9 and wounding 14.	Jordanian attack on bus in the Negev, killing 11 Israelis.	No condemnation.	
Gaza 28 Feb. 1955	Israeli forces attacked Egyptian military camp, killing 37 soldiers and 2 civilians.	Previous attacks across A.D.L. by Egyptian regular and irregular forces, Egyptian continuing assertion of a state of war and of belligerent rights. Defense of legitimate retaliation.	Unanimous condemnation. S/3378	Provocation by Egypt afforded no justification for reprisal action.
Patish, Gaza and Nahal Oz March/April 1955	Israeli complaint of attacks by Egyptian forces on village of Patish and on Israeli patrols.	Egypt invoked right of retaliation of Gaza inhabitants and denied that Egyptian forces were responsible.	No condemnation.	No useful purpose served by establishing a balance-sheet of responsibility and Council not to be a review authority on M.A.C. decisions.
Gaza Sept. 1955	Israeli attack on Khan Yunis, killing 10 soldiers and 25 civilians.	Self-defense after long chain of acts of murder and destruction originating from Gaza.	No condemnation but called on all parties to observe the Armistice Agreement.	No purpose served in striking a balance of responsibilities.
Lake Tiberias 11/12 Dec. 1955	Israeli forces attacked Syrian positions, killing 49 Syrian soldiers and civilians.	Self-defense and reprisal for Syrian artillery fire on Israeli police launch and fishing vessels: cumulative effect of such acts ensured proportionality.	Unanimous condemnation. S/3538	Provocations no justification for large-scale, deliberate reprisal.

34   THE AMERICAN JOURNAL OF INTERNATIONAL LAW   [Vol. 66

SYNOPSIS OF SELECTED REPRISAL INCIDENTS—*Continued*

Incident	Nature	Arguments in justification	Security Council Action	Basis
Negev and Gaza 14/16 August 1956	Israeli truck and other vehicles ambushed and mined: 4 killed, 8 wounded. Israeli counter-raid, attacking military post and ambushing jeep, killing 9 Egyptians.	No formal complaint to Security Council.		
Sharafi and Qalquilya Sept./Oct. 1956	Israeli attacks on police and army posts in Jordan, killing 39 (Sharafi) and 22 (Qalquilya).	Self-defense, background of accumulation of incidents between Israeli and Jordanian patrols.	No action.	
Suez Crisis October 1956	Large-scale Israeli invasion of Gaza and Sinai, involving heavy fighting.	Self-defense against repeated fedayeen attacks from bases across A.D.L.	No condemnation.	British and French intervention in Suez also involved therefore veto frustrated action. Provocations did not justify Israeli reprisals.
Lake Tiberias 11/17 March 1962	Israeli and Syrian counter-allegations of aggression, culminating in Israeli mortar attack on two Syrian villages.	Self-defense required silencing of Syrian gun positions.	Unanimous resolution deplored hostile exchanges and determined Israeli attack to be flagrant violation of resolution of 19 January 1956. S/5111	
Yemen March/April 1964	U.K. charged Yemen with air attacks and other violations of territory of S. Arabian Federation. British aircraft counter-attacked after prior warning to minimize risk of injury to civilians.	Self-defense designed to ward off further attacks.	Resolution deploring British military action. S/5649	Retaliation condemned in general and British action in particular.
Kibbutz Dan 13 Nov. 1964	Syrian fire on Israeli patrol and on Kibbutz Dan, killing 3 Israelis and wounding 11. Israeli attack by aircraft, killing 7 and wounding 26.	Airstrike the only effective means to halt the shelling of Israeli villages: an act of self-defense, not reprisal.	Proposal to condemn Israel *not* adopted. (6:0:9 abst.)	While deploring Israeli action, majority felt the more useful approach was to reactivate the M.A.C.
Jordan 14 Nov. 1966	Brigade of Israeli troops crossed A.D.L., supported by jets and heavy artillery, attacking villages south of Hebron with heavy civilian casualties.	Increase of terrorist and sabotage raids from Jordan (alleged 71 raids since 1965) imposed on Israel the need to protect her borders.	Unanimous condemnation of reprisal. S/7598	Disproportionate large-scale military action.

SYNOPSIS OF SELECTED REPRISAL INCIDENTS—*Continued*

Incident	Nature	Arguments in justification	Security Council Action	Basis
Samu Incident Nov. 1966	Following series of incidents with Syria and increased terrorist activities by Al Fatah, Israeli vehicle mined, killing 3 and wounding 6. Israel mounted large-scale, battalion attack on Samu, destroying houses, killing 18 and wounding 34 including many civilians.	Warning and deterrent to villages harboring Al Fatah and legitimate self-defense against terrorism and indirect aggression.	Unanimous condemnation. S/7598	Reprisals illegal and this reaction large-scale and disproportionate.
Eilat Incident 21 Oct. 1967	Israeli destroyer sunk by Egyptian missile-firing craft. Disputed whether inside or outside Egyptian territorial waters. Israel responded with bombardment of Suez oil refineries on 24 Oct.	Egypt argued self-defense in face of violation of her territorial waters. Israel justified retaliation on grounds that cease-fire demanded reciprocity.	Neutral resolution condemning "the violation of the cease-fire." S/Res/240 (1967).	
Karameh Incident 21 March 1968	Israeli bus struck mine in Negev, killing 2 and injuring several school children. Large-scale Israeli attack with tanks, aircraft and helicopters on Karameh and nearby villages in Jordan, followed by claims to have killed 150 terrorists.	Israel alleged armed attacks from Jordan violated the cease-fire: necessary action taken to protect territory, and people under Israel's jurisdiction.	Unanimously condemned Israel. S/Res/248 (1968)	Reprisals illegal and this action disproportionate.
Es-Salt Raid 4 Aug. 1968	Israeli aircraft attacked village in Jordan claimed to be base for terrorist activities.	Claim of self-defense.	Unanimously condemned Israel. S/Res/256 (1968)	Reprisals illegal and this action disproportionate.
Beirut Raid 28 Dec. 1968	Arab terrorist attack on El Al aircraft in Athens. Killing 1 passenger, Israeli reprisal raid on Beirut airport destroying 13 Arab registered aircraft.	Some claim of self-defense in Security Council but outside Council regarded as reprisal.	Unanimously condemned Israel. S/Res/262 (1968)	Reprisals illegal, misdirected against Lebanon and wholly disproportionate
Es-Salt Raid 26 Mar. 1969	Israeli aircraft attacked illegal Al-Fatah base, killing 18 and wounding 25.	Self-defense against attacks on Israeli civilian population by terrorists.	Condemns Israel. S/Res/265 (1969) 11:0:4 U.K. and U.S. abstaining because of lack of censure of terrorist activities.	Reprisals illegal.

36 THE AMERICAN JOURNAL OF INTERNATIONAL LAW [Vol. 66

SYNOPSIS OF SELECTED REPRISAL INCIDENTS—*Continued*

Incident	Nature	Arguments in justification	Security Council Action	Basis
Portugese attack on Zambia 28 July 1969	Portugese armed forces attacked Zambesian village, destroying property and killing 2 civilians.	Claim of self-defense in face of repeated incursions of armed groups from Zambia.	Resolution condemns Portugal. S/Res/268 (1969)	Reprisals illegal.
South Lebanon Raid 26 August 1969	Israeli air attack on villages in S. Lebanon alleged to be bases for guerrilla activities: 4 civilians killed.	Claim of self-defense in face of repeated incursions of terrorists into Israel from Lebanese territory.	Resolution condemns Israel. S/Res/270 (1969)	Reprisals illegal.
Portugese attack on Senegal 25 November and 7 December 1969	Artillery attack on village of Samine, destroying property and killing civilians	Claim of self-defense as to the attack of 25 November, on the ground that necessary to protect Portuguese territory from repeated incursions by armed bands from Senegal. As to the alleged attack on 7 December, Portugal denied any complicity in this.	Resolution condemns Portugal. S/Res/272 (1969) U.S. and Spain abstaining.	Not characterized as reprisals but simply as illegal attack on territory.
Israeli invasion of Lebanese territory 12 May 1970	Large-scale attack on Lebanese border villages alleged to be bases for terrorist organizations. Damage to property and loss of civilian life.	Israel claimed self-defense against repeated acts of terrorism perpetrated from Lebanese territory against Israel.	Resolution condemns Israel. S/Res/280 (1970) 11-0-4 abstentions.	Not characterized as reprisals but condemned as a large-scale, premeditated military attack against Lebanon.
Israeli invasion of Lebanese territory 2 September 1970	As above.	As above.	Resolution calls for withdrawal of Israel armed forces. S/Res/285 (1970) 14-0-1 abstention.	
Portugese attack on Guinea 22/23 November 1970	Invasion by sea-borne forces.	Portugal denied all responsibility for the invasion. Fact-finding mission refuted this denial.	Resolution condemns Portugal. S/Res/290 (1970) Four abstentions.	Not characterized as reprisals but simply as an illegal attack on territory.

[13]

ARMED REPRISALS

Roberto Barsotti

1. THE ABSOLUTE PROHIBITION OF ARMED REPRISALS AND ATTEMPTS AT REINTRODUCING THEM

According to the most widely-accepted interpretation, the United Nations Charter – and in particular the general prohibition of the threat or use of force contained in Art. 2(4) – has made armed reprisals illegal[1]. A great deal of significant evidence has been drawn (and still can be drawn) from international practice to support this conclusion.

The Security Council, which is the most competent body to pronounce on the subject, has repeatedly condemned acts of reprisal involving the use of armed force, not only with reference to the particular features of the individual actions considered, but also in absolute terms. For example, Resolution 188 (1964)

> 1. '*Condemns* reprisals as incompatible with the purposes and principles of the United Nations'

Similarly, the resolutions adopted by the Council on January 19th 1956 and April 9th 1962 contain an absolute condemnation and reject the idea, on principle, that the retaliatory nature of the action considered should make it lawful. The Council

> '*Condemns* Israeli military action [...] whether or not undertaken by way of retaliation[2]'

The Secretary-General underlined the continuity and consistency of the resolutions passed on the subject, by declaring

> 'fully justified the stand of the Security Council on *all* acts of violence, including those which reflected a policy of retaliation[3]'

The declarations made by the various delegates during the debates in the Council are also of the greatest interest. They reveal not only a radical rejection of the very idea of armed reprisals[4], but also the grounds on which

80

they are held to be unlawful, which lie both in the principles of the Charter and in more general considerations. One of the most significant is the view that it is inadmissible for

'any State, especially any Member of the United Nations [...] to take the law into its own hands through reprisal and retaliation[5]'.

This is evidence that there has been a radical change in the traditional view of self-help as the major instrument of law enforcement in the international order:

'no Government, *even under extreme provocation*, [is] justified in taking the law into its own hands[6]'.

On October 24th 1970, the General Assembly also formulated a blanket prohibition permitting of no exceptions, in Resolution 2625 (XXV) ('Declaration on Principles of International Law Concerning Friendly Relations'):

'States have a duty to refrain from acts of reprisal involving the use of force'.

As has rightly been stressed[7], the categorical nature of this statement rules out the possibility, entertained by some writers, of interpreting the concluding phrase of Art. 2(4) as an escape clause. But another more significant point should be added: during the work of the Sixth Committee, no delegate questioned the absolute nature of the ban, as applied to armed reprisals. Only on the question of extending the ban to reprisals not involving the use of armed force was there any disagreement[8]. It was held by some that the right of retaliation should be preserved, limited to this particular category of acts of self-help, to make up for the shortcomings of the system of peaceful settlement of disputes[9].

The more recent General Assembly Resolution 36/103, adopted on December 9th, 1981 ('Declaration on the Inadmissibility of Intervention and Interference in the Internal Affairs of States') contained an equally unequivocal reassertion of

'The duty of a State to refrain from armed intervention, subversion, military occupation [...] or any act of military [...] interference in the internal affairs of another State, including acts of reprisal involving the use of force' (Sect. II, lett. c).

According to an authoritative interpretation[10], the International Court of Justice itself stated the unlawfulness of armed reprisals in its judgment of April 9th 1949, regarding the *Corfu Channel Case*. It is held that by declaring 'Operation Retail' inadmissible the Court was condemning as contrary to international law any form of 'forcible self-help to obtain redress for rights already violated[11]'.

Even outside the United Nations system important evidence can be found to confirm the existence of a widespread conviction that forcible reprisals are unlawful. A particularly significant example of this is the 1975 Final Act of the Conference on Security and Co-operation in Europe:

'they [the participating States] will also refrain in their mutual relations from any act of reprisal by force[12]'.

With so much evidence to the same effect in international practice and legal interpretations, it would seem reasonable to conclude that reprisals do constitute a forbidden use of force and that all that remains to be done is to clarify the characteristics which distinguish them from the only lawful use of force: self-defence. During the past decade, however, this view has been increasingly subjected to argued criticism; it has been held that, in the present state of international society, to qualify reprisals as unlawful is unrealistic, of only marginal significance or even dangerous and counter-productive.

This critical attitude is based essentially on two considerations: on the one hand, the inefficiency of the system of collective security (and in particular of the Security Council, which is now incapable of imposing its rules of conduct on States); on the other, the widespread resort to forcible reprisals by States (which makes for a 'credibility gap' with respect to the norm forbidding them). Starting from here the reasoning has developed, initially rather cautiously, but becoming progressively more decided in tone and eventually reaching radical conclusions which are in outright contrast with the previously recorded facts.

To start with, in fact, it was admitted that U.N. practice rejects the idea of reprisals, and merely held that the crisis in the mechanism of enforcement of the Charter 'leads to a kind of *second-order level* of legal inquiry', inspired by the more permissive attitude of customary international law[13]. This interpretation, while on the one hand it opens up a possibility of recourse to armed reprisals (in so far as it appears to deny that the relative ban has become a customary rule), on the other imposes serious limitations to this possibility of lawful use of forcible self-help[14].

Subsequently, however, the view developed that the prohibition of reprisals based on the Charter was 'rapidly degenerating to a stage where its normative character is in question[15]'. It appeared, in fact, that the Security Council was not only incapable of stopping the practice of reprisals, but also inclined to a partial acceptance of 'reasonable' reprisals. This discrepancy between the formal principle (which should be recognized as having the status of *jus cogens*) and actual practice, makes it possible to identify certain criteria whereby the condemnation of the Security Council can be avoided

82

'even though the Council will maintain the general proposition that all armed reprisals are illegal[16]'.

This second interpretation, at a first glance, might appear to be more rigorous that the preceding one in excluding armed reprisals, in so far as it classifies the principle of the illegality of all reprisals involving the use of force as *jus cogens*, giving it therefore general authority in positive international law. In practice, the effects of this theory on the general ban on any resort to unlawful force are more serious. By suggesting that there may be reprisals which by virtue of their 'reasonableness' will avoid condemnation by the Security Council, this interpretation brings retaliatiory use of force back *inside the framework of the United Nations system*, which would thus be shown up not only as incapable of functioning, but also as contradictory and inconsistent[17].

A third, even more radical interpretation openly defends the legitimacy – and indeed utility – of reprisals, above all on the strength of the argument that an effective mechanism of collective security has failed to materialize, either on a universal or a regional level. This makes it necessary 'not to re-interpret arbitrarily the Charter but to read experience into it': and experience has shown that the use of coercion can be indispensable to protect the overall objectives of the Charter; a prohibition of violence 'is not an absolute virtue; it has to be weighed against other values as well[18]'. Hence the explicitly formulated conclusion: 'There is a need perhaps, for some kind of reinstitution of reprisal – if not in the most classical sense, then in a more limited sense – as some kind of sanctioning instrument under international law[19]'.

This type of argument, concerning the process of formation of a norm (that is, the rule on the reinstitution of reprisals) can only be evaluated by going beyond a mere analysis of positive law to considerations of legislative policy, to find the solution which comes closest to the realities of contemporary international relations.

All these interpretations[20], aimed at limiting or even eliminating the unqualified proscription of reprisals involving force, are part and parcel of a general tendency on the part of States to extend the exceptions to the ban on force contained in Art. 2(4).

The most significant expressions of this tendency are to be found in the debates which preceded the adoption of General Assembly Resolution 2625 (XXV) ('Declaration on Principles of International Law Concerning Friendly Relations and Cooperation Among States in Accordance with the Charter of the United Nations') in October 1970, and Resolution 3314 (XXIX) ('Definition of Aggression') on December 14th 1974. As is well-known, on both these occasions the socialist countries and a majority of third world countries upheld the view that national liberation movements act in self-defence and that military intervention in their aid is therefore possible[21]. While the western States denied the legitimacy of the exception claimed for peoples under colonial rule, they asserted that the use of forces is lawful if authorized by a regional agency, even without the prior consent of the Security Council[22].

Another important instance of this trend is to be seen in the practice concerning the resort to armed force in defence of nationals abroad. Most western countries have shown that they consider this conduct to be in accordance with international law, either by using it themselves or by approving its use by others[23].

The alleged lawfulness of any kind of use of force other that self-defence, however, can only be tested by an appropriate analysis of practice. The relevant norms of the Charter are so categorical that adequate conclusions cannot be reached simply by means of a literal interpretation of their content.

Now, with regard to reprisals, verification through an examination of practice turns out to be a particularly elaborate and complex business, because there are so many theories on the subject, based on so many different types of argument.

As we have seen, some of these theories claim that armed reprisals are lawful. There are essentially two possible justifications for holding this view: either one maintains that the customary right of reprisal has survived the ban imposed by Art. 2(4), or one shows that although the system of the Charter annulled this right, a more recent particular customary rule has reestablished it.

To assess the validity of these two claims, it is necessary to look in international practice for two distinct types of evidence: one, of a higher level, which could prove the formation – in the framework of the U.N. system – of a particular customary rule creating an exception to Art. 2(4); the other, of a much lower level, which would simply show that the customary norm permitting the retaliatory use of force has remained positive international law.

With this end in mind we shall first attempt to ascertain the volume of the relevant practice, that is, the frequency of resort to armed reprisals by States (section 2). This will permit us, on the one hand, to give an exact definition of the type of conduct to be taken into consideration, and, on the other, to ascertain if the frequency of such conduct is sufficient to put in doubt the normative value of ban in the Charter. We will then analyse the major features of this practice (section 3), to establish whether it bears witness to the formation of a particular customary rule, or, if not, at least to the survival of the traditional customary rule. Even if the conclusions are negative, however, the inquiry cannot be considered complete. Since there are those who hold the view that although armed reprisals are unlawful, they may on occasions have certain features which exempt them from condemnation by the Security Council[24], it will then be necessary to carry out a sepa-

84

rate study of the conduct of States *inside* this body, in the course of the debates held on the subject of reprisals (section 3 *in fine*).

Finally, since the lawfulness of reprisals has also been upheld *de jure condendo*, we must go beyond a simple examination of practice. Of course it is
not for the commentator to discuss the *advisability* or *utility* of a reinstitution
of reprisals: to say anything on this subject would simply be to express a personal 'political' view of international relations. We will therefore do no
more here than assess the consistency of this new hypothesis of a lawful use
of force with the general ban contained in Art. 2(4) and with the system of
peaceful settlement of disputes and the mechanism of collective security of
the Charter (section 5). The coexistence in a single legal order of obligations and rights which were radically conflicting and mutually exclusive
would in fact be inadmissible.

2. SOCIAL IMPACT OF THE RETALIATORY USE OF FORCE
ON THE WORLD COMMUNITY: THE RELEVANT PRACTICE

Going on now to analyse the cases of retaliatory use of force by States, an
important point should be borne in mind: the features which distinguish the
customary right of reprisal are anything but clear and unambiguous. It is
quite understandable, in fact, that, at the time when resort to war was unconditionally permitted, the need to define and distinguish between the
single measures short of war was not felt, since their lawfulness was never in
doubt. Thus when the necessity to make this distinction arose (in consequence of the prohibition of war and even of the threat or use of force), it
became apparent that there was some uncertainty as to the essential characteristics of the reprisal[25]. This has had a negative effect on the interpretation
of practice, leading quite frequently to actions being classified as reprisals
which do not really come into the same category as this form of self-help.

There have, for instance, been occasions when an action has been classified as a retaliatory use of force without it being demonstrated that the conduct of the claimant State possesses the necessary features. The *Corfu
Channel incident*, to give one example, has often been referred to in works
on reprisals, figuring even as a double example of forcible self-help: first,
for the passage of four British Navy vessels on October 22nd 1946, and secondly for the subsequent sweeping of the Strait (known as 'Operation Retail'). In fact neither of these actions technically qualifies as an act of reprisal.

The former does not because the action concerned was not one which is
normally unlawful, but, on the contrary, consisted of excercise of the right
of innocent passage. As the International Court of Justice recognized, the
fact that

'the passage 'was made with ships at action stations in order that they might be able to re-taliate quickly if fired upon again' [..] cannot, in itself, be regarded as unreasonable [...]. Having regard [..] to all the circumstances of the case [..] the Court is unable to charac-terize these measures [..] as a violation of Albania's sovereignty[26]'.

'Operation Retail', too, was not a case of 'forcible self-help to obtain redress for rights already violated[27]', because while it is true that the U.K. agent, in his speech in reply before the Court, classified the Operation as one of self-help, it is equally undeniable that he was referring to a right of self-help that was entirely different from reprisal:

'I am asking the Court [...] to say that, at any rate, one type of case where the right of self-help applies, is where an injured State takes action to secure and preserve evidence, as a measure preparatory to submitting its grievance to the appropriate international orga-nization[28]'.

In other cases another necessary precondition of reprisal is overlooked: the commission by the target State of a *prior international delict* against the claimant State. This has led to the inclusion in recent practice on reprisals, of incidents such as the French air raid on Sakhiet – Sidi – Youssef (Feb-ruary 8th 1958), and the Portuguese attacks on Zambia (between May 18th 1966 and June 30th 1969), on Senegal (November 25th and December 7th 1969) and on Guinea (November 1969 and November 1970). The retalia-tory character of these actions is extremely doubtful, in view of the fact that they were all reactions on the part of colonial powers against neighbouring States accused of sheltering and assisting national liberation movements. Any action taken by third party States which favours the exercise of the right of self-determination, so long as it is limited to the concession of bases in their territory and assistance of a not directly military kind, is definitely lawful and, indeed, has been encouraged repeatedly in General Assembly resolutions[29]. According to the Afro-Asian States, the socialist States and some Latin American States, direct military action in favour of national lib-eration movements is also lawful. However, the opposition of western States to this idea makes the development of such a widely permissive cus-tomary rule unlikely[30].

In the cases under examination, however, the claimant States themselves stressed that they were reacting above all against the authorization – by the target States – of the organization of subversive forces operating from their territory[31]. The further accusation that the armed forces of the target States were directly involved (made only by Portugal against Zambia and Senegal) was neither proved nor taken into consideration by the member States dur-ing the Council's discussions. The members of the Security Council have never accepted the existence of any prior responsibility on the part of the States that were victims of the armed attacks. During the debates in the Se-curity Council and in the resolutions condemning the actions, they are never

86

described as reprisals; on the contrary, Resolution 268 (1969) speaks explicitly of 'unprovoked raids'.

Finally, there is a third group of cases to which the name of reprisals has been improperly applied (or, at least, where there is some doubt on the question), because there has not been an adequate assessment of the *subjective element (animus)*, which is necessary to distinguish armed reprisal from war proper[32]. It is common knowledge that this distinction has always been a complex one to make and has become still more elusive in the ambiguous situations common in recent international experience (guerrilla activities, prolonged quasi-belligerency, series of terrorist incidents[33]). In some cases, however, convincing evidence can be found to demonstrate the true intent of the State resorting to armed force. For example, in the case of the above mentioned attack by Portugal on Guinea in 1970, evidence that Portugal's aim was much more far-reaching than that of sanctioning and deterring which is typical of retaliatory action, was provided by an *impartial international body*. The Special Mission's report to the Security Council on December 3rd 1970 makes it plain that the main objective of the operation was to overthrow the government and replace it with dissident elements[34]. Hence, the target of the violence was in this case the independence of the attacked State and its very existence as an autonomous entity: which is the characteristic aim of war, not of reprisal.

Where other forcible actions are concerned, it is clear that the intent is not that of reprisal from the fact that these actions are *linked, both in time and purpose*, with a *war in the true sense of the word*, involving the same States. If the alleged measure short of war is followed (or preceded) by hostilities which are indubitably acts of war, it is reasonable to suppose – at least as a rebuttable presumption – that the *animus bellandi* extends to all connected conduct.

We should make clear that our intention here is not to put forward the theory of 'accumulation of events', which tries to justify every forcible action as self-defence and which the Security Council has invariably rejected[35]. In the type of situation to which we are referring, it is not a question of summing individual actions and attributing a different significance to them as a whole from that which each one has when taken singly. We mean, rather, to infer the intent behind a lesser action from that inherent in the larger action to which it is linked. The evidence of the facts – and not a mere process of logical interpretation – is used here to provide proof of intent, which would be impossible otherwise to ascertain objectively.

Consider, for example, the Gulf of Tonkin and Pleiku incidents (August 1964 – February 1965), which were defined, by the Secretary of Defense and the White House, respectively as 'retaliation' and 'appropriate reprisal action[36]'. Although the two U.S. bombing raids were carried out in reply to specific North Vietnamese attacks, their true nature would appear to be that of war operations proper (it is of no concern here whether they were attacks or acts of self-defence). The true nature of the action is not to be deduced from the *nomen juris*, which is variable (for instance, in the United Nations these same air strikes were defended by the United States Government as measures of self-defence), but from the actual conduct of the States concerned, before and after these operations.

If we look at the question from this point of view, it can be noted, first, that *by late 1964* the United States had recognized the existence of a level of subversion and infiltration in South Vietnam amounting to armed attack[37], and stated explicitly that

'the acts of aggression by the North Vietnamese [...] make no sense whatsoever standing alone[38]'.

The United States reaction was not therefore directed only against the North Vietnamese action immediately preceding it, but was a reply to more complex conduct which, in its opinion, constituted armed attack. To stop here, however, would be tantamount to acritical acceptance of the 'accumulation of events' theory, and would lay one open to the relative objections (the first of these being that the classification of an action cannot be left to the State concerned, but must be deduced from the evidence of objective circumstances).

But in the cases in point there is another factor which seems to provide decisive proof that these forcible actions had a more far-reaching aim than reprisals: the fact, that is, that they were followed – as a logical development – by operations which were undoubtedly acts of war. The objective evidence of these further developments shows that the preceding declarations were not mere verbal expedients, but expressed the true *animus:* the later actions were in fact quite consistent and consequential.

The same can be said about the incidents between Israel and the neighbouring Arab States which were most directly connected with wars (the Six Day war in 1967 and the Israeli-Lebanese war in 1981). For example, it would seem unrealistic to attribute a retaliatory aim to the Israeli bombing of seven Syrian areas on July 14th 1966 and the shelling of industrial installations in Suez on October 24th 1967[39]. More probably, these operations were respectively the prelude to and the natural extension of the Six Day war of June 1967. In fact, while Israel claimed that it was reacting to 'acts of aggression and threats of war', Syria said that

'the frequency of Israel's acts of aggression [...] pointed to a fundamental Israeli policy [...] (that) stemmed from Zionist ideology [...] based on a policy of constant aggression against neighbouring Arab States[40]'.

88

The United Arab Republic, in a letter dated October 24th to the Security Council, stated unequivocally that

> 'Those military operations could not be justified as a retaliatory measure [...] because they were conducted against civilian and industrial installations, not military targets';

and during the debate termed the bombing of Suez as an 'act of war' and 'aggression [...] totally unprovoked[41]'.

All the States in conflict, judging from their own statements, felt themselves to be engaged in hostilities of a warlike nature. These statements might, however, be held not to reflect the truth but to have been made for reasons of political expediency: by Israel to provide grounds for a plea of self-defence and by the Arab States to make Israel's position more serious. But, once again, decisive proof can be inferred from the objective circumstances already mentioned: the connection, that is, between these incidents and what was undeniably a war between the same States. It was explicitly recognized by some members of the Security Council that the connection between these events was not only temporal but also functional[42].

Still on the subject of the features which are essential if an action is to be considered a reprisal according to general international law, and the need to verify that these features are in fact present, one further point can be made.

The military operations carried out over the last thirty years by Israel against the neighbouring Arab States are generally taken to constitute the main nucleus of modern practice on armed reprisals. There is no such agreement, however, either among States or among commentators, as to what are the indispensable preconditions for a correct definition of such forcible actions.

For example, the juridical nature of the whole Middle Eastern situation is quite unsettled. Some commentators consider there to be formally a state of peace (because of the existence of Armistice Agreements and successive cease-fire resolutions[43]), whereas others see the relationship between these States as one of quasi-belligerency[44], or even as a state of war[45]. And yet, only by defining this situation is it possible to establish if these military operations are to be evaluated by reference to peacetime reprisals doctrine, or by reference to the status of belligerency.

There is disagreement, too, as to the lawfulness of the actions against which Israel is reacting: are they acts of terrorism[46], or is there a war of national liberation in course[47]? Is the Israeli presence in the occupied territories now lawful by virtue of the principle of effectiveness, or, having come about illegally by force, does it have no legal standing? Whether the Israeli actions are to be classified as armed reprisals or not (independently of the further question of whether they are legally justifiable), depends on which of these views one favours. If one view is taken, the conduct of the Arab

States becomes entirely lawful, in which case the indispensable precondition that an act of reprisal must be directed against a prior international delict is missing. Besides, convincing proof of the fact that it is impossible to classify the Israeli military operations without first finding an answer to these questions is to be found in the objective circumstances that there is serious disagreement among States as to whether these forcible actions are armed reprisals.

Israel has always put forward the justification that it was acting in self-defence, whereas the Arab States have repeatedly called for the Israeli attacks to be condemned, defining them as 'aggression[48]' – sometimes more specifically as 'armed aggression according to Art. 51[49]' – and even as an 'act of war[50]'.

As regards the third party States represented on different occasions in the Security Council, there is a clear contrast between the position taken by the western countries, on the one hand, and the socialist and third world countries, on the other. The United States and almost all the western countries[51], although rejecting Israel's justifications for her policy, never fail to express their disapproval of violence *regardless of the direction* from which it comes, to make it plain that they consider the conduct of the Arab countries unacceptable too[52]. Indeed, the condemnation of Israeli military actions as reprisals is conceived as a guarantee of a balanced evaluation by the Security Council: so much so that when a resolution makes no reference to Arab actions or ommissions the western States mostly abstain[53], or, in extreme cases, use their right of veto[54].

By contrast, the States belonging to the socialist bloc and the third world[55] invariably deny that Israel's actions against the Arab countries can be considered as acts of reprisal. To call them reprisals is unacceptable, in the words of the Soviet delegate in the debate on the Karameh incident of March 21st 1968[56], because this would 'place the aggressor and the victim of the aggression on the same footing'. Still more explicitly, criticizing the position taken by the western countries, the same delegate said:

> 'the so-called even-handed approach of those countries amounts to an attempt to justify aggression and to prevent an unconditional condemnation of Israel'.

When the resolution of condemnation expressly defines the Israeli action as reprisal, or refers to prior violations on the part of the Arabs, the socialist and third world countries as a general rule either abstain[57], or justify their failure to vote against the draft by the need for a unanimous condemnation of Israel's conduct[58], or interpret the relevant paragraphs of the resolution as assigning total responsibility to Israel[59].

The present inquiry is not the place for an in-depth analysis of the various legal problems involved in Arab-Israeli relations. However, from what we

90

have seen so far we can usefully draw at least one (if only partial) conclusion. Whether the conflict between Arabs and Israelis is relevant to practice on armed reprisals is a hypothetical (or at least doubtful) question, not being preceded by verification of the existence of certain indispensable preconditions, which, even now, are subject to conflicting interpretations, and, in any case, giving rise to serious disagreement between the main components of the international community. As a result, any determination of the present status of reprisals which is based essentially, if not exclusively, on the relations between Israel and the Arab countries, is to be evaluated with caution, if not scepticism.

If the critical evaluation of practice so far carried out is correct, it must be recognized that the actual number of cases of reprisals involving force in the period since the second world war is much lower than that usually given in traditional studies. A first conclusion can therefore already be drawn: at least from a *quantitative* point of view (that is, judging from the frequency of relevant actions) the divergence between the prohibition of armed reprisals, embodied in the Charter, and actual practice, is not so serious as to give grounds to the belief that there is a process of degeneration of the ban in question.

This conclusion is confirmed if we proceed from our consideration of the *quantity* of cases actually relevant to consider their *quality*, that is, the inherent characteristics of conduct of this kind by States.

3. IMPACT OF RECENT PRACTICE ON CUSTOMARY LAW
AND THE U.N. CHARTER

Let us suppose now that the points so far raised are unfounded, and that all the incidents traditionally considered as examples of armed reprisals really are just that. We must now assess the importance of this practice on the basis of the characteristics it presents with respect to the two logical alternatives on which the theories mentioned previously are based: that the customary rule which permits resort to forcible reprisals has survived the general ban laid down in Art. 2(4), or that a particular customary norm has developed, within the system of the Charter, which extends the exceptions to the prohibition of the threat or use of force.

The first and most apparent feature of this practice is that the States which have carried out acts of reprisal are without exception western States (Great Britain, Israel, United States, France, Portugal). In other words, only members of one sector of the international community have actually resorted to this type of measure short of war. The fact that conduct of this kind has not been generalized does not bear witness to the formation of a customary rule creating an exception to the prohibition of the use of force.

91

Furthermore, the States which have had recourse to forcible actions of this kind have themselves always tried to justify their conduct by qualifying it as self-defence (either individual or collective[60]). It is therefore reasonable to suppose that they are aware of the illegality of their conduct if it is described in any other way.

It is true that, in official declarations, there are sometimes variations in the terminology used. For example, the United States bombing raids in reply to the Gulf of Tonkin incident were spoken of in Senate Hearings by Secretary of Defense McNamara as "retaliation"; and the U. S. air strikes following the North Vietnamese attacks at Pleiku were described by the White House as "appropriate reprisal action"[61]. The Israeli Chief of Staff, General Bar Lev, defined both the Israeli commando attack against Egyptian installations in the Nag Hamadi area and the Beirut raid in 1968 as reprisals[62]. These variations in terminology do not appear to be significant, however, first because they are only to be found in declarations made by two States (Israeli and the United States), and secondly because they were only used in political statements, for propagandistic or descriptive purposes, and were certainly not intended as legal definitions.

It is significant, rather, that in the United Nations, acts of reprisal – including those mentioned above[63] – have invariably been defended as measures of self-defence. When they have had to give a legal definition of their conduct, that is, the States concerned have made it clear that they do not consider it to be in accordance with any rule of international law, if presented as reprisal. But this is not all: sometimes the State which resorts to force – in the course of the debate concerning the action it has taken – explicitly declares its conviction that reprisals are illegal. The British delegate Sir Patrick Dean, for example, in a statement in explanation of the United Kingdom abstention on Resolution 188 (1964) (which, in its initial operative clause *"Condemns* reprisals as incompatible with the purposes and principles of the United Nations"), declared as follows:

> "I do not object to the (first operative paragraph) since, as I explained in my speech on April 7, the action which my Government took on March 28 was not a reprisal or a retaliation"[64].

It could be objected that the recognition by the claimant States of the unlawfulness of armed reprisals, in the United Nations, can only show that these forcible actions are held to be contrary to the Charter, but not necessarily to general international law. In fact, this does not appear to be the opinion of the States concerned. In the first place, during debates in the United Nations, they have repeatedly expressed their unreserved condemnation of reprisals carried out by other States. In 1954 in the Security Council the delegates of France, Britain, and the United States expressed the concern of their respective governments

92

"When any State, especially [but not exclusively] any Member of the United Nations [. . .]
presumed to take the law into its own hands through reprisal and retaliation[65]".

In 1962, when presenting their joint draft resolution, Great Britain and the
United States declared that – in their opinion – there could be "no justification" for a policy of retaliation[66]. In 1968, on two separate occasions[67], the
French delegate said that "the very idea of military reprisals" was unacceptable to the French Government.

Moreover, the same States have condemned armed reprisals in general
outside the United Nations also, making no reference to the Charter. In
1973, for example, the U. S. Department of State rejected Professor Rostow's proposal that the United States endorse the right of reprisal as a measure of self-help, "when a State cannot or will not fulfill its international legal obligations to prevent the use of its territory for unlawful exercise of
force[68]".

Finally, States which have carried out armed reprisals have not only defined their forcible actions as self-defence inside the United Nations organs,
but sometimes outside them too, thus demonstrating that they are not making use of this definition merely to avoid condemnation under U. N. law. To
take the case of France, for example, the report sent by General Salan to
the Minister of National Defence on February 9th 1958, defines the raid on
Sakiet – Sidi – Youssef as an "action aérienne de légitime défense"[69].

In conclusion, then, not only is there absolutely no sign of an *opinio juris*
in the conduct of the States in question, but there is even evidence of an
awareness of the unlawfulness of reprisals, which is stated explicitly above
all when other States carry out retaliatory actions. This being the case, it is
improbable either that the old permissive customary rule has survived or
that a particular customary rule derogating from Art. 2(4) of the Charter has
recently developed.

Similar conclusions can be drawn from an examination of the attitude of
third party States (that is, States other than the claimant State and the target State[70]), with regard to cases of retaliatory use of force. No such State –
either in the United Nations or elsewhere – has ever openly maintained that
armed reprisals were lawful. On the contrary, all those States which have
had occasion to express an opinion during debates in the Security Council,
have invariably condemned military reprisals, both in general terms, as a
form of self-help[71], and with reference to the particular forcible action in
discussion. Moreover, the illegality of such actions is affirmed without reservations or exceptions; western, socialist and third world countries alike have
frequently stressed – with approval – that the *principle* and *policy* of retaliation
have been constantly rejected and condemned by the Security Council[72].

There is one feature of Security Council practice, however, which does
not seem consistent with the view that armed reprisals are absolutely unlaw-

ful: that is, the frequent reference to their disproportionate character as a motive for the condemnation of the claimant State[73]. It has been pointed out[74] that if *all* reprisals are illegal, the reference to the criterion of proportion is strictly irrelevant; and it is on the grounds of this apparent logical contradiction that the existence of reprisals likely to avoid condemnation has been argued[75].

In fact, this emphasis on the disproportionate nature of the act of reprisal under consideration can be seen to be entirely consistent with the conviction that armed reprisals are illegal in any event, so long as we bear in mind this fundamental point. The definition of an action as reprisal always presupposes the recognition of the existence of a prior international delict on the part of the target State. As we have already had occasion to note[76], this necessary implication has led to differences of opinion among members of the Council as to the nature of Israel's military actions against the neighbouring Arab States. Where there have been two instances of unlawful conduct (that is, the armed reprisal and the act or omission to which this was a reaction), it is necessary – not only for legal but also for political reasons – to specify the reason for condemning only one of them in a formal resolution. This has been stressed repeatedly by Israel, which has challenged the U. N.'s condemnation of its raids on the grounds that it is evidence of a double standard of evaluation with regard to the conduct of the Arab States[77]. The Security Council has held that to say that the reprisal action was disproportionate was the most appropriate answer to objections of this kind made by Israel, and the most adequate justification for the discrepancy in its treatment of the claimant and target States.

To summarise, then, there is no evidence either in State or U. N. practice to prove the existence of a customary rule legitimating armed reprisals. On the one hand, only a few States, all belonging to one section of the international community (that is, the west), have *in practice* resorted to this form of forcible self-help. Third party States, for their part, have not approved these specific actions nor have they affirmed the lawfulness of armed reprisals in principle; on the contrary, they have expressed their unconditional condemnation of such actions, thus ruling out any suggestion of acquiescence on their part. One of the essential elements in the process of formation of a customary norm is therefore entirely absent: that is, widespread resort to the conduct in question.

On the other hand, States which have made retaliatory use of force themselves have demonstrated that they do not hold this type of conduct to be in accordance with any general rule of international law by describing their own actions as acts of self-defence and condemning as reprisals similar actions carried out by other States. Third party States have been even more explicit on this point: they have radically and consistently expressed the opinion that such acts are unlawful – chiefly in Security Council debates.

94

Thus another essential factor in the formation of a customary rule – the psychological element (*opinio juris*) – is absent.

On the evidence of international practice, it appears extremely difficult to demonstrate the survival of the old permissive customary rule; and quite impossible, in view of the greater amount of evidence necessary, to prove the subsequent formation of a particular customary rule derogating from Art. 2(4) of the Charter.

We cannot, however, conclude our examination of practice here. As we have had occasion to note[78], there is an authoritative interpretation which holds that the Security Council, while restating the principle of the illegality of all armed reprisals, shows a clear reluctance to condemn *certain* reprisals. According to this view, the principal organ in the system of collective security, aware of its own incapacity to prevent resort to force, is moving in the direction of a partial acceptance of this form of self-help. An examination of Security Council debates makes it possible even to identify certain criteria of reasonableness likely to avoid condemnation. In other words, according to this interpretation, the Council would be acting counter to the role laid down for it in the Charter and favouring the possibility of armed reprisals which, although illegal *de jure*, become accepted *de facto*.

In fact there seems to be no need to reach such a pessimistic conclusion, which would open up the possibility of dangerous developments. It cannot be denied that some military operations capable of characterization as reprisals (more numerous, incidentally, than those traditionally taken into consideration[79]) have not been formally condemned. Nevertheless, it appears equally clear that this has never been because the Security Council regarded the action taken as a "reasonable" reprisal. The failure to adopt a resolution has always been determined by one of the following types of cause: either the (legal or political) need to delay putting a definitive label or passing judgment on the military operations in question; or, however paradoxical this may seem, the firm desire to condemn these operations precisely (and exclusively) as armed reprisals.

As regards the first type of cause, it should be pointed out that in some cases the decision to suspend judgment is entirely dictated by technical legal reasons. For example, the debate on the Israeli attack on the Jordanian village of Nahhalin (March 1954) was interrupted because the target State was not a member of the United Nations and the preconditions for the Security Council to deal with the question did not exist. As is well known, paragraph 1 of Art. 35 (relating to the possibility of a complaint being presented by a member State on behalf of a non-member State, as in the case in point) is held to be inapplicable without the authority and consent of the State concerned[80]. On the other hand, paragraph 2 (concerning the possibility of a complaint being presented by a non-member State) can be applied only if the non-member State accepts in advance the obligations of peaceful settlement laid down in the Charter. Neither of these conditions was met in the case in point because of the attitude taken by the Jordanian Government.

"On 26 May 1954 the representative of Jordan, upon instruction from his Government, informed the President that he was not empowered to represent his Government before the Council or to take part in the current discussion[81]".

In other cases the failure to adopt a resolution is due to reasons of an essentially political or diplomatic nature: that is, the Council holds that it is necessary to refrain from putting a definitive legal label on the action (and not from condemning an action already classified as a reprisal) so as not to compromise negotiations for a solution between the States concerned. In the case of the incidents at Sakiet-Sidi-Youssef (8th February 1958), the Council decided to adjourn the meeting in order to allow the parties to avail themselves of the good offices offered by the Governments of the United States and the United Kingdom[82]. Similary, on the occasion of the Israeli bombing of civilian targets in the Nag Hamadi area (October 31st 1968), the Security Council accepted the United Kingdom's suggestion to adjourn the discussion since the Foreign Ministers of the parties concerned were currently engaged in discussions[83].

In all the cases so far examined it is clear that the Council did not take into consideration the supposed reasonableness of the armed operations carried out, in so far as it consciously declined even to define them.

As regards the second type of cause for the non-adoption of a resolution (that is, the desire to condemn the action strictly *as an armed reprisal*) we need only recall certain observations made in the previous section. As we said the members of the Security Council have taken strongly contrasting positions, above all when considering Israeli raids on neighbouring Arab States. The States belonging to the socialist and Third World groups (with the exception of the Latin-American countries), wishing to stress the exclusive responsibility of Israel, which they accused of a policy of aggression, called for the Israeli military operations to be classified as armed attacks. The aim of this was to provide the grounds for the adoption of appropriate measures under Chapter VII of the U. N. Charter, and for Israel being made to pay compensation for the loss of life and damage to property caused by the attacks[84].

The western States, on the other hand, although deploring the Israeli reaction, were anxious to bring out the fact that the Arab countries attacked also bore their share of responsibility, and insisted that the actions should be labelled as reprisals. This solution, presupposing as it did the existence of a prior wrongful act on the part of the target State, lessened the negative consequences for Israel, reducing the need for resort to sanctions and weakening the claim for compensation.

In a majority of cases this disagreement between the member States has not prevented the adoption of a resolution. For the most part the socialist

96

and third world countries have agreed to the raids being classified as reprisals in order to make sure that some kind of condemnation of Israel's action
was passed[85]. Less frequently, and only in the most serious cases, the western countries have withdrawn their claim, being satisfied with the mention –
at least in the preamble of the resolution – of *"any and all* violations" of the
ceasefire and the specification that *all* violent incidents should be prevented[86].

Sometimes, though, the gap between the contrasting positions has been
unbridgeable, and no resolution has been adopted, either because there was
not the required majority (Kibbutz Dan incident, November 1964: Moroccan draft resolution; shelling of seven Syrian areas, July 1966[87]), or owing to
the negative vote of a permanent member of the Security Council (Kibbutz
Dan incident, November 1964: United Kingdom-United States draft resolution; bombing of the Syrian coast and of communities in Lebanon, September 1972; air attacks against refugee camps and villages in Lebanon,
1975[88]).

In all the cases just mentioned, however, even those States which are
closest to Israel politically expressed unequivocal disapproval of its military
operations. These States have repeatedly made the point in their declarations that their only concern is that a balanced resolution should be passed,
not one which condemns "only one form of violence[89]".

Even when there has not been a big enough majority in the Council for it
to formulate a final judgment, then, the disagreement has not been about
whether the military action of self-help was lawful (or even only admissible), but rather about the degree of unlawfulness – and hence of responsibility. In other words, a resolution of condemnation was not adopted in the
cases under examination, not because the Council regarded the actions as
"reasonable" reprisals, but because a number of States held that to classify
them as armed reprisals was not commensurate with the gravity of the action considered.

Further confirmation of this conclusion can be drawn from the fact that in
one of the cases of non-adoption of a resolution which is usually cited as evidence of alleged willingness on the part of the Council to condone the
armed operations complained of, its declared intention was quite the opposite. I am referring to the debate on the Pattish, further Gaza and Nahal Oz
incidents (March-April 1955), in the course of which the Chairman said
that:

> "The majority seemed to be of the opinion that there was no need for any new action by
> the Council, inasmuch as the facts brought to the Council's notice had been fully covered
> in the resolutions adopted by the Council on 29 and 30 March. He trusted that he was ex-
> pressing the general view of the Members of the Council in appealing to both sides to give
> full effect to those resolutions[90]".

This reference to previous resolutions of condemnation makes it clear that the Council's opinion of the actions was negative, and in a sense gave formal status to this opinion.

In conclusion, then, there is no indication – in the debates of the principal organ of the United Nations security system – of the existence of "reasonable" reprisals, likely to avoid condemnation. There is, in effect, no discrepancy between the formal principle of the illegality of armed reprisals and the actual practice of the Council; the Council can be accused of inefficiency, but not of inconsistency. Thus we have furter confirmation of the absolute nature of the ban on retaliatory use of force in positive international law.

Establishing exactly what the present legal status of armed reprisals is, is not the only, nor, apparently, the most complex problem which this type of forcible self-help poses. With reprisals, as with any alleged exception to the ban on the use of force other than self-defence, it is also necessary to carry out a further, rather delicate enquiry. Since there is an increasing tendency, both in the literature and in practice[91], to bring in new exceptions to obviate the failings of the system of collective security, it is necessary to establish whether, and to what extent, these can serve to correct the system, or if they do not in fact have the effect of breaking it up and nullifying the general prohibition laid down by article 2(4).

The significance and overall bearing of this tendency is not a thing which can be rapidly estimated by simply demonstrating that a particular exception to the ban imposed by the Charter is not – or is not yet – lawful under the present state of the law. Already in diplomatic circles – as has been said previously[92] – significant efforts have been made to extend the cases of individual use of force permitted; even if *consensus* has not so far been reached, these attempts demonstrate a fundamental dissatisfaction on the part of States with the absolute nature of the prohibition in Art. 2(4). This could lead to the evolution of the psychological element *(opinio juris)* in their conduct; with the result that the frequent cases of resort to the various kinds of forcible self-help – now justified with the plea of self-defence – would come to represent the beginning of the formation of rules creating exceptions to the present system.

It is because there is debate at present about a fundamental question affecting the overall balance of the international community (that is, the choice between a return to individual self-help or reinforcement of the social sanction), that we need to be fully aware of the implications of the possible alternatives and their compatibility with the present system. States may opt for the "reinstitution" of certain forms of forcible self-help (whether acts of reprisal, humanitarian intervention, intervention to protect nationals abroad or others), but only when they have fully understood what the effect of this choice would be and to what extent it is compatible with the collective security system which was established by general consent and

98

which nobody has ever explicitly suggested weakening or replacing.

4. SHOULD THE LAW BE CHANGED?
THE NEED FOR CONSISTENCY
WITH THE COLLECTIVE SECURITY SYSTEM

Before being able to proceed correctly to the further analysis we propose to make with particular reference to armed reprisals, we must first make one preliminary point clear.

When it is said that retaliatory use of force should be made lawful because the United Nations security system does not function or because it is inefficient, it should be borne in mind that the possibility of a paralysis of the system had already been envisaged when the Charter was drawn up. Significant confirmation of this is given – implicitly – by the tenor of the treaty which established the United Nations Organization, and in particuar Art. 51. To allow for an exception to the principle on which the whole mechanism of collective security hinges (that is, the principle that the Organization should have a monopoly of the use of force) clearly presupposes the recognition that the Council may – even if only temporarily – be unable to keep the peace; the possibility of an armed attack against a member State is conceivable only as a consequence of this incapacity. Further – explicit – confirmation is to be found in the preparatory discussions; all the proposals concerning lawful use of force put forward by the delegation of the great powers mentioned this eventuality. The United States draft even put it as a premise to the rule:

"Should the Security Council not succeed in preventing aggression...[91]"

The British draft foresaw the possibility of inefficiency not only prior to the attack, but after it too:

"If the Security Council should be unable to make a decision on the measures to be undertaken to restore the situation...[94]"

The Soviet proposal saw the Council's failure to take action not only as a precondition for lawful individual reaction, but also as the criterion for determining the permitted length of this reaction:

"if prior to taking the necessary measures for the maintenance of international peace and security by the Security Council an armed attack against a member State occurs[95]".

If the inefficiency of the mechanism established by the Charter was not an unexpected development, but had, on the contrary, been clearly foreseen by the States which created the mechanism, there are only two possible conclusions which can be reached without radically contradicting the initial choice. The first, more uncompromising one is to deny the possibility of new exceptions to the system other than those explicitly formulated in the Charter. This, however, is to take an excessively formalistic approach, which does not allow sufficiently for the fundamental fact that the degree of inefficiency of the system of collective security has turned out in actual practice to be much greater than that foreseen, on the basis of which the exceptions were allowed. Consequently, we cannot rule out the possibility that the greater seriousness of the situation may make further steps to correct and integrate the system advisable.

The second possible conclusion, which is more flexible and realistic, being based on consideration of what international society is really like and the recent trends in practice previously mentioned, is to admit the introduction of new exceptions, providing the same criterion of consistency with the system are used as was the case when the original exceptions were framed. The existence of the latter shows how the United Nations' monopoly of the use of force (established by Art. 2(4) and Chapter VII) can coexist with individual use of force - in exceptional circumstances only. We must now establish what fundamental principle was followed to make this coexistence possible. So long as the same principle is kept to when creating new exceptions, the system will maintain its initial spirit unaltered and its original structure will be strengthened.

If we are to be able to deduce what this principle is from the Charter, we must first consider the norms concerning the explicit exceptions to the general rule: in these we will be sure to find the requisites and conditions which are behind the principle and which will have to be extended to any new norm of the same kind if we want to avoid the absurdity of subjecting those very forms of individual use of force which cannot be denied (those which States have recognized and accepted from the start) to the most serious conditioning.

On careful examination we can see that the only relevant rule is Art. 51. Art. 107 was conceived as a transitory rule and meant to operate *outside* the system; in any case it appears to have been based on considerations of a contingent nature which are no longer applicable. Two points emerge from Art. 51 which seem to transcend the particular nature of the institution of self-defence and to be the conditions on which the consistency of the whole mechanism of collective security rests.

The first is to be identified in one of the preconditions for lawful self-defence: armed attack, or, in other words, an unlawful use of force on the part of the aggressor State. That this has a more general and extensive role than that played in relation to Art. 51 can be proved by systematic interpreta-

100

tion. After a long process of evolution beginning in the first half of the twentieth century[96], the condemnation of violence in international relations has become deeply rooted in the international social conscience. There may be some doubt as to whether it now has absolute character, but there can be no denying the fact that its influence is sufficient to limit the use of force to cases of the utmost gravity. No State could now consider force as a regular, everyday means of furthering its rights and interests. Moreover, now that the protection of human rights has become a primary value and fundamental obligation of States, it is impossible to put the sacrifice of individual life and integrity implied by armed violence on the same plane as damage to less important values (territorial interests, for example, or even moral interests such as national dignity and honour). It does not seem unreasonable, therefore, to affirm that any form of individual force which is not a reaction to an unlawful act of the same kind is now inadmissible – as is already the case with reference to self-defence.

The first condition is fully satisfied in the case of armed reprisals. In the instances we have examined there is not one case in which the military reprisal did not follow an unlawful use[97] of force, directly carried out by, or at least with the consent of, the target State (for example in the case of actions carried out by guerrillas with bases in a neighbouring State). From this point of view, one might at most suggest that, to be lawful, armed reprisals should be more closely proportionate than traditionally allowed.

This condition, however, although undeniably important, can sometimes prove insufficient to determine – beyond all reasonable doubt – whether a new exception is compatible with the collective security system. Take, for instance, those cases in which force is used to further national self-determination or to protect human rights from particularly serious violations (genocide, inhumane treatment of the citizens of a country): in such cases the values at stake are held by quite a few States and some commentators to be as fundamental as the maintenance of peace. While this view may be open to objection and is certainly not universally accepted in international society, it does undoubtedly carry a lot of emotional weight and may lead to some uncertainty as to whether exceptions such as self-defence for peoples under colonial rule and humanitarian intervention are not admissible, if only *de jure condendo*.

There must therefore be some other evaluative criterion to guide legislative choice; to find out what it is, we need to turn to Art. 51 again. This restates the various preconditions for lawful action in self-defence already required by customary law, but seems to stress one of these in particular, singling it out and developing it: this is the requirement that there should be a lack of alternative means. General international law establishes that armed defence must not only be generically inevitable (it is not possible not to react), but also specifically inevitable (it is not possible to react in any other way[98]). Art. 51 adds that the action of self-defence must cease as soon as "the Security Council has taken the measures necessary to maintain international peace and security". First, then, it is presumed that an alternative means does exist, namely action on the part of the Security Council; secondly, a time limit is fixed for the exercise of self-defence – again with reference to the action of the Council. These provisos and conditions lead to the conclusion that for the framers of the Charter the condition that there should be no possible alternative means does not only apply to the case of self-defence, but has the broader function of ensuring that an exception is compatible with the mechanism of collective security. This explains the provisos, which have the aim of coordinating the exercise of the exception with the action of the principal organ of this mechanism.

Once again, confirmation of this interpretation can be drawn from consideration of the general characteristics – or even the rationale – of the system. As this is based on the prohibition of the use of force, it follows that resort to force can only be permitted in exceptional circumstances, when it cannot be avoided by other means. It would therfore seem correct to conclude that this condition must be extended to any kind of individual use of force which is put forward as lawful to obviate the failings of the system of collective security.

It is in the light of this second criterion that the "reinstitution" of armed reprisals no longer appears compatible with the mechanism established by the Charter for the maintenance of international peace. If retaliatory use of force serves as a sanction for an unlawful act which has already taken place (and which actually constitutes one of the legitimating preconditions for it), then resort to military violence is no longer the only reaction possible. The aim of the reprisal – that is, to penalize and obtain immediate compensation for damage done – can be pursued by other means (unarmed reprisals, economic pressure etc.) It does not matter that these are less rapid and perhaps even less efficacious means of achieving these ends: since the damage deriving from the use of force is no longer otherwise inevitable (in fact, it has already taken place), reaction by force would no longer be justifiable because the values at stake would not be equivalent.

The correctness of this conclusion is indirectly confirmed by practice concerning attempts to introduce new exceptions to the ban imposed by Art. 2(4) or to extend the one contained in Art. 51. The only exception for which there is evidence of a process of formation – perhaps even completed – of a legitimating norm, is that concerning intervention to protect nationals abroad. And it is significant that in all the more recent cases in which action of this kind has been taken, there was no alternative to the use of force because of the immediate threat of otherwise inevitable and irreparable harm to the lives of citizens of the intervening State, as a consequence of violence carried out (or not prevented) by the host State[99].

102

All the other exceptions put forward are not only forbidden by positive rules of law but are also challenged by large sections of the international community: I am referring in particular to the self-defence of peoples under colonial rule[100] and humanitarian intervention[101]. It is no accident that in both these types of use of force it is not the case – in practice – that alternative means of action are lacking[102]. Experience has shown that other forms of reaction did exist and were reasonably effective. The process of decolonization has virtually reached completion without direct military intervention by third party States in favour of national liberation movements being permitted; and in Southern Rhodesia an end was put to the government's inhumane use of power without resort to armed force.

The admissibility of armed reprisals would appear, then, to be ruled out even *de jure condendo*, by reference to the obligations deriving from the Charter[103]. Obviously the reinstitution of this type of forcible self-help as a customary rule would be technically possible; not, however, to integrate and correct the system of collective security but as *an alternative* to it. Having thus clarified the implications of what is a political legislative choice, it becomes clear that to make reprisals lawful once more would be to return to an unorganic and primitive model of society from which the spirit of cooperation and a growing belief in the importance of social values have brought us progressively further away.

NOTES

1. See Jessup, *A Modern Law of Nations* (New York, 1948), p.175 Goodrich-Hambro, *Charter of the United Nations. Commentary and Documents*, 2nd ed. (Boston, 1949), pp. 102-104; Calogeropoulos Stratis, *La Souveraineté des Etats et les limitations au droit de guerre*, 2 Revue Hellénique de Droit International (1949), p. 164; Wehberg, *L'interdiction du recours à la force. Le principe et les problèmes qui se posent*, 78 Hague Recueil (1951-I), p. 72; Waldock, *The Regulation of the Use of Force by Individual States*, 81 Hague Recueil (1952-II), p. 493; Guggenheim, *Traité de Droit International public*, t. II (Genève, 1954), p. 91; Bowett, *Self-Defence in International Law (Manchester, 1958)*, pp. 13-14; Sørensen, *Principes de Droit international public*, 101 Hague Recueil (1960-III), p 219; Venezia, *La notion de représailles en droit international public*, 44 Revue générale de droit international public (1960), pp 493-494; Brierly, *The Law of Nations. An Introduction to the International Law of Peace*, 6th ed (Oxford, 1963), pp. 401-415; Higgins, *The Development of International Law through the Political Organs of the United Nations* (Oxford, 1963), pp. 217-218; Brownlie, *International Law and the Use of Force by States* (Oxford, 1963), p. 281; *Id., Principles of Public International Law*, 2nd ed. (Oxford, 1973), p. 452; Schwarzenberger, *A Manual of International Law* 5th ed. (London, 1967), pp. 185-186; Visscher, *Théories et réalités en droit international public*, 4th ed (Paris, 1970), p. 333-334; Greig, *International Law*, 2nd ed. (London, 1976), p. 888; Mosler, *The International Society as a Legal Community* (Alphen aan den Rijn, 1980), pp. 280-281; Gross (L. M.), *The Legal Implications of Israel's 1982 Invasion into Lebanon*, 13 California Western International Law Journal (1983), p. 475.

2. Res S/3538, January 19th 1956, para 2; Res S/5111, April 9th 1962, para. 2 See also S/Res/288 (1966), para. 3: *'Emphasizes* [...] that actions of military reprisal cannot be tolerated'.

3. Secretary General's Report of 27th September 1956 to the Security Council: summary in yearbook of the United Nations (hereafter cited as Y.U.N.) (1956), pp. 13-14.

4. See the declarations of France, Ethiopia, China, Y.U.N. (1968), p. 194 (Karameh incident, March, 1968); France, *ibid.*, p. 208 (Es Salt raid, August, 1968); Brazil, Canada, China, Denmark, France, Paraguay and Senegal, *ibid.*, p. 230 (Beirut raid, December, 1968); Paraguay, Y U.N. (1969), p 191 (Es Salt raid, March, 1969).

5. This argument has been put forward by Denmark, France, New Zealand, Turkey, the United Kingdom and the United States, Y U.N. (1954), pp 66-67 (Nahhalin incident, March, 1954); China, Y.U N (1968), pp. 194, 209 (Karameh incident, March, 1968; Es Salt raid, August, 1968)

6. Declaration by the representative of China, Y.U N. (1968), p 194 (Karameh incident, March, 1968).

7. Rosenstock, *The Declaration of Principles of International Law Concerning Friendly Relations a Survey*, 65 AJIL (1971), p. 179

8. See, for instance, the declaration made by the delegate of Hungary, GAOR, 23rd sess., Sixth Committee, 1094th meeting, para 2 ('his delegation would have preferred greater clarity of wording, since the present formulation left open the long-debated problem whether or not it implied the prohibition of reprisals not involving the use or armed force'); see also GAOR, 23rd sess , A/7326, *Report of the Special Committee on Principles of International Law Concerning Friendly Relations and Cooperation among States*, para. 64.

9. See the convincing reasons given for this view by the delegate of the Netherlands, GAOR, 23rd sess., Sixth Committee, 1094th meeting, par. 9-11.

10. Brierly, *op.cit supra*, note 1, p 245; Waldock, *op.cit. supra*, note 1, p. 493.

11. The authors mentioned in note 10 are of the opinion that another important principle concerning armed reprisals and the possibility of retaliatory use of force 'to affirm a legal right against an expected unlawful attempt to prevent its exercise' can be derived from the same decision (see also the quotation in note 26). For a critical evaluation of the view put forward by these authors see the comments made below at the beginning of section 2.

12. See *Conference on Security and Cooperation in Europe: Final Act* (August 1, 1975), Sect. 1(a) ('Declaration of Principles Guiding Relations between Participating States'), subsect. II ('Refraining from the threat or use of force'), XIV International Legal Materials (1975), p. 1294.

13. Falk, *The Beirut Raid and the International Law of Retaliation*, 63 AJIL (1969), pp. 430-431, note 39.

14. First, it places this use of force entirely *outside the framework of the United Nations system*, thus protecting the overall normative consistency of the latter. Furthermore, the fact that this legal inquiry different from the Charter approach is put on a second-order level implies the prior demonstration that the Charter approach has already proved ineffectual. Thus the space left open to forcible reprisals is not going to contribute to the weakening of the enforcement mechanism of the United Nations, but simply presupposes the recognition of a state of paralysis already in course. Finally, this second-order legality of reprisals, because of its subsidiary character, does not prescind entirely from the principles of the Charter: in fact this theory draws certain general policy lines from the Charter to supplement the customary norms, held to be too categorical and rigidly formulated to permit a retaliatory use of force 'at variance with community perceptions of lawful conduct' (Falk, op.cit., p. 440 ff.).

15. Bowett, *Reprisals Involving Recourse to Armed Force*, 66 AJIL (1972), p 2.

104

16. Bowett, *op.cit.*, p. 26.

17. The criterion of reasonableness put forward by the author of this interpretation no longer intervenes – as a second-order level of inquiry – to limit, in a subordinate way, conduct which is already unlawful according to the Charter, but rather to give it a shape which makes it somehow acceptable even to the Charter approach. In other words, 'reasonable' reprisals, which by the first intepretation were merely a *remedy for the inefficiency* of the enforcement mechanism of the United Nations now become *instrumental to the paralysis* of this mechanism. The principles of the Charter still play some part in determining whether conduct is 'reasonable' or not, but with the paradoxical effect of favouring the contradictions inside the system of collective security: that is, preventing the Security Council from condemning armed reprisals, although judging them 'all illegal'.

18. Lillich, *Forcible Self-Help under International Law* 62 U.S. Naval War College – International Law Studies (1980), *Readings in International Law from the Naval War College Review 1947-1977* (edited by R. B. Lillich and J. N. Moore), vol. II: *The Use of Force, Human Rights and General International Legal Issues*, pp 130, 136, 138.

19. Lillich, *op.cit.*, p. 133. Although this theory ascribes the legitimacy of armed reprisals more to *jus condendum* than positive law, it is in fact the one which most contradicts the Charter status of retaliatory use of force, described at the beginning of this section On the basis of it, resort to reprisals would not normally be unlawful and only admissible (or tolerated) in exceptional circumstances, but is to be considered advisable, even necessary, by virtue of the 'principle of major purposes' (*Id.*, p. 138.).

20. To these can be added those along very similar lines put forward by McHugh, *Forcible Self-Help in International law*, Readings in International Law from the Naval War College Review 1947-1977, *cit.* note 18, pp. 148, 150-151, 153-154, 158-159 (McHugh's views are based to a considerable extent, if with some modifications, on Falk's criteria, which he deems 'a framework for evaluating and managing the use of force'); and by Levenfeld, *Israeli Counter Fedayeen Tactics in Lebanon: Self-defense and Reprisal under Modern International Law*, 21 Columbia Journal of Transnational Law (1982), p. 35 (by reference to arguments put forward by Bowett, Waldock and Falk, Levenfeld concludes that 'arguments can be advanced that resort to reprisals is both legal and desirable under the Charter'). See also Wengler, *L'interdiction de recourir à la force. Problèmes et tendances*, 7 Revue belge de droit interational (1971-72), p. 449. According to Colbert, *Retaliation in International Law* (New York, 1948), p. 203; Stone, *Aggression and World Order*, (London, 1958), pp. 94-98, the lawfulness of armed reprisals can be derived from interpretation of the Charter.

21. For the debate concerning the Resolution on Friendly Relations, see the declarations made by Czechoslovakia, the USSR, Jugoslavia, Rumania, India, the UAR, Ghana, Syria, Cameroun, quoted by Ronzitti, *Il ricorso alla forza armata a protezione dei cittadini all'estero e per ragioni d'umanità* (Pisa, 1980), p. 37, note 60. For the preparatory work concerning the Resolution on the Definition of Aggression, see the saving clauses proposed by the Soviet draft (A/AC.134/L.12) and by the Thirteen-Power draft (A/AC.134/L.16 and Add. 1 and 2), and comment thereon by Schwebel, *Aggression, Intervention and Self-Defence in Modern International Law*, 136 Hague Recueil (1972-II), p. 483 ff.

22. See the statements made by Australia, Canada, the USA and the United Kingdom before the Special Committee on Principles of International Law concerning Friendly Relations and Co-operation among States (A/AC.125/L.22). See also the draft presented by the western countries in the Special Committee on the Question of defining aggression (A/AC.134/L.16 and Add. 1, 2), in connection with the Thirteen-Power draft (A/AC.134/L16 and Add. 1, 2) and comment thereon by Ronzitti, *op.cit.*, pp. 37-38, note 60.

23. We refer here above all to the following cases: British intervention at Suez (Oct.-Nov. 1956: France, which also took part in this military operation, justified its intervention differently); Belgian intervention in the Congo (July 1960); U.S. intervention in the Dominican Republic (April 1965; at least in the early stages the intervention was defined as 'an emergency action taken to protect lives'), the Israeli raid on Entebbe (July 1976); French intervention in the western Sahara, which involved air attacks on the troops of the Polisario (December 1977). One example of intervention to protect nationals abroad, carried out by a State not belonging to the western bloc, is the Egyptian raid on Larnaca (February 1978). For an in depth analysis of this topic, see above all Bowett, *The Use of Force for the Protection of Nationals Abroad*, in this volume.

24. See the authors quoted above, in notes 15 and 20.

25. See thereon Tucker, *Reprisals and Self-Defense: the Customary Law*, 66 AJIL (1972), p. 586 ff.; Greig, *op. cit.*, *supra*, not 1, p. 887.

26. I. C. J. Reports, *The Corfu Channel Case (Merits)*, 1949, p. 31. See, however, Brierly, *op.cit.*, *supra*, note 1, p. 421; Waldock, *op.cit.*, *supra*, note 1, p. 501; Mc Hugh; *op.cit. supra*, note 20, p. 151.

27. The Operation has been so characterized by Brierly, *op.cit. supra*, note 1, p. 425, and by Mc Hugh, *op.cit. supra*, note 20, p. 151

28. I. C. J. Pleadings, *The Corfu Channel Case - Oral Proceedings*, IV, p. 582.

29. See the examples of practice mentioned by Farer, *The Regulation of Foreign Intervention in Civil Armed Conflict*, 142 Hague Recueil (1974-II), p. 365 ff. See also the interpretation put forward by Schwebel, *op.cit.*, not 21, p 486, with reference to the 'Friendly Relations' Declaration, which would appear to be the most correct conclusion with regard to the problem in question.

30. See above note 21.

31. See France's complaint to the President of the Security Council (February 14th 1958), 42 Revue générale de droit international public (1958), pp. 177-178; and the following declarations by Portugal: Y.U.N. (1969), p. 136 (attacks on Zambia); *ibid.*, p 138 (attacks on Senegal: 'The crux of the problem [. .] was that all such incidents resulted from armed attacks by anti-Portuguese organizations that were allowed to operate from bases inside Senegal'); *ibid.*, p. 141 (attack on Guinea, November, 1969).

32. See the Report by the Secretary-General of the League of Nations, May 17th, 1927, VII S. d. N. Journal Officiel (1927), p 834. See also Quadri, *Diritto internazionale pubblico*, 5th ed. (Napoli, 1968), p. 267: Guggenheim, op cit., *supra*, note 1, at p. 92.

33. Compare Falk, *op.cit.*, *supra*, note 13, at p. 434.

34. Y.U.N. (1970), p. 189 (the other objectives, according to the report, were: to strike at the headquarters of the African Independence Party of Guinea and Cape Verde and to free Portuguese prisoners held in Guinea)

35. See cases quoted by Bowett, *op.cit*, *supra*, note 1, at pp. 5-7.

36. 73 AJIL (1979), p. 491.

37. Statement by the Department's Legal Adviser Stevenson, 73 AJIL (1979), p. 491.

38. Security Council, Official Records, 19th Year, 1141st Meeting.

39. Y.U.N. (1966), p. 168; Y.U.N. (1967), p 231.

40. Y.U.N. (1966), p. 169.

41. Y.U.N. (1967), p. 231.

42. See the statements by: Syria and Iraq, Y.U.N. (1966), p. 168; Jordan and Syria, Y.U.N. (1967), p. 233.

43. Bowett, *op.cit.*, *supra*, note 15, at p. 14, note 9

44. Falk, *op.cit.*, *supra*, note 13, at p. 434.

45. Blum, *The Beirut Raid and the International Double Standard*, 64 AJIL (1970), pp. 77-78.

46. This view has been adopted by the following States: Uganda, Y.U.N. (1966), p. 175 (at-

106

tack on Jordan, November 1966); U. S. A., Y.U.N. (1968), p. 206 (Es Salt raid, August 1968); U. S A. and Denmark, Y.U.N. (1968), pp. 229, 231 (Beirut raid, December 1968); Israel, Y.U.N. (1969), p. 187 (Es Salt raid, March 1969), Y.U N. (1972), pp. 158, 162 (invasion of Lebanese territory, February, 1972; air and ground attack on Lebanon, June 1972); United Kingdom and United States of America, Y.U.N. (1972), p. 163 (air and ground attack on Lebanon, June 1972); U.S.A., U.K., Australia, India, Panama, Peru, Y.U.N. (1973), p. 180 (Beirut raid, April 1973); United Kingdom, Y.U.N. (1974), p. 208 (attack on southern Lebanon, April 1974); Israel, Y.U.N. (1979), pp. 329, 332 (attacks on Lebanon, May-June 1979); Israel, 18 ONU-Chronique mensuelle, n. 9 (sept.-oct. 1981), p. 10 ff., 19 ONU-Chronique mensuelle, n. 8 (sept. 1982), p. 15 (attacks on Lebanon, July, 1981; June 1982)

47. This is the view endorsed by: Hungary, Y.U.N. (1968), p. 198 (Karameh incident, March 1968), Algeria, USSR, Y.U.N. (1968), p. 206 (Es Salt raid, August 1968); China, Y.U.N. (1973), p 180 (Beirut raid, April 1973); Y.U.N. (1979), p. 331 (attack on Lebanon, May 1979); USSR, Y.U.N. (1979), p 335 (attack on Lebanon, June 1979); German Democratic Republic, 18 ONU-Chronique mensuelle, n. 9 (sept.-oct. 1981), p. 15 (attack on Lebanon, July 1981).

48. See, for instance, Jordan, Y.U.N.(1953), p. 220; Y.U.N. (1954), pp. 66-67; Egypt, Y.U.N. (1955), p. 32; Jordan (and also Egypt, Lebanon and Syria), Y.U N (1956), p. 15; Syria, Y.U N. (1962), p. 135; Y U N. (1964), p. 175; Jordan, Y U N. (1966), p. 174; Syria, Y.U.N. (1966), pp. 168-169; the U.A.R., Y.U N. (1967), pp 231-232; Jordan, Y U N. (1968), p. 192; Lebanon, Y.U.N. (1968), po. 228-229; Jordan, Y.U.N (1969), p. 186; Lebanon, Y.U.N. (1970), p. 238; Y U.N. (1972), pp. 157, 162, Y.U.N. (1973), p. 179; Y.U.N. (1974), p. 207; Y.U N (1979), p. 333; 19 ONU-Chronique mensuelle, n. 8 (sept. 1982), p. 16.

49. See, for example, Syria, Y.U N. (1964), p. 175, Jordan, Y.U.N. (1966), p. 174; Lebanon, Y.U.N. (1970), p. 229.

50 U A.R., Y.U.N. (1967), p. 231 ('Israel's act of war of 24 October').

51. The line taken by the western States is generally supported by whichever of the Latin American States are represented on the Security Council on different occasion Other Third World States express their condemnation of Israeli military operations in terms which are at times quite analogous to those used by western States. see, for instance, Nigeria and Mali, Y.U.N. (1966), p. 174 (attack on Jordan, November 1966); Uganda, Y.U.N. (1966), p. 169 (shelling of seven Syrian areas, July 1966); Nigeria Y.U.N. (1967), pp 233-234 ('Eilat destroyer incident, October 1967); Pakistan, Y U N. (1968), p. 196 (Karameh incident, March 1968); Senegal, Y.U.N. (1968), p. 230 (Beirut raid, December 1968); India, Y.U.N. (1973), p. 180 (Beirut raid, April 1973).

52. See, above all, the general statement of the U.S.A. during the Security Council's debate concerning Israeli attack on Lebanon (June 1972), Y.U.N. (1972), pp. 162-163: 'To obtain United States concurrence, any draft resolution before the Council would have to be balanced and show concern about terrorist acts as well as Israeli attacks' See also the declarations by the U.S.A. (draft resolution), Y.U.N. (1967), p. 233 ('Eilat' destroyer incident, October 1967); the U.S A. and the U.K., Y.U.N. (1968), pp 193, 198 (Karameh incident, March 1968); the U.S A., the U.K. and Denmark, Y U N. (1968), pp. 206-207 (Es Salt raid, August 1968); the U.S.A. and Paraguay, Y.U.N. (1969), pp. 188, 191-192 (Es Salt raid, March 1969); Colombia, Finland, the U.K. and the U.S A., Y.U.N. (1970), p. 236 (attack on Southern Lebanon, May 1970); Italy, Belgium, France and the U.K. (draft resolution, preambular part), Y.U.N. (1972), p 159) (invasion of Lebanese territory, February 1972); the U.S.A., Belgium and Panama, Y.U.N. (1972), pp 162-163 (air and ground attack on Lebanon, June 1972); U.S.A., Australia, Panama, Peru and the U.K.-France draft resolution, Y U.N. (1973), pp. 180-181 (Beirut raid, April 1973); the

U.K., France and Australia, Y.U.N (1974), p. 208 (attack on southern Lebanon, April 1974); the U S A , Sweden and Costa Rica, Y.U.N. (1975), pp. 227-229 (air attack on Lebanon, December 1975).

53. See, for instance, France (who abstained in the vote on the U.S.A.-U.K. joint draft resolution (!), because it did not adequately apportion the responsabilities), Y.U.N. (1962), p. 137 (Lake Tiberias incident, March 1962); Colombia, Paraguay, the United Kingdom, the United States (who abstained in the vote on the three-power draft resolution S/9120/Rev.1, adopted by the Council as Res. 265 (1969)), Y.U.N. (1969), pp. 191-192; Colombia, Nicaragua, Sierra Leone, the United States (who abstained in the vote on Zambia draft resolution, S/9807, adopted by Council as Res. 280 (1970)), Y.U.N. (1970), p. 236; Panama and the U.S.A. (who abstained in the vote on the three-power draft resolution S/10722, adopted by the Security Council as Res. 316 (1972)), Y.U.N. (1972), p. 163.

54. See the following declaration by the U.S A. prior to (or in explanation of) the negative vote: on the three-power draft resolution S/10784, Y.U.N. (1972), p. 168 (attacks on Syrian Arab Republic and Lebanon, September 1972); on the five-power draft resolutions S/11898, Y.U N. (1975), p. 229 (air attack on Lebanon, December 1975); on France draft resolution S/15255/Rev. 2, 19 ONU-Chronique mensuelle, n. 8 (sept. 1982), p. 18 (air attack on Lebanon, June 1982).

55. With the exception of the States mentioned in note 51. In some cases the language used by the socialist and Third World States does not appear to be entirely consistent. For example Israel's military operations are described – in the course of the same debate – both as 'aggression' and as 'reprisals': see, for example, Syria, Y.U.N. (1964), p. 175 (Kibbutz Dan incident, November 1964); Syria, Y.U.N. (1966), pp. 168-169 (shelling of seven Syrian areas, July 1966); the U.S.S.R , Y.U.N (1968), p. 230 (Beirut raid, December 1968); Pakistan, Y U.N. (1969), p. 189 (Es Salt raid, March 1969).

56. Y.U.N (1969), pp. 195, 198.

57. See, for instance, Lebanon and the USSR (who abstained in the vote on the joint draft resolution S/3139/Rev.2, adopted by the Council on November 24th 1953), pp. 221-222; China, Guinea and USSR (who abstained in the vote on the two-power draft resolution S/10916/Rev 1, adopted by the Security Council as Res. 332 (1973)), Y.U.N. (1973), pp. 179-180; Czechoslovakia and the USSR (who abstained in the vote on the draft resolution S/13392, adopted by the Council as Res 450 (1979)), Y.U.N. (1979), pp. 331-332.

58. See the declarations by: the USSR, Y.U.N. (1962), p. 137 (vote on the two-power draft S/5110 and Corr. 1, adopted by the Security Council on April 9th 1962); Nigeria and the USSR, Y.U.N. (1967), pp. 233-234 (vote on the agreed text adopted by the Council as Res 240 (1967); Hungary and Pakistan, Y.U.N. (1968), p. 198 (vote on the agreed text adopted by the Council as Res. 248 (1968); Hungary and the USSR, Y.U.N. (1968), p. 232 (vote on the agreed text adopted by the Council as Res. 262 (1968); Pakistan and the USSR, Y.U.N. (1968), p. 213 (vote on the agreed text adopted by the Council as Res. 256 (1968)); Indonesia and the USSR, Y.U.N. (1974), p. 209, (vote on the agreed text adopted by the Council as Res. 347 (1974)).

59. See, for instance, the declarations by the USSR, Algeria and Jordan, Y.U.N. (1968), pp. 198-199: explanations of vote on Res. 248 (1968); Mauritania, Y.U.N. (1974), p. 209: explanation of vote on Res. 347 (1974).

60. More specifically, only the British attack on fort at Harib, in Yemen (March 1964), was described as collective self-defence, by the United Kingdom representative in the Security Council: 'a defensive response [...] in order to preserve the territorial integrity of the Federation of South Arabia for whose defence we are responsible [...] the action was taken in response to an urgent request from Ministers of the Federation to protect the interests and integrity of their country'; see the text of the statement in British Practice in

108

International Law (1964-I), edited by E. Lauterpacht, p. 109 ff.

61. See 73 AJIL (1979), p. 491.
62. See Falk, *op.cit. supra*, note 13, at pp. 416, 429 (note 38); but see Blum, *op cit. supra*, note 45, at p. 76.
63. See 73 AJIL (1979), p. 491.
64. British Practice in International Law (1964-I), p. 112.
65. Y.U.N. (1954), p. 67 (Nahhalin incident, March 1954).
66. Y.U.N. (1962), p. 137 (Lake Tiberias incident, March 1962).
67. Y.U.N. (1968), p. 194 (Karameh incident, March 1968); *ibid.*, p. 208 (Es Salt raid, August 1968).
68. 73 AJIL (1979), p. 490.
69. See the text in 42 Revue générale de droit international public (1958), pp. 171-172.
70. There seems to be no point in considering the attitude of the target States, in so far as they tend to call the armed action taken against them by a stronger name than 'reprisal' – or at any rate a different one – (e.g. 'armed attack', 'aggression' etc). In any case they have invariably called for the condemnation of the claimant State on the grounds that its conduct was unlawful and unjustifiable.
71. See above, notes 4 and 5. See also the declarations by India, Y.U.N (1967), p 233 ('Eilat' destroyer incident, October 1967); Ethiopia and the U.A.R.. Y U N. (1968), p. 196 (Karameh incident, March 1968); Zambia, Y.U.N. (1970), p. 232 (invasion of Lebanese territory, May 1970).
72. See France, the United Kingdom and the USA (joint draft resolution), Y.U.N (1955), p. 33 (Gaza incident, February 1955); Jordan, Y.U.N. (1956), p. 16 (Sharafi-Qalqilya incident, October 1956); Syria, Y.U.N. (1964), p. 174 (Kibbutz Dan incident, November 1964); Pakistan, Y.U.N. (1969), P. 189 (Es Salt raid, March 1969); the U.S.S R., Y.U.N. (1974), p 208 (attack on Southern Lebanon, April 1974).
73. See the declarations quoted by Bowett, *op.cit.*, *supra*, note 15, at p. 7 note 23; and by Lamberti Zanardi, *La legittima difesa nel diritto internazionale* (Milano, 1972), p. 271 note 222.
74. Bowett, *op.cit.*, *supra*, note 15, at p. 7.
75. Bowett, *op. cit.*, *supra*, note 15, at p. 28; Tucker, *op. cit. supra*, note 25, at p. 595; Mc Hugh, *op. cit.*, *supra*, note 20, at p. 154.
76. See above, section Two, text and notes 51-59.
77. See the Israeli statement quoted by Bowett, *op. cit.*, *supra*, note 15, at p 23 note 90; see also the declaration by the representative of Israel in the Security Council, Y.U.N., (1970), p. 237 (attack on Lebanon, May 1970).
78. See above, section One, text and notes 13-17.
79. The following cases should be added to those quoted by Bowett, op cit *supra*, note 15, at p. 11 ff.: Sakiet-Sidi-Youssef incident of February 1958, Y.U.N. (1958), pp. 77-78; attack on U.A.R. control stations of July 1967, Y.U.N. (1967), pp. 226 ff.; air attack on the Nag Hamadi area of October 1968, Y.U.N. (1968), p. 225 ff.; attacks on Lebanon and on the Syrian Arab Republic of September 1972, Y.U.N. (1972), p. 165 ff.; attack on Lebanon of December 1975, Y.U.N. (1975), p. 226 ff.
80. See the statement of the President of the Security Council at the outset of the meeting on May 12th 1954, Y.U.N. (1954), pp. 68-69.
81. Y.U.N. (1954), p. 69.
82. Y.U.N. (1958), pp. 77-78.
83. Y.U.N. (1968), pp. 227-228.
84. See, for instance, the declarations by: Lebanon and Pakistan, Y.U.N. (1953), pp. 222-223; Lebanon (draft resolution), Y.U.N. (1954), p. 68; Egypt, Y.U.N. (1955), p. 32; Syria (draft resolution), Y.U.N. (1955), p. 35; Syria, Y.U.N. (1964), p. 174; Jordan,

Y.U.N. (1966), p. 174; the U.A.R. and the USSR, Y.U.N. (1967), pp. 232-233; Jordan, the USSR, the UAR and Hungary. Y.U.N. (1968), pp. 192, 195, 196, 198; Jordan, Y.U.N. (1968), p. 205; Lebanon, the USSR, Algeria, India, Hungary and Pakistan, Y.U.N. (1968), pp. 229, 230, 231, 232; Jordan, Y.U.N. (1969), p. 186; Lebanon, Y.U.N. (1970), p. 229; Lebanon and the USSR, Y.U.N. (1972), pp. 157, 159.

85. See the declarations quoted above, note 58.
86. See Res. S/3139/Rev. 2, November 24th 1953, para. B; Res. S/5110, April 9th 1962, para 1; Res. 248 (1968), preamble and para. 3; Res. 316 (1972), preamble and para. 2; Res. 332 (1973), preamble and para. 1; Res; 347 (1974), para. 2. See also the declarations by: Finland, Y.U.N. (1970), p. 236; the U.K., Y.U N. (1972), p. 163, Y.U.N. (1973), p. 180; the U.S.A., Y.U.N. (1974), p. 209.
87. Y.U.N. (1964), p. 175; Y.U.N. (1966), p. 169.
88. Y.U.N. (1964), p. 175; Y.U.N. (1972), p. 168; Y.U.N. (1975), p. 229.
89. Y.U.N. (1973), p. 168; see also the declarations quoted above, note 52.
90. Y.U.N. (1955), p. 34.
91. See above, the final part of section One and notes 21-23. The fundamental premise underlying this view is the conviction that the ban on the use of force is closely connected and necessarily conditional to the working of the mechanism for the peaceful settlement of disputes and collective security. This conviction is shared by the Super Powers, as is apparent from the fact that they use the same expression to describe the concept: see the statement by Secretary of State Dulles, quoted by Lillich. op cit. *supra*, note 18, p. 138 ('Peace is a coin which has two sides; one is the avoidance of the use of force, and the other is the creation of the conditions of justice'); and the declaration by the U.S.S.R. in the Special Committee on Enhancing the Effectiveness of the principle of Non-Use of Force in International Relations (First sess., August-September 1978'): 'the two questions constituted two sides of the same coin' (Y.U.N. (1978), p. 171).
92. See above, notes 21-22.
93. U.S. For Rel. 1945-I, *General: The United Nations*, (Washington, 1967), p. 685.
94. U.S. For. Rel., 1945-I, p. 699.
95. U.S. For. Rel , 1945-I, p. 812.
96. See art. 1 of the Porter Convention (1907) and the following legal developments considered by Brownlie, *International Law and the Use of Force by States, cit., supra*, note 1, Chapters II, XI, XII.
97. Or at any rate a use of force which was *held to be* unlawful; for the purpose in hand it is of no concern if it really was unlawful or merely deemed to be so by the claimant State.
98. For the precondition of the *lack of alternative means* see the statements of: China, S.d N., Journal Officiel (1937), p. 655; Sweden, S.d.N., Journal Officiel, Supplément spécial n. 85, p. 69; Great Britain, India, New Zealand, S.d.N., Conférence pour la codification du droit international. Bases de discussion, III (C.75.M.69.1929.V), p. 1251.
99. Reference is made here to the cases quoted above, note 23.
100. See above, Section One, text and note 22.
101. See the declarations quoted by Ronzitti, *op. cit., supra*, note 21, at pp. 127-132.
102. Obviously, the existence of alternative means is to be recognized and admitted even when the political will to make use of such means does not actually exist, so that they cannot in practice lead to a solution to the situation. Thus, for instance, in the case of Namibia (South West Africa), the system of apartheid and colonial domination practised by the Pretoria government could be eliminated without resort to force, if States really applied the forms of economic pressure listed in Namibia Decree No. 1, issued by the U.N. Council for Namibia on 27th September 1974 (G.A.O.R., 29th sess., Suppl. No. 24 A, A/9624/Add.1, pp. 27-28): for more detailed consideration of the question, see Barsotti, *In tema di amministrazione diretta di territori non autonomi da parte dell'ONU: il caso*

110

della Namibia, 16 Comunicazioni e Studi dell'Istituto di diritto internazionale e straniero dell'Università di Milano (1980), p. 83 ff.

103. The conclusion that armed reprisals are utterly incompatible with the obligations imposed by the Charter makes a precise definition of the features which distinguish retaliatory use of force from self-defence essential. This, however, is beyond the scope of the present inquiry, since it implies an in depth analysis of the notion of self-defence contained in the Charter. Here we need only point out that to make this distinction it is not enough to consider the general characteristics of these two forms of self-help (the method generally used by legal writers: see Zourek, *La notion de légitime défense en droit international* (Rapport provisoire). 56 Annuaire de L'Institut de Droit International - Session de Wiesbaden 1975, pp. 60-61). We should rather consider the specific characteristics of unlawful reprisals: that is, of armed reprisals carried out in response to a prior unlawful use of armed force on the part of the target State. By reference to these characteristics the distinction is a complex one, but not impossible to make (as Tucker maintains, *op.cit.,* note 25, p. 586), above all if we concentrate on two features: the immediacy of the danger posed to the State and the lack of alternative means; and if we exclude the lawfulness of so-called preventive self-defence.

Part IV
Terrorism, Weapons of Mass Destruction and Information Warfare

[14]

On the Necessity of Pre-emption

Abraham D. Sofaer*

Abstract

The attacks of September 11, 2001 led President Bush to declare a 'war' on terrorism. Terrorists are capable of inflicting grave damage, and are not susceptible to the deterrent pressures felt by states. Pre-emption and prevention of attacks have become part of the US national security strategy to deal with this danger. International lawyers claim that pre-emption must be limited to actions in response to an attack that is imminent and unavoidable by any other means. This paper examines the background of the requirement that pre-emption is restricted to imminent attacks, and argues that the narrow standard properly applies only when a potential victim state can rely on the police powers of the state from which a prospective attack is anticipated. A more flexible standard for determining necessity is appropriate for situations in which the state from which attacks are anticipated is either unwilling or unable to prevent the attacks, or may even be responsible for them. The situation posed by Al Qaeda, operating from Afghanistan, was one in which the Taliban explicitly refused to prevent attacks on the US by that terrorist organization. The question of the applicability of the rule regarding necessity to Saddam Hussein's Iraq is more complicated, but a strong case can be made for the necessity of pre-emptive action.

President George W. Bush responded to the attacks of September 11, 2001 with dramatic actions and even more dramatic rhetoric. He promised to stop known terrorists from harming Americans. To this end, he declared 'war' on terrorism,[1] thereby refocusing the nation's strategic posture from one that targeted terrorists as criminals to one that treats terrorists and supporting states capable of threatening the US and its allies, as threats to national security.

This shift in perspective stems from important strategic realities. The civilized world faces a grave threat from terrorism, especially from groups supported by states. The current threat goes beyond conventional threats from terrorist groups. Globalization has facilitated the capacities of terrorists to travel, move money, and communicate. Technology has enhanced their ability to inflict damage with powerful explosives, modern weapons, and potentially through the use of weapons of mass destruction.

---

* George P. Shultz Senior Fellow, The Hoover Institution, Stanford University; Professor of Law (by Courtesy), Stanford Law School. All rights reserved.

[1] See, e.g., Address to a Joint Session of Congress and the American People (20 Sept. 2001) and Presidential Address (7 Oct. 2001), available at www.whitehouse.gov.

Typical criminal law enforcement is insufficient to reach and stop terrorists located in states that allow them to operate; prosecutions of low-level operatives, willing to die, cannot be expected to deter attacks. Indeed, deterrence is far less effective in dealing with modern terror (individuals or groups) than it has been with regard to conventional threats from state conduct.

States can attempt to avoid responsibility for attacks by using terrorists to carry them out. States can also enable terrorists to attack other states by refusing to prevent such attacks, as the Taliban did. In either situation, establishing responsibility for attacks is a formidable problem, greatly complicating national defence. Terrorist groups avoid detection by dispersing their members in highly decentralized cells; many are prepared to face death in pursuing their objectives. Success or victory for such people has a meaning alien to rational thought. Finally, no amount of preparation and technological sophistication will enable the US and other target states to prevent all serious terrorist attacks, or even to limit such attacks to a tolerable level. Technology should increasingly enhance security at key locations and for critical infrastructures. But the US remains target rich, and extremely vulnerable, because it is a large, thriving, open society unwilling to compromise its fundamental freedoms for security.

For these reasons, the US has advanced, more forcefully than ever, the need for pre-emptive actions.[2] In a speech on 1 June 2002, at West Point, President Bush explained that the 'gravest danger to freedom lies at the crossroads of radicalism and technology'.[3] He promised to oppose 'with all our power' efforts by terrorists and states to use modern weapons to advance radical aims by attacking the US or its allies. Where necessary, he would resort to pre-emptive actions, rather than permit the

---

[2] The need to act pre-emptively was clearly set out by former Secretary of State George P. Shultz in several speeches during the early 1980s. His advocacy of an 'active defense' was strongly opposed at that time, but it is now, once again, national policy. See generally the discussion in his *Turmoil and Triumph* (1993), at 645–653. He specifically states: 'We cannot allow ourselves to become the Hamlet of Nations, worrying endlessly over whether and how to respond. A great nation with global responsibilities cannot afford to be hamstrung by confusion and indecisiveness. Fighting terrorism will not be a clean or pleasant contest, but we have no choice ... We must reach a consensus in this country that our responses should go beyond passive defense to consider means of active prevention, preemption, and retaliation. Our goal must be to prevent and deter future terrorist acts ... The public must understand before the fact that occasions will come when their government must act before each and every fact is known — and the decisions cannot be tied to polls.' 648–649.

[3] Remarks by the President at 2002 Graduation Exercise of the United States Military Academy, West Point, New York. This explanation echoed statements of Secretary of Defense Donald Rumsfeld, who said on 31 January 2002 that when terrorists have weapons capable of inflicting grave damage, 'we have no choice':

> [D]efending the U.S. requires prevention, self-defense and sometimes preemption. It is not possible to defend against every conceivable kind of attack in every conceivable location at every minute of the day or night. Defending against terrorism and other emerging 21st century threats may well require that we take the war to the enemy. The best, and in some cases, the only defense is a good offense.

See 'Secretary Rumsfeld Speaks on "21st Century Transformation" of U.S. Armed Forces' (remarks delivered at the National Defense University, Fort McNair, Washington D.C. on 31 Jan. 2002), available at www.defenselink.mil/speeches/2002/s20020131-secdef.html.

devastating consequences that can flow from attacks such as occurred on September 11, 2001.

On 17 September 2002, this approach became part of the National Security Strategy for the nation's defence. The Strategy states the general goal of preventing 'our enemies from threatening us, our allies, and our friends, with weapons of mass destruction . . . .'[4] In Part V of the Strategy, this objective is explained as 'proactive counterproliferation' of weapons of mass destruction: 'We must be prepared to stop rogue states and their terrorist clients before they are able to threaten or use weapons of mass destruction against the United States and our allies and friends.' The Strategy states that the US 'will not use force in all cases to preempt emerging threats, nor should nations use preemption as a pretext for aggression'. But it asserts that the US

> has long maintained the option of preemptive actions to counter a sufficient threat to our national security. The greater the threat, the greater is the risk of inaction — and the more compelling the case for taking anticipatory action to defend ourselves, even if uncertainty exists as to the time and place of the enemy's attack.[5]

US policy therefore appears at this point to reserve the option of pre-emption where a grave threat is posed to it or its allies, especially by the threat or use of weapons of mass destruction in the hands of states or terrorists, that cannot be stopped or deterred through means short of the use of force.

The Strategy explicitly addresses the legality of pre-empting attacks. It notes that international law has long recognized the right to defend against 'imminent danger', and it argues that the concept of what constitutes an imminent threat must be adapted to reflect the capabilities and aims of terrorist groups and rogue states:

> For centuries, international law recognized that nations need not suffer an attack before they can lawfully take action to defend themselves against forces that present an imminent danger of attack. Legal scholars and international jurists often conditioned the legitimacy of preemption on the existence of an imminent threat — most often a visible mobilization of armies, navies, and air forces preparing to attack.
>
> We must adapt the concept of imminent threat to the capabilities and objectives of today's adversaries. Rogue states and terrorists do not seek to attack us using conventional means. They know such attacks would fail. Instead, they rely on acts of terror and, potentially, the use of weapons of mass destruction — weapons that can be easily concealed, delivered covertly, and used without warning.[6]

Can the Administration's policy of pre-emption be justified under international law? May the US properly cite current, unprecedented strategic necessities as a basis for satisfying international legal requirements? If not, can and should the doctrine of pre-emption be expanded to reflect new technological and strategic realities? Can the concept of self-defence accommodate a role for pre-emption that satisfies the need of leaders to protect their people, without providing a ready basis for states to use pre-emption as an excuse for aggression?

---

[4] National Security Strategy (USG 2002), Part I [hereinafter 'Strategy'], available at www.usinfo.state.gov.

[5] *Ibid.*

[6] *Ibid.*, at Part V.

212   *EJIL* 14 (2003), 209–226

Answering these questions requires examination of the legal and political precedents relevant to the use of pre-emptive force. These precedents establish that the rigid and limited view of the propriety of pre-emptive action has no valid historical basis, and is unsound, artificial and futile in attempting to restrict resort to the use of force. The current and proper standard remains necessity, but what is necessary must be determined on the basis of all the relevant circumstances, in light of the purposes of the UN Charter.

1 The Use of Force in International Law and Practice

The United Nations Charter governs the legality of the use of force under international law. Most international lawyers construe the Charter to limit the situations in which force is permissible. Professor Michael Bothe's contribution to this Symposium is representative of this approach.[7] They read the Charter, Article 2(4), as prohibiting all uses of force, regardless of purpose, except for two narrow categories: (1) specific authorization by the Security Council under Chapter VII, Article 42, or (2) actions of self defence under Article 51 in response to attacks on the territory of a member state. They then apply each of these grounds independently, requiring — with limited exceptions for minor uses of force — that at least one ground is satisfied. If not, the use of force is considered illegal, however strong the moral and practical case for using force might be under the circumstances.

This reasoning led most international lawyers to consider illegal NATO's action to stop the mass deportations and murders of ethnic Kosovars by the Serbs, even though virtually all conceded the action was both morally justified and politically necessary.[8] Many international lawyers who considered the action illegal nonetheless supported the use of force against the Serbs, declaring that it was a 'special case' that should not be regarded as a precedent.[9]

Some proposed that such uses of force could be justified as humanitarian intervention, and called for a Charter amendment to make this clear.[10] Some, recognizing that the conventional categories for justifying the use of force are far too limited, dramatically announced the proposition that international law is no longer capable of governing use-of-force decisions in a world of terrorism and rogue leaders.[11]

These issues are hardly new. Myres McDougal and Florentino Feliciano addressed them in 1961. They rejected as unwarranted and artificially narrow the mechanical

---

[7]   'Terrorism and the Legality of Pre-emptive Force,' 14 *EJIL* (2003) 227.

[8]   See, e.g., 2 TRANSLEX (Transnational Law Exchange) 5 (Special Supp. May 1999) (report of law professors' opinions).

[9]   This appears to be the official view of the European Union, and of many scholars. E.g., Simma, 'NATO, the UN and the Use of Force: Legal Aspects: Kosovo: A Thin Red Line' www.ejil.org/journal/Vol10/No1/ab1–2.html.

[10] See, e.g., Bettina Clark, *NATO, the UN, and the Use of Force — Policy Roundtables* http://www.unausa.org/issues/sc/nyrapporteur.html

[11] See Glennon, 'The New Interventionism: The Search for a Just International Law', *Foreign Affairs* (May–June 1999) 2, at 4.

reading of the Charter's use-of-force provisions; and they condemned as dangerous the notion — already by then advanced by scholars and statesmen — that international law has no proper role in governing the use of force by states.[12] They rejected the proposition that the Charter is a value-free document that prohibits all uses of force, regardless of purpose. The very language of Article 2(4) makes this obvious,[13] as do the history and purposes of the United Nations.[14] They considered as historically baseless, and logically unwarranted, the construction of Article 51 limiting the 'inherent' right of self-defence.[15] Most significantly, they rejected an approach toward use-of-force issues that artificially limits the relevant categories and considerations that may be weighed. They joined Julius Stone in rejecting this 'push button' approach to legal analysis, stating (over-optimistically): 'There is, however, increasing recognition that the requirements of necessity and proportionality . . . can ultimately be subjected only to that most comprehensive and fundamental test of all law, reasonableness in particular context.'[16]

While scholars in general have refused to accept this view, the US Government, including every State Department Legal Adviser on record, has done so. Abram Chayes, for example, specifically relied on McDougal and Feliciano in calling for a 'common lawyer' approach to use-of-force issues, that takes into account all relevant factors, rather than applying narrow and rigidly separate categories.[17] This view has repeatedly and consistently been followed by the US, among other states, in evaluating the propriety of using force under the Charter.[18]

Those committed to the narrow and mechanical construction of the Charter invariably claim that applying a reasonableness standard is subjective and therefore lawless. This argument, too, is old hat. Of course governments will strain to justify their uses of force. But a reasonableness standard will not cause any greater abuse than now occurs in the application of accepted categories. As McDougal and Feliciano

---

[12] M. S. McDougal and F. P. Feliciano, *Law and Minimum Public Order: The Legal Regulation of International Coercion* (1961), at 238 note 263, criticizing the view that policy-makers must choose between the standards of the UN Charter and protecting American security and preserving Western interests.

[13] Article 2(4) provides that Members shall refrain 'from the threat or use of force against the territorial integrity or political independence of any state, or in any other manner inconsistent with the Purposes of the United Nations'.

[14] The Charter was adopted by states that had used force to defeat the Axis powers, which were able to gain power in part because the League of Nations had failed to use force to stop their aggressions. President Truman, who presided over the Charter's birth, was prepared to use force if necessary without Security Council approval in assisting South Korea against the North's aggression.

[15] The best treatment is McDougal, 'The Soviet-Cuban Quarantine and Self-Defense', 57 *ASILJ* (1963) 597. It is clear that Art. 51 was intended to safeguard the right to collective self-defence, but the drive to limit all uses of force led scholars, astonishingly, to claim that the language of Art. 51 so clearly limited the use of force in self-defence to armed attacks against a member state that the purposes of its language and legislative history should be disregarded. E.g. Kunz, 'Individual and Collective Self-Defense in Article 51 of the Charter of the United Nations', 41 *ASILJ* (1947) 872, at 873.

[16] McDougal and Feliciano, *supra* note 12, at 217. In their book, McDougal and Feliciano develop a set of criteria by which to evaluate the legitimacy of self-defence.

[17] 'A Common Lawyer Looks at International Law,' 78 *Harvard Law Review* (1965) 1396. Chayes later changed his position on this and on other issues.

[18] See generally Sofaer, 'International Law and the Use of Force,' *The National Interest* (1988).

214   *EJIL* 14 (2003), 209–226

wrote: '[R]easonableness in particular context does not mean arbitrariness in decision but in fact its exact opposite, the disciplined ascription of policy import to varying factors in appraising their operational and functional significance for community goals in given instances of coercion.'[19]

The narrow, mechanical approach to use-of-force issues is perhaps nowhere applied more strictly than in connection with the concept of pre-emption. Despite the long acceptance as a legitimate aspect of self-defence in all legal systems, international lawyers widely assert that, after the UN Charter, no use of pre-emptive force (also called 'anticipatory self-defence') is allowed until after an 'attack' under Article 51, which some claim must be on the territory of the state seeking to defend itself.[20] The only possible, very narrow exception to this rule, they contend, is Secretary of State Daniel Webster's statement in 1842, arguing that the need to exercise self-defence within the territory of another state must be 'instant, overwhelming, and leaving no choice of means, and no moment for deliberation'.

The standard articulated by Secretary Webster deals with pre-emptive attacks on the territory of a state that is both willing and able to use its police powers to prevent the attack sought to be pre-empted. It is inapposite to situations such as the threat posed by Saddam Hussein's regime, which has refused to comply with Security Council resolutions aimed at preventing a new chapter in its repeated history of aggression, and in particular yet another violation of humanitarian law through the use of weapons of mass destruction. Webster's words have been torn from their context and applied to all uses of force. In any event, Webster's artificially narrow, nineteenth-century standard has never been treated as restrictively in practice as international lawyers generally claim.

It cannot rationally be claimed to apply *in haec verba* to the possibility of an attack with modern technology and advanced weapons of mass destruction, launched by terrorists acting secretly with state support.

2 *The Caroline* and International Law

The key facts in *The Caroline* incident are these. A rebellion by Canadians against their government was underway in 1837; many Americans openly supported the rebels with supplies and by enlisting as fighters for an invasion of Canada. Neither the US Government nor the state governments that bordered Canada acted effectively to stop Americans from supporting the rebels; the federal government claimed it lacked legislative authority to enforce neutrality.

On 13 December 1837, a group of rebels, led by an American, took control of Navy

---

[19]   *Ibid.*, at 218.
[20]   According to some commentators, moreover, the right to act only exists until the Security Council takes action, even if the Council's action is insufficient to assure the state's safety from further attacks. See the arguments raised by scholars at the symposium 'The United States and International Law — The Effects of U.S. Predominance on the Foundations of International Law', Göttingen, Germany, 25–27 October 2001, and cogently rejected by Professor Thomas M. Franck in 'Terrorism and the Right of Self-Defense,' 95 *AJIL* (2001) 839.

Island, located in Canadian territory in the Niagara River, and began using it as a place from which to attack Canadian boats and facilities. The rebel base on Navy Island began to receive supplies from *The Caroline*, operating as a ferry from the US shore. On 29 December, at night, a British force crossed the river in boats with the specific objective of destroying *The Caroline*. The British commander found that the American vessel had moved from Navy Island to Fort Schlossberg, in US territory. Later that night, the British attacked the vessel, killed at least one American, dragged the boat into the river's current, set it on fire; its remains were carried over Niagara Falls.

The Van Buren Administration was aware that many Americans supported the so-called Patriots who were attempting to foment rebellion in Canada. In December 1837, before the attack on *The Caroline*, both Secretary of State John Forsyth and Treasury Secretary Levi Woodbury wrote letters to federal officials near the US/Canadian border instructing them to prevent Americans from meddling in Canadian disputes. Officials in the Buffalo area wrote, however, that 'only an armed force along the Niagara border could stop the supply of Patriots on Navy Island'.[21] Not until *The Caroline* incident did the federal government send General Winfield Scott to the area, and even then without any forces. Americans continued to assist the rebels in their cross-border activities.

The debate over the legality of the British action began with a note dated 5 January 1838, from Secretary Forsyth to the British Minister in Washington, D.C., Henry S. Fox, calling the attack on *The Caroline* 'an extraordinary outrage', requesting a full explanation, predicting a future request for 'redress', and calling for the aggressors to be punished. Forsyth demanded redress on 19 January, enclosing affidavits. Fox responded promptly. His affidavits and arguments were based squarely on the failure of the US to enforce its own laws on the frontier, which he said forced the British subjects involved to 'consult their own security'. A 'necessity of self defence and self preservation', he argued, gave them the right to destroy the 'piratical' vessel within US territory. Forsyth responded on 13 February, challenging the assertion that the US had failed to prevent American interference in the Canadian insurrection.[22]

When word of *The Caroline* incident reached London, the facts were submitted to the law officers of the Crown, who concluded that the action was justified. The vessel had acted as a belligerent, and was not therefore 'entitled to the privileges of a neutral territory'. British forces were justified as a matter of 'self preservation' in attacking the vessel wherever it was found. Stevenson sent a complaint to Foreign Secretary Palmerston on 22 May, rejecting the notion that the vessel was 'piratical' as lacking support in international law. He agreed that Americans involved in the rebellion could be punished in Canada, but argued that Britain had no right to enter another 'sovereign and independent state' to arrest them. He acknowledged that a nation could justify entering another state's territory on grounds of necessity, but the standard for allowing such action in international law required that 'the necessity

[21]   K. R. Stevens, *Border Diplomacy* (1989), at 12–13.
[22]   *Ibid.*, at 24–25

216   *EJIL* 14 (2003), 209–226

must be imminent, and extreme, and involving impending destruction'.[23] These arguments, later repeated by Webster, were based on the writings of Grotius,[24] Pufendorf[25] and Vattel,[26] among others, all of whom supported a right to pre-empt attacks, but only when the circumstances made such action necessary.

Both, in short, agreed on the existence of a right to pre-empt attacks, when necessary in the circumstances. The principal difference between them was the claim by the British that the US was either unable or unwilling to stop the rebels within its

---

[23]   *Ibid.*, at 35.

[24]   Grotius regarded as the 'first cause' of a just war 'an injury not yet done which menaces body or goods'. H. Grotius, *De Jure Belli: et Pacis* (1853), at 206. If a person is 'menaced by present force with danger of life not otherwise evitable, war is lawful, even to the slaying of the aggressor . . . as a matter of "self-protection". This right of self-defence exists only when necessary; where the danger can be avoided, delay is proper to allow recourse to other remedies.' *Ibid.*, at 2101. It is lawful, Grotius opined, for those whose duty is to protect others from force, to 'kill him who is preparing to kill . . . ', even if it may be more laudable to forbear and be killed. Other issues he examined reflect the importance he (and the authorities he cites) gave to the particular facts of each situation, such as whether a robber enters a home at day or night, and whether one may be killed who appears merely to be preparing to strike but not kill, as opposed to one who has already struck a non-lethal blow. Grotius commented on whether a state is entitled to use force to avoid the 'possibility' of suffering an attack. He regarded as 'an intolerable doctrine' the notion that a state 'may rightly take arms against a power which is increasing, and may increase, so as to be dangerous'. Such a circumstance may be taken into account as a practical matter where the right to use force properly exists, but it is otherwise 'contrary to all notion of equity'. *Ibid.*, at 224–225.

[25]   Pufendorf wrote that a 'discerning judge' should have no problem determining the propriety of acts in self-defence based on 'the circumstances of each case'. S. Pufendorf, *De Jure Naturae et Gentium* (1688, reprinted 1964), at 264–294. As a general rule, he concluded, a man may, without fear of punishment, kill another in self-defence, once 'the aggressor, showing clearly his desire to take my life, and equipped with the capacity and the weapons for his purpose, has gotten into the position where he can in fact hurt me, the space [within which self-defence is permitted] being also reckoned as that which is necessary, if I wish to attack him rather than to be attacked by him'. Pufendorf, like Grotius, adds other observations that reflect the need to weigh a variety of relevant circumstances, including whether the danger could be avoided in any other way (which 'should be interpreted not too strictly'); whether the defender is obliged to attempt to escape when an attack is anticipated; or whether the defender may respond with lethal force to attacks that are intended only to 'mutilate' rather than kill.

[26]   Vattel comments directly on the power of states to act when threatened by other states, supporting in general the right to defend against a threat of force, when its use is necessary. His comments on pre-emptive (and preventive) uses of force are especially significant. An increase of power by one state, he wrote, is not grounds for using force to avoid the possibility of a future attack. We must 'have good grounds to think ourselves threatened by him [a leader who is arming for war], before we can lawfully have recourse to arms.' Monsieur de Vattel, *The Law of Nations* (1852) 308. Power alone does not 'threaten an injury', he concludes, but taken together with other evidence of improper intent or inclination, power can justify demands by another state for reassurance and ultimately the use of force to avoid injury:

> When once a state has given proofs of injustice, rapacity, pride, ambition, or an imperious thirst of rule, she becomes an object of suspicion to her neighbours, whose duty it is to stand on their guard against her. . . . [O]n occasions where it is impossible or too dangerous to wait for an absolute certainty, we may justly act on a reasonable presumption. If a stranger levels a musket at me in the middle of a forest, I am not yet certain that he intends to kill me; but shall I, in order to be convinced of his design, allow him time to fire? But presumption becomes nearly equivalent to certainty, if the prince who is on the point of rising to an enormous power has already given proofs of imperious pride and insatiable ambition . . . . [Would not requiring restraint in such situations deprive] mankind of the right to regulate their conduct by the dictates of prudence, and to act on the ground of probability?

territory from attacking Canada. The US, on the other hand, insisted that it was adequately fulfilling its obligation to prevent the rebels from attacking Canada from US territory.

The evidence established that US actions against the rebels were inadequate. President Tyler openly complained that he lacked adequate authority to move against the rebels. He asked Congress to increase his power by allowing the seizure of any vessel violating neutrality, not just privateers and warships, and by permitting arrests on 'probable cause' even before any improper action occurred. Congress did so on 10 March 1838, two months after *The Caroline* incident. Furthermore, additional attacks by rebels operating from within the US took place throughout 1838, undermining Forsyth's claim that the US was preventing all significant rebel activities. Finally, domestic politics began by 1839 to interfere with the US Government's incentive to cooperate with Canada. Van Buren, faced with the need to secure re-election, ordered a Canadian rebel released from US custody after being warned that he would lose states if he failed to do so. The British concluded that the US could not be trusted to act effectively, and specifically warned the US that it could not tolerate 'ruffians and brigands . . . again and again, to issue forth from within the jurisdiction of the United States, for the ruin of Her Majesty's subjects'.[27] Fox complained that the US refused to extradite rebels for punishment in Canada, and at one point informed his government that the US continued an 'unreasonable, unjust and inadmissible position' by insisting on the sanctity of its territory.[28]

Matters came to a head after November 1840, when New York officials arrested a Canadian deputy sheriff from Niagara named Alexander McLeod, and charged him with arson and murder in connection with *The Caroline*. The British protested, but Secretary Forsyth responded that the federal government could not intervene in a state criminal prosecution. The British insisted that McLeod was innocent, and that in any event he could not be prosecuted as a private individual, since what he had done was officially sanctioned. After William Harrison took office as President, Daniel Webster became Secretary of State. In March 1841, he invited the British to avow *The Caroline* incident and on that basis to request McLeod's release. The British Minister Fox obliged immediately, and Webster set about securing McLeod's release, with the approval of President Tyler, who assumed power upon Harrison's death.

It was at this point, 24 April 1841, that Webster wrote the letter to Fox containing his famous words concerning self-defence. Webster began the letter by assuring the British that, now that they had avowed the incident, McLeod would be released either by habeas corpus, or by the courts in due course. Turning to self-defence, Webster confirmed that it is available to states, not only to individuals, 'and is equally

---

On the other hand, he wrote, the mere fact that a neighbouring state prepares extensively for war is not enough to justify defensive action. 'The answer [in such situations] greatly depends on the manners and character of that neighbour.' If that state's leader has given no evidence of baseness or perfidy, then his word must be taken as sufficient, and the risk must be dealt with through preparations rather than action in self-defence. *Ibid.*, at 308–309.

[27] Stevens, *supra* note 21, at 52.

[28] *Ibid.*, at 62.

necessary for the preservation of both'. But, he wrote, 'the extent of this right is a question to be judged of by the circumstances of each particular case; and when its alleged exercise has led to the commission of hostile acts, within the territory of a Power at peace, nothing less than a clear and absolute necessity can afford ground for justification'.[29]

The circumstance upon which the British relied to justify destroying *The Caroline*, he noted, was 'defending the British Territory from the unprovoked attack of a bank of British rebels and American pirates, who, have been "permitted" to arm and organize themselves within the territory of the United States, [and] had actually invaded a portion of the territory of Her Majesty'. Webster rejected this claim, stating that the President would not assume that Britain meant by using the word 'permitted' to suggest that "those acts, violating the laws of the United States, and disturbing peace of the British territories, were done under any degree of countenance from this Government, or were regarded by it with indifference; or, that under the circumstances of the case, they could have been prevented, by the ordinary course of proceeding.' He argued that the US had shown exemplary leadership by adopting neutrality laws and enforcing them along a long border. Unlike other states, the US was averse to maintaining a large, standing force, he wrote. 'All that can be expected, from either government, in these cases, is good faith, a sincere desire to preserve peace and do justice, the use of all proper means of prevention, and, that if offences cannot, nevertheless, be always prevented, the offenders shall still be justly punished. In all these respects, this Government acknowledges no delinquency in the performance of its duties.' It was Britain, not the US, that owed a justification, not just for attacking, but for doing so in the manner, place, and time chosen, without exhausting other potential avenues. He returned, in concluding, to the basic point of the dispute: the US 'cannot admit, that its Government has not both the will, and the power to preserve its own neutrality, and to enforce the observance of its own laws upon its own citizens.'[30]

The British rejected Webster's position, because they believed the actual circumstances differed from those claimed to exist by the US. They viewed the US as either unable or unwilling to prevent the rebels and their American allies from attacking

---

[29]   Webster, 'Letter to Henry Stephen Fox', in K. E. Shewmaker (ed.), *The Papers of Daniel Webster: Diplomatic Papers, vol. I, 1841–1843* (1983) 62.

[30]   Webster's analysis of the issues related to establishing the necessity for sinking *The Caroline* is far more relevant to today's issues than his sweeping generalities: Even supposing the need to enter the territory of the US, he wrote, Britain must show it 'did nothing unreasonable or excessive; since the act justified by the necessity of self-defence, must be limited by that necessity, and kept clearly within it. It must be shown that admonition or remonstrances to the persons on board the "Caroline" was impracticable, or would have been unavailing; it must be shown that daylight could not be waited for; that there could be no attempt at discrimination, between the innocent and the guilty; that it would not have been enough to seize and detain the vessel; but that there was a necessity, present and inevitable, for attacking her, in the darkness of the night, while moored to the shore, and while unarmed men were asleep on board, killing some and wound[ing] others, and then drawing her into the current, above the cataract, setting her on fire, and, careless to know whether there might not be in her the innocent with the guilty, or the living with the dead, committing her to a fate, which fills the imagination with horror. A necessity for all this the Government of the United States cannot believe to have existed.' *Ibid.*, at 67–68.

Canada. Palmerston recounted the many hostile acts that had taken place on Canadian territory that originated in New York and included Americans. Either New York 'knowingly and intentionally permitted' the rebels and Americans to arm and make war against British territory, or the State Government 'had lost its authority over the Border Districts' which were in open defiance. Either way, the British had the right to enter US territory, since the area entered 'had ceased at that time to preserve that Neutral and Peaceful character, which every part of the United States was bound to maintain . . . .'[31]

Webster and Secretary Ashburton settled *The Caroline* issue about a year later, in an exchange of notes. Webster described the incident as an offence for which no apology had been given. Ashburton replied that the attack had in fact been required by 'overwhelming necessity', and that the circumstances satisfied Webster's test. After unexpectedly discovering *The Caroline* on the US side of the river, the British expedition had 'no moment for deliberation', and so went ahead with the attack. Ashburton wished to bring the matter to a close, however, since McLeod had been released and the US had dropped any claim for compensation. So, he regretted that 'some explanation and apology for this occurrence was not immediately made: this with a frank explanation of the necessity of the case might and probably would have prevented much of the exasperation and subsequent complaints and recriminations to which it gave rise'. Webster replied that the issue was closed, without challenging Ashburton's analysis.[32]

The historical setting of *The Caroline* incident makes clear that Webster's formulation for determining the legality of self-defence was based on his assumption that the attack was unnecessary, because the US was both willing and able to satisfy its obligation to prevent and punish attacks from within its borders. On that assumption, Webster reasonably claimed the British could use force within the US if the need to act was 'instant, overwhelming, leaving no choice of means and no moment for deliberation'. The British, Webster in effect argued, should have relied on the US to stop Americans and *The Caroline* in particular from violating its neutrality laws. On the assumption that the US could and would act appropriately to prevent attacks on Canada, the threat posed by a small supply vessel was not so imminent that it required the British to violate US territory.

The British rejected Webster's premise, contending (with good cause) that they could not rely on the US to neutralize the threat posed by the rebels and by *The Caroline* in particular, so that a delay would have served no purpose. The British position was therefore in principle consistent with prior US conduct in analogous situations, where the US claimed it was entitled to use force to defend itself on the territory of a state that failed to prevent attacks on US targets. Webster (like Forsyth before him) no doubt was aware that the US regarded itself as justified in using force in foreign territory to

---

[31]   Stevens, *supra* note 21, Webster, 'Lord Palmerston to Andrew Stevenson, September 18, 1941 (enclosure in Andrew Stevenson to Webster, August 27, 1841.)' in Shewmaker, *supra* note 30, at 133–134.

[32]   Stevens, *supra* note 21, at 165.

220   *EJIL* 14 (2003), 209–226

prevent attacks on US ships and nationals by pirates, Indians or others, where the state involved was either unable or unwilling to prevent such attacks.[33]

A *The Standard for Pre-emptive Self-defence*

Given this background, by what standard is a pre-emptive attack justifiable? The standard of necessity proposed by Webster is 'so abstractly restrictive as almost, if read literally, to impose paralysis'.[34] In the context Webster intended — where the state from which attacks are anticipated is not responsible for the threat, and is both able and willing to suppress them — a strict standard is appropriate. For example, the US, although attacked several times by Al Qaeda from its sanctuary in Afghanistan, at first demanded that the Taliban Government arrest and extradite Al Qaeda leaders. Only when the Taliban refused to fulfil their obligation to stop attacks by Al Qaeda, did the US use force within Afghanistan to end Al Qaeda's sanctuary there.

Webster's language should not, however, be applied as a general rule for all pre-emptive actions. *The Caroline* incident, in full context, makes clear that Webster's stated rule was meant to apply to situations in which the state on whose territory pre-emptive action is contemplated is not responsible for the threat involved, and is both able and willing to act appropriately to prevent the threat from being realized. The standard generally applicable to pre-emptive self-defence is, rather, the same general rule applicable to all uses of force: necessity to act under the relevant circumstances, together with the requirement that any action be proportionate to the threat addressed. This was in fact explicitly recognized in the arguments made by both Webster and his British interlocutors, as well as by the legal writers upon whom they relied.

Under such an approach, necessity cannot properly be established through an arbitrary assertion that a threat exists requiring pre-emption in the view of the party being threatened. Nor is a state free to attack another merely because the latter develops the capacity to inflict even grave damage in a military encounter. Rather, necessity must be established on the basis of factors and circumstances related to establishing the legitimacy of using force under international law principles and UN Charter values, including: (1) the nature and magnitude of the threat involved; (2) the likelihood that the threat will be realized unless pre-emptive action is taken; (3) the availability and exhaustion of alternatives to using force; and (4) whether using pre-emptive force is consistent with the terms and purposes of the UN Charter and other applicable international agreements.

Applying these criteria to the current crisis concerning Iraq demonstrates their utility in ensuring that those required to consider such matters have rigorously addressed the relevant concerns.

---

[33] The US had, for example, relied on Spain's incapacity or unwillingness to protect US territory from attacks emanating from islands in the West Indies during the very first years of the Republic, and from Spanish Florida in 1818 and 1819 by Seminole Indians. Stevens, *supra* note 21, at 26; A. D. Sofaer, *War, Foreign Affairs, and Constitutional Power: The Origins* (1976), at 276–278, 349–350, 370–373.

[34] McDougal and Feliciano, *supra* note 12, at 217.

1 The Threat

Threats vary according to their nature and magnitude. The types of weapons likely to be used in an attack is an aspect of the nature of a threat, as well as whether the weapons would be delivered by conventional forces or terrorist groups. Iraq has developed chemical and biological weapons. They are difficult to detect and their use could inflict massive casualties. Iraq also has a history of supporting terrorists, particularly Abu Nidal and his organization, and it used terrorists in an attempt to assassinate the first President Bush. The potential use of terrorists by Iraq makes it especially difficult to know when and where an attack will occur.

Iraq also poses a continuing threat to use conventional forces or weapons of mass destruction in light of its prior conduct and avowed motives. It has twice attacked states in the Gulf area in pursuit of its avowed aim of 'reestablishing' an 'Arab Nation' with its capital in Baghdad. If allowed to continue to develop weapons of mass destruction, including nuclear arms, Iraq could use or threaten to use those arms to disrupt or disrail international efforts to prevent Iraq from achieving its geopolitical objectives.

The magnitude of the threat posed by Iraq is potentially very great, both physically and economically. Its forces and weapons programmes could inflict massive casualties and cause grave disruption. The effects of a major attack on Iraq's most likely targets, Kuwait and Israel, are potentially horrendous, given their vulnerability and relatively limited, geographically concentrated populations. Iraq could also jeopardize the world's energy supply, not only by withholding its own oil, but by attacking and disrupting other sources of supply.[35]

2 Likelihood of Threat being Realized

A threat may be very great but unlikely to occur. While military preparations may be probative of intent to use force aggressively, for example, it is an insufficient basis in itself for inferring an intent to attack. A state may not attack a second state or a group within it merely to prevent the possibility of a future attack. For example, the US could not lawfully attack China merely because China is certain to become strong enough to threaten the US or even to challenge the US for strategic superiority. Pre-emption requires proof of an anticipated attack.

Any doctrine that allowed states to use force to prevent the potential development of a threat would wreak havoc in international security. It would allow a state to attempt to ensure its own security by attacking other states without proof that those other states have planned or would even consider an attack. The stand-off between the US and the Soviet Union for some 50 years was premised on the notion that neither state should or could lawfully attack the other in the absence of satisfactory proof that the attack was necessary to respond to an attack by the other state that was underway and unavoidable through diplomacy or other means short of force.

On the other hand, a potential attack may be treated as very likely to occur, even though it is not imminent. Israel's June 1981 attack on the Osirik nuclear reactor near

---

[35]   See generally Governmment of Britain, 'Iraq's Weapons of Mass Destruction', www.pm.gov.uk

222   *EJIL* 14 (2003), 209–226

Baghdad was condemned in a Security Council resolution as failing to meet the test of necessity.[36] Ambassador Jeanne Kirkpatrick has since repudiated the arguments she made in voting to condemn the attack. While Iraq's use of the plant to create material for a nuclear device had not begun, and any attack was therefore not 'imminent', Israel believed that a nuclear attack on its population by Iraq was eventually highly likely if Iraq were allowed to put the reactor into service and develop nuclear weapons. Israel justified this conclusion on the grounds that Iraq had refused to accept a disengagement with Israel at the end of the 1948 War; that Iraq had twice before attacked Israel in other wars; that Iraq had repeatedly expressed the view (in violation of the Charter) that Israel has no right to exist; that Iraq had no need for nuclear-fuelled power plants; and that Iraq's high degree of animosity for Israel created a real possibility of an attack with nuclear weapons that a small and geographically concentrated population could not survive. Iraq's missile attacks on Israel during the Persian Gulf War of 1991, in which Israel did not participate, and its aggression against others, tends to justify Israel's unwillingness to face the high degree of risk Iraq's prior conduct and positions created.

Considerable evidence supports the likelihood of another Iraqi aggression if it is allowed to continue to develop weapons of mass destruction. Iraq's leader, Saddam Hussein, has attacked both Iran and Kuwait with the aim of conquering them and assuming control over their resources. His goals have long been known to include consolidating under his control the vast areas parcelled out by the Western powers after the First World War. Iraq should in principle be averse to confronting superior forces, but Saddam's policies have not been based on rational calculation. Ambassador Joseph Wilson, for example, a former US diplomat who had extensive contact with Saddam Hussein and Iraq, reports that he 'learned firsthand . . . what the CIA psychiatrists have said for years: Saddam is an egomaniacal sociopath whose penchant for high-risk gambles is exceeded only by a propensity for miscalculation'.[37] In recent statements, Saddam acknowledges that he cannot win a war with the US, but he asserts that Iraq must nonetheless resist being forced to submit to US or UN pressure. He equates his situation to that of a Muslim hero, being tested along with the Iraqi people by God to demonstrate their willingness to confront evil. All this from one of the most determined and demented aggressors in modern history.

The likelihood of the threat posed by Iraq someday becoming real is also based on Saddam's perversity, as reflected in his willingness to inflict wanton destruction having no rational purpose. His egregious violations of human rights are well known. He used chemical weapons against Kurdish Iraqis, killing thousands of civilians, and against Iranian troops. He deliberately spilled tens of millions of barrels of oil into the Kuwaiti desert and into the Gulf, and set fire to 720 Kuwaiti oil wells, when he realized

---

[36]   See UN SC Res. 487, 36 UN SCOR, 2288th mtg., UN Doc. S/RES/487 (1981). An excellent description of this issue, by a scholar who defended the attack from the start, is Anthony D'Amato, 'Israel's Air Strike against the Osiraq Reactor: A Retrospective', *10 Temple Int'l Comp. L.J.* (1996) 259.

[37]   'How Saddam Thinks', *San Jose Mercury News*, 13 Oct. 2002, Sec. P, at 1. See generally US White House Background Paper, 'A Decade of Deception and Defiance', http://usinfo.state.gov/regional/nea/iraq.

he had been defeated in the Gulf War. It is true that he appears to have been deterred from using unconventional weapons in that war. But he may simply have been unable to use such weapons at that time, or been unprepared to do so directly rather than through surrogates, or he may have refrained from attempting to do so because he was left in power. President Bush has reasonably concluded on this record that the future threat from Saddam is both grave and highly likely to be realized, even though it is not imminent.

3 Exhaustion of Alternatives

To prove necessity requires exhaustion of all reasonable means of avoiding the threat involved without recourse to the use of force. This is a continuing duty, based on the realization that force is rarely unaccompanied by collateral damage to non-combatants and property. The Security Council imposed economic sanctions on Iraq and other penalties for over ten years, in some 16 Resolutions. It gave Iraq a 'last' opportunity in Resolution 1441 to comply with outstanding Security Council resolutions, including those related to the development of weapons of mass destruction. It is difficult to claim the US failed to exhaust all reasonable, alternative means for securing compliance short of force. Even if some states genuinely believed that Iraq's disarmament could be achieved through inspections and pressure, this view was based on very little evidence and on the impractical assumption that the US and its allies could afford indefinitely to position their armed forces in preparation for an attack.

4 Consistency with Charter Purposes

Article 2(4) of the UN Charter calls on Members to refrain from the threat or use of force against the territorial integrity or political independence of any state, or 'in any other manner inconsistent with the Purposes of the United Nations'. This principle has generally been claimed to apply to all uses of force, whatever their purpose. But that position has never made sense in light of the need to achieve the Charter's purposes. Pressure has repeatedly arisen for treating as legitimate uses of force that advance those purposes, without compromising the territorial integrity or political independence of the states involved. The increasing recognition being given to the legitimacy and need for humanitarian intervention is one reflection of the fact that actions that advance the Charter's purposes are necessarily more justifiable than those inconsistent with its purposes.

The use of force to disarm an established aggressor, without altering the territory of that member state, or depriving it of its sovereign status, is an end that is consistent with the 'Purposes' of the United Nations.

Another factor that should be taken into account in evaluating the consistency with the Charter of disarming Iraq by force is the many Security Council resolutions adopted on the subject. International lawyers agree that force can lawfully be used under the Charter if the Security Council, acting under Chapter VII, explicitly authorizes it. Many contend, moreover, that if authority is not clearly conferred by the

224   *EJIL* 14 (2003), 209–226

Council on Member States to use force, the Council's other actions, findings and conclusions cannot be relied upon to justify or even support a use of force.

In fact, however, while explicit grants of authority to use force are always effective, the Council can and has implicitly recognized the propriety of using force.[38] Anyway, it is unreasonable to refuse to give weight to Security Council actions in evaluating the need (and hence the legality) for using force, merely because the Council may not have granted explicit authority. In the case of Kosovo, for example, it was significant that the Council had found Serbia to have acted illegally in several respects, in ways that were a threat to international peace and security under Chapter VII; that Serbia had failed to comply with the Council's orders to stop such actions; that the Council had imposed economic and other sanctions on Serbia for its violations of Council resolutions and international law; and that it had set up a tribunal to try cases against leaders who violated important humanitarian prohibitions. All these findings and conclusions supported the propriety of NATO's resort to force.[39]

If the Council fails to grant Members explicit authority to use force against Iraq, the findings, conclusions, and other actions of the Council should nevertheless be given proper weight in evaluating the propriety of enforcement actions. Resolutions adopted by the Council to end the Gulf War were explicitly conditioned on Iraq's agreeing to give up its weapons programmes and to comply with other demands. Arguably, the breach by Iraq of those resolutions restores in full force the original authorization by the Council for the use of force in 1990.[40] In addition, numerous findings in resolutions, including Resolution 1441, condemn Iraq for violating Council resolutions and for egregious breaches of international law, including fundamental principles of human rights. Iraq has also violated other international agreements, including those prohibiting the development of chemical and biological weapons. When these considerations are taken into account, the case for disarming Iraq without further UN authorization is strong under the approach espoused by McDougal and Feliciano, and widely supported by government lawyers and statesmen.

5 Parchment Barriers and the Use of Force

The determined support of the international-law community for Webster's formulation as the basis for using force in self-defence rests, ultimately, not on its historic validity or cogency, but on the view that a very narrow, rigid rule is needed to prevent states from using force too liberally. Their concern is that allowing states to rely on a general rule that permits them to take into account the many relevant circumstances

---

[38] In dealing with the Taliban Government, the Council condemned its failure to arrest and punish or extradite Al Qaeda members responsible for attacks on the US, and at the same time recognized that such attacks triggered the right of self-defence. The international community has treated this formula as conferring Council approval for the military action that destroyed Al Qaeda's sanctuary and removed the Taliban from power.

[39] See the discussion in Sofaer, 'Kosovo and International Law', 36 *Stanford Journal of International Law* (2000) 1, at 12–15.

[40] See Shultz, 'Act Now', *Wash. Post,* 6 Sept. 2002, at A25.

and considerations that underlie uses of force will result in subjective, self-serving, lawless decisions.

This concern is perfectly legitimate. States are hardly models of objectivity in seeking to advance and protect their interests. It is illusory, though, to expect Webster's formulation to achieve any greater objectivity in international legal analysis than a more general but more coherent rule. States prepared to use force in bad faith are undeterred by restrictive legal rules. Japan, for example, claimed its occupation of Manchuria in 1931 satisfied the 'standard principle laid down in the *Caroline* case'. German leaders on trial at Nuremberg claimed their invasion of Norway in 1940 was an act of self-defence.[41] Conversely, an approach that requires a thorough analysis of necessity and proportionality, on the basis of considerations rationally and morally related to the reasonableness of using force, is unlikely to encourage uses of force that would not otherwise occur. Statesmen acting in good faith to protect their nations do not take artificial rules seriously; if anything, as McDougal and Feliciano noted long ago, they are more likely to respect standards rationally related to concerns they recognize as appropriate.

It is no less true today than it was when McDougal and Feliciano wrote, that artificial rules cannot bear the burden of the real world pressures that underlie use-of-force issues. Today, moreover, the need to enforce rules to advance human rights and to limit the power of tyrants and terrorists is greater than ever. To deprive the international community of a reasoned basis for using force threatens Charter interests and values, rather than supporting and advancing them.[42]

3 Conclusion

The use of force to pre-empt threats is a matter of considerable complexity, and requires a more nuanced evaluation than that implied by Webster's pronouncement in *The Caroline* case. Properly applied, pre-emption is an aspect of a state's legitimate self-defence authority. The power to act in self-defence after an attack is based on the need to prevent further attacks, not on any right to exact revenge. Therefore, just as pre-emption was to Grotius the first ground for the 'just' war, it is the key justification for using force in the post-Charter era.

Looking at the 'war' on terrorism thus far, the concept of pre-emption is being applied in a responsible manner, though some statements made by the current Administration might have suggested a broader application. Osama bin Laden and Al Qaeda had, prior to September 11, 2001, attacked the US and killed many Americans several times. They had also announced their intention to attack US nationals and targets until the US withdrew its forces from Saudi Arabia. Bin Laden issued a *fatwa* purporting to authorize (or even to mandate) the killing of Americans. It was certainly reasonable under the circumstances for the US to assume that further attacks were being planned. President Bush attempted to convince the Taliban Government in

---

[41] See discussion in Stevens, *supra* note 21, at 166–168.
[42] See generally the discussion in Sofaer, *supra* note 39, at 16–20.

226   *EJIL* 14 (2003), 209–226

Afghanistan to turn over Bin Laden and other Al Qaeda leaders, on the express promise that force would in that event not be used in Afghan territory. This warning was disregarded, and the Taliban made clear in numerous public statements that they regarded Bin Laden as a hero and supported his objectives.[43] It is, if anything, astonishing that the US allowed such a record to develop before acting forcefully to stop Al Qaeda from further implementing their destructive plans.

The President's 'axis of evil' phrase in his January 2002 State of the Union speech generated widespread comment, allegedly on the ground that he might be claiming the right to attack North Korea, Iran and Iraq. The speech makes no such claim, and President Bush has made clear that he has no plan based on present circumstances to attack either North Korea or Iran. Iraq is another matter entirely.[44]

Pre-emption must be considered responsibly, on a case-by-case basis, but it remains one aspect of every government's duty to protect its people. Weapons of mass destruction (the very possession of which may be illegal) can now be fashioned by many states, and delivered in many ways. When such weapons are likely to be used by a state, and all reasonable means short of force have been exhausted, it is reasonable to expect target states to consider pre-emption. Where such circumstances exist, pre-emption is necessary, and should therefore properly be regarded as part of the 'inherent right' of self-defence.

---

[43]   For instance, on 28 September 2001, Taliban leader Mohammed Omar strongly rejected the overtures of Pakistani religious leaders seeking extradition of Bin Laden to the US. Omar 'rebuffed . . . any negotiated settlement . . . between the United States and Afghanistan over bin Laden', saying that 'the Taliban was willing to fight to the death to protect bin Laden from U.S. military forces', and remarking on the virtues of going to war with the infidels because it was 'imposed upon us. . . .' See Chandrasekaran and Khan, 'Taliban Denies Clerics' Call for Bin Laden; Pakistani Visitors Hear Vow to "Fight Until the End"', *Wash. Post*, 29 Sept. 2001, at A01, available at 2001 WL 28360679.

[44]   For a summary case for the legality of enforcing Resolution 1441 by force see Sofaer, 'Iraq and International Law', *Wall St. J.*, 31 Jan. 2003, at A10.

[15]

International Law and the Pre-emptive Use of Force: Afghanistan, Al-Qaida, and Iraq

CHRISTOPHER GREENWOOD*

TABLE OF CONTENTS.

* CMG, QC; Professor of International Law, London School of Economics and Political Science. The author acknowledges with gratitude the assistance of Mr. Jonathan Drakeford, LLM, in checking references. He also wishes to express particular gratitude to the editorial team of the Journal in preparing this Article for the press and for the patience with which they bore the last minute changes necessitated by events in Iraq.

I.   INTRODUCTION

The question whether international law permits the use of force not in response to existing violence but to avert future attacks has taken on added significance in the aftermath of the events of September 11, 2001 and with the debate about Iraqi weaponry. Referring both to the threat of terrorist attack and the dangers posed by "rogue States", the National Security Strategy document, issued by President Bush in September 2002, warns:

> The United States has long maintained the option of pre-emptive actions to counter a sufficient threat to our national security. The greater the threat, the greater is the risk of inaction—and the more compelling the case for taking anticipatory action to defend ourselves, even if uncertainty remains as to the time and place of the enemy's attack. To forestall or prevent such hostile acts by our adversaries, the United States will, if necessary, act pre-emptively.
>
> The United States will not use force in all cases to pre-empt emerging threats, nor should nations use pre-emption as a pretext for aggression. Yet in an age where the enemies of civilization openly and actively seek the world's most destructive technologies, the United States cannot remain idle while dangers gather.
>
> . . .
>
> The purpose of our actions will always be to eliminate a specific threat to the United States or our allies and friends. The reason for our actions will be clear, the force measured, and the cause just.[1]

Nor have such sentiments been confined to the U.S. administration. Members of the Australian government, for example, have called for a reconsideration of the U.N. Charter provisions on self-defense to permit greater latitude for pre-emptive action.[2]

To some commentators, such statements are symptomatic of a disturbing willingness on the part of certain governments to disregard international law; others see them as indications of the need for a fundamental reconsideration of that law—possibly even including an amendment of the U.N. Charter—to meet a wholly new type of threat. Before embracing either school of thought, however, it is appropriate to examine whether, and if so under what circumstances, existing international law permits the use of force to prevent an attack that has not yet materialized. To that end, Part II. of this Article will review the legal framework on the use of force and suggest that there are cases in

---

1.   President George W. Bush, *The National Security Strategy of the United States of America*, 15–16 (Sept. 17, 2002), *at* http://www.whitehouse.gov/nsc/nss.pdf.

2.   *See, e.g.*, Senator Robert Hill, The John Bray Memorial Oration, 4, 6–8 (Nov. 28, 2002), *available at* http://www.minister.defence.gov.au/2002/694281102.doc (last visited Feb. 6, 2003); Doorstop   Interview, 4–5 (Nov. 28, 2002), *at* http://www.minister.defence.gov.au/HillSpeechtpl.cfm?CurrentID=2120; *see also* Interview by Neil Mitchell with Prime Minister John Howard, 5–6 (Nov. 29, 2002), *available at* http://www.pm.gov.au/news/interviews/2002/interview2013.htm (last visited Feb. 6, 2003).

[VOL. 4: 7, 2003]

Pre-emptive Use of Force
SAN DIEGO INT'L L.J.

which the use of "pre-emptive force" may be justified, provided that certain important conditions are satisfied. Parts III. and IV. will then apply this analysis to the two cases that have focused attention on the whole issue of pre-emptive action, namely, the threat from international terrorism (Part III.) and the situation in Iraq (Part IV.). The writer's conclusions are summarized in Part V.

At the outset, however, it is important to sound three notes of caution. First, there is no agreement regarding the use of terminology in this field. As a result, some commentators distinguish between "anticipatory" military action (which they generally use to describe military action against an imminent attack) and "pre-emptive" force (normally employed to describe the use of force against a threat that is more remote in time). Although this approach offers the appearance of precision, the appearance is deceptive because so many others use the two terms interchangeably. Statements about "pre-emptive" or "anticipatory" action need, therefore, to be treated with some caution. The present Article tries to avoid treating such words as though they were terms of art.

Secondly, publication deadlines meant that this Article was written at the end of January 2003, at the time that that the chief weapons inspector, Dr. Hans Blix, and the Director-General of the International Atomic Energy Agency, Dr. Mohammed El Baradei, made their first reports to the U.N. Security Council on the extent of Iraqi compliance with Security Council resolution 1441 (2002).[3] The proofs of the Article were revised on March 22, 2003, three days after the United States, United Kingdom, and other States commenced military operations against Iraq. While it has been possible to take account in the text of some developments between late January and the outbreak of fighting in mid-March 2003, it has not been possible to discuss these developments in detail or to amend the footnotes to give full references to the relevant documentation.[4]

Finally, it is of course well-established that the use of force in international relations is lawful only if it satisfies two requirements. The recourse to force, and the degree of force employed, must be lawful under the legal regime codified in the U.N. Charter (the *ius ad bellum*).

---

3. U.N. SCOR, 58th Sess., 4692nd mtg., U.N. Doc. S/PV.4692 (2003), *at* http://ods-dds-ny.un.org/doc/UNDOC/GEN/N03/224/61/PDF/N0322461.pdf?OpenElement [hereinafter U.N. Doc. S/PV.4692].

4. The United Kingdom Government Papers, IRAQ (Cm 5769, Feb. 2003); and IRAQ: UN DOCUMENTS OF EARLY MARCH 2003 (Cm 5785, Mar. 2003) contain invaluable collections of the later documents.

In addition, the conduct of hostilities must meet the requirements of international humanitarian law (the *ius in bello*).[5] Space, however, does not permit discussion of the *ius in bello* here and the present Article is therefore confined to *ius ad bellum* questions.

II. THE LEGAL FRAMEWORK OF THE USE OF FORCE IN INTERNATIONAL RELATIONS

There is broad agreement on the main principles that make up the international law on the use of force. The starting point is the Preamble to the U.N. Charter, which affirms that the "Peoples of the United Nations" are "determined to save succeeding generations from the scourge of war, which twice in our lifetime has brought untold sorrow to mankind", and Article 1(1), which gives, as the first purpose of the United Nations:

> To maintain international peace and security, and to that end: to take effective collective measures for the prevention and removal of threats to the peace, and for the suppression of acts of aggression or other breaches of the peace, and to bring about by peaceful means, and in conformity with the principles of justice and international law, adjustment or settlement of international disputes or situations which might lead to a breach of the peace.

These provisions make clear the importance, in the legal order embodied in the Charter, of maintaining international peace but also the readiness to use force to combat aggression and to prevent threats to the peace from materializing into acts of aggression or breaches of the peace—the Charter is about keeping the peace not about pacifism.

Article 2(4) then introduces into international law the most far-reaching limitation ever adopted on the use of force by States against one another:

> All Members shall refrain in their international relations from the threat or use of force against the territorial integrity or political independence of any State, or in any other manner inconsistent with the Purposes of the United Nations.

This provision was an innovation in 1945 and is cast in terms of an obligation binding only upon Members of the United Nations, but it has long been recognized as stating a principle that has become part of customary international law and, indeed, a rule of *ius cogens*, binding all States.[6] Although it has sometimes been suggested that it states only a partial prohibition and that some instances of recourse to force between States fall wholly outside its scope,[7] this is very much a minority view and most States

---

5. *See* Christopher Greenwood, *The Relationship of Ius ad Bellum and Ius in Bello*, 9 REV. INT'L STUD. 221 (1983).

6. *See, e.g.*, Military and Paramilitary Activities (Nicar. v. U.S.), 1986 I.C.J. 14, 99–100 (June 27).

7. *See, e.g.*, Anthony D'Amato, *Israel's Air Strike Upon the Iraqi Nuclear Reactor*, 77 AM. J. INT'L L. 584 (1983).

and commentators treat Article 2(4) as prohibiting all use of force by one State against another, or on the territory of another, unless that use of force is justified by one of the limited exceptions provided for in international law.[8]

The Charter expressly provides for two such exceptions: military action in self-defense, the right to which is preserved by Article 51, and military action taken or authorized by the U.N. Security Council under the collective security provisions of Chapter VII of the Charter.[9]

This section will focus on two questions. First, to what extent, if at all, does either the right of self-defense or the collective security powers of the Security Council permit military action to avert a threat that has not yet materialized in the form of actual violence? Secondly, do these powers permit a military reaction against threats emanating from terrorist groups or are they confined to threats from States?

A. Self-Defense

The right of self-defense is not created by the Charter—it is a customary law right of some antiquity and is said to be inherent in the concept of Statehood—but the conditions for its exercise are mostly to be found in the provisions of Article 51, which states that:

> Nothing in the present Charter shall impair the inherent right of individual or collective self-defense if an armed attack occurs against a Member of the United Nations, until the Security Council has taken measures necessary to maintain international peace and security. Measures taken by members in the exercise of this right of self-defense shall be immediately reported to the Security Council and shall not in any way affect the authority and responsibility of the Security Council under the present Charter to take at any time such action as it deems necessary to maintain or restore international peace and security.

The exercise of the right of self-defense is not subject to any requirement of prior authorization by the U.N. Security Council; it is an aspect of the sovereignty of the State (although subject to the limitations imposed by

---

8. *See* Bush, *supra* note 1, at 15; IAN BROWNLIE, INTERNATIONAL LAW AND THE USE OF FORCE BY STATES 112 (1963); D.W. BOWETT, SELF-DEFENCE IN INTERNATIONAL LAW 112–13 (1958); OSCAR SCHACHTER, INTERNATIONAL LAW IN THEORY AND PRACTICE 110 (1991). For discussion of these issues *see also* CHRISTINE GRAY, INTERNATIONAL LAW AND THE USE OF FORCE (2000); YORAM DINSTEIN, WAR, AGGRESSION AND SELF-DEFENCE (3rd ed., Cambridge Univ. Press 2001).

9. The present writer is one of those who asserts that there is also a right to take military action in extreme cases of humanitarian need, such as that which existed in Kosovo in 1999; *see* the writer's evidence to the House of Commons Foreign Affairs Committee, reproduced as Christopher Greenwood, *International Law and the NATO Intervention in Kosovo*, 49 INT'L & COMP. L.Q. 926 (2000).

11

international law, as will be seen). Self-defense may be individual (in response to an armed attack upon the State exercising the right) or collective (where a State or group of States go to the assistance of a State that is the victim of an armed attack, even though they have not themselves been attacked and are not directly threatened).[10]

It is noteworthy that Article 51 preserved the "inherent right" of self-defense, rather than creating a right, which otherwise would not have existed. Moreover, it was a comparatively late addition to the Charter, for most States initially assumed that "the right of self-defense was inherent in the proposals and did not need explicit mention in the Charter".[11] The customary law status of the right of self-defense and the close relationship between the customary principle and the provisions of Article 51 have been confirmed by the International Court and are not a matter of controversy.[12] That provision does not, however, state all of the requirements for a lawful resort to force in self-defense, for it is generally agreed that, to be lawful, the use of force must not exceed what is necessary and proportionate in self-defense.

1.   Self-Defense Against Threatened Attacks

Although Article 51 refers to the right of self-defense "if an armed attack occurs", the United Kingdom[13] and the United States[14] have consistently maintained that the right of self-defense also applies when an armed attack has not yet taken place but is imminent. This view of self-defense can be traced back to the famous *Caroline* incident of 1837.[15] That incident involved action taken by U.K. forces in Canada against the *Caroline*, a merchant vessel that was being used by Canadian rebels and their American supporters in attacks against Canada. British forces attacked the *Caroline* while she was on the U.S. side of the Great Lakes and destroyed her, killing some members of her crew. One of the British officers involved, a Lieutenant McLeod, was subsequently arrested in the United States on charges of murder arising out of the incident. The British government maintained that its forces had acted in

---

10.   For the limits of the right of collective self-defence *see* Military and Paramilitary (Nicar. v. U.S.), *supra* note 6, at 104–06.

11.   United Kingdom Commentary on the United Nations Charter, Cmd. 6666, at 9.

12.   Military and Paramilitary (Nicar. v. U.S.), *supra* note 6, at 102–03.

13.   *See, e.g.*, the statements by the U.K. government regarding the 1986 attack by the United States on Libya, 57 Brit. Y.B. Int'l L. 494, 639–41 (1986).

14.   *See, e.g.*, the statements by the U.S. government at the time of its attack on Libya, *Legal Regulation of Use of Force*, 1980–88 Digest § 1 at 3405–06.

15.   The correspondence between the two governments is set out in 2 J.B. Moore, Digest of International Law 412–29 (1906); 29 B.F.S.P. 1137–38; 30 B.F.S.P. 195–96. *See also* R.Y. Jennings, *The Caroline and McLeod Cases*, 32 Am. J. Int'l L. 82 (1938).

exercise of the right of self-defense and demanded McLeod's release. Secretary of State Daniel Webster's reply has long been regarded as a definitive statement of the right of self-defense in international law. Webster recognized that the right of self-defense did not depend upon the United Kingdom having already been the subject of an attack but accepted that there was a right of anticipatory self-defense in the face of a threatened armed attack, provided that there was "a necessity of self-defense, instant, overwhelming, leaving no choice of means and no moment for deliberation."[16] McLeod was subsequently released. The Caroline test was applied by the International Military Tribunals at Nuremberg[17] and Tokyo.[18] This suggests that a right of anticipatory self-defense against imminent threats of armed attack was part of the customary law right preserved by Article 51 of the Charter.

Practice[19] since 1945 (though not always unequivocal by any means) tends to support that conclusion and confirms that the right of self-defense in the Charter era continues to include a right to use force to avert imminent armed attack. The practice of the United Kingdom and the United States has already been mentioned. As Sir Derek Bowett has pointed out, even the Soviet Union, which was initially strongly opposed to any concept of anticipatory self-defense, itself relied on such a right at various times.[20] Two particularly revealing instances of State recognition of a right of anticipatory self-defense are the debates in the Security Council on the 1967 six-day war between Israel and the Arab States, as well as the 1981 Israeli attack on Iraq's nuclear reactor.

In the first case, although Israel's recourse to force against Egypt has sometimes (unconvincingly) been explained as a response to an actual attack or as the exercise of belligerent rights stemming from a war that

---

16. Letter from Daniel Webster to Henry S. Fox (Apr. 24, 1842), 29 BRIT. AND FOREIGN STATE PAPERS 1129, 1138 (1857), *quoted in* LORI DAMROSCH, INTERNATIONAL LAW: CASES AND MATERIALS 923 (2001).

17. 13 ANN. DIG. & REP. PUB. INT'L L. CASES 203, 210; *International Military Tribunal (Nuremberg), Judgment and Sentences*, 41 AM. J. INT'L L. 172, 205 (1947); Cmd. 6964, at 28–30.

18. *See* International Military Tribunal at Tokyo (1948), *in* 2 THE LAW OF WAR: A DOCUMENTARY HISTORY 1029, 1157–59 (Leon Friedman ed., 1972).

19. There has been no conclusive statement by the International Court of Justice on this subject. *See, e.g.*, Military and Paramilitary Activities (Nicar. v. U.S.), *supra* note 6, at 99–100 (noting that the question of anticipatory self-defense did not arise on the facts of the case and expressly left the matter open).

20. D.W. Bowett, *The Use of Force for the Protection of Nationals Abroad*, *in* THE CURRENT LEGAL REGULATION OF THE USE OF FORCE 39, 40, n.8 (Antonio Cassese ed., 1986).

had not formally been terminated, as Professor Franck has indicated, Israel's "words and actions clearly asserted a right of anticipatory self-defence against an imminent armed attack".[21] In Professor O'Brien's words, it was "a model case for anticipatory self-defense".[22] Moreover, the international reaction suggests that this claim struck a chord with other States. A Soviet draft resolution, which would have condemned Israel for an unlawful resort to force, achieved only four votes in the Security Council and was thus roundly defeated.[23] In the General Assembly, a similar resolution was also voted down.[24] The reaction of other States led Franck to conclude:

> [Israel's] attack on Egypt was in anticipation of an armed attack, not a reaction to it. Most States, on the basis of the evidence available to them, did however apparently conclude that such an armed attack was imminent, that Israel had reasonably surmised that it stood a better chance of survival if the attack were pre-empted, and that, therefore, in the circumstances, it had not acted unreasonably. This does not amount to an open-ended endorsement of a general right to anticipatory self-defence, but it does recognize that, in demonstrable circumstances of extreme necessity, anticipatory self-defence may be a legitimate exercise of a State's right to ensure its survival.[25]

Although international reaction to the 1981 Israeli attack on Iraq's nuclear reactor, on the other hand, was generally condemnatory of Israel,[26] in most cases that reaction was based on a conclusion that Israel had failed to demonstrate that there was an imminent threat from Iraq and had thus failed to satisfy the Caroline requirements for anticipatory self-defense, rather than on any rejection of anticipatory self-defense as such.[27] Indeed, the emphasis on this failure to demonstrate the existence of an imminent threat tends, if anything, to confirm the existence of a right of self-defense in cases where such an imminent threat was shown to exist.

Academic opinion on this question is divided. Brownlie,[28] Gray,[29] and Henkin,[30] among others, have argued that there is no right of self-defense until an armed attack has actually commenced. Dinstein[31] also

---

21. THOMAS FRANCK, RECOURSE TO FORCE 103 (2002); *but see* GRAY, *supra* note 8, at 112.
22. WILLIAM V. O'BRIEN, THE CONDUCT OF JUST AND LIMITED WAR 133 (1981).
23. 1967 U.N.Y.B. 190.
24. A/L.521 was rejected on July 4, 1967 by seventy-one votes against to twenty-two in favor, with twenty-seven abstentions. G.A. Draft Res. A/L.521, U.N. GAOR. 5th Emergency Special Sess., U.N. Doc. A/6717 (1967). For vote verification *see* 1967 U.N.Y.B. 209, U.N. Sales No. E.68.I.1.
25. FRANCK, op. cit., *supra* note 21, at 105.
26. *See* S.C. Res. 487, U.N. SCOR, 36th Sess., 2288th mtg., U.N. Doc. S/RES/487 (1981) (adopted unanimously, condemning the Israeli action).
27. FRANCK, op. cit., *supra* note 21, at 105–07.
28. BROWNLIE, *supra* note 8, at 257–76.
29. GRAY, *supra* note 8, at 112.
30. LOUIS HENKIN, HOW NATIONS BEHAVE 141–44 (1979).
31. DINSTEIN, *supra* note 8, at 182.

The Use of Force in International Law   315

[Vol. 4: 7, 2003]   *Pre-emptive Use of Force*
                                           SAN DIEGO INT'L L.J.

rejects anticipatory self-defense but accepts that there is a right of "interceptive self-defense", where a State has "committed itself to an armed attack in an ostensibly irrevocable way", an approach that differs but little from that in the *Caroline* case. On the other hand, in addition to Franck (whose work has already been cited), Waldock,[32] Fitzmaurice,[33] Bowett,[34] Schwebel,[35] and Jennings and Watts[36] have all argued that there is a right of anticipatory self-defense against an imminent armed attack.[37] The position is, perhaps, best summed up by Judge Higgins, who said:

> [I]n a nuclear age, common sense cannot require one to interpret an ambiguous provision in a text in a way that requires a state passively to accept its fate before it can defend itself. And, even in the face of conventional warfare, this would also seem the only realistic interpretation of the contemporary right of self-defence. It is the potentially devastating consequences of prohibiting self-defence unless an armed attack has already occurred that leads one to prefer this interpretation—although it has to be said that, as a matter of simple construction of the words alone, another conclusion might be reached.[38]

In the present writer's opinion, this view accords better with State practice and with the realities of modern military conditions than with the more restrictive interpretation of Article 51, which would confine the right of self-defense to cases in which an armed attack had already occurred.

Nevertheless, that practice also shows that the right of anticipatory self-defense is confined to instances where the armed attack is imminent. Not only was this limitation a central feature of the *Caroline* correspondence, it was the basis on which the Nuremberg Tribunal, while affirming the Caroline test, rejected the defense plea that the German invasion of Norway had been an act of anticipatory self-defense. It was also the basis for rejection of the Israeli claim in the reactor case. In so far as talk of a doctrine of "pre-emption" is intended to refer to a broader right of self-defense to respond to threats that might materialize at some time in the future, such a doctrine has no basis in law.

---

32. 81 RC (1952–II) 496–98.
33. 92 RC (1957–II) 171.
34. BOWETT, *supra* note 8, at 187–92.
35. 136 RC (1972–II) 478–83.
36. 1 OPPENHEIM'S INTERNATIONAL LAW 421 (Sir Robert Jennings and Sir Arthur Watts eds., 9th ed. 1992).
37. Waldock, Schwebel, and Jennings are all past Presidents of the International Court of Justice; Fitzmaurice was a Judge of that Court.
38. ROSALYN HIGGINS, PROBLEMS AND PROCESS: INTERNATIONAL LAW AND HOW WE USE IT 242 (1994).

In assessing what constitutes an imminent armed attack, however, it is necessary to take into account two factors that did not exist at the time of the *Caroline* incident. The first is the gravity of the threat. The threat posed by a nuclear weapon, or a biological or chemical weapon, if used against a city, is so horrific that it is in a different league from the threats posed (as in the *Caroline*) by cross-border raids conducted by men armed only with rifles. Where the threat is an attack by weapons of mass destruction, the risk imposed upon a State by waiting until that attack actually takes place compounded by the impossibility for that State to afford its population any effective protection once the attack has been launched, mean that such an attack can reasonably be treated as imminent in circumstances where an attack by conventional means would not be so regarded. The second consideration is the method of delivery of the threat. It is far more difficult to determine the time scale within which a threat of attack by terrorist means would materialize than it is with threats posed by, for example, regular armed forces. These would be material considerations in assessing whether, in any particular case, an attack should be treated as imminent.

Nevertheless, the requirement that the attack be imminent cannot be ignored or rendered meaningless. Even when taking into account the issues considered in the preceding paragraph, the right of self-defense will justify action only where there is sufficient evidence that the threat of attack exists. That will require evidence not only of the possession of weapons but also of an intention to use them.

2. Self-Defense Against Threats from Terrorists

In the aftermath of the events of September 11, 2001, it is also necessary to ask whether the concept of "armed attack" in Article 51 of the Charter is capable of including a terrorist attack. The concept of "armed attack" is, it is true, generally used with reference to the employment of regular armed forces by states. There is, however, no *a priori* reason why the term should be so confined. There is no doubt that terrorist acts by a state can constitute an armed attack and thereby justify a military response.[39] The U.N. General Assembly included certain types of terrorist activity committed by States in its definition of aggression in 1974.[40] Similarly, the International Court of Justice, in its judgment in the *Nicaragua* case in 1986, considered that covert military

---

39. For a discussion of this issue *see* Christopher J. Greenwood, *International Law and the United States' Air Operation Against Libya*, 89 W. VA. L. REV. 933, 939–45 (1987) (discussing whether pre-emptive force against anticipated terrorist attacks is justifiable).

40. G.A. Res. 1334, U.N. GAOR, 29th Sess., Supp. No. 31, U.N. Doc. A/9631 (1974) [hereinafter G.A. Res. 1334]. Article 3 lists a series of acts that are to be considered as aggression and includes, in sub-paragraph (g), "the sending by or on behalf of a state of armed bands, irregulars or mercenaries which carry out acts of armed force against another state of such gravity as to amount to the acts listed [earlier in the paragraph]."

[VOL. 4: 7, 2003]   *Pre-emptive Use of Force*
                                               SAN DIEGO INT'L L.J.

action by a state could be classified as an armed attack if it was of sufficient gravity.[41] The level of violence employed on September 11, 2001 undoubtedly reached that level of gravity. There is, therefore, no doubt that had those attacks been the work of a state, rather than a terrorist organization like Al-Qaida, they would have been classified as an armed attack for the purposes of Article 51 and the right of self-defense. It would be a strange formalism that regarded the right to take military action against those who caused or threatened such actions as dependent upon whether or not their acts could be imputed to a state.

There is, however, no reason to think that international law adopts such a formalistic approach. On the contrary, the famous *Caroline* dispute,[42] itself shows that an armed attack need not emanate from a state. The threat in the *Caroline* case came from a non-state group of the kind most would probably call terrorist today. The United States was not supporting the activities of that group and certainly could not be regarded as responsible for their acts. Yet, nowhere in the correspondence or in the subsequent reliance on the Webster formula on self-defense is it suggested that this fact might make a difference and that the Webster formula might not apply to armed attacks that did not emanate from a state.

The international reaction to the events of September 11, 2001 confirms the commonsense view that the concept of armed attack is not limited to State acts. The U.N. Security Council, in its resolutions 1368 and 1373 (2001), adopted in the immediate aftermath of the attacks, expressly recognized the right of self-defense in terms that could only mean it considered that terrorist attacks constituted armed attacks for the purposes of Article 51 of the Charter,[43] since it was already likely, when these resolutions were adopted, that the attacks were the work of a terrorist organization rather than a state. Moreover, the Security Council's subsequent characterization of those acts as "armed attacks" was echoed by other international bodies. Thus, the North Atlantic Council, the governing body of NATO, stated on September 12, 2001:

> If it is determined that this attack was directed from abroad against the United States, it shall be regarded as an action covered by Article 5 of the Washington Treaty, which states that an armed attack against one or more of the allies in Europe or North America shall be considered an attack against them all.[44]

---

41. Military and Paramilitary (Nicar. v. U.S.), *supra* note 6, at 102–03.
42. *See* text accompanying *supra* notes 15–18.
43. S.C. Res. 1368, U.N. SCOR, 56th Sess., 4370th mtg., pmbl. & para. 3, U.N. Doc. S/RES/1368 (2001); S.C. Res. 1373, U.N. SCOR 56th Sess., 4385th mtg., pmbl. & para. 4, U.N. Doc. S/RES/1373 (2001) [hereinafter S.C. Res. 1373].
44. Press Release, North Atlantic Council (Sept. 12, 2001), *available at* http://usinfo.state.gov/topical/pol/terror/01091205.htm (last visited Feb. 11, 2003).

The Foreign Ministers of the Organization of American States, meeting in consultation, likewise invoked the 1947 Inter-American Treaty of Reciprocal Assistance in declaring that "these terrorist attacks against the United States of America are attacks against all American States".

B. Collective Security

The power of the Security Council to take military action is based on Chapter VII of the U.N. Charter. For the Council to exercise its powers under this Chapter it must first make a determination under Article 39, which provides:

> The Security Council shall determine the existence of any threat to the peace, breach of the peace, or act of aggression and shall make recommendations, or decide what measures shall be taken in accordance with Articles 41 and 42, to maintain or restore international peace and security.[45]

Once the Council has made such a determination, it can take decisions binding on all Member States of the United Nations.[46] Those decisions may require States to take non-military measures, such as the imposition of sanctions.[47] They may also require States to take actions such as withdrawal from territory occupied in a conflict,[48] surrender of suspects for trial,[49] or disarmament.[50]

The Council may not require States to take military action but it can authorize them to do so.[51] That power stems from Article 42 of the Charter, which provides:

> Should the Security Council consider that measures provided for in Article 41 would be inadequate or have proved to be inadequate, it may take such action by air, sea, or land forces as may be necessary to maintain or restore international peace and security. Such action may include demonstrations, blockade, and other operations by air, sea, or land forces of Members of the United Nations.

---

45. Although Article 39 does not say so, it is clear from the context that references to "peace and security" mean "international peace and security; *see, e.g.*, the use of that term in U.N. CHARTER art. 42.

46. U.N. CHARTER art. 25.

47. U.N. CHARTER art. 41.

48. *See, e.g.*, S.C. Res. 660, U.N. SCOR, 45th Sess., 2392th mtg., U.N. Doc. S/RES/660 (1990) (requiring Iraq to withdraw from Kuwait).

49. *See, e.g.*, S.C. Res. 827, U.N. SCOR, 48th Sess., 3217th mtg., U.N. Doc. S/RES/827 (1993) (on the International Criminal Tribunal for the Former Yugoslavia); S.C. Res. 1214 U.N. SCOR 53rd Sess., 3952nd mtg., U.N. Doc. S/RES/1214·(1998) (requiring the Taliban regime in Afghanistan to surrender for trial those responsible for the attack on the U.S. embassies in East Africa in 1998).

50. *See, e.g.*, S.C. Res. 687, U.N. SCOR, 47th Sess., 2981st mtg., U.N. Doc. S/RES/687 (1991) (on Iraq, discussed *infra* in Part IV.) [hereinafter S.C. Res. 687].

51. U.N. Charter art. 43, para. 1 (stating that States shall conclude agreements with the United Nations regarding which parts of their armed forces they will make available to the Security Council for collective security operations has never been implemented). In the absence of such agreements, the decision whether or not to make forces available for a collective security operation is entirely in the discretion of each State.

Although this provision speaks of the Security Council "taking" military action, it has been used since the 1990–91 Gulf Conflict to authorize military action by groups of States to restore international peace and security.

1. Collective Security and Pre-emptive Action

There is no doubt that this power can be used pre-emptively. Indeed, the reference in Article 39 to "threat to the peace" (as distinct from "breach of the peace" and "act of aggression") as one of the three grounds on which the Council could exercise its Chapter VII powers, demonstrates that pre-emptive action was always intended to be a major feature of the regime of collective security created by the Charter.[52]

Nor does the Charter limit the pre-emptive power of the Security Council to threats that are "imminent". There is no trace of such a limitation anywhere in the Charter. On the contrary, the historical background against which the Charter was drafted—in particular, the importance of the lack of pre-emptive action against Hitler in the 1930's in contributing to the causes of World War Two—strongly suggests that the pre-emptive power of the Security Council was intended to be much more far-reaching than the power of individual States to take action by way of self-defense against threats of armed attack.

2. Collective Security and Terrorism

That leaves the question whether the concept of threat to the peace is broad enough to embrace not only threats emanating from States but also those created by a terrorist group like Al-Qaida. Although those who drafted the Charter were undoubtedly (and, given the historical background, understandably) concerned with threats posed by States, nothing in the language of Article 39 or the rest of the Charter suggests that only threats emanating from States can fall within its scope. In recent years, the Security Council has had no hesitation in treating acts of international terrorism, whether or not "State-sponsored", as threats to the peace for the purposes of Chapter VII of the Charter. Thus, even before September 11, 2001, the Council had characterized as a threat to international peace and security Libyan support for terrorism,[53] the

---

52. Jochen A. Frowein, *Article 39*, *in* THE CHARTER OF THE UNITED NATIONS: A COMMENTARY 720–21, paras. 6, 9 (Bruno Simma ed., 2nd ed. 2002).

53. S.C. Res. 748, U.N. SCOR, 47th Sess., 3063rd mtg., U.N. Doc. S/RES/748 (1992); S.C. Res. 883, U.N. SCOR, 48th Sess., 3312th mtg., U.N. Doc. S/RES/883 (1993); S.C. Res. 1192, U.N. SCOR, 53rd Sess., 2930th mtg., U.N. Doc. S/RES/1192 (1998).

attempted assassination of President Mubarak of Egypt,[54] and the attacks on the U.S. embassies in East Africa.[55] Although the first case involved State action, there was no clear indication of State involvement in either of the other incidents. In addition, the Council adopted a number of resolutions condemning international terrorism in general as a threat to international peace.[56]

The resolutions adopted by the Council in the aftermath of September 11, 2001 have been unequivocal in their condemnation of international terrorism and their characterization of it as a threat to international peace and security, which entitles the Council to exercise its Chapter VII powers. Resolution 1268 (2001), adopted unanimously on September 12, 2001, expressed the determination of the Council "to combat by all means threats to international peace and security caused by terrorist acts" and condemned "the horrifying terrorist acts which took place on 11 September 2001" as being, "like any act of international terrorism . . . a threat to international peace and security". In resolution 1373 (2001), which was also adopted unanimously, the Council repeated that characterization and, acting under Article 41 of the Charter, went on to require States to take extensive measures against the perpetrators and States suspected of assisting them. In addition, meetings of the Security Council held at ministerial level in November 2001 and January 2003 adopted declarations on terrorism, which were again based on the characterization of international terrorism as a threat to international peace and security.[57]

It seems clear, therefore, that under the collective security regime in the U.N. Charter, a State or group of States can be empowered to take military action to pre-empt threats of military action or terrorist activity and that the right to take such pre-emptive action is more extensive than is the case when a State acts in self-defense. It must be remembered, however, that the power to take action under the collective security regime can be conferred only by a decision of the Security Council. No state is entrusted under the Charter with the power to take military action to preserve or restore international peace and security without such a decision. In the absence of such a decision, only the more limited power to act in self-defense—individual or collective—remains.

---

54. S.C. Res. 1044, U.N. SCOR, 51st Sess., 3627th mtg., U.N. Doc. S/RES/1044 (1996).

55. S.C. Res. 1189, U.N. SCOR, 53rd Sess., 3915th mtg., U.N. Doc. S/RES/1189 (1998); S.C. Res. 1267, U.N. SCOR,54th Sess., 4051st mtg., U.N. Doc. S/RES/1267 (1999) [hereinafter S.C. Res. 1267].

56. *See, e.g.,* S.C. Res. 1269, U.N. SCOR, 54th Sess., 4053rd mtg., U.N. Doc. S/RES/1269 (1999).

57. S.C. Res. 1377, U.N. SCOR, 56th Sess., 4413th mtg., U.N. Doc. S/RES/1377 (2001); S.C. Res. 1456, U.N. SCOR, 58th Sess., 4688th mtg., U.N. Doc. S/RES/1456 (2003).

[VOL. 4: 7, 2003]　　　　　　　　　　　　*Pre-emptive Use of Force*
SAN DIEGO INT'L L.J.

III. THE USE OF FORCE AGAINST INTERNATIONAL TERRORISM

An analysis of the military action which followed September 11, 2001 in the light of the legal framework set out in Part II., the first point to note is that the United States and its allies consistently based their justification for military action in Afghanistan, and against Al-Qaida more generally, on the right of self-defense and not on any collective security mandate from the Security Council.

The reliance on self-defense is evident in the letters sent by, for example, the governments of the United States and the United Kingdom to the Security Council reporting on the measures that they were taking in Afghanistan.[58] On October 7, 2001, the U.S. Ambassador to the United Nations, John Negroponte, wrote to the President of the Security Council "to report that the United States of America, together with other States, has initiated actions in the exercise of its inherent right of individual and collective self-defense following the armed attacks that were carried out against the United States on September 11, 2001".[59] The letter went on to state that the United States had "clear and compelling information that the Al-Qaida organization . . . had a central role in the attacks" and further stated that the United States might find "that our self-defense requires further actions with respect to other organizations and states". The letter continued:

> The attacks on September 11, 2001 and the ongoing threat to the United States and its nationals posed by the Al-Qaida organization have been made possible by the decision of the Taliban regime to allow the parts of Afghanistan that it controls to be used by this organization as a base of operation. Despite every effort by the United States and the international community, the Taliban regime has refused to change its policy. From the territory of Afghanistan, the Al-Qaida organization continues to train and support agents of terror who attack innocent people throughout the world and target United States nationals and interests in the United States and abroad.
>
> In response to these attacks, and in accordance with the inherent right of individual and collective self-defense, United States armed forces have initiated actions designed to prevent and deter further attacks on the United States. These actions include measures against Al-Qaida terrorist training camps and military installations of the Taliban regime in Afghanistan. In carrying out these actions, the United States is committed to minimizing civilian casualties and damage to civilian property.

---

58. U.N. CHARTER art. 51. The second sentence of Article 51 of the Charter requires states taking action in self-defense to make such reports.

59. U.N. SECURITY COUNCIL, LETTER DATED 7 OCTOBER 2001 FROM THE PERMANENT REPRESENTATIVE OF THE UNITED STATES OF AMERICA TO THE UNITED NATIONS ADDRESSED TO THE PRESIDENT OF THE SECURITY COUNCIL, U.N. Doc. S/2001/946 (2001).

The U.K. *chargé d'affaires* wrote to the Security Council in similar terms on the same day. His letter stated that U.K. forces were engaged in military operations in Afghanistan and continued:

> These forces have now been employed and exercised the inherent right of individual and collective self-defence, recognised in Article 51, following the terrorist outrage of 11 September, to avert the continuing threat of attacks from the same source. My Government presented information to the United Kingdom Parliament on 4 October which showed that Usama bin Laden and his Al-Qaida terrorist organisation have the capability to execute major terrorist attacks, claimed credit for past attacks on United States targets, and have been engaged in a concerted campaign against the United States and its allies. One of the stated aims is the murder of United States citizens and attacks on the allies of the United States.

> This military action has been carefully planned and is directed against Usama bin Laden's Al-Qaida terrorist organisation and the Taliban regime that is supporting it. Targets have been selected with extreme care to minimise the risk to civilians.[60]

Did the right of self-defense in fact provide a satisfactory legal basis for military action in Afghanistan? In answering this question, four issues require examination. First, should the United States and its allies have obtained Security Council authorization before resorting to force? The answer is that there is clearly no legal requirement for them to do so. The right of self-defense preserved by Article 51 of the Charter is vested in states and its exercise requires no prior permission from the Security Council. The only sense in which the exercise of the right of self-defense is dependent upon the Security Council is found in the provision, in the first sentence of Article 51, that when the Security Council has "taken measures necessary to maintain international peace and security", the right of self-defense lapses. That clause in Article 51 has, however, generally been the subject of restrictive interpretation.[61] Moreover, although resolution 1373 (2001) adopted a wide range of non-military measures for the purpose of restoring international peace and security, the Council expressly reaffirmed the right to self-defense and thus made clear that it did not regard the resolution as in any way restricting the United States in the exercise of that right.[62]

Secondly, was the action by the United States and its allies a response to an armed attack within the meaning of Article 51? It has already been suggested that the concept of armed attack is not limited to State action and that the attacks of September 11, 2001 undeniably met the requirement of gravity identified by the International Court of Justice in

---

60. U.N. SECURITY COUNCIL, LETTER DATED 7 OCTOBER 2001 FROM THE CHARGE D'AFFAIRES A.I. OF THE PERMANENT MISSION OF THE UNITED KINGDOM OF GREAT BRITAIN AND NORTHERN IRELAND TO THE UNITED NATIONS ADDRESSED TO THE PRESIDENT OF THE SECURITY COUNCIL, U.N. Doc. S/2001/947 (2001).

61. *See generally* Christopher Greenwood, *New World Order or Old?: The invasion of Kuwait and the Rule of Law*, 55 MODERN L. REV. 153, 164–65 (1992).

62. *See* S.C. Res. 1373, *supra* note 43, at para. 4.

the *Nicaragua* case. Nevertheless, the attacks of September 11, 2001, terrible as they were, took place some weeks before the U.S. military response was commenced. Self-defense, which is lawful in international law, has to be carefully distinguished from reprisals, which, if they involve the use of armed force, are no longer lawful under the U.N. Charter. The requirement of necessity in self-defense means that it is not sufficient that force is used after an armed attack, it must be necessary to repel that attack. The use of force in response to an armed attack that is over and done with does not meet that requirement and looks more like a reprisal. The U.S. action has therefore been criticized for constituting what some consider to have been a reprisal, rather than a genuine action in self-defense.

That criticism is unconvincing. The events of September 11 cannot be considered in isolation. Taken together with other events, such as the attacks on the U.S. embassies in East Africa in 1998 and the attack on the *USS Cole* for which Al-Qaida had claimed responsibility, there were the clearest possible indications of further outrages to come. Moreover, in these circumstances there seems little difficulty in regarding the threat of future attacks from Al-Qaida as meeting the criteria of imminence. That was clearly the view of the governments of the United States and the United Kingdom, whose letters to the Security Council both spoke of averting future attacks from Al-Qaida. Whatever criticism this may have evoked from commentators,[63] it appears to have met with no hostility from states, even from those normally opposed to U.S. positions. Therefore, as long as the military action in Afghanistan is viewed as a forward looking measure to prevent an imminent threat from materializing into violence, rather than as a backward looking act of retaliation for the events of September 11, 2001, this criterion of self-defense appears to be satisfied.

Thirdly, did the threat of armed attack from Al-Qaida justify military action against Afghanistan? This is a more difficult question for several reasons. Had the relationship between Al-Qaida and the state of Afghanistan been such that Afghanistan could be held responsible in international law for the attacks of September 11, and other threats from Al-Qaida, there would have been no difficulty. The United States would then have been employing force against the state responsible for past

---

63. *See* Michael Byers, *Terrorism, the Use of Force and International Law After 11 September*, 51 INT'L & COMP. L.Q. 401 (2002).

armed attacks and the threat of future armed attacks upon it. However, the criteria for determining the responsibility of a state for the acts of a private organization are not altogether clear. In the *Nicaragua* case, the International Court held that the relationship between the United States and the *Contra* rebel movement in Nicaragua was not close enough to render the United States responsible for illegal acts committed by the *Contras*. The Court held:

> For this conduct to give rise to legal responsibility of the United States, it would in principle have to be proved that that state had effective control of the military or paramilitary operations in the course of which the alleged violations were committed.[64]

That test has largely been adopted by the International Law Commission in its Articles on State Responsibility,[65] although the International Criminal Tribunal for the Former Yugoslavia in its second decision in *Tadic*[66] suggests a looser standard. However, the evidence of the relationship between Al-Qaida and Afghanistan makes it difficult to conclude that either test had been satisfied.

A further complication is that the Taliban regime in Afghanistan was not recognized as the government of Afghanistan by the United States or the vast majority of other countries. That, however, makes no substantial difference. There is no doubt that the Taliban regime was the *de facto* government in Afghanistan at the relevant time and that the state of Afghanistan bore responsibility for its actions.[67] The most important point, however, is that the state of Afghanistan, through the acts of the Taliban regime, had undoubtedly violated international law in permitting Al-Qaida to operate from its territory. There is a general duty under international law for a state not to allow its territory to be used as a base for attacks on other states, whether by regular armed forces or terrorists.[68] In addition, Afghanistan violated specific obligations imposed by the Security Council following the embassy attacks in 1998.[69] At the very least, its position was analogous to that of a neutral

---

64.   Military and Paramilitary Activities (Nicar. v U.S.), *supra* note 6, at 65.

65.   INTERNATIONAL LAW COMMISSION, ARTICLES ON STATE RESPONSIBILITY, art. 8. *See* JAMES CRAWFORD, THE INTERNATIONAL LAW COMMISSION'S ARTICLES ON STATE RESPONSIBILITY: INTRODUCTION, TEXT, AND COMMENTARIES 110–13 (2002).

66.   International Criminal Tribunal for the Former Yugoslavia—Appeals Chamber: *Prosecutor v. Tadic*, 38 I.L.M. 1518, 1541 (1999).

67.   Rüdiger Wolfrum & Christiane E. Philipp, *The Status of the Taliban: Their Obligations and Rights Under International Law*, 6 MAX PLANCK Y.B. OF UN L. 559 (2002).

68.   United Nations General Assembly definition of aggression, resolution 3314 (XXIX), and numerous other resolutions of the Security Council and the General Assembly bear witness to such a duty.

69.   *See* S.C. Res. 1267, *supra* note 55; S.C. Res. 1333, U.N. SCOR, 55th Sess., 4251st mtg., U.N. Doc. S/RES/1333 (2000).

[VOL. 4: 7, 2003]   *Pre-emptive Use of Force*
SAN DIEGO INT'L L.J.

state that unlawfully allows a belligerent to mount military operations from its territory. Even though the neutral is not held responsible for those operations as such, it exposes itself to the risk of lawful military action to put a stop to them. Similarly, where a state allows terrorist organizations to mount concerted operations against other states from its territory, and refuses to take the actions required by international law to put a stop to such operations, the victims of those operations are entitled to take action against those terrorists. The Caroline formula on self-defense clearly permitted such action and the undoubted changes in international law since that time have not abolished this aspect of the right of self-defense. Because the Taliban regime made it clear throughout that it would vigorously oppose any foreign forces entering its territory to root out Al-Qaida bases, it exposed its own forces to lawful attack in exercise of the right of self-defense.

Finally, the action taken in self-defense needed to be necessary and proportionate. Faced with the prospect of more attacks as devastating as those of September 11, it is difficult to see how the United States went beyond what was necessary. It was also proportionate. Although the effect of United States and allied intervention in Afghanistan was to change the balance of the civil war taking place in that country and lead to the overthrow of the Taliban regime and its replacement by a new government, it is difficult to see how the intervention could have succeeded in its aims of removing the Al-Qaida bases in Afghanistan without going that far. Indeed, there would rightly have been much criticism of the United States and its allies had their intervention been accomplished while leaving the people of Afghanistan in the same plight as they were in beforehand.

The pre-emptive action that the United States and its allies took against Al-Qaida in Afghanistan was, therefore, a lawful exercise of the right of self-defense. It would, however, be a mistake to assume that self-defense would cover every military action that the United States or an ally might want to take against Al-Qaida (or other terrorist groups) in other countries. The use of force in Afghanistan fell within the concept of self-defense because the threat from Al-Qaida was imminent and because Afghanistan was quite openly affording sanctuary to large numbers of Al-Qaida personnel. These considerations will not necessarily be present in every case.

IV. IRAQ [70]

The military action against Iraq, which commenced in March 2003 also raises questions about the scope for pre-emptive military action in international law. Before those questions can be addressed, however, it is necessary to examine the background to the present situation because the legal position in 2003 can be understood only in the context of the actions taken by the U.N. Security Council over the years since the Iraqi invasion of Kuwait in August 1990.[71]

A.   The Security Council Resolutions on Iraq

That invasion, which was a flagrant violation of international law, was condemned by the Security Council in resolution 660 (1990), which required Iraq to withdraw from Kuwait. In common with most of the subsequent resolutions on Iraq, this resolution was adopted under Chapter VII of the U.N. Charter and its provisions were therefore legally binding on Iraq. When Iraq ignored the requirement that it withdraw, the Security Council adopted a series of further resolutions. For present purposes, the most important is resolution 678 (1990) by which the Council authorized:

> Member States co-operating with the Government of Kuwait, unless Iraq on or before January 15, 1991 fully implements, as set forth in paragraph 1 above, the [earlier Security Council resolutions on Kuwait] to use all necessary means to uphold and implement resolution 660 (1990) and all subsequent relevant resolutions *and to restore international peace and security in the area.* (Emphasis added.)

The reference to "all necessary means" was clearly understood to be an authorization of military action.[72] The passage emphasized shows that that authorization was not limited to the liberation of Kuwait but included an authority to use all necessary means for the purpose of restoring peace and security in the area.

The fighting that ensued was brought to an end at the beginning of March 1991 with the adoption of resolution 686 (1991). In April 1991, the Council went on to lay down an exhaustive list of requirements Iraq had to meet as the conditions for a permanent ceasefire. It did so in resolution 687 (1991), which referred to all of the earlier resolutions on Iraq, including resolution 678. In paragraph 1 of resolution 687, the

---

70. For discussion of this topic *see* Report of the United Kingdom House of Commons Foreign Affairs Committee, Foreign Policy Aspects of the War against Terrorism, H.C. (2002–03) No. 196, para. 129-61; Memoranda by Professors Brownlie and Greenwood reprinted with the Appendices to the report; Judgment of Professor Vaughan Lowe for the BBC hearing on the legality of use of force against Iraq, *at* http://www.bbc.co.uk/cgi-bin/education/betsie/parser.pl.

71. For a discussion of the 1990–91 conflict with Iraq *see* Greenwood, *supra* note 61.

72. *Id.* at 165–67.

[Vol. 4: 7, 2003]

Pre-emptive Use of Force
SAN DIEGO INT'L L.J.

Council "affirms all thirteen resolutions noted above, *except as expressly changed below* to achieve the goals of the present resolution, including a formal cease-fire." (Emphasis added.) One of those goals (as noted in preambular paragraph 25) was the restoration of peace and security in the area, something that had not been brought about simply because Kuwait had been liberated. Resolution 687 laid out what the Council determined Iraq had to do to achieve that goal. The Council required that Iraq:

[U]nconditionally accept the destruction, removal, or rendering harmless, under international supervision, of:

(a) all chemical and biological weapons and all stocks of agents and all related subsystems and components and all research, development, support and manufacturing facilities related thereto;

(b) all ballistic missiles with a range greater than one hundred and fifty kilometres, and related major parts and repair and production facilities.[73]

In addition, paragraph 12 of resolution 687 required Iraq "not to acquire or develop nuclear weapons or nuclear weapon usable material or any subsystems or components or any research, development, support or manufacturing facilities related to the above." The onus was on Iraq to demonstrate that it had complied with these requirements and to that end the Council established a weapons inspectorate (UNSCOM) and empowered the IAEA to fulfill the same role as UNSCOM with regard to Iraq's nuclear program.[74] Other provisions of resolution 687 required Iraq not to commit or support any act of terrorism and not to permit any terrorist organization to operate from its territory.[75] All of these requirements went directly to what the Council regarded as necessary to ensure a restoration of peace and security in the area.

Iraq formally accepted these requirements but resolution 687 was legally binding because of the obligations imposed on Iraq by Article 25 and Chapter VII of the U.N. Charter, not because of Iraq's acceptance of the resolution. The resolution was not the equivalent of an agreement.

In fact, Iraq never complied with the ceasefire conditions and was repeatedly found by the Security Council to be in breach of the requirements of resolution 687 regarding international peace and security. For example, resolutions 707 (1991), 949 (1994), 1060 (1996),

---

73. S.C. Res. 687, *supra* note 50, at para. 8.

74. The IAEA was charged with responsibility for investigating Iraq's nuclear weapons program. Responsibility for investigating all other relevant weapons programs was entrusted to UNSCOM, a body later replaced by UNMOVIC in 1999; *see* discussion *infra* Part IV.A.

75. S.C. Res. 687, *supra* note 50, at para. 32.

1115 (1997), and 1137 (1997) all condemned Iraqi violations of provisions of resolution 687. In 1998 the U.N. Secretary-General drew up a Memorandum of Understanding with Iraq regarding weapons inspections. The Security Council then, in resolution 1154 (1998) stressed:

> [C]ompliance by the Government of Iraq with its obligations, repeated again in the Memorandum of Understanding, to accord immediate, unconditional and unrestricted access to the Special Commission and the IAEA in conformity with the relevant resolutions is necessary for the implementation of resolution 687 (1991), but that any violation would have severest consequences for Iraq.

Nevertheless, Iraq continued to violate its obligations, a fact demonstrated, for example, by resolution 1205 (1998). After yet another attempt to resume inspections, UNSCOM reported to the Security Council on December 15, 1998:

> As is evident from this report, Iraq did not provide the full cooperation it promised on November 14, 1998.
>
> In addition, during the period under review, Iraq initiated new forms of restrictions upon the Commission's work. Amongst the Commission's many concerns about this retrograde step is what such further restrictions might mean for the effectiveness of long-term monitoring activities.
>
> In spite of the opportunity presented by the circumstances of the last month, including the prospect of a comprehensive review, Iraq's conduct ensured that no progress was able to be made in either the fields of disarmament or accounting for its prohibited weapons programs.
>
> Finally, in the light of this experience, that is, the absence of full cooperation by Iraq, it must regrettably be recorded against [sic] that the commission is not able to conduct the substantive disarmament work mandated to it by the Security Council and, thus, to give the assurances it requires with respect to Iraq's prohibited weapons programs.[76]

This report was followed by the withdrawal of the UNSCOM inspectors and a period of military action (Operation Desert Fox) by the United Kingdom and United States against targets in Iraq connected with unlawful Iraqi weaponry.[77] Resolution 1284 (1999) replaced UNSCOM with a new body, UNMOVIC, and required that Iraq allow UNMOVIC unrestricted access. Iraq, however, refused to permit UNMOVIC to operate within Iraq until it suddenly changed tack in September 2002 and agreed that the inspectors could return.

---

76. U.N. SECURITY COUNCIL, LETTER DATED 15 DECEMBER 1998 FROM THE SECRETARY GENERAL, ADDRESSED TO THE PRESIDENT OF THE SECURITY COUNCIL, U.N. Doc. S/1998/1172 (1998).

77. *See* United Kingdom Statement at U.N. SCOR, 53rd Sess., 3939th mtg., at 10, U.N. Doc. S/PV.3939 (1998), *at* http://ods-dds-ny.un.org/doc/UNDOC/PRO/N98/863/20/PDF/N9886320.pdf?OpenElement. Operation Desert Fox should not be confused with the quite separate Anglo-American actions to maintain "no-fly zones" established in northern and southern Iraq. The legal basis for the "no-fly zones" is humanitarian action in support of Security Council resolution 688 (1991). *See* Christopher Greenwood, *Is there a Right of Humanitarian Intervention?*, 39 WORLD TODAY 34 (Feb. 1993).

It was against this background that the Security Council unanimously adopted resolution 1441 (2002) on November 8, 2002. That resolution again expressly recalled resolution 678 (1990) and deplored the fact that Iraq had not complied with resolution 687 (1991). The Council recalled that resolution 687 had stated that "a ceasefire would be based on acceptance by Iraq of the provisions of that resolution, including the obligations on Iraq contained therein."[78] The resolution then stated that the Council:

> Decides that Iraq has been and remains in material breach of its obligations under relevant resolutions, including resolution 687 (1991), in particular through Iraq's failure to cooperate with United Nations inspectors and the IAEA, and to complete the actions required under paragraphs 8 to 13 of resolution 687 (1991).[79]

The term "material breach" has a special meaning in the law of treaties. In Article 60(3) of the Vienna Convention on the Law of Treaties, 1969, material breach is defined as:

> (a) a repudiation of the treaty not sanctioned by the present Convention; or,
>
> (b) the violation of a provision essential to the accomplishment of the object or purpose of the treaty.

At the Security Council meeting that adopted resolution 1441, Ireland stated that it understood the term "material breach" in the resolution to have the meaning set out in this Article.[80] Of course, resolution 687 is not a treaty but a unilateral act of the Security Council, more akin to a legislative instrument, which binds Iraq irrespective of its agreement. However, it is unlikely that anything will turn on this point. The object and purpose of resolutions 687 and 1441 is plainly to restore international peace and security and a material breach of its terms is therefore one that involves a violation of a provision essential to the accomplishment of that object. That includes the possession by Iraq of prohibited weapons, or the failure to cooperate actively with the inspectors, because the inspection mechanism is itself essential to the accomplishment of the purpose of the resolution. As a leading text on the law of treaties has stated, "material breach" is not the same as "fundamental breach" but can include the breach of an important ancillary provision such as one providing for monitoring and verification.[81]

---

78. S.C. Res. 1441, U.N. SCOR 57th Sess., 4644th mtg., pmbl., U.N. Doc. S/RES/1441 (2002) [hereinafter S.C. Res. 1441].

79. *Id.* at para. 1.

80. U.N. SCOR 57th Sess., 4644th mtg., at 7–8, U.N. Doc. S/PV.4644 (2002), *at* http://ods-dds-ny.un.org/doc/UNDOC/PRO/N02/680/99/PDF/N0268099.pdf?OpenElement.

81. ANTHONY AUST, MODERN TREATY LAW AND PRACTICE 238 (2000) (referring to the inspection provisions of the Chemical Weapons Convention).

The Council, however, decided "to afford Iraq . . . a final opportunity to comply with its disarmament obligations" under resolution 687 and the other resolutions.[82]   Iraq was required to submit "a currently accurate, full and complete declaration of all aspects of its programs to develop chemical, biological and nuclear weapons, ballistic missiles, and other delivery systems" as well as allow unrestricted access to inspectors from UNMOVIC and the IAEA.[83] The Council decided:

> [T]hat false statements or omissions in the declarations submitted by Iraq pursuant to this resolution and failure by Iraq at any time to comply with, and cooperate fully in the implementation of, this resolution shall constitute a further material breach of Iraq's obligations and will be reported to the Council for assessment in accordance with paragraphs 11 and 12 below;[84]
>
> . . . further that Iraq shall not take or threaten hostile acts directed against any representative or personnel of the United Nations or the IAEA or of any Member State taking action to uphold any Council resolution.[85]

Paragraph 9 required Iraq to cooperate "immediately, unconditionally and actively". In the event of Iraqi non-compliance, paragraphs 11 to 13 of the resolution provided that the Council:

> 11.   *Directs* the Executive Chairman of UNMOVIC and the Director-General of the IAEA to report immediately to the Council any interference by Iraq with inspection activities, as well as any failure by Iraq to comply with its disarmament obligations, including its obligations regarding inspections under this resolution;
>
> 12.   *Decides* to convene immediately upon receipt of a report in accordance with paragraphs 4 or 11 above, in order to consider the situation and the need for full compliance with all of the relevant Council resolutions in order to secure international peace and security;
>
> 13.   *Recalls*, in that context, that the Council has repeatedly warned Iraq that it will face serious consequences as a result of its continued violations of its obligations.

Resolution 1441 was based on a draft resolution sponsored by the United Kingdom and the United States. The draft was the subject of extensive informal consultations over a period of weeks before any text was made public. It is, therefore, impossible to be certain what changes may have been made in these informal negotiations or what understandings expressed about the meaning of different provisions in the resolution.   A draft resolution, which reflected these informal consultations, was published on November 6, 2002.[86] The text finally adopted differed from that draft in that the reference in paragraph 12 of the draft to the Council meeting "in order to consider the situation and the

---

82.   *Id.* at para. 2.
83.   *Id.* at para. 3.
84.   *Id.* at para. 4.
85.   *Id.* at para. 8.
86.   U.N. SECURITY COUNCIL, UNITED KINGDOM OF GREAT BRITAIN AND NORTHERN IRELAND AND UNITED STATES OF AMERICA: DRAFT RESOLUTION, U.N. Doc. S/2002/1198 (2002).

The Use of Force in International Law 331

[VOL. 4: 7, 2003]   *Pre-emptive Use of Force*
                                      SAN DIEGO INT'L L.J.

need for full compliance with all of the relevant resolutions in order to *restore* international peace and security" was changed by substituting the word "secure" for "restore". It has been suggested that this change weakens the argument that the resolution could provide an authority for the use of force because the change meant that the language of the resolution no longer tracked so closely the language of resolution 678 (1990).[87] The minor alteration in the language, however, seems a very slender basis for any such conclusion.

As required by resolution 1441, Iraq produced on December 7, 2002 a declaration relating to all its relevant weapons programs. It also admitted teams of inspectors from UNMOVIC and the IAEA. On January 27, 2003, the Executive Chairman of UNMOVIC, Dr. Hans Blix, and the Director-General of the IAEA, Mr. Mohammed El Baradei presented reports to the Security Council detailing the activities and findings of their teams during the first sixty days of inspections.[88] Dr. Blix's report showed that Iraq was still not in compliance with resolution 1441 and the other relevant resolutions. Although noting that Iraq had generally cooperated in terms of access (though he noted some problems), Dr. Blix found Iraq's cooperation on matters of substance wanting. Iraq had not provided the kind of active cooperation that resolution 1441 required; in particular, Iraq had not volunteered evidence from which unresolved questions about weaponry raised in previous inspections might be resolved. Specifically, Dr. Blix expressed concern about:

(1) evidence that Iraq had made greater progress in purifying and weaponizing VX nerve gas than it had admitted;[89]

(2) documents relating to the use of chemical bombs in the Iran-Iraq war, which suggested that some 6500 chemical bombs, with approximately 1000 tonnes of chemicals, were unaccounted for;[90]

(3) the discovery of a small number of chemical rocket warheads, which highlighted the issue of rockets, had not been accounted for;[91]

---

87. Frederic Kirgis, *Security Council Resolution 1441 on Iraq's Final Opportunity to Comply with Disarmament Obligations*, ASIL INSIGHTS, Nov. 2002, *available at* http://www.asil.org/insights/insigh92.htm (last visited Feb. 3, 2003).
88. U.N. Doc. S/PV.4692, *supra* note 3.
89. *Id.* at 5.
90. *Id.*
91. *Id.*

(4) indications that Iraq had produced more anthrax than it had declared and that it might have retained some bacterial growth media possibly sufficient to produce 5000 liters of anthrax;[92]

(5) evidence that Iraq had continued to develop missiles with a range of more than 150 kilometers;[93]

(6) a discovery of documents in the home of an Iraqi scientist, which suggested that other documents might, have been placed in private homes so as to make their detection more difficult;[94]

(7) the unwillingness of Iraqi scientists to meet inspectors other than in the presence of Iraqi officials.[95]

The Blix Report also noted that UNMOVIC had built up its capabilities, which were at the disposal of the Security Council.[96] Dr. El Baradei also noted certain matters that his team was investigating but stated that "to date we have found no evidence that Iraq has revived its nuclear weapons programme since the elimination of the programme in the 1990s".[97]

Dr. Blix and Dr. El Baradei briefed the Council again on February 14[98] and March 7, 2003.[99] In addition, UNMOVIC produced on March 6, 2003 a detailed document entitled "Unresolved Disarmament Issues".[100] Although these reports referred to progress and a number of concessions on the part of the Iraqi government, they also established that, four months after the adoption of resolution 1441, Iraq had still not taken all the steps required to put an end to the continuing breach identified in paragraph 1 of resolution 1441. At the meeting of the Security Council on March 7, 2003, when Iraq's representative contended that Iraq had no weapons of mass destruction and was cooperating fully with the inspectors,[101] not one member of the Council agreed that Iraq had yet put an end to the material breach of resolution 687, which the Council had earlier identified and most made express statements that Iraq was still in breach, although there were evident differences about the extent of that breach and about the best way in which to respond to it.[102]

---

92.   *Id.* at 6.
93.   *Id.*
94.   *Id.* at 7.
95.   *Id.* at 8.
96.   *Id.*
97.   *Id.* at 12.
98.   The briefings are set out in Cm 5769, *supra* note 4, at 79, 85.
99.   The briefings are set out in Cm 5785, *supra* note 4, at 4, 8.
100. Cm 5785, *supra* note 4, at 15.
101. U.N. Doc. S/PV.4714, at 34–35.
102. *Id.* at 9 (Germany), 13 (Mexico), 14 (United States of America), 17 (Russian Federation), 19 (France), 21 (China), 22 (Chile), 23 (Spain), 25 (United Kingdom), 28 (Angola), 29 (Cameroon), 30 (Bulgaria), 32 (Pakistan), 33–34 (Guinea).

[Vol. 4: 7, 2003]   *Pre-emptive Use of Force*

SAN DIEGO INT'L L.J.

The differences over whether to resort to force or whether to continue with the inspections meant, however, that the Council was effectively deadlocked. By March 16 it had become clear that neither a resolution that would authorize military action (or one which would be perceived as doing so) or a resolution that the inspectors should continue with their work would be adopted. In these circumstances, the United States, the United Kingdom, and a number of other States decided to take military action without a further resolution, relying on the authorization granted by resolution 678 (1990).[103] That action began on March 20, 2003.

B. The Legality of Military Action Against Iraq

Was that resort to force lawful? This question certainly aroused controversy with several States expressing the view that it was not, while others strongly defended the action.[104] In the light of the Blix Reports and the "Unresolved Issues" document published by UNSCOM,[105] it is plain that, at the date military action commenced, Iraq continued to be in material breach of resolution 1441 (2002) and resolution 687 (1991). The debate in the Council on March 7, 2003 showed that, with the possible exception of Syria, all the members of the Council accepted that this was the case.[106] Moreover, that breach was no technicality but meant that, on the basis of the existing Security Council resolutions, Iraq posed a threat to international peace and security as determined by the Security Council.

In those circumstances, there is no doubt that the Council could lawfully have adopted a fresh resolution authorizing military action. Resolution 1441 (2002) did not, in and of itself, constitute such a fresh mandate. The text of that resolution made clear that any breach by Iraq was to be reported to the Council, which would then "convene ... in order to consider the situation and the need for full compliance with all of the relevant Council

---

103. The British government's exposition of this argument was set out in an answer by the Attorney-General, Lord Goldsmith, to a parliamentary question on March 17, 2003, 646 PARL. DEB. H.L. WA 2, and a longer paper on the legal basis for action sent by the Secretary of State for Foreign and Commonwealth Affairs to the Foreign Affairs Committee of the House of Commons, *at* http://www.fco.gov.uk/servlet/Front?pagename=OpenMarket/Xcelerate/ShowPage&c=Page&cid=1007029394383&a=KArticle&aid=1047661460790.

104. *See also* the differing views expressed in the United Kingdom Parliament, *e.g.*, in the debate on the Legality of the Use of Force in the House of Lords on March 17, 2003, 646 PARL. DEB. H.L. WA cols. 68 et seq.

105. *See* discussion *supra* note 100.

106. *See* the statements cited *supra* note 102.

resolutions in order to secure international peace and security".[107] Moreover, several States made clear when the resolution was adopted that there was no "automaticity" involved,[108] so that any violation by Iraq would have to be discussed by the Council before any recourse to force.

A new resolution expressly authorizing military action was not, however, necessary as a matter of international law. The authorization to use "all necessary means" contained in resolution 678 (1990) had not been terminated by the Security Council. On the contrary, as demonstrated above, it was reaffirmed, as recently as November 2002, in the preamble to resolution 1441 (2002). Contrary to what is frequently suggested,[109] resolution 678 was not solely about the liberation of Kuwait. The authorization for the coalition to use force went beyond the goal of liberating Kuwait by authorizing military action for the purpose of restoring international peace and security in the area.

Resolution 687 (1991) then determined that the restoration of international peace and security required the partial disarmament of Iraq. Resolution 687, paragraph 1, affirmed Resolution 678 except to the extent that the other provisions of resolution 687 expressly changed resolution 678. The text of resolution 687 contained nothing that expressly (or impliedly) indicated that the Council either considered that the mandate contained in resolution 678 had been discharged or that it could not be relied upon in the event of Iraq continuing to pose a threat to international peace and security. The imposition of a ceasefire by resolution 687 (1991) suspended hostilities and thus suspended the authority to use force but, by reaffirming resolution 678, resolution 687 left open the possibility of further military action to achieve the objectives of resolution 678 in the event of Iraqi violation of the ceasefire terms.

It is, of course, true that resolution 678 was not intended to remain in force indefinitely.[110] But that fact is not decisive. The same could be said of resolution 661 (1990) imposing economic sanctions. The Council plainly intended that neither resolution should remain in force longer than was necessary to ensure Iraqi compliance with the various resolutions on Kuwait and to restore peace and security in the area. Following the liberation of Kuwait, resolution 687 (1991) set out exactly what the Council considered had to be done by Iraq to ensure that peace and security was restored but Iraq did not do what was required of it. That resolution 678 (1990) remained in force, therefore, was due solely to Iraq's persistent violation of its obligations under

---

107. S.C. Res. 1441, *supra* note 79, at para. 12.
108. *See, e.g.*, Statement by the United States, S/PV.4644, at 3; Statement by the United Kingdom, *id.* at 5. *See also* U.N. SECURITY COUNCIL, LETTER DATED 8 NOVEMBER 2002 FROM THE REPRESENTATIVES OF CHINA, FRANCE AND THE RUSSIAN FEDERATION TO THE UNITED NATIONS ADDRESSED TO THE PRESIDENT OF THE UNITED NATIONS, U.N. Doc. S/2002/1236 (2002).
109. *See, e.g.*, answer by Professor Brownlie in response to Question 89, *supra* note 70.
110. Lowe, *supra* note 70, at para. 115.

resolution 687. Moreover, the recent reaffirmation of resolution 678 (1990) in the preamble to resolution 1441 (2002) cannot be dismissed as mere verbiage; the only possible interpretation of that paragraph in the preamble was that the Council (unanimously) considered that the earlier resolution was still in force.

The principle that the authorization of force contained in resolution 678 could revive in the event of Iraqi violation of the ceasefire conditions in resolution 687 was relied on by the United Kingdom and the United States in January 1993.[111] That action—and the legal justification advanced for it—received support from the Secretary-General of the United Nations, who said:

> The raid yesterday, and the forces that carried out the raid, have received a mandate from the Security Council according to resolution 678 and the cause of the raid was the violation by Iraq of resolution 687 concerning the ceasefire.
>
> So, as the Secretary-General of the UN, I can say that this action was taken and conforms to the resolutions of the Security Council and conforms to the Charter of the United Nations.[112]

This principle was also invoked by the United Kingdom and the United States in December 1998 at the time of Operation Desert Fox.[113]

The decision by the Council, in paragraph 1 of resolution 1441 (2002), that Iraq was guilty of a continuing material breach of the conditions of resolution 687 (1991) showed that the conditions for the revival of the authority to use force existed. The use of the term "material breach" in resolution 1441 was particularly significant as it was the term that had been used by the Council at the time of the 1993 recourse to force. The decision to grant Iraq a final opportunity to comply, however, together with the requirement that any failure on the part of Iraq to take that opportunity had to be reported to the Council for consideration under paragraph 12 of resolution 1441, meant that resolution 1441 did not automatically revive the authorization of military action.[114] Nevertheless, the requirement in paragraph 12 of resolution 1441 that the Council consider the matter, did not mean that no action could be taken under resolution 678 unless the Council decided on such a course. As the British government's statement on the legal basis for military action made clear:

---

111. *See, e.g.,* the statements by the U.K. government reproduced in 64 BRIT. Y.B. INT'L L. 736 (1993).

112. IRAQ AND KUWAIT: THE HOSTILITIES AND THEIR AFTERMATH 741–42 (Marc Weller ed., Cambridge 1993).

113. *See supra* text accompanying notes 77–78. For criticism of this reliance on resolution 678 *see* Christine Gray, *From Unity to Polarisation: International Law and the Use of Force Against Iraq,* 13 EUR. J. INT'L L. 1 (2002).

114. Hence the statements about there being no automaticity. *See* discussion *supra* note 108 and accompanying text. *See also* Foreign Secretary's statement, *supra* note 103, at para. 11.

> Had that been the intention, [resolution 1441] would have provided that the Council would decide what needed to be done to restore international peace and security, not that it would consider the matter. The choice of words was deliberate; a proposal that there should be a requirement for a decision by the Council, a position maintained by several members, was not adopted. Instead the members of the Council opted for the formula that the Council must consider the matter before any action is taken.[115]

In accordance with paragraph 12 of resolution 1441, the Council did consider the matter at several formal meetings and in numerous informal consultations between its members. Those meetings and consultations showed that the members of the Council were agreed that Iraq remained in material breach of its disarmament obligations but disclosed that the members were divided about what to do with the result that no decision could be taken. In these circumstances, although it must be recognized that others have taken a different view, the present writer believes that those governments who resorted to force were right to conclude that they could rely on the authorization of military action in resolution 678, read together with resolutions 687 and 1441.

V. CONCLUSIONS

In his State of the Union address on January 28, 2003, President George W. Bush highlighted the importance of pre-empting attacks such as the one that occurred on September 11, 2001. In doing so, he made the following remark:

> Some have said that we must not act until the threat is imminent. Since when have terrorists and tyrants announced their intentions, politely putting us on notice before they strike. If this threat is permitted to fully and suddenly emerge, all actions, all words and all recriminations would come too late.[116]

This Article has sought to demonstrate that international law does not require that States wait until it is too late but nor does it give a broad general license for pre-emptive military action. The following conclusions seem warranted:

(1) All States have the right of self-defense against an armed attack, actual or imminent;

(2) There is, however, no right to take military action in self-defense against a threat that is not imminent;

(3) In determining whether an attack is imminent, the gravity of the threat and the means by which it would materialize in

---

115.   *See* Foreign Secretary's statement, *supra* note 103, at para. 11.
116.   President's State of the Union Address (Jan. 28, 2003), *available at* http://www.whitehouse.gov/news/releases/2003/01/20030128-19.html (last visited Mar. 3, 2003).

violence are relevant considerations and mean that the concept of imminence will vary from case to case;

(4) The Security Council can authorize States to use pre-emptive military force against a threat to the peace in circumstances where an attack is not yet imminent;

(5) The scope for pre-emptive action under the collective security regime is therefore more extensive than under the right of self-defense;

(6) Neither the right of self-defense nor the collective security regime is confined to threats emanating from States.

[16]

The Use of Force against Terrorists

Christian J. Tams*

Abstract

Whether states can use force against terrorists based in another country is much discussed. The relevant provisions of the UN Charter do not provide a conclusive answer, but have to be interpreted. The present article suggests that in the course of the last two decades, the Charter regime has been re-adjusted, so as to permit forcible responses to terrorism under more lenient conditions. In order to illustrate developments, it juxtaposes international law as of 1989 to the present state of the law. It argues that the restrictive approach to anti-terrorist force obtaining 20 years ago has come under strain. As far as collective responses are concerned, it is no longer disputed that the Security Council could authorize the use of force against terrorists; however, it has so far refrained from doing so. More controversially, the international community during the last two decades has increasingly recognized a right of states to use unilateral force against terrorists. This new practice is justified under an expanded doctrine of self-defence. It can be explained as part of a strong international policy against terrorism and is part of an overall tendency to view exceptions to the ban on force more favourably than 20 years ago. Conversely, it has led to a normative drift affecting key limitations of the traditional doctrine of self-defence, and increases the risk of abuse.

1 Introduction

The legal rules governing the use of force form the core of modern international law. The ban on the use of force is widely held to be peremptory in nature, and has often been described as the 'cornerstone' of the modern international system.[1] The latter

---

* Professor of International Law, University of Glasgow. Email: c.tams@law.gla.ac.uk.

[1] *Armed Activities on the Territory of the Congo* (DRC–Uganda case), [2005] ICJ Rep 201, at para. 148 ('The prohibition against the use of force is a cornerstone of the United Nations Charter'); *Military and Paramilitary Activities in and against Nicaragua (Nicaragua v. United States)* (Nicaragua case) [1986] ICJ Rep 14, separate opinion of President Singh, at 153 ('the very cornerstone of the human effort to promote peace in a world torn by strife'); *Case concerning Oil Platforms (Islamic Republic of Iran v. United States of America)*

360 *EJIL* 20 (2009), 359–397

statement in particular suggests a sense of immutability: cornerstones not only cannot be removed (if the edifice resting on them is to stand), but they should better not be moved at all. In that respect, the 'cornerstone image', despite its popularity, may convey a wrong impression. The precise scope of the legal rules governing the use of force is by no means beyond debate. It is much discussed whether particular forms of conduct (such as severe coercion not involving military force, low-level military violence, or indirect forms of aggression) are covered by the prohibition. More importantly, there have been protracted debates about exceptions to the prohibition, that is, about justifications that should be available to states using force in order, e.g., to implement a decision by the UN Security Council, to protect human rights of their or of foreign nationals, to fight insurgents operating from foreign territory, or – admittedly one of the more ambitious claims[2] – to enforce judgments of international courts.

The UN Charter (UNC) lays down the parameters of these debates. Article 2(4) UNC obliges UN members to 'refrain in their international relations from the threat or use of force against the territorial integrity or political independence of any State, or in any other manner inconsistent with the Purposes of the United Nations'. In Articles 42, 43 and Article 51, the Charter recognizes two exceptions to this prohibition: forcible enforcement measures within the framework of the organization's collective security system, and the right of self-defence against armed attacks. These provisions lay down an ambitious regime of rules against force. In some cases, states have apparently considered the regime to be too ambitious and have deliberately stepped out of it. These are rare instances, however, and in the clear majority of cases arguments about the legality of forcible conduct are tailored to fit the Charter regime.[3] Conversely, the Charter regime on the use of force, notwithstanding its fundamental importance or even its role as a cornerstone, has been anything but static. Faced with challenges such as those referred to in the preceding paragraph, the international community has not formally amended the Charter rules, but has re-appraised them through interpretation.[4] In many respects, the interpretation has produced clear and stable results, but it has also led to processes of adaptation and adjustment in the light of new realities or perceptions.[5]

The following considerations address one particular challenge to the system, and analyse how the international community has responded to it during a particular period of time. The particular period is the years 1989–2009, coinciding with the first

---

(Oil Platforms case), Judgment of 6 Nov. 2003, [2003] ICJ Rep 161, dissenting opinion of Judge Elaraby, at 291 ('The principle of the prohibition of the use of force in international relations ... is, no doubt, the most important principle in contemporary international law to govern inter-State conduct; it is indeed the cornerstone of the Charter'); ibid., separate opinion of Judge Simma, at 328; C. Joyner, *International Law for the 21st Century* (2005), at 165.

[2] Cf. Schachter, 'The Enforcement of International Judicial and Arbitral Decisions', 54 *AJIL* (1960) 1.

[3] For references, insofar as they are relevant to the question of anti-terrorist force, see *infra*, section C.

[4] Cf. Cassese, 'Return to Westphalia?', in A. Cassese (ed.), *The Current Legal Regulation of the Use of Force* (1986), at 514 (distinguishing 'normative' and 'interpretative' changes).

[5] Tom Franck's *Recourse to Force* (2002) offers an excellent analysis of the evolving nature of the Charter's regime governing force.

20 years of the *European Journal of International Law*. The particular challenge is that of terrorism. It will be argued that in the course of two decades the legal rules governing the use of force have been re-adjusted so as to permit forcible responses against terrorism under more lenient conditions. To bring out those developments, the subsequent sections juxtapose the law governing anti-terrorist force as perceived in 1989 ('The Past')[6] and the present legal regime of 2009 ('The Present').[7] In order to put developments between 1989 and 2009 in perspective and to avoid the impression that the present state of the law marked an 'end of history', a final section briefly speculates how the law may develop in the two decades to come ('The Future').[8] Before we begin this journey through time, four caveats seem in order:

(i) In line with the overall goal of the symposium, the present article focuses on the rules governing the use of force. It is not a study of terrorism, but assesses the application of the *jus ad bellum* to the particular problem of terrorism.[9] No attempt is made to analyse in any detail what activities can be subsumed under the concept of 'terrorism'.[10] As a working definition, 'terrorism' shall be understood to mean an activity 'intended to cause death or serious bodily harm to civilians or non-combatants with the purpose of intimidating a population or compelling a government or an international organization to do or abstain from doing any act.'[11] While leaving open many issues, that working definition seems sufficient for present purposes to describe the type of activity against which states might claim to respond by forcible means. As will be shown, the definitional problem has not paralysed the international community. It has not stopped states from asserting a right to use force against persons or groups they claimed were 'terrorists', and it has not stopped others from reacting to those assertions.[12]

(ii) Focusing on the use of force, the following considerations present only one aspect of the fight against terrorism, and by no means the most relevant. No attempt is made to describe the ever-growing network of international obligations requiring states to, for example, criminalize terrorist activities, prosecute or extradite terrorist offenders, freeze bank accounts of terror suspects,[13] or attempt to address causes of

---

[6]   *Infra*, section 2.

[7]   *Infra*, section 3.

[8]   *Infra*, section 4B.

[9]   Cf. the distinction drawn by Higgins, 'The General International Law of Terrorism', in R. Higgins and M. Flory (eds.), *Terrorism and International Law* (1997), at 13.

[10]   Cf. Saul, 'Attempts to Define "Terrorism" in International Law', 52 *Netherlands Int'l L Rev* (2005) 57; Walter, 'Defining Terrorism in National and International Law', in C. Walter *et al.* (eds), *Terrorism as a Challenge for National and International Law: Security versus Freedom?* (2004), at 23; and C. Wandscher, *Internationaler Terrorismus und Selbstverteidigungsrecht* (2006), at 27 ff, for detailed discussions.

[11]   Annan, 'In Larger Freedom. Towards development, security and human rights for all', Report of the Secretary-General, UN Doc. A/59/2005, at para. 91.

[12]   See Dupuy, 'State Sponsors of Terrorism', in A. Bianchi (ed.), *Enforcing International Law against Terrorists* (2004), at 5, for a similar remark.

[13]   For comprehensive perspectives on the international fight against terrorism see the contributions to M. Glennon and S. Sur (eds.), *Terrorism and International Law/ Terrorisme et droit international* (2008), at chs 7, and 13–14; Higgins and Flory (eds.), *supra* note 9 (especially Part II: 'Cooperation against Terrorism'); and Bianchi (ed.), *supra* note 12.

362   *EJIL* 20 (2009), 359–397

terrorism. Non-forcible responses to terror will be taken into account only in the most general way, insofar as their existence reduces the need to resort to force (or their absence increases it).

(iii)   In line with the structure of legal rules governing the use of force (which, as will be explored below,[14] require states to refrain from the use of force 'in their international relations'[15]), the subsequent discussion deals with the extraterritorial, cross-border use of force against terrorists. As a consequence, measures addressed involve the use of force which, even though it may target terrorists, also affects another state's territorial sovereignty.[16] In contrast, no attempt is made to scrutinize the legal limits restricting the right of states to employ force against terrorists based in their own territory – a question regulated largely by rules of national law, international human rights law, or possibly also humanitarian law. Furthermore, the less likely scenario of forcible measures directed against terrorists based in neutral areas outside any state's jurisdiction (the High Seas, possibly Antarctica, etc.[17]) will equally not be covered.

(iv)   Finally, in at least one respect, the subsequent analysis will adopt a broad approach. It addresses the different aspects of the international regime governing recourse to force, beginning with the ban on force, but also covering exceptions justifying multilateral as well as unilateral forcible conduct. Of course, some issues (such as the question of self-defence against terrorist acts) will require a broader treatment than others, simply because they have proved so controversial. Yet it is believed that in order to assess the legal regime governing anti-terrorist force in a balanced way, a broader approach is required which helps place that particular controversy in perspective.

2 The Past: Anti-terrorist Force 1989

A *The Heyday of a Restrictive Analysis*

In order to assess legal developments, it is necessary to revisit the starting-point. For present purposes, that starting-point is the year 1989. It is a starting-point chosen to allow reflection on development during the lifespan of the *European Journal*. Yet it is also a convenient starting-point because the year 1989 (or, more broadly, the period of the late 1980s) seems to have been the heyday of a particular understanding of the *jus ad bellum*. Of course, few aspects of the law in this area are ever universally agreed, and it would be wrong to suggest that, 20 years ago, the scope of the international rules on force had been uncontroversial. However, some of the big debates of

---

[14] *Infra*, section 2A.

[15] Art. 2(4) UNC.

[16] This reasoning of course does not apply if force is used with the consent of the territorial state. That aspect is not addressed in the following either.

[17] See Davis, 'The Phantom of the Neo-Global Era: International Law and the Implications of Non-State Terrorism on the Nexus of Self-Defense and the Use of Force', in R. Miller and R. Bratspies (eds), *Progress in International Law* (2008), at 637, n. 19.

the time – about wars of national liberation, about the Brezhnev doctrine – have lost (much of) their relevance. If these are left to one side, then, in retrospect, the late 1980s appear to have been the high point of what might be called a 'restrictive analysis' – an approach seeking to limit the availability of military force to the largest possible extent. This restrictive analysis was not invented in 1989 nor formulated as a coherent strategy. Yet, 20 years ago it represented the mainstream approach to the *jus ad bellum* which was arguably more dominant than ever before or thereafter. The mainstream approach was reflected in many of the influential writings of the time, such as the treatment of Articles 2(4), 39–43, and 51 UNC in the first editions of Charter commentaries by Cot/Pellet[18] and Simma,[19] in the majority of contributions to Antonio Cassese's 1986 collection of essays,[20] or in the 1985 proceedings of the German Society of International Law.[21] These writings could build on the gradual consolidation of a Charter regime which in 1945 had been revolutionary, but over time had been reinforced through landmark ICJ rulings (such as *Corfu Channel* and *Nicaragua*[22]) and important General Assembly resolutions.[23] Of course states, especially the more powerful, were suspicious of the limits placed upon them by the Charter and felt that the drafters had gone too far in their quest to ban force, but ideological confrontation typically precluded agreement on a more flexible re-interpretation.[24]

For present purposes, the restrictive analysis is crucial not only as a general approach to the *jus ad bellum* but because it informed the international community's approach to anti-terrorist force. International terrorism of course was a very real threat to many states in the late 1980s. However, the international community typically approached this threat in a 'contextual' way, taking account of the causes of terrorism, and was unwilling to condemn it in an unequivocal way.[25] Not surprisingly, it failed to adopt a comprehensive anti-terrorism convention.[26] While sectoral conventions on specific types of terrorist activities were ratified,[27] these tended to approach terrorism as a problem of criminal law to be addressed by means short of (international) military

---

18 J.P. Cot and A. Pellet (eds.), *La Charte des Nations Unies* (1985) (contributions by Virally, Cohen Johnathan and Fischer, and Cassese).

19 B. Simma (ed.), *Die Charta der Vereinten Nationen* (1991) (contributions by Randelzhofer and Frowein).

20 Cassese (ed.), *supra* note 4.

21 K. Hailbronner and D. Schindler (eds.), *Die Grenzen des völkerrechtlichen Gewaltverbots. Berichte der Deutschen Gesellschaft für Völkerrecht* vol. 19 (1986).

22 [1986] ICJ Rep 14; [1949] ICJ Rep 4.

23 See, e.g., GA Res. 2131 (XX); GA Res. 2625 (XXV); GA Res. 3314 (XXIX); GA Res. 42/22 (1987).

24 Hence Cassese concludes his (admittedly more sceptical) evaluation by recognizing that it would be 'difficult to contend that ... a general agreement had been reached concerning [a broader] interpretation of crucial provisions of the U.N. Charter on the use of force': Cassese, *supra* note 4, at 513.

25 See the excellent summary by Klein, 'Le droit international à l'épreuve du terrorisme', 321 *Recueil des Cours* (2006) 203, at 309.

26 *Cf. ibid.*, at 312 ff.

27 See the list of conventions available at www.un.org/terrorism/instruments.shtml. Cf. further Gioia, 'The UN Conventions on the Prevention and Suppression of International Terrorism', in G. Nesi, *International Cooperation in Counter-terrorism. The United Nations and Regional Organizations in the Fight Against Terrorism* (2006), at 3; Röben, 'The Role of International Conventions and General International Law in the Fight against International Terrorism', in Walter *et al.* (eds), *supra* note 10, at 789.

364 *EJIL* 20 (2009), 359–397

force. Given this lack of consensus, it comes as no surprise that the traditional *jus ad bellum* viewed assertions of a right to use anti-terrorist force rather sceptically. In line with the dominant, restrictive, analysis of the legal rules governing resort to force, international law as at 1989 effectively ruled out the possibility that states could law-fully resort to forcible measures against terrorists based in another country. This in turn was reflected in the prevailing interpretation of the ban on force (section B), as well as the construction of exceptions to it (sections C and D).

B *A Robust Interpretation of the Prohibition on Force*

By the late 1980s, there had emerged a broad consensus that the prohibition against the use of force was comprehensive in scope, and that it declared *every* use of force in the international relations of a state to be *prima facie* illegal.[28] As a consequence, the extraterritorial use of force, by one state, against terrorists operating within another state inevitably violated the rule.[29]

This interpretation of the prohibition marked a compromise between competing schools of thought: on the one hand, it maintained the 'military' understanding of force, resisting attempts to open Article 2(4) UNC to other forms of coercion;[30] on the other, it interpreted the ban on military force robustly. This robust inter-pretation flowed naturally from the text of Article 2(4) UNC, but had been chal-lenged in the UN's early days, notably by states and authors insisting that uses of force not directed against another state's territorial integrity or political inde-pendence were in line with Article 2(4).[31] That argument however (which some-times was adapted to the use of anti-terrorist force[32]) was difficult to bring in line with the wording and history of the provision: a cursory reading was sufficient to note that forcible conduct 'in any other manner inconsistent with the Pur-poses of the United Nations' would also be outlawed, and the *travaux préparatoires* clearly showed that the subsequent inclusion of other elements of the text (such as the reference to 'political independence' and 'territorial integrity') had not been intended to restrict the scope of the prohibition.[33] On that basis, narrow readings of the prohibition had been convincingly dismissed by the ICJ in its *Corfu Channel*

---

[28] Lachs, 'General Course on Public International Law', 169 *Recueil des Cours* (1980-IV) 162 (Article 2(4) as a 'residual catch-all provision'); A. Verdross and B. Simma, *Universelles Völkerrecht* (3rd edn, 1984), at para. 469; Randelzhofer, *supra* note 19, Art. 2(4), marginal note (MN) 34.

[29] Schachter, 'The Lawful Use of Force by a State against Terrorists in another Country', 19 *Israel Yrbk on Human Rights* (1989) 209, at 213–214.

[30] See, e.g., Verdross and Simma, *supra* note 28, at para. 476; Virally, 'Commentary on Article 2(4)', in Cot and Pellet, *supra* note 18, at 120.

[31] Most prominently by the UK in the Corfu Channel case, ICJ Pleadings, Corfu Channel, Vol. III, 296. See further D. Bowett, *Self-Defence in International Law* (1958), at 142; W. Wengler, *Das völkerrechtliche Gewaltverbot. Probleme und Tendenzen* (1967), at 13–14; and cf. the summary by T. Gazzini, *The Changing Rules on the Use of Force in International Law* (2005), at 125–126.

[32] See, e.g., Kühn, 'Terrorism and the Right of Self-Defence', 6 *S African Yrbk Int'l L* (1980) 42.

[33] See Franck, *supra* note 5 at 12–13, and Randelzhofer, *supra* note 19, Art. 2(4) MN 36, for clear summa-ries of debates; subsequent discussions are conveniently summarized by C. Gray, *International Law and the Use of Force* (3rd edn, 2008), at 31–33.

judgment,[34] and had lost support ever since. The Court's *Nicaragua* judgment[35] applied this robust interpretation of the Charter-based prohibition to the sphere of customary international law, which according to the Court was very similar in scope.[36] It followed that states seeking to use force extraterritorially, as part of an anti-terrorist campaign, required some legal justification.

It deserves to be mentioned though that terrorists were covered by the ban on force merely indirectly. The use of force, by a state, against individuals or groups was *as such* not sufficient to violate the prohibition.[37] That prohibition, as Article 2(4) UNC made clear, only obliged states not to use force 'in their international relations'. As a consequence, anti-terrorist force could be used as long as it did not concern the scope of states' international relations. That term, in turn, was read to cover inter-state relations, with cautious extensions to cover the use of force in relations between states and *de facto* regimes or states and arguably national liberation movements. In the present context, the use of force against terrorists based in another state clearly came within the scope of a state's 'international relations', but the indirect way in which Article 2(4) addressed the matter would be relevant to the discussion of exceptions.

C *The Security Council's Inability to Respond to Terrorist Attacks*

Under the Charter system as originally envisaged, collective enforcement action under Chapter VII was to be the main exception to the prohibition on force.[38] States seeking to rely on that exception in the fight against terrorism were, however, bound to be disappointed. The main reason for this was obvious. Between 1945 and the late 1980s the Security Council failed to use its authority.[39] Even though its decision-making procedures had been applied with considerable flexibility,[40] block confrontation paralysed the collective security system of Chapter VII during the

---

[34] *Supra* note 22, at 35, where the Court stressed that even temporary infringements constituted a violation of Art. 2(4) UNC. See further I. Brownlie, *International Law and the Use of Force* (1963), at 265 ff; Randelzhofer, *supra* note 33, Art. 2(4) MN 35–37.

[35] *Supra* note 1.

[36] *Ibid.*, at paras 187–190 (but contrast the ambiguous statement in para. 175, where the Court observes that the two rules were not 'identical').

[37] Verdross and Simma, *supra* note 28, at para. 469; Virally, *supra* note 30, at 121–122. Cf. also the commentary to principle 6 of the *Principles of International Law on Self-Defence* set out by Chatham House (ed. Elisabeth Wilmhurst, 2005, at 12): 'The right of states to defend themselves against ongoing attacks, even by private groups of non-state actors, is not generally questioned. What is questioned is the right to take action against the state that is the presumed source of such attacks, since it must be conceded that an attack against a non-state actor within a state will inevitably constitute the use of force on the territorial state.'

[38] Franck, *supra* note 5, at 20–21.

[39] Cohen, 'Commentary on Art. 39', in Cot and Pellet, *supra* note 18, at 649; Gray, *supra* note 33, at 254–255.

[40] See notably the re-interpretation of Art. 27(3) UNC according to which abstentions by permanent members did not preclude the adoption of resolutions. In the *Namibia* opinion, the ICJ accepted this adaptation of the Charter rules: see *Legal Consequences for States of the Continued Presence of South Africa in Namibia (South West Africa) notwithstanding Security Council Resolution 276 (1970)* [1971] ICJ Rep 16, at para. 22.

366   *EJIL* 20 (2009), 359–397

first four decades of the UN's existence.[41] In no instance had the Security Council qualified a specific act of terrorism (let alone terrorism as such) as a threat to, or breach of, the peace in the sense of Article 39 UNC; as a consequence, it did not take any enforcement action against terrorists.[42]

The Security Council's paralysis, however, overshadowed another problem: it was by no means clear that, even if it agreed, the Security Council would have been entitled to adopt forcible measures against terrorists. As regards the conditions of Security Council action, it remained at least doubtful whether terrorist attacks could have amounted to a threat to, or breach of, the peace in the sense of Article 39 UNC. Having become used to the Security Council's ever-broadening approaches during two sanctions decades, in retrospect one can hardly fail to be amazed by the caution with which commentators approached Articles 39–42 UNC in the late 1980s. Admittedly, the Council's discretion in interpreting the notion of 'threat to peace', of which SC Resolutions 217 and 221 had provided early examples, was widely stressed.[43] Yet many writers seemed concerned not to make too much of these precedents. Some even went so far as to read Articles 39–42 UNC in line with the inter-state prohibition on force, requiring at least a threat of force in the sense of Article 2(4) UNC[44] – which meant that terrorist acts, unless attributed to a state,[45] were outside the Security Council's competence. Furthermore, it seemed clear that states, not non-state actors (such as terrorist organizations), were to be the targets of sanctions.[46] Finally, with respect to sanctions involving the use of force, the relationship between Articles 42 and 43 UNC remained uncertain.[47] The Charter's drafters had probably intended to couple both provisions, envisaging military enforcement action by UN forces in the sense of Article 43, not by member state forces implementing a Security Council mandate. As is well known, special agreements were not concluded. According to many, this meant that the whole system of military enforcement action under Chapter VII remained 'inoperative'.[48] In any event, commentators writing in the late

---

[41]   The subsequent discussion remains focused on the Security Council's conduct under Ch. VII UNC. Other 'institutional' exceptions to the ban on force (notably GA authorizations pursuant to the 'Uniting for Peace' resolution or measures directed against former enemy states) are not addressed, as they have not been relevant in the fight against terrorism.

[42]   P. van Krieken, *Terrorism and the International Legal Order* (2002), at 141. Some cautious statements on cooperation against hostage-taking as a form of international terrorism could be found in SC Res. 589 (1985), but this was not adopted under Ch. VII.

[43]   See, e.g., Frowein in Simma, *supra* note 19, Art. 39 MN 17; Cohen, *supra* note 39, at 649 and 654.

[44]   See, e.g., Wengler, *supra* note 31, at 13–14, and many further references in Arntz, *Der Begriff der Friedensbedrohung in Satzung und Praxis der Vereinten Nationen* (1975), at 21 ff.

[45]   *Cf. infra*, section 2D1

[46]   See, e.g., Frowein, *supra* note 43, Art. 42 MN 14.

[47]   *Cf.*, e.g., the detailed analysis by Fischer, in his treatment of Art. 42 in the first edition of the Cot and Pellet commentary, *supra* note 18, at 710–714. For a summary of debates see Gazzini, *supra* note 31, at 35–36; Frowein and Krisch, in Simma, *supra* note 33, Art. 42 MN 20.

[48]   See, e.g., L. Goodrich and A. Simons, *The United Nations and the Maintenance of International Peace and Security* (1955), at 398 ff, for the most influential comment. For further references see Fischer in Cot and Pellet, *supra* note 18, at 710–714.

1980s were by no means agreed that the two provisions could be easily uncoupled, thus permitting the use of force by states implementing a Security Council mandate.

D *The Rejection of a Right to Use Anti-terrorist Force Unilaterally*

Security Council enforcement action being effectively unavailable, the legal regime governing anti-terrorist force crucially depended on the scope of other exceptions permitting the *unilateral* use of force. Whether the 'use of force by a State against terrorists in another country' could ever be 'lawful'[49] was much discussed. As regards international practice, a number of incidents – among them Israel's anti-terrorist raids since the 1950s, the South African incursions into neighbouring ('frontline') states during the 1970s and 1980s, or the United States' 1986 attacks on Libya – focused international attention. They also helped clarify the legal parameters of the debate in that responding states invoked different legal justifications. The following sections address their claims, distinguishing between the principal argument based on self-defence and additional justifications such as reprisals or hot pursuit.

1 *A Narrow Construction of Self-defence*

Self-defence was the principal ground on which states relied in order to justify their use of anti-terrorist force.[50] The underlying argument was straightforward: setting out a broad construction of self-defence, states claimed a right to respond to attacks even if these were not carried out by another state. While these claims were made frequently, they were never received favourably by the international community. In fact, during the 1970s and 1980s, the international community rejected them almost systematically.[51] To give but some examples, Israel's 1985 raid on the PLO Headquarters outside Tunis was 'condemn[ed] vigorously' by the Security Council, which declared it an 'act of armed aggression … in flagrant violation of the Charter of the United Nations' and urged other states 'to take measures to dissuade Israel from resorting to such acts against the sovereignty and territorial integrity of all States'.[52] Similarly, the United States' 1986 raid on targets in Libya, while controversially discussed by commentators, was roundly rejected by the General Assembly as 'a violation of the Charter of the United Nations and of international law'.[53] South Africa's incursions into neighbouring states, if anything, met with stiffer resistance.[54]

Of course, the international reaction (both the limited support and the overwhelming condemnation) was at least partly motivated by ideological divisions – for political

---

[49]　To adapt the title of Schachter's influential article, *supra* note 29, at 209.

[50]　See Gray, *supra* note 33, at 136–140, for a summary of incidents involving Israel, South Africa, Portugal, and the US.

[51]　*Cf.* Klein, *supra* note 25, at 375 ('*quasi systématiquement*'); for similar statements see Corten and Dubuisson, 'Opération "liberté immuable": une extension abusive du concept de légitime défense', 106 *RGDIP* (2002) 59; and Gazzini, *supra* note 31, at 191, who accepts that 'for decades the United Nations has rejected self-defence claims related to military measures against alleged terrorists'.

[52]　SC Res. 573 (1985). For earlier condemnations see SC Res. 313 (1972), and SC Res. 508 and 509 (1982).

[53]　GA Res. 41/38.

[54]　See notably SC Res. 527 (1982), SC Res. 546 (1984), and SC Res. 568 (1985).

368   *EJIL* 20 (2009), 359–397

reasons, the international community was likely to reject each and every argument put forward by a then-pariah state such as South Africa. Crucially, however, resolutions such as GA Resolution 41/38 or SC Resolution 573 were *also* based on legal principle. They applied the restrictive construction of the right of self-defence prevailing at the time to the particular problem of anti-terrorist force. As far as the substantive conditions of self-defence are concerned, the restrictive construction depended on three arguments which, taken together, made self-defence effectively unavailable as a justification for forcible anti-terrorist measures.

First, self-defence against armed attacks by non-state actors was admitted in principle, but only under narrow conditions.[55] For an attack to qualify as an 'armed attack' in the sense of Article 51 (or its customary equivalent[56]), the direct attack by a non-state actor had to be attributed to another state under rather stringent rules on attribution. The law on this point was shaped by the ICJ's judgment in the *Nicaragua* case, which concerned the relationship between a state and rebel forces, but came to define the rules on attribution generally.[57] In that decision, the Court (drawing on the General Assembly's *Definition of Aggression*[58]) accepted that the *jus ad bellum* could be violated by 'the sending by or on behalf of a state of armed bands, groups, irregulars or mercenaries, which carry out acts of armed force against another state'.[59] Yet for the conduct of irregular forces to be attributable to a state, that state had to exercise 'effective control [over] the military or paramilitary operations' in question,[60] whereas logistical or other support was insufficient.[61] Self-defence thus depended on complex, and typically fact-dependent, questions of attribution, and required responding states to show a substantial involvement of the territorial state in the very attacks of a terrorist organization against which the response was directed (referred to as 'effective control' test).[62] As a consequence, only terrorist

---

[55] For further comment on this point see Bruha and Tams, 'Self-Defence Against Terrorist Attacks. Considerations in the Light of the ICJ's *Israeli Wall* Opinion', in K. Dicke *et al.* (eds.), *Weltinnenrecht. Liber Amicorum Jost Delbrück* (2005), at 92 ff.

[56] As the ICJ clarified in the Nicaragua case, *supra* note 1, conventional and customary rules of self-defence both presupposed an armed attack; the Court's interpretation of that term thus came to shape the law of self-defence irrespective of the source of law. The Court thereby implicitly rejected the view that a broader, customary right of self-defence had survived the Charter's adoption, or had even been preserved as an 'inherent right' in the sense of Art. 51 UNC. See further Verdross and Simma, *supra* note 28, at para. 470; Gray, *supra* note 33, at 117–118; Kenny, 'Self-Defence', in R. Wolfrum (ed.), *United Nations: Law, Policies and Practice* (1995), at 1163–1164.

[57] As noted by Murphy, that judgment was critically received by many, but 'over time … seems to have passed into the corpus of accepted jurisprudence, to the point where the United States itself now cites to the judgment as authority': Murphy, 'Protean Jus ad bellum', in T. Giegerich and A. Zimmermann (eds), *A Wiser Century? Judicial Dispute Settlement, Disarmament and the Laws of War 100 Years after the Second Hague Peace Conference* (forthcoming 2009), at 9–10 of the manuscript.

[58] *Cf.* GA Res. 3314 (XXIX) (Art. 3(g)).

[59] Nicaragua case, *supra* note 1, at para. 195.

[60] *Ibid.*, at paras 109 and 115; as well as para. 17 of Judge Ago's separate opinion.

[61] *Cf.* the critical comment in Judge Jennings' dissent, at 533.

[62] The effective control test has been the subject of much debate. In addition to the dissent of Judge Jennings (at n. 61), See the more flexible approach developed by the ICTY in its *Tadic* judgment (Case IT-94-1,

attacks effectively controlled by another state triggered a right of self-defence. By adopting a restrictive approach to attribution the Court effectively restricted self-defence to the inter-state context. This approach seemed in line with an inter-state reading of the *jus ad bellum*, took into account the scepticism among UN members against broader readings of self-defence (which would have allowed the abuse of the concept), and for a while was hardly attacked as a matter of principle.[63] It should be noted however that the Court's approach really depended on a re-reading of the text of Article 51 UNC: rather than accepting that that provision recognized the right of states to use self-defence 'if an armed attack occurs', the Court's *Nicaragua* judgment (insofar as it shaped the interpretation of that provision) effectively reformulated the provision to allow for responses 'if an armed attack *by another State* occurs'.[64] The implications of this re-reading would come to haunt the Court some 15 years later.

Secondly, the right of self-defence was narrowly construed in another respect as well. The Court's *Nicaragua* judgment confirmed that self-defence should be available only in response to grave infractions of the prohibition against the use of force. Again, just as with issues of attribution, such a threshold requirement was not easily applied and specific incidents remained controversial.[65] Yet as a matter of principle, the Court's clear message that it would 'be necessary to distinguish the most grave forms of the use of force (those constituting an armed attack) from other less grave forms'[66] was clear, and came to shape the dominant understanding of self-defence as a defence against qualified uses of force.[67] This narrow interpretation could draw on the differences in wording between Article 2(4) UNC on the one hand ('any ... use of force') and Article 51 UNC on the other ('armed attack').[68] Yet it seemed to imply

---

Prosecutor v. Tadic, 38 ILM (1999) 1518, at paras 116–145). In the light of subsequent discussions, it bears repeating that both Jennings and the ICTY accepted that some form of attribution was required. For further comment on the required degree of involvement see de Hoogh, 'Articles 4 and 8 of the 2001 ILC Articles on State Responsibility, The Tadic Case and Attribution of Acts of Bosnian Serb Authorities to the Federal Republic of Yugoslavia', 72 *British Yrbk Int'l L* (2003) 255.

[63] In fact, pursuant to Judge Kooijmans (writing in 2004), the inter-state reading 'has been the generally accepted interpretation for more than 50 years': *Legal Consequences of the Construction of a Wall in the Occupied Palestinian Territory*, Advisory Opinion, 9 July 2004, [2004] ICJ Rep 131, Separate Opinion of Judge Kooijmans, at para. 35. For further detail on the different arguments see Tams, 'Swimming with the Tide, or Seeking to Stem It? Recent ICJ Rulings on the Law of Self-defence', 18 *Revue Québécoise de Droit International* (2005) 275, at 278–280.

[64] This was made very clear in Judge Higgins' separate opinion in the Israeli Wall case, *supra* note 63, at her para. 33): 'there is, with respect, nothing in the text of Article 51 that thus stipulates that self-defence is available only when an armed attack is made by a state. That qualification is rather a result of the Court so determining in Military and Paramilitary Activities in and against Nicaragua'.

[65] See Randelzhofer, *supra* note 33, Art. 51 MN 20–31, for a discussion of relevant scenarios. According to some commentators, the 'threshold requirement' was only relevant to armed attacks carried out by irregular forces; see Raab, '"Armed Attack" after the Oil Platforms Case', 17 *Leiden J Int'l L* (2004) 719, at 724–725; Taft, 'Self-Defense and the *Oil* Platforms Decision', 29 *Yale J Int'l L* (2004) 295. This reading does not affect the argument on terrorists made in the text. It should be noted however that it cannot be reconciled with the Court's subsequent jurisprudence addressed *infra*, at section 3D2c.

[66] *Supra* note 1, at para. 191.

[67] Randelzhofer, *supra* note 33, Art. 51 MN 4–5.

[68] Verdross and Simma, *supra* note 28, at para. 472; Murphy, *supra* note 57, at 10 of the manuscript.

that states would have to turn the other cheek, or at least forgo forcible responses, when faced with lesser breaches of Article 2(4) UNC – an apparent implication which remained controversial.[69] With respect to extraterritorial anti-terrorist violence, the threshold requirement was crucial as attacks by terrorists were likely (although not necessarily) to be of lesser intensity than attacks by organized state military forces, and thus might fail to meet the required threshold.[70] To avoid that conclusion, notably Israel took the view that 'continuous pin-prick assaults', if part of a general strategy, could be 'apprais[ed] … in their totality as an armed attack'.[71] But, by and large, the accumulation doctrine was received unfavourably and Israel's reliance on it was not accepted in discussions in the Security Council.[72]

Finally, under the traditional approach, the right of self-defence was limited by a 'functional argument':[73] Article 51 and customary international law entitled states to 'resort to force only defensively, in the presence of an armed attack and to the extent necessary to repel it'.[74] While the special problem of anticipatory responses was much discussed,[75] it was accepted in principle that 'self-defence [was] not an open-ended instrument but only has the aim of repelling armed attacks and provisionally guaranteeing the security of states'.[76] This functional reading implied requirements of necessity and proportionality limiting the scope of the right, but also meant that there had to be a temporal link between the measures of self-defence and the attack against which they were directed, sometimes referred to as the requirement of 'immediacy'.[77] Unless the 'accumulation doctrine' was accepted (which, by and large, it was not[78]), this meant that responses against terrorist attacks of an instant character could not easily

---

[69] For criticism over time see, e.g., Dahm, 'Das Verbot der Gewaltanwendung nach Art. 2(4) der UNO-Charta', 10 *Jahrbuch für Internationales Recht* (1961–1962) 48, at 54–56; Gazzini, *supra* note 31, at 133 ff; Randelzhofer, *supra* note 33, Art. 51 MN 5.

[70] Guillaume, 'Terrorisme et droit international', 215 *Recueil des Cours* (1989-III) 287, at 406.

[71] *Cf.* Y. Dinstein, *War, Aggression and Self-Defence* (4th edn, 2005), at 230–231; and further Feder, 'Reading the U.N. Charter Connotatively: Toward a New Definition of Armed Attack', 19 *NYU J Int'l L & Pol* (1987) 395, at 414–418.

[72] See Wandscher, *supra* note 10, at 170 ff and 270; Levenfeld, 'Israel's Counter-Fedayeen Tactics in Lebanon: Self-Defense and Reprisal Under Modern International Law', 21 *Columbia J Transnat'l L* (1982/83) 1 (but contrast Gray's more cautious interpretation of Security Council practice, *supra* note 33, at 155). The ICJ's jurisprudence on the matter is ambiguous: *cf.* the Nicaragua case, *supra* note 1, at para. 231, as well as the more recent pronouncements addressed *infra* in Section 3D2c.

[73] See Cannizaro, 'Contextualizing Proportionality: Jus ad bellum and jus in bello in the Lebanese War', 88/864 *Int'l Rev Red Cross* (2006) 782.

[74] *Ibid.* For similar statements see Bowett, 'Reprisals Involving Recourse to Armed Force', 66 *AJIL* (1972) 1, at 3; Randelzhofer, *supra* note 33, Art. 51 MN 42; Gazzini, *supra* note 31, at 129.

[75] Contrast, e.g., Brownlie, *supra* note 34, at 275–278, and Cassese, *supra* note 18, at 774–778 on the one hand, and Bowett, *supra* note 31, at 188–189; Schachter, 'The Right of States to Use Armed Force', 82 *Michigan L Rev* (1984) 1620, at 1634–1635, on the other. In the Nicaragua case, *supra* note 1, at para. 194, the ICJ avoided a pronouncement on the matter.

[76] Cannizaro, *supra* note 73, at 782.

[77] Gazzini, *supra* note 31, at 143; a similar point is made by Gill, 'The Temporal Dimension of Self-Defence: Anticipation, Pre-Emption, Prevention and Immediacy', 11 *J Conflict & Security L* (2006) 361, at 368–369.

[78] *Cf. supra*, note 67. On the dual effects of the 'accumulation doctrine' see also Gazzini, *supra* note 31, at 144, and further *infra* section 3d2.

qualify as self-defence, as 'coming after the event and when the harm has already been inflicted', they could not 'be characterized as a means of protection'.[79]

Taken together, these factors meant that under the traditional understanding dominant in the late 1980s, states seeking to justify the extraterritorial use of force against terrorists faced almost insurmountable hurdles.

2 Exclusion of Other Justifications

Finally, the traditional *jus ad bellum* narrowed to options for states to use force against terrorist attacks because it tended to view self-defence and Security Council enforcement action as the *only* available exceptions to the ban on the use of force. Insofar as states invoked other grounds, they were likely to be accused of undermining the Charter regime specifically recognizing two exceptions only. The underlying approach – one might speak of the 'exclusivity thesis' – flowed naturally from the text and spirit of the UN Charter.[80] Admittedly, it seemed more difficult to accept in practice: when looking at forcible conduct relevant in the fight against terrorism, humanitarian interventions to rescue nationals held captive abroad were the most obvious exception,[81] yet the legality of such actions remained controversial, and the practice was sometimes explained as an aspect of self-defence, so as to accommodate the exclusivity thesis.[82] On balance, however, the exclusivity thesis was a strong factor leading to the progressive exclusion of traditionally accepted exceptions to the ban on the use of force, and also precluded the acceptance of new exceptions.

As regards potential new exceptions invoked to justify anti-terrorist measures, South Africa's attempt to introduce an expanded doctrine of hot pursuit by land may serve to illustrate the point.[83] The doctrine, in South Africa's argument, justified limited breaches of Article 2(4) UNC, namely incursions into foreign territory as part of an ongoing pursuit of offenders. Hot pursuit was introduced as a novel justification permitting responses where reliance on self-defence failed, e.g., for lack of attribution. Yet, as Christine Gray noted rather benevolently, 'this doctrine was not well-received'[84] – in fact it was resoundingly rejected in SC Resolution 568 (1985), in which the Council 'denounce[d] and reject[ed] racist South Africa's practice of "hot pursuit"' as an attempt to 'destabilize and terrorize Botswana and other countries'. This denunciation of course was part of a general condemnation of apartheid South Africa, yet it was based on the legal principle that the Charter's exceptions to Article 2(4) UNC were exhaustive.[85]

---

[79] Bowett, *supra* note 74.

[80] Randelzhofer, *supra* note 19, Art. 51 MN 3.

[81] See N. Ronzitti, *Rescuing Nationals Abroad Through Military Coercion and Intervention on Grounds of Humanity* (1985) for a comprehensive account.

[82] See the cautious assessment by Gray, *supra* note 33, at 156–160.

[83] For details see *ibid.*, at 136–137; and further Kwakwa, 'South Africa's May 1986 Military Incursions into Neighbouring African States', 12 *Yale J Int'l L* (1987) 421. A similar argument was made by Rhodesia in the 1970s: see Luttig, 'The Legality of the Rhodesian Military Ocrations inside Mozambique – the Poblem of Hot Pursuit on Land' 3 *S African Yrbk of Int'l L* (1977) 136.

[84] Gray, *supra* note 33, at 137.

[85] For more on the doctrine see N. Poulantzas, *The Right of Hot Pursuit in International Law* (2002), at 11 ff; Singh, 'The Right of Hot Pursuit on Land: an Inaccurate and Unfortunate Analogy from Law of Sea', 42 *Civil & Military LJ on Rule of Law, Military Jurisprudence and Legal Aid* (2006) 71.

With respect to formerly accepted exceptions, the doctrine of armed reprisals (sometimes described as 'forcible self-help') probably has been the most prominent 'victim' of the exclusivity thesis.[86] Under the pre-Charter rules, the right to take armed reprisals had been part of the regular rules on countermeasures – accepted in principle, subject to the requirements of necessity and proportionality, and to be distinguished from self-defence by its character as an enforcement measure aimed at inducing compliance with international law.[87] Not requiring an 'armed attack' and not limited to defensive reactions, the concept of armed reprisal of course would have been a convenient tool in the fight against terrorism; it might have justified forcible responses to the use of force below the threshold of an armed attack, where the threat was no longer immediate, or where the real purpose of the response was to deter future attacks, or even to punish offenders.[88] Convenient though it was, the doctrine plainly could not be squared with the Charter's comprehensive ban on force, and was denounced 'on every possible occasion'.[89] Actual instances of state practice (such as the British bombing of Fort Harib in Yemen in 1964) were condemned from the 1960s;[90] from 1970 onwards, important documents such as the Friendly Relations Declaration[91] or the Helsinki Final Act[92] almost inevitably contained generalized exclusionary clauses, e.g., obliging states 'to refrain from acts of reprisal involving the use of force'.[93] It does not come as a surprise that states, even when they took anti-terrorist measures the real aim of which was to retaliate hardly ever portrayed their conduct as an 'armed reprisal', but instead invoked self-defence, even where that on the facts seemed less plausible.[94]

E *The Past: Taking Stock*

The terrorist threat for many states was very real 20 years ago. The problem existed and was addressed by an emerging regime of international rules against terrorism. Yet within that regime the use of force against terrorism did not play a central role. Insofar as the international community engaged in the fight against terror, it largely followed a 'criminal law strategy',[95] seeking to criminalize certain

---

[86] See the detailed account by Barsotti, 'Armed Reprisals', in Cassese, *supra* note 4, at 79. For an earlier and more positive assessment of the doctrine *cf.* Bowett, *supra* note 74.

[87] Gazzini, *supra* note 31, at 163 ff.

[88] On the relation between both concepts see *ibid.*, at 203; Bowett, *supra* note 74, at 3.

[89] Gazzini, *supra* note 31, at 166.

[90] On the Harib incident see SC Res. 188 (1964); and further SC Res. 111 (1956), 171 (1962), 316 (1972), 332 (1973), 573 (1985); as well as GA Res. 41/38 (1986).

[91] GA Res. 2625 (XXV) (principle I.6). By the same token, the restrictive analysis could not accept the use of force based on a broadly-construed doctrine of necessity. Notwithstanding academic debate (e.g. Schachter, *supra* note 29, at 225 ff), states did not invoke necessity as a self-standing legal justification.

[92] 14 ILM (1975) 1292 (Declaration on Principles Guiding Relations between Participating States (Basket 1), Principle II.3).

[93] GA Res. 2625 (XXV) (principle I.6).

[94] To give but one example, the US was at pains to portray its 1986 attacks on Libya as an act of self-defence. Most other states (and commentators) rather saw it as an armed reprisal: see Franck, *supra* note 5, at 89–91; Gray, *supra* note 33, at 196.

[95] The term is borrowed from S. Neff, *War and the Law of Nations* (2005), at 382.

terrorist activities and to improve cooperation between states. The 'military mode of operation',[96] approaching terrorism by cross-border military force, remained exceptional. To give but one illustration, Gilbert Guillaume's 1989 Hague Lecture on '*Terrorisme et droit international*' addressed sectoral conventions, issues of humanitarian law, and criminal cooperation at some length, and then treated forcible responses against terror in a mere five pages.[97]

It could do so because, as far as forcible responses were concerned, states had agreed on a general ban, but were unwilling to apply the existing exceptions to the fight against terrorism. There was little to expect from a collective security system paralysed by block confrontation. The Security Council was incapable of addressing terrorist threats, let alone doing so by forcible means. This left the unilateral option, which some states – notably Israel, South Africa, and the United States – did assert. However, their claims, whether based on self-defence or some other legal construction, were never accepted. To the clear majority of states, 20 years ago, to admit the unilateral use of force against terrorists meant to invite abuse. The restrictive approach was easy to bring in line with the wording of the UN Charter. Influenced by experience of two world wars, the drafters had excluded 'the unilateral use of force ... as far as possible'.[98] Article 2(4) UNC placed a heavy onus on states using force. Self-defence as the only relevant exception allowing for unilateral force was accepted as a temporary right aimed at repelling armed attacks. Subsequent practice and jurisprudence, true to the drafters' intention to minimize the availability of lawful force, construed this exception narrowly, and rejected attempts to maintain or introduce unwritten exceptions.

Admittedly, in some respects, the seemingly rigid rules were handled rather flexibly. During the 1960s and 1970s, freedom from colonial domination seemed a 'legitimate cause', and the fight against it arguably could be pursued by means of force.[99] But for obvious reasons that argument was not applied to the fight against terrorism. Divided by political ideology, the international community did not consider 'freedom from terrorism' a legitimate cause which would have required a flexible application of the rules against force or should be fought by military means. In some instances, it may have lacked the power actually to prevent the use of force against terrorists, but it was not prepared to give blessing to such conduct.

3 The Present: Anti-terrorist Force 2009

A *The Restrictive Analysis under Pressure*

The last two decades have presented states with ample opportunity to revisit the rules governing anti-terrorist force. On the face of it, the Charter regime is the same: Articles 2(4), 42/43, and 51 UNC still apply. As often, states have shown a remarkable

---

[96] *Ibid.*, at 383.
[97] Guillaume, *supra* note 70, at 287. Forcible responses are dealt with at 402–407.
[98] As put by Randelzhofer, *supra* note 33, Art. 51 MN 4.
[99] *Cf.* Gray, *supra* note 33, at 59 ff for a clear summary of debates.

374   *EJIL* 20 (2009), 359–397

reluctance formally to change existing rules. In fact, even reform initiatives set up to study initiatives such as the High Level Panel on Threats, Challenges and Change deny the need for reform.[100] However, the restrictive regime dominant 20 years ago has come under strain. Within the collective security system, the Security Council has reinvented itself and has used its powers creatively.[101] While that development has mostly been welcomed, states and commentators increasingly question whether the drafters of the Charter were wise to exclude 'the unilateral use of force ... as far as possible'.[102] Outside the anti-terrorism context, this is brought out by renewed debates about humanitarian intervention or force against pirates just as new discussions about intervention in failed states or forcible interdiction at sea: sceptics upholding the restrictive view may still draw support from the text of the Charter rules (as traditionally interpreted), but by and large seem to be on the defensive.

Legal debates about anti-terrorist force bear distinctive features, but by and large fit in with the general development. An increasing number of states considers terrorist activities to be a threat which has to be addressed through multilateral or unilateral action, including by forcible means. There is still no comprehensive anti-terrorism convention, but special sectoral treaties have mushroomed, and have been complemented by far-reaching anti-terrorism rules enacted as part of secondary United Nations law.[103] These new rules are informed by a new 'a-contextual' approach which is willing to ignore the root causes of terrorism and denounce it as criminal irrespective of its motives.[104] 'Freedom from terrorism' thus is increasingly regarded as a universal community value.[105] Conversely, the fight against terrorism is increasingly regarded as a legitimate cause which might warrant a 'military approach'[106] and allow readjustments to the *jus ad bellum*. To analyse this development in a more nuanced way it is necessary to revisit the three different aspects of the traditional regime – the ban on force, the collective security option, and the exception(s) allowing for unilateral force.

B *The Robust Interpretation Affirmed*

Very little needs to be said on the ban on force. Notwithstanding the introductory comments just made, in this respect there have been few developments. To begin with, the ban on force still, as 20 years ago, does not prohibit the use of force against terrorists as such, but only in international relations between states. As such it covers the extraterritorial use against terrorists based in another country, but does so only indirectly.

---

[100] See High-Level Panel Report, 'A More Secure World: Our Shared Responsibility. Report of the High-level Panel on Threats, Challenges and Change' (UN Doc. A/59/565), Annex I (Recommendations), at para. 53: 'Article 51 of the Charter of the United Nations should be neither rewritten nor reinterpreted'.

[101] See *infra*, section 3C.

[102] As put by Randelzhofer, *supra* note 33, Art. 51 MN 4. For similar observations see Davis, *supra* note 17, at 635–636; Kenny, *supra* note 56, at 1164.

[103] See further *infra*, section 3C.

[104] Klein, *supra* note 25, at 319 ('*condemnation "décontextualisée" du terrorisme*').

[105] This is well captured in Kofi Annan's much-cited statement that 'a terrorist attack on one country is an attack on humanity as a whole': UN Doc. S/PV.4370.

[106] *Cf.* Neff, *supra* note 95, at 382–383.

As regards the scope of the prohibition, even though the traditional regime has come under strain, the comprehensive ban on force has not been seriously questioned. Admittedly, in heated exchanges (both within and outside the anti-terrorism context), some commentators have rehearsed old arguments about the allegedly limited scope of the prohibition,[107] while others (notably in the United States) have suggested the Charter system had become obsolete.[108] But these claims have been few and far between, and the argument underlying them has met with the very limited amount of attention that it deserved.[109] As under the old law, the contemporary *jus ad bellum* of course is capable of distinguishing between grave and minor infractions of the prohibition against force. International lawyers however seem as unwilling as before to read into Article 2(4) UNC any *de minimis* exception. Instead, the robust interpretation continues to enjoy the support of the large majority of states and commentators.[110]

C *The Security Council's New Activism (and Its Limits)*

In contrast, the collective security system has confronted the problem of terrorism; as a consequence, it is today a real possibility that states using force against terrorists should be in a position to do so with the blessing of the Security Council. This is a result of (i) the Security Council's *renaissance* since 1989 and (ii) its active role in the fight against terrorism. As far as the use of force against terrorists is concerned, the new potential has however not been fully used to date (iii).

(i)   As is well-known, in the last two decades the Security Council has asserted its role in the international system and has adopted a very liberal interpretation of its powers under Chapter VII UNC.[111] In fact, so completely has it re-invented itself that worries about the Council's paralysis have quickly given way to concerns about the limits of its powers.[112] While indeed worrying in many respects, the

---

[107]   See with respect to terrorism, e.g., Travalio, 'Terrorism, International Law, and the Use of Military Force', 18 *Wisconsin Int'l LJ* (2000) 145. *Cf.* Gray, *supra* note 33, at 31 ff for a summary of further debates.

[108]   *Cf.* Glennon, 'Why the Security Council Failed', *Foreign Affairs*, May/June 2003, 16; and *ibid.*, 'How International Rules Die', 93 *Georgia LJ* (2005) 939, for the boldest assertions.

[109]   For a rebuttal see, e.g., Wandscher, *supra* note 10, at 127–128; and the refreshingly 'sober' remarks by Wood, 'The Law on the Use of Force: Current Challenges', 11 *Singapore Yrbk Int'l L* (2007) 1, at 2–5.

[110]   See Randelzhofer, *supra* note 33, Art. 2(4) MN 35–37 (with many further references). Note also that the 2005 World Summit Outcome reaffirms the scope of the prohibition without mentioning 'territorial integrity' and 'political independence' (i.e., the two aspects of Art. 2(4) UNC which had served to justify restrictive interpretations): '[w]e reiterate the obligation of all Member States to refrain in their international relations from the threat or use of force in any manner inconsistent with the Charter': GA Res. A 60/1, at para. 77.

[111]   For a clear assessment of this process see Frowein and Krisch in Simma, *supra* note 19 (2nd ed.), Introduction to Chapter VII, MN 7–10; Cortright *et al.*, 'The Sanctions Era : Themes and Trends in UN Security Council Sanctions since 1990', in V. Lowe *et al.* (eds), *The United Nations Security Council and War: The Evolution of Thought and Practice since 1945* (2007), at 205; Delbrück, 'Staatliche Souveraänitaät und die neue Rolle des Sicherheitsrates der Vereinten Nationen' [1993] *Verfassung und Recht in Übersee* 6.

[112]   See with respect to anti-terrorist sanctions van Herik, 'The Security Council's Targeted Sanctions Regimes: in Need of Better Protection of the Individual', 20 *Leiden J Int'l L* (2007) 797; Bothe, 'Security Council's Targeted Sanctions Against Presumed Terrorists: the Need to Comply with Human Rights Standards', 6 *J Int'l Criminal Justice* (2008) 541.

Security Council's practice has quickly disposed of two legal problems which might in the past have limited the potential for collective action against terrorism. First, the Council has 'uncoupled'[113] Articles 42 and 43 UNC.[114] It is beyond doubt today that on the basis of Article 42 UNC, the Council can authorize military measures by coalitions of the willing, and that this authorization should justify the – otherwise illegal – use of force. Secondly, no one seriously questions the Council's right to qualify as a 'threat to peace' situations which have nothing to do with the use of inter-State force,[115] Chapter VII has thus been uncoupled from Articles 2(4) and 51 UNC. Both developments, it is submitted, are fully in line with the text and spirit of the Charter. Especially the second development has made it possible for the Security Council to take a leading role in the fight against terrorism.

(ii)   A leading role it has indeed assumed. There are two aspects to this. First, practice since 1989 makes it abundantly clear that acts of terrorism can amount to threats to peace in the sense of Article 39 UNC.[116] The Council has stated so time and again, both with respect to concrete instances of terrorist violence[117] and in a more principled manner.[118] With respect to the former, it may be noted that it has addressed acts of terrorism without an evident international element.[119] As regards statements of principle, SC Resolution 1566 (2004) is particularly clear; in it the Council, acting under Chapter VII, '[c]ondemns in the strongest terms all acts of terrorism irrespective of their motivation, whenever and by whomsoever committed, as one of the most serious threats to peace and security'.[120] Practice thus has clarified the substantive conditions for Security Council enforcement action, and leaves no doubt that the Security Council can adopt sanctions against terrorists and terrorism.

Secondly, as far as actual sanctions are concerned, the picture is more nuanced. Of course, once the Security Council has qualified an act of terrorism as a threat to the peace, the road towards sanctions under Articles 41 and 42 UNC is in principle open. Yet the Council has used these provisions rather differently. Its new activism is based on enforcement measures of a non-military character. In fact, with respect to Article 41 UNC, there is very little the Council has *not* done, and it may have exceeded its competences more than once in the process. To give just some examples, during the last two decades, as part of a fight against terrorism, the Council has

---

[113] Franck, *supra* note 5, at 24.

[114] *Cf.* Gazzini, *supra* note 31, at 35 ff, 43 ff; Frowein and Krisch, *supra* note 111, Art. 42 MN 20–22.

[115] See references *supra*, at note 111.

[116] *Cf.* Gazzini, *supra* note 31, at 33: 'in a string of resolutions ... the Security Council without hesitation declared international terrorism a threat to peace'. See Klein, supra note 25, at 328 ff for a detailed account.

[117] See, e.g., SC Res. 1368 and 1373 (concerning 9/11 attacks), SC Res. 1438 (Bali), SC Res. 1530 (Madrid). *Cf.* Gray, *supra* note 33, at 227–228, for further detail, and www.un.org/terrorism/sc-res.shtml for a list of resolutions.

[118] See, e.g., SC Res. 1377 ('Declaration on the Global Effort to Combat Terrorism'), SC Res. 1456 ('Declaration on the Issue of Combating Terrorism').

[119] See, e.g., the presidential statement of 1 Sept. 2004 condemning terrorist activities in Russia (UN Doc. S/PRST/2004/31).

[120] SC Res. 1456, second preambular para.

set up a special anti-terrorism committee;[121] it has ordered member states to freeze bank accounts of terror suspects,[122] to prosecute specific terrorist acts,[123] and to extradite terror suspects;[124] and it has even assumed the role of a legislator fast-tracking the usual, and cumbersome, treaty-making process.[125] With regard to non-military sanctions, the fight against terrorism indeed has become a catalyst for an ever-broader understanding of the Security Council's competences.

(iii)   In contrast, the Security Council has not so far authorized the use of anti-terrorist force as a military sanction.[126] While stretching the interpretation of Article 41 UNC, it has refrained from applying Article 42 UNC in the fight against terrorism. This does not mean that it has not contemplated military sanctions. In SC Resolutions 1368 and 1373, the Council expressly noted that the attacks of 9/11 had triggered a right of self-defence – an issue to be addressed below[127] – but this amounted to a multilateral endorsement of a claim to use force unilaterally, rather than multilateral enforcement action in the sense of Article 42.[128] The reasons for this absence of practice under Article 42 UNC remain a matter for speculation. With respect to the 9/11 attacks, there is little doubt that the Council would have authorized enforcement action had the United States wanted to adopt a 'multilateral' approach.[129] In most other cases, military measures were not considered useful, and not contemplated by the victim state. Insofar as the Security Council has adopted general 'law-making' resolutions, its conduct has not concerned specific violent acts, and thus military sanctions have simply not been called for. Finally, although developments during the last two decades have removed the legal obstacles which might have previously prevented collective action against terrorists, the political hurdles for Security Council sanctions remain the same: in particular, sanctions require the support (or at least acquiescence) of all five permanent members (the P5). And while the consensus among the P5 during the last decade has been astonishing, the issue of military enforcement measures remains sensitive, and agreement cannot be taken for granted.

To sum up, unlike 20 years ago, it is beyond doubt today that the Security Council can authorize military measures against terrorists, and thereby justify the extraterritorial use of force by a state implementing that mandate. To date, however, such military enforcement action has remained a theoretical possibility. Recent practice

---

[121]   SC Res. 1267.

[122]   See, e.g., SC Res. 1373, para. 1c; SC Res. 1735, para. 1a.

[123]   See, e.g., SC Res. 1373, para. 2e.

[124]   SC Res. 731, para. 3; SC Res. 748, para. 1.

[125]   See notably SC Res. 1373.

[126]   Gray, *supra* note 33, at 227.

[127]   *Infra*, section 3D.

[128]   Eisemann, 'Attaques du 11 septembre et exercise d'un droit naturel de légitime défense', in O. Corten *et al.* (eds), *Le droit international face au terrorisme* (2002), at 239.

[129]   For critical comments on the US decision not to follow a multilateral approach see Delbrück, 'The Fight Against Global Terrorism: Self-Defense or Collective Security as International Police Action?', 44 *German Yrbk Int'l L* (2001) 9. See Fassbender, 'The UN Security Council and International Terrorism', in Bianchi, *supra* note 12, at 83, 88–89, for further detail on the debates preceding the adoption of SC Res. 1373.

378 *EJIL* 20 (2009), 359–397

has clarified that international law permits it, but also shows that it remains at best an exceptional option.[130]

D A Broader Right to Use Force Unilaterally?

The key developments during the last two decades affect the rules governing the *unilateral* use of force against terrorists. Unlike with respect to the multilateral option, there has been a considerable body of practice – states exercising force against terrorists have, expressly or by implication, moved beyond the traditional regime. This body of recent practice needs to be briefly surveyed (1) before it can be evaluated, especially in the light of recent jurisprudence (2).

1 International Practice: Beyond the Traditional Approach

As noted above, ever since 1945, states have used force against terrorist threats; yet their practice for a long while was sparse, and typically critically received by the international community. The last two decades have seen a considerable shift. The number of states which claim a right to take forcible anti-terrorist measures has markedly increased, while the willingness of other states to condemn such measures has decreased. The situations in which force has been used (or a corresponding right has been asserted) vary considerably, but have almost exclusively been explained as exercises in self-defence.

(i)   To begin with the most obvious piece of evidence, there was general agreement that the United States could resort to measures of self-defence in response to the 9/11 attacks.[131] This it did from October 2001 by launching *Operation Enduring Freedom*.[132] That operation has now been on-going for 7½ years and has served as a justification for forcible measures against Al-Qaeda and Taleban targets, but also includes a 'maritime component'. While initial debates about the conditions of self-defence have ebbed away, over the years there has been growing concern that *Operation Enduring Freedom* overstretched the limits of self-defence.[133] Still, a series of international relations continues to underline the importance of the operation as part of the international efforts to stabilize the situation in Afghanistan.[134]

(ii)   The response against the 9/11 attacks is not an isolated incident.[135] Quite to the contrary, in a variety of instances, states have reacted against terrorist attacks by

---

[130] Gray, *supra* note 33, at 228.

[131] For details see Eisemann, *supra* note 128, at 239; Franck, 'Terrorism and the Right of Self-Defense', 95 *AJIL* (2001) 839; Stahn, 'Nicaragua is Dead, long live Nicaragua!', in Walter *et al.* (eds.), *supra* note 10, at 827.

[132] *Cf.* Gray, *supra* note 33, at 203 ff (including comments on whether Operation Enduring Freedom could now be justified on grounds other than Art. 51 UNC).

[133] For an early critique see Corten and Dubuisson, *supra* note 51.

[134] See, e.g., SC Res. 1510, 1589, 1659, 1707.

[135] See Bruha and Tams, *supra* note 55, at 95–97; and the very detailed survey of state practice by G. Wettberg, *The International Legality of Self-Defence against Non-State Actors* (2007), at 139 ff.

using massive military force, including the invasion of states from which terrorists were operating.[136]

Just as in the past, Israel has remained one of the most ardent supporters of a broad right to self-defence. In 2003, in response to a suicide bombing in Haifa it bombed Palestine camps north of Damascus.[137] In the summer of 2006, following rocket attacks against it by the Lebanon-based Hezbollah, Israel responded first with bombardments and then an invasion of Lebanon.[138] The international community's reaction to the raids of October 2003 as well as to the July War of 2006 was mixed. There was broad agreement (with respect to both conflicts) that Israel's use of force had been disproportionate. However, a considerable number of states, especially with respect to the July 2006 war, in principle accepted Israel's right to use force against terrorist organizations such as Hamas or Hezbollah. Israel itself was at pains to attribute Hezbollah's conduct to Lebanon and Syria, but did not claim that these states had controlled and directed Hezbollah's conduct.

Furthermore, since the 1990s, Turkey has repeatedly invoked a right to use force against Kurdish PKK bases in northern Iraq.[139] The 1990s saw frequent incursions. A decade later, cross-border attacks of October 2007 led to an unprecedented escalation, culminating in 'Operation Sun', a ground offensive during which several thousand Turkish troops invaded northern Iraq in late February 2008. The international community's reaction was characterized by a 'mixture of sympathy and concern'[140] for Turkey's conduct. Just as with respect to the July War, states stressed the need for reactions to be proportionate, and on that basis criticized the Turkish use of force. Most reactions however 'carefully refrained from formally condemning Turkey's behaviour'.[141]

(iii)   When looking at uses of force below the threshold of invasions proper, the number of instances in which states have used force against terrorist attacks increases considerably. Not all of them are well documented, but to support the argument made here, it may be sufficient briefly to refer to the following incidents:

- In 1998, in response to attacks on US embassies in Kenya and Tanzania, the United States bombarded a pharmaceutical plant in the Sudan (allegedly used by terrorists) and a terrorist base in Afghanistan.[142] To justify its conduct, the United

---

[136] In addition to the examples addressed in the following, the Ethiopian invasion in Somalia deserves to be mentioned. For contrasting perspectives on the conflict see Yihdego, 'Ethiopia's Military Action Against the Union of Islamic Courts and Others in Somalia: Some Legal Implications', 56 *ICLQ* (2007) 666; and Corten, 'La licéité douteuse de l'intervention militaire éthiopienne en Somalie et ses implications sur l'argument de l'"intervention consentie"', 111 *RGDIP* (2007) 513.

[137] Cf. Wandscher, *supra* note 10, at 196–197; Gray, *supra* note 33, at 234–237.

[138] For details see Zimmermann, 'The Second Lebanon War: Jus ad bellum, jus in bello and the Issue of Proportionality', 11 *Max Planck Yrbk UN L* (2007) 99; and Cannizaro, *supra* note 73, at 779.

[139] See the detailed account by Ruys, 'Quo Vadit Jus ad Bellum? A Legal Analysis of Turkey's Military Operations against the PKK in Northern Iraq', 12 *Melbourne J Int'l L* (2008) 334; and cf. Wettberg, *supra* note 135, at 144–151, for details on the Turkish raids of the 1990s.

[140] Ruys, *supra* note 139, at 344.

[141] *Ibid.* (where this statement is made to describe the EU's response. As Ruys notes subsequently, '[o]ther reactions from the international community were generally analoguous to the EU approach': *ibid.*).

[142] See Lobel, 'The Use of Force to Respond to Terrorist Attacks: The Bombing of Sudan and Afghanistan', 24 *Yale J Int'l L* (1999) 537.

380   *EJIL* 20 (2009), 359–397

States referred to Article 51 UNC but did not allege any substantial involvement of Afghanistan and/or Sudan in the activities. The international community's reaction was mixed, ranging from condemnation (especially of the attacks on Sudan) to open or tacit approval. Similarly (though involving an instance of alleged 'state terrorism'), the United States had fired missiles on the headquarters of the Iraqi Intelligence Service in Baghdad in 1993, in response to an alleged assassination attempt on President Bush.[143]

- From the mid-1990s, Iran on several occasions invoked Article 51 UNC to justify the use of force against bases of the Mujahedin-e Khalq Organization (MKO) on Iraqi territory.[144] While Iraq denounced the use of force as an act of aggression, the international community did not condemn it. Equally 'uncommented'[145] remained Iran's incursions into Iraqi territory in pursuit of Kurdish armed bands (labelled 'organized terrorist mercenaries'). There was little evidence suggesting that the conduct of the MKO (let alone that of Kurdish insurgents) could have been attributed to Iraq under the traditional 'direction and control' test.

- In 2000 and again in 2004, Russia asserted a right to respond extraterritorially to Islamic terrorists.[146] In 2007, following attacks by Chechen rebels, it conducted air strikes against Chechen bases in the Pankisi Gorge in Georgia, claiming that Georgia 'had been unable to establish a security zone in the area of the [Russian–Georgian] border, continues to ignore Security Council Resolution 1373 and does not put an end to the bandit sorties and attacks on adjoining areas of Russia'.[147] Responses were mixed, but again there was no principled condemnation that would have denied Russia's right to use force extraterritorially.

- In March 2008, Colombian forces moved into Ecuadorian territory in pursuit of rebels belonging to FARC (which it considers a terrorist organization).[148] The OAS qualified the operation as a 'violation of [Ecuador's] sovereignty';[149] other international organizations were largely silent; the United States expressed support.

(iv)   The examples mentioned so far involve the actual use of force by states. The new trend they reflect is confirmed by statements. Russia's assertion of a broad right to use force extraterritorially has been referred to already.[150] Along similar lines, Australia claimed a right to use force extraterritorially against terrorists threatening to attack Australia or its citizens following the Bali bombings of October 2002.[151] As for more principled statements, the 2005 African Union Non-Aggression and Common

---

[143] See Reisman, 'The Raid on Baghdad: Some Reflections on Its Lawfulness and Implications', 5 *EJIL* (1994) 120; Condorelli, 'A propos de l'attaque américaine contre l'Iraq du 26 juin 1993', 5 *EJIL* (1994) 134; Kritsiotis, 'The Legality of the 1993 U.S. Missile Strike on Iraq and the Right of Self-Defence in International Law', 45 *ICLQ* (1996) 162.

[144] Wandscher, *supra* note 10, at 148–149; Wettberg, *supra* note 135, at 151–152.

[145] *Cf. ibid.*, at 152; and see also Franck, *supra* note 5, at 64.

[146] *Cf.* Wandscher, *supra* note 10, at 197–198.

[147] UN Doc. S/2002/1012. *Cf.* Gray, *supra* note 33, at 230.

[148] See Murphy, *supra* note 57, at 25–26 of the manuscript.

[149] OAS CP/Res 930 (1632/08) (5 Mar. 2008).

[150] *Supra* note 147.

[151] Ruys, *supra* note 139.

Defence Pact expressly qualifies the harbouring of terrorists, as well as any provision of support for them, as an act of aggression.[152] Finally, the United States' 2002 National Security Strategy went well beyond these claims; it famously asserted a right of pre-emptive self-defence against non-imminent threats, in particular those by terrorist organizations.[153]

(v)　Finally, these instances seem part of a broader trend among states to exercise force against attacks by non-state actors – attacks which would have been difficult to justify under the traditional approach. While not specifically relying on a right to use force against terrorist attacks, states like Rwanda, Tajikistan, or Burma/Myanmar have all responded to cross-border attacks by insurgents or rebels. For that purpose, they have all moved troops into neighbouring states even though these, under the traditional rules of attribution, could hardly be said to have directed or controlled the insurgents.[154]

The brief summaries provided in the previous paragraphs of course cannot replace a detailed assessment, but clearly point in one direction: the international community today is much less likely to deny, as a matter of principle, that states can invoke self-defence against terrorist attacks not imputable to another state. Instead debate has shifted towards issues of necessity and proportionality (i.e. the scope of self-defence measures). This is particularly clear in the international community's responses to Israel's repeated claims to use self-defence, in particular the July War of 2006.[155] The vigorous and principled condemnation of the 1970s and 1980s has been replaced by concerns that Israel's actions should remain proportionate (which often they have not been). The traditional approach seeking to minimize the availability of lawful force in that respect has come under pressure – as Tom Franck noted already in 2002, assertions of a right to exercise self-defence against terrorist and other non-state attacks 'are no longer exceptional claims'.[156]

2 Assessing Recent Practice

While Franck's observation is shared by many commentators, it is much more difficult to assess how recent practice can be fitted into the traditional legal regime. This is

---

[152]　*Cf.* Art. 1(c)(xi): '[t]he following shall constitute acts of aggression: ... the encouragement, support, harbouring or provision of any assistance for the commission of terrorist acts and other violent trans-national organized crimes against a Member State': available at: www.africa-union.org/root/AU/Documents/Treaties/text/Non%20Aggression%20Common%20Defence%20Pact.pdf.

[153]　White House, *The National Security Strategy of the United States of America*, available at: www.whitehouse.gov/nsc/nss.pdf. For extensive debates see Reisman and Armstrong, 'The Past and Future of the Claim of Preemptive Self-Defense', 100 *AJIL* (2006) 525; Hoffmeister, 'Preemptive Strikes: a New Normative Framework', 44 *Archiv des Völkerrechts* (2006) 187; Murphy, 'The Doctrine of Preemptive Self-defense', 50 *Villanova L Rev* (205) 699; Bothe, 'Terrorism and the Legality of Pre-emptive Force', 14 *EJIL* (2003) 227.

[154]　*Cf.* Franck, *supra* note 5, at 64; Gray, *supra* note 33, at 140 (qualifying these instances as 'more straightforward claims to self-defence against irregular forces'); and Wettberg, *supra* note 135, at 190–192 and 204.

[155]　Cannizaro, *supra* note 73, at 782. Even Pierre Klein, otherwise very sceptical of a more flexible approach to self-defence, describes recent responses as '*pour le moins contrastées*': Klein, *supra* note 25, at 406.

[156]　Franck, *supra* note 5, at 64.

382 *EJIL* 20 (2009), 359–397

mainly due to two factors. First, the more recent practice affects many central features of the traditional, restrictive approach. Secondly, the new trends emerging in practice are clearly discernable, but may require further consolidation before bringing about a readjustment of the law. This is in particular because recent rulings by the international courts have addressed many aspects of the *jus ad bellum* and need to be taken into account. The current law thus is in many respects in a state of flux. That said, in at least one respect states and courts have been clear: they have treated the new practice under the rubric of self-defence, and have not 'invented' new exceptions to the use of force. This aspect needs to be addressed before the challenges to the traditional understanding of self-defence can be evaluated.

a. The 'Ritual Incantation'[157] of Self-Defence

The new practice summarized above is marked by its diversity. States have used anti-terrorist force in very different situations, ranging from 'on the spot' reactions to cross-border violence to long-term campaigns with broadly defined objectives (notably *Operation Enduring Freedom*). In addition to repelling attacks, their use of force has typically served non-defensive purposes, notably as a means of retaliation (e.g., in the United States' raid on Baghdad) or as a means of enforcing international rules against terrorism (e.g., Russia's attacks on Georgian territory). Given this diversity, it is interesting to note that, almost inevitably, states seeking to justify their conduct have invoked the right of self-defence. In contrast, they have not re-opened debates about the permissibility of armed reprisals, even where their actions seemed to follow the logic of retaliation.[158] What is more, although there has been much talk about the 'enforcement paradigm',[159] states have not asserted a right to enforce international law against terrorists as a self-standing exception to the ban on force, but considered it as a sub-set of self-defence.[160] The diversity of new, anti-terrorist practice thus stands in stark contrast to the almost monotonous assertions of self-defence. Anti-terrorist practice thus supports Christine Gray's more general observation that references to self-defence today may almost amount to the 'ritual incantation of a magic formula'.[161]

On the face of it, the 'ritual incantation' of self-defence may be comforting. For present purposes, it narrows down the field of inquiry considerably. If states do not invoke other grounds (even though they may better reflect their actual conduct), they do not seem to consider that these other grounds would afford justification. To take but one example, if states resort to what may look like reprisals, but then do all they can to explain their conduct as an act of self-defence, they – quite correctly[162] – do

---

[157] Gray, *supra* note 33, at 119.

[158] Gazzini, *supra* note 33, at 203–204; Gray, *supra* note 133, at 197–198.

[159] See, e.g., W. Lietzau, *Combating Terrorism: Law Enforcement or War*, in *Terrorism and International Law. Challenges and Responses* (2003), at 75; Dinstein, *supra* note 71, at 247.

[160] *Ibid.*, at 247 ('Extra-territorial law enforcement is a form of self-defence').

[161] Gray, *supra* note 33, at 119.

[162] In fact, official condemnations of armed reprisals remain *en vogue*: see, e.g., Art. 50(1)(a) of the ILC's Articles on State Responsibility (Annex to GA Res. 56/83), which provides: '[c]ountermeasures shall not affect: (a) The obligation to refrain from the threat or use of force as embodied in the Charter of the

not seem to think that a plausible case for the legality of armed reprisals can be made out.[163] In that respect, it may be said that, notwithstanding the new practice, at some level the traditional *jus ad bellum* continues to function. States do not publicly question the main pillars on which it rests. Discussion still takes place within the parameters of the traditional system; that system has not lost its capacity to channel debates.

On the other hand, while the pillars of the system still stand, they may be eroding rather fast. Invocations of Article 51 UNC (or even 'ritual incantations') may indicate compliance with the system's logic, but could also be signs of its degeneration. The point was very clearly made by Daniel Bethlehem, who noted '[t]he reliance by States on self-defence in virtually every conceivable circumstance', which in turn had led 'to normative drift, as attempts have been made to stretch the concept'.[164] As will be shown, this 'normative drift' indeed affects key features of the regime of self-defence. The subsequent sections address three aspects of the traditional regime which have come under particular strain, and in so doing seek to give a balanced account of the present state of the law governing anti-terrorist force.

b. What Remains of the Strict Rules on Attribution?

Much of the discussion so far has centred on the inter-state reading of self-defence. Given the number of responses to terrorist attacks, many commentators have queried whether the 'effective control' test of attribution was still valid. The issue has prompted rather heated exchanges among commentators,[165] especially after the International Court of Justice had seized the opportunity to address the matter. In retrospect, some claims made during these debates appear exaggerated. Especially in the immediate aftermath of the 9/11 attacks, many commentators proclaimed a radical re-reading

---

United Nations'. Summarizing comments by governments, the ILC's Special Rapporteur had observed that 'the first and uncontroversial exclusion is forcible countermeasures', and further noted: 'there is, in any event, no basis in modern international law for countermeasures involving the use of force as prohibited by the Charter': Third Report on State Responsibility, UN Doc. A/CN.4/507, at para. 335.

[163] See Gray, *supra* note 33, at 197. Contrast Gazzini's more nuanced view (*supra* note 31, at 204); and the very positive assessment put forward by O'Brien, 'Reprisals, Deterrence and Self-defence in Counterterror Operations', 30 *Virginia J Int'l L* (1990) 421.

[164] Bethlehem, 'International Law and the Use of Force: the Law as It Is and as It Should Be' (written evidence to the Select Committee on Foreign Affairs – Minutes of Evidence, 8 June 2004), available at: www.publications.parliament.uk/pa/cm200304/cmselect/cmfaff/441/4060808.htm, at para. 21.

[165] See, e.g., Cassese, 'Terrorism Is also Disrupting Some Crucial Legal Categories of International Law', 12 *EJIL* (2001) 993; Stahn, *supra* note 131, at 827; Kammerhofer, 'The Armed Activities Case and Non-State Actors in Self-Defence Law', 20 *Leiden J Int'l L* (2007) 89; Tomuschat, 'Der 11. September und seine rechtlichen Konsequenzen', 28 *Europäische Grundrechte-Zeitschrift* (2001) 535; Murphy, 'Self-defense and the Israeli Wall Opinion – An Ipse Dixit from the Court?', 99 *AJIL* (2005) 62 and 'Terrorism and the Concept of "Armed Attack" in Article 51 of the U.N. Charter', 43 *Harvard Int'l LJ* (2002) 41; Krajewkski, 'Selbstverteidigung gegen bewaffnete Angriffe nicht-staatlicher Organisationen', 40 *Archiv des Völkerrechts* (2002) 183; Ruys and Verhoeven, 'Attacks by Private Actors and the Right of Self-Defence', 10 *J Conflict & Security L* (2005) 289; Antonopoulos, 'Force by Armed Groups as Armed Attack and the Broadening of Self-defence', 55 *Netherlands Int'l L Rev* (2008) 159; Klein, *supra* note 25, at 386 ff. For earlier assessments by the present writer see Tams, 'Light Treatment of a Complex Problem: The Law of Self-Defence in the Wall Case', 16 *EJIL* (2005) 963 and *supra* note 63; Bruha and Tams, *supra* note 55, at 85.

384   *EJIL* 20 (2009), 359–397

of Article 51 UNC, which completely dispensed with the need for attribution as set out in the *Nicaragua* judgment.[166] Following this new approach, states could resort to self-defence against all types of armed attacks, irrespective of any state involvement. Predictably, this radical re-reading has prompted much discussion, not least by the International Court of Justice.

The ICJ's New Uncertainty

Faced with these new challenges, the International Court of Justice initially seemed willing to defend its traditional approach. In the *Israeli Wall* case, in a 'telegraphic'[167] statement 'startling in its brevity',[168] it observed that 'Article 51 of the Charter … recognizes the existence of an inherent right of self-defence in the case of armed attack *by one State against another State*', and hence did not justify Israeli measures aimed at preventing attacks by terrorists operating from within the occupied territories.[169] One year later, the Court's majority was far more equivocal. It rejected Uganda's reliance on self-defence as a response to armed attacks by a rebel movement operating from within the Democratic Republic of the Congo (DRC), since these could not be attributed to the DRC.[170] In a curious turn of argument, the Court then however expressly left open the question 'whether and under what conditions contemporary international law provides for a right of self-defence against large-scale attacks by irregular forces'.[171] Both pronouncements were criticized by individual judges. Predictably, a number of judges were not convinced by the majority's (lack of) reasoning in the *Israeli Wall* opinion and drew attention to the more recent practice. More importantly, Judges Buergenthal, Kooijmans, and Simma expressly accepted that self-defence was available against armed attacks 'even if [these attacks] cannot be attributed to the territorial State'.[172]

Towards a More Lenient Standard of Attribution

Given the Court's new uncertainty and the amount of new state practice, the better view indeed is that the traditional rules have been modified. This in fact seems to have

---

[166] See, e.g., Murphy, 'Self-defence and the Israeli Wall Opinion', *supra* note 165, at 62 and 'Terrorism and the Concept of "Armed Attack"', *supra* note 165, at 41; Krajewski, *supra* note 165, at 183; Greenwood, 'International Law and the Pre-emptive Use of Force: Afghanistan, Al-Quaeda, and Iraq', 4 *San Diego Int'l LJ* (2003) 17; Franck, *supra* note 131, at 839.
  As noted above (section 2D1), this approach indeed could point to the wording of Art. 51 UNC, which speaks of an 'armed attack' without any further qualification.

[167] Scobbie, 'Words My Mother Never Taught Me – In Defence of the International Court', 99 *AJIL* (2005) 76, at 87.

[168] Murphy, '"Self-defense and the Israeli Wall Opinion', *supra* note 165, at 62.

[169] *Supra* note 63, at para. 139. For comment on the Court's (lack of) reasoning see Murphy, '"Self-defense and the Israeli Wall Opinion', *supra* note 165, at 62; Tams, 'Light Treatment of a Complex Problem', *supra* note 165.

[170] *Supra* note 1, at para. 147: 'the legal and factual circumstances for the exercise of a right to self-defence by Uganda against the DRC were not present'.

[171] *Ibid.*

[172] *DRC-Uganda case*, *supra* note 1, separate opinion of Judge Simma, at para. 12. For similar statements see the separate opinion of Judge Kooijmans in the same case (at para. 30), and Judge Buergenthal's declaration in the *Israeli Wall* opinion, *supra* note 63, at para. 6.

become the prevailing understanding.[173] There is, however, much discussion about the way the new developments can be accommodated. In this respect, the academic debate, suggesting a clear distinction between state attacks and non-state attacks, may have been based on false premises. As noted above, the *Nicaragua* case did not rule out that attacks by non-state actors could be promoted to the level of state attacks, if only the state was sufficiently involved in them; as a consequence, it may have been more flexible than defenders of the traditional approach acknowledged.[174] Conversely, the radical re-reading, by focusing on non-state attacks as such, seemed to take self-defence out of its regulatory context and fails to recognize that it serves as an exception to the comprehensive ban on the *inter-state* use of force.[175] The radical re-reading of self-defence may have provided a justification for the attack on terrorists, but could not explain why states were entitled to violate the territorial sovereignty of the state in which they were based.[176]

In between strict adherence to tradition and radical departure, the more convincing way to accommodate the new practice is to opt for an approach which retains the traditional understanding of self-defence as a justification for the use of force *between states*, but recognizes the existence of special rules on attribution of terrorist activities.[177] This more moderate (but still important) re-reading indeed seems to be borne out by state practice: states invoking self-defence do make an effort to identify links between the territorial state and the terrorist organization in question.[178] What they no longer seem to do is to identify links that are strong enough to amount to 'effective control' as required by the *Nicaragua* test. Instead, contemporary practice suggests that a territorial state has to accept anti-terrorist measures of self-defence directed against its territory where it is responsible for complicity in the activities of terrorists based on its territory – either because of its support below the level of direction and control or because it has provided a safe haven for terrorists. In short, pursuant to this more moderate re-reading, modern practice points towards a special standard of imputability in relations between terrorist groups and host states, arguably most closely resembling international rules against 'aiding and abetting' illegal conduct.[179] The contours

---

[173] See, e.g., Ruys and Verhoeven, *supra* note 165; Stahn, *supra* note 165; Murphy, "Self-defense and the Israeli Wall Opinion', *supra* note 165, at 62; and the references in Bruha and Tams, *supra* note 55, at 94 ff. For different perspectives, contrast Pierre Klein's defence of the traditional approach (*supra* note 25, at 396 ff) and Christine Gray's more cautious assessment (*supra* note 33, at 193 ff). It is submitted that both however fail to appreciate the breadth of new practice.

[174] *Supra*, section 2D1.

[175] *Cf. supra*, section 2B. If states attack terrorists in another country, the ban on force is violated because foreign territory is attacked, not because terrorists as such are targeted.

[176] Antonopolous, *supra* note 165, at 168. To overcome this problem, commentators typically refer back to the arguments about the unwillingness (or even inability) of the territorial state to prevent terrorist activities – conduct which in turn means that the territorial state had to accept the use of force against its territory. This however means that at some level issues of state involvement re-enter the debate.

[177] For a balanced and convincing account of the move towards this 'nuanced position' see Ruys and Verhoeven, *supra* note 165, at 309 ff.

[178] *Ibid.*, at 312.

[179] The 'aiding and abetting' test is explored by Ruys and Verhoeven, *supra* note 165, at 315 ff.

386   *EJIL* 20 (2009), 359–397

of this new test have yet to be firmly established, and it lies in the nature of things that the broadening of attribution standards increases the risk of abuse. However, it is submitted that the concept of 'aiding and abetting' in terrorist activities captures the essence of new practice while still maintaining some degree of predictability. Notably, it broadens the forms of support which trigger a territorial state's responsibility, but does not lose sight of its intention. At the same time, the test seems flexible enough to accommodate issues such as the international condemnation of a state's conduct (e.g. through Security Council resolutions calling on a state to repress terrorists operating on its territory), but also clarifies that where a state is unaware of terrorist conduct it will not be exposed to forcible responses.[180]

The gradual recognition of this new standard of attribution indeed marks a departure from the restrictive test enunciated in *Nicaragua*. Curiously, this departure comes at a time when the *Nicaragua* test has matured into a general (residual) rule of attribution affirmed in the ILC's work on state responsibility[181] and confirmed in the Court's jurisprudence.[182] However, the novelty of the approach should not be overstated. Rules on attribution are not set in stone; Article 51 UNC does not lay down a particular approach. The traditional approach requiring 'effective state control' may have become accepted over time, but it was a standard developed by the Court, not God-given.[183] As a consequence, a move towards a more lenient standard of attribution should not be seen as revolutionary (let alone as blasphemy), but as a process of reform. It brings the new law in line with views expressed in Judge Jennings' dissent, notably his plea for more flexible standards of attribution,[184] and in that respect may have been another illustration of minority views slowly gaining ground. What is more, the more lenient standard of attribution can be said to reflect the growing determination of the international community's fight against terrorism.[185] Finally, by employing the notion of complicity, it builds on a form of involvement which, pursuant to

---

[180] *Ibid.*

[181] See especially Art. 8 ('Conduct directed or controlled by a State'). In the commentary thereto, the ILC makes extensive reference to the Nicaragua judgment, thus acknowledging the origin of the effective control test.

[182] See the ICJ's judgment in *Application of the Convention on the Prevention and Punishment of the Crime of Genocide (Bosnia and Herzegovina v. Serbia and Montenegro)*, Judgment of 26 Feb. 2007, not yet reported (the Bosnian Genocide case), at paras 396 ff.

[183] *Cf.* also Gill, *supra* note 77, at 365: 'the Nicaragua decision, while authoritative, should not be seen as solving once and for all the question of what forms of armed action, and involvement and support for insurgencies, terrorist acts and the like, constitute an armed attack that would trigger the right of self-defence'.

[184] *Cf. supra* note 1, at 533.

[185] In that respect, new developments confirm Oscar Schachter's remarks, made 20 years (*supra* note 29, at 218) that when assessing the required degree of state involvement in terrorist activities, one 'should take account of the strong international policy against terrorism'. As has been noted, in 1989, the international community seemed not (yet) willing to accept this reasoning, and indeed its policy against terrorism may not yet have been that strong after all. Two decades on, Schachter's statement seems to have become an adequate description of the new approach to attribution. What is more, if rules on attribution are capable of reflecting the international community's condemnation of particular conduct (such as terrorism), then this may also explain why the ICJ, in DRC–Uganda, *supra* note 1, at para. 160, seemed to adhere to the traditional test when addressing the attribution of acts committed by irregular bands.

Article 16 of the ILC's Articles and the ICJ's jurisprudence, qualifies as wrongful,[186] and which the African Union's Non-Aggression and Common Defence Pact describes as an aggression.[187]

None of this suggests that the move towards a more lenient rule of attribution is a beneficial development. However, it is a move which the international community seems willing to accept and which should be seen as a process of reform rather than a revolution.

c. What Remains of the Threshold Requirement?

The second element of the traditional understanding – the threshold requirement – has received less attention. Still, the brief survey of practice suggests that states have claimed a right to respond to breaches which, in themselves, may not have qualified as a 'most grave for[m] of the use of force'. By way of example suffice it to mention the responses, by Israel and Turkey, which were prompted by cross-border attacks below the threshold of an armed attack.[188] These developments indicate that the threshold requirement distinguishing armed attacks from 'lesser sins' may need to be re-visited. In this respect, two observations are in order.

Affirmation in Principle

While state practice suggests a more lenient approach, the distinction as such has been defended rather vigorously. In fact, the recent jurisprudence of international courts and tribunals if anything affirms it. While the ICJ seems to have second thoughts about the 'state attack requirement', it has reaffirmed the threshold requirement on various occasions. In the *Oil Platforms* case, it expressly affirmed the distinction between 'most grave' and 'less grave forms' of the use of force in the context of inter-state conflicts.[189] In *DRC–Uganda*, insofar as it left open whether states could respond to 'attacks by irregular forces',[190] it contemplated self-defence only if directed against 'large scale attacks'.[191] When looking beyond the ICJ, the threshold requirement was equally decisive for the award of the Eritrea/Ethiopia Boundary Commission, whose decision hinged on the distinction between 'geographically limited clashes' and armed attacks triggering a right of self-defence.[192] Recent jurisprudence thus suggests

---

[186] Pursuant to Art. 16, 'A State which aids or assists another State in the commission of an internationally wrongful act by the latter is internationally responsible for doing so if: (a) that State does so with knowledge of the circumstances of the internationally wrongful act; and (b) the act would be internationally wrongful if committed by that State.' In the Bosnian Genocide case, *supra* note 182, the ICJ accepted that Art. 16 reflected customary international law and, more importantly, that the ILC's considerations could be applied to situations involving state assistance to private actors (*ibid.*, at paras 418 ff).

[187] See *supra* note 152.

[188] With respect to the former case see, e.g., Cannizaro, *supra* note 73 (stating that the Hezbollah attacks 'immediately preceding the Israeli reaction against Lebanon seem to be very similar to the type of conduct which, according to the Court's [Nicaragua] ruling, does not justify recourse to an armed response').

[189] *Supra* note 1, at paras 51 and 62. *Cf.* further Raab, *supra* note 65, at 724, who notes that 'the Court [in Oil Platforms] relied almost exclusively on the authority provided in the *Nicaragua* case'.

[190] *Supra* note 1, at para. 147.

[191] *Ibid.*

[192] Award on Ethiopia's Jus ad bellum Claims, 45 ILM (2006) 430, 1–8.

that the distinction between armed attacks and more limited uses of force is still very relevant.[193]

A More Flexible Application (and Its Risks)

On closer scrutiny, there may have nevertheless been some development. When applying the threshold requirement, states seem to have shown a new willingness to accept the 'accumulation of events' doctrine which previously had received little support.[194] This doctrine of course affects many aspects of the law on self-defence.[195] With respect to the threshold requirement, it must be assessed whether a series of minor incidents, taken together, can be said to reach the threshold of an armed attack. In reacting to Israel's and Turkey's practice, few states have *expressly* endorsed this doctrine. By implication, the large number of states accepting Turkey's and Israel's claim to self-defence however seemed to accept it, at least in situations involving constant terrorist attacks which are part of a deliberate policy of violence.[196] As regards recent jurisprudence, the doctrine was much discussed by the litigants in the *Cameroon–Nigeria*, *DRC–Uganda*, and *Oil Platforms* cases. The Court did not expressly pronounce on the matter, but equally seemed inclined to accept it – hence its statement, in *Oil Platforms*, that 'even taken cumulatively' a series of incidents did not qualify as an armed attack on the United States.[197]

These statements suggest a trend towards the recognition of the 'accumulation doctrine', but may require further consolidation. Clearly, the doctrine appeals to those who have long criticized the gap between Articles 2(4) and 51 UNC, implying that states had to accept low-level uses of force.[198] By recognizing the possibility of accumulation, the international community might close this gap. However, recognition of the accumulation doctrine is not the only way to achieve that goal. In his separate opinion in the *Oil Platforms* case, Judge Simma favoured an alternative approach, admitting 'proportionate defensive [forcible] measures' against uses of force not qualifying as an armed attack; this in turn may have been one factor leading him to reject the 'accumulation doctrine'.[199]

Both arguments suggest that while the threshold requirement is maintained as such, it is increasingly being re-interpreted – either by admitting the possibility of accumulation or by recognizing a right of low-level counterforce. Both approaches indicate increased opposition to the narrow construction of self-defence set out in *Nicaragua* and to the gap resulting from it. On policy grounds, that gap indeed seems difficult to defend, and attempts to close it should be viewed favourably. In terms of the law, the argument in favour of 'proportionate defensive measures' is difficult to

---

[193] See the very clear assessment by Gray, *supra* note 33, at 148.

[194] *Cf. supra* note 72.

[195] *Cf.* Gazzini, *supra* note 33, at 144.

[196] See Cannizaro, *supra* note 73.

[197] *Supra* note 1, at para. 64. See also Gazzini, *supra* note 33, at 144; Gray, *supra* note 33, at 156; and Raab, *supra* note 65, at 732, for similar readings of the Court's ambiguous statement.

[198] *Cf. supra* section 2D1.

[199] *Supra* note 1 separate opinion Simma, at paras 13–14.

square with the comprehensive ban on force and requires the abandonment of the 'exclusivity thesis'. In contrast, to re-interpret the threshold requirement in the light of the accumulation doctrine may present the more feasible approach. However, as will be shown in the next section, the 'accumulation doctrine', while closing the gap between Articles 2(4) and 51 UNC (and doing so in an elegant way), produces serious side-effects: it undermines the temporal dimension of self-defence and risks turning a temporal right into an open-ended licence to use force. For that reason, it can only be hoped that the international community will not embrace it and, if anything, accept a more limited right to use low-level counterforce against cross-border violence.

d. The Scope of the Right

Debates about the re-interpretation of the 'armed attack' requirement have occupied most of the academic discussion. However, the real 'normative drift'[200] discernable in recent practice on self-defence concerns not the conditions under which states can invoke self-defence, but the scope of the right. In particular, recent practice seems to have largely abandoned the functional understanding of self-defence as a protective means of 'repelling armed attacks'.[201] This in turn raises doubts not only about the temporal limits of self-defence, but also about the inherently defensive character of the right.

The Temporal Limitation

The temporal limitation of self-defence has come under pressure from different directions. States' assertions of a right of pre-emptive self-defence (e.g., in the United States' 2002 National Security Strategy) present the most obvious challenge. That challenge has led to a more flexible handling of the immediacy criterion, but in its radical form seems to have been resisted. By and large, few states were willing to accept the United States' assertion of a right of pre-emptive self-defence.[202] The United Kingdom's Attorney General, not otherwise known principally to oppose the United States' position, was adamant that 'international law permits the use of force in self-defence against an imminent attack but does not authorise the use of force to mount a pre-emptive attack against a threat that is more remote'.[203] In his report *In Larger Freedom*, Kofi Annan equally made it clear that Article 51 UNC 'covers an imminent attack', but '[w]here threats are not imminent but latent, the Charter gives full authority to the Security Council to use military force, including preventively, to preserve international peace and security'.[204] Finally, the ICJ's judgment in *DRC–Uganda* points in the same direction: in response to Uganda's assertion of a right to defend security interests (i.e.,

---

[200] Bethlehem, *supra* note 164.

[201] Cannizaro, *supra* note 73.

[202] In addition to the statements cited in the text see, e.g., the views of Malaysia, Iran, Lebanon, Yemen, and Vietnam during the Security Council debate on Operation Iraqi Freedom (4726th meeting, 2003). See further Gray, *supra* note 33, at 209 ff; Bothe, *supra* note 153 (each with many further references).

[203] Statement in HL Debs, 21 April 2004, vol. 660, cols. 370–371. See Wood, *supra* note 109, at 7–8 for further details.

[204] UN Doc. A/59/2005, at paras 124–125 (based on para. 188 of the High Level Panel Report, UN Doc. A/59/565).

390 *EJIL* 20 (2009), 359–397

interests not under an imminent threat), the Court observed: 'Article 51 ... does not allow the use of force by a State to protect perceived security interests .... Other means are available to a concerned State, including, in particular, recourse to the Security Council.'[205] These statements suggest that the doctrine of pre-emptive self-defence has been rejected, and with it the boldest attempt so far to turn Article 51 UNC into a *carte blanche* for forcible intervention.

This rejection may however have come at a price. While rejecting pre-emptive self-defence, the international community – almost as part of a 'bargain' – seems to move towards accepting the doctrine of anticipatory self-defence. The statements just cited[206] are evidence of a more flexible approach. Admittedly, the matter is far from settled,[207] but when looked at from a distance the price to pay seems small, and a re-adjustment of the rules would not necessarily conflict with the wording of Article 51 UNC.[208] Perhaps more importantly, recent practice suggests that the problem of anticipatory self-defence is increasingly overshadowed by debates about the 'accumulation of events' doctrine.[209] As noted above, that doctrine may serve to broaden the notion of armed attack. Yet it also, and much more fundamentally, affects the temporal dimension of self-defence. If attacks can be accumulated, then a response will satisfy the immediacy requirement even if it comes too early or too late to repel the single incident which prompted it. The risks of such an approach are readily apparent – in the extreme scenario, a state facing continuous 'pin prick attacks' by a terrorist movement can rely on self-defence to justify the use of force *sine die*. While understandable as a means of re-defining the gravity of armed attacks, the 'accumulation doctrine' thus effectively undermines the immediacy requirement characterizing the temporal right of self-defence.

As noted above, the 'accumulation doctrine' has received increased support in recent practice, but has not officially been endorsed.[210] The preceding considerations suggest that its growing acceptance presents grave risks. The risks are borne out particularly clearly by *Operation Enduring Freedom*, an operation initially based on a broad, yet defensible reading of Article 51 UNC, which has turned into a self-perpetuating military campaign serving a range of objectives. It is submitted that that campaign has clearly overstretched the boundaries of even the broadest understanding of self-defence.[211] One can only hope that the international community's willingness to accept a 'quasi-permanent' state of self-defence will remain an isolated deviation from the general rule, perhaps to be explained by the singular impact of the 9/11 attacks which triggered it.

---

[205] *Supra* note 1, at para. 148.

[206] *Supra* at notes 203–205.

[207] For example, the Non-Aligned Movement expressed concern about the High Level Panel Report's assessment: see UN Doc. A/59/PV.85, at 14–15. *Cf.* further Hamid, 'The Legality of Anticipatory Self-Defence in the 21st Century World Order', 54 *Netherlands Int'l L Rev* (2007) 441; and Gray, *supra* note 33, at 160 ff.

[208] 'In Larger Freedom', UN Doc. A/59/2005, at para. 124.

[209] See Gray, *supra* note 33, at 165: '[i]n practice States prefer to argue for an extended interpretation of armed attack and to avoid the fundamental doctrinal debate [about anticipatory self-defence]'.

[210] *Supra* section 2D2c.

[211] For early criticism see Corten and Dubuisson, *supra* note 51; and further Gray, *supra* note 33, at 203 ff.

The Defensive Character of Measures

Equally worrying is the tendency of the international community to accept claims based on self-defence which in reality do not serve a defensive purpose. As noted above, under the traditional, restrictive, doctrine, self-defence was not available against 'instant' terrorist attacks which were completed before the victim state could react.[212] The 'accumulation doctrine', if accepted, of course might help avoid that result. Still, even under that doctrine, measures of self-defence in principle would have to serve a 'defensive' purpose. The survey of practice suggests that this requirement today is applied very flexibly. States have labelled as self-defence a whole range of measures which did not serve a defensive purpose. For example, when justifying its 1993 attack on Baghdad or the 1998 bombardment of Sudan/Afghanistan, the United States invoked Article 51 UNC, but argued in terms of retaliation, not protection.[213] Similarly, Russia, explaining its attacks on the Pankrisi Gorge, invoked a right to enforce international law, not to defend itself.[214] By the same token, Iran's pursuit of Kurdish fighters into Iraqi territory did not serve to 'repel an attack' (whether grave enough/imminent or not) but to arrest criminals.[215] Of course it is often difficult to re-establish the motives prompting a state to use force, and the line between defence and retaliation may at times be difficult to draw. Yet one cannot fail to note that in recent years states have invoked self-defence to justify conduct which primarily served non-defensive purposes.

Again, it may be too early to tell whether recent practice will modify the existing standards. In the light of claims to 'retaliatory self-defence', the dangers of the recent trend need to be recalled. By accepting that states merely 'pay lip-service to the need to act in self-defence'[216] while in reality pursuing other objectives, the international community seems to give up an inherent feature of the right of self-defence, namely its defensive character. The result may be rather paradoxical: while unequivocally condemning the doctrine of armed reprisals, the international community seems indeed – as Pierre Klein aptly noted – gradually to accept armed reprisals disguised as self-defence.[217] In so doing, it may re-introduce an altogether flexible exception to the ban on force which had been considered illegal for decades, and abandon an inherent feature of the right of self-defence.

E *The Present: Taking Stock*

The preceding considerations suggest that in many respects the last two decades have transformed the rules governing forcible responses against terrorism. The international community's growing determination to fight terrorism has not left the *jus ad bellum* unaffected. The extraterritorial use of force remains *prima facie* illegal, but

---

[212] *Cf. supra* section 2D1.

[213] Kritsiotis, *supra* note 143, at 169; Gazzini, *supra* note 33, at 204.

[214] UN Doc. S/2002/1012.

[215] *Cf. supra* note 144.

[216] Gray, *supra* note 33, at 166.

[217] Klein, 'Vers la reconnaissance progressive d'un droit à des représailles armées?', in Corten *et al.* (eds), *supra* note 128, at 249. See also the brief comments by Franck, *supra* note 5, at 91 (his n. 84).

392   *EJIL* 20 (2009), 359–397

justification seems much more readily available than 20 years ago. Insofar as the UN's collective security system is concerned, this has been uncontroversial. It is beyond doubt today that the Security Council can authorize the use of force against terrorists. However, the political limits remain. Even in times of worldwide consensus, individually affected states may prefer to act unilaterally. More importantly, even a 'legislating' Security Council seems to lack the political will to decide on military enforcement against terrorists.

As far as forcible measures are concerned, the contemporary 'strong international policy against terrorism'[218] therefore has been implemented outside the Security Council framework. This has brought about new uncertainty about the scope of exceptions to the ban on force. Whether the new practice is a temporary aberration or ushers in a new era in which the *jus ad bellum* is applied with greater flexibility may in some respects be too early to tell. Yet three points can be made: (i) the new practice is more than a response to the 9/11 attacks. On frequent occasions, during the last two decades, many different states have asserted a right to use force against terrorists, and their conduct has been viewed rather favourably by the international community. (ii) The new practice is exclusively justified under an expanded doctrine of self-defence, even though it may bear little resemblance to classical forms of self-defence. (iii) As far as possible re-adjustments of the law of self-defence are concerned, the debate about the state or non-state origin of the attack seems overstated. While there seems to emerge a new, lower standard of attribution, the new practice can be explained as a reform of the previous, restrictive approach set out in *Nicaragua*. The real 'normative drift'[219] concerns two other aspects of the law on self-defence: the immediacy test and the requirement that measures be defensive in character. By increasingly abandoning these limitations, the international community runs the risk of transforming a temporary defensive right into an open-ended instrument for forcible intervention.

4 Conclusion and Coda

A *Concluding Observations*

The preceding discussion suggests that the law governing anti-terrorist force is in a process of change. This process may be looked at from different angles. The growing international consensus against terrorism has entailed far-reaching legal consequences. International rules requiring state cooperation or active state conduct against terrorism have multiplied. More important, at least for present purposes, is the militarization of the fight against terrorism. International law now accepts that the fight against terror may require the use of extraterritorial force – certainly within the multilateral context, but possibly also outside it. To return to a point made earlier,

---

[218] *Cf.* Schachter, *supra* note 29, at 218.

[219] Bethlehem, *supra* note 164.

a Hague Lecture on '*Terrorisme et droit international*' today would have to devote more than five pages to the problem of forcible measures.[220]

As regards the *jus ad bellum*, developments during the last two decades indicate that the law is capable of adaptation. The growing consensus against terrorism has put pressure on the traditionally restrictive regime. This pressure has affected the interpretation of exceptions to the ban on force. These are increasingly construed broadly, so as to take account of the denunciation of terror. The broad construction can be easily accommodated within the United Nations system of collective security. With respect to unilateral force, it requires a far more difficult adjustment of the traditional rules, and is proving much more controversial. Yet the process of adjustment seems well under way. The point can by illustrated by reference to a statement made some 25 years ago, in Security Council debates on one of the more high-profile instances of anti-terrorist force. To justify his country's raid on Tunis, Israel's representative then argued that 'Tunisia knew very well what was going on in this extraterritorial base, the planning that took place there, the missions that were launched from it, and the purposes of those missions: repeated armed attacks against my country and against innocent civilians around the world. Tunisia, then, actually provided a base for murderous activity against another State and, in fact, the nationals of many States who are the objects and victims of this terrorist organization.' And, further, '[a] country cannot claim the protection of sovereignty when it knowingly offers a piece of its territory for terrorist activity against other nations'.[221]

Twenty-five years ago that statement was roundly rejected, partly because Security Council members evaluated the facts differently, but partly because they did not accept Israel's legal argument. As a consequence, 14 members of the Security Council agreed to condemn Israel's conduct in the strongest terms, with only the United States abstaining.[222] How the Security Council would respond were it to hear the same argument again today remains a matter for speculation. Much depends of course on the facts and the credibility of a state's claim. Yet the underlying legal claim argument – that states aiding and abetting terrorists abuse their sovereignty and must accept some form of counter-action – has become a standard formula of modern debates and would probably meet with approval of some and tacit agreement of many states.

The consequences, and implications, of the new, flexible approach are readily apparent. By recognizing a broad construction of the exception, the international community, in a specific field of international relations, increasingly seems to free states from constraints imposed by the ban on force.[223] In that respect, developments in the law governing anti-terrorist force fit in well with a new willingness to accept (or at least

---

[220] Contrast George Guillaume's more succinct treatment in his 1989 lectures (*supra* note 70). In fact, in Pierre Klein's 2006 Hague course ('Le droit international à l'épreuve du terrorisme', 321 *Recueil des Cours* (2006) 287) questions relating to cross-border force occupy roughly one third of the written version.

[221] UN Doc. S/PV.2615, at 86–87.

[222] SC Res. 573. *Cf. supra*, section 2D.

[223] Conversely, to adapt an expression used by Antonio Cassese, states seem to have successfully 'reappropriate[d]' a right that they had 'lost as a result of the creation of the U.N.' and the traditional, restrictive analysis of the Charter regime (*Cf.* Cassese, *supra* note 4, at 511).

394   *EJIL* 20 (2009), 359–397

consider justifiable) the use of force where it serves a legitimate cause, notably borne out by renewed debates about the legality of humanitarian interventions. This new flexibility of course comes at a price: the broadly construed exceptions to the ban on force can be abused – a risk which is much increased by the worrying tendency to extend self-defence in time or even to accept 'retaliatory self-defence'. Yet the preceding discussion also suggests that during the last two decades the international community has been prepared to take that risk. Readjustments of the *jus ad bellum* are not deduced from some legal principle, but borne out by the actual practice of states, which at least during the last two decades has recognized the right of states to use anti-terrorist force if this served to avert threats and no other means seemed available. Whether this flexible approach persists will depend not least on the prudence of states in making use of their 'reappropriated'[224] right.

B *Coda – The Future: Anti-terrorist Force 2029*

If the *jus ad bellum* has evolved during the last 20 years, then it is likely to evolve further over time. If it is accepted that some aspects of the rules on anti-terrorist force are in a process of readjustment, then they may even require some further development, either confirming recent trends or reversing them. So how might the law develop? How might commentators, 20 years from now (possibly in a symposium celebrating the 40th anniversary of the *European Journal*), reflect on 'the use of force against terrorists'? Prediction, as has been observed,[225] 'is very difficult, especially if it's about the future', so the subsequent paragraphs are speculative. However, three scenarios can be envisaged.

1 *A Return to the Criminal Law Strategy*

The first scenario is that of a de-militarization of the fight against terrorism and of a return to the criminal law strategy. This would presuppose further progress in the move towards a criminalization of terrorism and the establishment of a much more effective system of international cooperation. As part of an ever 'strong[er] international policy against terrorism',[226] states would need to accept – whether in international conventions or through Security Council legislation – a broader range of obligations relating to the treatment of terrorists and terrorist organizations. If existing treaties are to serve as a model, the future multilateral regime is likely to include enhanced duties to criminalize and prosecute terrorist activities, arrangements for cooperation in criminal matters, as well as in the fight against financiers of terrorism; in addition, one might hope that it also includes safeguards protecting individual rights of terror suspects. As a residual option, the international community might also establish international judicial bodies competent to prosecute terrorist activities – maybe eventually even a 'terrorism chamber' of the International Criminal Court. Just as it has done with respect to other international tribunals, the Security Council

---

[224] *Cf. ibid.*

[225] Allegedly by the Danish physicist Niels Bohr.

[226] *Cf.* Schachter, *supra* note 29, at 218.

would be well-placed to assume the role of an enforcement agent, e.g., by requiring states to hand over terror suspects, failing which they might face sanctions. In fact, the (no doubt reformed) Security Council of 2029 might even call upon a standing anti-terrorist force to arrest terror suspects and hand them over to the ICC's terrorism chamber. While the latter development may require some imagination, the criminal law scenario could build on the groundwork laid in existing anti-terrorism conventions and on precedents of previous Security Council action.[227] In contrast, an effective criminal law strategy, backed up by Security Council sanctions, would reduce the need (perceived or real) for unilateral force. The broad construction of self-defence emerging during the 1990s and 2000s might in retrospect then appear as no more than a temporary aberration.

2 A More 'Protean' Jus ad bellum

The second scenario is less optimistic, but may be more likely. It is based on the assumption that the trend towards unilateral anti-terrorist force consolidates. If states continue to exercise anti-terrorist force, how would this consolidated body of practice affect the state of the law? On one level the answer is clear: many aspects of the *jus ad bellum* are flexible enough to accommodate change (and indeed may have accommodated it already). It is submitted that the Charter does not preclude the recognition of a right to use self-defence against states harbouring terrorists, if that is required to avert an imminent armed attack. By the same token, the Charter does not rule out the 'accumulation doctrine', although that doctrine presents grave risks. In fact, the Charter may even tolerate the trend towards retaliatory defence, even though one might hope that states abusing the self-defence concept for non-defensive purpose would be more open about their real intentions. In short, if the international community agrees on the broader reading of Article 51 UNC emerging during the last two decades, then that re-interpretation will become accepted over time. Commentators writing in 2029 might in retrospect point to the 1990s and 2000s as the crucial period in which the broader reading had gained ground. Perhaps they might even view the flexible approach to anti-terrorist force as one of the key elements of a general move towards what Sean Murphy has labelled a 'protean *jus ad bellum*'.[228] The gradual recognition of a right to use anti-terrorist force from the 1990s may in retrospect have paved the way towards a new understanding of the rules on force – a 'protean' approach striking a new balance between the absence of force and the protection of common values, permitting states to disregard constraints of the Charter in defence of community goals. If this is to happen (and one may dread the thought), then the commentator writing in 2029 might describe the fight against terror as a catalyst of indeed revolutionary change.

3 Extraterritorial Enforcement Jurisdiction over Terrorists

Finally, there may be a third scenario transcending the dichotomy between criminal and military anti-terrorism strategies. A commentator writing in 2029 might be

---

[227] See, e.g., SC Res. 731 and 748 (requiring Libya to hand over terror suspects); and SC Res. 1593 (referring the situation in Darfur to the ICC prosecutor).

[228] Murphy, *supra* note 57.

396   *EJIL* 20 (2009), 359–397

able to report on the emergence of a regime of international enforcement jurisdiction over terrorists. That regime may be based on international conventions or Security Council authorisations, or both. It would allow states to use force extraterritorially as a designated measure of law enforcement. It may have drawn inspiration from long-established rules governing enforcement measures against pirates on the high seas,[229] or controversial attempts to re-write the principles governing the interdiction of ships,[230] but would need to move beyond these so as to allow for enforcement *on foreign soil*. Presumably, the right of states to enforce anti-terrorist rules would be subject to rather strict conditions: for example, it could require the responding state to provide evidence of the territorial state's failure to act (thus taking up considerations of necessity and complementarity), and to respond only against individuals or organizations included on an internationally-agreed 'black list'.

The new regime of extraterritorial enforcement jurisdiction over terrorists would be based on the conviction that the fight against terrorism requires a military component, but it would channel military measures into a regime of enforcement jurisdiction established in the interest of the international community. As such, it would recognize that forcible measures against terrorists in recent years have typically been based on the logic of enforcement, not defence. Unlike other possible scenarios, a regime of extraterritorial jurisdiction would address terrorists directly (just as Article 110 of the Law of the Sea Convention (LOSC) addresses pirate ships directly) rather than indirectly applying the inter-state rules on force to them.

Evidently, the prospects for such an enforcement regime are rather slim. It presupposes a willingness of states to accept a far-reaching exception to present-day rules governing enforcement jurisdiction. Still, the possibility should not be completely ruled out. Recent Security Council resolutions have revived and broadened the long-dormant rules governing enforcement jurisdiction over pirates, so as to permit enforcement measures within sovereign spaces of another state.[231] The fate of the 'proliferation security initiative' abandoning the principle of exclusive flag state jurisdiction in favour of some form of 'public interest enforcement' is by no means sealed. It is entirely possible that these developments should signal a broader approach to enforcement jurisdiction generally which, by 2029, could be applied to terrorists as well.

***

The different options are not mutually exclusive. Twenty years from now, the fight against terror may still be fought, as today, with criminal *and* military means, possibly complemented by an internationalized enforcement regime of limited application (e.g., in failed states). In fact (and that might be scenario 4), the fight against terror

---

[229] See Art. 110 (1)(a) LOSC.

[230] *Cf.* Guilfoyle, 'Interdicting Vessels to Enforce the Common Interest: Maritime Countermeasures and the Use of Force on the High Seas', 56 *ICLQ* (2007) 69, for an excellent discussion.

[231] SC Res. 1816 and 1851 (2008).

may have effectively been abandoned if different factions within the international community again revert to the rhetoric of 'our' versus 'your' terrorists, the former fighting for legitimate causes, the latter engaging in criminal activities. If there is one lesson to draw from developments during the last two decades, then it is that no scenario can be excluded. Who, in the 1980s, would have expected the international community to move towards an unconditional condemnation of terrorist activities? Who, in 1989, would have expected the Security Council to adopt a comprehensive, non-military, anti-terrorism programme through a series of resolutions? If the international community is capable of maintaining a strong stance against terrorism, then there is no reason to expect that the *jus ad bellum* should be immune from (further) change.

[17]

Computer Network Attack and the Use of Force in International Law: Thoughts on a Normative Framework

MICHAEL N. SCHMITT*

This Article explores the acceptability under the jus ad bellum, *that body of international law governing the resort to force as an instrument of national policy, of computer network attack. Analysis centers on the United Nations Charter's prohibition of the use of force in Article 2(4), its Chapter VII security scheme, and the inherent right to self-defense codified in Article 51. Concluding that traditional applications of the use of force prohibition fail to adequately safeguard shared community values threatened by CNA, the Article proposes an alternative normative framework based on scrutiny of the consequences caused by such operations.*

* Professor of International Law, George C. Marshall European Center for Security Studies, Garmisch-Partenkirchen, Germany. Faculty Member, International Institute of Humanitarian Law, San Remo, Italy. The author expresses his appreciation to Dean Robert Wood and the Naval War College's Center for Naval Warfare Studies for a generous grant supporting this research, and to the following individuals for sharing their thoughts on subject: Ms. Louise Doswald-Beck, International Committee of the Red Cross; Dr. Dieter Fleck, German Ministry of Defense; Professor Christopher Greenwood, London School of Economics; Dean Françoise Hampson, University of Essex; Professor Adam Roberts, Oxford University; Commander Jim Scorer, Royal Navy; and Commander Jeffrey Stieb, U.S. Coast Guard. Of course, all views and opinions expressed in this article are those of the author alone and do not necessarily reflect those of any other individual, the Department of Defense, the United States Air Force, or any other government agency. E-mail: schmitt@aya.yale.edu

886 *COLUMBIA JOURNAL OF TRANSNATIONAL LAW* [37:885

As the next millennium approaches, the global community's dependence on computers and the networks that connect them, such as the Internet, is growing exponentially. This dependency amounts to a significant vulnerability, for computer networks underlie key societal functions as diverse as finance, military command and control, medical treatment, and transportation. Great attention is already being placed on the methods and means by which computer network attacks ("CNA") might be conducted, and significant resources are being devoted to developing offensive and defensive CNA capabilities.

This Article explores the acceptability under the *jus ad bellum*, that body of international law governing the resort to force as an instrument of national policy, of computer network attack. Analysis centers on the United Nations Charter's prohibition of the use of force in Article 2(4), its Chapter VII security scheme, and the inherent right to self-defense codified in Article 51. Concluding that traditional applications of the use of force prohibition fail to adequately safeguard shared community values threatened by CNA, the Article proposes an alternative normative framework based on scrutiny of the consequences caused by such operations. By contrast, the Chapter VII security regime is assessed as sufficiently flexible to adapt to the new threats represented by CNA. Finally, the Article argues for a rather restricted understanding of the right to self-defense, suggesting that it be limited to operations which are *de facto* armed attacks, or imminently preparatory thereto. The net result is a limitation on both state resort to CNA techniques which might threaten global stability and on individual responses which might themselves prove destabilizing.

The global community is fast becoming "wired." By the beginning of the next millennium some 100 million individuals will enjoy access to the Internet.[1] Indeed, over the past decade the number of users has almost doubled annually.[2] Today, students attend virtual

---

1. *See* CHARLES SWETT, STRATEGIC ASSESSMENT: THE INTERNET (July 17, 1995), *available at* <http://www.fas.org/cp/swett.html>. To illustrate the global nature of the phenomenon, consider the number of computers linked to the worldwide net per ten thousand persons for selected countries: Finland, 500+; U.S., 300+; Norway, Australia, New Zealand, Sweden, 200+; Denmark, Switzerland, Canada, Netherlands, Singapore, 100+; United Kingdom, nearly 100. *See* Office of the Assistant Secretary of Defense for Command, Control, Communications and Intelligence, Directorate for Information Operations, Presentation at National Defense University (Jan. 1998).

2. *See Information Security: Computer Attacks at Department of Defense Pose Increasing Risks: Testimony Before the Permanent Subcomm. on Investigations of the Senate Comm. on Governmental Affairs*, 104th Cong. (1996) (statement of Jack L. Brock, Director, Defense Information and Financial Management Systems Accounting and Information, General Accounting Office) [hereinafter Brock]; ACCOUNTING AND INFORMATION MANAGEMENT DIVISION, INFORMATION SECURITY: COMPUTER ATTACKS AT DEPARTMENT OF DEFENSE POSE INCREASING RISKS (GAO/T-AIMD-96-92, May 22, 1996).

universities continents away from their computer terminals; shoppers buy on-line from their living room, and lawyers perform complex legal research without ever opening a law book. More significantly, the use of computers, and the networks that link them to one another, has become far more than a matter of mere convenience—in some cases survival may be at stake. International air traffic control relies on linked computer nets, as do such diverse, and critical, functions as telephone operations, emergency response, medical record management, oil distribution, municipal sewage treatment, electrical generation, and railway switching.

Military reliance on computers has grown in lock-step fashion with reliance on computers in the civilian sector. Today, the United States Department of Defense (DOD) employs well over two million computers and operates more than ten thousand local area networks. Moreover, some two hundred command centers are computer-dependent. These figures do not account for the two million plus computer users that regularly do business with the DOD.[3] While the armed forces of other nations are less dependent on computer resources and connectivity than those of the United States, the trend towards military computerization, with varying degrees of fervor, approaches universality. After all, the 1990-1991 Gulf War aptly demonstrated the determinative effect of technology, particularly computer-enabled logistics, communications, intelligence, and force application, on the modern battlefield. It was a lesson lost on few military thinkers or operators.[4]

Paradoxically, most capabilities carry within them the seeds of vulnerability, a truism well-illustrated by the new cyber dependencies, both civilian and military. Whether quantitative or qualitative in nature,

---

3. *See* Brock, *supra* note 2.

4. On the changing face of war and its relationship to the law of armed conflict, *see generally* Michael Schmitt, *Bellum Americanum: The U.S. View of Twenty-First Century War and Its Possible Implications for the Law of Armed Conflict, in* THE LAW OF ARMED CONFLICT: INTO THE NEXT MILLENNIUM 389 (Michael Schmitt & Leslie Green eds., 1998). For more general discussion of the "revolution in military affairs," see WILLIAM S. COHEN, SECRETARY OF DEF., ANN. REP. TO THE PRESIDENT AND CONGRESS, ch. 13 (1998); Dennis M. Drew, *Technology and the American Way of War: Worshipping a False Idol?*, AIR FORCE J. LOGISTICS, Winter 1987, at 21; James R. Fitzsimonds, *The Coming Military Revolution: Opportunities and Risks*, PARAMETERS, Summer 1995, at 30; Dan Gouré, *Is There a Military-Technical Revolution in America's Future?*, WASH. Q., Autumn 1993, at 175; Andrew F. Krepinevich, Jr., *Cavalry to Computer: The Pattern of Military Revolutions, in* STRATEGY AND FORCE PLANNING 582 (Naval War College Faculty ed., 1995); Andrew F. Krepinevich, Jr., *Keeping Pace with the Military-Technical Revolution*, ISSUES IN SCIENCE & TECHNOLOGY, Summer 1994, at 23; Kenneth F. McKenzie, Jr., *Beyond Luddites and Magicians: Examining the MTR*, PARAMETERS, Summer 1995, at 15; Abhi Shelat, *An Empty Revolution: MTR Expectations Fall Short*, HARVARD INTERNATIONAL REVIEW, Summer 1994, at 52.

888   *COLUMBIA JOURNAL OF TRANSNATIONAL LAW*   [37:885

the extraordinary advances made possible by breakthroughs in computer technology represent dangerous vulnerabilities exploitable by opponents ranging from economic, political, and military competitors, to terrorists and criminals. These threat sources are familiar. However, the unique nature of the cyber threats they pose differs in four interrelated ways from those traditionally faced. First, computer networks comprise a new *target category*. It is no longer necessary, for example, to physically destroy electrical generation facilities to cut power to a foe's command and control system; instead, the computer network that drives the distribution system can be brought down to accomplish the same result. Second, whereas the *means* of "attack" in centuries past usually presupposed the use of kinetic force, in the twenty-first century an attack may be nothing more than the transfer of cyber commands from one computer to others. Third, while the *result* of a cyber attack may be physical destruction, such as the "meltdown" of a nuclear reactor following interference with its control systems, it need not be. The objective may simply be to shut off a particular service or function (e.g., disrupting telecommunications) or to alter or misdirect data (e.g., unauthorized electronic funds transfer or transmittal of false intelligence information). Finally, cyber attacks stretch traditional notions of territorial integrity. In most cases they will not involve the crossing of political borders by any tangible instrument of the attacker, such as military forces, equipment, or projectiles.[5]

This article explores the *jus ad bellum* implications of one such cyber threat—"computer network attack"—in a state-on-state context. Computer network attack consists of "[o]perations to disrupt, deny, degrade, or destroy information resident in computers and computer networks, or the computers and networks themselves."[6] After briefly

---

5. Bibliographies on information operations are available on-line. *See, e.g., An IW Bibliography* (visited Feb. 24, 1999) <http:// www.infowar.com/RESOURCE/IWBIB1.html-ssi>; Air University, *Information Warfare* (visited Feb. 24, 1999) <http://www.au.af.mil/au/aul/bibs/infowar/if.htm>; Naval War College, *Library Notes* (visited Feb. 24, 1999) <http://www.nwc.navy.mil/library/libinfwf.htm>. For an introduction to the subject, see generally THE INFORMATION AGE: AN ANTHOLOGY ON ITS IMPACT AND CONSEQUENCES (David S. Alberts & Daniel S. Papp eds., 1997); CYBERWAR : SECURITY, STRATEGY, AND CONFLICT IN THE INFORMATION AGE (Alan Campen ed., 1996); CYBERWAR 2.0: MYTHS, MYSTERIES AND REALITY (Alan Campen & Douglas Dearth eds., 1998); MARTIN C. LIBICKI, THE MESH AND THE NET: SPECULATIONS ON ARMED CONFLICT IN A TIME OF FREE SILICON (1995); MARTIN C. LIBICKI, WHAT IS INFORMATION WARFARE? (1995); WINN SCHWARTAU, INFORMATION WARFARE: CHAOS ON THE ELECTRONIC SUPERHIGHWAY (1994). A number of these works and others on information warfare are available on-line at the National Defense University's electronic books website. *See National Defense University Press Books On-line* (visited Feb. 24, 1999) <http://www.ndu.edu/inss/books/books.html>.

6. JOINT CHIEFS OF STAFF, JOINT PUB. 3-13, JOINT DOCTRINE FOR INFORMATION OPERATIONS GL-5 (Oct. 9, 1998) [hereinafter JOINT PUB. 3-13].

setting forth the technical and doctrinal framework for CNA, analysis will turn to the issue this new potential technique of international coercion poses: When does a computer network attack conducted by, or on behalf of, a state constitute a wrongful use of force under international law? Though it is not the focus of this essay, a brief discussion of the responses available to a state victimized by CNA will follow.

Such issues arise in two scenarios. In the first, State A conducts CNA operations against State B with no intention of ever escalating the conflict to the level of armed engagement. The advantages gained through the CNA are ends in themselves. In the second scenario, State A conducts CNA operations in order to prepare the battle space for a conventional attack. The goal is to disorient, disrupt, blind, or mislead State B so as to enhance the likelihood that conventional military operations will prove successful.

Although not limited to the security scheme set forth in the United Nations Charter, analytical emphasis will be placed on the prohibition on the use or threat of force in Article 2(4), Chapter VII's authorization of community responses in the face of aggression, and the right to self-defense codified in Article 51. The intent is to survey the existing normative architecture for prescriptive fault lines, those points where the *jus ad bellum,* as understood in prevailing cognitive paradigms, fails to adequately safeguard and foster shared global values.[7] To the extent such fault lines are identified, suggestions as to how either causative normative lacunae might best be filled, or cognitive paradigms might profitably shift, will be offered for consideration. The Article will conclude with tentative thoughts on the policy implications of differing approaches to addressing the fault lines.

---

7. For surveys on information operations and the law, see generally Office of the Judge Advocate General, Headquarters United States Air Force, A Primer on Legal Issues in Information Warfare (3d ed., 1997); David J. DiCenso, Information Operations: An Act of War? (Oct. 7, 1998) (unpublished report for the Institute of National Security Studies, U.S. Air Force Academy); Charles Dunlap, *The Law of Cyberwar: A Case Study from the Future, in* CYBERWAR 2.0: MYTHS, MYSTERIES AND REALITY (Alan Campen & Douglas Dearth eds., 1998); LAWRENCE GREENBERG ET AL., INFORMATION WARFARE AND INTERNATIONAL LAW (1998); Sean P. Kanuck, *Information Warfare: New Challenges for Public International Law,* 37 HARV. INT'L L.J. 272 (1996); Mark R. Shulman, *Discrimination in the Laws of Information Warfare,* 37 COLUM. J. TRANS. L. 939 (1999).

890   *COLUMBIA JOURNAL OF TRANSNATIONAL LAW*   [37:885

I.   UNDERSTANDING COMPUTER NETWORK ATTACK

Computer network attack is but one form of a relatively new category of warfare, information operations ("IO").[8]   Information operations comprise "[a]ctions taken to affect adversary information and information systems while defending one's own information and information systems."[9] The term must be understood very expansively. For instance, the United States military defines information as "facts, data, or instructions in *any* medium or form" and an information system as the *"entire* infrastructure, organization, personnel, and components that collect, process, store, transmit, display, disseminate, and act on information."[10] Thus, information operations would encompass, among an array of other activities, virtually any nonconsensual actions intended to discover, alter, destroy, disrupt, or transfer data stored in a computer, manipulated by a computer, or transmitted through a computer network. To the extent these operations, whether occurring during times of peace or armed conflict, intend interference with a country's national defense by targeting defense premises or resources, including human and natural resources, they constitute "sabotage."[11] It should also be noted that the

---

8. Although efforts to affect an opponent's information base and protect one's own have characterized warfare throughout history, it is only in the last decade that IO has been recognized as a distinct form of warfare meriting its own separate doctrine, policy, and tactics.

9. JOINT PUB. 3-13, *supra* note 6, at GL-7. For the IO policy of U.S. forces, see generally INFORMATION OPERATIONS, U.S. DEP'T OF DEF. DIRECTIVE (DODD) S-3600.1 (Dec. 9, 1996); JOINT INFORMATION OPERATIONS POLICY, CHAIRMAN OF THE JOINT CHIEFS OF STAFF INSTRUCTION (CJCSI) 3210.01A (Jan. 1996). Other official IO-related guidance includes: DEFENSIVE INFORMATION WARFARE OPERATIONS IMPLEMENTATION, CHAIRMAN OF THE JOINT CHIEFS OF STAFF INSTRUCTION (CJCSI) 6510.01 (Aug. 22, 1997); JOINT CHIEFS OF STAFF, JOINT PUB. 3-13.1, JOINT DOCTRINE FOR COMMAND AND CONTROL WARFARE, (Feb. 7, 1996) [hereinafter JOINT PUB. 3-13.1]; JOINT CHIEFS OF STAFF, JOINT PUB. 3-53, DOCTRINE FOR JOINT PSYCHOLOGICAL OPERATIONS (July 10, 1996) [hereinafter JOINT PUB. 3-53]; JOINT CHIEFS OF STAFF, JOINT PUB. 3-58, JOINT DOCTRINE FOR MILITARY DECEPTION (May 31, 1996) [hereinafter JOINT PUB. 3-58]; U.S. DEP'T OF THE NAVY, CHIEF OF NAVAL OPERATIONS INSTRUCTION 3430.26, IMPLEMENTING INSTRUCTION FOR INFORMATION WARFARE COMMAND AND CONTROL (Jan. 18, 1995); U.S. DEP'T OF THE NAVY, NAVAL DOCTRINE PUBLICATION 6, NAVAL COMMAND AND CONTROL (May 19, 1995); U.S. DEP'T OF THE AIR FORCE, AIR FORCE DOCTRINE DOCUMENT 2-5, INFORMATION OPERATIONS (Aug 5, 1998); U.S. DEP'T OF THE ARMY, U.S. ARMY FIELD MANUAL 100-6, INFORMATION OPERATIONS (Aug. 27, 1996); U.S. DEP'T OF THE MARINES, MARINE CORPS ORDER 3430.1, POLICY FOR INFORMATION OPERATIONS (May 19, 1997). *See also* U.S. DEP'T OF THE AIR FORCE, THE CORNERSTONES OF INFORMATION WARFARE (1995). Many U.S. military publications are available on-line. *See Joint Electronic Library* (visited Feb. 24, 1999) <http://www.dtic.mil/doctrine/jel/>.

10. JOINT PUB. 3-13, *supra* note 6, at GL-7 (emphasis added).

11. *See* U.S. DEP'T OF DEFENSE, JOINT PUB. 1-02, DICTIONARY OF MILITARY AND ASSOCIATED TERMS 387 (March 23, 1994, as amended through June 10, 1998), *available at DODD   Dictionary   of   Military   Terms* (visited   Feb.   24,   1999) <http://www.dtic.mil/doctrine/jel/doddict/> [hereinafter JOINT PUB. 1-02].   The key

term "information warfare" ("IW") is often incorrectly used as a synonym for "information operations." In fact, IW accurately refers only to those information operations conducted during times of crisis or conflict intended to effect specific results against a particular opponent.[12] Thus, IW would not include information operations occurring during peacetime.

As suggested, IO is subdivided into defensive and offensive information operations.[13] CNA lies within the latter grouping, together with such varied activities as military deception,[14] psychological operations,[15] electronic warfare,[16] physical attack, and special information operations.[17] Its defining aspect is that it operates on data existing in computers or computer networks. That being so, computer network attack cuts across many categories of offensive IO—is intended result, for instance, might be deception or psychological effect. It is a technique, rather than a particular genre of objective. CNA operations can be used to facilitate strategic, operational, and tactical ends.[18] Further, because physical destruction seldom results from CNA,

---

distinguishing characteristic of sabotage is its design to interfere with the national defense. Thus, an attack on the banking system would not constitute sabotage, but one on a factory manufacturing military equipment would.

12. *See id.* at 217. Information operations must also be distinguished from command and control warfare (C2W), a form of IO with the specific purpose of influencing, degrading, or destroying an opponent's ability to direct its forces. On C2W, see JOINT PUB. 3-13.1, *supra* note 9.

13. Defensive IO "integrate[s] and coordinate[s] policies and procedures, operations, personnel, and technology to protect and defend information and information systems." Activities that support defensive IO include "information assurance (IA), OPSEC [operations security], physical security, counterdeception, counterpropoganda, counterintelligence (CI), EW [electronic warfare], and SIO [special information operations]." JOINT PUB. 3-13, *supra* note 6, at I-10. Each of these terms is defined in the Glossary to JOINT PUB. 3-13, *supra* note 6. Offensive IO, by contrast, is intended to "affect adversary decision makers and achieve or promote specific objectives." *Id.* at I-10.

14. "Actions executed to deliberately mislead adversary military decision makers as to friendly military capabilities, intentions, and operations, thereby causing the adversary to take specific actions (or inactions) that will contribute to the accomplishment of the friendly mission." JOINT PUB. 1-02, *supra* note 11, at 281.

15. "Planned operations to convey selected information and indicators to foreign audiences to influence their emotions, motives, objective reasoning, and ultimately the behavior of foreign governments, organizations, groups, and individuals. The purpose ... is to induce or reinforce foreign attitudes and behavior favorable to the originator's objectives." *Id.* at 358.

16. "Any military action involving the use of electromagnetic and directed energy to control the electromagnetic spectrum or to attack the enemy." *Id.* at 151.

17. "Information operations that by their sensitive nature, due to their potential effect or impact, security requirements, or risk to the national security of the United States, require a special review and approval process." JOINT PUB. 3-13, *supra* note 6, at GL-10.

18. [19] Strategic objectives are those at the national or multinational level. Operational objectives lie at the level of major military campaigns or of a military theater of operations. Tactical objectives arise at the individual battle or engagement level.

892   COLUMBIA JOURNAL OF TRANSNATIONAL LAW   [37:885

decision-makers find it a particularly attractive option in situations short of armed conflict.[19]

CNA techniques vary widely. Perhaps best known is the transmission of computer viruses into an adversary's computer network to destroy or alter data and programs. Logic bombs can also be introduced that sit idle in a system, awaiting activation at the occurrence of a particular event or set time. A logic bomb might be set to "explode" upon the call-up of reserve forces. Other techniques for disrupting information systems range from simply flooding it with false information to using "sniffer" programs to collect access codes that allow entry into a targeted system. In some cases, such attacks may occur without revealing the source, or even the fact, of the attack. In others, the identity of the attacker might be "spoofed" so as to convince the victim that the attack originated elsewhere.

Hypothetical examples of CNA, some realistic, others stretching credulity, abound in the literature. Consider just a few.

(1)   Trains are misrouted and crash after the computer systems controlling them are maliciously manipulated.[20]

(2)   An information blockade is mounted to limit the flow of electronic information into or out of a target state.[21]

(3)   Banking computer systems are broken into and their databases corrupted.[22]

(4)   An automated municipal traffic control system is compromised, thereby causing massive traffic jams and frustrating responses by emergency fire, medical, and law enforcement vehicles.[23]

---

19. In fact, IO has been characterized as possibly having its "greatest impact in peace and the initial stages of crisis." JOINT CHIEFS OF STAFF, INFORMATION WARFARE: A STRATEGY FOR PEACE... THE DECISIVE EDGE IN WAR 5 (n.d.). This is because many, if not most, of its effects are other than physical destruction. Indeed, according to the JCS, "IW [sic] can make an important contribution to defusing crises; reducing the period of confrontation and enhancing the impact of informational, diplomatic, economic, and military efforts; and forestalling or eliminating the need to employ forces in a combat situation." *Id.*

20. *See* ROGER C. MOLANDER ET AL., STRATEGIC INFORMATION WARFARE: A NEW FACE OF WAR 66 (1996).

21. *See* Kanuck, *supra* note 7, at 289.

22. *See* Molander, *supra* note 20, at 74.

23. *See* PRESIDENT'S COMMISSION ON CRITICAL INFRASTRUCTURE PROTECTION, CRITICAL FOUNDATIONS: PROTECTING AMERICA'S INFRASTRUCTURES A-48 (Oct 1997).

> (5)   Intrusion into the computer system controlling water distribution allows the intruder to rapidly open and close valves. This creates a hammer effect that eventually causes widespread pipe ruptures.[24]
>
> (6)   A logic bomb set to activate upon initiation of mass casualty operations is imbedded in a municipal emergency response computer system.

Lest such scenarios seem implausible, computer networks have already proven remarkably vulnerable. For instance, the Defense Information Systems Agency (DISA) identified fifty-three attacks on military and DOD systems in 1992. By 1995 that number had grown to 559, and an astonishing fourteen thousand incidents are anticipated in 1999. In addition, DISA estimates that only one attack in 150 is detected.[25] In what is perhaps the best known incident, two hackers penetrated the Air Force's Rome Laboratory in 1994 by using software that allowed them to appear legitimate. The intruders entered the system over 150 times, established links with foreign Internet sites, copied sensitive data, and attacked other linked government facilities and defense contractor systems.[26]

Particularly problematic is the fact that the source of the vulnerability is the very interconnectedness that renders networks so powerful. Most significantly, interconnectivity exacerbates the consequences of CNA due to the likelihood of reverberating effects. An incident in 1996 illustrates how this phenomenon can occur. When a single power line in Oregon short-circuited, other power lines were

---

24. *See id.* at A-46.

25. *See* TED UCHIDA, SCHOOL OF ADVANCED MILITARY STUDIES, U.S. ARMY COMMAND AND GENERAL STAFF COLLEGE, BUILDING A BASIS FOR INFORMATION WARFARE RULES OF ENGAGEMENT 8 (1997). In order to test computer security, DISA periodically uses typical "hacker-tools" to attack DOD computers. During a test of over twenty-six thousand unclassified computers in 1995, only 2% of the intrusions were detected, and of those only 5% were properly reported to the appropriate authorities. *See* DEFENSE SCIENCE BOARD TASK FORCE, INFORMATION WARFARE: DEFENSE (IW-D) 2-15 (Nov. 1996). In another study looking at the results of fifty-nine assessments involving 37,518 computers, 3.6% had easily exploitable "back-doors," 65% could be penetrated once the intruder was inside the network, 96% of professionally conducted penetrations go undetected by systems administrators and users, and 73% of detected penetrations were not reported. *See* Paul A. Strassmann, Information Terrorism: The Ultimate Infosec Challenge, Briefing at National Defense University (Jan. 5, 1998).

26. *See* OFFICE OF SCIENCE AND TECHNOLOGY POLICY, EXECUTIVE OFFICE OF THE PRESIDENT, CYBERNATION: THE AMERICAN INFRASTRUCTURE IN THE INFORMATION AGE (Apr. 1997).

894   *COLUMBIA JOURNAL OF TRANSNATIONAL LAW*   [37:885

forced to assume its load. Unable to cope with the increased demand, they too became overloaded and were shut down. The situation continued to snowball. By the time it was brought under control, a power blackout had spread to portions of fifteen states, as well as parts of Canada and Mexico.[27] Although not the product of a computer network attack, an identical result could easily have been caused by one.

The danger is that interrelationships cut across critical components of the national infrastructure. The Office of Science and Technology Policy, likening it to Mrs. O'Leary's cow and the Great Chicago Fire, highlighted this dilemma in an assessment of infrastructure vulnerability:

> The public telephone network, for example, relies on the power grid, the power grid on transportation, and all the sectors on telecommunications and the financial structure . . . . Most of today's cybernetic networks are actually combinations of networks, interconnected and interdependent. Interactions among these subsystems are critical to overall network performance, indeed they are the essence of network performance. Because the system also interacts with the real world environment, the interactions among subsystems are not necessarily predictable and sequential, like the steps of an assembly process, but can be essentially random, unsynchronized, and even unanticipated.[28]

Obviously, this complex national infrastructure web contains within it the likeliest CNA targets, both because of its national import, and because it offers an opponent countless avenues of attack. Our energy, communications, industrial, financial, transportation, human

---

27. *See id.*

28. *Id.* The Defense Science Board Task Force also noted this point.

> Our Task Force had many enlightening discussions about the potential for effects to cascade through one infrastructure (such as the phone system) into other infrastructures. This example is particularly important because most of our other infrastructures ride on the phone system. No one seems to know quite how, where, or when effects actually would cascade; nor what the total impact would be.

DEFENSE SCIENCE BOARD TASK FORCE, *supra* note 25, at 2-14.

services, and defense systems are brimming with computer dependencies.[29] Predictive efforts centering on potential targets and the methods that might be used to attack them lie at the core of defensive planning (and offensive brainstorming). Although such labors at times

---

29. The President's Commission on Critical Infrastructure Protection focused on the existence of infrastructures and the vulnerabilities they represent.

> Life is good in America because things work . . . We are able to assume that things will work because our infrastructures are highly developed and highly effective . . . By *infrastructure* we mean more than just a collection of individual companies engaged in related activities; we mean a network of independent, mostly privately owned, manmade systems and processes that function collaboratively and synergistically to produce and distribute a continuous flow of essential goods and services.

It noted the criticality of certain aspects of the infrastructure.

- Transportation . . . moves goods and people within and beyond our borders, and makes it possible for the United States to play a leading role in the global economy.
- Oil and gas production and storage . . . infrastructure fuels transportation services, manufacturing operations, and home utilities.
- The water supply infrastructure assures steady flow of water for agriculture, industry (including various manufacturing processes, power generation, and cooling), business, fire fighting, and our homes.
- Government services . . . consists of federal, state, and local agencies that provide essential services to the public.
- Banking & finance . . . manages trillions of dollars, from deposit of our individual paycheck to the transfer of huge amounts in support of major global enterprises.
- Electrical power infrastructure . . . [includes] generation, transmission, and distribution systems that are essential to all other infrastructures and every aspect of our economy.
- Telecommunications [have] . . . been revolutionized by advances in information technology in the past two decades to form an information and communications infrastructure, consisting of the Public Telecommunications Network (PTN), the Internet, and the many millions of computers in home, commercial, academic, and government use . . . connected to one another . . . . Networking is essential to a service economy as well as to competitive manufacturing and efficient delivery of raw materials and finished goods. The information and communications infrastructure is basic to responsive emergency services. It is the backbone of our military command and control system. And it is becoming the core of our educational system.

PRESIDENT'S COMMISSION ON CRITICAL INFRASTRUCTURE PROTECTION, *supra* note 23, at 3-4.

approximate random speculation, consider a representative attempt in the form of a notional list of the "Top 10" Information Warfare targets:

1. Culpeper, Virginia electronic switch which handles all Federal funds and transactions;

2. Alaska pipeline which currently carries 10 percent of all U.S. domestic oil;

3. Electronic switching system which manages all telephones;

4. Internet;

5. Time distribution system;

6. Panama Canal;

7. Worldwide Military Command and Control System (WMCSS);

8. Air Force satellite control network;

9. Strait of Malacca, the major maritime link between Europe-Arabian Peninsula and the Western Pacific and East Asia;

10. National Photographic Interpretation Center (Washington).[30]

Of course, these are information *warfare* targets designed to enhance an attacker's relative military position in times of crisis or conflict. Target sets would certainly differ for CNA conducted as part of a peacetime operation not intended to prepare the battle space for future conflict. However, the list illustrates specific examples of targets that serious thinkers have contemplated. Actual targets would, of course, depend on the overall political-military objective sought by the attacking state.

---

30. Arsenio T. Gumahad II, *The Profession of Arms in the Information Age*, JOINT FORCE Q., Spring 1997, at 14, 18, citing WIRED MAGAZINE, July-Aug. 1993. An interesting IO scenario was used during a war game at National Defense University. Set in the year 2000, it involved an OPEC meeting that goes awry when Saudi Arabia opposes Iranian demands for an oil production cutback in order to drive prices up. Iran mobilizes and conducts several attacks on Saudi warships. It also begins to conduct information warfare operations to destabilize the Saudi regime and keep the United States and United Kingdom out of the fray. A Saudi refinery is destroyed when computer malfunctions in its control mechanisms cause a fire; a "logic bomb" placed in the computer system running U.S. railways causes a passenger train to derail; computer "worms" begin to corrupt the U.S. military's classified deployment database, and a "sniffer" disrupts fund transfers in the Bank of England. *See* Steve Lohr, *Ready. Aim. Zap*; *National Security Experts Plan for Wars Whose Targets and Weapons are all Digital*, N.Y. TIMES, Sept. 30, 1996, at D-1.

The emerging information age generates new vulnerabilities that are likely to be exploited. Opponents of developed, first-world states cannot hope to prevail on the battlefield, or even in the boardroom. The technological and fiscal wherewithal of the developed states underlies an unprecedented level of military and economic supremacy. Moreover, as between these preeminent states (primarily the United States, its NATO allies, and Japan), the likelihood of armed conflict is *de minimus*. Thus, opponents of any particular state cannot hope to turn to a peer competitor of that state for support.

Facing these realities, a lesser-advantaged state hoping to seriously harm a dominant adversary must inevitably compete asymmetrically. It must seek to counter the strengths of the opponent not head-on, but rather, circuitously, employing unorthodox means to strike at centers of gravity. For instance, possession of weapons of mass destruction (WMD) can offset conventional military weakness. This is precisely why the United Nations Security Council takes the UNSCOM effort to deprive Iraq of WMD so seriously. Iraq cannot possibly hope to successfully confront the U.S. and its allies on the battlefield, but a credible threat to employ chemical or biological weapons in pursuit of national objectives would give it disproportionate (and malevolent) influence on the world scene. Similarly, asymmetry also undergirds most state or state-sponsored terrorism. It presents a relatively inexpensive means of striking a superior opponent in a very visible, yet relatively cost-free manner.[31]

CNA offers analogous asymmetrical benefits. In the first place, and as will be explored *infra*, in many cases a computer network attack will either not merit a response involving the use of force, or the legality of such a response will be debatable (even if the victim is able to accurately identify the fact, much less the source, of attack). Thus, because of the potentially grave impact of CNA on a state's infrastructure, it can prove a high gain, low risk option for a state outclassed militarily or economically. Moreover, to the extent that an opponent is militarily and economically advantaged, it is probably technologically-dependent, and, therefore, teeming with tempting CNA targets.

To further complicate matters, the knowledge and equipment necessary to mount a computer network attack are widely available; CNA is quite literally "war on the cheap." One expert has asserted that with one million dollars and twenty individuals, he can "bring the U.S.

---

31. On asymmetry, see generally Schmitt, *supra* note 4.

to its knees."[32] Another maintains that the defense information infrastructure (DII) can be disrupted for weeks by ten individuals with $10,000, while still others claim that for $30,000,000, one hundred individuals could so corrupt the country's entire information infrastructure that recovery would take years.[33] To place these figures into context, a single F-16 aircraft cost $26,000,000 in fiscal year 1997.[34] Unfortunately, the ability to conduct such operations is widespread. The President's Commission on Critical Infrastructure Protection has projected that by the year 2002, some nineteen million individuals will have the know-how to launch cyber attacks.[35] Today, over 120 countries are in the process of establishing information operations competence.[36] In particular, the Chinese have discovered information warfare, and organized research in the subject proceeds apace.[37] So too, not surprisingly, has the United States. Each of the armed services, as well as the Central Intelligence Agency, currently operates an information operations center.[38]

The centrality of information assets to national security, and therefore the need to safeguard them from CNA, cannot be overstated, a point well-recognized in official doctrine. The U.S. National Security Strategy for 1997, states that:

---

32. Planning Considerations for Defensive Information Warfare, Task Order 90-SAIC-019, Dec. 16, 1993 (*prepared for* The Defense Information Systems Agency, Joint Interoperability and Engineering Organization, and Center for Information Systems Security) (citing Robert D. Steele, War and Peace in the Age of Information, Superintendent's Guest Lecture, Naval Postgraduate School (August 1993)) [hereinafter Planning Considerations].

33. *See* Planning Considerations, *supra* note 32, at 17.

34. *See* JANE'S ALL THE WORLD'S AIRCRAFT 676 (Paul Jackson et al. eds., 1997-98).

35. *See* PRESIDENT'S COMMISSION ON CRITICAL INFRASTRUCTURE PROTECTION, *supra* note 23, at 9. Moreover, there will be approximately 1,300,000 "telecommunications systems control software specialists with tools and know how to disrupt or take down the public telecommunications network." *Id.*

36. *See* Brock, *supra* note 2, at 5.

37. *See* HAI LUNG & CHANG FENG, CHINESE MILITARY STUDIES INFORMATION WARFARE, (Hong Kong PTS Msg 210225Z Feb. 96, Subj: PLA Undertakes Study of Information Warfare) (Publications Translations Section, U.S. Consulate General, Hong Kong trans.). According to the report, preparations are underway for the establishment of an Information Warfare Institute, a non-governmental entity that will be responsible for "strategic planning . . ., theoretical studies, and technological development. Its aim is to enable high-technology advances from the nonmilitary sector to be applied to the military sector under the guidance of military theory." *Id.* Russia is also interested in enhancing IO capabilities. *See, e.g.,* Mary C. FitzGerald, *Russian Views on Electronic and Information Warfare, in* NATIONAL DEFENSE UNIVERSITY, PROCEEDINGS OF THE THIRD INTERNATIONAL COMMAND AND CONTROL RESEARCH AND TECHNOLOGY SYMPOSIUM: PARTNERS FOR THE 21ST CENTURY 126 (1997).

38. *See* Mark Walsh, *U.S. Military Expands Information Warfare Defense*, DEF. NEWS, Apr. 28-May 4, 1997, at 25; Lohr, *supra* note 30, at D4.

> The national security posture of the United States is increasingly dependent on our information infrastructures. These infrastructures are highly interdependent and are increasingly vulnerable to tampering and exploitation. Concepts and technologies are being developed and employed to protect and defend against these vulnerabilities; we must fully implement them to ensure the future security of not only our national information infrastructures, but our nation as well.[39]

Similarly, the most recently published National Military Strategy provides:

> Success in any operation depends on our ability to quickly and accurately integrate critical information and deny the same to an adversary. We must attain information superiority through the conduct of both offensive and defensive information operations. . . . Superiority in these areas will enable commanders to contend with information threats to their forces, including attacks which may originate from outside their area of operations. It also limits an adversary's freedom of action by disabling his critical information systems.[40]

In light of this centrality, *jus ad bellum* issues loom large. The information infrastructure and its multitudinous components comprise an attractive target set, and because of the ease with which CNA can be conducted, a critical, and difficult to defend, vulnerability. It is to the legal milieu in which such operations might occur that analysis shall now turn.

---

39. OFFICE OF THE PRESS SECRETARY, THE WHITE HOUSE, A NATIONAL SECURITY STRATEGY FOR A NEW CENTURY (May 17, 1997) (visited Feb. 23, 1999) <http://www1.whitehouse.gov/WH/html/library-plain.html>.

40. JOINT CHIEFS OF STAFF, NATIONAL MILITARY STRATEGY: SHAPE, RESPOND, PREPARE NOW, A MILITARY STRATEGY FOR A NEW ERA (1997) (visited Feb. 23, 1999) <http://www.dtic.mil/jcs/nms>.

II.	COMPUTER NETWORK ATTACK AS A USE OF FORCE

As noted, any number of purposes might motivate a state to conduct computer network attacks. Perhaps the CNA is designed to lay the groundwork for a subsequent conventional attack. Alternatively, it may be intended to stand alone, to cause damage and disruption without any desire to facilitate latter traditional military operations. Regardless of its aim, normative evaluation of the actions that occur will center on whether or not the actions constituted a wrongful use of force, or threat thereof, in violation of international law.

Article 2(4) of the UN Charter expresses the key prescription in international law regarding the use of force. By that provision, "All Members shall refrain in their international relations from the threat or use of force against the territorial integrity or political independence of any state, or in any other manner inconsistent with the Purposes of the United Nations."[41] Purposes of the United Nations expressly cited in the Charter include the maintenance of international peace and security.[42] Therefore, uses (or threats) of force which endanger international stability fall within Article 2(4)'s prescriptive envelope. It is a prohibition reiterated in numerous international instruments, both binding and aspirational.[43] Lest the provision be misinterpreted, it is important to recall that Article 2(4) is prohibitive rather than remedial in nature. It does not, in and of itself, authorize any response to a use or threat of force. Rather, the Charter delineates the bases for response to the wrongful use of force, as will be discussed *infra*, in Chapters VI and VII. Article 2(4) merely serves to render particular uses of force wrongful in the Charter scheme.

---

41. U.N. CHARTER art. 2, para 4.

42. *See id.* art. 1, para 1.

43. For instance, the General Assembly, in its resolution regarding the Declaration on Principles of International Law Concerning Friendly Relations and Cooperation Among States in Accordance with the Charter of the United Nations, has provided that,

> Every State has a duty to refrain in its international relations from the threat or use of force against the territorial integrity or political independence of any State, or in any other manner inconsistent with the purposes of the United Nations. Such a threat or use of force constitutes a violation of international law and the Charter of the United Nations and shall never be employed as a means of settling international issues.

> G.A. Res. 2625 (XXV), U.N. GAOR, 25th Sess., Supp. No. 28, at 121, U.N. Doc. A/8082 (1970), *reprinted in* KEY RESOLUTIONS OF THE UNITED NATIONS GENERAL ASSEMBLY, 1946-1996, at 3 (Dietrich Rauschning et al. eds., 1997) [hereinafter Declaration on Friendly Relations]. The resolution was adopted by acclamation.

Before turning to the specific query of when CNA might violate Article 2(4), it is first necessary to briefly consider the reach of Article 2(4).[44] The most significant issue surrounds the seemingly restrictive phrase "territorial integrity or political independence, or in any other manner inconsistent with the Purposes." Are there uses of force not otherwise authorized within the Charter that fall beyond Article 2(4)'s gamut because they do not threaten the territorial integrity or political independence of a target state or otherwise violate some specifically articulated prohibition found elsewhere in the Charter? Although the precise wording of the article generated much controversy as the Charter was being negotiated,[45] the mainstream view among international law experts is that the "other manner" language extends coverage to virtually any use of force not authorized within the Charter.[46] Thus, applying the prevailing positivist approach, analysis of use of force scenarios proceeds from the premise that an authorization for the use has to be found within the four corners of the Charter, not from the postulate that force is permissible unless a specific Charter prohibition thereon applies.[47] In the CNA context, this understanding would limit the scope of inquiry to whether the operation amounts to a use of force.

---

44. The analysis which follows will address uses of force, but applies equally to *threats* to use force. In other words, to the extent that CNA constitutes a use of force, the threat to commit such an attack will also be prohibited. On threats, see Romana Sadurska, *Threats of Force*, 82 AM. J. INT'L L. 239 (1988).

45. Originally, the draft of the Charter did not contain the terms territorial integrity or political independence, and the proposal for their inclusion was controversial. However, the travaux make it clear that the "other manner" language filled any possible voids in coverage. *See* Doc. 1123, I/8, 6 U.N.C.I.O Docs. 65 (1945); Doc 784, I/1/27, 6 U.N.C.I.O. Docs. 336 (1945); Doc. 885, I/1/34, 6 U.N.C.I.O. Docs. 387 (1945). *See also* IAN BROWNLIE, INTERNATIONAL LAW AND THE USE OF FORCE BY STATES 265-69 (1963) [hereinafter BROWNLIE, USE OF FORCE]. For a brief discussion of this issue in the context of information operations, see James N. Bond, Peacetime Foreign Data Manipulation as One Aspect of Offensive Information Warfare: Questions of Legality under the United Nations Charter Article 2(4), at 55-56 (June 14, 1996) (Advanced Research Project, United States Naval War College).

46. *See, e.g.,* YORAM DINSTEIN, WAR, AGGRESSION AND SELF-DEFENSE 86 (2d ed. 1994); Josef Mrazek, *Prohibition of the Use and Threat of Force: Self-Defence and Self-Help in International Law*, 27 CAN. Y.B. INT'L L. 81, 90 (1989); Albrecht Randelzhofer, *Article 2(4)*, *in* THE CHARTER OF THE UNITED NATIONS: A COMMENTARY 106, 117-18 (Bruno Simma et al. eds., 1995).

47. Unfortunately, this approach occasionally leads to tortuous efforts to justify operations, such as those in response to terrorist attacks, in Charter (usually self-defense) terms. A classic example would be the 1986 raid (Operation El Dorado Canyon) on Libya by U.S. aircraft in response to the terrorist bombing intended to kill U.S. servicemen at a disco in Berlin. On the operation and its justification, see *President's Address to the Nation, Apr. 14, 1986, reprinted in U.S. Exercises Right of Self-defense Against Libyan Terrorism*, DEP'T ST. BULL., at 1 (June 1986). Much attention has been paid to the fact that Libya was planning attacks on up to thirty U.S. diplomatic facilities worldwide. *See Joint News Conference by Secretary Schultz and Secretary Weinberger, April 14, 1986, reprinted in U.S. Exercises Right of Self-defense Against Libyan Terrorism, supra*, at 3 (June 1986).

Of course, the meaning of "force" may prove a matter of some dispute, as may the precise boundaries of the Charter's use of force sanctions, but if a CNA operation constitutes force, it will be deemed wrongful unless Charter-based. No further analysis is necessary.

Although textually sound, the positivist approach fails to reflect the realities underlying uses of force. It evidences misguided fidelity to the failed constitutive endeavor to establish a Charter security schema that would generally dispense with the need for unilateral uses of force, except in aberrant situations necessitating immediate self-defense. The envisioned normative architecture presupposed an effective enforcement mechanism—collective response under Security Council control—that has only slowly, and somewhat haphazardly, begun to be realized in the last decade. Absent an authoritative coercive enforcement mechanism, strict adherence to the plain text meaning of Article 2(4) can actually operate as a counterpoise to the Charter's world order aspirations. Specifically, adherence to a textual interpretation of the Charter security regime only allows either collective responses under Security Council mandate or defensive actions. During the Cold War, the Security Council was rendered impotent by bipolar competition. Despite the demise of bipolarity, the international community continues to struggle to forge consensus in the face of glaring acts of aggression, breaches of peace, or threats to peace. Inflexible understandings of Article 2(4)'s relationship to uses of force risk foreclosing unilateral or multilateral responses to deleterious situations that desperately demand community action, but upon which the Security Council has failed to act.

Fortunately, the international community has not allowed itself to be crippled by the relative desuetude of the Charter security system. On the contrary, in many cases states have responded to situations, either individually or in concert, in which community interests were served by taking coercive measures not specifically provided for in the Charter. Such incidents combine to map out a complex operational code as to those coercive acts the international community, or at least the politically relevant members thereof, accepts as lawful. Over a decade ago, Professor Michael Reisman identified nine basic categories of unilateral uses of force which enjoy some degree of community support:

> [S]elf-defense, which has been construed quite broadly; self-determination and decolonization; humanitarian intervention; intervention by the military instrument within spheres of influence and critical defense zones; treaty-sanctioned interventions within the territory of

another State; use of the military instrument for the gathering of evidence in international proceedings; use of the military instrument to enforce international judgements; and counter measures, such as reprisals and retorsions.[48]

The majority of these actions would be difficult to justify under the Charter, absent a strained interpretive effort.

As Professor Reisman notes, the categories themselves are not determinative.[49] Instead, every threat or use of force is evaluated on its own merits based upon the context in which it occurs. Thus, for example, while the operational code acknowledges the lawfulness of humanitarian intervention in certain circumstances, in others it might be deemed unlawful—the operational code is contextual. Moreover, the categories in which uses of force are sometimes considered appropriate evolve. New categories, such as use of the military in cross border counter-terrorist operations, may emerge, while shifts in the nature and effectiveness of the Charter security scheme may diminish the acceptability of others, such as the unilateral use of the military instrument to gather evidence. Many criteria of lawfulness operate synergistically to contribute to the final assessment of legality, such as the imminence and severity of the situation being addressed, less coercive or less violent alternatives and the viability of community responses. Ultimately, though, such extra-Charter uses of force will fall outside the operational code if they fail to advance shared world order values. The point here is not to index the operational code vis-à-vis uses of force, but rather to simply highlight the fact that a Charter analysis cannot be performed in isolation of the constantly developing and evolving operational code.[50]

Article 2(4) continues to enjoy predominant prescriptive valence, and it remains appropriate to view the provision as a general prohibition on non-Charter uses of force. That said, it must be recognized that certain forceful acts that lie outside the narrow options available in the

---

48. W. Michael Reisman, *Criteria for the Lawful Use of Force in International Law*, 10 YALE J. INT'L L. 279, 281 (1985) [hereinafter Reisman, *Criteria*]. *See also* W. Michael Reisman, *Article 2(4):The Use of Force in Contemporary International Law*, 78-79 AM. SOC. INT'L L. PROC. 74, 79-84 (1984-85); W. Michael Reisman, *War Powers: The Operational Code of Competence*, 83 AM. J. INT'L L. 777 (1989).

49. *See* Reisman, *Criteria, supra* note 48, at 282.

50. For an interesting projection of factors likely to affect the use of force in the future, see Anthony D'Amato, *Megatrends in the Use of Force, in* THE LAW OF ARMED CONFLICT, *supra* note 4, at 1.

Charter nevertheless comport with the operational code. A useful approach may well be to apply a rebuttable presumption to uses of force not specifically consistent with the Charter security system. A presumption of unlawfulness would attach to any such use. The burden would then shift to the actor to justify its actions within the relevant international community.

Given this analytical framework, the dispositive question is whether CNA constitutes use of force. Since the drafting of the UN Charter, the reach of the term "force" has proven contentious. The Vienna Convention on the Law of Treaties sets forth the core interpretive principle that international instruments are to be interpreted "in accordance with the ordinary meaning to be given to the terms of the treaty in their context and in light of its object and scope."[51] But what is the plain meaning of the term "force"? Does it only extend to "armed" force, i.e. force applied by military units, or does it encompass other forms of coercion? In addressing this issue, some commentators point to the Charter itself,[52] an approach consistent with the Vienna Convention's inclusion of a treaty's preamble, text, and annexes in its "context."[53] For instance, the Preamble includes among Charter purposes the goal that "*armed* force . . . not be used save in the common interest . . . ." If the Article 2(4) prohibition were intended to extend beyond armed force, then presumably the preamble, for reasons of internal consistency, would not have included the term "armed." After all, the Charter's articles are designed to effectuate its preambular aspirations. Thus, preambular terminology is logically interpreted more broadly than that contained in the articles. The wording of Article 44 further supports a restrictive interpretation. It states, "When the Security Council has decided to use force it shall, before calling upon a Member not represented to provide armed forces . . . ." "Force" appears, as in Article 2(4), without the qualifier "armed," but, as demonstrated by the reference to "armed forces," clearly contemplates that the force used be armed.

---

51. Vienna Convention on the Law of Treaties, May 23, 1969, art. 31(1), 1155 U.N.T.S. 331 (1969). This point was reiterated by the International Court of Justice in *The Competence of the General Assembly for the Admission of a State to the United Nations* case. In that case, the ICJ noted that "the first duty of a tribunal which is called upon to interpret and apply the provisions of a treaty is to endeavor to give effect to them in their natural and ordinary meaning in the context in which they occur." General List No. 9, 1950 I.C.J. 4, 8 (Mar. 3) (advisory opinion).

52. *See* Randelzhofer, *supra* note 46, at 112; Hans Wehberg, "L'Interdiction du Recours á la Force: Le Principe et les Problèmes qui se Posent," 78 R.C.A.D.I. 1, 69 (1951).

53. Vienna Convention, *supra* note 51, art. 31(2).

The Charter uses the term "armed force" twice,[54] a fact which might seem to suggest the drafters intended to distinguish it from unqualified force after all. However, both cases involve Chapter VII enforcement, in which armed force is but one of multiple options available to the Security Council in responding to threats to the peace, breach of the peace, or acts of aggression. Read in context, they clearly refer to a particular point along the continuum of coercion. By contrast, because Article 2(4) precludes nothing but "force," there was no need to distinguish it through qualification.

While textual analysis is often telling, it is based on the somewhat suspect premise that a diverse group of diplomatic teams was thoroughly aware of the subtle nuances of language. This is so despite the fact that many members of the teams do not share English (or for that matter any language of the other authoritative texts—Chinese, French, Russian, and Spanish) as their first language.[55] Of course, negotiating teams do obsess over terminological precision in order to avoid committing their state to unintended and undesired obligations. However, should ambiguity or obscurity remain, interpretive recourse may be made to "the preparatory work of the treaty and circumstances of its conclusion."[56]

In the case of Article 2(4), the *travaux préparatoires*[57] do shed considerable light on the subject. At the San Francisco Conference, the Brazilian delegation submitted amendments to the Dumbarton Oaks proposals that would have extended Article 2(4)'s range to economic coercion.[58] Though the proposition received a majority vote in committee, the Conference declined adopting it by a vote of 26-2. [59] Thus, analysis based on both UN Charter *travaux* and text leads to an interpretation excluding economic, and for that matter political, coercion from Article 2(4)'s prescriptive sphere.

---

54. *Id.* arts. 41, 46.

55. U.N. CHARTER art. 111.

56. Vienna Convention, *supra* note 51, art. 32. ("Recourse may be had to supplementary means of interpretation, including the preparatory work of the treaty and the circumstances of its conclusion, in order to confirm the meaning resulting from the application of article 31, or to determine the meaning when the interpretation according to article 31: (a) Leaves the meaning ambiguous or obscure; or (b) Leads to a result which is manifestly absurd or unreasonable").

57. "Legislative history," specifically the record of negotiations leading to final adoption of the Convention.

58. *See* Doc. 784, I/1/27, 6 U.N.C.I.O. Docs. 331, 334, 609 (1945). Originally, the Dumbarton Oaks Proposal for the prohibition read as follows: "All members of the Organization shall refrain from the threat or use of force in any manner inconsistent with the purposes of the Organization." Doc. 1123 I/8, 6 U.N.C.I.O. Docs. 65, 68 (1945).

59. *See* Doc. 2, G/7 (e)(4), 3 U.N.C.I.O. Docs. 251, 253-54 (1945).

Other international instruments of the time also used the term "force" without qualification.[60] In none of them does any support for inclusion of economic or political pressure appear. In fact, the terminological approach in one of the key constitutive documents of the time implies just the opposite. The Charter of the Organization of American States (as subsequently amended) avoids use of the naked term "force" altogether, instead separately referring to "armed force" and "coercive measures of an economic or political character."[61] Its drafters appear to have been sensitive to the normative import of the distinction, an unsurprising fact in light of Brazil's membership in the organization.[62]

In fairness, the restrictive interpretation has not enjoyed universal acceptance. The desire for a broader definition resurfaced twenty-five years after the San Francisco Conference during the drafting of the General Assembly's Declaration on Friendly Relations. The Declaration expresses the use of force prohibition in terms identical to Article 2(4).[63] During committee handling of the draft, differences of opinion again arose over whether the term "force" should extend to "all forms of pressure, including those of a political or economic character, which have the effect of threatening the territorial integrity or political

---

60. *See, e.g.,* Inter-American Treaty of Reciprocal Assistance, Sept. 2, 1947, art. 1, T.I.A.S. No. 1838, 21 U.N.T.S. 77: ". . . undertake in their international relations not to resort to the threat or the use of force in any manner inconsistent with the provisions of the Charter of the United Nations or of this Treaty." *See also* Pact of the League of Arab States, March 22, 1945, art. 5, 70 U.N.T.S. 238, which only speaks of force; "Any resort to force in order to resolve disputes arising between two or more member States of the League is prohibited." This instrument was drafted contemporaneously with the U.N. Charter.

61. Charter of the Organization of American States, Apr. 30, 1948, T.I.A.S. No. 2361, 119 U.N.T.S. 3.

> Article 18: No State or group of States has the right to intervene, directly or indirectly, for any reason whatever, in the internal or external affairs of any other State. The foregoing principle prohibits not only armed force but also any other form of interference or attempted threat against the personality of the State or against its political, economic, and cultural elements,

> Article 19: No State may use or encourage the use of coercive measures of an economic or political character in order to force the sovereign will of another State and obtain from it advantages of any kind.

62. Recall that Brazil had proposed that Article 2(4) of the U.N. Charter encompass economic coercion. *See supra* text accompanying note 58.

63. *See* Declaration on Friendly Relations, *supra* note 43, prin. 1, annex (The General Assembly "[s]olemnly proclaims the following Principles: 1. The Principle that States shall refrain in their international relations from the threat or use of force against the territorial integrity or political independence of any State, or in any other manner inconsistent with the purposes of the United Nations.").

independence of any State."[64] Most Western States sought to limit the expression to armed force, in some cases linking the prohibition to the right to respond in self-defense pursuant to Article 51 of the Charter to an armed attack. In contrast, the bulk of African and Asian nations advocated a purpose-based interpretive analysis. By their reasoning, a desire to assure the political independence of States through protection of sovereign prerogative and territorial inviolability permeated Article 2(4). To the extent that economic and political coercion constituted a threat to those principles, the article, as well as the Declaration, should be interpreted to preclude such misdeeds. For proponents, interpretative endeavors, particularly when text is ambiguous, should not be foreclosed by *travaux*, but rather should reflect the underlying purposes of the article in the current international context. Latin American countries split on the issue.

Ultimately, the debate proved impossible to resolve—the Declaration's Principles, and the textual explication thereto, do not directly address the differences. However, much of the explanation of the Principle prohibiting resort to force is cast in terms relevant only to armed force.[65] That the Declaration fails to cite economic or political measures in the Principle on the use of force, but does so with regard to the Principle imposing a duty not to "intervene in matters within the domestic jurisdiction of any State,"[66] strengthens the restrictive argument. Tellingly, a second General Assembly Resolution on the subject, this one issued in 1987, takes an analogous approach. In the Declaration on the Enhancement of the Effectiveness of the Principle of Refraining from the Threat or Use of Force in International Relations, "armed intervention" is tied to "interference or attempted threats against the personality of the State or against its political, economic and cultural elements," whereas economic and political coercion are cited in the context of "the subordination of the exercise of . . . sovereign rights" and securing "advantages of any kind" from the target state.[67] Again, while the Declaration does not definitively resolve the reach of the term

---

64. U.N. GAOR Special Comm. On Friendly Relations, 24th Sess., 114th mtg., U.N. Doc. A/AC.125/SR.114 (1970). *See also Report of the Special Comm. on Friendly Relations*, U.N. GAOR, 24th Sess., Supp. No. 19, at 12, U.N. Doc. A/7619 (1969); Derek W. Bowett, *Economic Coercion and Reprisals by States*, 13 VA. J. INT'L L. 1 (1972).

65. *See, e.g.*, "[a] war of aggression," "irregular forces or bands," "acts of civil strife or terrorist acts," "military occupation," "disarmament," etc. Declaration on Friendly Relations, *supra* note 43, prin. 1, annex.

66. *Id.* For example, "[n]o State may use or encourage the use of economic, political or any other type of measures to coerce another State in order to obtain from it the subordination of the exercise of its sovereign rights and to secure from it advantages of any kind. *Id.*

67. G.A. Res. 42/22, U.N. GAOR, 42d Sess., 73d plen. mtg., Agenda Item 131, annex, art. I ¶ 7-8 (1988), *reprinted in* KEY RESOLUTIONS, *supra* note 43, at 7.

"force," its general tenor, and the varying contexts in which armed, economic, and political coercion arise, suggest that although economic and political coercion may constitute threats to international stability and therefore are precluded by the principle of non-intervention (discussed *infra*), the concept of the use of force is generally understood to mean armed force.[68]

The foregoing analysis shows that the prohibition of the threat or use of force includes armed, but not economic or political coercion.[69] However, it does not demonstrate that the borders of "force" precisely coincide with armed force, i.e., physical or kinetic force applied by conventional weaponry. This reality has only recently proven of applicative import. Until the advent of information operations, most coercion could be handily categorized into one of several boxes, for few coercive options existed that could not be typed as political, economic, or armed in nature. Because there was little need to look beyond these genera, discourse about the lawfulness of State coercion, as illustrated *supra,* tended to revolve around them. If the act in question fell within the armed force box, it violated the prescription banning the use of force; if not, questions of legality had to be resolved by looking elsewhere.[70]

On rare occasions, the relatively bright line test for wrongful use of force proved inutile. For instance, in the *Nicaragua* Case the International Court of Justice (ICJ), held that:

---

68. As to both declarations, recall that by Article 31(3) of the Vienna Convention subsequent agreement regarding interpretation of a Treaty is an appropriate interpretive consideration. *See* Vienna Convention, *supra* note 51, art. 31(3).

69. On economic sanctions, see Paul Szasz, *The Law of Economic Sanctions, in* THE LAW OF ARMED CONFLICT, *supra* note 4, at 455.

70. This is not to say that international law scholars missed the distinction; it is only to say that it has attained particular significance in the last decade. For instance, Hans Kelsen noted:

> There are two kinds of force not exercised by use of arms: (1) an action of a state directed against another state which constitutes a violation of international law but which is not performed by use of arms; (2) a reprisal which does not involve the use of armed force. Article 2, paragraph 4, refers to the "use of force." It therefore prohibits both kinds of force. Hence, not only is the use of force prohibited but any action of a member state illegal under general international law which is directed against another state is prohibited by the Charter, and the member states are forbidden to resort not only to war but also to reprisals.

HANS KELSEN, COLLECTIVE SECURITY UNDER INTERNATIONAL LAW 57 n.5 (49 Naval War College International Law Studies 1954, 1956). Ian Brownlie disagrees with this assessment, arguing that "there is no evidence . . . that it bears the meaning suggested by Kelsen." BROWNLIE, USE OF FORCE, *supra* note 45, at 362.

> [W]hile arming and training of the *contras* can certainly be said to involve the threat or use of force against Nicaragua, this is not necessarily so in respect of all assistance given by the United States Government. In particular, the Court considers that the mere supply of funds to the *contras*, while undoubtedly an act of intervention in the internal affairs of Nicaragua . . . does not itself amount to a use of force.[71]

Assuming the Court accurately characterized the state of the law, the dimensions of the armed force box grew slightly. In what was tantamount to an application of agency theory, the Court determined that force apparently includes actively and directly preparing another to apply armed force, but not merely funding the effort. Nevertheless, despite the subtle shift in the understanding of force, prescriptive ratiocination continues to transpire within a familiar paradigm, that of distinguishing armed force from other tools of coercion.

At least since promulgation of the Charter, this use of force paradigm has been instrument-based; determination of whether or not the standard has been breached depends on the type of the coercive *instrument*—diplomatic, economic, or military—selected to attain the national objectives in question. The first two types of instruments might rise to the level of intervention, but they do not engage the normatively more flagrant act of using force. However, despite instrument classing, in actual practice it does not follow that coercive acts involving armed force necessarily operate at counter-purposes with community values (they are condoned when consistent with the operational code). Even when they do, it is not always the case that they do greater violence thereto. For instance, a temporally and spatially limited border incursion is probably a lesser threat to either international peace and security or the right of states to conduct their affairs free from outside interference than was the 1973-1974 Arab oil embargo.[72] Yet,

---

71. Military and Paramilitary Activities (Nicar. v. U.S.), 1986 I.C.J. 4,119, (June 27). Note that the ICJ was not actually applying Article 2(4) *qua* 2(4) because application of the Charter was barred by the U.S. acceptance of jurisdiction (pursuant to Article 36(2) of the Court's Statute) only on the condition that all States involved in the case be party to any multilateral treaty used by the Court to adjudicate the issue. Therefore, the Court applied the customary international law prohibition on the resort to force.

72. For a discussion of force as extending beyond armed force, see Jordan J. Paust & Albert P. Blaustein, *The Arab Oil Weapon: A Threat to International Peace*, 68 AM. J. INT'L L. 410 (1974).

910   *COLUMBIA JOURNAL OF TRANSNATIONAL LAW*   [37:885

the prescriptive framework would proscribe the former, but not the latter.[73]

In order to understand the distinction, one must first inquire into why the limitation exists at all. International law regarding coercion seeks to foster or frustrate consequences. Although, as noted in the discussion of operational codes, normative architectures evolve over time as community aspirations shift in one direction or another, certain shared community values, albeit often aspirational, permeate world order prescription. They include, *inter alia*, physical survival and security for both individuals and the tangible objects on which they rely, human dignity (particularly that expressed in human rights norms), social progress and quality of life, and "the right of peoples to shape their own political community."[74] In a sense, these aspirations echo a human hierarchy of need. International law seeks to advance them to a degree largely determined by both their position in the hierarchy of need and the nature of the systemic constraints that the international system imposes on their pursuit.

The primary constraint, the determinative reality, is that these aspirations must be pursued within a state-based international structure. This structure contains many obstacles, not the least of which is interstate rivalry rift with zero-sum thinking.[75] The UN Charter reflects this understanding by including in its purposes the maintenance of international peace and security, development of friendly relations among nations, achievement of international cooperation in solving

---

73. On the appropriateness of applying the economic instrument, see Clinton E. Cameron, *Developing a Standard for Politically Related State Economic Action*, 13 MICH. J. INT'L L. 218 (1991).

74. These aims derive from those expressed in the Preamble to the U.N. Charter:

> [T]o save succeeding generations from the scourge of war, which twice in our life-time has brought untold sorrow to mankind, and to reaffirm faith in fundamental human rights, in the dignity and worth of the human person, in the equal rights of men and women and of nations large and small, and to establish conditions under which justice and respect for the obligations arising from treaties and other sources of international law can be maintained, and to promote social progress and better standards of life in larger freedom.

U.N. CHARTER preamble, art. X, para. X. The final aim was perceptively articulated in W. Michael Reisman, *Allocating Competences to Use Coercion in the Post-Cold War World: Practices, Conditions, and Prospects, in* LAW AND FORCE IN THE NEW INTERNATIONAL ORDER 26, 45 (Lori Fisler Damrosch & David J. Scheffer eds., 1991). To a very great extent, these shared values overlap.

75. Of course, the aims are perhaps at greater risk from internal sources, but Westphalian state-centrism, with its emphasis on the principle of sovereignty, has held back the progress of international law in responding to internal threats. Fortunately, the effort to limit inter-state conflict usually advances community-wide aspirations without imperiling the internal autonomy that sovereignty cherishes.

international problems, and harmonization of the actions of nations.[76] While these appear to be goals in and of themselves, they are actually intermediate goals in the attainment of the ultimate ends just articulated. They are community value enablers.

The prohibition on the use of force is designed to advance these intermediate objectives (and occasionally the ultimate aims) by restricting those acts most likely to endanger them—uses of force. In fact, the international community is not directly concerned with the particular coercive instrumentality used (force in this case), but rather the consequences of its use. However, it would prove extraordinarily difficult to quantify or qualify consequences in a normatively practical manner. Undesirable consequences fall along a continuum, but how could the criteria for placement along it be clearly expressed? In terms of severity? Severity measured by what standard of calculation? Harm to whom or what?[77]

The difficulty in looking to consequences themselves as criteria for calculating lawfulness led the Charter drafters to use prescriptive short-hand to achieve their goals. Because force represents a consistently serious menace to intermediate and ultimate objectives, the prohibition of resort to it is a relatively reliable instrument-based surrogate for a ban on deleterious consequences. It eases the evaluative process by simply asking whether force has been used, rather than requiring a far more difficult assessment of the consequences that have resulted.

Of course, the use of force can cause widely divergent results depending on the weapon used, scale of attack, and nature of the target, as can economic coercion, which may result in everything from financial uneasiness to the collapse of an economy. Nevertheless, instrument-based evaluation is merited in the case of the former, but not the latter, by virtue of its far greater consequence-instrument congruence. Armed coercion usually results in some form of physical destruction or injury, whereas economic (or political) coercion seldom does. Additionally, the risk of an escalating conflict from a use of force ordinarily exceeds the risk from economic or political coercion because force strikes more directly at those community values at the top of the human hierarchy of need, in particular survival. The fact that the consequences of the use of force are almost immediately apparent,

---

76. U.N. CHARTER art. 1.

77. Moreover, a purely consequence-based standard would risk falling prey to dissonant (e.g., cultural) valuation paradigms. On the subject of valuation paradigms, see Michael N. Schmitt, *War and the Environment: Fault Lines in the Prescriptive Landscape,* ARCHIV DES VÖLKERRECHTS (1999) (forthcoming).

912   *COLUMBIA JOURNAL OF TRANSNATIONAL LAW*   [37:885

whereas economic or political consequences, although severe, emerge much more slowly, and thereby allow opportunity for reflection and resolution, compounds the danger of escalation. An even more basic problem is pinning down the cause and effect relationship when applying economic and political coercion. During the time lag between the initiation of the coercion and the emergence of consequences, intervening factors may enter the picture without which the consequences would not have occurred.

Because the results of applying economic and political instruments generally constitute lesser threats to shared community values, the use of force standard serves as a logical break point in categorizing the asperity of particular coercive acts. Any imprecision in this prescriptive short-hand is more than outweighed by its clarity and ease of application.

What matters, then, are consequences, but for a variety of reasons prescriptive shorthand based upon the instrument involved classifies coercive acts into two categories—those the community most abhors (force), and all others (which may in themselves violate less portentous community prescriptions). Computer network attack challenges the prevailing paradigm, for its consequences cannot easily be placed in a particular area along the community values threat continuum. The dilemma lies in the fact that CNA spans the spectrum of consequentiality. Its effects freely range from mere inconvenience (e.g., shutting down an academic network temporarily) to physical destruction (e.g., as in creating a hammering phenomenon in oil pipelines so as to cause them to burst) to death (e.g., shutting down power to a hospital with no back-up generators). It can affect economic, social, mental, and physical well-being, either directly or indirectly, and its potential scope grows almost daily, being capable of targeting everything from individual persons or objects to entire societies.

Note that Article 41 of the Charter cites "interruption of . . . communication" as a "measure not involving armed force."[78] Certainly, some forms of computer network attack would fall in the ambit of this characterization. However, many forms would not. More to the point, the Charter drafters did not contemplate CNA. Therefore, to reason that CNA is a "measure not involving armed force" by virtue of Article 41 is over-reaching. So how should computer network attack best be characterized? As a use of armed force? As force? As some nascent modality of inter-State coercion which exists in a normative void?

---

78. U.N. CHARTER art. 41.

One narrow category of computer network attack is easily dealt with. CNA specifically intended to directly cause physical damage to tangible property or injury or death to human beings is reasonably characterized as a use of *armed* force and, therefore, encompassed in the prohibition. Thus, in the examples above, the pipeline destruction and the shutting of power to the hospital are examples of CNA which the actor knows can, and intends to, directly cause destruction and serious injury. Armed coercion is not defined by whether or not kinetic energy is employed or released, but rather by the nature of the direct results caused, specifically physical damage and human injury. Instrumentalities that produce them are weapons. There is little debate about whether the use of chemicals or biologicals falls within the meaning of armed force, even though the means that cause the injury or death differ greatly from those produced by kinetic force. [79] Similarly, there was little doubt that neutron bombs constitute weapons, nor has controversy over the classification as weapons of the new varieties of non-lethals (many of which do not release kinetic energy as a mode of effect) surfaced.[80] That computer network attack employs electrons to cause a result from which destruction or injury directly ensues is simply not relevant to characterization as armed force. The dilemma lies beyond this limited category of computer network attacks. How should computer network attacks which do not cause physical damage or injury, or do so indirectly, be classed vis-à-vis the prohibition on the use of force?

Unless the international community is willing to adopt a *de novo* scheme for assessing the use of inter-state coercion, any justification or condemnation of CNA must be cast in terms of the use of force paradigm. In that computer network attack cuts across the instrument-based distinction employed as prescriptive short-hand, it becomes necessary to shift cognitive approach if one wishes to continue to operate within the existing framework. The key to doing so lies in revisiting the "force" box. As the discussion has illustrated, the controversy surrounding the meaning of the term was not so much whether the concept was limited to armed force, but rather whether it included economic coercion. To the extent that the qualifier "armed" was cited, it was done in order to counter the argument for extension. There was no need to look beyond armed force because intermediate forms of coercion such as CNA were not generally contemplated. Yet, the holding of the ICJ in the *Nicaragua* Case with regard to arming and

---

79. *See* BROWNLIE, USE OF FORCE, *supra* note 45, at 362.

80. On non-lethal weapons, see James C. Duncan, *A Primer on the Employment of Non-Lethal Weapons,* 45 NAVAL L. REV. 1 (1998).

914   *COLUMBIA JOURNAL OF TRANSNATIONAL LAW*   [37:885

training the contras suggested that other forms of "force" were not necessarily excluded. Therefore, the use of force line must lie somewhere between economic coercion and the use of *armed* force. The question becomes how to locate the point of demarcation, at least with regard to this new genre of coercion.

Perhaps the best approach is to start by reflecting upon the underlying motivation for the instrument-based distinctions: consequences. This is an imprecise endeavor, for, as discussed, the instruments do not precisely track the threats to shared values which, ideally, the international community would seek to deter. Nevertheless, if commonalities between typical consequences for each category can be articulated, perhaps CNA can be classed according to consequence affinity with the current prescriptive distinguishers.

Economic and political coercion can be delimited from the use of armed force by reference to various criteria. The following number among the most determinative:

1) *Severity*: Armed attacks threaten physical injury or destruction of property to a much greater degree than other forms of coercion. Physical well-being usually occupies the apex of the human hierarchy of need.

2) *Immediacy*: The negative consequences of armed coercion, or threat thereof, usually occur with great immediacy, while those of other forms of coercion develop more slowly. Thus, the opportunity for the target state or the international community to seek peaceful accommodation is hampered in the former case.

3) *Directness*: The consequences of armed coercion are more directly tied to the *actus reus* than in other forms of coercion, which often depend on numerous contributory factors to operate. Thus, the prohibition on force precludes negative consequences with greater certainty.

4) *Invasiveness*: In armed coercion, the act causing the harm usually crosses into the target state, whereas in economic warfare the acts generally occur beyond the target's borders. As a result, even though armed and economic acts may have roughly similar consequences, the former represents a greater intrusion on the rights of the target state and, therefore, is more likely to disrupt international stability.

5) *Measurability*: While the consequences of armed coercion are usually easy to ascertain (e.g., a certain level of destruction), the actual negative consequences of other forms of coercion are harder to measure. This fact renders the appropriateness of community condemnation, and the degree of vehemence contained therein, less suspect in the case of armed force.

6) *Presumptive Legitimacy*: In most cases, whether under domestic or international law, the application of violence is deemed illegitimate absent some specific exception such as self-defense. The cognitive approach is prohibitory. By contrast, most other forms of coercion—again in the domestic and international sphere—are presumptively lawful, absent a prohibition to the contrary. The cognitive approach is permissive. Thus, the consequences of armed coercion are presumptively impermissible, whereas those of other coercive acts are not (as a very generalized rule).

These consequence commonalities can serve as the ties between CNA and the prevailing instrument-based prescriptive shorthand.[81] By this scheme, one measures the consequences of a computer network attack against the commonalities to ascertain whether they more closely approximate consequences of the sort characterizing armed force or whether they are better placed outside the use of force boundary. This technique allows the force box to expand to fill lacunae (that became apparent upon the emergence of coercive possibilities enabled by technological advances) without altering the balance of the current framework—the growth is cast in terms of the underlying factors driving the existing classifications.

How might this technique operate? In determining whether an opponent's computer network attack (or threat thereof) fell within the more flexible consequence–based understanding of force (or whether an action being considered by one's own information warriors does), the

---

81. Arguably, *responsibility* is a seventh commonality. Armed coercion is the exclusive province of states; only they may generally engage in uses of force across borders, and in most cases only they have the ability to do so with any meaningful impact. By contrast, non-governmental entities are often capable of engaging in other forms of coercion (propaganda, boycotts, etc.). Therefore, with armed coercion the likelihood of blurring the relative responsibility of the State, a traditional object of international prescription, and private entities, usually only the object of international administration, narrows. In sum, the consequences of armed coercion are more susceptible to being charged to the State actor than in the case of other forms of coercion. However, this is an issue of assessing State responsibility, not lawfulness. It is a practical challenge, not a normative one.

nature of the act's reasonably foreseeable consequences would be assessed to determine whether they resemble those of armed coercion. If so, extension of the use of force prohibition to the act would be justified. If not, wrongfulness under international law would have to be determined by resort to prescriptive norms other than that prohibiting force.

Consider two apposite examples. In the first case, computer network attacks disable a busy air traffic control (ATC) system during horrendous weather. An airliner crashes and deaths result. No kinetic force has been used to destroy the airliner, but CNA was plainly the proximate cause of the tragedy. This action would be considered a use of force. The severity of the consequences, multiple deaths and physical destruction, rises to a level equal to that of armed coercion. The technique did not permit sufficient opportunity to defuse the crisis before the consequences occurred, and, although CNA did not directly target the aircraft's on-board systems, the crash would not have occurred but for the attack on the ATC assets. Furthermore, in order to cause the damage, signals had to be transmitted across political borders. The consequences of the attack are easily measurable (in terms of human and property loss), and, although attempts to harm others through their computers and computer networks is a relatively new technique, there is a growing body of law in many countries criminalizing such activities.[82]

Contrast this analysis with that addressing an attack on a university computer network designed to disrupt military related research occurring in campus laboratories. Severity, considered in the context of shared values, falls significantly below that of armed coercion. No physical damage or measurable suffering occurs, at least in the short term. The desired outcome, diminished capability on the battlefield, is remote from the act, and it is indirect in that it will depend on a number of indeterminacies—the ability to regenerate data, the possible existence of other research efforts moving towards the same conclusions, the

---

82. For summaries of applicable domestic law, see JOINT CHIEFS OF STAFF, INFORMATION ASSURANCE: LEGAL, REGULATORY, POLICY AND ORGANIZATION CONSIDERATIONS (3d ed. 1997), § 4; Roger D. Scott, *Legal Aspects of Information Warfare: Military Disruption of Telecommunications,* 45 NAVAL L. REV. 57, 64-75 (1998). As to responsibility (*see supra* note 78 and accompanying text), in the macro sense it will be difficult to assess because most computer network attacks can be conducted by non-governmental individuals with access to the requisite hard and software; it requires no special infrastructure available only to a government. However, though this factor would augur against characterizing computer network attack in the abstract as a use of force, because it is technologically-dependent, technological means may be able to reliably ascertain the source of the attack as a specific sate or agent thereof. To the extent this is true of a particular method of attack, it increases the appropriateness of labeling it a use of force.

likelihood the project would have been funded through entry into the inventory, etc. Although the transmission of the signal is intrusive and presumptively illegitimate, metering the consequences will prove difficult. In sum, the underlying nature of the consequences resulting from this particular information operation fails to sufficiently resemble that characteristic of uses of armed force. Extension of the instrument-based use of force distinguisher would be inappropriate.

It may appear torturous to use the prescriptive shorthand (instrument-based classification) as a point of departure, rather than simply ask to what degree the consequences of computer network attack threaten shared community values. One might simply look no further than the severity of consequences.[83] Indeed, at conferences and among those who have considered the subject in any depth, there is a tendency to take this stance when struggling with the dilemma of how to account for non-kinetically based harm with a system designed to regulate kinetic activities. The flaw in doing so lies in the fact that it calls for a new normative architecture altogether to handle such actions, an architecture that amounts to more than an interpretive dilation of the use of force standard. It would constitute a new standard.

By contrast, reference to the instrument-based shorthand facilitates greater internal consistency and predictability within the preexisting framework for inter-state coercion. It allows determinations on the inclusivity of the use of force to more closely approximate the current system than analysis based solely on consequentiality would allow. As a result, subscription by the international community is more likely, and application should prove less disruptive and controversial. This is not to say that greater focus on core objectives, on consequentiality in its pure form, is not to be sought. It is only a recognition that until the international community casts off its current cognitive approach, community values are, for practical reasons, best advanced in terms of that which is familiar and widely accepted.

It should be noted that schema-imbuing consequences, rather than acts, with normative valence are nothing new. In the *jus in bello*, consequence-based analysis predominates. The principle of proportionality, for instance, balances positive consequences (military advantage) against harmful ones (collateral damage and incidental

---

83. Consequences should not be confused with motivation (justification). The operational code operates based primarily on the latter; it looks to the rationale for the use of force to justify it, not what its consequences are.

918   COLUMBIA JOURNAL OF TRANSNATIONAL LAW   [37:885

injury).[84] Additionally, Protocol I to the Geneva Conventions prohibits starvation of civilians, causation of "widespread, long-term and severe damage" to the environment, and attacks on works and installations containing dangerous forces which "may cause the release of dangerous forces and consequent severe losses among the civilian population."[85] Similarly, the Environmental Modification Convention forbids the use of any hostile environmental modification technique that has "widespread, long-lasting or severe effects."[86]

More to the point, consequentiality arguably dominates analysis of inter-state coercion short of the use of force, for once an act slips out of the force box into a category containing other coercive methods, the issue of the instrument fades in favor of consequences, specifically the consequence of intervention in the affairs of other states. Of course, armed coercion can constitute intervention, but the modality of coercion rather than the fact of intervention is determinative. By contrast, in considering non-forceful coercion, the start point is whether it amounts to prohibited intervention. For instance, the Declaration on the Inadmissibility of Intervention provides that "[n]o State may use or encourage the use of economic, political or any other type of measures to coerce another State in order to obtain from it the subordination of the exercise of its sovereign rights or to secure from it advantages of any kind . . . ."[87] It is not the fact of economic coercion, but rather its consequence that matters. Thus, while certain techniques may be prohibited by a particular international agreement,[88] the encompassing norm is consequence-based.

---

84. Proportionality is a customary international law principle, codified in 1977 Protocol Additional to the Geneva Conventions of 12 Aug. 1949, and Relating to the Protection of Victims of International Armed Conflicts, June 8, 1977, arts. 51.5(b) &57.2(iii), *reprinted in* 3 HAROLD S. LEVIE, PROTECTION OF WAR VICTIMS: PROTOCOL 1 TO THE 1949 GENEVA CONVENTIONS 174, 337 (1980). [hereinafter ADDITIONAL PROTOCOL I]. It is defined as "[t]he principle that seeks to limit damage caused by military operations by requiring that the effect of the means and methods of warfare used must not be disproportionate to the military advantage sought." PIETRO VERRI, DICTIONARY OF THE INTERNATIONAL LAW OF ARMED CONFLICT 90 (Edward Markee & Susan Mutti trans., 1992).

85. Additional Protocol I, *supra* note 84, arts. 54, 55 & 56.

86. Convention on the Prohibition of Military or Any Other Hostile Use of Environmental Modification Techniques, Dec. 10, 1976, art. I. para. 1, 31 U.S.T.S. 333, 1108 U.N.T.S. 151, 16 I.L.M. 88, 91 (1977).

87. Declaration on the Inadmissibility of Intervention in the Domestic Affairs of States and the Protection of Their Independence and Sovereignty, G.A. Res. 2131, U.N. GAOR,20th Sess., Supp. No. 14, at 12, U.N. Doc. A/6220 (1965), *reprinted in* KEY RESOLUTIONS, *supra* note 43, at 26.

88. For example, regarding international telecommunications law *see* International Telecommunication Convention (with Annexes, Final Protocol, Additional Protocols, Resolutions, Recommendations and Opinions), Oct. 25, 1973, 28 U.S.T. 2495, 1209 U.N.T.S. 32; International Telecommunication Convention, Nov. 6, 1982, S. TREATY DOC. NO. 99-6.

Arguably the approach to CNA and the use of force suggested in this essay falls within the camp of "radical teleological interpretation," for ultimate purposes are being identified in order to lend prescriptive substance to a treaty provision.[89] Yet, this is not a case of crafting new prescriptions, but rather one of simply determining how to address activities not contemplated at the time the Charter was promulgated by resort to Charter norms. Clearly, had CNA posed a significant threat in 1945, the drafters would have crafted a standard against which it could be prescriptively measured. Moreover, because the Charter is the constitutive instrument of an international organization, flexibility in interpretive spirit is apropos. Such documents must remain malleable if the organization in question is to remain relevant to changing international circumstances. As one distinguished commentator has noted, "[T]his [flexible] approach has been used as a way of inferring powers, not expressly provided for in the relevant instruments, which are deemed necessary in the context of the purpose of the organization."[90]

Finally, since the approach is consequence, vice instrument, based, it will forfeit much of the clarity that the latter mode of analysis offered; more gray area cases will occur. This is particularly true in the absence of state practice, and the responses thereto necessary to permit an operational code to emerge from the fog of inter-State relations. In assessing individual instances of CNA, then, the question is how to resolve the unclear cases. Should a presumption operate in favor of inclusion *or* exclusion of CNA in the use of force box?

While policy concerns may impel a particular state towards one position or the other, the security framework of the Charter would be best effected by application of an inclusivity presumption. If the debate is about whether a particular information operation is or is not a use of force, then the consequences of that operation are likely such that they would be violative of the prohibition on intervention at any rate. The issue is probably not legality, but rather illegality by what standard. Therefore, to the extent that treaty prohibitions have any deterrent effect, inclusivity would foster shared community values. The contrary position would assert that labeling uncertain cases as a use of force

---

89. *See* IAN BROWNLIE, PRINCIPLES OF PUBLIC INTERNATIONAL LAW 631-32 (4th ed. 1990).

90. MALCOLM N. SHAW, INTERNATIONAL LAW 659 (4th ed. 1997). The comment is made with particular regard to subsequent practice. Professor Shaw cites, as support for his proposition, Reparations for Injuries Suffered in the Service of the United Nations, 1949 I.C.J. 174 (Apr. 11); Competence of the General Assembly for the Admission of a State to the United Nations, 1950 I.C.J. 4 (Mar. 3); Certain Expenses of the U.N., 1962 I.C.J. 151 (July 20); Legal Consequences for States of the Continued Presence of South Africa in Namibia (South West Africa) Notwithstanding Security Council Resolution 276 (1970), 1971 I.C.J. 16 (June 21).

would be destabilizing, for the victim would be more likely to respond forcefully. However, as to be discussed, it is not the use of force, but rather "armed attack" which gives a state the right to respond in self-defense. An operation that generates doubt as to its status under use of force typology would surely not rise to the level of an armed attack. Moreover, this position does not leave the international community remedy-less. Under Article 39, the Security Council may mount forceful responses even to events that threaten the peace. Most gray area cases would at least rise to this level.[91]

The prohibition on the use of force enjoys normative valence beyond its Charter context. It also constitutes customary international law.[92] Customary law has both objective and subjective components: it must evidence consistent state practice over time by a meaningful group of states and *opinio juris sive necessitatis*[93] must exist.[94] In evaluating the actions of the United States in the *Nicaragua* case, the International Court of Justice held that a prohibition on the use of force did exist in customary law (and that the U.S. had violated it).[95] In light of both the Court's conclusory finding regarding state practice[96] and its heavy reliance on non-binding General Assembly Resolutions to establish the requisite *opinio juris*,[97] the legal reasoning underlying the judgement is suspect. Nevertheless, a majority of commentators concur in the ultimate finding that the prescription enjoys customary status.[98]

The problem in application of the customary standard to CNA is that the customary and Charter prescriptions, while similar, do not coincide.

---

91. The obvious danger, though, is that the international community will not react, possibly because the actor is a member of the P-5 and vetoes any action. This would encourage states to respond unilaterally at lower levels of force.

92. *See* Statute of the International Court of Justice, June 26, 1945, art. 38.1(b), 832 U.S.T.S. 993, 1978 Y.B.U.N. 1197. Customary law is a "general practice accepted as law." *Id.*

93. Belief that compliance with the practice is out of a sense of legal obligation.

94. *See* North Sea Continental Shelf (F.R.G. v. Den.; F.R.G. v. Neth.), 1969 I.C.J. 3, 44 (Feb. 20).

95. On the issue of the customary nature of the prohibition, see 1986 I.C.J. 4, 98-101, 147.

96. *Id.* at 100. The Court did not actually catalogue state practice; instead, it merely noted that state conduct was generally consistent with the rule. Randelzhofer labels this line of argument "highly disputable." Randelzhofer, *supra* note 46, at 126.

97. The Court cited the unanimous adoption in 1970 of the Declaration on Friendly Relations, *supra* note 43. *See* 1968 I.C.J. 4, 100. Recall that the Declaration reiterated the language of Article 2(4). For criticism of this approach, see Anthony D'Amato, *Trashing Customary International Law*, 81 AM. J. INT'L L. 101 (1987). On the relationship between the Charter and the Declaration, see F.L. Kirgis, *Custom on a Sliding Scale*, 81 AM. J. INT'L L. 146, 147 (1987).

98. *See* BROWNLIE, USE OF FORCE, *supra* note 45, at 113; Dinstein, *supra* note 46, at 93; PETER MALANCZUK, AKEHURST'S MODERN INTRODUCTION TO INTERNATIONAL LAW 311 (7th rev. ed. 1997).

The ICJ itself acknowledged this point in the *Nicaragua* case when it opined:

> [O]n the question of the use of force, the United States itself argues for a complete identity of the relevant rules of customary international law with the provisions of the Charter. The Court has not accepted this extreme contention . . . . However, . . . the Charter gave expression in this field to principles already present in customary international law, and that law has in the subsequent four decades developed under the Charter to such an extent that a number of the rules contained in the Charter have acquired a status independent of it.[99]

While state consent to be bound by a treaty can be interpreted as consent to reasonable application of accepted rules of interpretation, the state practice and *opinio juris* requirements of customary international law may lead over time to divergence among formerly coincident norms. Treaty law is both more and less flexible than its customary law counterpart. On the one hand, it is flexible in its susceptibility to interpretation in accordance with evolving context; such context is consequential even in the absence of any shift in state practice (perhaps the opportunity for state practice has not presented itself). On the other hand, it is inflexible in the sense that the prescription itself is frozen beyond interpretation thereof; new norms require new consent. Customary law, by contrast, is unlimited in scope, but limited by the fact that it cannot react to evolving context absent practice and *opinio juris*.

Of course, customary law responds to change in some degree. For instance, the prohibition of the use of force would extend to employment of any new weaponry that fell within the general ambit of *armed* force, for in the same way that Article 2(4) always contemplated armed coercion, so too has the customary standard. Indeed, because the *Nicaragua* decision was based on customary international law, it is reasonable to extend the concept of force to the direct support (arming/training) of those who employ it. Nevertheless, there is no basis in state practice for extension beyond the immediate periphery of armed force. In particular, the absence of any significant CNA practice renders it inappropriate to do so. A customary norm may develop over time, but it does not exist at present. Neither practice, nor *opinio juris*, is in evidence.

---

99. 1968 I.C.J. 4, 96-97.

922   COLUMBIA JOURNAL OF TRANSNATIONAL LAW   [37:885

This is not to say that CNA exists wholly beyond the customary international law governing the use of force. However, whereas the approach proposed in this essay would extend the treaty application to computer network attacks causing consequences which approximated the nature of those involving armed force, application of the customary norm to CNA would require it to be characterized as a new technique of armed force. In order to rise to this level, it must cause not *analogous* consequences, but identical results, specifically direct human injury or physical damage to tangible property. Thus, it must fall within the narrow category of computer network attacks that are appropriately characterized as an application of armed force.[100]

A final prospective point regarding customary international law lies in its greater potential scope. In responding to incidents of computer network attack, the effect of Article 2(4) can never advance beyond the interpretive boundaries of the existing use of force cognitive paradigm. However, over time a new customary norm may emerge that addresses CNA in and of itself, quite aside from its use of force implications. Such a norm may very well prove more restrictive than current prescriptions. At the present, the possibility is purely speculative.

Note that the prohibition on resort to force enjoys more than customary standing. It has been identified by both the International Law Commission[101] and the International Court of Justice[102] as *jus cogens*—"a norm accepted and recognized by the international community of States as a whole as a norm from which no derogation is permitted and which can be modified only by a subsequent norm of general international law having the character."[103] In essence, *jus cogens* norms are customary norms writ large, for they are not susceptible to avoidance through party consent (e.g., in the form of a later treaty). Given their customary character, the treatment of computer network attack in the *jus cogens* context mirrors that with regard to customary international law. Therefore, this specific peremptory norm extends to CNA rising to the level of a *de facto* use of armed force, but not to other forms of computer network attack.

---

100. *See supra* text accompanying notes 77-80.

101. In the Commission's commentary on the draft articles of the Law of Treaties (Vienna Convention), the Charter's prohibition of the use of force was cited as "a conspicuous example" of jus cogens. *See* Report of the International Law Commission, 18th Sess., 1966 (II) I.L.C.Y.B. 247. When such peremptory norms emerge, any existing treaty in conflict with them become void and terminate. *See* Vienna Convention, *supra* note 51, art. 53.

102. *See* 1968 I.C.J. 4, 100.

103. Vienna Convention, *supra* note 51, art. 53.

Finally, although this essay centers on the use of force, it must be understood that the fact that a computer network attack does not violate peremptory, customary, or conventional use of force norms does not necessarily render CNA consistent with international law. In particular, an attack may amount to prohibited intervention in the affairs of other states. As noted by the ICJ in the *Nicaragua* case, "[t]he principle of non-intervention right of every sovereign State to conduct its affairs without outside interference . . . it is part and parcel of customary international law."[104] The obligation to refrain from intervention finds further expression in various General Assembly Resolutions, most notably the Declaration on the Inadmissibility of Intervention in the Domestic Affairs of States and the Protection of their Independence and Sovereignty[105] and the Declaration on Friendly Relations.[106] CNA may be particularly appropriate for consideration in the context of intervention, due to its reliance on technology. Although the technology necessary to commit computer network attack is increasingly widespread, technologically advanced states still maintain an edge in their ability to use it. This disparity in access to the technique heightens its inadmissibility as a form of coercion.[107]

---

104. 1968 I.C.J. 4, para. 202.

105. Declaration on Inadmissibility of Intervention, *supra* note 87.

> 1. [N]o State has the right to intervene, directly or indirectly, for any reason whatever, in the internal or external affairs of any other State. Consequently, armed intervention and all other forms of interference or attempted threats against the personality of the State or against its political, economic and cultural elements, are condemned.
>
> 2. No State may use or encourage the use of economic, political or any other type of measures to coerce another State in order to obtain from it the subordination of the exercise of its sovereign rights or to secure from it advantages of any kind . . . .
>
> 5. Every State has an inalienable right to choose its political, economic, social and cultural systems, without interference in any form by another State.

Id. at 26. Note that although the United States voted in favor of the resolution, it stated that the resolution was "only a statement of political intention and not a formulation of law." U.N. GAOR, 20th Sess. at 436, U.N. Doc. A/C.1/SR.1423. That said, the Declaration on Friendly Relations purports to articulate basic principles of international law, including that of non-intervention. *See* Declaration on Friendly Relations, *supra* note 43. The United States offered no statement challenging that characterization.

106. *See* Declaration on Friendly Relations, *supra* note 43.

107. In the Corfu Channel case, the International Court of Justice held, in response to the United Kingdom's argument that it had entered Albanian waters to seize evidence, that, "[i]ntervention is perhaps still less admissible in the particular form it would take here; for, from the nature of things, it would be reserved for the most powerful states and might easily lead to perverting the administration of international justice itself." The Corfu Channel Case (U.K. v. Alb.),1949 I.C.J. 4, 35 (Apr. 9).

924   *COLUMBIA JOURNAL OF TRANSNATIONAL LAW*   [37:885

III.   RESPONDING TO COMPUTER NETWORK ATTACKS WITH FORCE

While an in-depth analysis of the appropriateness of responding to computer network attack with force is beyond the purview of this essay, a brief outline of the subject is useful to help place the use of force prohibition in context. With the exception of the operational code discussed *supra,* the framework for appropriate uses of force generally resides within the UN Charter.   The Charter admits of only two situations allowing the use of force—Security Council authorized operations pursuant to Chapter VII and self-defense in accordance with Article 51.

Under Chapter VII, the Security Council has the authority to "determine the existence of any threat to peace, breach of peace, or act of aggression."[108] When the Council does so, it may call upon member states of the United Nations to apply "measures not involving the use of armed forces" to resolve the situation.[109] Note that the measures contemplated include "complete or partial interruption of . . . telegraphic, radio, or other means of communication," techniques likely to involve CNA. If non-forceful measures have proved inadequate, or if the Council believes that they would be futile, it may "take such action by air, sea, or land forces as may be necessary to maintain or restore international peace and security."[110] Responses may include information operations falling into either the "not involving armed force" or "armed force" category, as long as they are conducted in accordance with methods and means limitations.[111] To the extent that the type of operation falls squarely within the mandate of the Security Council Resolution authorizing the action, the distinction between the two categories is not particularly relevant.

---

108. U.N. CHARTER art. 39. For an excellent commentary on the article, see Jochen Frowein, *Article 39, in* THE CHARTER OF THE UNITED NATIONS: A COMMENTARY, *supra* note 46, at 605.

109. U.N. CHARTER art. 41 (According to the article, "[t]hese may include complete or partial interruption of economic relations and of rail, sea, air, postal, telegraphic, radio, and other means of communication, and the severance of diplomatic relations.").

110. U.N. CHARTER art. 42 ("Such action may include demonstrations, blockade, and other operations by air, sea, or land forces of Members of the United Nations.").

111. When engaged as combatants, U.N. forces follow the Guidelines for U.N. Forces Regarding Respect for International Law (FAD/TM, May 1996, 005797) (on file with Author). On the applicability of the law of armed conflict to peace operations, see Umesh Palwankar, *Applicability of International Humanitarian Law to United Nations Peace-Keeping Forces,* INT'L REV. RED CROSS, May-June 1993, at 227; Memorandum of the ICRC to the Governments of the States Party to the Geneva Conventions and Members of the United Nations on the Applicability of the Geneva Conventions by the Military Units Placed at the Disposal of the United Nations, Nov. 10, 1961, *reprinted in* INT'L REV. RED CROSS, Dec. 1961, at 490.

However, when does a computer network attack amount to a threat to peace, breach of peace, or act of aggression such that the Council may authorize a response by armed force? The answer can only be provided by the Security Council, for despite attempts by some states to imbue the provision with greater clarity during drafting of the Charter, the member states decided to allow the Council wide discretion by leaving the terms relatively undefined.[112]

In 1974, the General Assembly defined the term aggression as "the use of armed force by a State against the sovereignty, territorial integrity or political independence of another State, or in any manner inconsistent with the Charter of the United Nations . . . ."[113] Cast in terms of "armed" force, acts of aggression would only include those forms of CNA that rise to the level of armed force by virtue of their intent to cause direct damage or injury.[114] However, while all acts of

---

112. Proposals were made by Bolivia [*see* Doc. 2 G/14 (r), 3 U.N.C.I.O. Docs. 585 (1945)], the Philippines [*see* Doc. 2 G/14 (k), 3 U.N.C.I.O Docs. 538 (1945)], and Czechoslovakia [*see* Doc. 2 G/14 (b), 3 U.N.C.I.O Docs. 469 (1945)]. The Bolivian proposal was supported by Columbia, Egypt, Ethiopia, Guatemala, Honduras, Iran, Mexico, New Zealand, and Uruguay. *See* Doc. 442 III/3/20, 12 U.N.C.I.O. Docs. 341 (1945). The U.S. and U.K. opposed a delineation of acts of aggression on the ground that doing so might force responses by the Security Council that would not otherwise be justified. *Id.* at 341-42. Ultimately, the proposal for defining aggression was rejected by a 22-12 vote. *See* Doc. 502/3/22, 12 U.N.C.I.O. Docs. 349 (1945).

113. Definition of Aggression, G.A. Res. 3314 (XXIX), art. 1, U.N. GAOR, 29th Sess., Supp. No. 31, at 142, U.N. Doc. A/9631 (1975), 13 I.L.M. 710 (1974), *reprinted in* KEY RESOLUTIONS, *supra* note 43, at 13. Judge Schwebel of the United States addressed the significance of the resolution in his dissent in the *Nicaragua* case.

> The significance of the Definition of Aggression—or of any definition of aggression—should not be magnified. It is not a treaty. It is a resolution of the General Assembly which rightly recognizes the supervening force of the United Nations Charter and the supervening authority in matters of aggression of the Security Council. The Definition has its conditions, its flaws, its ambiguities and uncertainties. It is open ended. Any definition of aggression must be, because aggression can only be ultimately defined and found in the particular case in light of its particular facts. At the same time, the Definition of Aggression is not a resolution of the General Assembly which purports to declare principles of customary international law not regulated by the United Nations Charter . . . . This resolution rather is an interpretation by the General Assembly of the meaning of the provisions of the United Nations Charter governing the use of force . . . .

1968 I.C.J. 4, 345.

114. In Article 3, the General Assembly offered examples of aggression:

> Any of the following acts, regardless of a declaration of war, shall be subject to and in accordance with the provisions of Article 2, qualify as an act of aggression:
> a) The invasion or attack by the armed forces of a State of the territory of another state . . . or any annexation . . . ;

aggression constitute breaches of the peace, or threats thereto, the obverse is not true; threats to the peace do not necessarily amount to aggression. Aggression is a pejorative term that implies fault; it imposes responsibility. A threat or breach of the peace, by contrast, may or may not be susceptible to the determination of blame, but nevertheless may merit a forceful community response. Moreover, while attaching responsibility by labeling an act aggressive requires that armed force have occurred, threatening or breaching of the peace need not. The mere fact that the peace is threatened is enough for the Security Council to engage the matter.

But what is meant by "peace"? Is it the absence of inter-state violence or does it envision something broader, such as human well-being or community cooperation? Article 1(2), for instance, speaks of "develop[ing] friendly relations among nations based on respect for the principle of equal rights and self-determination of peoples . . . " in order to "strengthen universal peace."[115] Nevertheless, an overly expansive understanding of the concept would fly in the face of the sovereignty notions that pervade international law. That being so, the better interpretation seeks consistency with the Charter provision in which sovereignty concerns have already been balanced against shared community values, Article 2(4)'s prohibition on the use of force. In the Charter context, then, peace may best be defined as the absence of the use of force, whether the use of that force is legitimate or not. Article 39 represents a value choice in favor of community, vice unilateral, replies to uses of force.

---

b) Bombardment . . . against the territory of another State or the use of any weapons by a State against the territory of another State;

c) . . . blockade . . . ;

d) An attack by the armed forces of a State on the land, sea or air forces, or marine and air fleets of another State;

e) The use of armed forces of one State which are within the territory of another State with the agreement of the receiving State, in contravention of the conditions provided for in the agreement or any extension of their presence in such territory beyond term of the agreement;

f) The action of a State in allowing its territory, which it has placed at the disposal of another State, to be used by that other State for perpetrating an act of aggression against a third State;

g) The sending by or on behalf of a State of armed bands, groups, irregulars or mercenaries, which carry out acts of armed force against another State of such gravity as to amount to the acts listed above, or its substantial involvement therein.

Definition of Aggression, *supra* note 43, art. 3.

115. U.N. CHARTER art. 1, para. 2.

By the breach of peace standard, the Security Council could react forcefully pursuant to Article 42 to a computer network attack that amounted to a use of force as described above in the Article 2(4) context. Of much greater significance to information operations is the threat to the peace standard. It allows the Security Council to authorize a response by force to any situation that might provoke a breach of the peace (use of force). Legality, or lack thereof, of the prospective forceful response (the breach of the peace) to the provocation is not determinative as to whether a threat to the peace exists.[116] The question of threat is factual, not juridical. To complicate matters, the Security Council finds such threats with a fair degree of ease. For example, in 1991, the Council characterized fighting between the Yugoslavian government and the break-away states of Croatia and Slovenia as a threat to peace, most likely due to fear that this internal armed conflict might eventually risk involvement from outside the country.[117] Other examples of the Security Council finding threats to the peace in the last decade include, *inter alia*, the anarchy in Somalia,[118] civil war in Liberia,[119] and even the refusal of the Libyan government to turn over suspects in the Pan Am Flight 103 bombing.[120]

Given this liberality, many forms of computer network attack, whether a use of force or not, could comprise a threat to the peace. Each would have to be evaluated in context, the permutations of which are infinite—time, place, target, actor, consequence, etc. What might cause one target state to react forcefully at a certain time or in particular

---

116. *See* Frowein, *supra* note 108, at 612.

117. *See* S.C. Res. 713, U.N. SCOR, 3009th mtg., U.N. Doc. S/RES/713 (1991). This resolution, and all other Security Council Resolutions are available online at <http://www.un.org/Docs/sc.htm>.

118. *See* S.C. Res. 733, U.N. SCOR, 3039th mtg., U.N. Doc. S/RES/733 (1992).

119. *See* S.C. Res. 788, U.N. SCOR, 3138th mtg., U.N. Doc. S/RES/788 (1992).

120. *See* S.C. Res. 748, U.N. SCOR, 3063rd mtg., U.N. Doc. S/RES/748 (1992). Until the demise of the Cold War, the Council, due to the existence of off-setting bloc vetoes, proved impotent in responding to threats to the peace. In only one case (Rhodesia) did it find a threat to the peace and authorize forceful measures in response. In Security Council Resolution 221, the Council authorized the United Kingdom to deny ships carrying oil destined for Rhodesia access, by force if necessary, to the Port of Beira in Mozambique. *See* S.C. Res. 221, U.N. SCOR, 1277th mtg., U.N. Doc. S/RES/221 (1966). The impotence of the Security Council led the General Assembly to adopt the Uniting for Peace Resolution in 1950. It provides that:

> [I]f the Security Council, because of the lack of unanimity of the permanent members, fails to exercise its primary responsibility for the maintenance of international peace and security in any case where there appears to be a threat to the peace, breach of the peace or act of aggression, the General Assembly shall consider the matter immediately with a view to making appropriate recommendation to Members for collective measures, including . . . the use of armed force.

G.A. Res. 377(V), para. 1, 1950 U.N.Y.B. 193-95.

928   COLUMBIA JOURNAL OF TRANSNATIONAL LAW   [37:885

circumstances might be perceived as relatively unimportant by another. Certainly, any serious CNA conducted by contenders in long-standing global flash-points (e.g., India-Pakistan, Turkey-Greece) risks ignition. On the other hand, it is possible to envision computer attacks among major Western economic powers (perhaps in the form of economic espionage) that would clearly not threaten the peace if discovered. Reduced to basics, though, Security Council discretion in Chapter VII matters would be at its apex when determining whether a particular computer network attack amounts to a threat to the peace sufficient to justify a forceful community (or community-authorized) response.

Article 51 expresses the second UN Charter authorization of the use of force:

> Nothing in the present Charter shall impair the inherent right of individual and collective self-defence if an armed attack occurs against a Member of the United Nations, until the Security Council has taken measures necessary to maintain international peace and security. Measures taken by Members shall be immediately reported to the Security Council and shall not in any way affect the authority and responsibility of the Security Council under the present Charter to take at any time such action as it deems necessary in order to maintain or restore international peace and security.[121]

The sole authorization of unilateral use of force outside the Charter security system, this provision responds to the reality that the international community may not be able to react quickly enough to armed aggression[122] to forestall attack on a victim state. It therefore permits states and their allies to defend themselves until the international "posse" arrives pursuant to Chapter VII.

Note that Article 51 restricts a state's right of self-defense to situations involving *armed* attack, a narrower category of act than Article 2(4)'s use of force.[123] Although coercion not involving armed

---

121. U.N. CHARTER art. 51. For an excellent survey of the article, see Albrecht Randelzhofer, *Article 51, in* THE CHARTER OF THE UNITED NATIONS: A COMMENTARY, *supra* note 46, at 106.

122. The French text of the Charter uses the term "agression armée."

123. The limit of self-defense to response to an armed attack is not universally accepted. *See* Tom J. Farer, *Political and Economic Coercion in Contemporary International Law*, 79 AM. J. INT'L L. 405 (1985). Professor Schachter has responded to such assertions forcefully and convincingly:

force may violate Article 2(4) and result in action under Article 39, it does not follow that states may also react unilaterally pursuant to Article 51. This narrowing plainly reflects the Charter's preference for community responses (e.g., even to threats to peace) over individual ones. In the case of a computer network attack, it is also a prudent approach due to the difficulty states may have in identifying the correct source of an attack.

Thus, faced with CNA that does not occur in conjunction with, or as a prelude to, conventional military force, a state may only respond with force in self-defense if the CNA constituted armed force by the standard enunciated *supra* for armed force, i.e., that it is intended to directly cause physical destruction or injury. The victim state could repair to the Security Council and allege that other acts of CNA threaten the peace and merit a Chapter VII response, but it could not respond forcefully thereto on its own accord. Additionally, computer network attacks falling short of armed attack might nevertheless violate Article 2(4)'s prohibition on the use of force, thereby subjecting the actor to international opprobrium, but not to a response in self-defense.

The foregoing analysis applies only to situations in which the computer network attack occurs in total isolation. What of computer network attacks launched to prepare the battle space? The possibilities abound. CNA disables intelligence gathering assets such as satellites. An opponent "attacks" the Global Positioning Satellite System (GPS) to confound targeting and maneuver. Computerized military medical records are corrupted to complicate provision of medical treatment upon the outbreak of hostilities. A logic bomb is implanted in the reserve activation system, programmed to operate upon call-up. Concerted CNA brings down large sections of the military communications network.

Some commentators have gone so far as to contend that economic action of such intensity and magnitude would justify forcible self-defense by the target state, and collective defense by its allies. I disagree. Even egregious economic aggression whether or not illegal, does not constitute an armed attack or a use of force in the Charter sense. Allowing forcible reprisal to non-military coercion would broaden the grounds for use of force to an intolerable degree.

Oscar Schachter, *In Defense of International Rules on the Use of Force*, 53 U. CHI. L.REV. 113, 127 (1986). *See also* Report of the International Law Commission on the Work of its Thirty-Second Session (1980), U.N. Doc. A/35/10, *reprinted in* [1980] II(2) Y.B.I.L.C. 53, n.176.

It is often said that acts of unarmed aggression also exist (ideological, economic, political, etc.), but even though they are condemned, it cannot be inferred that a state which is a victim of such acts is permitted to resort to the use of armed force in self-defense. Hence, these possibly wrongful acts do not fall within the purview of the present topic, since recourse to armed force, as analysed in the context of self-defence, can be rendered lawful only in the case of armed attack.

In none of these situations does the attack, in and of itself, constitute an *armed* attack. However, each may very well be an essential step in just such an attack. In certain circumstances, they would merit a forceful response. The prevailing standard maintains that an attack must be "imminent" before the right to self-defense matures. In the nineteenth century, Secretary of State Daniel Webster crafted the classic articulation of this "anticipatory" right with regard to the now famous *Caroline* incident. He opined that self-defense should "be confined to cases in which the necessity of that self-defense is instant, overwhelming, and leaving no moment for deliberation."[124] Mere preparation failed the test. Following World War II, the Nuremberg Tribunal spoke approvingly of the *Caroline* standard.[125]

Unfortunately, a conundrum surfaces in the application of the imminence criterion. Some commentators assert a high standard for imminence, reading the *Caroline* principle narrowly.[126] Indeed, on its face, it appears to impose a fairly restrictive temporal test. The force used in self-defense must occur just as the attack is about to be launched.

A better approach asks what the principle seeks to achieve. Obviously, it hopes to stave off violence so as to allow maximum opportunity for peaceful alternatives to work. However, at the same

---

124. Letter from Daniel Webster to Lord Ashburton (Aug. 6, 1842), *reprinted in* 2 JOHN MOORE DIGEST OF INTERNATIONAL LAW 411-12 (1906). The Caroline incident involved a Canadian insurrection in 1837. After being defeated, the insurgents retreated into the United States where they recruited and planned further operations. The Caroline, a naval vessel, was being used by the rebels. British troops crossed the border and destroyed the vessel. Britain justified the action on the grounds that the United States was not enforcing its laws along the frontier and that the action was a legitimate exercise of self-defense. *Id.* at 409-11.

125. *See* International Military Tribunal (Nuremberg), Judgement and Sentences, 41 AM. J. INT'L L. 172, 205 (1947). There is significant state practice regarding assertions of anticipatory self-defense. Professor Bowett has noted a number of the earlier examples:

> Pakistan justified the entry of her troops into Kashmir in 1948 on this basis before the Security Council, an argument opposed only by India. Israel's invasion of Sinai in October, 1956, and June, 1967, rested on the same argument. The OAS has used the same argument in relation to the blockade of Cuba during the 1962 missile crisis. Several states have expressed the same argument in the Sixth Committee in connection with the definition of aggression and the UN itself invoked the principle of anticipatory self-defense to justify action by ONUC in Katanga in December, 1961, and December, 1963. Following the invasion of Czechoslovakia by the USSR in 1968, it is permissible to assume that the USSR now shares this view, for there certainly existed no "armed attack."

Derek W. Bowett, *Reprisals Involving Resort to Armed Force*, 66 AM. J. INT'L L. 1, 4 n.8 (1972).

126. *See, e.g.,* Oscar Schachter, *The Right of States to Use Armed Force*, 82 MICH. L. REV. 1620, 1634-35 (1984).

time, it recognizes that states need not risk destruction through inaction. The principle balances the desire to avoid inter-state violence against the right of a state to exist unharmed. This being so, imminence is best understood as relative. For instance, as defensive options become more limited or less likely to succeed, the acceptability of preemptive action grows. A weak state may be justified in acting sooner than a stronger one, when facing an identical threat, simply because it is at greater risk in having to wait. The greater the relative threat, the more likely preemptive actions are to be effective, and, therefore, the greater the justification for acting before the enemy can complete preparations and mount its aggressive attack.

Conceptually, each victim state has a different window of opportunity within which it must act to counter the impending attack. In some cases, the window is wide, extending even to the point of attack itself. In others, it may be much narrower. Unless international law requires the potential victim to simply suffer the attack before responding,[127] the proper standard for evaluating an anticipatory operation must be whether or not it occurred during the last possible window of opportunity. Hence, the appropriate question relates more to the correct timing of the preemptive strike than to the imminence of the attack that animates it.

It is not sufficient to look entirely to the victim state. The likelihood of the pending attack should also determine the appropriateness of forceful response in self-defense. Focusing on this point, Professor Yoram Dinstein has (despite rejecting the "anticipatory" terminology) suggested the admissibility of "interceptive" defense under Article 51.

> Interceptive . . . self-defence takes place after the other side has committed itself to an armed attack in an ostensibly irrevocable way. Whereas a preventive strike anticipates an armed attack which is merely "foreseeable" (or even just "conceivable"), an interceptive. strike counters an armed attack which is "imminent" and practically "unavoidable."[128]

---

127. Professor Dinstein perceptively notes that Article 2 of the Definition of Aggression Resolution refers to the first use of force as prima facie evidence of aggression. In other words, the burden is upon the actor to demonstrate that its use of force was not aggression. But this necessarily means that there are first uses of force that do not amount to aggression and are, therefore, not wrongful. *See* Dinstein, *supra* note 46, at 187.

128. *Id.* at 190.

932   *COLUMBIA JOURNAL OF TRANSNATIONAL LAW*   [37:885

Anticipatory self-defense most effectively realizes the presumption against violence, the preference for community responses, and the right of a State to survival by combining the two elements. Defense in advance of the attack is legitimate if the potential victim must immediately act to defend itself in a meaningful way and if the potential aggressor has irrevocably committed itself to attack. Without the first requirement, anticipatory self-defense risks missing opportunities to resolve the situation peacefully; without the second, a danger exists of responding to an attack that is speculative at best.

A wide array of computer network attack operations executed to prepare the battle space may meet this standard. By the anticipatory self-defense standard, the right of a state to respond forcefully to them would depend not so much on the nature of the information operation, as on its significance vis-à-vis the coming armed attack. Does the CNA appear merely preparatory or is it more likely an irreversible step in the final chain of events? Placement of a logic bomb in an air defense sector's warning network does not demand an immediate retort. Attempting to corrupt the system as troops are massed along the border and the enemy's air force has just completed a 48-hour stand-down represents a much more serious threat and may well merit an immediate defensive response. How capable is the state of defending itself in the event the attack does come? The logic bomb is only a potential interference with future operations, whereas corruption of the air defense system may require a prompt response lest the opponent be able to destroy the victim State's air force on the ground without warning. Is the CNA the sort of act that logically fits into a near-term attack sequence? Attacking supply and transportation computer networks fits because it would hinder reinforcement and resupply efforts. So too do attacks on communication systems, as C3 attacks are highly likely immediately preceding any attack.[129] By contrast, attacking defense research facility networks does not fit into a near-term attack sequence because the benefits of most such operations are likely to be reaped long after the computer attack occurs.

Essentially, the right to respond forcefully in self-defense to a computer network attack that does not in and of itself constitute an armed attack arises upon the confluence of three factors:

---

129. "C3" refers to command, control, and communications systems. Similar terms of art include "C2," command and control, and "C3ISR," command, control, communications, intelligence, surveillance, and reconnaissance. "C2W," command and control warfare, would include attacks on systems encompassed by each of these terms. *See supra* note 11 and accompanying text.

1) The CNA is part of an overall operation culminating in armed attack;

2) The CNA is an irrevocable step in an imminent (near-term) and probably unavoidable attack; and

3) The defender is reacting in advance of the attack itself during the last possible window of opportunity available to effectively counter the attack.[130]

Note that it is not the CNA that is actually being defended against, but instead the overall armed attack, complete with its information operation component. Thus, compliance with the requirement that acts in self-defense be proportional is measured against the armed attack, not the CNA.[131] For the same reason, the attack need not be against the facility that launched the CNA or even designed to counter this or other computer network attacks. Again, the armed attack is the normative driver, not the information operation.

The final issue surrounding self-defense is whether Article 51 subsumes the "inherent right" to self-defense, in other words whether a separate and distinct right exists in customary international law. Clearly, a customary law right to self-defense exists, a fact recognized by the ICJ in the *Nicaragua* case. But is that right only meaningful to states which are not party to the UN Charter (or those which would exercise collective defense to come to their assistance) or does the right exist altogether separately? Is it limited to armed attack, and does it evolve in different directions and at a different pace? This debate has permeated scholarship and practice regarding the law of self-defense for

---

130. Michael Walzer has suggested a similar line of reasoning:

> The line between legitimate and illegitimate first strikes is not going to be drawn at the point of imminent attack but at the point of sufficient threat. That phrase is necessarily vague. I mean it to cover three things: a manifest intent to injure, a degree of active preparation that makes that intent a positive danger, and a general situation in which waiting, or doing anything other than fighting, greatly magnifies the risk.

MICHAEL WALZER, JUST AND UNJUST WARS 81 (2d ed. 1992).

131. Self-defense must be both necessary and proportional. "There is a specific rule whereby self-defence would warrant only measures which are proportional to the armed attack and necessary to respond to it, a rule well established in customary international law." 1968 I.C.J. 4, 94 *cited with approval in* Legality of the Threat or Use of Nuclear Weapons, 1996 I.C.J. 4, 226, at para. 41, 31 I.L.M. 809, 822 (1996). *See also* RESTATEMENT (THIRD) OF THE FOREIGN RELATIONS LAW OF THE UNITED STATES § 905 (1987). Professor Brownlie labels proportionality "the essence of self-defence." BROWNLIE, USE OF FORCE, *supra* note 45, at 279 n.2.

the last five decades.[132] However, in the context of the Charter security scheme, the right clearly appears limited to defense against armed attacks. If a less restrictive customary international law norm would permit responses to situations other than armed attacks, parties to the Charter would still be bound by their treaty obligation. Of course, an operational code regarding defensive responses to CNA which varies from the armed attack standard could develop that is less-restrictive than Article 51. That would not alter the content of the standard, but simply relegate it to the positivist myth system.

IV.   CONCLUDING THOUGHTS ON THE APPROPRIATE NORMATIVE
       FRAMEWORK

Computer network attack represents a new tool of coercion in the international arena, one that is fundamentally different from those previously available. Arguably, its distinctiveness merits consideration of a new and unique normative framework to specifically address computer network attack or, more broadly, information operations. However, consensus on the need for such an effort, let alone its substantive content, is unlikely to be achieved at any time in the near future.

Cognizant of this reality, and of the fact that efforts to develop and field computer network attack capability are being pursued vigorously, the essay considers this new coercive technique within the current prescriptive environment. It suggests an analysis of computer network attack under international law, particularly as framed with the U.N. Charter, that would proceed as follows.

1) Is the technique employed in the CNA a use of *armed* force? It is if the attack is intended to directly cause physical damage to tangible objects or injury to human beings.

---

132. In 1980, the International Law Commission catalogued some of the more important and influential positions on the subject. Among those advocating limiting the right to situations involving armed attack were: J.L. Kinz, *Individual and Collective Self-Defense in Article 51 of the Charter of the United Nations*, 41 AM. J. INT'L L. 872 (1947); Hans Kelsen, *Collective Security and Collective Self-Defense under the Charter of the United Nations* 42 AM. J. INT'L L. 783, 791-92 (1948); PHILIP JESSUP, A MODERN LAW OF NATIONS 165 (1948); Quincy Wright, *The United States Intervention in Lebanon*, 53 AM. J. INT'L L. 112 (1959). Taking the contrary approach were JAMES BRIERLY, THE LAW OF NATIONS 416 (1963); L.C. Green, *Armed Conflict, War and Self-Defence*, 6 ARCHIV DES VÖLKERRECHTS 387 (1957); MYRES MCDOUGAL & FREDERICO FELICIANO, LAW AND MINIMUM WORLD PUBLIC ORDER 263 (1961). The ILC took no position on the issue.

2) If it is not armed force, is the CNA nevertheless a use of force as contemplated in the U.N. Charter? It is if the *nature* of its consequences track those consequence commonalities which characterize armed force.

3) If the CNA is a use of force (armed or otherwise), is that force applied consistent with Chapter VII, the principle of self-defense, or operational code norms permitting its use in the attendant circumstances?

   a) If so, the operation is likely to be judged legitimate.

   b) If not and the operation constitutes a use of armed force, the CNA will violate Article 2(4), as well as the customary international law prohibition on the use of force.

   c) If not and the operation constitutes a use of force, but not armed force, the CNA will violate Article 2(4).

4) If the CNA does not rise to the level of the use of force, is there another prohibition in international law that would preclude its use? The most likely candidate, albeit not the only one, would be the prohibition on intervening in the affairs of other States.

Assuming a CNA occurs, the appropriateness of a response by armed force may be analyzed in the following manner:

1) If the computer network attack amounts to a use of armed force, then the Security Council may characterize it as an act of aggression or breach of peace and authorize a forceful response under Article 42 of the Charter. To constitute an armed attack, the CNA must be intended to directly cause physical damage to tangible objects or injury to human beings.

2) If the CNA does not constitute an armed attack, the Security Council may nevertheless find it to threaten the peace (the absence of inter-state violence) and authorize a use of force to prevent a subsequent breach of peace. The CNA need not amount to a use of force before the Council may determine that it threatens peace.

3) States, acting individually or collectively, may respond to a CNA amounting to armed attack with the use of force pursuant to Article 51 and the inherent right of self-defense.

4) States, acting individually or collectively, may respond to a CNA not amounting to armed attack, but which is an integral part of an operation intended to culminate in armed attack when:

   a) The acts in self-defense occur during the last possible window of opportunity available to effectively counter the attack; and

   b) The CNA is an irrevocable step in an imminent (near-term) and probably unavoidable attack.

The indeterminacies in this scheme are the evolution of customary law and the emergence of operational code norms. It is entirely possible that customary law norms restricting the use of CNA beyond Charter levels could emerge. However, any such process would be incremental. Much more likely is emergence of new operational codes, either enhancing or relaxing existing norms, in response to the exploding possibilities of information operations.

To the extent that such codes reflect the expectations of the politically effective actors on the international scene, policy vectors assume normative valence. The United States, unfortunately, faces a dilemma with regard to an appropriate policy stance vis-à-vis computer network attack. Its technological wherewithal renders it the state most capable of conducting information operations, but also the one most vulnerable, particularly to CNA. The temptation to exploit one's strengths drives much of the serious attention paid by U.S. government agencies, both military and civilian, to offensive information operations. However, as time goes on our relative advantage will inevitably slip as IO know-how diffuses to increasing numbers of states. Moreover, it will prove an attractive asymmetric option to states unable to field forces to the level of the United States and its closest allies.

Given this likely unfolding of events, perhaps the policy approach that best fosters U.S. interests is one advocating a restrictive view of the permissibility of computer network attack. Since the Charter use of force prohibition reflects a fair degree of imprecision in the CNA context, this approach would favor greater inclusivity in gray area applications of the norm. This predilection to restrictions on CNA operations should not be interpreted as a suggestion that the criteria for armed attack be relaxed. On the contrary, maintaining a relatively high threshold for triggering the right to respond to CNA in self-defense, although not enhancing its deterrent effect, serves to maintain constraints on the usually more disruptive act of unilateral resort to armed force. Furthermore, should an information operation be mounted that raises the question of whether an act of armed force has occurred, it would in all likelihood amount to a threat to the peace and thereby seize the Security Council of the matter. This may be faint consolation for the state facing a serious computer network attack, but from a world order perspective it represents the optimal alternative. As Myres McDougal and Federico Feliciano eloquently noted nearly four decades ago,

> The overwhelming common interest in basic order, and the exorbitant potential costs of exercise of force by contemporary weapons would appear to counterbalance losses states may occasionally incur from lesser wrongs left inadequately redressed because of deficiencies in available remedial procedures or the limited ability of a poorly organized community to create effective remedies for all wrongs.[133]

Ultimately, of course, it is achievement of world order that best fosters the shared community values underlying the *jus ad bellum*.

---

133. McDougal & Feliciano, *supra* note 132, at 207-08.

[18]

Information Warfare as International Coercion: Elements of a Legal Framework

Christopher C. Joyner* and Catherine Lotrionte**

Abstract

Worldwide interconnectivity through massive computer networks now makes states vulnerable to new threats. Foreign governments can launch computer-based assaults, or acts of information warfare, on another state's domestic systems such as energy grids, telecommunications, and financial facilities that could severely damage or disrupt national defence or vital social services. Even realizing the new forms of computer-generated weapons and changing concepts of sovereignty and territory brought about by global interdependence, international law is likely to rely on UN Charter principles to define the legal boundaries of cyberspace. While perhaps not armed force literally, resort to cyberforce may be viewed as a form of intervention that can produce harmful or coercive effects, and put at risk the national security of another state. There is need for modern international law to define more precisely the criteria used to distinguish which state actions are permissible as normal computer-generated transborder data flow from those cyberactivities that might qualify as an 'armed attack' against a state. Clearer rules are also needed for what responses are permissible as self-defence by a state targeted in an information warfare situation and how international institutions might facilitate the attainment of these objectives.

1 Introduction

Alvin and Heidi Toffler's *The Third Wave* proclaimed in 1991 the dawn of the Information Age. They depicted the history of the world in three waves — the

*   Professor of International Law, Department of Government, Georgetown University.
** Assistant General Counsel, Office of the General Counsel, Central Intelligence Agency; Adjunct Professor, National Security Studies Program, Georgetown University. The authors would like to thank Anthony Clark Arend, Professor Dorothy Denning and Phillip Johnson for assistance and comments made during the preparation of this study. The views expressed in this article are those of the authors alone and do not necessarily reflect the position of the United States Government.

agricultural wave, the industrial wave, and the information wave.[1] A decade later, the Information Age has fundamentally transformed the way in which the world operates. Global proliferation in computer interconnectivity, most notably the profound growth in use of the Internet, has revolutionized the way governments, societies and much of the world communicates and conducts business.[2]

At the same time, the technology-intensive Information Age brings with it opportunities for 'cyber-crime', 'cyber-war' or, as more aptly put, the prosecution of 'Information Warfare'. Western societies have spent years building information infrastructures that are interoperable, easy to access and easy to use. Attributes such as openness and ease of connectivity that promote telecommunications efficiency and expedite customer service also now render a society's information infrastructure vulnerable to attacks from other computerized systems.[3] The implications of these developments are clear. Particularly regarding how governments conduct wars and use military force, the Information Age promises profound changes in the future. The manners and means in which states interact internationally are dramatically changing.[4] Given such realities, international legal rules also must be dramatically adapted if new cyberspace technologies are to be regulated, or even managed, in their increasingly pervasive transnational applications.

This study examines known techniques of Information Warfare (IW) and the international legal implications generated by their use. For purposes of definition, our study considers IW to be a subset of Information Operations that is 'conducted during time of crisis or conflict to achieve or promote specific objectives over a specific

---

[1]   See Alvin and Heidi Toffler, *The Third Wave* (1991). See also Alvin and Heidi Toffler, *War and Anti-War: Survival at the Dawn of the 21st Century* (1993) (the emerging knowledge-based society will use knowledge-based systems to conduct warfare).

[2]   Stocks are purchased on-line. Applications for employment are made on-line. Work is done on-line. University degrees are earned on-line. Airplane tickets are bought on-line. Communications with friends occur on-line. People even register to vote on-line. The benefits of the computer-based Internet system are enormous. Vast amounts of information are literally at the fingertips, facilitating research on virtually every topic imaginable. Financial and other business transactions can be executed almost instantaneously. Electronic mail, Internet websites and computer bulletin boards allow instantaneous communications quickly and easily with virtually an unlimited number of persons or groups.

[3]   A General Accounting Office report stated that the Defense Department was subjected to 250,000 information warfare attacks in 1995. See US General Accounting Office, 'Information Security: Computer Attacks at Department of Defense Pose Increasing Risks', Report No. GAO/T-AIMD-96–92 (1996) www.access.gpo.gov/su_docs/aces/aces160.shtml?/gao/index.html (visited 18 July 2001). The Pentagon asserts that there were only 500 incidents this year. See Maier, 'Is US Ready for Cyberwarfare?', *Insight on the News*, 5 April 1999, at 18. Today, financial institutions can be defrauded on-line. Trade secrets can be stolen on-line. Extortion and blackmail can be committed on-line. People can be impersonated on-line. Commerce can be disrupted on-line. Persons can be stalked on-line. Even a war can be started on-line. See Cilluffo *et al.*, 'Cybercrime … Cyberterrorism … Cyberwarfare, Averting an Electronic Waterloo' (Center for Strategic and International Studies Task Force Report, 1998).

[4]   See Alvin and Heidi Toffler, *War and Anti-War* (1993) 2. See Security in Cyberspace: Hearings Before the Permanent Subcommittee on Investigations of the Senate Commission on Government Affairs, 104th Cong. (1996) 150, at 155 (testimony of Jamie S. Gorelick, Deputy Attorney-General, describing how technology generally, and information networks specifically, play critical roles in the functioning and development of these important areas).

adversary or adversaries'.[5] The realistic potential of instigating IW underscores the changed nature of the globalized world environment, as well as the technological revolution in how transnational conflict might be conducted in the twenty-first century. Coincidentally, both these developments highlight the need to develop or amend the rules and criteria on which factual assertions are based for a state to employ force against another state. The transnational nature of IW suggests that, while international legal norms found in contemporary UN Charter law are helpful, they may not be sufficient for reaching acceptable solutions.[6]

[5] Traditional means of conducting IW include psychological operations, electronic warfare, military deception, physical destruction and information attack. For example, in using IW a government could manipulate the enemy's reasoning (i.e. psychological operations), deny accurate information to the enemy (i.e. electronic warfare), mislead the enemy about its own capabilities and intentions (i.e. military deception), use conventional bombs or electromagnetic pulse weapons targeting information systems of the enemy (i.e. physical destruction) and corrupt information without visibly changing the physical entity within which it resides (i.e. information attacks). The US Air Force defines information warfare as 'any action to deny, exploit, corrupt, or destroy the enemy's information and its functions; protecting ourselves against those actions; and exploiting our own military information functions'. Department of the Air Force, 'Cornerstones of Information Warfare' (visited 18 July 2001), www.af.mil/lib/corner.html. See also Chairman of the Joint Chiefs of Staff, Joint Publication 1–02, *Dictionary of Military and Associated Terms* (1998) 422, available at www.dtic.mil/doctrine/jel/new_pubs/jp1–02.pdf; Office of the Chief of Naval Operations, Department of the Navy, OPNAVINST 3430.26, at 1 (18 January 1995) ('Information warfare is the action taken in support of national security strategy to seize and maintain a decisive advantage by attacking an adversary's information infrastructure through exploitation, denial, and influence, while protecting friendly information systems'); Dorothy E. Denning, *Information Warfare and Security* (1999) 23 ('Information warfare consists of offensive and defensive operations against information resources of a "win–lose" nature'). For some general discussions on Information Warfare, see Alrich, 'The International Legal Implications of Information Warfare' (US Air Force Institute for National Security Studies Occasional Paper 9, April 1996) 3–5; Martin C. Libicki, *What Is Information Warfare?* (Center for Advanced Command Concepts and Technology, Institute for National Strategic Studies, National Defense University, August 1995) (identifying seven forms of Information Warfare); Stein, 'Information Warfare', *Airpower Journal* (Spring 1995) 31–39; Colonel Richard Szafranski, USAF, 'Theory of Information Warfare: Preparing for 2020', *Airpower Journal* (Spring 1995) 56–65; Winn Schwartau, *Information Warfare: Chaos on the Electronic Highway* (1994) (defining IW into three categories according to the nature of the defence); and Arquilla and Ronfeldt, 'Cyberwar is Coming!', 12 *Comp. Strategy* (April–June 1993) 141 (introduces the concept of 'cyber-war' for the purpose of examining knowledge-based conflict at the military level). See also Haeni, 'An Introduction to Information Warfare' (visited 19 July 2001), www.tangle.seas.gwu.edu/reto/infowar/info-war.html.

[6] These Charter-based rules were designed for a world where military conflict mainly involved large-scale armed attacks by one state against the territory of another, such as those in the First World War, the Second World War and on smaller scales throughout the Cold War. During those conflicts, governments could count an enemy's planes, tanks and ships. From these assessments, a government could decide how to organize its defence based upon its calculations of the enemy's offensive threat capabilities. The use of cyber-space technologies makes the determination of an enemy's assets more difficult and thus complicates arrangements for setting up adequate defensive strategies. See generally Vizard, 'War.Com: A Hacker Attack Against NATO Uncovers a Secret War in Cyberspace', *Popular Science*, 1 July 1999, at 80. It is difficult to manage risks in conflict or to know what assets must be spent on defence, especially when who, where or what IW weapons an enemy possesses remain unknown factors. See also Rattray,

828   *EJIL* 12 (2001), 825–865

The rise of IW technologies in post-Cold War conflicts[7] provokes questions about the legal definitions of 'armed attack' and 'self-defence' as articulated in the UN Charter, the norms for contemporary state behaviour, and the factual basis involved in IW activities. Claims that a government has surreptitiously penetrated another country's information infrastructure and caused great physical harm raise complex factual issues not previously present when states confronted and openly attacked each another with armies, planes, ships, tanks and conventional weapons. It may be difficult to attribute an IW attack to any particular foreign state, or to characterize that government's motive or intent. An IW attack might be initiated by a foreign private entity or person without state sponsorship. Or a foreign state could hire mercenary-like individuals to carry out an IW attack without attribution to state sponsorship. A cyber-attacker may not be physically near the locations where the attack is launched or where its effects impact. The means of a cyberspace attack may not be readily detectable. A virus sent to a computer via an e-mail attachment will not be readily apparent, as missiles are when they are launched. Under all these circumstances, what lawful action may a state take to respond? The recent availability of IW requires reconsideration of the fact-finding processes and criteria used by governments to make assessments concerning if or when force may be used transnationally through their computer systems.

This article examines how IW is regarded within the context of contemporary international legal rules. It assesses the vulnerabilities of state information infrastructures to these cyberspace technologies, including threats to their national security,[8] and the reality of their international applications. International legal rules regulating the use of force are then analyzed as they apply to the use of IW techniques. This analysis also seeks to determine whether and when cyber-based IW activities might qualify as permissible uses of force. Finally, suggestions are made for criteria that contribute to clarifying the legal nature of IW and to designing a more appropriate regulatory framework. At bottom this study evaluates which legal rules applicable to IW might be used by governments to conduct their foreign policies in compliance with international law and which applications of cyberspace activities present serious legal challenges to maintaining order in contemporary relations among states.

'The Emerging Global Information Infrastructure and National Security', *Fletcher Forum on World Affairs* (Summer–Fall 1997) 81, at 93–95 (describing the need for multilateral efforts to control information warfare and positing several different international mechanisms); see also Anthony Lake, 6 *Nightmares* (2000) 57 (citing Deputy Secretary of Defense John Hamre's statements on the difficulties of dealing with the lack of borders in cyberspace).

[7]   See Allard, 'The Future of Command and Control: Towards a Paradigm of Information Warfare', in L. Benjamin Ederington and Michael J. Mazarr (eds), *Turning Point: The Gulf War and US Military Strategy* (1994) 161, at 166; Department of Defense, 'Conduct of the Persian Gulf Conflict: Final Report to Congress' (1992); Swalm, 'Joint STARS in Desert Storm', in Alan D. Campen (ed.), *The First Information War* (1992) 167.

[8]   For a more extensive discussion of the threats to the national security from abroad see James Adams, *The Next World War* (1998); and Lake, *supra* note 6.

2 Defining the Threat

The pace of developing cyber-technologies and the Internet's ubiquity have brought not only advances in the quality of life, but also new international threats to governments. As nation-based cyber-systems assume increasingly complex, more intricate roles in international commerce, daily life and national defence, these computer networks have become more vulnerable to transnational threats. Interconnectivity aggravates the risk that disabilities affecting one system will also infect other interconnected systems.[9] Massive computer networks provide multiple pathways between and among systems that, if not properly secured, can be operated from remote locations to gain unauthorized access to data and operations in other states. The resultant damage can vary, depending on the type and extent of the IW threat. Critical system operations can be disrupted or otherwise sabotaged, sensitive data can be read and copied, and data or processes can be altered. There is today significant concern that hostile foreign governments could launch computer-based attacks on critical national or regional systems — such as those supporting energy distribution, telecommunications and financial services — that severely damage or disrupt national defence or other vital social services and result in serious harm to the public welfare.[10]

Western societies are particularly cognizant of cyber-based security concerns.[11]

---

[9] See Defense Science Board Task Force, *Information Warfare: Defense* (IW-D) (November 1996) 2–15 ('Our task force had many enlightening discussions about the potential for effects to cascade through one infrastructure (such as the phone system) into other infrastructures. No one seems to know quite how, where, or when effects actually would cascade; nor what the total impact would be'). The Office of Science and Technology Policy, Executive Office of the President, highlighted the dilemma: 'The public telephone network, for example, relies on the power grid, the power grid on transportation, and all the sectors on telecommunications and the financial structure ... Most of today's cybernetic networks are actually combinations of networks, interconnected and interdependent. Interactions among these subsystems are critical to overall network performance. Because the system also interacts with the real world environment, the interactions among subsystems are not necessarily predictable and sequential, like the steps of an assembly process, but can be essentially random, unsynchronized, and even unanticipated.' IW-D, *ibid.*, at 2–14.

[10] See Graham, 'US Studies New Threat: Cyber Attack', *Washington Post*, 24 May 1998, A1. In mid-1997, a National Security Agency 'hacker team' broke into Defense Department computers and the US electric power grid system as part of the 'Eligible Receiver' exercise. The team simulated a series of rolling power outrages and 911 emergency telephone systems overloads and foiled FBI and Pentagon efforts to trace the attackers. The success of the simulated attack spurred efforts by the government to overcome the vulnerabilities, which still exist. For a detailed description of 'Eligible Receiver', see Denning, *supra* note 5, at 23.

[11] President Clinton recently highlighted the escalating threat posed by IW when he averred that: 'Our security is challenged increasingly by nontraditional threats from adversaries, both old and new, not only hostile regimes, but also international criminals and terrorists who cannot defeat us in traditional theaters of battle, but search instead for new ways to attack by exploiting new technologies and the world's increasing openness.' President Clinton's commencement address to the US Naval Academy, May 1998. See also Woolsey, 'Resilience and Vulnerability in the Information Age', in Stuart J.D. Schwartzstein (ed.), *The Information Revolution and National Security* (1996) 79, at 82–83 (describing

830 *EJIL* 12 (2001), 825–865

Similarly, the intelligence community is seriously concerned.[12] In the event a state's vital information network infrastructure stops functioning, an Information Age society could be paralyzed and collapse into chaos.[13] Industries that benefit from cyber-technological advances could be immobilized if critical networks providing power, transportation, national defence and medical services are attacked and brought down.[14] The pervasively destructive potential of cyber-based IW presents new international military implications and invites new analytical considerations of where IW fits into the body of contemporary international legal rules pertaining to the use of force.[15]

---

incentives rogue states and terrorist groups have to engage in information warfare); Mann, 'Cyber-Threat Expands with Unchecked Speed', *Aviation Week and Space Technology*, 8 July 1996, 63, at 64 (reporting that CIA Director John Deutch ranks threats of information warfare as 'a close third behind the threats from weapons of mass destruction ... and the proliferation and terrorist use of nuclear, biological, and chemical ... weapons').

[12] In June 1998 and February 1999, the Director of Central Intelligence (DCI) testified in Senate hearings that several governments now recognize that computer attacks against civilian computer systems represent an option that foreign enemies could use to 'level the playing field' during an armed crisis against the United States. As DCI George Tenet observed: 'Who would consider attacking our nation's computer systems? Yesterday, you received a classified briefing answering this question in some detail. I can tell you in this forum that potential attackers range from national intelligence and military organizations, terrorists, criminals, industrial competitors, hackers, and disgruntled or disloyal insiders.' See Cyber Attack: Is the Nation at Risk?, Hearing before the Senate Committee on Government Affairs, 105th Cong. (24 June 1998) 10 (testimony by Director of Central Intelligence George J. Tenet), www.odci.gov/cia/public_affairs/speeches/dci_testimony_062498.html. See also Mann, *supra* note 11, at 64 (reporting that former DCI, John Deutch, ranked threats of information warfare as 'a close third behind the threats from weapons of mass destruction ... and the proliferation and terrorist use of nuclear, biological, and chemical ... weapons'). More instructively, former Deputy Attorney-General Jamie S. Gorelick provided real world examples that demonstrated the vulnerabilities of US computer systems: 'In 1992, a computer intruder was arrested for tampering with the Emergency 911 systems in Virginia, Maryland, and New Jersey in order to introduce a virus and bring down the systems. Also in 1992, a fired employee of an emergency alert network sabotaged the firm's computer system by hacking into the company's computers, causing them to crash for about 10 hours. During that time, there was an emergency at an oil refinery. The disabled system was therefore unable to alert thousands of nearby residents to a noxious release from the refinery. Finally, a sniffer was introduced into computers of NASA's Goddard Space Flight Center, permitting someone to download a large volume of complex calibration telemetry calculations transmitted from satellites. The sniffer remained undetected for an unprecedented length of time.' The Honorable Jamie S. Gorelick, Deputy Attorney-General of the United States, at the US Air Force Academy, Colorado Springs, Colorado, 29 February 1996, available at www.lawyernet.com/members/jimfesq/wca/1996/28/deep.html.

[13] See Schwartau, *supra* note 5, at 308–310 (describing how a concerted attack against critical financial and communication networks could result in widespread panic and lead to a situation resembling anarchy).

[14] See Laqueur, 'Postmodern Terrorism', *Foreign Affairs*, September–October 1996, at 14 (arguing that a computerized, information-warfare-based attack initiated against the Federal Reserve's main switching terminal in Culpepper, Virginia, would be disastrous to the United States); see also Schwartau, *supra* note 5, at 308–310 (describing the spiralling confusion and panic a concerted series of information-warfare attacks could cause).

[15] The conflict in the Persian Gulf illustrates the importance of infrastructures to US national defence — our domination of Iraq's information and communications ensured victory over a well-armed military force with minimum allied losses. As the Soviet General S. Bogdanov, Chief of the General Staff Center for Operational and Strategic Studies, noted after the end of the Gulf War: 'Iraq lost the war before it even

Several states are pursuing government-sponsored offensive cyber-programs. These states now include IW in their military doctrine, as well as their war college curricula. Their governments recognize the value of attacking adversary computer systems in order to counter other states' military superiority. The President's Commission on Critical Infrastructure Protection projects that, by the year 2002, 19 million individuals will have the knowledge with which to launch cyber-attacks.[16] Today, more than 120 countries are in the process of establishing information operations competence.[17] While most analyses by the intelligence community regarding IW capabilities of various states is classified, the body of unclassified information regarding the perspectives on and potential use of IW by other states is growing considerably.[18] Many of these governments may pose a sophisticated electronic intrusion threat to national security and emergency preparedness telecommunications and information systems.[19] Russia, China and France have acknowledged developing IW programs; and, according to one estimate, at least 33 other

---

began. This was a war of intelligence, electronic warfare, command and control and counter intelligence. Iraqi troops were blinded and deafened ... Modern war can be won by *informatika* and that is now vital for both the US and the USSR.' Briefing by Martin S. Hill, OASD C3I. Presented at the Worldwide PSYOP Conference, November 1995.

[16] See President's Commission on Critical Infrastructure Protection, Critical Foundations: Protecting America's Infrastructure A-48, 9 (October 1997).

[17] See Information Security: Computer Attacks at Department of Defense Pose Increasing Risks: Testimony Before the Permanent Subcommittee on Investigations of the Senate Committee on Governmental Affairs, 104th Cong. (1996) (statement of Jack L. Brock, Director, Defense Information and Financial Management Systems Accounting and Information, General Accounting Office). According to the US National Security Agency, more than 100 governments are capable of accessing, attacking, and conceivably disabling America's computers. *60 Minutes*, 9 April 2000.

[18] Both China and Russia have been very active in developing information warfare competence. See Hai Lung and Chang Feng, 'Chinese Military Studies Information Warfare' (Hong Kong PTS Msg 210225Z, February 1996, Subject: PLA Undertakes Study of Information Warfare) (Publications Translations Section, US Consulate General, Hong Kong). See also FitzGerald, 'Russian Views on Electronic and Information Warfare', in National Defense University, *Proceedings of the Third International Command and Control Research and Technology Symposium: Partners for the 21st Century* (1997) 126.

[19] National security and emergency preparedness ('NS/EP') telecommunications and information systems are used to maintain a state of readiness to respond to and manage any event or crisis. NS/EP telecommunications and information systems include the public network and all designated National Communications System primary assets. In testimony before Congress, an intelligence expert testified to the growing threats from foreign nations: 'We are detecting, with increasing frequency, the appearance of doctrine and dedicated offensive cyber-warfare programs in other countries. We have identified several, based on all-source intelligence information that are pursuing government-sponsored offensive cyber-programs. Foreign nations have begun to include information warfare in their military doctrine, as well as their war college curricula, with respect to both defensive and offensive applications. They are developing strategies and tools to conduct information attacks. Those nations developing cyber-programs recognize the value of attacking adversary computer systems, both on the military and domestic front. Just as foreign governments and the military services have long emphasized the need to disrupt the flow of information in combat situations, they now stress the power of cyber-warfare when targeted against civilian infrastructures, particularly those that could support military strategy.' Statement for the Record by John A. Serabian Jr, Information Operations Issue Manager, Central Intelligence Agency, before the Joint Economic Committee on Cyber Threats and the US Economy, 23 February 2000, Washington, DC, available at www.odci.gov/cia/public_affairs/speeches/ cyberthreats_022300.html.

countries have established sophisticated electronic intrusion programs for intelligence collection.[20] The Russians have stated: 'An attack against the telecommunications and electronic power industries of the United States would, by virtue of its catastrophic consequences, completely overlap with the use of weapons of mass destruction.'[21] More ominously, Chinese newspaper reports suggest that: 'An adversary wishing to destroy the United States only has to mess up the computer systems of its banks by high-tech means. This would disrupt and destroy the US economy.'[22]

Compared to the military forces and weapons that threatened Western societies in the past, modern technology has made the tools of IW cheap, readily available and easily obtainable.[23] The ubiquity of Internet access and the easy availability of hacker tools on underground Internet sites have significantly reduced both financial and intellectual barriers to launching attacks against critical computer systems. Little special equipment is needed to launch such attacks. The basic attack tools consist of computers, modems, telephones and software, essentially the same instruments used by hackers and cyber-criminals. IW, unlike nuclear warfare, is not just the province of the industrial nation-state. Terrorist groups, whether state-sponsored or independent, domestic or international, as well as organized crime syndicates and individuals, have cyber-technologies at their disposal to launch these attacks.[24]

The first step for any effective response to growing threats is to establish an

---

[20]   National Intelligence Council, 'The Foreign Information Warfare Threat to US Telecommunications and Information Systems' (undated briefing); testimony of Dan Kuehl, National Defense University, before the Joint Economic Committee, 23 February 2000 (depicting China and Russia as two nation-states that are cyber-threats to the US) (hereinafter 'Kuehl testimony'); and Madsen, 'Intelligence Agency Threats to Computer Security', 6 *International Journal of Intelligence and Counter Intelligence* (Winter 1993) 446–487.

[21]   See FitzGerald, *supra* note 18, at 126.

[22]   Speech by Jim Mackey, Department of Energy, International Association for Counterterrorism and Security Professional Briefing, 8 October 1999, Tysons Corner, VA (unpublished transcript on file with the authors). In an interview on *60 Minutes*, on 9 April 2000, Bill Triplett, a senior staffer on Capitol Hill monitoring cyber-warfare and a specialist on the Chinese military, stated that 'the Chinese probably have the biggest program from the standpoint of being able to attack our infrastructure'. In a recent book published by two Chinese colonels in the People's Liberation Army of China, the two colonels state: 'If we want to have victory in future wars, we must be fully prepared intellectually for this scenario, that is, to be ready to carry out a war which, affecting all areas of life of the countries involved, may be conducted in a sphere not dominated by military actions.' See Kuehl testimony, *supra* note 20, at 31. For a detailed discussion of Chinese views on future warfare and the national security environment, see Mike Pillsbury, *Chinese Views of Future Warfare* (National Defense University Press, 1998) and Mike Pillsbury, *China Debates the Future Security Environment* (National Defense University Press, 1999), available at www.ndu.edu; and Gertz, 'China Plots Winning Role in Cyberspace', *Washington Post*, 17 November 1999, A1.

[23]   See Denning, *supra* note 5, at 17 (in comparison to the exorbitant amount of money required to fund conventional forces, Denning suggests that between US$1 million and US$10 million could fund an adept IW team of about 10–20 hackers). See also Schwartau, *supra* note 5, at 308–310.

[24]   In April 2000, in an interview with *60 Minutes*, Richard Clarke, the White House's national coordinator for security, infrastructure protection and counterterrorism, described a real possibility for the future. 'One morning we're told by the drug cartel in Colombia, "Either the United States pulls out of Colombia, either the United States stops killing the cocaine plants, or else there'll be an information warfare attack on Houston".'

awareness of the problem's magnitude.[25] Among Western governments, the United States has a leading role in this respect, with executive guidance coming most specifically in Presidential Decision Directive 63 (PDD-63) signed by President Clinton in April 1998.[26] Entitled 'Critical Infrastructure Protection', PDD-63 calls for a national effort to ensure the security of increasingly vulnerable and interconnected infrastructures in the United States, and emphasizes the importance of the partnership between the government and private sectors and the importance of international cooperation. PDD-63 also creates the National Infrastructure Protection Center (NIPC) under the Federal Bureau of Investigation (FBI). The NIPC's mission is to act as the focal agency for gathering information on threats to infrastructure, providing timely warning of attacks, analysis and law enforcement investigation and response.[27] The defence community also created its own crisis reaction centres to monitor its computer networks and react to indications of unauthorized penetration of US defence systems.[28]

As sectors of an industrialized society become increasingly aware of national vulnerabilities and dependence on information infrastructures, a number of counter-measures to minimize threats to these infrastructures have been proposed: information-sharing about incidents, legislation to better define computer crimes, improved law enforcement capabilities, and more focused research and development efforts. While these measures are significant, further action (both legal and technological) is needed for mitigating international threats posed by IW technologies.

---

[25] For the United States, this public awareness campaign was initiated in July 1996, when the President's Commission on Critical Infrastructure Protection (PCCIP) was established to develop a strategy for protecting and ensuring the continued operation of the nation's computer systems and networks, particularly those governing telecommunications, oil and gas, electricity, bank and financial operations, transportation, water supplies, critical emergency response and government. Executive Order No. 13010, 61 Fed. Reg. 37, 347 (1996). The PCCIP's chairman, Robert Marsh, along with his team of 18, which included former Deputy Attorney-General Jamie Gorelick and former Chairman of the Senate Armed Services Committee Sam Nunn, spent a year investigating the nation's vulnerabilities from computer attacks and formulating policy proposals for how the US was going to protect its infrastructure. In its October 1997 report, 'Critical Foundations: Protecting Americas Infrastructures', the PCCIP described the potentially devastating implications of poor information security from a national perspective and discussed recommendations. While the Report of the PCCIP proposed numerous broad measures of infrastructure security such as IW early warning systems and a cooperative relationship between public and private sector entities, the report makes no mention of the international dimension of the problem of security in cyberspace. 'Critical Foundations, Protecting America's Infrastructures' (Report of the President's Commission on Critical Infrastructure Protection, Washington, DC, October 1997), available at www.pccip.ncr.gov/report_index.html.

[26] White Paper, The Clinton Administration's Policy on Critical Infrastructure Protection: Presidential Decision Directive 63, 22 May 1998, available at www.CIAO.gov/press_release/whitehousefactsheet_pdd63.html.

[27] The White House, 'Protecting America's Critical Infrastructures', PDD-63, The White House, Washington, DC, 22 May 1998.

[28] In 1993, the US Air Force created the Air Force Information Warfare Center (AFWIC), which is responsible for the Air Force's defensive and offensive IW capability. The Navy's equivalent centre is the Fleet Information Warfare Center (FIWC) and the US Army's is called Land Information Warfare Center (LIWC).

834   *EJIL* 12 (2001), 825–865

So the problem expands. New technologies generate new opportunities, which include options to conduct IW. Paradoxically, greater dependence upon new technologies also breeds enhanced vulnerabilities for technologically advanced societies. To exploit vulnerabilities in information resources, more sophisticated tools are becoming available. For these reasons, IW must be regarded seriously — not merely to know when a cyber-based attack might occur, but more critically to know how to react if such an information attack does occur.

For the interconnected global community to prepare for a cyber-based future, questions pertaining to international law must be addressed: what is the permissibility of IW under international law? Does the use of IW constitute a violation of the proscription against 'use of force' under contemporary international legal norms? Relatedly, under what circumstances may governments permissibly use IW under international law? Does IW engender only the right of self-defence under international law, or can IW engender other legal rights or restrictions beyond that right? This essay treats these questions within the confines of state-sponsored cyber-activities[29] because states remain the fundamental units of the international system, and as such are the actors principally affected by international legal rules.[30] However, as non-governmental organizations, groups and even individuals gain more recognized political and legal status in the international system, those actors will warrant special consideration under a legal analysis of IW.

3 IW as Information Operations

Contemporary international law must adapt to the rapidly changing nature of transnational communications systems. The broad sweep of advanced military technologies and the new ways in which they affect states are labelled 'Information Operations' (IOs),[31] within which IW is considered a subset. These Information Operations provide commanders with the ability to observe the battle space, analyze events and direct forces. Information Operations provide logisticians with the ability

---

[29] For instance, this article will not address the issue of non-state actors' use of IW under international law, nor will it address the issue of the use of force by states against non-state actors such as recreational hackers, terrorists, organized criminals and other non-state actors.

[30] See Ian Brownlie, *Principles of Public International Law* (4th ed., 1990) 58–59 (noting that international law concerns itself primarily with states). See *ibid.*, at 59.

[31] The US Government has defined 'information operations' as: 'Actions taken to affect adversary information and information systems, while defending one's own information and information systems. IO require the close, continuous integration of offensive and defensive capabilities and activities, as well as effective design, integration, and the interaction of C2 [command and control] and intelligence support. IO are conducted through the integration of many capabilities and related activities. Major capabilities to conduct IO include, but are not limited to, OPSEC [Operations Security], PSYOP [Psychological Operations], military deception, EW [Electronic Warfare], and physical attack/destruction, and could include CAN [Computer Network Attack]. IO-related activities include, but are not limited to public affairs (PA) and civil affairs (CA) activities.' Chairman of the Joint Chiefs of Staff, Joint Publication 3–13, *Joint Doctrine for Information Operations* (1988) 1-9 and 1-10, available at www.dtic.mil/doctrine/jel/new_pubs/jp3_13.pdf. See also Department of the Air Force, 'Cornerstones of Information Warfare', *supra* note 5, at 12 (information operations are 'any action involving the

to know what weapons are in their inventories and where to focus attention, as well as the information necessary to know where a target is, what the target's defences are, and which weapon will most effectively destroy that target.[32] Four interrelated processes support defensive information operations: information environment protection, attack detection, capability restoration, and attack response. They 'are conducted across the range of military operations at every level of war to achieve mission objectives'.[33] Offensive Information Operations could include the active collection of intelligence about information systems, unauthorized intrusions into information systems, the introduction of vulnerabilities into computer systems, corruption or denial of data, and disabling or destroying information systems.[34]

The implications of exotic IW technologies for the future of warfare is uncertain. Even so, it is clear that the new forms of attack enabled by information technology are qualitatively different from previous forms of military assaults. Some cyber-tools — such as computer intrusions and computer viruses — may push military conflict from the physical world into an electronic universe. Some new weapons may produce scant physical effects on an enemy, while others can cause massive destruction or loss of life. Some instruments require no physical intrusion beyond national borders, while others might be construed as military intervention. Finally, some cyber-weapons impact solely on military targets, while others in the process of disabling military targets also produce collateral damage on civilians. Damage from various forms of IW cyber-attack today is only speculative and remains dependent on what technologies are used when, against what facilities and for what duration. In an IW event, however, severe damage could range from pervasive military and civilian deaths and

---

acquisition, transmission, storage, or transformation of information that enhances the employment of military forces'); Joint Chief of Staff, *Information Assurance: Legal, Regulatory, Policy and Organization Considerations* (Department of Defense, 3rd ed., 1997). For an alternative definition of information warfare, see Denning, *supra* note 5 (Denning provides a theory of information warfare based on the value of information resources to an offence and defence and not necessarily based upon physically destructive acts).

[32] Information operations are both defensive and offensive. Defensive information operations 'ensure the necessary protection and defense of information and information systems upon which joint forces depend to conduct operations and achieve objectives'. Joint Publication 3–13, *supra* note 31, at III-1. For Denning, defensive information operations seek to protect information resources from attack by countering the potential for loss of value. See Denning, *supra* note 5, at 10.

[33] Joint Publication 3–13, *supra* note 31, at II-1. Computer network attacks (CNA) are a subcategory of information operations. CNAs consist of '[o]perations to disrupt, deny, degrade, or destroy information resident in computers and computer networks, or the computers and networks themselves'. See Report of the PCCIP, *supra* note 25. Such computer attacks are a form of offensive information operations. For a general discussion of computer network attacks, see Schmitt, 'Computer Network Attack and the Use of Force in International Law: Thoughts on a Normative Framework', 37 *Columbia Journal of Transnational Law* (1999) 885. Offensive information operations seek to increase the value of a target resource by altering the availability and integrity of the information resources to the benefit of the offence and to the detriment of the defence.

[34] See Colonel Phillip A. Johnson, USAF, Associate Deputy General Counsel (IA), Office of General Counsel, DOD, in 'Opening Shots: Information Warfare and the Law', brief to FY 98, US Air Force Judge Advocate-General School, Legal Aspects of Information Operations Symposium, Maxwell AFB, Alabama, Appendix F, 'Principal DOD Information Warfare Organizations', at F-33–F-34.

extensive computer system malfunctions, to destruction or loss of sensitive government information or national economic crisis, to the denial-of-service of important
military or government systems in time of emergency, or merely inconvenience for
civilian personal and business populations.

Information Warfare Weapons

A wide variety of IW tools are at present available, both defensively and offensively, for
carrying out IW attacks.[35] Such weapons include the following:

- a 'sniffer', executed from a remote site by an intruder that would allow the
  intruder to retrieve user IDs and passwords as they traverse a network; with user
  IDs and passwords intruders may gain access to sensitive information related to
  national defence, corporate proprietary information or trade secrets;[36]
- a 'Trojan horse', remotely installed into the controlling switching centres of the
  Public Switched Network, which allows an outsider to control the network and
  causing it to malfunction on command;[37]
- a 'trap door', used to gain unauthorized access and control of air traffic control
  systems, thereby creating the potential to cause pandemonium and violence in
  the skies;[38]
- a 'logic bomb', placed within a rail computer system, causing trains to be
  misrouted and crash;[39]

---

[35] See Lawrence T. Greenberg *et al.*, *Information Warfare and International Law: Introduction* (National
      Defense University, 1998).

[36] See *infra* in the text at notes 51–54 for a description of the Solar Sunrise case describing an attack on US
      national defence computers. See also John Fialka, *War by Other Means* (1997) (discussing corporate
      espionage).

[37] A 'Trojan horse' contains hidden code that executes potentially malicious acts such as recording
      passwords entered by legitimate users, installing a virus, and collecting system connectivity information
      when triggered by an external event. The code can engage in any malicious act within the privileges of
      the host program, or break out to operate with any other program or by itself. Roger C. Molander *et al.*,
      Strategic Information Warfare: A New Face of War (1996) 64. An example of a 'Trojan horse' was a
      compromised copy of the 'Dansie Shopping Cart'. See www.securityfocus.com.

[38] Also known as a 'backdoor', a trapdoor provides an undocumented way of gaining access to a computer
      system or particular software program. A 'backdoor' may be a legitimate feature, installed by a vendor to
      allow remote maintenance of the system, or a system programmer who wants to break into that
      computer after he has put it in or after the company no longer employs her. Intruders can use remote
      network dial-up to access a backdoor and gain unauthorized access to a system.

[39] A 'logic bomb' is a program that lies dormant until a trigger condition causes it to activate and destroy the
      host computer's files. The execution is usually triggered by a date or time. A 'logic bomb' can be hidden
      within a 'Trojan horse' or carried by a 'virus'. See Denning, *supra* note 5, at 258.

- 'video morphing', used to make the news broadcasts of a state indistinguishable from an enemy's creation of its version of that same broadcast;[40]
- a 'denial of service attack',[41] executed to prevent critical networks from being able to exchange data with other systems supporting functions such as emergency services, flight safety and war readiness;[42]
- a 'computer worm'[43] or 'virus',[44] which travels from computer to computer across a hospital's computer network, damaging medical data and disrupting vital systems;

---

[40] See Grier, 'Information Warfare', *Air Force Magazine*, March 1995, 34, at 35; and Graham, 'Military Grappling with the Guidelines for Cyber War', *Washington Post*, 8 November 1999, A1.

[41] In a 'denial-of-service' attack, an intruder executes a program from a remote site that congests or disables the service on the victim computer. By sending forged Internet control message protocol (ICMP) echo request packets (i.e. 'ping' packets) to IP broadcast addresses, the attack can cause network congestion or outage because of the large number of ICMP echo reply packets being sent to the victim site. An overload of this process congests the system, resulting in degraded network performance, or may render the system inoperable. CERT, SEI, CMU, CERT Advisory CA-98.01.smurf, Pittsburgh, PA: CERT, 5 January 1998.

[42] In February 2000, Yahoo, Cable News Network, eBay, Buy.com and ZDNet were all hit with what appeared to be coordinated denial-of-service attacks.

[43] A 'worm' is a self-replicating program that moves from one system to another along a network, as opposed to a virus that attaches itself to legitimate programs or files either destroying them or co-existing with them. A worm does not destroy software or compromise data. A 'worm' uses all available computing resources and saturates communications links, similar to a denial-of-service attack. See Charles P. Pfleeger, *Security Computing* (2nd ed., 1996) 179. In November 1998, a program called the Morris Internet Worm caused the disruption of service to thousands of computers and their users across the Internet. Robert Morris was charged with unleashing this 'worm' and was convicted under 18 USC 1030(a)(5)(A). See *United States v. Morris*, 928 F 2d 504 (2nd Cir.), cert. denied, 502 US 81 (1991) (defining a 'worm' as a program that travels from one computer to another but does not attach itself to the operating system of the computer it 'infects'). See also Spafford, 'The Internet Worm: An Analysis', at ftp://coast.cs.purdue.edu/pub/Doc/morris_worm/spaf-Iworm-paper-CCR.ps.Z. GAO provided an overview of this worm incident. See ftp://coast.cs.purdue.edu/pub/Doc/morris-worm/GAO-rpt.txt. In a recent worm incident, a malicious VBS script program developed by a Filipino student from Manila flooded network systems, degrading mail, file and web traffic, effecting hundreds of thousands of systems. See www.cert.org/advisories/CA-2000-04.html.

[44] A 'virus', like a 'worm', is a program that infects other programs. The virus becomes active when users access the infected program or file. Once active, the virus has two basic functions: replication and execution. Pfleeger, *supra* note 43, at 179. For a general discussion of computer viruses, see David Ferbrache, *Pathology of Computer Viruses* (1991). In March 1999, a Microsoft Word macro virus (the so-called 'Melissa' virus) developed by 30-year-old David Smith of Aberdeen, New Jersey, propagated itself via e-mail attachments causing system overloads and mail servers to crash. Although the Melissa virus disrupted operations at thousands of companies and some government agencies, it reportedly did not compromise sensitive government data. However, it illustrated the speed with which malicious software can spread in today's interconnected computing environment. See www.cert.org/advisories/CA-99-04-Melissa-Macro-Virus.html.

838   *EJIL* 12 (2001), 825–865

- an 'infoblockade', which blocks all electronic information from entering or leaving a state's borders;[45]
- 'spamming',[46] which floods military e-mail communication systems preventing field communications from reaching the troops; and
- 'IP spoofing',[47] which fabricates messages whereby an enemy masquerades as an authorized command authority giving false military information to troops in the field.

Some of these tools can have devastating results if used by criminals or terrorists. For example:

- computer intruders divert funds from bank computers and corrupt data in bank databases, causing disruption or panic, as banks need to shut down to address their problems;[48]
- computer intruders steal and disclose confidential personal, medical or financial information, as a tool of blackmail and extortion, and cause widespread social disruption or embarrassment;[49]
- spies steal classified information from secure government databases and gain information vital to national security;[50] and

---

[45]   Kanuck, 'Recent Development, Information Warfare: New Challenges for Public International Law', 37 *Harvard International Law Journal* (1996) 272, at 289. Interestingly, the UN Charter appears to contemplate these types of electronic interference with a country's communications as 'infoblockades'. Article 41 provides that, in its effort to address breaches of the peace, the UN Security Council may call upon UN members to disrupt an aggressor's 'rail, sea, air, postal, telegraphic, radio, and other means of communication'.

[46]   'Spamming' is an IW tool that clogs the victim's e-mail box with unwanted mail that can interfere with the delivery of desirable messages. See Denning, *supra* note 5, at 122–124. Simply put, it is junk mail sent via e-mail. In 1998, a defendant was held liable to AOL for sending over 60 million pieces of unauthorized bulk e-mail advertisements to customers of AOL. The defendant was found guilty of trespass to chattel under Virginia common law, false designation of origin under the Lanham Act for using 'aol.com' in the spam headers, and dilution by tarnishment because of negative associations with AOL's mark. See 1998 US Dist. LEXIS (ED Va 1998).

[47]   'IP spoofing' is an IW tool that allows an intruder to forge the e-mail 'from' address of a user so that the message appears to becoming from somewhere other than its actual source. In spoofing, the victim receiving the forged message will accept the message believing that it is coming from a trusted source. See Denning, *supra* note 5, at 255–256.

[48]   Molander, *supra* note 37, at 74.

[49]   Some of these scenarios have been described by James Adams in his book, *The Next World War* (1998) 156–158: 'A CyberTerrorist will remotely access the processing control systems of a cereal manufacturer, change the levels of iron supplement, and sicken and kill the children of a nation enjoying their food ... A CyberTerrorist will attack the next generation of air-traffic control systems, and collide two large civilian aircraft ... A CyberTerrorist will remotely alter the formulas of medication at pharmaceutical manufacturers.'

[50]   In 1994, two hackers penetrated the US Air Force's Rome Laboratory by installing seven 'sniffer' programs that allowed them to read, copy and delete e-mail and read and copy sensitive information. The intruders entered the system over 150 times, copied sensitive data and attacked other linked government facilities and defence contractor systems. Eventually, two British hackers, co-named Kuji and Datastream Cowboy, were determined to be the guilty hackers. See Jim Christy, Rome Laboratory Attacks, Prepared Testimony Before the Senate Governmental Affairs Committee Permanent Investigations Subcommittee, 22 May 1996. In Dorothy E. Denning and Peter J. Denning (eds), *Internet Besieged: Countering Cyberspace*

● terrorists cause an aircraft to crash through the use of a pulse device that disrupts and permanently corrupts the information system components within the aircraft.

These technological tactics may appear more science fiction than actual fact. Today, however, the science is real and the technology is fact. Stock markets and commodity exchanges, electronic power grids, municipal traffic control systems, air traffic control or navigation systems and classified national security information systems can be manipulated or disrupted by any one or a combination of these IW tools, with accompanying economic or societal disruption, physical destruction or loss of life. The status of international law, however, lags behind cyber-technology. Two recent incidents spotlight this disparity and suggest that serious consideration should be given to ways and means that international legal rules may apply to a cyber-attack as a transnational use of force.

A *Solar Sunrise*

In January 1998, tensions flared between the United States and Iraq over United Nations weapons inspections. Saddam Hussein expelled the UN inspectors from Iraq, precipitating a crisis and pushing the US to the brink of renewed military action in the Persian Gulf. On the first Monday in February, analysts at the Air Force's national computer monitoring centre detected an unusual series of red warning flags pop up on their screens, indicating unauthorized intrusions into at least six electronic networks across the country. Several dozen computer systems in US military installations and government facilities were successfully compromised by the intruders, which prompted a full-scale Department of Defense (DOD) response now known as Operation Solar Sunrise.[51]

The attack against DOD computer systems ultimately violated systems belonging to the US Navy and Air Force, as well as federally funded research laboratories. Although no classified systems reportedly were compromised, the attackers obtained system privileges used to read password files, delete files and create 'back doors' for subsequent re-entry. The intruders hid their electronic tracks by routing their attack through computer systems in the United Arab Emirates. They accessed unclassified

---

Scofflaws (1998). In 1992, the Defense Information Systems Agency (DISA) identified 53 attacks on military and DOD systems. In 1995, that number had grown to 559. By the year 2000, the number of attacks was estimated to approach 500,000 a year. See Correll, 'War in Cyberspace', *Air Force Magazine*, January 1998; see also Ted Uchida, School of Advanced Military Studies, US Army Command and General Staff College, *Building a Basis for Information Warfare Rules of Engagement* (1997) 8. 'Cyberespionage' is the term that has been coined to describe the use of computers and networks to obtain secret information. Some foreign governments recruit malicious hackers to help them conduct espionage against the US Government. According to Clifford Stoll in his book, *The Cuckoo's Egg* (1990), the German hackers caught in attacks against the US Government systems were actively conveying information to Russian agents.

51   See Graham, 'US Studies New Threat: Cyber Attack', *Washington Post*, 24 May 1998, at A1.

840 *EJIL* 12 (2001), 825–865

logistics, administration and accounting systems that control the US ability to manage and deploy military forces. They gained privileged access to computers by using tools available from a university website and installed 'sniffer' programs to collect user passwords. They created a 'backdoor' to re-enter the system and then used a patch available from a university website to close the vulnerability and prevent others from repeating their exploit.[52]

Despite potentially grave consequences, these attacks were orchestrated neither by an organized terrorist group nor a foreign government; rather, an Israeli teenager code-named 'The Analyzer' and two 16-year-old high school students in Cloverdale, California, broke into these systems, simply to prove that they could.[53] The incident made clear to government policy-makers that such intrusions pose real threats to national security.[54]

B *Moonlight Maze*

In October 1999, Michael A. Vatis, Director of the FBI's National Infrastructure Protection Center (NIPC), testified before a Senate subcommittee in the first public confirmation about the year-long FBI investigation code-named Moonlight Maze.[55] Moonlight Maze revealed the most extensive computer attack aimed at the US Government. According to reports, hackers working from Russia penetrated DOD computers for more than a year and stole vast amounts of sensitive information.[56] Security experts first spotted the intrusions in January 1998 when Air Force and Army computer crime investigators tracked the attacks to an Internet service provider in Russia. According to Pentagon and FBI officials, the Russian hacking was a

---

[52] Testimony before the House Joint Committee on Preventing Economic Cyber Threats by John A. Serabian Jr, 23 February 2000.

[53] The Israeli National Police, working with US authorities, arrested Ehud Tanedaum and charged him with illegally accessing US and Israeli government computers. The two teenagers, who have been publicly identified, were charged and tried in juvenile court. See Reed and Wilson, 'Suspected Pentagon Hacker Found — FBI Arrests Israeli Teen Who Had Bragged He Couldn't Be Caught', *Seattle Times*, 19 March 1998, at A7.

[54] The United States was then contemplating military action in the Gulf because of Iraqi non-compliance with UN inspection teams. The timing of these cyber-intrusions raised particular concerns in the United States that they were the initial stages of a computer-generated attack by a hostile government. The incident galvanized US Government agencies with foreign and domestic missions alike to coordinate their efforts in response, which required a massive cooperative effort by the FBI, the Justice Department's Computer Crimes Section, the Air Force Office of Special Investigations, NASA, the Defense Information Systems Agency, the National Security Agency, the CIA and various computer emergency response teams from the military services and government agencies. See Drogin, 'Yearlong Hacker Attacks Net Sensitive US Data: Technology: The Systematic Assault on Pentagon Computers Originates in Russia, Officials Say', *Los Angeles Times*, 7 October 1999.

[55] The NIPC is the FBI unit responsible for coordinating the federal response to computer threats. President Clinton made the FBI the lead agency for protecting the nation's computer systems when he signed Presidential Decision Directive 63 on 22 May 1998. See PDD-63, *supra* note 26.

[56] Testifying before a Senate subcommittee on technology and terrorism, Michael A. Vatis, Director of the FBI's NIPC, stated that 'the intrusions appear to have originated in Russia', and that the intruders stole 'unclassified but still sensitive information about essentially defence technical research matters'. See generally the discussion about Moonlight Maze in Drogin, *supra* note 54, at A1.

state-sponsored Russian intelligence campaign to secure US technology,[57] which targeted not just DOD, but also the Department of Energy, NASA, military contractors and military-linked civilian universities.[58]

The Moonlight Maze intrusions were 'distributed coordinated attacks', a style of penetration that is particularly effective at compromising existing defences. Distributed coordinated attacks can employ thousands of servers to attack and overwhelm a single server. Because so many servers are used, each attack can be camouflaged as a legitimate connection attempt, making it difficult for the victim's intrusion software to know that it is under attack, and disguising the identity of who is attacking.[59] The lesson learned from Moonlight Maze is that the United States and Western societies have become 'extraordinarily vulnerable' to penetration and sabotage of critical computer systems.[60] Left unattended is what lawful recourse government officials may take in response to state-sponsored attacks such as that by Moonlight Maze.

[57] Kimery, 'The Russians Are Coming', in 3 *Military Information Technology*, which is available online at www.MIT-kmi.com.

[58] No classified computers were reported to have been breached and no networks were reported destroyed or damaged. Notwithstanding that no classified databases were compromised, the US Government's unclassified networks contain significant amounts of confidential and sensitive data that might be valuable to foreign governments. DOD computer databases, for example, contain information about military logistics, planning, purchases, payroll and personnel, as well as routine e-mails between Pentagon personnel. Pentagon officials reportedly said that this was the first time Russia made a 'sophisticated, patient, and persistent' attempt to penetrate US computer networks. As the NASA Inspector General Roberta Gross said in an interview: 'It's difficult to tell what the damage is ... They weren't shutting down systems. They were taking file listings, looking to see what's in people's directories.' *Ibid.* Kimery, *supra* note 57. Gross said that the intruders also installed 'parking tools that they can use to get back in later'. Such electronic 'trapdoors' may be used to evade detection devices and to secretly regain access to a computer system.

[59] Kimery, 'Moonlight Maze', in 3 *Military Information Technology*, online at www.MIT-kmi.com. A number of commentators have publicly acknowledged the gravity of these incidents. 'The kids [responsible for the Solar Sunrise attack last year into DISA and other DOD computer networks] essentially found a well-known vulnerability of the operation system and came in that way'. Arthur L. Money, the Assistant Secretary of Defense for Command, Control, Communications and Intelligence, disclosed in October 1999 at the National Information Systems Security Conference in Arlington, VA. But Moonlight Maze brings 'a whole different, much more sophisticated approach ... it also brings another dimension — no longer with hackers, but with the problem of a state-sponsored attack'. Drogin, *Los Angeles Times*, 7 October 1999, at A1. According to Money: 'It's the magnitude of the extraction that is alarming to us.' *Ibid.* In the same vein, Vatis opined that: 'The greatest potential threat comes from foreign state actors who might choose to engage in information warfare against the United States, because they realize that they can't take us on in conventional military terms and would seek to go after what they perceive as our Achilles heel ... which is our reliance on information technology, more than any other country to control our critical operations.' Vatis testimony, *supra* note 56.

[60] As Richard Clark posited on *60 Minutes* in April 2000: 'An enemy could systematically disrupt banking, transportation, utilities, finance, government functions and defense. We know other countries that are developing information technology and are doing reconnaissance of our computer networks.' Clark sees the Moonlight Maze intrusions as 'pre-war reconnaissance' where half a dozen nations are busy scanning each other's networks to get a good map of where the key things are and what the key vulnerabilities are of those networks. He describes these circumstances as ones where, for the first time, the US has a 'potential foreign threat ... where the military can't save us'. *Ibid.*

842   *EJIL* 12 (2001), 825–865

The Kosovo Crisis

Experiments with the use of IW occurred during the Kosovo crisis. On 30 March 1999, three days after NATO began its bombing missions over Serbia and Kosovo, hackers initiated a coordinated programme to disrupt NATO's e-mail communications system by overloading it.[61] While the hackers' identities were not determined, Western authorities suspect they were members of the *Crna Ruka* (Black Hand) that attacked the Kosovo Information website earlier in October 1998.[62]

According to US officials, the United States also resorted to cyber-attacks during the Kosovo conflict. President Clinton reportedly approved a top secret plan to destabilize Yugoslavian leader Slobodan Milosevic by using computer hackers to infiltrate and attack foreign bank accounts held by Yugoslavia in order to siphon off funds that might be used for military purposes.[63] Public reports also suggest that the United States instigated a coordinated attack to disrupt the Yugoslav command and control network in order to protect NATO warplanes from being targeted by the air defence command and to confuse Yugoslav military messages.[64] The degree of success stemming from these US efforts at cyber-war against the Milosevic regime remains unclear, however.

4 The Legal Setting: Understanding the Implications

A Sovereignty Considerations

The realistic threat of cyber-attacks resurrects the need to consider fundamental international legal rules. Contemporary international law gives to each state a right to liberty within the international arena — that is, a certain right to be free, independent and unfettered from foreign control and forcible influence. This general principle of exclusive sovereignty over national territory is firmly fixed in customary international law.[65] This principle implies that each state is autonomous, free from coercion, and able to preserve the corporate integrity of its territory. Each state exercises control

---

[61] See Vizard, *supra* note 6, at 80.

[62] *Ibid.*

[63] See Vistica, 'Cyberwar and Sabotage', *Newsweek*, 31 May 1999, at 38; and Sullivan, 'Cyberwar? The US Stands to Lose', 28 May 1999, www.msnbc.com/news/274526.asp.

[64] Hoffmann, 'US Opens the Door to Cyberwar Technology: The Kosovo Conflict Saw the First Electronic Attacks on Enemy Computer and Communications Systems', *Orange Reg.*, 24 October 1999, at A35.

[65] See *Restatement (Third) of the Foreign Relations Law of the United States* (1987) para. 102; see also the Statute of the ICJ, 26 June 1945, Article 38(1)(b), 832 USTS 993, *Yearbook of the United Nations* (1978) 1197 (customary law is a 'general practice accepted as law'). See *Military and Paramilitary Activities In and Against Nicaragua (Nicaragua v. US)*, ICJ Reports (1986) 1, at 93–99, para. 202 (noting '[t]he principle of non-intervention right of every sovereign State to conduct its affairs without outside interference ... [I]t is part and parcel of customary international law'.). See also the 'Declaration on the Inadmissibility of Intervention in the Domestic Affairs of States and the Protection of Their Independence and Sovereignty', General Assembly Resolution 2131, UN GAOR. 20th Session, Supp. No. 14, at 12, UN Doc. A/6220 (1965) 26; the 'Declaration on Principles of International Law Concerning Friendly Relations and Cooperation Among States in Accordance with the Charter of the United Nations', General Assembly Resolution 2625 (XXV), UN GAOR, 25th Session, Supp. No. 28, at 121, UN Doc. A1 8082

over its national territory to the exclusion of all other states, and any limitation of this authority is subject to the consent of the territorial state. In particular, no state may use armed force to invade the territory of another state, no state may conduct a physical assault against another state by land, sea or air, and no state may carry out strategic observation in or over the national territory of another state. The territorial scope of sovereignty covers all national spaces. International law establishes qualifications of state jurisdiction on the high seas, in outer space, and through national airspace.[66] Critical is whether these same principles of territorial sovereignty apply as legal rules for governing the international use of cyberspace. Consider the following scenarios.

Suppose a foreign government, in an attempt to influence the political process in a target state, sends thousands of random e-mail messages to the citizens of that target state, criticizing the policies of the party in power. Would this form of e-mail propaganda violate the sovereignty of the foreign state? Or, what if a government launches an IW attack against another state by routing a corrupted e-mail message containing a computer virus through an Internet service provider that is located in a third state. Has the sovereignty of the target state been violated? Has that of the third state been violated? Does it matter that there was no physical damage done to the third state? What if, unintentionally, the computer virus does harm to the computer systems of the third state? Does it matter that the attacking state did not intend to cause harm to the third state? Such questions strike at core issues compounding the lawfulness of IW transborder data flow as it relates to the sovereignty of states.

The new technological capability of governments to employ IW instruments across international networks or through the atmosphere as electromagnetic waves challenges the viability of territorial sovereignty as a legal construct.[67] Sovereignty, a fundamental principle of international law since the Treaty of Westphalia of 1648, holds that each state retains exclusive authority over activities within its borders. Under this principle, so long as physical boundaries of jurisdiction exist and objects and activities can be precisely located, the legal concepts of possession, sovereignty and inviolability make sense. Each new medium that is accessed through technological advancement can be possessed, divided and held as sovereign territory (e.g. land and airspace) or shared in common (e.g. the high seas and outer space).

To punctuate these precepts, such customary rules of territorial sovereignty are

---

(1970). For a discussion of what customary international law is, see Anthony Clark Arend, *Legal Rules and International Society* (1999) 47–48 (customary international law consists of two elements: it must reflect consistent state practice over time by a significant group of states and there must be a belief on behalf of the state that the practice is required by law (*opinio juris*)).

[66] See United Nations Convention on the Law of the Sea, 10 December 1982, UN Doc. A/CONF.62/122, 21 ILM 1261; Treaty on Principles Governing the Activities of States in the Exploration and Use of Outer Space, Including the Moon and Other Celestial Bodies, 27 January 1967, 18 UST 2410; TIAS No. 6347; 610 UNTS 205; Convention on International Civil Aviation, Chicago, 7 December 1944, 59 Stat. 1693, 84 UNTS 289 ('The contracting States recognize that every state has complete and exclusive sovereignty over the airspace above its territory.').

[67] See Kanuck, *supra* note 45, at 275–276 (discussing the challenges that IW presents to an international paradigm based on territorial sovereignty).

844   *EJIL* 12 (2001), 825–865

codified by modern conventional law.[68] UN Charter law in Article 2(4) uses the term
'territorial integrity' to substantiate these modern legal concerns, which makes
immanent legal sense. The meaning of these terms appears plain and simple:
'Territorial' means limited to a specific territory. 'Integrity' means an unimpaired or
unmarred condition, original perfect state, entireness, completeness, undivided or
unbroken.[69] However, as tested by state practice and legal interpretation over the past
half-century, the parameters of the terms are less clear and may suggest wider latitude
in meaning. Such seems the case for what interpretation best suits these terms within
the modern purposes of Article 2(4). The traditional concept of sovereignty may not be
suitable for an increasingly interdependent and globalized world. This seems
especially true for a world that is becoming electronically interconnected as billions of
signals travel between national networks, as electromagnetic waves cross national
borders instantaneously, unsupervised and with impunity, thereby creating conditions that allow individuals or groups in one place to affect systems transglobally,
while the legal authority of the state to regulate those activities generally stops at its
national borders.

In an international technological milieu where the globe is shrinking and
cooperation and interaction across national boundaries are increasingly essential, the
isolation of any state or its society becomes impractical. New rules to govern
technological advancements and their international deployment may be required to
keep interstate co-existence peaceful. Every day, more individuals, societies and
governments plug into the global electronic, digital network simply because they have
determined that for their activities to be successful, they must be 'connected'. Thus,
the concept of sovereignty no longer is static. It appears to be evolving into a construct
made more porous by the twin forces of interdependence and globalization. Similarly,
the intangible penetration of borders carried by electronic signals might not be the sort
of violation traditionally thought to constitute an 'attack' under UN Charter law.
These features in post-industrial technological society complicate the development of
international legal rules that might deal more effectively with transnational activities
in cyberspace.

Rigid notions of Westphalian sovereignty and territorial integrity yield to a more
porous, dynamic set of technological realities. For a legal regime to account for
pervasive activities within the realm of cyberspace, where massive amounts of data
flow unchecked as electronic signals across national borders, the legal paradigm must
reach beyond the dimension of local events. Interactions and consequences, not mere
physical territory, must be treated more as legal bases of a new legal system. It is
reasonable to surmise, therefore, that, if the notion of sovereignty is becoming

---

[68]   The first step to codify this principle of territorial sovereignty was taken in 1919 in the Covenant of the
       League of Nations, Article 10 of which provides for the protection of territorial integrity: 'The Members of
       the League undertake to respect and preserve as against external aggression the territorial integrity and
       existing political independence of all members of the League.' Covenant of the League of Nations, Article
       10, Versailles, 28 June 1919 (Treaty Series, 1919/4, 25). The Charter of the United Nations reaffirms the
       principle of territorial integrity in its Article 2(4).
[69]   *Webster's Third New International Dictionary*, vol. II (1966) at 1174 and 1148.

antiquated, so too might be traditional interpretations of 'use of force' and 'armed attack' under contemporary UN Charter law as they relate to IW. We now turn to address this point.

Cyber-Force as an Armed Attack

The United Nations was founded 'to save succeeding generations from the scourge of war' and 'to suppress acts of aggression or other breaches of the peace'.[70] At the heart of the UN Charter lies Article 2(4), which asserts the key prescription under modern international law regarding the 'use of force' and reaffirms the principle of 'territorial sovereignty'.[71] The provision simply declares that: 'All members [of the United Nations] shall refrain in their international relations from the threat or use of force against the territorial integrity or political independence of any state, or in any other manner inconsistent with the purposes of the United Nations.' The choice of using the term 'force', as opposed to 'war', 'aggression' or 'military conflict', is significant in that it encompasses situations which include hostile acts that fall short of the technical state of belligerency. This fundamental proscription against the use of interstate force is traditionally regarded as being confined to the use or threat of 'armed' force, meaning the possible resort to a violent weapon that inflicts human injury.[72] Obviously, computers are neither troops nor tanks. In the case of cyber-force, fundamental questions arise over what weapons might be covered within the legal scope of Article 2(4). Indeed, it is not off the mark to assert that modern technologies defy attempts to set out as exhaustive a list of which weapons may or may not be used within the legal meaning of UN Charter law. Even so, an international consensus admits that such a prohibition on the use force extends to conventional weapons, as well as to bacteriological, biological and chemical devices and nuclear and thermonuclear weapons. The issue remains, however, as to whether instruments of IW such as 'Trojan horses', 'viruses', 'worms' or 'sniffers' qualify as weapons of 'force' as construed under contemporary international legal rules.

While the 'threat or use of force' may be interpreted broadly to mean both armed

---

[70] UN Charter, Preamble. See also Schachter, 'International Law: The Right of States to Use Armed Force', 82 *Michigan Law Review* (1984) 1620 ('When the UN Charter was adopted it was generally considered to have outlawed war.'). The drafters of the Charter intended that instrument to resolve shortcomings in the Kellogg–Briand Pact regarding the prohibition on war. See Pact of Paris, 26 August 1928, Stat. 46:2343, TS No. 796, UNTS 94:57 (signatories condemned recourse to war and agreed to resolve all disputes by peaceful means); see also Yoran Dinstein, *War, Aggression and Self-Defence* (2nd ed., 1994) 83–84. The Kellogg–Briand Pact was an attempt to prohibit the use of war as an instrument of national policy.

[71] See Ian Brownlie, *Principles of Public International Law* (4th ed., 1990) 58–59 and 112; Ingrid Detter De Lupis, *The Law of War* (1987) 56; and Dinstein, *supra* note 70, at 84 (explaining that the expression 'use of force' includes war, measures short of war, and even threats of force).

[72] D.W. Bowett, *Self-Defence in International Law* (1958) 148; and Ian Brownlie, *International Law and the Use of Force by States* (1963) 361.

846   *EJIL* 12 (2001), 825–865

and non-armed force,[73] pragmatism tends to restrict this interpretation to armed interventions.[74] Indeed, the primary purpose promoting the formation and function of the United Nations is to prevent war. Seen from this vantage point, UN Charter law clearly prohibits international intervention through the use of *armed* force, but withholds comment on other, more subtle forms of 'subversive' coercion that do not involve, at the very least, a perceived threat of armed force.[75] The Age of Information Warfare invites reconsideration of the restrictive scope of this prohibition. The fact that one government today can use IW instruments transnationally through cyberspace to inflict damage on cyber-based facilities in another state suggests the need to consider a broader interpretation of the prohibition on the use of force.

Article 2(4) stipulates a clear prohibition on a state's right to use force, which presumably would include cyber-force. Yet, exceptions to this proscription are evident, two of which find explicit mention in Charter language, although others have also evolved into acceptance through state practice. First, there is the well-known self-defence exception to the proscription on use of force contained in Article 51 of the Charter.[76] Secondly, the Security Council retains the authority to authorize the use of force to respond to 'any threat to the peace, breach of the peace or act of aggression'.[77]

Coupled with these Charter-based exceptions are certain UN resolutions that maintain the permissibility to use force in support of self-determination movements.[78] Similar consideration accrues to the possibility that a norm of humanitarian intervention exists within the realm of the customary right of self-defence.[79] Nonetheless, disagreement persists over what these challenges to the scope and application of Articles 2(4) and 51 mean for the UN Charter and contemporary

---

[73]   See, e.g. Kelsen, 'General International Law and the Law of the United Nations', in Gesina H.J. Van Der Molen *et al.* (eds), *The United Nations: Ten Years Legal Process* (1956) 4–5; see also Ahmed M. Rifaat, *International Aggression: A Study of the Legal Concept, Its Development and Definition in International Law* (1979) 120, at 234.

[74]   Wright, 'Subversive Intervention', 54 *AJIL* (1960) 521, at 529.

[75]   While some have attempted to classify covert action as a form of aggression, see Report of the International Law Commission to the General Assembly, 2 *Yearbook of the International Law Commission* (1950) 123, at 123–133, UN Doc. A/CN.4/SER.A.

[76]   UN Charter, Article 51. See *infra* note 94.

[77]   UN Charter, Articles 39 and 42.

[78]   See Brownlie, *supra* note 71 (describing how it may be lawful for a self-determination movement to seize territory and for other states to use force in support of it). See also Reisman, 'Criteria for the Lawful Use of Force in International Law', 10 *Yale Journal of International Law* (1985) 279, at 281; and Reisman, 'Article 2(4): The Use of Force in Contemporary International Law', 78–79 *American Society of International Law Proceedings* (1984–1985) 74, at 79–84.

[79]   See Joyner and Arend, 'Anticipatory Humanitarian Intervention: An Emerging Legal Norm?', 10 *Journal of Legal Studies* (2000) 27; see also Bowett, *supra* note 72; Lillich, 'Forcible Self-Help by States to Protect Human Rights', 53 *Iowa Law Review* (1967) 325; Moore, 'The Control of Foreign Intervention in International Conflict', 9 *Virginia Journal of International Law* (1969) 205, at 261–264; W. O'Brien, *The Law of Limited International Conflict* (1965) 29–30; Reisman, 'Humanitarian Intervention to Protect the Ibos', in R. Lillich (ed.), *Humanitarian Intervention and the United Nations* (1973) 167, at 177 (Reisman notes that a 'close reading of [Article 2(4)] will indicate that the prohibition is not against the use of coercion per se, but rather the use of force for specified unlawful means').

international legal rules.[80] Even so, the lack of agreement on the precise formulation of obligations contained in Article 2(4) and the principle of non-intervention is not cause for them to be rejected as irrelevant. To do so jettisons the modern basis upon which legal restraints on forcible interstate violence rest.

Other instruments vehemently confirm the prohibition against intervention by one state into the affairs of other states, and make relevant the need to devise legal restrictions on the use of cyber-force. Pre-eminent among these, the 1965 Declaration on the Inadmissibility of Intervention in the Domestic Affairs of States[81] avers that:

> No state has the right to intervene, directly or indirectly, for any reason whatsoever, in the internal or external affairs of any other state. Consequently, armed intervention and all other forms of interference or attempted threats against the personality of the state or against its political, economic and cultural elements, are condemned.

This prohibition was reaffirmed in the 1970 Declaration on Principles in International Law,[82] with the proviso that not only were such interferences condemned, but they were held to be in breach of international legal rules.[83] Intervention is prohibited when it interferes in matters in which each state is permitted to decide freely by virtue of the principle of state sovereignty. Respect for the principle of the sovereignty of states closely allies to legal rules that prohibit the use of force and interstate intervention.[84] At first blush, then, the unmistakable inference is that any transnational cyberspace activities that affect the internal affairs of a state might well breach general legal principles upholding respect for sovereignty and non-intervention. Other considerations, however, call for caution in reaching that conclusion.

Widespread international agreement upholds the prohibition on intervention by

---

[80] At least three major schools of thought assert disparate views on the efficacy of Articles 2(4) and 51. One group, which has been labelled the 'legalists', argues that Article 2(4) is still good law. The reasoning here rests upon the fact that the UN Charter is a treaty and, until the parties have withdrawn from the treaty, the treaty terms are still binding. The second and most accepted view is espoused by so-called 'core-interpretationists', who argue that, while the core of Article 2(4) is still good law, state practice has gone beyond a literal interpretation of Article 2(4). According to this approach, Article 2(4) does not prohibit all forms of force; for instance, force is allowed to rescue nationals and for humanitarian intervention. Finally, a third group of commentators, called the 'rejectionists', contend that, because states have chosen to ignore Article 2(4) when it suits their policy objectives, the inescapable conclusion is that Article 2(4) is not controlling of state behaviour. For this group, if a norm fails to reflect state behaviour and a state's belief that it has a legal obligation to follow the norm, then the norm is less than law. See Arend and Beck, *Use of Force* (1993) 82–92.

[81] General Assembly Resolution 2131 (XX).

[82] General Assembly Resolution 2625 (XXV).

[83] More than two decades earlier, the International Court of Justice in the *Corfu Channel Case* had declared specifically that 'the alleged right of intervention [was] the manifestation of a policy of force, such as has, in the past, given rise to serious abuses and as such cannot . . . find a place in international law'. The Court noted that to allow such a right as a derogation from a state's territorial sovereignty would be even less admissible. The Court concluded that the essence of international relations lay in the respect by independent states of each other's territorial sovereignty. ICJ Reports (1949) 4, at 35; 16 ILR 155, at 167. See also Brownlie, *supra* note 72, at 283–289.

[84] ICJ Reports (1986) 111; 76 ILR 445.

848   *EJIL* 12 (2001), 825–865

one state into the sovereign affairs of another.[85] However, legal opinion diverges over
the scope of the non-intervention rule. Indeed, few topics prompt greater legal
controversy than the duty not to intervene, or the alleged right under certain
circumstances of states to intervene. The debate is compounded in the quest to define
which types of intervention by which actors might be acceptable under what
particular circumstances.[86]

The line separating unlawful intervention from legitimate interference is often
difficult to draw. It is easy to argue that incursions by military forces across national
borders violate international norms, and that mere economic and diplomatic forms of
coercion are more likely to fall within the realm of permissive behaviour. The dilemma
becomes apparent, however, when attempts are made to distinguish between more
subtle kinds of intervention, such as naval interdiction, massive economic sanctions,
humanitarian intervention, and computer-directed forms of cyber-assault. Legal logic
suggests that a government-sponsored computer attack involving transnational
networks and telecommunications might trigger legal implications arising from the
prohibitions in Article 2(4). So it becomes necessary to ascertain what activities
involving use of the Internet constitute 'force' or 'the use of force' as prohibited by

---

[85]   See Emerich de Vattel, *The Laws of Nations or the Principles of Natural Law* (1758) Book I, chapter III,
      section 37 (testifying to the universal consensus against 'intermeddl[ing] in the domestic affairs of
      another Nation'); and *Restatement (Third) of the Foreign Relations Law of the United States* (1987) para.
      102.

[86]   Various views on intervention tend to fall into four rules, over which there is still debate. First, there is the
      'neutral non-intervention' rule, which holds that aid from a foreign state is permissible when requested
      and when there exists a low level of civil strife. According to this rule, aid is not permissible in the event of
      an insurgency or belligerency, and should never be given to the rebel forces. Secondly, a 'self-
      determination' rule permits a foreign state to provide aid to any group seeking self-determination, the
      government or the rebels. Thirdly, the 'proportionate counter-intervention' rule permits offsetting
      assistance to the government of a state if a third state has already given aid to the rebels. Aid is limited to
      the territory involved in the civil strife; and, if the aid to the rebels is equivalent to an armed attack, the
      outside state providing assistance to the government can respond against the third state. And, finally, the
      'limited counter-intervention' rule permits offsetting assistance to the government of a state if a third
      state has already given aid to the rebels, aid must be limited to the territory experiencing the conflict, and
      the aiding state can never take action against the third intervening state giving aid to the rebels. See
      Arend and Beck, *supra* note 80, at 82–92. Cf. Jackamo, 'From the Cold War to the New Multilateral World
      Order: The Evolution of Covert Operations and the Customary International Law of Non-Intervention',
      32 *Virginia Journal of International Law* (1991) 929 (discussing the contemporary customary law of
      non-intervention). The International Court of Justice recently flushed out one factor that distinguishes
      between permissible and impermissible intervention. In *Military and Paramilitary Activities In and Against
      Nicaragua*, the ICJ found that the United States violated the customary international law of
      non-intervention by training, encouraging and arming the Contra forces in Nicaragua. See *Military and
      Paramilitary Activities In and Against Nicaragua (Nicaragua v. US)*, ICJ Reports (1986) 1, at 93–99 (noting
      that the United States recognized Article 2(4) as both a 'universal norm' and a 'universal international
      law'). The Court in this case determined that Article 2(4)'s prohibition of the use of force was a principle of
      customary international law, 'to be thenceforth treated separately from the provisions, especially those of
      an institutional kind, to which it is subject to the treaty-law plane of the Charter'. *Ibid.*, at 100. The ICJ
      also held that overflights by US aircraft violated customary international law regarding the violation of
      the territorial sovereignty of states. *Ibid.*, at 147.

Article 2(4). Arguably, this provision applies only to 'armed force'.[87] Yet, a use of force implies unlawful violence threatened or committed against persons or property, and, if cyber-force qualifies as a form of violence, it involves swift, injurious impacts on a targeted facility.

The critical point is this: though perhaps not 'armed force' in the literal sense, resort to cyber-force may be viewed as a form of intervention that can produce certain harmful or coercive effects in other states. Serious legal questions thus arise: does a denial-of-service attack against a foreign Internet site breach the legal rule prohibiting use of transnational force? Is the denial of service an act of coercion that fits within the legal ambit of acts prohibited by relevant UN declaratory instruments? Does a government's intentional interference with or interruption of another state's Internet service violate international legal rules? Or, should it be regarded as more legally akin to the lawful domestic decision of a government to instigate a legal economic embargo of another state? Would such interference be sufficiently 'coercive' so as to construe breach of the international legal rule that prohibits the use of force? Suppose a government 'attacks' another state's computer systems. Would such an attack against a bank or defence industry in another state constitute an unlawful 'use of force' or an 'armed attack' against that latter state? What form or repercussions must that cyber-generated assault take before the target state can respond? What degrees or kinds of cyber-force would be permissible? Clear answers to these quandaries are provided neither by UN Charter law nor by contemporary international legal rules.

Similar difficulties arise in defining what should constitute a 'use of force' with regard to biological and chemical weapons.[88] Chemical and biological weapons, it can be argued, should be viewed as forms of force because, if used, such weapons can destroy life and property.[89] Certain, though not all, weapons of IW also present real threats of widespread destruction. If, for example, a 'worm' were released and it incapacitates a hospital's computer network or an emergency 911 computer system, hundreds of lives might be put at risk. Equally plausible are circumstances that involve the cyber-instigated downing of computers that control chemical and nuclear power plants or oil refineries, which could cause massive releases of deadly gases or toxic effluents.[90] Such attacks could produce social impacts as devastating as those caused

---

[87] See Brownlie, *supra* note 72, at 265–278. Brownlie concludes that Article 2(4) includes force besides 'armed force', but he does not indicate the nature of these other uses of force.

[88] See Brownlie, *supra* note 72, at 362. Much like information operations, chemical and biological weapons do not have to involve the physical explosions and violence associated with traditional conceptions of armed force.

[89] *Ibid.*, at 362.

[90] See Constantini, 'Information Warriors Form New Army', International Press Service, 9 August 1996, available in 1996 WL 10768646. See also Lake, *supra* note 6 (examining six real scenarios that threaten the US, including cyber-terrorism).

850 *EJIL* 12 (2001), 825–865

by chemical weapons.[91] Using similar technologies, some computer attacks could destroy property, but spare harm to people. For example, a computer virus might be used to compromise Wall Street's electronic power supply and telecommunication infrastructures, thereby shutting down the financial markets. Chaos and panic could ensue, perhaps cascading even into dramatic repercussions for the economic stability of the United States and other Western financial markets. In the event, however, no human lives likely would be lost. Still, the real possibility that computer-based information operations in one state could destroy lives and damage property in other states points up the legal rationale for concluding that such activities should be prohibited as a 'use of force' under UN Charter law.

The argument seems persuasive that cyber-based activities that directly and intentionally result in non-combatant deaths and destruction — such as the premeditated disruption of an air traffic control system that results in the crash of a civilian airliner or the corruption of a medical database that causes civilians or wounded soldiers to receive transfusions of the wrong blood type — breach modern prohibitions on the use of force. Less clear is the case of other cyber-based activities, for example the disruption of a financial or social security system or the disclosure of confidential personal information, which produces no human injuries or property damage. These activities clearly intrude into the internal affairs of another state, but do not exceed any visible threshold of harm against which customary international law protects civilians. While certainly impermissible, one might argue whether such acts of subversive intervention are legally sufficient for automatically triggering forms of retaliation involving use of armed force by the targeted state.

B Resort to Self-defence

Contemporary international legal rules prohibit the threat or use of force except when authorized by the Security Council, or when undertaken by individual states in self-defence and in response to 'an armed attack'.[92] At least two important exceptions apply to these prohibitions on the use of force. First, in accordance with Chapter VII provisions of the Charter, the United Nations may use force, including military force, as a means to enforce decisions of the Security Council.[93] Secondly, individual

---

[91] See Laqueur, *supra* note 14, at 14 (arguing that a computerized, information warfare-based attack initiated against the Federal Reserve's main switching terminal in Culpepper, Virginia, would be disastrous to the United States); see also Schwartau, *supra* note 5, at 308–310 (describing the spiralling confusion and panic a concerted series of information-warfare attacks could cause); see also Wilson, 'The Precipice Problem: A Guide to the Destabilization of Western Civilization', www.infowar.com/class3/class3.html-ssi (visited on 17 March 1997). Wilson describes a concerted campaign which is geared towards catastrophically disrupting critical functions of society controlled by technology such as phone, power, financial, transportation, communication and law enforcement information networks. Wilson concludes that, after such an attack, 'some things are clear — there will be immediate chaos. The amount of damage that will be done will total into the trillions; this does not take into account the long-term economic effects, which will not be correctable. The West will be suffering from near-fatal internal strife.'

[92] See UN Charter, Articles 2(4) and 51.

[93] Under Article 39 of the UN Charter, the Security Council can determine whether there has been a 'breach of the peace' and can authorize the use of force under Article 42.

governments may take forcible action, including the use of military measures, in self-defence.[94]

In the world of cyberspace, however, serious issues of law and policy concerning self-defence persist. Suppose a state is the targeted victim of a computer network attack from a private terrorist organization located within another country. The IW attack takes the form of sophisticated intrusions into top-secret military databases of the victim state. Classified military information is stolen, destroyed and altered. When the victim state's intrusion-detection mechanisms fail to give warning of these intrusions, the victim state erroneously relies on false data in making foreign policy and military decisions. The goal of the attack is successful. The result is the death of 20 servicemen who perish when a military unit conducting training operations launches a missile into their military unit, rather than the vacant training grounds because they relied on the compromised data.

Under this scenario, does the victim state have any recourse against the state from which the IW attack originated, or just the private terrorist organization? Could the victim state launch an attack in self-defence in order to stop the computer intrusions into its computer systems? Is the victim limited to destroying the computer virus that has penetrated its system, or can the victim state attack back in self-defence with conventional forces, destroying the structural facilities from where the computer viruses were launched? Does the victim state have first to gain permission from the government of the state where the terrorists are located before acting in self-defence using armed force?

Finally, does the victim state's inability to detect the compromise of its computer system in some way detract from its right to act in self-defence? What if the victim state did not have any intrusion-detection system in place? And would the victim state's right of self-defence under international law be different if the result of the attack was not loss of life, but only the theft of classified information?

Contemporary international legal rules provide few definitive answers to these considerations. In instances where a state can link cyber-attack to a foreign government, a forcible response may be necessary, either to defend that state against an ongoing attack or to prevent future attacks. Provided that the attack is actual or the threat is imminent and without any alternative choice of means, the victim state may lawfully invoke self-defence to justify reasonable, necessary and proportional measures to safeguard its security. This, in essence, embodies the right of self-defence.[95] The victim state would justify its response as part of its right of self-defence as set out in contemporary UN Charter law. Less obvious, however, is that these UN Charter rules provide legal support for taking military action against a state or its agents that conduct cyber-based information attacks against another state.

The exercise of self-defence, clearly a right of states, remains subject to legal

---

[94] As provided for in Article 51: 'Nothing in the present Charter shall impair the inherent right of individual or collective self-defence if an armed attack occurs against a member of the United Nations until the Security Council has taken measures necessary to maintain international peace and security.'

[95] Bowett, *supra* note 72, at 269; O'Brien, *supra* note 79, at 23–32, a comprehensive summary of various views on the meaning of self-defence.

852   *EJIL* 12 (2001), 825–865

restrictions, even in cases of cyber-attack. On the one hand, only actions taken in self-defence are permitted; reprisals and retaliation are proscribed under contemporary UN Charter law.[96] This being the case, a government can respond to an IW attack by using some kind of force.[97] Once the cyber-attack ends, however, it is questionable whether international legal rules allow the target state to retaliate forcibly against the attacker. If a state is under a continuous, foreign-instigated IW attack and is suffering physical, financial and potentially mortal harm, that government is not expected to tolerate events that are destroying its national infrastructure. It seems reasonable that a government subjected to such a cyber-attack would be permitted to respond immediately by taking action in self-defence to thwart the attack. But suppose a government discovers several weeks afterwards that it has been victimized by a cyber-assault on its computer systems. Is that government granted any right of subsequent retaliation? The rules of modern international law generally suggest that this should not be the case, and instances of cyber-assault should be treated no differently than an act of foreign espionage. Forcible retaliation as retribution is not permitted. Compensation or reparations may be sought through diplomatic channels from the offending government, but acts of reprisal are not lawfully acceptable, largely because they could perpetrate a circle of persistent violence.[98] Retaliation by means of IW should be treated no differently.

A second limitation on the right to self-defence mandates that not all uses of force, inclusive of cyber-force, necessarily qualify as 'armed' attacks. As the International Court of Justice concluded in *Nicaragua v. United States*, governments do not perforce have the right of armed response to acts that fall short of constituting an 'armed attack'. Only military attacks, and not every isolated armed incident, rise to the level of an 'armed attack'.[99] The point to be made here is that certain acts of intrusion may be unlawful, but that fact does not necessarily give a state the right to respond by using armed force in self-defence. Simply put, some illegal actions taken by a government against another state rise to the level of violating prohibitions of the use of force, but not every act of intervention rises to the level of an 'armed attack', nor necessarily triggers a state's right to respond in self-defence, resorting to military force.

The traditional limitation on armed force to measures taken strictly in self-defence upholds world community standards contributing to a more stable international

---

[96] Brownlie, *supra* note 72, at 281–283; Schachter, *supra* note 70, at 1620.

[97] See Arend, 'International Law and the Recourse to Force: A Shift in Paradigms', 27 *Stanford Journal of International Law* (1990) 1, at 14 (referring to the 'typical action taken in self-defense' as one in which the state must immediately act to protect itself from an ongoing attack).

[98] See, e.g. Security Council Resolution 188, UN SCOR, 19th Session, 188th Meeting, UN Doc. AA/5751 (1964); *Restatement (Third) of the Foreign Relations Law of the United States* (1987) para. 905. For a review of the legality of reprisals in the context of the US missile raid on Baghdad in 1993 in response to the alleged assassination attempt on President Bush, see Reisman, 'Self-Defence or Reprisal? The Raid on Baghdad: Some Reflections on Its Lawfulness and Implications', 5 *European Journal of International Law* (1994) 120, at 125; and Ratner and Lobel, 'Bombing Baghdad: Illegal Reprisal or Self-Defense?', *Legal Times*, 5 July 1993, at 24.

[99] See *Military and Paramilitary Activities In and Against Nicaragua (Nicaragua v. US)*, ICJ Reports (1986) 1, at 93–99.

order. First, the restriction tends to dissuade the scenario of the vicious cycle of escalating violence from occurring. Secondly, it ensures that force is used only as an emergency measure — as a necessary last resort. Thirdly, it functions as a restraint against uses of force that are based on pretext, misunderstanding and erroneous factual determinations. Professor Louis Henkin put it well when he observed that the United Nations 'recognize[s] the exception of self-defense in emergency, but limit[s] [it] to actual armed attack, which is clear, unambiguous, subject to proof, and not easily open to misinterpretation or fabrication'.[100] In the post-Second World War era of conventional military weapons and international war, such considerations were particularly apt.

The legal and technological situations have changed radically today. When one state attacks another state with tanks, air strikes or missiles, the factual predicate for self-defence stands clear and manifest. Such is hardly the present case. In a time earmarked by pervasive unchecked transnational electronic interactions, techniques of cyber-based IW can be used by a government to disrupt (or 'attack') facilities in another state. A computer-network-based attack involving software weapons such as viruses or 'Trojan horses' is far less apparent than Professor Henkin's observation suggests. It seems untenable that international rules require a government that is being subjected to an electronic attack — the results of which may inflict catastrophic social and economic damage on its society — to delay responding until the factual predicate or the intent of the perpetrators are made clear. Similarly untenable is the case for a government to launch an armed attack on another state, merely because it suspects that the latter state is using the Internet subversively. Irrefutable evidence must exist to support that suspicion or justify a retaliatory response. Such a licence eviscerates legal prohibitions against the use of force, and invites unsubstantiated accusations of 'cyber-aggression' as a new legal predicate for states to retaliate forcibly. These undesirable scenarios suggest the need to construct new international rules that hold factual predicates to a less ambiguous legal standard.

A first step towards shaping new rules is to clarify what constitutes an 'armed attack' in the context of cyber-generated IW. As noted earlier, the right of self-defence may be permissible against an armed attack or its imminent threat. But neither contemporary UN Charter law nor general international legal rules furnish adequate answers for what actions constitute an 'armed attack' or its imminent threat. Moreover, the issue of whether 'armed attack' is legally synonymous with 'aggression' has never been satisfactory resolved.[101] This conundrum remains no less conflicted in cases of cyber-attack that disrupt vital military, industrial or public healthcare facilities.

Certain misconceptions surround contemporary interpretations of self-defence.

---

[100] Louis Henkin, *How Nations Behave* (2nd ed., 1979) 142 (emphasis added).

[101] The definition of 'aggression' put forward by the UN General Assembly in 1974 contributes little to clarifying the legal status of cyber-based acts by one state against facilities in another state: 'Aggression is the use of armed force by a state against the sovereignty, territorial integrity or political independence of another state, or in any other manner inconsistent with the Charter of the United Nations, as set out in this Definition.' United Nations Press Release, GA/5194, 20 December 1974.

854   *EJIL* 12 (2001), 825–865

One surmises that UN Charter law restricts the right of self-defence to a delict committed by one state, which constitutes an 'actual' armed attack.[102] While sometimes true, considerable legal support resides in the proposition that a state has an inherent right to use force in self-defence against acts that do not constitute a classic armed attack.[103] Another misconception about self-defence is the supposition that an 'armed attack' can only occur if the military forces of a state carry it out. That may not always be the case. Paramilitary forces, irregular forces, border security forces, police forces or even armed civilians might take actions that amount to such an attack. Moreover, an armed attack may take either direct or indirect forms. It assumes a direct character if a state employs armed forces straight away against another state. Armed attack can take an indirect form if a state launches an attack from a third state, or uses irregular or foreign forces as its surrogates. Finally, the misconception persists that a state must be attacked before the right to defend its territorial integrity can be exercised. The notion of pre-emptive or anticipatory self-defence permits a state to defend itself in the event of imminent danger or an actual threat of armed attack. The legal caveat is that the threat must be real and credible and create an imminent need to act, with a genuine probability of attack. As succinctly expressed in the well-known *Caroline* doctrine, the threat must be 'instant, overwhelming, leaving no choice of means, and no moment for deliberation'.[104] The reasonable conclusion is that

---

[102] See Brownlie, *supra* note 72, at 265–278. For more detailed argument rejecting this view, see Bowett, *supra* note 72, at 187–193; J. Brierly, *The Law of Nations: An Introduction to the International Law of Peace* (6th ed., 1963) 417–418; and O'Brien, *supra* note 79, at 23–32.

[103] This view is supported by the inclusion in the General Assembly's definition of aggression of acts that do not entail armed attacks by a nation's armed forces, such as the unlawful extension of the presence of visiting forces, or allowing a nation's territory to be used by another state 'for perpetrating an act of aggression against a third State'. See United Nations Press Release, GA/5194, 20 December 1974, Article 3, which states that the following qualify as acts of aggression: '(a) The invasion or attack by the armed forces of a State of the territory of another State, or any military occupation, however temporary, resulting from such invasion or attack, or any annexation by the use of force of the territory of another State or part thereof; (b) Bombardment by the armed forces of a State against the territory of another State or the use of any weapons by a State against the territory of another State; (c) The blockade of the ports or coasts of a State by the armed forces of another State; (d) An attack by the armed forces of a State on the land, sea or air forces, or marine and air fleets of another State; (e) The use of armed forces of one State which are within the territory of another State with the agreement of the receiving State, in contravention of the conditions provided for in the agreement or any extension of their presence in such territory beyond the termination of the agreement; (f) The action of a State in allowing its territory, which it has placed at the disposal of another State, to be used by that other State for perpetrating an act of aggression against a third State; (g) The sending by or on behalf of a State of armed bands, groups, irregulars or mercenaries, which carry out acts of armed force against another State of such gravity as to amount to the acts listed above, or its substantial involvement therein.' Definition of Aggression, General Assembly Resolution 3314, UN GAOR, 29th Session, Supp. No. 19, 2319th Plenary Meeting, at 392, UN Doc. A/9890 (1974).

[104] See *The Caroline Case*, in J.B. Moore, *Digest of International Law*, vol. 2 (1906) 409. Bowett, *supra* note 72, at 59; R.Y. Jennings, 'The Caroline and McLeod Cases', 32 *AJIL* (1938) 89.

international law is not a suicide pact among states, and thus a society does not have to wait until it is physically harmed to defend itself.[105]

Computer-generated intrusions and cyber-communication disruptions elude easy classification as being 'attacks'. In evaluating the propriety of taking defensive action, it seems more useful to consider the legal consequences of such a computer-generated action rather then the mechanism used to launch the attack. That is, computer intrusions committed to steal data or disrupt air traffic control may be equally intrusive, but the more extensive destruction and death caused by disruption of a public air traffic control system render that action more susceptible to the equivalent of an 'armed attack' than an attempt at data theft. It seems reasonable to qualify cyber-assaults that are sufficiently destructive as 'armed attacks', regardless of the level of intrusion. Difficulty persists in asserting that an unauthorized cyber-based intrusion into an unclassified information system *ipso facto* always meets the legal threshold of being an armed attack. If, however, the same act resulted in shutting down a state's air traffic control system, as well as in collapsing banking institutions, financial systems and public utilities, and opened the floodgates of dams that caused deaths and property damage, considerable merit would reside in alleging that such an attack inflicted damage equivalent to that caused by an 'armed attack'. Although those information systems do not contain classified information, such computer-generated acts would obviously imperil that state's society and threaten its national security.

The nature of the information stolen or compromised also contributes to determination of whether an action rises to the level of legally being considered 'an attack'. If certain data are considered vital to national security (i.e. information that is 'classified'), that information may be afforded special protections under the regime of self-defence. For instance, if a foreign government attacks the computer databases of another state's department or ministry of defence, and steals classified information related to troop locations during a time of armed conflict, or the codes to nuclear weapons' launch instruments, such actions could qualify as being tantamount to 'armed attacks', even though no immediate loss of life or destruction results. If a state's government discovers that these computer attacks against its defence ministry's classified databases were continuous, and evidence exists to support that the perpetrators are planning future cyber-attacks (and the government's claims are accepted as true and accurate), a reasonable deduction is that the computer intruders were engaged in an ongoing attack against the defence establishment of that state.

The government's assertions, if in fact true, could thus give rise to a right of

---

[105] Whether an imminent danger of an armed attack actually exists depends on the individual circumstances of each case. For an armed attack to occur, some level of actual or potential physical destruction, combined with some level of intrusion into a target state's borders or violation of its sovereignty rights, should be evident. Some actions, such as aerial bombardment of a state's military command and control centres, will clearly constitute 'armed attacks', as they inflict high levels of both forcible intrusion and destruction. Other acts, such as radio and television propaganda broadcasts, are not considered 'armed attacks' and are usually relegated to forms of subversive intervention.

856   *EJIL* 12 (2001), 825–865

self-defence against the cyber-intruders and the government intentionally sponsoring those IW activities. Such a right permits the target state to take necessary and proportionate countermeasures, including the use of force intended to halt those actions and to prevent similar future assaults.[106] Perhaps the targeted computers are unclassified military logistics systems containing information about the management of spare parts, troop mobilization and medical supplies, the corruption of which would seriously interfere with a state's ability to conduct military operations and defend its national security. Such a cyber-attack on unclassified systems may still give rise to a right of self-defence. As suggested earlier, the consequences of the cyber-attack on the targeted programs may be more important than the means used to implement it.

Discussion of deterrence often arises from advocates of strong and swift military responses to terrorist attacks. They argue that force is necessary as 'an effective counterweight to extremism'.[107] Even so, some experts question the deterrent value of military responses to attacks.[108] They identify the risks of error and lack of a prompt military response in military self-defence attacks as not justifying any gains in deterrence value. They are also concerned with provoking the original attackers, thereby causing an escalation of violence and a cycle of retaliation.[109]

Under these circumstances, IW may actually serve as an effective tool for dissuading self-defence, as well as deterring military responses. In using IW a government could react immediately through use of computers that can be accessed instantaneously. Once an intrusion is detected, only minutes are needed for a state to collect enough computer generated evidence to meet the predicate factual threshold for lawfully initiating a response. The time to respond is thus significantly less than that required for military equipment and personnel to be readied and deployed abroad for a conventional strike. Targeting the attackers, moreover, can be more precise and is less likely to inflict human casualties. Finally, cyber-based actions taken in self-defence can be prosecuted instantaneously and covertly, thus avoiding public acts that expose a state to a breach of international legal rules and to any action taken in self-defence by the targeted government. This covert process allows the opportunity for an offending state, once it realizes that it has been found out, to halt its aggressive

---

[106] See *Military and Paramilitary Activities In and Against Nicaragua (Nicaragua v. US)*, ICJ Reports (1986) 1. However, the target state would not have the right to launch a computer attack through a third state's territory in order to react in self-defence without that third state's permission.

[107] See Schultz, 'Low Intensity Warfare: The Challenge of Ambiguity', 25 ILM (1986) 204, at 205.

[108] As former CIA Director James Woolsey testified, an effective military response is often 'at odds with its being prompt'. Hearings on Counterterrorism Policy Before the Judiciary Committee of the Senate, 105th Cong. (1998) (testimony of James Woolsey, former Director of the CIA), 1998 WL 564420.

[109] See Scherman, 'US Fury on 2 Continents: Pros and Cons', *New York Times*, 21 August 1998, at A11 ('Experts say, it is most likely that the targets of the action and their supporters will lash back'). Some believe that the bombing of Pan Am Flight 103 over Lockerbie, Scotland in 1988 was Libya's response to the US air strike against Libya in 1986 after the Libyans allegedly ordered the bombing of a nightclub in West Berlin that killed a US Army sergeant and injured 50 American military personnel. Newman *et al.*, 'Clinton Raises the Stakes in the War Against Terrorism', *US News and World Report*, 31 August 1998, at 38 ('The bombing of Pan Am Flight 103 in 1988 is widely believed to have been an act of revenge for the US bombing of Libya in 1986').

actions without being subjected to international criticism. This avoids humiliating the attacking state. At the same time, this process might persuade the perpetrator not to retaliate, thus alleviating that government from its felt need to escalate its response on account of national security or national interests, which probably would avoid exacerbating the level of violence.[110]

C *Implications for Anticipatory Self-defence*

Some contemporary legal theories support the premise that customary international law does not limit a state simply to reacting to traditional armed attack,[111] and that cyber-force might be used lawfully as an instrument of pre-emptive self-defence. According to general legal rules for self-defence, not only may a government respond to an attack launched against its territory, but a government can also take self-defensive military action in anticipation of such an armed attack.[112] This principle of 'anticipatory self-defence' asserts that the use of force by one state against another is permissible as self-defence if the force used to respond is both really necessary and not excessive in relation to the perceived threat. Even so, such a principle of 'pre-emptive' self-protection does not sanction acts of self-defence under any and all circumstances. To do so might invite committing acts in circumstances that actually constitute aggression. Moreover, while the right of self-defence may at times seem ambiguous, accepted legal criteria have evolved under customary international law that set limits for determining the legitimacy of action taken in self-defence.

These concerns directly relate to cyber-warfare. For instance, suppose a government's military officials locate a 'trapdoor' within their computers that control that

[110] We would like to thank Phillip Johnson for his helpful insights on this point.

[111] For a discussion of the various views of international scholars regarding the legitimacy of anticipatory self-defence under Article 51, see Arend and Beck, *supra* note 80, at 73 and the accompanying footnotes. According to Arend and Beck, most international legal scholars can be divided into two schools of thought regarding the legitimacy of anticipatory self-defence: the 'restrictionists', who take the position that anticipatory self-defence violates Article 51; and the 'counter restrictionists', who argue that, for various reasons, anticipatory self-defence does not violate Article 51.

[112] See Dinstein, *supra* note 70, at 172 (explaining the customary right of self-defence as a preventive measure and not only as a responsive measure). The *Caroline Case* of 1837 is often cited as legitimizing the right of anticipatory self-defensive action taken in response to an imminent armed attack by another state or other entity. See *The Caroline Case*, in J.B. Moore, *Digest of International Law*, vol. 2 (906) 412. In 1837, British forces took action against an insurgency by Canadian rebels who had mounted several attacks from islands in the Niagara River. The British sought to capture the US steamboat *Caroline* that the rebels had chartered to maintain their supply lines. The British seized the *Caroline* while it was moored in US territory, burned the vessel and sent it downstream where it plunged over the Falls. During the incursion the British killed several US citizens. The US Government complained that the British had violated US sovereignty while the British countered that they had simply acted 'in self-defence'. In a letter to Henry Fox, the British minister in Washington, DC, Secretary of State Daniel Webster wrote that the British could only justify the use of force in self-defence so long as the British could prove 'a necessity of self-defence, instant, overwhelming, leaving no choice of means, and no moment for deliberation'. Letter from Secretary Webster to Mr Fox, 24 April 1981, *British and Foreign State Papers* (1857) 1129, at 1138. The traditional principle of anticipatory self-defence was first enunciated by Secretary of State Daniel Webster in his response to a Canadian attack on the American ship *Caroline*, which had been assisting Canadian rebels in their efforts against the Canadian Government. See Jennings, *supra* note 104.

858 *EJIL* 12 (2001), 825–865

state's missile defence systems. They identify the source of a computer intrusion to be the ministry of defence of a foreign government. The victim state is able to verify the theft of at least a dozen passwords, and undertakes the necessary action to have the entire missile launch passwords immediately changed. However, because of the nature of the trapdoor, the targeted government cannot know for sure what sensitive information was stolen, including whether the codes to deactivate the defence system were compromised. Without sufficient time to change the codes, the victim government must decide whether to react in a pre-emptive fashion, i.e. to act against the foreign state that intruded into the victim state's missile defence computer systems. Would the victim state be justified in attacking the foreign state to pre-empt an IW attack that would deactivate their missile defensive system?

Contemporary international law supports the possibility of such a response. As a traditional international rule, however, for recourse to anticipatory self-defence to be lawful, it must be limited by specific considerations. First, such action must be necessary. In this respect, necessity requires that a state undertake self-defence only as a last resort. At the same time, the law requires that a state demonstrate that actions taken in response are proportional to the threat being directed against its territory. Plainly put, cyber-force used in anticipatory self-defence must be neither unreasonable nor excessive. This notion of proportionality implies that the degree of cyber-force employed be limited in magnitude, intensity and duration to that which is reasonably necessary to counter the threat actually posed against the target state. Proportionality applies both to whether a given level of cyber-force is appropriate as a response to a particular grievance (as part of the law of the use of force, *jus ad bellum*) and whether a given cyber-action is appropriate in light of its objectives and the damages/casualties that will result (as part of the law of armed conflict, *jus in bello*).[113] In short, the level of forcible response by a victim state must be proportionate to the force applied by the aggressor state in the initial attack. For example, a full-scale blitzkrieg across a broad front, accompanied by massive aerial bombardment, would obviously be disproportionate as a response to a patrol's border raid. Nor would a cyber-generated effort to bring down a society's financial or banking infrastructure be appropriate as a response to a computer intrusion that temporarily disrupted public telecommunications in the victim state.

Secondly, the cyber-generated response must strive to balance the damage it inflicts, especially to civilians, against the military objectives it aims to accomplish. In this regard, a cyber-attack directed against civilian healthcare facilities would not be permissible as an act of self-defence. For over 150 years these precepts drawn from the *Caroline* incident have influenced the interpretation of international legal rules. While an international consensus is still lacking to substantiate the applicability of anticipatory self-defence as a universally accepted principle of international law, no consensus actively opposes the concept either. It thus appears that no strict prohibition precludes a government using cyber-force pre-emptively as long as the perceived threat is demonstrated to be real and immediate, and the criteria of

---

[113] *Restatement (Third) of the Foreign Relations Law of the United States* (1987) para. 905.

proportionality and necessity as general legal rules are adhered to in the application of computer-generated coercion.

5 Rethinking Legal Thresholds for Information Warfare

We live in an era in which many countries possess instruments of IW and the peacekeeping function of the UN Security Council is less than fully effective. Many IW weapons are capable of instantaneous mass destruction with no forewarning of the impending destruction. Other IW tools, such as preset 'logic bombs' and 'Trojan horses', operate like mines floating in territorial waters as their cyber-programs lie in wait until activated. In this context, governments must ponder not only whether the UN Security Council will act on their behalf, but also whether any assistance if offered will be too little, too late. In the absence of genuine guarantees of collective security against conventional military threats, governments will have to weigh whether launching a pre-emptive cyber-based attack is warranted against another state's computer assets in order to preserve their own national security from a perceived threat of IW.[114] Given such circumstances, a broader reading of self-defence would permit cyber-generated forms of anticipatory self-defence to be conducted lawfully, presumably with fewer human casualties and less property damage.[115]

As a source of customary international law, state practice seems to sympathize with permitting some IW activities. For instance, espionage, universally criminal under domestic laws, does not *ipso facto* violate international law.[116] In this context, IW conducted as espionage activity might be considered lawful. Furthermore, ruses have long been part of warfare and their legitimacy is explicitly recognized in the laws of war.[117] Just as the original ancient Trojan Horse was legal, so too would the use of some 'Trojan Horse' pieces of software be permissible in times of armed conflict between two states.

If a target state cannot substantiate that a foreign-generated computer attack against its information systems meets the threshold of force necessary for an 'armed attack', then that government may not respond with conventional, kinetic military force, unless it is willing to risk that response being labelled the form of aggressive 'armed attack' prohibited under UN Charter law. International legal rules and customary state practice presently support a state's acting in self-defence against attacks on its national information infrastructure. However, a government's response

---

[114] One useful approach to the concept of self-defence in the context of IW is Michael Walzer's restatement of the *Caroline* principle. According to Walzer, a state has the right to self-defence when a nation perceives the following on the part of an aggressor: (1) an intent to injure; (2) active preparation making intent a positive danger; and (3) a general situation in which waiting or doing anything other than fighting greatly magnifies the risk. Michael Walzer, *Just and Unjust War: A Moral Argument with Historical Illustrations* (2nd ed., 1992) 81.

[115] See Walter G. Sharp Sr, *CyberSpace and the Use of Force* (1999) 43.

[116] See Kanuck, *supra* note 45; and Abram N. Shulsky, *Silent Warfare: Understanding the World of Intelligence* (2nd ed., 1993) 103.

[117] Protocol Additional to the Geneva Conventions of 12 August 1949; and Relating to the Protection of Victims of International Armed Conflicts, 12 December 1977, 1125 UNTS 3.

860 *EJIL* 12 (2001), 825–865

to a cyber-attack, like that to any force, must comply with the prescribed legal principles set down in the concepts of necessity, imminence and proportionality. Moreover, the perceived 'intent' behind a cyber-attack should be taken into account in making any decision to anticipate or respond to an offensive act. In this regard, certain factors serve as useful guidelines when considering whether to act in self-defence, among them the following: (1) a clear indication of intent by the offending state; (2) the availability and sufficiency of evidence to demonstrate that preparations for the attack have advanced to the point where it is imminent; and (3) the ability to make the advantage of a pre-emptive attack proportional to the risks of precipitating a war that might otherwise be avoided.[118] In any event, deciding whether a particular form of cyber-based attack meets the conditions of necessity and imminence depends on the particular perceptions of the threatened state. A targeted government's decision to respond also depends on that state's vulnerabilities and the potential for damage by a particular cyber-attack. Similarly, the perceived intent of the offending government may determine the level of response by a target state. If the government of a targeted state believes that another state's assault on its information systems merely serves as a prelude to a larger conventional attack, then it might view the 'non-armed' assault as the first phase in a war-making process. Similarly, a state victimized by cyber-assaults might absorb some degree of damage while reserving the right to act later in accordance with the doctrine of self-defence. Whether a government considers cyber-based danger 'imminent' depends on the intensity of the attack, the target of the attack, the reaction time required in order to successfully pre-empt the attack, and the speed with which the damage may move throughout the computer networks.

Just as it is not clear that an attack on information systems amounts to an 'armed attack' against a state's territorial integrity or political independence, neither is it obvious what types of action would be proportionate to such an attack, especially in cases where the attack inflicts little or no physical damage or loss of life. Where a computer intrusion disrupts or corrupts a database, or denies service for vital elements of a society's electronic infrastructure, thereby inflicting great hardship on the target country, that state must decide what form of response qualifies as being proportionate to the cyber-attack. In the absence of real physical destruction or human deaths — such as the crash of a passenger aircraft through manipulation of the air traffic control system — it remains polemical as to whether a conventional military attack would be proportionate. However, if a conventional response is deemed disproportionate to an IW attack, a response in kind may be an option as long as its effects remain proportionate to the offending state's 'armed attack'.

The dual-use quality of most telecommunications networks further complicates the feasibility of applying traditional international legal rules as constraints on the use of IW. These dual uses blur the distinctions between military and civilian systems. By doing so, confusion is introduced between military targets, which are legitimate to attack during conflict, and civilian facilities, which are protected under humanitarian

---

[118] William V. O'Brien, *The Conduct of Just and Limited War* (1981) 132–133.

rules of armed conflict. Some IW tools do not always allow their users to distinguish between military and civilian facilities. Additionally, Western military forces are particularly dependent on non-military systems for deployment and logistics.[119] Attacks having military objectives might be directed predominantly at civilian systems, with resultant collateral damage and injury to the civilians who operate and depend upon them.[120]

Cyber-attacks on military targets may cause civilian systems connected to those military systems to fail. Alternatively, a virus fed into an adversary's military computer might inadvertently or otherwise enter into civilian systems. In a related vein, electronic assaults on computer systems that otherwise might be considered legitimate targets may be impermissible also on account of the danger caused to civilians by malfunction of those systems. A cyber-attack on military power facilities, defence-related munitions factories, pharmaceutical plants or nuclear power plants could pose problems for society in general if the computer-generated failure of a facility leads to the release of toxic substances into the atmosphere. In this regard, the issue remains as to whether a state necessarily waives its rights to protection against cyber-attacks on civilian targets if it purposefully integrates military facilities into its civilian systems. Given the current rules of armed conflict, one would think that, yes, the rights to protection of civilian facilities are given up when those facilities are used for military purposes. A state may leave its civilian computer-based communications systems vulnerable to a legitimate attack if that government allows both military and civilian systems to run on the same networks.

As warfare capability evolves through fast, accurate and covert information weaponry, the requirement under the UN Charter of an 'armed attack' occurring before a government may act in self-defence becomes less pragmatic. Given the capabilities of IW techniques, this approach may prove too restrictive. In circumstances involving the possible use of IW weapons, a government simply may not be able to afford to wait until the necessity to act is so dire. Within this context, a more appropriate approach may be reliance upon the customary international rule of anticipatory self-defence, which would permit resort to force if the threat is instant and overwhelming, and leaves no choice of means or no moment for deliberation. In an age when many states possess instruments that can be employed transnationally to conduct IW, the instantaneous need to interpret other governments' intentions can mean the difference between peace and conflict. The potential for pervasive societal disruptions caused by a premeditated IW attack renders such a 'wait and see' approach overly risky for most technologically advanced states.

The instant quality of cyber-force suggests the need for a more practical approach to dealing with IW, one which would tolerate the pre-emptive use of cyber-force under the doctrine of anticipatory self-defence when a government perceives that there exists a significant and real threat to its national security, and responds to pre-empt

---

[119] See Sterner, 'Digital Pearl Harbor, National Security in the Information Age', 2 *National Security Studies Quarterly* (Summer 1996) 33, at 43.

[120] See Kanuck, *supra* note 45, at 284.

862   *EJIL* 12 (2001), 825–865

that threat in a reasonable and responsible manner. To be lawful, this modern theory of anticipatory self-defence to counter IW threats would rest upon the ability to determine the reality of the perceived threat and the reasonableness of the response in self-defence. The standard of reasonableness would have to meet both a subjective and an objective test. On the one hand, the subjective test would ascertain whether the purported target state has reasonable grounds for believing that a real threat exists. On the other hand, the objective test would determine whether third party states view the threat in the same light.[121] The objective test would also consider whether the cyber-force used to counter the perceived threat was reasonable relative to the threat posed.[122] When applied to the transnational use of cyber-force, anticipatory self-defence would allow governments to meet their minimum national security requirements and at the same time ensure that the use of force is necessary and proportional under the circumstances.

6 Legal Rules and Information Warfare Reconsidered

International legal rules provide the framework for organizing and processing political and military interaction among nation-states. Today, the Internet performs a critical role in this regard, as it provides a vast web of interlinked channels for instantaneous intergovernmental communication. More profoundly, the Internet makes possible new types of legal regimes. The Internet and international law thus can become partners in shaping new considerations and forms of sovereignty. International law can crystallize norms of behaviour in cyberspace. The Internet can provide the mechanism for giving these ideas form and substance through human activities.

At the same time, cyber-based activities can be used for unlawful purposes, in particular the pursuit of IW as examined in this study. No provision of modern international law explicitly prohibits IW.[123] This is significant because, as usually regarded under international law, that which international law does not prohibit it generally permits.[124] However, the absence of a prohibition against IW is not dispositive, since under international law general principles may apply to the use of

---

[121] In August 1998, US cruise missiles struck a terrorist training camp in Afghanistan and a chemical plant in Sudan. The rationale articulated for this action was self-defence.

[122] See generally Myers S. McDougal and Florentino Feliciano, *Law and Minimum World Public Order: The Legal Regulation of International Coercion* (1961).

[123] Because of the nature of certain IW activities such as jamming and spoofing, orbital assets are necessary to carry out IW activity, thus implicating rules and principles of outer space law. Yet no public law convention dealing with outer space prohibits the use of IW activities that make use of satellite assets. See the 1967 Treaty on the Principles Governing the Activities of States in the Exploration and Use of Outer Space, Including the Moon and Other Celestial Bodies, 27 January 1967, 18 UST 2410; TIAS No. 6347; 610 UNTS 205; the 1971 Agreement Related to the International Telecommunications Satellite Organization, 23 UST 3813; TIAS No. 7532; and the 1976 Convention on the International Maritime Satellite Organization, 31 UST 1; TIAS No. 9605.

[124] See *Legality of the Threat or Use of Nuclear Weapons*, Advisory Opinion, 8 July 1996, ICJ Reports (1996), at para. 21.

IW.[125] International law may pose constraints on the conduct of IW, just as it does on modes of warfare that use traditional forms of attack. Alternatively, international law may leave wiggle room for using many types of IW techniques in many circumstances. In some situations, international law might find that certain cyber-actions do not rise to the level of acts that count as indicators of hostile intent, nor of a use of force. It is neither possible nor necessary to create a comprehensive list of what cyber-techniques lay definitively beyond the bounds of acceptable acts under international law. State actions, like human behaviour generally, assume significance from their own particular context, not as generic stereotypes classified into a specific legal category.

The major legal issues for the future turn on whether and to what extent a state should be authorized to use information operations and whether a state can act in self-defence using information operations. The most important task confronting international lawyers is to clarify various criteria by which the legitimacy of a state's use of forcible measures in information operations situations can be appraised, with the ultimate goal of bringing the international system closer to a more orderly, predictable environment for interstate intercourse. To this end, certain criteria might be useful for designing a framework of legal rules affecting the use of force applicable to IW. For one, determination must be made as to what constitutes lawful force when information operations are used transnationally. A state could use information operations to defend itself from an imminent armed attack, or actions deemed equivalent to an armed attack (i.e. indirect aggression that rose to the level of an armed attack).

Secondly, a determination must be made as to what actions in information operations amount to an 'armed attack'. Such an assessment of the character of the information operations could be done based upon a critical evaluation of various interrelated factors, in particular the nature of the activities, the severity of the effect of the activities, and how long the activities persist. Gauging these factors would contribute much towards gauging the quality and quantity of a particular act of cyber-force, as well as its lawful character.

For a computer assault to qualify as an 'armed attack', its intensity and effects should be equivalent in severity to those inflicted by a traditional 'armed attack'. That is, a foreign-instigated computer action that temporarily interrupts service of another state's local phone company and causes a few hundred people to be without a phone service would not amount to an 'armed attack'. Conversely, a computer attack that intentionally compromises the control system of a chemical or biological plant, and, as a result, causes the release of toxic gases over large population centres, is more likely to be considered the legal equivalent of an armed attack.

A third factor to be weighed in determining whether a computer attack rises to the level of an 'armed attack' is the duration of the action. A one-time computer attack against the financial markets of Wall Street, causing a crash, or the penetration and theft of classified top-secret information from defence department databases, might by

---

[125] *Ibid.*, at para. 86.

864   *EJIL* 12 (2001), 825–865

itself be sufficient to constitute an armed attack. Yet, even a low intensity attack against a state's financial markets that produces intermittent interruptions or causes the theft of sensitive, albeit not top-secret information, could conceivably constitute an armed attack if done as part of an ongoing continuous attack. While the theft of secrets from one database may in and of itself not qualify as an armed attack, the persistent, premeditated theft of sensitive information may do so.

In addition, other standards can be applied to the process of evaluating the responsive use of information operations, particularly in self-defence. These would include: the degree to which a cyber-attack caused an immediate and extensive threat to human lives; an assurance that a proportional use of force will not threaten a greater destruction of values than those at stake; a demonstration that the action taken in response causes only minimal effects on authority structures; evidence that a prompt disengagement occurs consistent with the purpose of the action; and in the aftermath of the cyber-attack and its response, an assurance that the government of a targeted state furnish immediate and full reporting to the Security Council and any appropriate regional organizations.[126]

7 Conclusion

Western societies have invested trillions of dollars in building information infrastructures that are interpretable, easy to access and easy to use. Attributes like openness and the ease of systems' interconnectivity, which promote efficiency and expeditious customer service, are the same factors that make these systems vulnerable to attacks. Recent cyber-attacks in the United States underscore this point. Information warriors have taken the threat out of the realm of the abstract and made it real. Thus, a major challenge for national governments during the next decade will be to find ways to defend cyber-based infrastructure and to protect telecommunications commerce while maintaining an open society, all carried out through lawful means.[127]

To be relevant today, the rules of modern international law must define more sharply the criteria used to distinguish between which state actions are permissible as normal computer-generated transborder data flows for international communications, trade and financial assistance from those cyber-activities that might qualify as an 'armed attack', against which the use of force is permissible. Even with new forms of computer-generated weapons and changing concepts of sovereignty and territory, international law will continue to rely upon UN Charter principles and rules to define the legal boundaries of 'cyberspace'. Modern state practice is grounded in those norms, and they remain the foundation for guiding interstate behaviour in the Information Age. Yet, at the same time, international law must evolve and adapt.

---

[126] Moore, *supra* note 79, at 264.

[127] In the recent words of President Clinton, in the context of meeting the challenges of terrorism, the challenge of IW 'requires the confident will of the American people to retain our convictions for freedom and peace and to remain the indispensable force in creating a better world at the dawn of a new century'. 'Remarks by the President on American Security in a Changing World' at George Washington University, Washington, DC, Office of the Press Secretary, The White House, 5 August 1996.

Clearer rules for what kinds of IW action constitute an 'armed attack', what responses are permissible as self-defence by a state targeted in an IW situation, and how international institutions can facilitate processes aimed at reaching these objectives should be re-examined and re-evaluated. This ambition cannot help but remain a constant challenge, as international law struggles to keep pace with the all-too-rapid advancements in technology in general, but especially as more people in more societies add to the burgeoning worldwide use of cyber-technologies.

Part V
Humanitarian Intervention
and the Responsibility to Protect

[19]

THE CUSTOMARY INTERNATIONAL LAW DOCTRINE OF HUMANITARIAN INTERVENTION: ITS CURRENT VALIDITY UNDER THE U.N. CHARTER

JEAN-PIERRE L. FONTEYNE*

The Indian action in the 1971 Bangladesh crisis[1] has recently revived the debate among scholars on the question of the legality of unilateral[2] humanitarian[3] intervention[4] under the U.N. Charter.

* Lecturer in Law, University of the West Indies, Faculty of Law. J.D., State University of Ghent; LL.M., University of Virginia, School of Law.
The assistance of Professor Richard B. Lillich is gratefully acknowledged.
All textual translations were provided by the author.

1. *See generally* INT'L COMM'N OF JURISTS, THE EVENTS IN EAST PAKISTAN, 1971 (1972) [hereinafter cited as INT'L COMM'N OF JURISTS]; Nanda, *A Critique of the United Nations Inaction in the Bangladesh Crisis*, 49 DENVER L. J. 53 (1972) [hereinafter cited as Nanda, *Critique*]; Nanda, *Self-Determination in International Law: The Tragic Tale of Two Cities—Islamabad (West Pakistan) and Dacca (East Pakistan)* 66 AM. J. INT'L L. 321 (1972) [hereinafter cited as Nanda, *Self-Determination*]; *Documents: Civil War in Pakistan*, 4 N. Y. U. J. INT'L & POL. 524 (1971).

2. Throughout this article the term *unilateral* intervention will be used as a generic term to denote intervention either by a single State (*individual* intervention) or by a group of States (*collective* intervention). Recent examples of the former are provided by the 1956 Soviet intervention in Hungary, the 1958 U.S. intervention in Lebanon, the 1969 British "mini-intervention" in Anguilla, and the Indian intervention in East Pakistan. The latter can be illustrated by the joint French-British-Israeli intervention in the 1956 Suez crisis, the SEATO intervention in South Vietnam, the 1964 Stanleyville airdrop carried out in cooperation by Belgium, the United States, and the United Kingdom, the intervention by the Members of the Warsaw Pact in Czechoslovakia (1968), and the joint U S.-South Vietnamese intervention in Cambodia (1970). Unilateral intervention is essentially characterized by the lack of formal authorization from any competent international body, universal or regional, and in the case of collective unilateral intervention, by the non-institutionalized character of the association of States carrying out the intervention. Unilateral intervention must be distinguished on the one hand from intervention by armed forces *under the direct control of the United Nations* (Korea, UNEF, ONUC, Cyprus) *or of an appropriate regional organization* (1965 intervention in the Dominican Republic, in its second stage, after the "take-over" by the Organization of American States), and on the other hand from individual or collective intervention duly *authorized* by such an organization (first stage of the intervention in the Dominican Republic, carried out by the United States, but subsequently "ratified" by the Organization of American States).

3. Humanitarian intervention has been defined as:

204   CALIFORNIA WESTERN INTERNATIONAL LAW JOURNAL   Vol. 4

With the exception of some vague and controversial allegations of self-defense by Indian spokesmen,[5] India itself has not tried to justify its intervention in East Pakistan on international legal grounds. Specifically, she has not appealed to the doctrine of humanitarian intervention.[6] Nevertheless, the failure of the Indian government to refer openly to this theory does not alter the fact that its course of action in the Bangladesh situation probably constitutes the clearest case of forceful individual humanitarian intervention in this century. The question which the Indian

---

[T]he justifiable use of force for the purpose of protecting the inhabitants of another State from treatment so arbitrary and persistently abusive as to exceed the limits within which the sovereign is presumed to act with reason and justice.

E. STOWELL, INTERNATIONAL LAW 348 (1931). *Compare* Rougier, *La Théorie de l'Intervention d'Humanité*, 17 REVUE GENERALE DE DROIT INTERNATIONAL PUBLIQUE (REV. GEN. DR. INT'L PUBL.) 468, 472 (1910) [hereinafter cited as Rougier].

4. For the purposes of this article, the term *intervention* is defined as "dictatorial interference by a State [or group of States] in the affairs of another State for the purpose of maintaining or altering the actual conditions of things." 1 L. OPPENHEIM, INTERNATIONAL LAW 305 (8th ed. H. Lauterpacht 1955) [hereinafter cited as OPPENHEIM]. This emphasizes that "intervention proper is always *dictatorial* interference, not interference pure and simple." *Id.* This definition rejects as too broad Accioly's definition: "Intervenção pode ser definida com a ingerência de um Estado nos negócios internos ou externos de outro Estado não dependents dêle, com a intenção de lhe impor certa maneira de proceder." H ACCIOLY, MANUAL DE DIREITO INTERNACIONAL PUBLICO 50 (8th ed. 1968). As pointed out by M. GANJI, INTERNATIONAL PROTECTION OF HUMAN RIGHTS 14-15 (1962) [hereinafter cited as GANJI], and by Reisman, *Humanitarian Intervention to Protect the Ibos*, in HUMANITARIAN INTERVENTION AND THE UNITED NATIONS 167, 179 n.42 (R. Lillich ed. 1973) [hereinafter cited as Reisman], the term *dictatorial* does not necessarily require the actual use or threat of armed forces to allow an interference to be considered intervention, but can be taken to include other modalities of coercion as well. Nevertheless, this article will be primarily concerned with *armed* intervention.

5. *See, e.g.*, Prime Minister Gandhi's statement in the Indian Parliament, May 24, 1971, *cited in* Nanda, *Self-Determination, supra* note 1, at 334 & n.94; Prime Minister Gandhi's statement in The Motherland (New Delhi), Dec. 5, 1971, at 2, col. 1., *cited in* Nanda, *Critique, supra* note 1, at 65 & n.95.

6. A possible explanation for India's reluctance to invoke formally the theory of humanitarian intervention in what appears to have been an almost perfect setting to do so, may have been its desire to avoid inconsistency between its course of action in the Bangladesh situation and its previous position in theoretical debates in the United Nations, where it apparently favored a strict interpretation of articles 2(4) and 51 of the Charter, thereby rejecting any additional exceptions to the flat prohibition of the threat or use of force regardless of motive. *See, e.g.*, Statement by Mr. Krishna Rao (India), Special Committee on Principles of International Law Concerning Friendly Relations and Co-Operation Among States (Spec. Comm. on Fr. Rel.), 19 U.N. GAOR, U.N. Doc. A/A.C. 119/S.R.29, at 13 (1964).

operation raises is whether the present state of international law, as modified by the U.N. Charter, still permits unilateral resort to force in order to remedy a situation of large-scale deprivation of the most fundamental human rights, committed by a State against its own nationals.

In view of the serious doubts recently expressed by various scholars as to the existence of a "right" to intervene for humanitarian purposes as a generally recognized principle of customary international law (*even in the pre-Charter period*[7]), it will be necessary to analyze this particular contention before assessing the eventual survival of the doctrine in spite of the U.N. Charter prohibition of State-initiated force.

I. The Traditional Doctrine of Humanitarian Intervention: State Practice

Despite such early precedents as the Crusades, several of

---

7. Lauterpacht stated that: "The doctrine of humanitarian intervention has never become a fully acknowledged part of positive international law." Lauterpacht, *The Grotian Tradition in International Law*, 23 BRIT. Y.B. INT'L L. 46 (1946). *But see* note 125 *infra* and accompanying text. *Compare* Waldock, *The Regulation of the Use of Force by Individual States in International Law* (Hague Academy of International Law), 81 RECUEIL DES COURS 455, 461 (1952) [hereinafter cited as Waldock], who fails to mention humanitarian intervention in his list of traditional grounds of justification for intervention. *See also* J. BRIERLY, THE LAW OF NATIONS 403 (6th ed. H. Waldock 1966) [hereinafter cited as BRIERLY]; GANJI, *supra* note 4, at 42; R. REDSLOB, TRAITE DE DROIT DES GENS 258 (1950) [hereinafter cited as REDSLOB]; Franck & Rodley, *After Bangladesh: The Law of Humanitarian Intervention by Military Force*, 67 AM. J. INT'L L. 275, 277 ff., 299 & 302 (1973) [hereinafter cited as Franck & Rodley]; Humphrey, *Foreword*, in HUMANITARIAN INTERVENTION, *supra* note 4, at VII; Marshall, *Comment*, 3 INT'L LAWYER 435 ff. (1969). *Contra*, D. BOWETT, SELF-DEFENSE IN INTERNATIONAL LAW 95 (1958) [hereinafter cited as BOWETT]; L. CAVARE, LE DROIT INTERNATIONAL PUBLIC POSITIF 632 (3d ed. 1969); 1 P. GUGGENHEIM, TRAITE DE DROIT INTERNATIONAL PUBLIC 289 (1953); A. THOMAS & A. THOMAS, THE DOMINICAN REPUBLIC CRISIS 1965, at 19-20 (IXth Hammarskjöld Forum 1967) [hereinafter cited as THOMAS & THOMAS]; Aronéanu, *L'Intervention d'Humanité et la Déclaration Universelle des Droits de l'Homme*, 33 REVUE DE DROIT INTERNATIONAL, DE SCIENCE DIPLOMATIQUE ET POLITIQUE 126, 128 ff. (1955) [hereinafter cited as Aronéanu]; de Nova, *The International Protection of National Minorities and Human Rights*, 11 HOWARD L. J. 274 (1965); Lillich, *Forcible Self-Help to Protect Human Rights*, 53 IOWA L. REV. 325, 326 (1967) [hereinafter cited as Lillich, *Self-Help*]; Lillich, *Intervention to Protect Human Rights*, 15 McGILL L. J. 205, 209 ff. (1969) [hereinafter cited as Lillich, *Intervention*]; McDougal & Reisman, *Response*, 3 INT'L LAWYER 438 ff (1969); Röling, *On Aggression, on International Criminal Law, on International Criminal Jurisdiction (Part I)*, 2 NEDERLANDS TIJDSCHRIFT VOOR INTERNATIONAAL RECHT 167, 177 (1955) [hereinafter cited as Röling].

206   CALIFORNIA WESTERN INTERNATIONAL LAW JOURNAL   Vol. 4

which could be considered humanitarian interventions, or the 16th and 17th century religious wars,[8] it seems that the institution of humanitarian intervention is in fact largely a creation of the latter part of the 19th century. This is certainly true so far as State practice *explicitly* referring to this justification is concerned. Earlier instances of humanitarian intervention are too closely tied with a feeling of religious solidarity to allow them to be classified as genuinely humanitarian.

A large number of cases have occurred in which States in the 19th and early 20th century allegedly intervened on behalf of the local populations in other States. Examples include the United States' interventions in Cuba at the end of the 19th century,[9] and the protests by the European Major Powers against the cruel treatment of political prisoners in Morocco in the beginning of the 20th century.[10] These cases seem to lack either a *clear* humanitarian motive or the *highly coercive* character of an armed intervention.[11] Therefore, the analysis of pre-Charter precedents of

---

8. For examples of interposition by sovereigns in favor of religious minorities in other States, *see* 1 R. PHILLIMORE, COMMENTARIES UPON INTERNATIONAL LAW 621 et seq. (3d ed. 1879).

9. *But see* Reisman, *Humanitarian Intervention*, *supra* note 4, at 182-83. For the official U.S. justification for the first of this series of interventions, see President Grant's Message to the U.S. Congress, Dec. 7, 1874, *cited in* W. MANNING, COMMENTARIES ON THE LAW OF NATIONS 97, n.† (rev. ed. S. Amos 1875) [hereinafter cited as MANNING]. *See generally* 6 J. MOORE, DIGEST OF INTERNATIONAL LAW 211 ff. (1906) [hereinafter cited as MOORE]; de Lapradelle, *Chronique sur les Affaires de Cuba*, 1 REVUE DE DROIT PUBLIQUE ET DE SCIENCE POLITIQUE EN FRANCE ET A L'ETRANGER 74 (1900) [hereinafter cited as de Lapradelle]; Lefur, *Chronique sur la Guerre Hispano-Américaine*, 5 REV. GEN. DR. INT'L PUBL. 665 (1898). For a summary of the U.S. involvement in Latin America from the Spanish-American War to the creation of the Organization of American States, see H. DE VRIES & J. RODRIGUEZ-NOVAS, THE LAW OF THE AMERICAS 16-17 and 20 (1965).

10. *See* Rougier, *Chronique des Faits Internationaux*, 17 REV. GEN. DR. INT'L PUBL. 62, 98 ff. (1910). For a comprehensive treatment of 19th and early 20th century instances of humanitarian "intervention," both armed and diplomatic, see E. STOWELL, INTERVENTION IN INTERNATIONAL LAW 63-316 (1921) [hereinafter cited as STOWELL].

11. GANJI, *supra* note 4, at 41, n.124. Instances of *peremptory demands* by Major Powers, as occurred quite frequently in that period, should not be summarily discarded as not amounting to intervention. Often backed by an implicit threat of military or other measures, in case satisfaction was not given, they could be almost as coercive as actual armed intervention and retain a particular relevance as precedents in view of the prohibition in the U.N. Charter of not only the use but also the mere *threat* of force. *See* U.N. CHARTER, art. 2, para. 4. A good example of the threat to use force for humanitarian purposes is provided by the peremptory demands of France and Great Britain, backed by

forceful humanitarian intervention must be restricted to the notorious cases in Eastern Europe.[12]

A.   Intervention in Greece (1827-1830)

As a result of the numerous massacres perpetrated in previous years by the Sublime Porte, France, Great Britain, and Russia concluded the Treaty of London on July 6, 1827. In this treaty they resolved *unilaterally* to combine their efforts to put an end to the bloodshed in Greece and proposed a limited local autonomy for the region within the Ottoman Empire. Upon rejection of their proposal by the Turkish government, the three Major Powers undertook an armed intervention which on September 14, 1829, resulted in the *a posteriori* acceptance by the Porte of the provisions of the 1827 Treaty of London, and in the independence of Greece in 1830.

In his *International Protection of Human Rights*, Ganji contends that this intervention provides only a very limited precedent of humanitarian intervention, insofar as the armed intervention against Turkey was mainly carried out by Russia. It was his opinion that Russia could rely on certain concessions it obtained from the Sultan by the 1774 Treaty of Kutchuk-Kainardji for the protection of the Christian religion in the Ottoman Empire.[13]

It seems, however, that this approach is far too negative in view of the rather revolutionary character of the course of action of the European Powers, since this was an era where the absolute personal jurisdiction of the Prince over his subjects was still largely regarded as a central attribute of sovereignty. It appears clear that this course of action could certainly not have been envisaged as early as 1774, nor assented to beforehand by Turkey in the Treaty. It is indeed doubtful whether Russia could justify its *armed* intervention on the Treaty, for article VII merely provided that:

> The Sublime Porte pledges to protect the Christian religion and its churches constantly; and also it grants permission to the Ministers of the Imperial Court of Russia to make *representations* in all circumstances, in favor of the new church

---

the mobilization of their fleets, to the King of the Two Sicilies in 1856. Rougier, *supra* note 3, at 475.

12. The facts of these cases are taken primarily from GANJI, *supra* note 4, at 22 ff.; STOWELL, *supra* note 10, at 63 ff.; Rougier, *supra* note 3, at 473. *See also* J. MATTIOTT, THE EASTERN QUESTION (2d ed. 1930).

13. GANJI, *supra* note 4, at 23-24.

208   CALIFORNIA WESTERN INTERNATIONAL LAW JOURNAL   Vol. 4

in Constantinople . . . as well as in favor of those who service
it . . . [14]

Furthermore, as far as participation in the intervention by
France and Great Britain is concerned, it is even clearer that
this provision could not provide a treaty-basis, since the Treaty
was a purely bilateral agreement between Turkey and Russia.

Finally, in the 1827 Treaty of London the Major Powers
themselves indicated that their action was dictated "no less by
sentiments of humanity, than by interest for the tranquilty of
Europe;"[15] thus invoking, for the first time in history, humanitarian concern as a justification for intervention.

B.   Intervention in Syria (1860-1861)

Following the massacre of thousands of Christians in Syria
by the local Moslem population with the complicity of the Turkish
authorities, France, Great Britain, Prussia, and Russia met with
Turkey at the Conference of Paris and signed a Protocol on August
3, 1860.   In this agreement they gave France a mandate to intervene in Syria to restore order in the area.   Six thousand French
troops were sent to Syria, and on October 5, 1860, an International
Commission was created.   This commission adopted a set of rules
regulating the French presence in Syria and, on June 9, 1861, a
new Constitution for the Lebanon region.   Subsequently, the
French force, having completed its mission, left Syria.

Apparently, not too much importance should be given to the
fact that *formally* this operation did not amount to an intervention
since the Sultan gave his consent to the activities of the Concert
of Europe by signing the Protocol of Paris.[16]   One can reasonably

---

14. 1774 Treaty of Peace and Friendship Between Turkey and Russia (Kutchuk-Kainardji), 2 G. DE MARTENS, RECUEIL DES TRAITES 287-322 (2d ed. 1817),
cited in GANJI, *supra* note 4, at 18 (emphasis added). Articles XVII and XXIII
of the same treaty contain similar pledges. This persecution of Christians in
Turkey constituted a violation of these treaty commitments and, under the then
valid rule of legal resort to force for enforcement of treaty obligations, would
have justified Russian self-help in the form of intervention However, the inclusion in article VII of a specific permission for the Russian agents in Turkey to
make representations—and nothing more—could, *e contrario*, indicate that other,
more drastic measures by Russia in case of violation of these specific human rights
provisions had not been envisaged nor consented to in the treaty.

15. Treaty of London, July 6, 1827, 14 BRIT. & FOREIGN STATE PAPERS
633 (1826-1827), *cited in* GANJI, *supra* note 4, at 22.

16. "When consent is given by a state to foreign action of an interventionary character, in reality there is no intervention." THOMAS & THOMAS, *supra*
note 7, at 22. Although strongly opposed to any form of intervention for any

question the validity of that consent, for it seems clear that Turkey assented to the French expedition "only through constraint and a desire to avoid worse."[17]

Similarly, one should not place too much emphasis on the *official* ground of justification invoked by the Major Powers: article IX of the General Treaty of Paris of March 30, 1856, concluded between Austria, France, Great Britain, Prussia, Russia, Sardinia, and Turkey. The first paragraph of this article merely takes note of the promulgation by the Sultan, in February 1856, of the *Firman Hatti-Sherif*. This document was a domestic legislative instrument of utter vagueness in which he affirmed his generous intentions towards all his subjects without distinction as to religion or race. The second paragraph of the same article specifically provides that this reference to the *Firman*:

> [C]ould not, in any circumstance, give the right to the said Powers to intervene either collectively, or separately, in the relations of his Majesty the Sultan with his subjects, nor in the internal administration of his Empire.[18]

As Rougier, a contemporary, observes: "Their right to intervene cannot be based on this text, but only on the fact that the Turkish government had allowed six thousand of its subjects to be massacred."[19] And he concludes: "The Syrian intervention was thus a humanitarian intervention, and not an intervention aimed at enforcing execution of a convention."[20]

---

reason whatsoever, Mencer reaches a similar conclusion based on a formalistic logical reasoning:

> [S]i l'admissibilité de l'intervention humanitaire est conditionnée par un assentiment donné préalablement et expressément dans un traité, . . . d'une part . . . il ne s'agit pas d'une imposition de volonté au vrai sens de ce terme, d'une ingérence entreprise contre la volonté de l'Etat respectif (puisqu'il ne s'agit point d'une intervention au sens des règles de droit), et d'autre part, il s'y applique la règle selon laquelle il est possible . . . de donner, par la voie d'un traité valide et librement conclu, l'assentiment à toute ingérence et non seulement à l'intervention humanitaire.

Mencer, *La Coéxistence Pacifique et le Principe de la Non-Intervention*, 1 BOLETIN MEXICANO DE DERECHO COMPARADO 314 (1969) [hereinafter cited as Mencer].

17. STOWELL, *supra* note 10, at 66. Even those scholars who question the existence of a customary international law right of humanitarian intervention feel compelled to concede this point: "The state practice justifies the conclusion that no genuine case of humanitarian intervention has occurred, *with the possible exception of the occupation of Syria in 1860 and 1861*." I. BROWNLIE, INTERNATIONAL LAW AND THE USE OF FORCE BY STATES 340 (1963) [hereinafter cited as BROWNLIE]. *See also* GANJI, *supra* note 4, at 26 & 28.

18. 46 BRIT. & FOREIGN STATE PAPERS 12 (1855-1856), *cited in* GANJI, *supra* note 4, at 20.

19. Rougier, *supra* note 3, at 474.

20. *Id.*, at 474 n.4. It would seem that this provision of the Treaty of

C. *Intervention in the Island of Crete (1866-1868)*

As a result of several years of persecution and discrimination at the hand of the Turkish authorities in the island, the Christian population of Crete broke into open rebellion against the Ottoman rulers in 1866 and proclaimed *enosis* (union) with Greece. Following the brutal repression of the revolt by the Porte, the European Powers, with the exception of Great Britain, made various pressing demands upon the Sultan, ranging from Turkish consent to an on-the-spot investigation by an International Commission of Inquiry to free elections and independence of Crete. None of these proposals were accepted by the Porte, but upon British advice, the Sultan promulgated a new Constitution for the island, ameliorating the position of the Christians. The Sultan's reaction thus avoided the armed intervention which had been envisaged by the European Powers following his initial refusal.

In this particular instance, it seems that the diplomatic interposition of the European Powers could, as Ganji contends,[21] be based on the violation by Turkey of specific treaty obligations. The Powers invoked in justification various provisions of the London Protocol of February 20, 1830, whereby France, Great Britain, and Russia guaranteed the Greek independence, as well as article IX of the 1856 Treaty of Paris. While the latter, as has already been indicated, could not possibly provide a treaty basis for an intervention, albeit a purely diplomatic one, it seems that the tripartite London Protocol could justify, on conventional grounds, the nonforceful intercessions of France and Russia. This is true since the Protocol, as adhered to by Turkey in a note of April 24, 1830,[22]

Paris, if it has to have any relevance at all in this case, should be interpreted as a pledge by the Great Powers to refrain from intervening, rather than as allowing them to intervene. *Contra:* GANJI, *supra* note 4, at 30-31, who makes the rather controversial statement that the *firman* of the Sultan has to be considered an integral party of the treaty since several European Powers would have "hesitated" to accept the treaty, had those guarantees for the non-Moslem population not been given by Turkey. And he concludes:

> The principle of non-intervention in the second paragraph of article IX was embodied for the sole purpose of providing that, *as long as the Sultan was acting in good faith in implementing the Firman,* the European powers were to abstain from intervening. . . .

Id. (emphasis added).

21. GANJI, *supra* note 4, at 29.

22. 17 BRIT. & FOREIGN STATE PAPERS 203 (1827-1830), *cited in* GANJI, *supra* note 4, at 28.

contained a declaration by France, Great Britain, and Russia to
the extent that:

> [E]ach Allied Power . . . would consider it its duty to
> interpose its influence with the Porte, so as to ensure to the
> inhabitants of the above mentioned Isles [Candie[23] and Sa-
> mos], protection against oppressive and arbitrary acts.[24]

Whether this document would have equally justified the
armed intervention once envisaged by the European Powers, is
much more doubtful. Furthermore, it leaves unaltered the finding that the Protocol could not provide a conventional ground
for the participation of those European Powers not parties to it
(Austria, Italy, and Prussia).

D. Intervention in Bosnia, Herzegovina, and Bulgaria (1876-1878)

Following a formal declaration of war by Serbia and Montenegro against the Porte on June 30, 1876, in support of the
oppressed Christian populations of Bosnia, Herzegovina, and
Bulgaria, the European Powers met with Turkey at the Conference of Constantinople. When the Sultan refused to agree to
the establishment of an International Commission to control the
implementation of the reforms he proposed to carry out in the
Balkan, Austria-Hungary, France, Germany, Great Britain, Italy,
and Russia met separately and agreed upon the London Protocol of
March 31, 1877. In this Protocol, the European Powers reaffirmed
their concern for the Christians in the area and indicated their intention to watch the fulfillment of the reform promises made by the
Porte in the 1856 Treaty of Paris. They also stressed their determination to take all necessary measures in the event that the Sultan
failed to improve the condition of his Christian subjects in the
Balkan.

After rejection of the Protocol by Turkey on the grounds
of domestic jurisdiction in general, and of the restrictive terms
of article IX, paragraph 2, of the 1856 Treaty of Paris in particular,[25] Russia declared war upon the Porte. Subsequently, the
other Major Powers declared their neutrality and, on February

---

23. This is the ancient french name for Crete used in the treaty.
24. 17 BRIT. & FOREIGN STATE PAPERS 203 (1827-1830), *cited in* GANJI,
supra note 4, at 28.
25. *See* authority cited in note 18 *supra* and accompanying text.

19, 1878, the war came to an end with the signing of the Preliminary Treaty of San Stefano.

Following negotiations between Austria-Hungary, France,
Germany, Great Britain, Italy, Russia, and Turkey at the Congress of Berlin, the 1878 Treaty of Berlin was adopted. It provided for limited local autonomy of a Christian government under
Turkish suzerainty in Bulgaria, and for the occupation of Bosnia
and Herzegovina by Austria-Hungary. It further reaffirmed the
independence of Montenegro, Rumania, and Serbia, and imposed
specific obligations of religious and racial non-discrimination upon
Turkey, both in the Empire itself, and in the autonomous prin-
cipality of Bulgaria.[26]

The declarations of war by Serbia and Montenegro were officially justified by humanitarian solidarity with the oppressed
populations in the neighboring countries. On the other hand,
the demands by the European Powers, as well as the war waged
by Russia, were once more formally based upon an invocation
of article IX of the 1856 Treaty of Paris. As has been indicated
earlier, this provision could not provide a valid ground for intervention, armed or non-armed. Again, it seems that this is a case
which could only be justified by the underlying humanitarian concern of the Major Powers, as was clearly alluded to in the note
of the Russian government to the Sublime Porte of November
13, 1876:

> His Imperial Majesty does not want war . . . but is deter-
> mined not to hestiate as long as the principles that have been
> recognized as equitable, *humane,* necessary by the whole of
> Europe . . . have not received full execution in effective
> guarantees.[27]

E.   Intervention in Macedonia
(1903-1908, 1912-1913)

Following increasingly intense sporadic insurrections in Mac-
donia from 1893 onward, and more directly in response to the
atrocities committed by the Ottoman troops in mid-1903, Austria-
Hungary and Russia, acting as mandatories of the Concert of Europe, strongly urged the Porte to accept the Mürzsteg Program.

---

26. 69 BRIT. & FOREIGN STATE PAPERS 753 (1877-1878), *cited in* GANJI,
supra note 4, at 20-21.

27. 47 BRIT. & FOREIGN STATE PAPERS 321 (1856-1857), *cited in* GANJI,
supra note 4, at 31 (emphasis added).

This program included a series of far-reaching reform proposals for Macedonia, the introduction of which was to be controlled by Austrian and Russian diplomatic agents. Impressed by the European unity and determination, the Sultan, late in 1903, gave his consent to the Program.

After the outbreak of the Young Turk Revolution in June, 1908, the Powers withdrew their control agents, as the reformist ideology of the new rulers made it appear likely that application of the Program would be continued and foreign supervision seemed to have become unnecessary. This hope was soon shattered when the new regime embarked on a program of intense "Turkification" of the Christian population of Macedonia. In view of this unexpected development, and particularly of the extreme brutality with which the "Turkification" was carried out, Bulgaria, Greece, and Serbia, "unable to tolerate any longer the sufferings of their brethren in Turkey,"[28] declared war upon the latter. On May 30, 1913, after some seven months of fighting, this war came to an end with the conclusion of the 1913 Treaty of London, by which Turkey ceded the greater part of Macedonia for partition among the Balkan Allies.

In 1903, the peremptory demands by Austria-Hungary and Russia on behalf of the Concert of Europe were, again, formally based on the provisions of article IX of the 1856 Treaty of Paris, and on various parts of the 1878 Treaty of Berlin. As indicated above, article IX lacks relevance. However, reference to the latter treaty is more convincing. It is clear that articles 23 and 62 of the 1878 treaty imposed specific obligations on Turkey regarding the treatment of its non-Moslem subjects[29] and as a result the right of intervention to secure compliance with conventional obligations was generally accepted under international law at that time.[30]

It is noteworthy, that the three Balkan Allies, although not able to invoke any breaches of direct treaty commitments since they were not parties to, but only subjects of, the Berlin Treaty, did not hesitate to resort to force. Significantly, their justification for their course of action was their humanitarian concern with the treatment inflicted upon the Macedonian people.[31]

---

28. *Note Verbale* to the British Government, 106 BRIT. & FOREIGN STATE PAPERS 1059-60 (1913), *cited in* GANJI, *supra* note 4, at 36.

29. *See* authority cited in note 26 *supra* and accompanying text.

30. *See, e.g.*, Rougier, *supra* note 3, at 474.

31. *See* authority cited in note 28 *supra* and accompanying text.

214   CALIFORNIA WESTERN INTERNATIONAL LAW JOURNAL   Vol. 4

II. THE PRE-CHARTER DOCTRINE

A. *The Question of Principle: Is Humanitarian Intervention Permissible under International Law?*

While rather vague statements, to the extent that a sovereign is entitled to intervene on the basis of religious solidarity in the internal affairs of another when the latter mistreats his own subjects beyond the limits of what seems acceptable, can be found as early as the writings of St. Thomas Aquinas, it is only later[32] that this doctrine appears to have been secularised in the doctrine of lawful assistance to a people struggling against tyranny.

Albeit in general terms, Grotius accords his support to this view when he declares:

> There is also another question, whether a war for the subjects of another be just, for the purpose of defending them from injuries by their ruler. Certainly it is undoubted that ever since civil societies were formed, the ruler of each claimed some especial right over his own subjects. . . . [But] . . . [i]f a tyrant . . . practices atrocities towards his subjects, which no just man can approve, the right of human social connexion is not cut off in such case.[33]

Vattel, on the other hand, seems not to have been completely able to resolve what Mosler called "the problem of the friction between Sovereignty and the Law of Nations."[34] First, he observes:

> The sovereign is the one to whom the Nation has entrusted the empire and the care of government; it has endowed him with his rights; it alone is directly interested in the manner in which the leader it has chosen for itself uses his power. No foreign power, accordingly, is entitled to take notice of the administration by that sovereign, to stand up in judgment of his conduct and to force him to alter it in any way. If he buries his subjects under taxes, if he treats them harshly, it is the Nation's business; no one else is called upon to admonish him, to force him to apply wiser and more equitable

---

32. For an analysis of the writings of early scholars on this point, see Esmein, *La Théorie de l'Intervention Internationale chez Quelques Publicistes Français du XVIème Siècle*, 24 NOUVELLE REVUE HISTORIQUE DE DROIT FRANCAIS ET ETRANGER 563 (1900). *See generally* A. DUNNING, POLITICAL THEORIES FROM LUTHER TO MONTESQUIEU (1905).

33. H. GROTIUS, 2 DE JURE BELLI EST PACIS, Ch. XXV, at 438 (Whewell transl. 1853).

34. H. MOSLER, DIE INTERVENTION IM VÖLKERRECHT 3 (1938).

principles.[35]

Vattel immediately qualifies this general statement by the apparently contradictory contention that:

> [I]f the prince, attacking the fundamental laws, gives his people a legitimate reason to resist him, if tyranny becomes so unbearable as to cause the Nation to rise, any foreign power is entitled to help an oppressed people that has requested its assistance.[36]

Once the middle of the 19th century is reached, the decline of the Law of Nature and the rising of the contradictory values of nationalism, sovereign independence and nonintervention on the one hand, and humanitarianism on the other hand, influences the thinking on the subject. The statements become clearer; the scholars take positions; and, in general, a dichotomy appears between the champions of an expanding nonintervention norm and those who favor a more flexible rule permitting intervention on various grounds.

Kant, for instance, illustrates the first approach when he states:

> In general . . . the bad example given by a free person to the others does not result in any damage to the latter. One could thus not intervene for that motive alone without oneself giving an example of the very scandal one is trying to avoid and without endangering the autonomy of all States.[37]

Mamiani, the leader of the Italian nonintervention or neo-nationalist school, is quoted by Carnazza-Amari as saying:

> The actions and the crimes of a people within the limits of its territory do not infringe upon anyone else's rights and do not give a basis for a legitimate intervention. Truely, what positive right of the other peoples does one infringe upon? Have you ever heard it said that the law requires that one be only confronted with good example . . . .[38]

Carnazza-Amari himself summarizes the extreme position of the Italian school as follows:

> Neither can one justify intervention in the case where the

---

35. 2 E. DE VATTEL, LE DROIT DES GENS, Ch. IV, para. 55 (Pradier-Fodéré ed. 1863).

36. *Id.*, para. 56.

37. E. KANT, ESSAI PHILOSOPHIQUE SUR LA PAIX PERPETUELLE, art. V, *cited in* Rougier, *supra* note 3, at 482 n.1.

38. 1 CARNAZZA-AMARI, TRAITE DE DROIT INTERNATIONAL EN TEMPS DE PAIX 557 (Montanari-Revest transl. 1880).

local government does not respect *the most elementary laws of justice and humanity.*[39]

This rigid noninterventionism was not particular to Italy. In France, for example, Pradier-Fodéré states:

> The right to punish presupposes sovereign power, on the part of the one exercising it, over the one against whom it is being exercised. . . . While the sovereign can sanction crimes that disturb the social and political order of the people he governs, his authority expires at the border of the national territory, and he lacks the right to punish criminals whose acts would have affected public order abroad.   Accordingly, if he lacks this right as against criminals that would be mere individuals, *a fortiori* he cannot be so preposterous as to exercise it as against a State and a whole people.[40]

And he concludes:

> This [humanitarian] intervention is illegal because it constitutes an infringement upon the independence of States, because the powers that are not directly, immediately affected by these inhuman acts are not entitled to intervene. If the inhuman acts are committed against nationals of the country where they are committed, the powers are totally disinterested.   The acts of inhumanity, however condemnable they may be, as long as they do not affect nor threaten the rights of other States, do not provide the latter with a basis for lawful intervention, as no State can stand up in judgment of the conduct of others.   As long as they do not infringe upon the rights of the other powers or of their subjects, they remain the sole business of the nationals of the countries where they are committed.[41]

Heffter, in Germany, seems to espouse the doctrine of the Italian school when he writes:

> As far as no imminently threatening violations of the law

---

39. *Id.*, at 555 (emphasis added). *See also* E. CIMBALI, IL NON-INTERVENTO—STUDIO DI DIRITTO INTERNAZIONALE UNIVERSALE 262 (1889) *and* TANOVICEANO, LE DROIT INTERNATIONAL DE L'INTERVENTION 12-13 (1884). Strangely enough, the Italian school, while absolutely condemining intervention for humanitarian purposes as such, strongly supported the right of States to assist other nations struggling for independence. *Id.*, at 89. This approach is similar to the current double standard applied by the United Nations in dealing with human rights questions involving self-determination of colonial peoples, as opposed to human rights violations in a non-colonial setting.

40. 1 P. PRADIER-FODERE, TRAITE DE DROIT INTERNATIONAL EUROPEEN ET AMERICAIN 655 (1885).

41. *Id.* at 663. *See also* DE FLOECKHER, DE L'INTERVENTION EN DROIT INTERNATIONAL 18-19 (1896).

or [actual] perils are involved, even the most outrageous in-
equities, that are committed in a State, cannot provide another [state] with a legal ground for unilateral intervention
against the former; for no State is entitled to pass judgment
upon another.[42]

The Latin American scholars, traditional champions of the
nonintervention principle in view of their experience as victims
of repeated foreign intervention, took the same inflexible approach. For instance, Pereira states:

> Internal oppression, however odious and violent it may be,
> does not affect, either directly or indirectly, external relations
> and does not endanger the existence of other States. Accord-
> ingly, it cannot be used as a legal basis for use of force and
> violent means.[43]

Likewise in the Anglo-American literature, some resistance
against the notion of a permissible intervention for humanitarian
purposes can be found in this period. Halleck, for example,
writes:

> We have stated . . . that when a state is desolated by pro-
> tracted civil war, foreign interference, by way of pacific med-
> iation, in order *to stay the effusion of blood,* is not only justi-
> fiable, but is sometimes a duty imposed by humanity. But
> will the general interests of humanity justify interference to
> the extent of *war* of intervention?[44]

Quoting Phillimore, he answers this question negatively:

> This ground of intervention . . . urged on behalf of the gen-
> eral interests of humanity, has been frequently put forward,

---

42. A. HEFFTER, DAS EUROPÄISCHE VÖLKERRECHT DER GEGENWART AUF DER
BISHERIGEN GRUNDLAGEN 109-10 (7th ed. 1882) [hereinafter cited as HEFFTER].
He approves, however, the Italian support for the right of assistance to peoples
involved in a war of independence:

> Eine weitere Befugniss, nämlich zu einer thatlichen Cooperation eröf-
> fnet sich wenn in einem Staate ein innerer Krieg wirklich ausgebrochen
> ist und ein anderer Staat von dem im Recht befindlichen aber wider-
> rechtlich bedrängten Theile um Hilfe angerufen wird. Es ist schon
> das Recht jedes einzelnen Menschen, dem widerrechtlich Gekränkten zu
> seiner und seines Rechtes Erhaltung beizustehen; es muss auch das
> Recht der Staaten sein.

Id., at 110. Even more resolute in his condemnation of humanitarian intervention is Gareis: "Von der Anwendung des 'Prinzips der Nichtintervention' allge-
mein eine Ausnahme zu Gunsten der Humanität zu machen ist unzulässig. . . ."
K. GAREIS, INSTITUTIONEN DES VÖLKERRECHTS 96 (2d ed. 1901). *See also* H.
STRAUCH, ZUR INTERVENTIONSLEHRE 13-14 (1879).

43. 1 L. PEREIRA, PRINCIPIOS DE DIREITO INTERNACIONAL 97-98 (1902),
cited in 1 H. ACCIOLY, TRAITÉ DE DROIT INTERNATIONAL PUBLIC 283 (Goulé
transl. 1940) [hereinafter cited as ACCIOLY].

44. H. HALLECK, INTERNATIONAL LAW 340 (1861).

and especially in our own times, but rarely, if ever, without others of greater and more legitimate weight to support it. . . . As an accessory to others, this ground may be defensible, but, as a substantive and solitary justification of intervention in the affairs of another country, it can scarcely be admitted into the code of international law, since it is manifestly open to abuses, tending to the violation and destruction of the vital principles of that system of jurisprudence.[45]

More typically, however, a substantial body of writers espouse a double-level permissibility by refusing to grant humanitarian motivation the character of a formal *legal* justification of intervention, while at the same time recognizing that a violation of the nonintervention principle, though technically a breach of the law, might in certain circumstances be not only excusable, but even commendable. Bernard, for instance, states: "The law . . . prohibits intervention. . . . Nay, there may even be cases in which it becomes a positive duty to transgress it."[46] Specifically referring to humanitarian considerations, Harcourt argues: "Intervention is a question rather of policy than of law, and when wisely and equitably handled . . . may be the *higher policy* of justice and humanity."[47]

Another tendency in this period is to accept a *limited* right of humanitarian intervention, restricting its lawful application either to very specific circumstances or to situations involving certain categories of States only.

An example of the former type of qualification is provided by Creasy when, acknowledging that "intervention may be justifiable, and even a duty, in certain exceptional cases,"[48] he restricts the legality of humanitarian intervention to those cases only:

> [W]here we intervene in behalf of a grievously oppressed people, which has never amalgamated with its oppressors as one nation, and which its oppressors have systematically treated as an alien race, subject to the same imperial authority, but in other respects distinct . . . [or] where the King, or dominant party of a nation keeps up, in defiance

---

45. 1 R. PHILLIMORE, ON INTERNATIONAL LAW, paras. 394 ff., *cited in* HALLECK, *supra* note 44, at 340.

46. M. BERNARD, ON THE PRINCIPLE OF NON-INTERVENTION 33-34 (1860).

47. V. HARCOURT (HISTORICUS), LETTERS ON SOME QUESTIONS OF INTERNATIONAL LAW 14 (1863) (emphasis added). *Compare* the modern approach to retaliation of Falk and Bowett, note 194 *infra*. *See also* note 193 *infra* and accompanying text.

48. E. CREASY, FIRST PLATFORM OF INTERNATIONAL LAW 303 (1876).

of the State's fundamental Laws, a mercenary army of regular troops, especially if carefully organized and officered by
men who are of creed, of politics, and of feelings alien from
those held by the great majority of the population, and
where, by this being done, all effective manifestations of the
popular will, and the formation of a truly national force are
rendered utterly impossible, . . . [49]

thus requiring a racial element to transgress the *internal matter
aspect* of the treatment by a sovereign of his own subjects.[50]

More common, however, was the notion that the *right* to
intervene for humanitarian motives was to be restricted to the
relations between "civilized" and "non-civilized" nations.

de Martens, for instance, argues that:

Vis-a-vis non civilized nations . . . intervention by the civilized powers is in principle legitimate, when the Christian
population of those countries is exposed to persecutions or
massacres.   In those circumstances, it is justified by common religious interests and humanitarian considerations. . . .
These motives are not applicable to the relations between civilized powers . . .[51]

By so arguing, he links the notion of humanity with that of religious solidarity and with the existence of different categories of
States.   Often without the religious connotation, similar opinions
can be found in the works of a number of jurists of this period.[52]

Although their pronouncements usually remain vague and
are often qualified by considerations of Major Power supremacy
and outspoken predilection for collective action, from the 1860's
on, writers seem increasingly won to the idea of the lawfulness
of humanitarian intervention.

Following some rather revolutionary conceptions by Heiberg,[53] revealed as early as 1842, and shortly after the publication
of Berner's *Deutsche Staatswörterbuch*,[54] Dana's edition of Whea-

---

49. *Id.*, at 303-05.
50. *Compare* the current "double standard" generally applied by the United
Nations regarding human rights violations in accordance with the presence or
absence of a racial or colonial implication.
51. 1 F. DE MARTENS, TRAITE DE DROIT INTERNATIONAL 398 (Léo transl.
1883).
52. *See* BERNARD, *supra* note 46, at 7; STRAUCH, *supra* note 42, at 14;
GAREIS, *supra* note 42, at 85.   For a critique of this approach, see KEBEDGY,
INTERVENTION 85-86, *cited in* STOWELL, *supra* note 10, at 65, n.14.
53. HEIBERG, DAS PRINZIP DER NICHTINTERVENTION IN SEINER BEZIEHUNG
AUF DIE AUSSERE UND INNERE ORGANISATION DES STAATS 14-15 (1842).
54 BERNER, DEUTSCHE, STAATSWÖRTERBUCH 341 (1860).

ton's *Elements of International Law* notices in 1866 that:

> The interference of the Christian powers of Europe, in favor of the Greeks . . . affords a further illustration of the principles of international law authorizing such an interference . . . where the general interests of humanity are infringed by the excesses of a barbarous and despotic government.[55]

Referring primarily to civil strife situations, Bluntschli observes in 1874:

> One is authorized to intervene to ensure respect for the individual rights that have been recognized as necessary . . . whenever they happen to be violated in the struggles between citizens of a single state.[56]

Qualifying his position by the restriction that "[i]nterference on the score of humanity or of religion can be justified only by the extreme gravity of the case,"[57] Woolsey, in 1876, unambiguously asserts that:

> [I]nterference . . . can be justified . . . on . . . the . . . following [ground]: . . . [t]hat some extraordinary state of things is brought about by the crime of a government against its subjects.[58]

That same year, in a letter addressed to Rolin-Jacquemyns, Arntz developed the theory as follows:

> When a government, even acting within the limits of its rights of sovereignty, violates the rights of humanity, either by measures contrary to the interests of other States, or by excessive injustice or brutality which seriously injure our morals and civilization, the right of intervention is legitimate. For, however worthy of respect the rights of sovereignty and independence of States may be, there is something even more worthy of respect, namely the law of humanity, or of human *society*, that must not be violated. In the same way as *within* the State freedom of the *individual* is and must be restricted by the law and the *morals* of the *society*, the individual freedom of the *States* must be limited by the law of human society.[59]

---

55. H. WHEATON, ELEMENTS OF INTERNATIONAL LAW 113 (8th ed. R. Dana 1866).

56. J. BLÜNTSCHLI, LE DROIT INTERNATIONAL CODIFIE 272, art. 478 (Lardy transl. 1874).

57. T. WOOLSEY, INTRODUCTION TO THE STUDY OF INTERNATIONAL LAW 73 (1876).

58. *Id.*, at 57.

59. *Lettre de M. Arntz*, in Rolin-Jacquemyns, *Note sur la Théorie du Droit*

And he concludes I recognize the right of intervention *in an absolute way as against all* States."[60]

Some ten years later, Fiore, although basically a noninterventionist,[61] articulates the doctrine further:

> It is, indeed, unquestionable that, as a society cannot be imagined in the absence of laws, abidance by the natural laws of the society of States is of such capital importance for everybody's tranquilty that, if one of them was to be permitted to violate them with impunity, and the others were obliged to remain indifferent to that violation, without the right to prevent it, the society of States could not survive.
> . . .[62]

Specifically regarding humanitarian intervention he concludes:

> The violation of international law can also be a consequence of events occurring inside a State, and which results in the direct violation of international law. Let us assume, for instance, that a prince, in order to put down a revolution, violates all the generally recognized laws of war, has prisoners executed, authorises destruction, looting, arson, and encourages his supporters to commit those odious actions and others of the same kind; or, alternatively, let us suppose that it is the faction that [seized power] which engages in similar crimes. Inaction and indifference of other States would constitute an egocentric policy contrary to the rights of all; for whoever violates international law to the disadvantage of anybody, violates it not only to the detriment of the person directly affected, but as against all civilized States.[63]

The *legal* character, in the opinion of these writers, of the permissibility of humanitarian intervention is clearly apparent. For instance, de Lapradelle, commenting upon the U.S. intervention in Cuba, states:

> Whereas it is true that States are sovereign, that sovereignty . . . has its limits . . . in international *law* . . . in the fundamental rights of humanity.[64]

Despite similar views expressed in that same period by other

---

d'Intervention, 8 REVUE DE DROIT INTERNATIONAL ET DE LEGISLATION COMPAREE [REV. DR. INT'L & LEGISL. COMP.] 675 (1876).

60. *Id.*

61. Rougier, *supra* note 3, at 482 n.1.

62. 1 P. FIORE, NOUVEAU DROIT INTERNATIONAL PUBLIC 521-22 (Antoine transl. 1885).

63. *Id.*, at 524-25.

64. de Lapradelle, *supra* note 9, at 75 (emphasis added).

222   CALIFORNIA WESTERN INTERNATIONAL LAW JOURNAL   Vol. 4

scholars[65] as well as statemen,[66] it is only after the turn of the century that one is able to witness what Mandelstam called "the victory of the principle of humanitarian intervention over the rigid dogma of nonintervention."[67]   Of particular importance for this development, together with the precedents set by State practice primarily in Eastern Europe, was the fundamental refusal of many authors to allot to State sovereignty the character of an *ab-*

---

65. *See, e.g.*, S. AMOS, POLITICAL AND LEGAL REMEDIES FOR WAR 158 (1880) [hereinafter cited as AMOS]. "[G]ross acts of inhumanity . . . persisted in on either side . . . may, on grounds of humanity, properly precipitate intervention." *Accord*: Engelhardt, *Le Droit d'Intervention et la Turquie*, 12 REV. DR. INT'L & LEGISL. COMP. 365 (1880):

> A un point de vue plus large et en dehors des ingérences qu'autorisent d'une part le droit conventionnel proprement dit et d'autre part le droit international basé sur des maximes solennellement reconnues et communément observées, l'intervention peut être admise lorsqu'un Etat . . . se rend coupable d'une 'violation énorme' des droits de l'humanité.

Presumably as a result of the self-determination aspect of most precedents, a large number of scholars concentrate on situations involving civil strife when illustrating their plea in support of humanitarian intervention. For instance, Hall observes:

> While however it is settled that as a general rule a state must be allowed to work out its internal changes in its own fashion . . . intervention for the purpose of checking gross tyranny or of helping the efforts of a people to free itself is very commonly regarded without disfavour.

W. HALL, A TREATISE OF INTERNATIONAL LAW 265 (2d ed. 1884). *See also* A. RIVIER, LEHRBUCH DES VÖLKERRECHTS 233 (1899) [hereinafter cited as RIVIER]:

> Als ein fernerer Fall, wo Intervention rechtmässig ist, wird auch derjenige angegeben, wo die Rechte der Menschheit von einer grausamen, barbarischen Regierung verletzt werden durch flagrante Ungesetzlichkeiten, Verfolgungen u.s.w., wo gewiss noch hinzuzufügen ist der Fall ähnlicher Gewaltthatigkeiten von seiten einer revolutionären Faktion, welchen Namen sie auch tragen möge.

Compare MANNING, *supra* note 9, at 97:

> The only grounds on which interference with the affairs of a foreign State would now be held capable of justification are . . . (2) the continuance of a revolutionary state of affairs in the foreign State under circumstances in which it seems highly probable that, without such interference, either public order can never be restored at all; or can only be restored after such sufferings to humanity and such injuries to surrounding States as obviously overbalance the general evil of all interference from without.

66. *See, e.g.*, Statement by U.S. Secretary of State Fish *cited in* D. GRUBER, CRISIS DIPLOMACY 339 (1959):

> [T]he general rule of non-intervention in the domestic affairs of other countries does not apply if 'the grievance adverted to is so enormous, as to impart to it, as it were, a cosmopolitan character, in the redress of which all countries, governments and creeds alike are interested.'

See also Statement of President McKinley (1898), *cited in* Reisman, *supra* note 4, at 182-83 *and* President Grant's Message to Congress *cited in* MANNING, *supra* note 9.

67. Mandelstam, *La Protection des Minorités* (Hague Academy of International Law), 1 RECUEIL DES COURS 367, 391 (1923) [hereinafter cited as Mandelstam].

solute principle not susceptible of restrictions or exceptions. Consequently, nonintervention was seen as a flexible notion which could lawfully be disregarded for the defense of higher values in certain circumstances.[68]

In the period immediately preceding the first World War, it seems that the majority of the writers had been won to the idea of the legality of humanitarian intervention,[69] and that only a few scholars, albeit notorious ones, continued to reject the validity of the doctrine. Apparently, most of them did so on the basis of doubts as to the actual integration of the theory in the generally accepted body of customary international law, rather than because of fundamental philosophical, ideological, or political convictions regarding absolute sovereignty and nonintervention.[70]

A minority appeared still troubled by the contradiction between these basic notions and their personal humanitarian feelings. Lawrence, for instance, tried to reconcile both by emphasizing the difference between law and policy, giving priority to the latter in exceptional circumstances:

---

68. *See* notes 94-96 *infra* and accompanying text. *See generally* Brocher de la Fléchère, *Solidarité et Souveraineté*, 26 REV. DR. INT'L & LEGISL. COMP. 415 (1894).

69. For example, Basdevant urged that: "[L]'Etat qui ne remplit pas sa fonction de justice même à l'égard de ses nationaux perd son droit au respect et . . . les autres puissances sont autorisées à substituer leur action à la sienne." Basdevant, *Chronique*, 11 REV. GEN. DR. INT'L PUBL. 110 (1904). In an often quoted passage, Borchard notes that:

> [W]here a state under exceptional circumstances disregards certain rights of its own citizens, over whom presumably it has absolute sovereignty, the other states of the family of nations are *authorized by international law to intervene* on grounds of humanity.

E. BORCHARD, THE DIPLOMATIC PROTECTION OF CITIZENS ABROAD 14 (1916) (emphasis added). *See also* L. OPPENHEIM, INTERNATIONAL LAW 347 (1st ed. 1905); A. PILLET, PRINCIPES DE DROIT INTERNATIONAL PRIVE 171 (1903); Lingelbach, *Intervention in Europe*, 16 ANNALS AM. ACAD'Y POL. & SOC'L SCI. 25 (1900); Rougier, *supra* note 3; MOORE, *supra* note 9, at 347 ff.

70. The following statment by Hodges typifies this position: "As regards an intervention undertaken in the *cause of humanity* there seems to be a divergence of opinion among the most prominent writers . . ." H. HODGES, THE DOCTRINE OF INTERVENTION 87 (1915) [hereinafter cited as HODGES]. With a view towards the evolution of international law, he optimistically concludes:

> As the feeling of general interest in humanity increases, and with it a world-wide desire for something approaching justice and an international solidarity, interventions undertaken in the interests of humanity will also doubtless increase. . . . We may therefore conclude that future public opinion and finally international law will sanction an ever increasing number of causes for intervention for the sake of humanity.

Id. at 91.

There is a great difference between declaring a national act to be legal, and therefore part of the order under which states have consented to live, and allowing it to be morally blameless as an exception to ordinary rules. . . . An intervention to put a stop to barbarous and abominable cruelty is "a high act of policy above and beyond the domain of law." It is destitute of technical legality, but it may be morally right and even praiseworthy to a high degree.[71]

Hyde attempted to partially circumvent the domestic jurisdiction problem by a requirement of transnational racial connection between the intervenor and the victims:

In the treatment of its own citizens a state enjoys the largest freedom. Its conduct in that respect may be cruel and may visibly shock the sensibilities of the outside world. Nevertheless, the law of nations does not, by reason thereof, stamp it as illegal and of a character to justify interference. . . . It is conceivable, however, that the tyrannical conduct of a state towards its own subjects might directly affect a numerous class of subjects of another state, who were connected by blood with the victims of ill-treatment. If the injury thus sustained were of periodic recurrence and felt by large numbers of the population of the outside state, the latter would doubtless assert the right to intervene. In so doing it would find justification for its action on grounds closely analogous to those of self-defense.[72]

In the period separating the first World War from the creation of the U.N. Charter, the same dichotomy runs through the doctrine, with scholars such as Fauchille,[73] Stowell,[74] Mandelstam,[75] Seferiades,[76] Le Fur,[77] and Mosler[78] asserting that the

---

71. T. LAWRENCE, THE PRINCIPLES OF INTERNATIONAL LAW 129 (4th ed. 1910). *Compare* authorities in notes 46-47 *supra* and accompanying text.

72. Hyde, *Intervention in Theory and Practice*, 6 ILL. L. REV. 1, 6 (1911-12). *Compare* notes 204 ff. *infra* and accompanying text *See also* the Indian justification for intervening in East Pakistan, in Nanda, *Self-Determination, supra* note 1 at 334 & n.94 *and* Nanda, *Critique, supra* note 1, at 65 & n.95.

73. *See* 1 P. FAUCHILLE, TRAITE DE DROIT INTERNATIONAL PUBLIC 570 (8th ed. 1922).

74. *See* STOWELL, *supra* note 10, at 52.

75. *See* Mandelstam, *supra* note 67. *See also* A. MANDELSTAM, LA SOCIETE DES NATIONS ET LES PUISSANCES DEVANT LE PROBLEME ARMENIEN 1-32 & 307 ff. (1926).

76. *See* Séfériadès, *Principes Généraux du Droit International de la Paix* (Hague Academy of International Law), 34 RECUEIL DES COURS 381, 389 (1930).

77. *See* LEFUR, L'INTERVENTION POUR CAUSE D'HUMANITE (1935), *cited in* Aronéanu, *supra* note 7, at 129.

theory of humanitarian intervention has been assimilated by customary international law, while others such as Roxburgh,[79] Higgins,[80] Winfield,[81] Potter,[82] Strupp,[83] Trolliet,[84] and Accioly[85] ex-

78. *See* Mosler, *supra* note 34, at 63.

79. Roxburgh approximates Hodges' position (note 70 *supra*) in his statement that:

> But whether there is really a rule of the Law of Nations which admits such interventions may well be doubted. Yet, on the other hand, it cannot be denied that public opinion and the attitude of the Powers are in favour of such interventions, and it may perhaps be said that in time the Law of Nations will recognize the rule that interventions in the interest of humanity are admissible.

1 L. OPPENHEIM, INTERNATIONAL LAW 229 (3d ed. R. Roxburgh 1920) [hereinafter cited as OPPENHEIM].

80. Higgins adopts the Lawrence approach (note 71 *supra* and accompanying text), at least for unilateral humanitarian intervention in this statement that:

> Interventions, whether armed or diplomatic, undertaken either for the reason or upon the pretexts of cruelty, or oppression, or the horrors of a civil war, or whatever the reason put forward . . . would have . . . to justify themselves, when not authorized by the whole body of civilized states accustomed to act together for common purposes, as measures which, being confessedly illegal in themselves, could only be excused in rare and extreme cases in consideration of the unquestionable extraordinary character of the facts causing them, and of the evident purity of the motives and conduct of the intervening state.

W. HALL, A TREATISE ON INTERNATIONAL LAW 344 (8th ed. P. Higgins 1924) [hereinafter cited as HALL].

81. Winfield classifies *humanity* among the "alleged grounds of justification [of intervention] as to which international practice is uncertain." Winfield, *The Grounds of Intervention in International Law,* 5 BRIT. Y.B. INT'L L. 149, 161 (1924). He concludes: "But whether it is legal . . . must in the present state of practice be regarded as an unsolved point." *Id.,* at 162.

82. Potter follows Oppenheim's 3d ed. (*see* note 79 *supra*) and Winfield (*see* note 81 *supra*), in their doubts as to the integration in customary international law of the doctrine of humanitarian intervention, primarily due to insufficient State practice:

> Il ne semble pas que, dans la pratique internationale, ce droit ait jamais fait l'objet d'une reconnaissance indiscutable. Les cas où l'on s'en est prévalu sont trop peu nombreux, les divergences dans les thèses gouvernementales trop marquées—l'Etat qui subit l'intervention nie toujours l'existence de ce droit—et la question dans son ensemble encore trop débattue, pour qu'on puisse affirmer que le droit dont il s'agit s'est établi d'une manière positive.

Potter, *L'Intervention en Droit International Moderne* (Hague Academy of International Law), 32 RECUEIL DES COURS 611, 653 (1930).

83. Strupp unambiguously rejects any lawful humanitarian intervention:

> [P]artout où le droit des gens, valable entre l'Etat intervenant et celui contre lequel l'intervention est dirigée, n'accorde pas un droit spécial, l'intervention est illicite. Elle l'est aussi là où il y a a intervention collective . . . de même que là où l'humanité exige impérieusement ce que l'on a dénomme 'intervention d'humanité. Le *droit des gens* ne connait ni celle-ci, ni d'autres.

Strupp, *Les Règles Générales du Droit de la Paix* (Hague Academy of International Law), 47 RECUEIL DES COURS 263, 517 (1934).

84. *See* TROLLIET, ESSAI SUR L'INTERVENTION EN DROIT INTERNATIONAL PUBLIC 66-70 & 78 (1940).

85. *See* ACCIOLY, *supra* note 43, at 282-83.

pressed doubts as to whether this incorporation had actually taken place.

Nevertheless in 1946, shortly after the United Nations had become a reality, Sir Hartley Shawcross felt entitled to declare at the Nüremberg Trials that:

> [T]he right of humanitarian intervention, in the name of the Rights of Man trampled upon by the State in a manner offensive to the feeling of Humanity, has been recognized long ago *as an integral part of the Law of Nations.*[86]

B. *The Question of Norms: When is Humanitarian Intervention Permissible?*

Caught up in the theoretical debate on the preliminary principle question of whether international law recognized a right of humanitarian intervention in general, the 19th and pre-Charter 20th century scholars devoted little attention to the study of the conditions under which such interventions, if at all permissible, could lawfully take place. The majority focused on the philosophical or politico-ideological foundations of their basic position and generally failed to supplement their initial choice with a comprehensive set of norms for decision-making or appraisal of actual cases.

Some loosely articulated criteria—examples of which include a widely shared preference for collective forms of action,[87] insis-

---

86. H. SHAWCROSS, EXPOSE INTRODUCTIF AU PROCES DE NUREMBERG, *cited in* Aronéanu, *supra* note 7, at 127 (emphasis added).

87. Amos indicated that:
> It is in the highest degree desirable that the element of private interest should be entirely removed,—an object which can best be secured, in respect of such cases as these, by habits of combined policy among as great a number of States as possible.

AMOS, *supra* note 65, at 159. *Accord* RIVIER, *supra* note 65, at 233:
> Dies [nämlich Intervention zu Gunsten der Humanität] ist aber kein Fall berechtiger Intervention eines einzelnen Staates. Vielmehr lässt sich in solchen Fallen nur eine Kollektivintervention der Staaten, welche die Völkergemeinde bilden, rechtfertigen.

Compare, FIORE, *supra* note 62, at 522-23:
> Ce qu'il importe de bien établir, c'est que, comme le motif légitime supposé d'intervention dériverait du devoir qui incombe à l'association des Etats d'observer et de faire respecter le droit international, un Etat ne pourrait pas être seul juge, et justifier ensuite l'intervention en alléguant qu'il existait une atteinte réelle au droit des gens. La société des Etats devrait seule avoir ce droit, et l'on doit considérer par conséquent comme une chose bien certaine, que l'unique garantie solide et exempte de danger serait *la garantie collective* des Etats qui vivent en société de fait. Toutefois, rien ne s'opposerait à ce que, lorsque les Etats associés auraient reconnu dans certains faits le caractère d'attentats au droit des gens, et employé d'abord tous les moyens pour rétablir l'ordre, l'un ou

tence on disinterestedness of the intervenor,[88] or restriction of the scope of applicability of the doctrine to certain situations only—civilized *versus* non-civilized nations,[89] assistance to justified rebellion against tyranny,[90] extreme atrocities,[91] deprivation of certain specified, more fundamental human rights[92]—have been proferred. However, no integrated list of criteria of legality

> l'autre d'entre eux ne put être délégué pour exécuter le mandat de punir l'offense dans les limites préalablement établies sauf ensuite le droit pour les Etats associés de régulariser les conditions de fait qui pourraient résulter de l'intervention.

But see 1 P. FIORE, NOUVEAU DROIT INTERNATIONAL PUBLIC 225 (Pradier-Fodéré transl. 1868). *See also* HALL, *supra* note 80, at 344; HODGES, *supra* note 70, at 91; OPPENHEIM, *supra* note 79, at 229; Arntz, *supra* note 59, at 675; Winfield, *supra* note 81, at 162. *Contra*, Stowell, *supra* note 10, at 63, n.1: "[C]ollective intervention is often too unwieldy and too tardy to serve as a practical method of procedure."

88. Amos stated that "so far as [humanitarian] intervention is concerned, it is, above all, desirable that the purity of the motives should be conspicuous. . . ." AMOS, *supra* note 65, at 159. *See also* HALL, *supra* note 80, at 344; MANNING, *supra* note 9, at 96 & 97. *Contra*, STOWELL, *supra* note 10, at 63, n.1:

> Desirable as it may be that humanitarian intervention should be, whenever possible, both disinterested and collective, this cannot be made a condition for the justification of the action taken. . . . States are not generally willing to incur the burdens of intervention, even on the appealing ground of humanity, unless they are also actuated by other and more selfish considerations. . . .

89. *See* note 52 *supra* and accompanying text. *See also* J. BLÜNTSCHLI, LE DROIT INTERNATIONAL CODIFIE, arts. 5 & 280 (1870), *cited in* Rougier, *supra* note 3, at 505 *and* J. LORIMER, PRINCIPES DE DROIT INTERNATIONAL 69 (Nys transl. 1885).

90. *See* discussion in note 39 *supra*. *See also* CREASY, *supra* note 48, at 303 & 305; HEFFTER, *supra* note 42, at 109-10; MANNING, *supra* note 9, at 97; VATTEL, *supra* note 35, at 23.

91. Stowell urged that:

> Pour que l'intervention d'humanité ne serve pas de prétexte à une immixtion dans les affaires intérieures d'Etats voisins, la pratique internationale l'interdit pour le motif général de conduite inhumaine, sauf dans les cas où le traitement inhumain des particuliers, sujets des Etats voisins, résulte d'abus répétés ou continus, constituant une dénégation de certains droits reconnus aux particuliers dans toute communauté civilisée.

Stowell, *La Théorie et la Pratique de l'Intervention* (Hague Academy of International Law), 40 RECUEIL DES COURS 91, 141 (1932). *See also* HALL, *supra* note 80, at 344; HERSHEY, ESSENTIALS OF INTERNATIONAL PUBLIC LAW AND ORGANIZATION 239 (1927); MANNING, *supra* note 9, at 97; WOOLSEY, *supra* note 57, at 57 & 73.

92. Fauchille wrote that:

> Quels actes peuvent justifier une intervention d'humanité? Ce sont les actes attentatoires aux droits de l'homme, c'est-à-dire aux droits qui lui appartiennent en tant qu'homme, avant même qu'il fasse partie d'une société politique. Or, ces droits se résument en deux idées essentielles: droit à la vie et droit à la liberté.

FAUCHILLE, *supra* note 73, at 570. *Compare* LEFUR, *supra* note 77, *cited in* Aronéanu, *supra* note 7, at 128-29.

was presented until the publication of Rougier's *La Théorie de l'Intervention d'Humanité.*[93]

After an extensive critique of the traditional notions of absolute sovereignty and equality of States, particularly in connection with the resulting doctrine of nonintervention,[94] Rougier sets out what he calls "the theory of the law of humanity and of functional power."[95] Proceeding within the framework of this basic postulate,[96] he analyzes and rejects the legality of individual intervention[97] and eventually opts for collective intervention on various policy[98] and legal grounds.[99] Pointing out, however, that "in fact, the scholars only require collegiality so as to ensure, among the intervenors, the combination of two conditions: namely disinterestedness and the widest possible authority,"[100] he concludes that it is "the disinterestedness and the authority of the intervening States, and not their number, which provide legitimacy to the intervention."[101] Observing that, while these two basic require-

---

93. Rougier, *supra* note 3, at 497-525. For an outline and a short analysis of Rougier's criteria, *see* GANJI, *supra* note 4, at 9-11.

94. Rougier, *supra* note 3, at 480-89.

95. *Id.*, at 489-97. For a theoretical exposition, *see* Pillet, *Le Droit International Public*, 1 REV. GEN. DR. INT'L PUBL. 1 (1894); Pillet, *Les Droits Fondamentaux des Etats*, 5 REV. GEN. DR. INT'L PUBL. 66 & 236 (1898) *and* 6 REV. GEN. DR. INT'L PUBL. 503 (1899).

96. Rougier summarizes:

Cette théorie affirme l'existence d'une règle de droit générale s'imposant aux gouvernants comme aux gouvernés, supérieure au droit national et international qui n'en sont que des expressions particulières. Elle place sous la protection de cette règle les prérogatives essentielles de l'individu, ce qu'on appelle les *droits de l'homme*. Elle considère le pouvoir des gouvernants comme la contre-partie d'une fonction qu'ils ont à remplir, et conclut que le gouvernement qui manque à ses fonctions, partiellement déchu de son pouvoir, poet subir le contrôle d'un Etat étranger.

Rougier, *supra* note 3, at 489.

97. *Id.*, at 498-99.

98. Rougier enumerates the practical advantages of collective action as greater material and moral power, avoidance of conflict between intervenors acting independently without coordination, and increased impartiality due to the probable presence within the intervening collectivity of non-directly interested States. He argues that the inherent slowness of collective action could conveniently be remedied by delegation of the interventionary power to a single State. *Id.*, at 499-501.

99. Rougier summarizes his legal analysis as follows:

Le droit d'agir contre une gouvernement inhumain appartient proprement à la Société des nations, gardienne du droit humain, que les actes tyranniques lèsent dans ses prérogatives essentielles; les puissances intervenantes sont ses représentants. Or la Société des nations ne peut être représentée que par une collégialité d'Etats.

Id. at 501.

100. *Id.*, at 502.

101. *Id.*

ments are generally fulfilled in the case of collective action, and that this is *not necessarily* controlling,[102] Rougier formulates his own theory: "the system of disinterested and authorized intervention."[103]

Acknowledging the *de facto* inequality of States, even within the same "civilization," and refusing to ascribe to the traditional principle of equality the character of a fundamental *right* of every State, he claims that: "the law can only acknowledge the natural hierarchy of power, moral authority or civilization that occurs between nations,"[104] and that "protection of the collective interests requires the existence of rulers and ruled."[105] Considering the actual distribution of power in the world, he concludes that certain States—the United States in the Americas, as recognized by the Monroe doctrine, and the "concert des grandes puissances" in Europe, as ascertained by almost a century of State practice[106]—"take control of the direction of general affairs and possess over the others . . . a legitimate authority."[107] Insofar as their actions appear to be disinterested in that they tend to "ensure respect for the general rule of law and not to pursue the realization of an individual advantage,"[108] this special authority, he submits, will allow them, individually in the case of the United States and collectively in the case of the European Major Powers, to intervene lawfully in their capacity of trustees and defenders of the law of humanity whenever the latter is seriously violated in another State.

Turning finally to substantive requirements of legality, Rougier lists the following three criteria:

    1. that the event which . . . motivates [intervention] be an action of the public authorities, and not merely of private individuals;

    2. that this action constitute a violation of the law of humanity, and not merely a violation of national positive law;

    3. that the intervention fulfill certain [circumstantial] requirements.[109]

---

102. *Id.*
103. *Id.*
104. *Id.*, at 504.
105. *Id.*
106. *Id.*, at 507.
107. *Id.*, at 506-07.
108. *Id.*, at 502.
109. *Id.*, at 512.

Regarding the first[110] of these criteria, he specifies:

The fault [of the] government can consist either of a positive action, or of an abstention. In the former case, the tyrannical measures are carried out or ordered by the very agencies of the State, with whom sovereign power rests, or by agents of the public service. . . . In the latter case, the abuses are committed by private individuals, but they are tolerated by the government whereas it had the duty *and the capability* of preventing them.[111]

Regarding the second condition,[112] he makes a distinction between the *droits de l'homme*—"which he possesses in his capacity as man even before his membership of a political society, and which he would continue to possess if he ceased to be a member [of such a society] . . ."[113] and the *droits du citoyen*—"which the individual possesses as a result of his membership of a political society . . . "[114] Only the former could, if violated, provide a sufficient ground for intervention[115] since

[*h*]*uman* solidarity . . . requires protection of the human physical, moral and social personality, but does not demand that an individual be allowed to exercise, in his particular society, certain given activities or benefit from certain social advantages; determination of these advantages is within the purview of the rules of *national* solidarity.[116]

Analyzing what rights, specifically, are to be considered *droits de l'homme* as opposed to *droits du citoyen,* and, as such, are in principle susceptible of lawful protection by foreign intervention, he concludes that only the right to life,[117] the right to free-

---

110. *See generally id.,* at 512-15.

111. *Id.,* at 513 (emphasis added). *Compare,* discussion, note 248 *infra.*

112. *See generally* Rougier, *supra* note 3, at 512-23.

113. L. DUGUIT, MANUEL DE DROIT CONSTITUTIONEL 483 (1907), *cited in* Rougier, *supra* note 3, at 516.

114. *Id.*

115. Rougier noted that: "Seule la violation de ces droits essentiels serait une juste cause d'intervention." Rougier, *supra* note 3, at 517.

116. *Id.,* at 516 (emphasis added).

117. Regarding this right, Rougier states: "Tout homme a droit au respect de sa vie, de son intégrité physique et à la libre disposition de son individu." *Id.,* at 517. He furthermore considers the obligations of the State in this respect to be active as well as passive: "Il ne suffit même point que les gouvernements respectent la vie de l'individu; ils la doivent encore protéger." *Id.* He concludes:

Cette protection est une des fonctions primordiales qui s'imposent à toutes les sociétés politiques et dont le mauvais accomplissement peut justifier une intervention étrangère. L'application de cette idée la plus universellement admise en doctrine vise le cas où le Souverain fait massacrer ou laisse massacrer ses sujets.

Id. Compare notes 237 ff. *infra* and accompanying text.

dom[118] and the right to legality[119] can be included in the first category.

Finally, regarding his third criterion,[120] he acknowledges that considerations of opportunity should, and in practice usually will, play an important role in the decision of a State with respect to whether to intervene. As factors particularly relevant for this process, he mentions "the extent of the scandal,"[121] "a pressing appeal from the victims,"[122] "the very constitution of the guilty state,"[123] and "certain favorable conditions relating to the political

---

118. As to the substance of this right, Rougier observes: "La qualité d'être humain suppose la liberté physique et morale . . . ." Rougier, *supra* note 3, at 518. As to the latter, he specifies:

> La liberté morale, à la différence de la liberté physique, ne peut jamais être enlevée à l'individu. . . . Le gouvernement le plus tyrannique peut seulement interdire les manifestations extérieures de cette liberté. . . . De telles mesures peuvent être contraires aux droits du citoyen, notamment au droit d'égalité, mais on ne saurait y voir des atteintes au droit humain, aussi longtemps du moins qu'elles ne s'accompagnent pas de persécutions violentes et d'attentats contre la vie et la liberté des individus.

Id., at 519.

119. Rougier defines this right as:

> [L]e droit pour tout individu d'être protégé dans son activité par un certain ordre légal, d'échapper au pur arbitraire de ses gouvernants, et de n'être frappé dans sa vie et dans ses biens que conformément à la loi, par une autorité juridictionelle régulière suivant des formes établies.

Id., at 521. He justifies the inclusion of this right among the *droits humains* by asserting that:

> [L]'homme es un être social ne pouvant vivre isolément et . . . l'existence d'une société quelconque suppose l'establissment d'un ordre légal . . . . Le droit humain veut que tout regroupement d'hommes soit régi par une règle de droit.

Id. But he immediately qualifies this statement by adding:

> Quant au choix et à la détermination de cette règle, c'est l'affaire de chaque société particulière. . . . Si donc l'individu a un droit théorique à la légalité, l'établissement de cette légalité est une question d'ordre national. La droit de chaque homme se confond ici avec le droit du citoyen.

Id. He nevertheless argues that intervention for the protection of that right could lawfully take place "ou bien lorsque les institutions légales d'un Etat apparaissent inhumaines, ou bien lorsqu'un Etat viole les formes légales qu'il a édicté [*sic*] lui-même. . . ." *Id.*, at 522. But he concludes, particularly in view of of the principle of opportunity: "[I]l semble que . . . le droit à la légalité doive rester un droit purement théorique. . . ." *Id.*, at 523.

120. *See generally id.*, at 523-25.

121. *Id.*, at 524. Rougier explains this requirement by specifying that intervention should be resorted to only:

> [D]ans des cas exceptionellement graves, soit que la vie d'une population entière se trouve menacée, soit que les actes barbares se répètent habituellement, soit que leur caractère horrible choque plus violemment la conscience universelle.

Id. Compare notes 239 ff. *infra* and accompanying text.

122. Rougier, *supra* note 3, at 524.

123. *Id.* Rougier articulates this point by adding that States should refrain

balance, the economic rivalries, the financial interests . . . [of the] intervenors . . ."[124]

III. CONCLUSION AS TO THE CUSTOMARY LAW

Regarding the incorporation of the doctrine of humanitarian intervention as an established principle in customary international law, it has been demonstrated in the preceding analysis that, while historically there has never been unanimity on this point, there has, nevertheless, been some consistency since the latter part of the 19th century. As Lauterpacht points out there has been:

> a substantial body of opinion and practice in support of the view that there are limits to [the] discretion [of states in the treatment of their own nationals] and that when a State renders itself guilty of cruelties against and persecutions of its nationals in such a way as to deny their fundamental human rights and to shock the conscience of mankind, intervention in the interest of humanity is legally permissible.[125]

Furthermore, it seems that a correct interpretation of the pre-Charter precedents corroborates neither Ganji's[126] nor Potter's conclusions.[127] Doubts may indeed be cast as to the *sincerity* of the humanitarian motivation of some of these cases. Examples of these include the unilateral large-scale military operations carried out by Russia against the Porte in 1877-1878 and the Macedonian war of 1912-1913. In spite of the formal treaty rights of a clearly questionable nature usually invoked by the intervening States, it seems irrefutable that their major underlying concern and true justification was the condition of the non-Moslem populations in the Ottoman Empire.

It is conceded that the precedents are not particularly num-

---

from intervening

> [D]'autant plus que [l'Etat coupable] possède une organisation politique plus parfaite garantissant plus efficacement les libertés des citoyens contre l'arbitraire gouvernemental. Aussi bien, dans un Etat semblable, les violations d'humanité seront rares et exceptionelles, liées à quelque convulsion politique profonde, et disparaitront d'elles-mêmes sans qu'il soit besoin d'une action internationale; celle-ci aurait plus de chances d'aggraver le mal que de le guérir.

Id. Compare authority cited in note 244 *infra.*

124. Rougier, *supra* note 3, at 525.

125. OPPENHEIM, *supra* note 4, at 312. *See also* H. LAUTERPACHT, INTERNATIONAL LAW AND HUMAN RIGHTS 120 ff. (1950) [hereinafter cited as LAUTERPACHT].

126. "[T]he practice of humanitarian intervention is limited to cases based on conventions." GANJI, *supra* note 4, at 43.

127. *See* discussion in note 82 *supra.*

erous, but the extent of State practice necessary to create a rule of customary international law is a debatable question. That they are actually so scarce should not come as a surprise. As Lauterpacht explains:

> The disinclination to take the responsibility for an international conflagration likely to follow upon such intervention or the consideration of the interests of the persecuted likely to suffer rather than to benefit from intervention unless fully backed by force, have been to some extent responsible for the relative infrequency of humanitarian intervention.[128]

In addition, customary international law is not created by State practice only. The opinions of the leading scholars, especially in an essentially non-institutionalized structure such as that of international law, have a significant impact upon the development of the legal norms of the system, as was reaffirmed in article 38(1)(d) of the Statute of the International Court of Justice.[129]

The continuous reference throughout the twentieth century to the theory of humanitarian intervention, in the doctrine and in State practice (as in the case of the 1964 Stanleyville airdrop[130] and in that of the initial stage of the intervention in the Dominican Republic in 1965[131]), and supplemented by its *de facto*

---

128. OPPENHEIM, *supra* note 4, at 313. Regarding the motives for the lack of *real* interest on the part of both foreign governments and public opinion for human rights violations abroad, *see* Bilder, *Rethinking International Human Rights: Some Basic Questions*, 1969 WIS. L. REV. 171.

129. The Statute provides that:
> The Court, whose function it is to decide in accordance with international law such disputes as are submitted to it, shall apply: . . . subject to the provisions of Article 59, judicial decisions and *the teachings of the most qualified publicists of the various nations, as a subsidiary* means for the determination of the rules of law.

I.C.J STAT., art. 38, para. 1(d) (emphasis added).

130. *See, e.g.,* Statement by President Johnson, *reprinted in* 51 U.S. DEP'T STATE BULL. 846 (1964). *See generally* De Schutter, *Humanitarian Intervention: A United Nations Task*, 3 CALIF. W. INT'L L. J. 21-22 (1972) [hereinafter cited as De Schutter]; Lillich, *Self-Help, supra* note 7, at 338 ff.; *The Congo Crisis 1964: A Case Study in Humanitarian Intervention*, 12 VA. J. INT'L L. 261 (1972) [hereinafter cited as *Congo Crisis*].

131. *See, e.g.,* Statement by President Johnson, *reprinted in* 53 U.S. DEP'T STATE BULL. 20 (1965). *See generally* THOMAS & THOMAS, *supra* note 7; Bogen, *The Law of Humanitarian Intervention: United States Policy in Cuba (1898) and in the Dominican Republic*, 7 HARV. INT'L L. J. 296 (1965) [hereinafter cited as Bogen]; Bohan, *The Dominican Case: Unilateral Intervention*, 60 AM. J. INT'L L. 809 (1966); Fenwick, *International Law, the O.A.S. and the Dominican Crisis*, 19 NAVAL WAR COLLEGE REV. 18 (1966) [hereinafter cited as Fenwick, *International Law*]; Fenwick, *The Dominican Republic: Intervention or Collective Self-Defense?*, 60 AM. J. INT'L L. 64 (1966) [hereinafter cited as Fenwick,

The Use of Force in International Law

utilization in the Bangladesh crisis seem indeed to undercut the Thomases' contention that:

> [Since u]nder the theory that to protest to a government would be to intervene in the internal political systems which recognize terror as a legitimate method of government, the democracies failed (prior to the advent of World War II) to protest the Nazi persecutions in Germany, the Franco persecutions in Spain and the Russian persecutions in Russia and satellite countries . . ., humanitarian intervention in the 20th century . . . retains but little vigor.[132]

The cases referred to constitute flagrant examples of failure to invoke the doctrine in situations where it was genuinely demanded.[133]   That this provides sufficient ground for the conclusion that the doctrine of humanitarian intervention has fallen in disuse and consequently lost any relevance or validity in present times, is a much more questionable contention.   It does not seem that international law requires *constant, faultless* utilization to avoid automatic abolition of a customary rule; many rarely used institutions of customary international law would otherwise have to be considered invalidated for lack of sufficiently frequent application.   For example, it is doubtful whether hot pursuit has been used that often in recent times, and yet this right is unquestionably still accepted as a valid part of the general law of nations as attested by its restatement in article 23 of the 1958 Geneva Convention on the High Seas.

Turning finally to the normative problem, it appears that some widely accepted criteria of legality of humanitarian intervention can be distillated from the abundant literature on the subject.   This can be done in spite of the overall vagueness and lack of structuration of the pronouncements by pre-Charter scholars:

Dominican Republic]; McLaren, *The Dominican Crisis: An Inter-American Dilemma*, 4 CAN. Y.B. INT'L L. 178 (1966); Meeker, *The Dominican Situation in the Perspective of International Law*, 53 U.S. DEP'T STATE BULL. 60 (1965); Nanda, *The United States Action in the 1965 Dominican Crisis: Impact on World Order (Part I)*, 43 DENVER L. J. 441 (1966).

132. A. THOMAS & A. THOMAS, NON-INTERVENTION 373-74 (1965).   *Compare*, BROWNLIE, *supra* note 17, at 340-41:

> With the embarassing exception provided by Germany ['s invocation of the doctrine in defense of its intervention in Czechoslovakia], the institution has disappeared from modern state practice.

133. *But see* Reisman, *supra* note 4, at 178, referring to "[T]he Allied effort against the Axis in the Second World War" as an extreme example of "inclusive participation" in humanitarian intervention.

(1) disinterestedness of the intervening Power(s), in the sense of a non-seeking of particular interests or individual advantages;[134]

(2) restriction of the applicability of the theory to extreme cases of atrocity and breakdown of order;[135]

(3) active participation or passive complicity or condonation of the violations by the sovereign;[136]

(4) general predilection for collective action,[137] by preference at the hands of the Major Powers,[138] who have a particular responsibility[139] for ensuring overall respect of minimal international standards of treatment of local populations.

As the foregoing study has shown, while divergences certainly existed as to the *circumstances* in which resort could be had to the institution of humanitarian intervention, as well as to the *manner* in which such operations were to be conducted, the *principle* itself was widely, if not unanimously, accepted as an integral part of customary international law. Indeed, "the doc-

---

134. *Compare* authorities in notes 249 ff. *infra* and accompanying text.

135. *Compare* authorities in notes 236 ff. *infra* and accompanying text.

136. *Compare* discussion in note 248 *infra*.

137. *Compare* authorities in notes 278 ff. *infra* and accompanying text.

138. As the Great Powers were then the only form of international "organization," this criterion is related to present day notions of primary responsibility of international organizations and the subsidiary character of humanitarian intervention. *See* authorities in notes 267 ff. *infra* and accompanying text.

139. This aspect is emphasized by Rougier who urges *formal* recognition by international law of this factual inequality. *See* text accompanying notes 94 & 104 *supra*. This position is not astonishing. This author concurs with Perez-Vera in her statement that "aujourd'hui le principe de l'égalité souveraine de tous les Etats, malgré ses défaillances, s'oppose à un raisonnement de ce genre . . ." Perez-Vera, *La Protection d'Humanité en Droit International*, [1969] REVUE BELGE DE DROIT INTERNATIONAL 401, 416 [hereinafter cited as Perez-Vera]. He would like to point out, however, that even today the principle of sovereign equality of States seems far from absolute in practice. The U.N. Charter declares that one of the purposes of the Organization is "to develop friendly relations among nations based on *respect for the principle of equal rights . . . of peoples, ...*" U.N. CHARTER, art. 1, para. 2 (emphasis added). The Charter also declares that "The Organization is based on *the principle of the sovereign equality of all its Members*." *Id.*, art. 2, para. 1 (emphasis added). The Charter nevertheless technically acknowledges the *de facto* inequality of its Member States by granting a veto power to the Permanent Members of the Security Council, thus recognizing that certain States are endowed with particular rights and responsibilities. *Id.*, art. 27, para. 3. Further reference can be made to the problem of micro-States in general, and in particular, to recent proposals which have been made in the Organization of American States to restrict or prevent membership of a potentially large number of small Caribbean island-States on the brink of independence.

trine of humanitarian intervention appears to have been so clearly established under customary international law that only its limits and not its existence is subject to debate."[140]

IV. PRESENT VALIDITY OF THE CUSTOMARY DOCTRINE

As many scholars have come to recognize in recent years,[141] there is a need in the area of human rights to shift the field of study from the substantive to the procedural side; in other words, from defining human rights standards to creating machinery for their implementation and enforcement.[142]   As article 4 of the Proclamation of Teheran of May 13, 1968, noticed:

> Since the adoption of the Universal Declaration of Human Rights the United Nations has made substantial progress in defining standards for the enjoyment and protection of human rights and fundamental freedoms . . . but much remains to be done in regard to the implementation of those rights and freedoms.[143]

The numerous international human rights instruments which have been adopted *by the U.N. General Assembly* during the last two decades on the one hand, and the lack of any significant number of ratifications of most major conventions *by the nations of the world*[144] on the other hand, seem to justify this conclusion and illustrate the problem of bridging the gap between mere theoretical lip-service dictated by political opportunism, and practical application of the acclaimed principles.   The fact that the

---

140. INT'L L. ASS'N, *The International Protection of Human Rights by General International Law*, Interim Report of the Sub-Committee, International Committee on Human Rights 11 (The Hague 1970).

141. The International Law Association concluded that:
   [T]he trend is now towards the establishment of international machinery and techniques for implementation . . . that is to say . . . some kind of supervision and control of the conduct of States in the observance of the standards now established.
INT'L L. ASS'N, Interim Report of the Committee on Human Rights, Report of the 52d Conference 754 (Helsinki 1966).

142. "The most difficult problem still confronting the framers of the United Nations' Human Rights Program is that of devising effective procedures for enforcement." McDougal & Bebr, *Human Rights in the United Nations*, 58 AM. J. INT'L L. 603, 629 (1964).

143. International Conference on Human Rights, Final Act, U.N. Doc. A/CONF. 32/41, art. 4 (1968).

144. As of November 1971, for instance, only thirteen ratifications had been deposited for the Covenant on Civil and Political Rights and the Covenant on Economic, Social and Cultural Rights and four for the Optional Protocol on Civil and Political Rights. D. HARRIS, CASES AND MATERIALS ON INTERNATIONAL LAW 531 n.40; 539 n.53; and 540 n.57 (1973).

U.N. Human Rights Commission has finally taken the important step of deciding, in its rules of procedure, to take into consideration individual petitions concerning human rights violations,[145] is but meager consolation. It is in those extreme cases where the most fundamental human rights are massively threatened, that the United Nations and the regional organizations, paralyzed by Major Power disagreements and the reluctance of the New States to accept any infringement upon the sacrosanct principles of sovereign independence and nonintervention[146] in a setting lacking colonial or para-colonial[147] aspects,[148] have been unable or unwilling to take any significant measures.[149] Biafra, Indonesia, Sudan, Burundi, Bangladesh, and, more recently, Uganda are but the most recent and bloody examples of the unfortunate passivity and ineffectiveness of the international organizations.[150]

In view of this state of affairs, one might have good reason to question the wisdom[151] of the now "classic" interpretation of

---

145. Sub-Commission on the Prevention of Discrimination and Protection of Minorities, Commission on Human Rights, Res. 1 (XXIV), U.N. Doc E/CN.4/ SUB.2 CRP.6, art. 2(a) (1971).

146. For statements by national representatives in the United Nations, *see* Fonteyne, *Forcible Self-Help by States to Protect Human Rights: Recent Views from the United Nations*, in HUMANITARIAN INTERVENTION AND THE UNITED NATIONS 197, at 205-06 & n.39; 209-11 & nn.53-58; 215-16 & nn. 74-76 (R. Lillich ed. 1973) [hereinafter cited as Fonteyne].

147. The term "para-colonial" is used here to indicate the situation in Rhodesia or South Africa where black-white racism is a remnant of a colonial past, as opposed to "colonial" which indicates an overseas government situation, or "racial" which indicates a situation of racism lacking colonial origin.

148. For statements by national representatives in the United Nations, *see* Fonteyne, *supra* note 146, at 208 n.50.

149. "[T]he United Nations has not so far proved an effective instrument for remedying flagrant violations of elementary rights and freedoms." BRIERLY, *supra* note 7, at 295-96. *See also* Komarnicki, *L'Intervention en Droit International Moderne*, 60 REV. GEN. DR. INT'L PUBL. 521, 566 (1956), observing after only a decade of U.N. activity, that:

> [D]ans les conditions actuelles, *les Nations Unies ne sont pas capables de s'acquitter de leur tâche principale*: contribuer au développement du droit international et à l'établissement de l'ordre international basée sur la justice, conformément aux buts et aux devoirs inscrits dans la Charte.

Compare, Remarks by Louis Henkin, in *Biafra, Bengal, and Beyond: International Responsibility and Genocidal Conflict*, 66 PROCEEDINGS AM. SOC'Y INT'L L. 89, 96-97 (1972) [hereinafter cited as Remarks by Louis Henkin]:

> [I]t is not possible in civil wars to isolate and act only upon genocide and other human rights violations. Indeed, usually the international community can not act at all, because of the national and international politics that dominate each civil war situation.

150. *See, e.g.,* INT'L COMM'N OF JURISTS, *supra* note 1.

151. Lillich advocated that:

> Surely to require a state to sit back and watch the slaughter of innocent people in order to avoid violating blanket prohibitions against the

the Charter regulation of use of force as illustrated for instance by Mr. Gomez Robledo (Mexico) in the U.N. 6th Committee:

> [U]nder article 2, paragraph 4, of the United Nations Charter it was clear that the use of force was permissible in only two cases: enforcement action ordered by the Security Council under article 42; and in conformity with article 51 individual or collective self-defence in the event of armed attack.[152]

A departure from this strict constructionism of the Charter provisions relating to the use of force, and from the traditional domestic jurisdiction limitation, raises serious problems of Charter interpretation. To quote Professor Lillich:

> [T]wo provisions make it "very doubtful" . . . whether forcible self-help to protect human rights is still permissible under international law. In the first place, all states by Article 2(4) renounce "the threat or use of force against the territorial integrity or political independence of any state," subject of course to the self-defense provision contained in Article 51. Secondly, Article 2(7) prevents intervention by the United Nations "in matters which are essentially within the domestic jurisdiction of any state," except for the application of enforcement measures under Chapter VII.[153]

A. The Domestic Jurisdiction Limitation and the Principle of Nonintervention[154]

The principle of nonintervention, rather surprisingly in view of its wide acceptance[155] at the time of the creation of the United Nations, is not explicitly provided for in the Charter regarding

---

use of force is to stress blackletter at the expense of far more fundamental values.
Lillich, *Self-Help, supra* note 7, at 344. *Compare,* J. STONE, AGGRESSION AND WORLD ORDER 99 (1968) [hereinafter cited as STONE].

152. Mr. Gomez Robledo (Mexico), 18 U.N GAOR, 6th Comm., U.N. Doc. A/C.6/S.R.806, at 133, para. 12 (1963). For further statements in the United Nations, *see* Fonteyne, *supra* note 146, at 209-11 & nn.53-58.

153. Lillich, *Intervention, supra* note 7, at 210-11.

154. *See generally* Ermacora, *Human Rights and Domestic Jurisdiction* (Hague Academy of International Law), 124 RECUEIL DES COURS 375 (1968) [hereinafter cited as Ermacora; *and* Fawcett, *Human Rights and Domestic Jurisdiction,* in THE INTERNATIONAL PROTECTION OF HUMAN RIGHTS 286 (E. Luard ed. 1967).

155. *See, e.g.,* BRIERLY, *supra* note 7, at 402: "[C]ertain principles were fairly clear in customary law. Intervention, being a violation of another state's independence, was recognized to be in principle contrary to international law. . . ."

inter-State relations.[156] While article 2(4) specifically prohibits the threat or use of force between *States*,[157] article 2(7) explicitly covers the relations between the United Nations and its Members only.[158] This precludes *the Organization* from intervening in matters essentially within the jurisdiction of any State with the important exception of actions in respect to threats to the peace, breaches of the peace, and acts of aggression.[159] However, this does not affect inter-State relations.

Notwithstanding some sporadic affirmations to the contrary,[160] it seems that the explicit references in articles 1(2) and 2(1) of the Charter[161] and the subsequent interpretation given to the nonintervention principle by a nearly unanimous doctrine and by the United Nations itself, justify the contention that the basic obligation of nonintervention in the domestic affairs of a State is equally,[162] if not more,[163] applicable on the level of inter-State relations.

---

156. Despite wide recognition as an integral part of customary international law, the principle of nonintervention was affected by vagueness and confusion. Lillich, *Self-Help, supra* note 7, at 330 & n.31. As Brierly observed: "The law of intervention . . . was also sometimes obscured under the cloak of a political doctrine such as the Monroe doctrine. . . ." *See* BRIERLY, *supra* note 7, at 402. This, perhaps, provides a partial explanation for the indicated omission.

157. With the exception of article 51 situations, action in pursuance of a Chapter VII decision, and the now obviously irrelevant Article 107.

158. For statements by national representatives in the United Nations, *see* Fonteyne, *supra* note 146, at 204 & n.31.

159. U.N. CHARTER, Ch. VII.

160. *See, e.g.,* Mr. Schwebel (U.S.A.):

[I]n the United States' delegation's view article 2(7) of the Charter applied only to intervention by the United Nations, and . . . intervention by one State in the affairs of another was illicit under the Charter only when it was accompanied by the threat or use of force. Article 2(7) was the only provision in the Charter which made express reference to non-intervention, and the scope of State intervention was defined only in Article 2(4).

19 U.N. GAOR, Spec. Comm. on Fr. Rel., U.N. Doc. A/A.C.119/S.R.32, at 25 (1964). For further statements in the United Nations, *see* Fonteyne, *supra* note 146, at 204-05 & n.33.

161. *But see* discussion and authorities at note 139 *supra.*

162. *See, e.g.,* Mr. Colombo (Argentina):

The Charter of the United Nations prohibited the Organization from intervening in matters which are essentially within the domestic jurisdiction of any State. The same principle must be laid down in explicit terms in regard to relations between the States themselves.

19 U.N. GAOR, Spec. Comm. on Fr. Rel., U.N. Doc. A/A C.119/S.R.28, at 7 (1964). For further statements in the United Nations, *see* Fonteyne, *supra* note 146, at 205 & n.37.

163. The Representative from Cyprus stated that: "A very clear distinction should . . . be drawn between the concept of absolute sovereignty of States in relation to each other and that of the limited sovereignty of States in relation

The Use of Force in International Law

Today the whole range of activities relating to human rights, both in and outside the United Nations, as exemplified by the large number of declarations and conventions[164] which have in recent years been adopted on the subject,[165] indicate that the scope of domestic jurisdiction is dwindling. Further examples include the almost daily involvement of various U.N. agencies and organs with actual human rights problems;[166] the repeated refusal by the General Assembly and the Security Council to accept article 2(7) of the Charter as preventing consideration by the United Nations of serious cases of human rights violations,[167] particularly in a colonial or para-colonial context;[168] and, the

---

to the United Nations." Mr. Rossides (Cyprus), 18 U.N. GAOR, 6th Comm., U.N. Doc. A/C.6/S.R.822, at 230, para. 9 (1963). Consequently, the nonintervention principle, as applicable to States, "had a much wider scope." Mr. El-Erian (United Arab Republic), U.N. Doc. A/C.6/S.R.811, at 164, para. 26 (1963). For further statements in the United Nations, see Fonteyne, *supra* note 146, at 205 & nn.35-36.

164. *See generally* BASIC DOCUMENTS ON HUMAN RIGHTS (I. Brownlie ed. 1971).

165. A large number of those conventions have failed to obtain a sufficient number of ratifications to come into force. This does not basically alter the conclusion that the whole area of human rights is presently the subject of, at least theoretical permanent international attention.

166. *See generally* J. CAREY, U.N. PROTECTION OF CIVIL AND POLITICAL RIGHTS (1970) [hereinafter cited as CAREY]; Ermacora, *supra* note 154; Higgins, *Compliance with United Nations Decisions on Peace and Security and Human Rights Questions*, in THE EFFECTIVENESS OF INTERNATIONAL DECISIONS 34 (S. Schwebel ed. 1971).

167. Consideration of such cases was addressed by the Representative from Cyprus:

> Since the adoption of the Charter, the general tendency had been . . . to extend the possibilities of intervention by the United Nations. Thus article 2, paragraph 7, of the Charter had repeatedly been interpreted by the General Assembly as allowing the United Nations to intervene in the internal affairs of a State in case of a flagrant violation of human rights or of the provisions of the Charter.

Mr. Rossides (Cyprus), 18 U.N. GAOR, 6th Comm., U.N. Doc. A/C.6/S.R.822, at 230, para. 10 (1963). Compare the lack of action by the United Nations in, for instance, the cases of human rights violations in Bulgaria, Hungary, Rumania, Tibet, Greece, and Haiti. *See generally* M. RAJAN, UNITED NATIONS AND DOMESTIC JURISDICTION 341 ff. (1958) [hereinafter cited as RAJAN]; Ermacora, *supra* note 154, at 415 ff. For statements by national representatives in the United Nations, see Fonteyne, *supra* note 146, at 206-09 & nn.40-49 & 51-52.

168. *See, e.g.,* Mr. Nachabe (Syria):

> [A] state should not, under cover of the principle of non-intervention in domestic matters, commit acts contrary to the peremptory rules of international law, such as those which outlawed the discredited practices of colonial domination and attacks on human rights.

20 U.N. GAOR, 6th Comm., U.N. Doc. A/C.6/S.R.884, at 265, para. 52 (1965). For further statements in the United Nations, see Fonteyne, *supra* note 146, at 207-08, nn. 46-48 & 50.

world-wide concern of the public opinion with extreme cases such as Biafra, Southern Africa, Rhodesia or Bangladesh.[169] These developments seem to substantiate Professor Ermacora's conclusion that:

> [T]he right to self-determination and the protection of human rights in matters of discrimination as far as "gross violations" or "consistent patterns of violations" are concerned are no longer essentially within the domestic jurisdiction of States. . . .[170]

Domestic jurisdiction is "an essentially relative question; it depends upon the development of international relations."[171] In view of the variable character of the concept,[172] it appears that the universal attention devoted to the way in which people are treated in their own country, and the practice of the United Nations in this field, must clearly be interpreted as indicating that human rights have finally been removed from the exclusive jurisdiction of States and lifted up into the realm of international concern.[173] As a consequence, human rights have been placed outside the reach of the article 2(7) intervention ban, even in cases not amounting to a threat to the peace.[174] This is true so

169. See generally P. JESSUP, A MODERN LAW OF NATIONS 91 (1949) [hereinafter cited as JESSUP]; LAUTERPACHT, supra note 125, at 177 ff.; OPPENHEIM, supra note 4, at 313; THOMAS & THOMAS, supra note 132, at 376; Lillich, Self-Help, supra note 7, at 338; McDougal & Bebr, supra note 142, at 612. Compare the treatment of this question in connection with the U.N. mandatory economic sanctions against Rhodesia in McDougal & Reisman, Rhodesia and the United Nations: The Lawfulness of International Concern, 63 AM. J. INT'L L. 1, 14 nn. (1969) [hereinafter cited as McDougal & Reisman]. See also Howell, A Matter of International Concern, 63 AM. J. INT'L L. 771 (1969). Contra, Acheson, The Arrogance of International Lawyers, 2 INT'L LAWYER 591 (1968) [hereinafter cited as Acheson]. Compare, REDSLOB, supra note 7, at 250.

170. Ermacora, supra note 154, at 436. For allegations to the contrary made on several occasions by South Africa in the United Nations, see CAREY, supra note 166, at 104 ff.

171. Tunis-Morocco Nationality Decrees Case, [1923] P.C.I.J., ser. B, No. 4, reprinted in 1 M. HUDSON, WORLD COURT REPORTS 143 (1943).

172. RAJAN, supra note 167, at 57 ff. Compare M. MOSKOWITZ, HUMAN RIGHTS AND WORLD ORDER 32 ff. (1958).

173. See Reisman, supra note 4, at 171 ff. Compare, The Question of Race Conflict in South Africa, Consideration by the General Assembly Between the 7th and 14th Sessions, 1952-1959, in SUMMARY OF THE PRACTICE OF THE UNITED NATIONS AND OF VIEWS EXPRESSED IN THE UNITED NATIONS BY MEMBER STATES IN RESPECT OF FOUR OF THE PRINCIPLES OF INTERNATIONAL LAW CONCERNING FRIENDLY RELATIONS AND CO-OPERATION AMONG STATES IN ACCORDANCE WITH THE CHARTER OF THE UNITED NATIONS, PREPARED BY THE SECRETARIAT, 19 U.N. GAOR, Spec. Comm. on Fr. Rel., U.N. Doc. A/A.C.119/L.2, at 141, para. 288 (1964) [hereinafter cited as SUMMARY]. Contra, id., at 141-42, para. 289.

174. See Reisman, supra note 4, at 189 & 190-91. Compare The Question

242   CALIFORNIA WESTERN INTERNATIONAL LAW JOURNAL   Vol. 4

far as measures by the United Nations are concerned, and probably regarding unilateral State action as well.[175]

B. *The Prohibition of the Threat of Use of Force*

As already indicated, what appears now to have become the "classic" view of the Charter prohibition of the threat or use of force in inter-State relations interprets article 2(4)[176] in a broad way intended to encompass the entire range of possible situations.[177]

Relying primarily upon the intentions of the framers, the proponents of this approach stress the fact that the qualifying terms "against the territorial integrity or political independence of any State" ought not to be taken as restricting the absolute scope of the prohibition. Acknowledging that an "unqualified" interpretation of article 2(4) in fact constitutes a twist of the plain meaning of the text, Professor Giraud notices that:

> This [restrictive] interpretation has not been retained. The

of Race Conflict in South Africa, Consideration by the General Assembly Between the 15th and 17th Sessions, 1960-1962, in SUMMARY, *supra* note 173, at 146, para 298; The Question of Race Conflict in South Africa, Consideration by the Security Council in 1963 and by the General Assembly During the 18th Session, 1963, in SUMMARY, *supra* note 173, at 149, para. 301.

175. *See generally* R. HIGGINS, THE DEVELOPMENT OF INTERNATIONAL LAW THROUGH THE POLITICAL ORGANS OF THE UNITED NATIONS 118-30 (1963). *Compare*, Wright, *Domestic Jurisdiction as a Limit on National and Supra-National Action*, 56 Nw. U.L. REV. 11 (1961). The conclusion which the present article reaches at this point does not mean that *armed* unilateral intervention for humanitarian purposes is permissible under the U.N. Charter, for there still remains the hurdle of the article 2(4) prohibition of use of force. This author contends only, at this stage, that, unless the position is taken that the nonintervention principle is stricter for States and should be distinguished from the article 2(7) limitation on U.N. jurisdiction, the preceding analysis justifies acceptance of less extreme forms of coercive unilateral action in situations of gross and persistent violation of the most fundamental human rights. This conclusion stands as long as one sticks to the "classic" interpretation of the term "force" in article 2(4), namely *armed* force, an approach suggested, among other things, by the Charter itself where it expressly lists, among the purposes of the Organization, the intention "[t]o ensure . . . that *armed* force shall not be used, save in the common interest. . . ." U.N. CHARTER, Preamble (emphasis added). *Compare* BRIERLY, *supra* note 7, at 415-16, concluding that "it is clear that article 2(4) does not preclude a state from taking unilaterally economic or other [measures] not involving the use of armed force." Arriving at a similar conclusion on the nonintervention point, but unwilling to go any further, the Thomases state:

> The general international law right of an individual nation or a group of nations to intervene for humanitarian purposes remains unchanged, except that this intervention may no longer be taken by means involving the use or threat of force.

THOMAS & THOMAS, *supra* note 132, at 384.

reason for it is that this interpretation does not correspond at all to the intentions of the drafters of the Charter. At the San Francisco Conference, that portion of the sentence referring to "the territorial integrity or the political independence" was added to the text merely to satisfy the small Powers who wished to see the guarantee of article 10 of the Pact of the League of Nations restated in the Charter, and not to restrict the scope of the prohibition of recourse to force.[178]

Similarly, regarding the final part of paragraph 4, Professor Wehberg points out:

The terms of the prohibition "in any other manner incompatible with the purposes of the United Nations," should not be interpreted as implying any other authorized use of force. . . . One can . . . refer [in this connection] to the statements of the American representative [at] the debates [of Committee I/1 of the San Francisco Conference], emphasizing that . . . the sentence "or in any other manner" was intended to guarantee "that there would be no loopholes . . . ."[179]

Looking at the article 2(4) prohibition within the framework of the Charter as a whole, Sir Humphrey Waldock concludes:

[A]rticle 2(4) prohibits entirely any threat or use of force between independent States except in individual or collective self-defense under article 51 or in execution of collective measures under the Charter for maintaining or restoring peace.[180]

This interpretation, which can properly be considered the generally accepted one in the United Nations itself,[181] views the Charter as a closed structure of self-sufficient norms, completely

---

176. The Charter provides that:

All Members shall refrain in their international relations from the threat or use of force against the territorial integrity or political independence of any state, or in any other manner inconsistent with the Purposes of the United Nations.

U.N. CHARTER, art. 2, para. 4.

177. See note 152 supra and accompanying text.

178. Giraud, L'Interdiction du Recours à la Force—La Théorie et la Pratique des Nations Unies, 67 REV. GEN. DR. INT'L PUBL. 501, 512-13 (1963). See also Brownlie, The Use of Force in Self-Defence, 37 BRIT. Y.B. INT'L L. 183, 235 (1961).

179. Wehberg, L'Interdiction du Recours à la Force (Hague Academy of International Law), 78 RECUEIL DES COURS 7, 70 (1951).

180. Waldock, supra note 7, at 493.

181. See note 152 supra and accompanying text.

divorced from the pre-existing body of rules under customary international law. This would ensure as a system of conflict-management in which articles 2(4) and 51 are inversely correlative and intended to cover the whole spectrum of possibilities.[182]

When supported by the contention that "if nations had wished to exclude humanitarian intervention from these prohibitions . . . they would have done so explicitly,"[183] this approach leads necessarily to the general conclusion that

> The landing of armed forces of one state in another state is a "breach of the peace" or "threat to the peace" even though under traditional international law it is a lawful act. It is a measure of forcible self-help, legalized by international law because there has been no international organization competent to act in an emergency. The organizational defect has now been at least partially remedied through the adoption of the Charter and a modernized law of nations should insist that the collective measures envisaged by art. 1 of the Charter shall supplant the individual measures approved by traditional international law . . . .[184]

---

182. *Compare,* Röling, *supra* note 7, at 177, who supports humanitarian intervention as an additional exception, not explicitly provided for in the Charter, on the basis that "a legal rule without exceptions does not exist." He further comments that: "It is impossible to formulate rules of law in such a way that the most extreme and rare situations would be dealt with. An endeavour to achieve such a rule would amount to perfectionism." *Id.*

183. THOMAS & THOMAS, *supra* note 7, at 22, referring to the Latin-American doctrine. Mencer noted that:

> L'institution de la soi-disant intervention humanitaire ne constitue, dans le droit international contemporain, aucune institution autonome, telle pour laquelle la donnent certains auteurs dans une certaine mesure. Elle ne constitue pas une exception de l'applicabilité générale et absolu [sic] de l'interdiction d'intervention. L'article 2, alinea 4, de la Charte interdit aux Etats la menace ou l'emploi de la force, et il se conçoit que l'intervention pour des raisons humanitaires n'est pas citée en tant qu'exception de cette interdiction générale. Elle ne figure pas non plus, en qualité d'exception, à l'article 2, alinéa 7.

Mencer, *supra* note 16, at 314-15. This contention raises the fundamental question as to whether the Charter must be construed as abolishing all pre-existing norms of customary international law which it does not specifically and explicitly save, or has left unaffected those traditional rules which are not necessarily in contradiction with its own provisions and purposes. This author tends to favor the latter position for a variety of reasons, including the widely shared principle of interpretation in domestic law, which could be applied here by analogy, in that the technique of implicit repeal of pre-existing laws must be restrictively interpreted, and applied only when contradiction with the new rules is unavoidable. *Compare,* Nanda, *supra* note 131, at 478. *See also* Report of the 6th Committee, 18 U.N. GAOR, Annexes, Vol. III, Agenda Item 71, U.N. Doc. A/5671, at 34, para. 61 (1963); Samuels, in HUMANITARIAN INTERVENTION AND THE UNITED NATIONS 43 (R. Lillich ed. 1973).

184. JESSUP, *supra* note 169, at 169-70.

Applying this approach specifically to humanitarian intervention, Dr. Brownlie logically concludes:

[I]t is extremely doubtful if this form of intervention has survived the express condemnations of intervention which have occurred in recent times[185] or the general prohibition of resort to force to be found in the U.N. Charter.[186]

Faced with the problem of the *de facto* inability and political unwillingness both of the United Nations[187] and of the regional organizations,[188] to take any significant action, other than

---

185. It seems, however, that there has never been a clear and unambiguous condemnation by the United Nations of a specific instance of humanitarian intervention *as such.* In connection with the 1964 Stanleyville airdrop, for example, Nanda concludes: "[T]he Council Resolution after the Stanleyville debate [does] not prohibit such action, nor . . . specifically permit it." Nanda, *supra* note 131, at 477-78. Similarly, Bastid sums up her evaluation of the same Security Council debates as follows:

Sous réserve du problème difficile de l'appréciation des conditions dans un cas concret il semble bien qu'au cours de ce débat le princ:pe même de l'intervention d'humanité n'ait pas été contesté. De ce point de vue la position des représentants des Etats d'Amérique latine, traditionnellement attachés au principe de non-intervention doit être spécialement relevée. Le Délégué du Brésil a déclaré que l'action humanitaire pour sauver la vie d'ôtages était légitime quant à ses motifs et aux moyens employés. Tel a été aussi l'avis du représentant de la Bolivie . . .

Bastid, *Remarques sur l'Interdiction d'Intervention,* in MELANGES OFFERTS A JURAJ ANDRASSY 13, 21 (1968). *Compare,* Statement by Mr. Bouattoura (Algeria), *cited in id.,* at 20. *See also* R. FALK, LEGAL ORDER IN A VIOLENT WORLD 329-31 & 334 (1968) [hereinafter cited as FALK]; *The Congo Crisis, supra* note 130, at 269 ff. & 273; De Schutter, *supra* note 130, at 23 & n.10.

186. BROWNLIE, *supra* note 17, at 342. Mencer rejects the usefulness of analyzing whether one could or should distinguish between permissible and impermissible interventions:

Il est . . . impossible de continuer utilement la recherche scientifique de cette questions [sic] au moyen d'une méthode qui, bien qu'elle se soit acclimatée est évidemment déjà dépassée et vieillie à présent, savoir [sic] au moyen de la méthode de distinction d'interventions . . . selon la forme (par exemple . . . intervention individuelle ou collective, économique, financ:aire, commerciale, idéologique, humanitaire ou autres [sic] . . . . Sous l'angle méthodolog:que et, d'autant plus, sous l'aspect théorique . . . non seulement la forme, mais aussi le *motif* de l'intervention est sans importance . . . . A présent, la théorie artificielle des soi-disants motifs légitimes est ensontenable [sic] . . . alle [sic] n'a aucune justification scientifique . . . Aucune de ces "justifications" n'affaiblit pas [sic] les conséquences de la *violation de la souveraineté* de l'Etat contre lequel l'intervention a été dirigée . . .

Mencer, *supra* note 16, at 304-05. He concludes: "La science progressiste de droit international s'oppose . . . à toutes les doctrines de l'intervention légitime." *Id.,* at 307.

187. *See* text accompanying note 150 *supra.*

188. Referring to the Organization of African Unity, Thapa observes:

The African Organization, a loose association of African States, lacks among its members a coherence of aims and principles, so that it has proven of little use in the handling of regional problems. Particularly, inhuman treatment, unless at the hands of white rulers, does not come among its list of immediate concerns; which casts doubts as to whether

246   CALIFORNIA WESTERN INTERNATIONAL LAW JOURNAL   Vol. 4

humanitarian relief measures,[189] to remedy even extreme situations of human rights deprivations other than those involving *apartheid* or racial discrimination in a colonial or para-colonial context,[190] an increasing number of scholars have been seeking legal and extra-legal arguments to justify unilateral humanitarian operations.[191]

The approach which they have taken towards this problem is not uniform and as a result two major strands can be distinguished. They can conveniently be described as the "double level" and the "legal" approach.

The proponents of the "double level" approach[192] accept the "classic" view on the Charter prohibition of unilateral use of force as a necessary corollary to the attainment of what they see as the United Nations' primary goal. That is, maintenance of in-

---

any collective action of the African organization for such purposes would be forthcoming if the necessity arose.

Thapa, *Humanitarian Intervention*, 75 (1968) (unpublished thesis in McGill University Law School Library) [hereinafter cited as Thapa].

189. On this level as well, the United Nations has encountered serious difficulties in performing its task. *See, e.g.*, on relief operations in Biafra: Remarks by Beverley May Carl, in *Biafra, Bengal, and Beyond: International Responsibility and Genocidal Conflict*, 66 PROCEEDINGS AM. SOC'Y INT'L L. 89, 103 ff. (1972); Address by Senator Edward M. Kennedy, *id.*, at 90. *See generally* Gottlieb, *International Assistance to Civilian Populations in Armed Conflicts*, 4 N.Y.U.J. INT'L L. & POL. 403 (1971) [hereinafter cited as Gottlieb].

190. Even in a para-colonial situation such as Rhodesia, where the United Nations has taken certain measures, their significance in terms of effectiveness in attaining their objective is, to say the least, questionable. *See, e.g.*, Statement of Senator Harry F. Byrd Jr., in *Hearings on S.1404, U.N. Sanctions Against Rhodesia—Chrome, Before the Senate Committee on Foreign Relations*, 92d Cong., 1st Sess. (1971). *See generally* SANCTIONS AGAINST SOUTH AFRICA (R. Segal ed. 1964).

191. Jenks advocates that:

[T]he world community must recognize the need . . . for external intervention in cases not covered by the right of self-defense as so defined [in Article 51 of the Charter] in which a world interest or the conscience of mankind is involved. The world community cannot tolerate acts of savagery on the ground that its civilised members have renounced the threat and use of force in their international relations.

JENKS, A NEW WORLD OF LAW? 30 (1969) [hereinafter cited as JENKS].

192. *See generally* the debates of the Charlottesville Conference on Humanitarian Intervention and the United Nations (March 11-12, 1972), *reprinted in* HUMANITARIAN INTERVENTION AND THE UNITED NATIONS 3-135 (R. Lillich ed. 1973). *See also* Brownlie, *Thoughts on Kind-Hearted Gunmen, id.*, at 139-48 [hereinafter cited as Brownlie, *Gunmen*]; Brownlie, *Humanitarian Intervention*, in LAW AND CIVIL WAR IN THE MODERN WORLD (J. Moore ed. 1973). For a rebuttal, *see generally* Lillich, *Humanitarian Intervention: A Reply to Dr. Brownlie and a Plea for Constructive Alternatives*, LAW AND CIVIL WAR IN THE MODERN WORLD (J. Moore ed. 1973).

ternational peace and security through elimination of *all* forceful
interactions between States that are not comprised among the
legal exceptions expressly mentioned in the Charter: individual
and collective self-defense and action in pursuance of a Chapter
VII decision. They feel compelled, in view of the already demonstrated inability or unwillingness of the international organizations to cope with such dramatic situations as Biafra or Bangladesh, to acknowledge that the absolute interpretation of the Charter prohibition on use of force by States is an unworkable and
unacceptable restriction upon last resort unilateral action in case
of extreme violation of the most fundamental human rights. Nevertheless, they are not prepared to depart from their allegiance to
their basic force-minimalization position and to consider an
eventually revived customary doctrine of humanitarian intervention which would fully legalize this kind of action as an additional
exception not explicitly provided for in the Charter. On the
other hand, they point to the lack of *formal* condemnation or
criticism *on principle* in the United Nations and in other international fora in such cases as the Stanleyville operation or the Indian
intervention in Bangladesh. From this they conclude that, in circumstances of extreme gravity, the world community, by its lack of
adverse reaction, *in practice* condones conduct which, although a
formal breach of positive legal norms, appears "acceptable" because of higher motives of a moral, political, humanitarian, or other
nature.[193] This lack of express condemnation in specific cases,
they submit, would in fact confer to such actions the character of
some kind of second-tier or sub-legality.[194]

Insofar as this approach purports to give an accurate description of the *lex lata* and its application,[195] not much can be raised

---

193. *See* Franck, in HUMANITARIAN INTERVENTION AND THE UNITED NATIONS
64 (R. Lillich ed. 1973); Frey-Wouters, *id.*, at 107-08; Friedmann, *id.*, at 114;
Wright, *The Legality of Intervention Under the United Nations Charter*, 51 PRO-
CEEDINGS AM. SOC'Y INT'L L. 77, 81 (1957); Remarks by Louis Henkin, *supra*
note 149, at 96.

194. *See* Lillich, in HUMANITARIAN INTERVENTION AND THE UNITED NATIONS
61-62 & 118 (R. Lillich ed. 1973); Falk, *id.*, at 68-69. *Compare*, on the subject
of reprisals which raises similar, if not stronger, problems of justification under
the U.N Charter: Falk, *The Beirut Raid and the International Law of Retaliation*, 63 AM. J. INT'L L. 415, 430 n.39 (1969); Bowett, *Reprisals Involving Recourse to Armed Force*, 66 AM. J. INT'L L. 1, 10-11 & 26 (1972).

195. *See, e.g.*, on the absence of formal condemnation of India in the Bangladesh context: Nanda, in HUMANITARIAN INTERVENTION AND THE UNITED NA-
TIONS 99 (R. Lillich ed. 1973). Among the numerous draft proposals submitted
between 1962 and 1970 by Member States of the United Nations on the question

The Use of Force in International Law

against it. When, however, its proponents condone it, so to say *de lege ferenda*, as the most suitable system for attaining a fair balance between the seemingly contradictory goals of protection of human rights in extreme cases and maintenance of a peaceful world order,[196] this author cannot agree.

The main arguments which have been advanced in support of this approach comprise:[197] fear of abusive invocation of a fully legalized doctrine of humanitarian intervention; practical restraints upon the conduct of States due to the necessity of, at least "technical" breach of the law; clarity and simplicity of the general rule of total prohibition of armed intervention, coupled with the fear that recognition of an exception for humanitarian motives might "erode the psychological constraints of the use of force for other purposes;"[198] and, concordance with the present

of further articulating Charter norms on the prohibition of force, both in the 6th Committee and in the Special Committee on Principles of International Law Concerning Friendly Relations and Co-operation Among States, none explicitly provided for any exceptions not specifically envisaged by the Charter. Only one such draft, submitted by the United Kingdom, specified in its written commentary that its paragraph 5, embodying the two Charter exceptions (article 51 and Chapter VII) in a broad interpretation, was intended to "set . . . out *in a non exhaustive manner* the principal circumstances in which the use of force is lawful." Commentary, United Kingdom Proposal, 19 U.N. GAOR, Sp. Comm. on Fr. Rel., U.N. Doc. A/A.C.119/L.8, at 4 (1964) (emphasis added).

196. *Compare*, Prof. Moore's distinction between the respective intellectual tasks of description of what the law *is* and recommendation as to what it *ought* to be. Moore, in HUMANITARIAN INTERVENTION AND THE UNITED NATIONS 120-21 (R. Lillich ed. 1973).

197. *See generally* Farer, *Humanitarian Intervention—The View from Charlottseville*, in HUMANITARIAN INTERVENTION AND THE UNITED NATIONS 149, 152 & 155-57 (R. Lillich ed. 1973) [hereinafter cited as Farer, *Humanitarian Intervention*]; Brownlie, *Gunmen, supra* note 192, at 147-48; Franck, in HUMANITARIAN INTERVENTION AND THE UNITED NATIONS 14, 64 & 89 (R. Lillich ed. 1973); Falk, *id.*, at 33; Frey-Wouters, *id.*, at 107-08; FALK, *supra* note 185, at 161; Gottlieb, *supra* note 189, at 415 & n.48.

198. Farer, *Humanitarian Intervention, supra* note 197, at 152. Another argument sometimes advanced is the likelihood of humanitarian intervention actually causing more harm than benefits to the people it is intended to assist. Franck, for instance, observes that:

> [T]here is a strong indication that more people died in Bangladesh during the two or three weeks when the Indian Army was liberating the country than had been killed previously.

Franck, in HUMANITARIAN INTERVENTION AND THE UNITED NATIONS 65 (R. Lillich ed. 1973). *See also* Farer, *Humanitarian Intervention, supra* note 197, at 152. Finally, it has been argued that a flat prohibition of humanitarian intervention might have the beneficial effect of inducing States to resort to (non-coercive) measures at an earlier stage so as to prevent the situation from deteriorating and reaching such proportions that armed intervention becomes the only effective remedy left. Franck, in HUMANITARIAN INTERVENTION AND THE UNITED NATIONS 104-05 (R. Lillich ed. 1973). *Contra*, Lillich, in *id.*, at 109.

state of the law.

So far as the fear of abuse is concerned, this author must confess that he is unable to see how a "double level" theory, recognizing the permissibility of certain illegalities, would in any respect reduce the opportunities for abusive utilization. It seems likely that a clearly stated rule, restricting by a set of precise criteria the lawfulness of humanitarian intervention to certain well-defind, specific situations, would provide a far stronger incentive for a State to refrain from intervening in a situation or in a manner falling short of the requirements set forth for its legality. This would be much more effective than would a system in which the prospective intervenor knows that, regardless of his motives, he breaches the law, but can hope that the world community will remain silent as a result of apathy or political division, and thus implicitly condone his intervention, however selfish its purposes may have been.[199]

Such a situation would certainly enhance neither clarity nor predictability. An absolute prohibition undermined by creeping exceptions puritanically called "acceptable breaches" seems hardly more straightforward in application than a rule which openly recognizes some limited and strictly defined exceptions, by permitting appraisal and eventual characterization of the conduct of an intervenor as unlawful.

In addition, "[i]t would indeed be wrong to unnecessarily brand conduct unlawful which is morally justified."[200] This could

---

199. Significant is Prof. Franck's rationale for opposing legal recognition of humanitarian intervention:

> [A]s a lawyer I would prefer to advise politicians contemplating such intervention to look to political rather than legal justifications and mitigation. Political leaders who are contemplating unilateral military intervention should not be encouraged to believe that international law is firmly on their side. It is not. At best, it is unclear. *They could still take their chances on a cogent political justification being accepted as genuine by the international community.*

Franck in HUMANITARIAN INTERVENTION AND THE UNITED NATIONS 64 (R. Lillich ed. 1973) (Emphasis added).

200. Bogen, *supra* note 131, at 303. This author does not wish to go as far as Bogen who, referring to the absence of any action by the world community prior to World War II regarding the persecutions of Jews in Nazi Germany, contends that law-abiding nations could be dissuaded from intervening for humanitarian reasons in situations genuinely requiring it, by the absence of an applicable legal exception to the general rule of prohibition of the use of force, and accordingly criticizes the "absolute" interpretation of article 2(4) on that ground. *Id. Compare,* Farer, *Humanitarian Intervention, supra* note 197, at 160 *and* Franck, in HUMANITARIAN INTERVENTION IN THE UNITED NATIONS 89 (R. Lillich ed. 1973).

only encourage States to run the risk, break the law, invoke some vague, plausible higher motive, and hope that the world community will fail to censor their conduct. In the long run such a situation must inevitably lead to an increasing authority deflation of international law in general, and of the Charter in particular.[201] If States can "acceptably" break the law for humanitarian reasons, why should it not be equally tolerable to violate it for other, perhaps morally less commendable motives as well?

Thus it seems that the only real advantage of the "double level" approach is its complete correspondence with the present state of the law, integrating at the same time the strict *theoretical* prohibition of unilateral use of force for any reason not amounting to self-defense, and the *practice* of non-condemnation of at least some types of "technical" violations of this norm. In view of the various disadvantages this theory entails, it might be advisable in assessing what the law *ought* to be, to frame the recommended rule in such a way as to attach the label of lawfulness to what is deemed acceptable.[202]

In view of the highly improbable character of a Charter revision expressly integrating unilateral use of force for humanitarian purposes as an additional exception to the general prohibition of use of force by States, those scholars who want the *legality* of past and future instances of humanitarian operations recognized, have tried to find bases in the Charter, as it presently stands, to support their contention.

The Thomases, in rather cautious terms, conclude that:

> In spite of a recognition of a right of humanitarian intervention by customary international law, strict principles of modern multilateral treaty law *may* have completely abolished the right . . . .[203]

Nevertheless, in connection with article 51 of the Charter, they contend that:

---

201. *See* Prof. Falk's description of this approach as "advocating civil disobedience on an international level." Falk, in HUMANITARIAN INTERVENTION AND THE UNITED NATIONS 108 (R. Lillich ed. 1973). *See also* the euthanasia and marijuana laws parallels referred to by Prof. Lillich in HUMANITARIAN INTERVENTION AND THE UNITED NATIONS 62, 117 & 118 (R. Lillich ed. 1973) *and* Dr. Brownlie, in Brownlie, *Gunmen, supra* note 192, at 146.

202. *Compare,* Farer, *Humanitarian Intervention, supra* note 197, at 160; Baxter, in HUMANITARIAN INTERVENTION AND THE UNITED NATIONS 54 (R. Lillich ed. 1973); Almond, *id.,* at 133 & 134.

203. THOMAS & THOMAS, *supra* note 7, at 20 (emphasis added).

A plea can be made that where it is legal to intervene to protect one's own nationals, it is an extension of this legality to protect the nationals of others. The so-called principle of nationality is not inflexible . . . [204]

They seemingly endorse the often invoked argument that self-help to protect one's own nationals can be deemed included in the "inherent" right of self-defense retained by article 51,[205] and go on to extend this permissibility through an "ancillarity-like" rationale to cover situations in which the nationality link is missing.[206]

Attractive though this reasoning might be, particularly in those cases where a State, intervening to rescue some of its own nationals, avails itself of the opportunity to save other foreigners as well,[207] this author has serious reservations regarding this approach. For one thing, it is by no means certain that even protection of nationals can properly be taken to fall within the purview of self-defense as defined in article 51.[208] Secondly, from a pol-

---

204. *Id.*

205. *See, e.g.*, BOWETT, *supra* note 7, at 91-105; D. GREIG, INTERNATIONAL LAW 673 (1970) [hereinafter cited as GREIG]; STONE, *supra* note 151, at 94-97; A. THOMAS & A. THOMAS, THE ORGANIZATION OF AMERICAN STATES 162 (1963); Fenwick, *International Law, supra* note 131, at 27; Fenwick, *Dominican Republic, supra* note 131, at 64. *See also* Report of the 6th Comm., 18 U.N. GAOR, Annexes, Agenda Item 71, U.N. Doc. A/5671, at 34, para. 61 (1963). This rationale has also been relied upon by the United Kingdom in support of its intervention in the 1956 Suez crisis. *See, e.g.*, Statement of Prime Minister Eden in the British House of Commons, *cited in* Fawcett, *Intervention in International Law* (Hague Academy of International Law), 103 RECUEIL DES COURS 347, 400 (1961).

206. *Compare, Responsibility of States for Damage Done in their Territories to the Person or Property of Foreigners,* Report of the League of Nations Committee of Experts for the Progressive Codification of International Law, Sub-Commitee on State Responsibility, 20 AM. J. INT'L L. 177, 182 (Spec. Supp. 1926), *cited in* THOMAS & THOMAS, *supra* note 7, at 20.

207. Particularly when the State whose nationals have been rescued by the intervenor supports or condones the latter's actions, very little can be asserted against the legality of this type of "simultaneous rescue" operation, provided the intervention of the acting State for the protection of its own nationals and is deemed legal in the first place. The operation might then be considered to have been carried out on behalf of all the States involved, and therefore within the scope of *collective* self-defense. *Compare*, statements cited in note 211 *infra*.

208. "The extent to which the right to self-defense includes a right of protection over nationals abroad . . . has been, and in a lesser degree remains, the subject of acute controversy." JENKS, *supra* note 191, at 30. *See also* BROWNLIE, *supra* note 17, at 429 ff. The terms of article 51, taken literally, require (1) an armed attack (2) directed against the State. This seems to make it rather difficult to "equate protection of nationals abroad with the preservation of the state itself." Lillich, *Self-Help, supra* note 7, at 336. On the other hand, the

The Use of Force in International Law

icy perspective, the inclusion of self-help to protect nationals abroad in the right of self-defense of the State itself, does raise some serious questions.   To the extent that this broad view of self-defense emphasizes the functional character of the State[209] as an institution whose goals and interests only acquire a real content through their relationship with the interests and security of its constituting elements, namely man, this author agrees.   The real danger of equating self-help to protect individuals abroad with self-defense of the State as a whole, however, lies in its potential to incite States to disregard any notion of proportionality and to resort to force as soon as even a very small group of their nationals is endangered.   Likewise, where the size of the threatened group would genuinely justify drastic measures of protection, to use an amount of force unrelated to the extent of the actual hardship to be prevented.[210]   And thirdly, this rationale seems hardly applicable to those situations in which the violations reach the most dramatic proportions, namely where the victims are nationals of the State committing the violations.   Foreign intervention will then by and large have to take place contrary to the wishers of that State's gov-

---

qualification of the term self-defense as an *"inherent right"* could be taken to indicate that article 51 merely restates the *customary* right to self-defense, which traditionally did include self-help in situations not amounting to an armed attack upon the State.   This is illustrated by the now classic formulation of self-help by Webster in relation to the incident of the steamer Caroline in 1837: "[A] necessity of *self-defense*, instant, overwhelming, leaving no choice of means and no moment for deliberation."   U.S. Secretary of State Webster, *cited in* Nanda, *supra* note 131, at 48 (emphasis added).   Some support for a broader interpretation of article 51 beyond the plain meaning of its terms can also be found in the I.C.J.'s qualified acceptance of the legality of the initial measures taken by the United Kingdom in the Corfu Channel incident.   Corfu Channel Case, [1949] I.C.J. 4, 30.   *Compare*, McDougal, *Authority to Use Force on the High Seas*, 20 NAVAL WAR COLLEGE REV. 19, 28-29, *cited in* Lillich, *Intervention, supra* note 7, at 217 n.58:

> I'm ashamed to confess that at one time I lent my support to the suggestion that article 2(4) and the related articles did preclude the use of self-help less than self-defense.   On reflection, I think that . . . article 2(4) and article 51 must be interpreted differently . . . .   In the absence of collective machinery to protect against attack and deprivation, I would suggest that the principle of major purposes requires an interpretation which would honor self-help against prior unlawfulness.

See generally BRIERLY, *supra* note 7, at 416 ff.; L. GOODRICH & E. HAMBRO, CHARTER OF THE UNITED NATIONS: COMMENTARY AND DOCUMENTS 229 nn. (1949); H. KELSEN, THE LAW OF THE UNITED NATIONS 791 (1950); STONE, *supra* note 151, at 98 ff.   For statements by national representatives in the United Nations, rejecting a broad interpretation of article 51, *see* Fonteyne, *supra* note 146, at 217 & nn.79-81.

209. *Compare*, notes 95-96 *supra* and accompanying text.
210. *Compare*, Lillich, *Self-Help, supra* note 7, at 337 & n.77.

ernment, thus eliminating any possibility of rational invocation of *collective* self-defense, however broadly one stretches the concept.[211] Unlike in a protection-of-nationals case, the absence of any transnational connection other than general international concern with human rights, excludes characterization of such cases as even minimally threatening, directly or indirectly, the intervening State's interests or security. Unless one transposes to the inter-State level the encouraging but somewhat artificial threat to the peace rationale utilized by the United Nations to justify mandatory sanctions against Rhodesia,[212] it appears extremely difficult to vindicate resort to measures of *self*-help in this context.

The more commonly taken approach combines three main arguments: restrictive interpretation of the article 2(4) prohibition; balancing out of the Charter's major purposes; and limited invocation of the non-realization of the basic expectations of the Members of the United Nations when they renounced their right under customary international law to use force unilaterally.[213]

Article 2(4) of the Charter, it is argued, should be interpreted in accordance with its plain language, so as to prohibit the threat or use of force *only when directed at the territorial integrity or political independence* of a State.[214] Taken in con-

---

211. *Compare,* statements by national representatives in the United Nations, justifying assistance to *colonial* peoples on the basis of an extended collective self-defense rationale, in Fonteyne, *supra* note 146, at 213-14, nn.67-69. *See also id.,* at 214 n.70. *See generally* Payne, *Sub-Saharan Africa: The Right of Intervention in the Name of Humanity,* 2 GA. J. INT'L & COMP. L. 77 (1972).

212. The Security Council, in declaring the Rhodesian situation to constitute a threat to the peace, recognized that deprivations of human rights and of the right to self-determination *on the internal level,* could threaten *international peace and security. These could trigger forceful reactions of neighboring or* other States. *See generally* Fenwick, *When Is There a Threat to the Peace?— Rhodesia,* 61 AM. J. INT'L L. 753 (1967); Franck, *Policy Paper on the Legality of Mandatory Sanctions by the United Nations Against Rhodesia,* CENTER FOR INT'L STUDIES, PUB. No. 1 (1968); McDougal & Reisman, *supra* note 169; Robinowitz, *U.N. Application of Selective Mandatory Sanctions Against Rhodesia: A Brief Legal and Political Analysis,* 7 VA. J. INT'L L. 147 (1967). *Contra,* Acheson, *supra* note 169.

213. *See* THOMAS & THOMAS, *supra* note 7, at 16; Lillich, *Self-Help, supra* note 7, at 334 ff.; Lillich, *Forcible Self-Help under International Law,* 22 NAVAL WAR COLLEGE REV. 56 (1970) [hereinafter cited as Lillich, *Forcible Self-Help*]; Lillich, *Intervention, supra* note 7, at 210 ff.; McDougal & Reisman, *supra* note 7; Perez-Vera, *supra* note 139; Reisman, *supra* note 4; Thapa, *supra* note 188. This author has attempted to integrate in one theory various arguments advanced by the above scholars. This does not mean, however, that each of them explicitly articulates the whole range of arguments in this article, or would necessarily agree with every contention made in the following exposition.

214. "A close reading of [article 2(4)] will indicate that the prohibition

nection with article 51, this would mean that these two provisions are not necessarily complementary, in that situations might arise in which armed force is utilized unilaterally neither against the political independence of territorial integrity of any State, nor in the exercise of the inherent right or individual or collective self-defense. Specifically, "[s]ince a humanitarian intervention seeks neither a territorial change nor a challenge to the political independence of the State involved,"[215] and particularly in view of the closing words of article 2(4) referring to the purposes of the Charter, this specific modality of the use of force is "not only not inconsistent with the purposes of the United Nations but is rather in conformity with the most fundamental peremptory norms of the Charter."[216]

This position does not overlook the various policy problems raised by this interpretation of article 2(4), one of the major ones being that this approach would necessitate a case by case appraisal of the alleged motivation and purposes of any action claimed to fall under the exception. This would not of course simplify the norm or its application in practice.[217]

---

is not against the use of coercion per se, but rather the use of force for specified unlawful purposes. . . ." Reisman, *supra* note 4, at 177. *Compare*, statements by national representatives in the United Nations, in Fonteyne, *supra* note 146, at 214 & n.71.

215. Reisman, *supra* note 4, at 177. *See also* Lillich, *Self-Help, supra* note 7, at 336; Lillich, *supra* note 213, at 63; Perez-Vera, *supra* note 139, at 415.

216. Reisman, *supra* note 4, at 177. He concludes: "[I]t is a distortion to argue that [humanitarian intervention] is precluded by article 2(4)." *Id. See also* Perez-Vera, *supra* note 139, at 415. Lillich argues that "[c]ertainly, if a construction of the Charter, namely article 2(4), will further human rights, it is a proper construction." Lillich, *supra* note 213, at 63. *Compare*, Claude, in HUMANITARIAN INTERVENTION AND THE UNITED NATIONS 42 (R. Lillich ed. 1973); statements by national representatives in the United Nations, in Fonteyne, *supra* note 146, at 215 & n.73. *Contra*, statements in the United Nations, *id.*, at 215-16, nn. 74-76; JENKS, *supra* note 191, at 29; GREIG, *supra* note 205, at 668. *See also* note 179 *supra* and accompanying text. The same apparent contradiction of purposes can be found in recent restatements of the nonintervention principle by the U.N. General Assembly, such as the Declaration on the Inadmissibility of Intervention in the Domestic Affairs of States and the Protection of their Independence and Sovereignty, G.A. Res. 2131 (XX), 20 U.N. GAOR, Supp. 14, U.N. Doc. A/6014, at 11 (1965), and the Declaration on Principles of International Law Concerning Friendly Relations and Co-opertaion Among States, G.A. Res. 265 (XXV), 25 U.N. GAOR, Supp. 28, U.N. Doc. A/8028, at 121 (1970). *See generally* Note, *A Proposed Resolution Providing for the Authorization of Intervention by the United Nations, a Regional Organization, or a Group of States in a State Committing Gross Violations of Human Rights*, 13 VA. J. INT'L L. 340, 342 (1973) [hereinafter cited as *Proposed Resolution*].

217. For statements by national representatives in the United Nations, *see*

From the standpoint of text interpretation as well, the argument can be criticized, for this approach takes the words "against the territorial integrity or political independence of any State" to refer to the *motives and goals* of the State resorting to force. Article 2(4), on the other hand, does not indicate that it relates to the intentions of the parties.[218] In fact, even in those limited cases of rescue of foreigners, where it is possible for the intervenor to pull out very quickly without really affecting the internal authority structures of the State intervened in, armed intervention will still inevitably constitute a temporary violation *de facto* of the latter's territorial integrity and, to a certain extent, of its political independence, if carried out against its wishes. In most instances of humanitarian intervention on behalf of peoples deprived of their most fundamental human rights by or with the approval of their own government, the infringement upon the State's territorial integrity and political independence will be far more serious. Achievement of a lasting solution in such cases will usually require a change of government or even a secession, so that the foreign intervention will have had to fundamentally influence the domestic political process and organization of the State intervened in.

Considering article 2(4) in the broader perspective of the major purposes of the Charter,[219] and specifically in view of the closing words of paragraph 4,[220] there is clearly a need for balancing the sometimes opposite goals of conflict-minimalization and protection of human rights.[221] Espousing Professor Lillich's view

---

Fonteyne, *supra* note 146, at 209-11 & nn.54-58. On the other hand, an appraisal of these and other subjective elements is already needed with the present "classic" approach towards the Charter prohibition of force. The validity of a claim that a certain conduct falls under the article 51 exception of self-defense cannot meaningfully be assessed by applying merely mechanical tests. *See, e.g.,* Statement by Mr. Chaumont (France), 25 U.N. GAOR, Spec. Comm. on Aggression, U.N. Doc. A/A.C.134/S.R.57, at 36 (1970). However, the traditional Soviet "chronological" approach towards the determination of acts of aggression could be adopted. *See, e.g.,* Draft U.S.S.R. Resolution, 9 U.N. GAOR, Annexes, U.N. Doc. A/C.6/L.332/Rev.1, at 6-7 (1954).

218. Jenks notes that:

The reference to 'territorial integrity or political independence' can be so construed as to introduce an element of ambiguity into the obligation [to refrain from the threat or use of force] but not reasonably so as to substitute a subjective test of intention for the objective test of the nature and effect of the action taken.

JENKS, *supra* note 191, at 28-29.

219. *See* U.N. CHARTER, Preamble, paras. 1 & 2, and art. 1, paras. 1 & 3.

220. *But see* authorities in notes 179 and 216 *supra*.

221. Reisman, however, advocates that:

The preamble and critical first Article of the Charter, framed in the awful shadow of the atrocities of the war, left no doubt as to the inti-

that "a prohibition of violence is not an absolute virtue"[222] and that "it has to be weighed against other values as well,"[223] Professors McDougal and Reisman contend that:

> The continuing authority of community expectations about the lawfulness of humanitarian intervention is greatly confirmed by all the contemporary developments associated with the United Nations. The repeated, insistent emphasis upon its underlying policies can only be regarded as strengthening, not weakening, the historic remedy.[224]

Referring in particular to articles 55[225] and 56[226] of the Charter, which they interpret as transforming the general commitment of U.N. Members to human rights into "an active obligation for joint and separate action,"[227] they submit that:

> [T]he cumulative effect of the Charter in regard to the basic policies of the customary institution of humanitarian intervention is to create a coordinate responsibility for the active protection of human rights: members may act jointly with the Organization in what might be termed a new organized, explicitly conventional humanitarian intervention or singly or collectively in the customary or international common law humanitarian intervention. Any other interpretation would be suicidally destructive of the explicit major purposes for which the United Nations was established.[228]

And conclude that:

> Insofar as it is precipitated by intense human rights deprivations and conforms to the general international legal regulations governing the use of force—economy, timeliness, commensurance, lawfulness of purpose, and so on—[humanitarian intervention] represents a vindication of interna-

---

mate nexus that the framers perceived to link international peace and security and the most fundamental human rights of all individuals. Reisman, *supra* note 4, at 171.

Compare authorities in note 292 *infra* and accompanying text.

222. Lillich, *Forcible Self-Help, supra* note 213, at 65.

223. *Id.*

224. McDougal & Reisman, *supra* note 7, at 442.

225. The Charter provides that: "[T]he United Nations shall promote . . . universal respect for, and observance of, human rights and fundamental freedoms for all without distinction as to race, sex, language or religion." U.N. CHARTER, art. 55.

226. "All Members pledge themselves to take *joint and separate action* in cooperation with the Organization for the achievement of the purposes set forth in Article 55." U.N. CHARTER, art. 56 (Emphasis added).

227. McDougal & Reisman, *supra* note 7, at 444.

228. *Id.*

tional law . . . [229]

Furthermore, since "[the] great expectations of the immediate postwar period have not materialized,"[230] in that the machinery for collective security and enforcement envisaged by the States ratifying the Charter has in fact not been established,[231] one might wonder whether a State would not be entitled to challenge the absolute validity of the Charter prohibition of force and fall back upon the traditional doctrine of humanitarian intervention in those exceptional cases of extreme human rights deprivations.[232]

As long as the necessity of strictly defining and limiting the circumstances in which States could rely upon this latitude is kept in mind, would it not be advisable to consider the present poten-

---

229. Reisman, *supra* note 4, at 177.

230. Lillich, *Self-Help, supra* note 7, at 335. These hopes have been cruelly deceived in that no article 43 agreements have been concluded, the Security Council is often paralyzed on important issues by the crippling and constant use of the veto, and the agenda of the General Assembly has been virtually monopolized by the "new" nations for discussion of colonial and para-colonial subjects. *Compare,* Baxter, in HUMANITARIAN INTERVENTION AND THE UNITED NATIONS 53-54 (R. Lillich ed. 1973); Lillich, *id.,* at 61.

231. Arguably, the establishment of machinery for collective security and enforcement was so basic a condition for the Members of the United Nations in surrendering their right under customary international law to use force for a variety of reasons, that failure by the Organization to create this machinery would partially relieve the Member States of their obligation of restraint under the Charter. *See, e.g.,* Statement of Mr. Shahi (Pakistan), 23 U.N. GAOR, 6th Comm., U.N. Doc. A/C.6/S.R.1080, at 9, para. 68 (1968). As Prof. Stone's views regarding the Charter prohibition of force indicate, an outright "contract-like" approach to the Charter could prove extremely hazardous in that this might totally undermine the conflict minimalization structure which, for the first time in history, has been established through the replacement of the criterion of "just war" by that of self-defense. *See generally* STONE, *supra* note 151. *Compare,* JENKS, *supra* note 191, at 30: "Injustice, subjectively determined, does not justify the threat or use of force to protect or enforce rights which the community has not yet evolved adequate means of securing." *See also* Henkin, *Force, Intervention, and Neutrality in Contemporary International Law,* 57 PROCEEDINGS AM. SOC'Y INT'L L. 147, 148-49 (1963).

232. In reference to this possibility, Thapa states that:

[A]n absolutist view, that the Charter has abolished the customary principle of humanitarian intervention, is not defensible—this principle continues to exist as an exception to all rules, whether set forth by customary or conventional international law, which bans forceful intervention for such purpose.

Thapa, *supra* note 188, at 13. Writing against the background in view of the Biafran crisis, and listing the various types of intervention permissible under the U.N. Charter, Adaramola concludes: "It seems that in extreme conditions humanitarian intervention will be justified." Adaramola, *The Nigerian Crisis and Foreign Intervention: A Focus on International Law,* 4 NIGERIAN L.J. 76, 78 (1970).

258 CALIFORNIA WESTERN INTERNATIONAL LAW JOURNAL Vol. 4

tials of the international organizations? Similarly, it seems reasonable to recognize *legally*, that in certain extreme situations, when neither the United Nations nor the competent regional organization can or wants to assume its responsibilities, a State may be temporarily relieved of its obligation of restraint under article 2(4)[233] so as to provide a form of "substitute or functional enforcement of international human rights."[234]

V. CRITERIA FOR APPRAISAL OF HUMANITARIAN INTERVENTION

Various scholars have, in recent times, formulated modernized criteria for appriasal of the legality of alleged cases of humanitarian intervention.[235] While overlapping on a large number of points, the proposed norms, nevertheless, show some significant variations. This author will attempt to reconcile and supplement them in three major groups: substantive, procedural, and preferential criteria.

A. Substantive Criteria

1. Characteristics of the Situation Warranting Humanitarian Intervention: limitation to ongoing or imminent large-scale deprivations of the most fundamental human rights.[236]

a) Fundamental character of the human rights involved: Without going as far as Professor Perez-Vera who considers only the right to life sufficiently essential to warrant a departure by a State from the principle of prohibition to force,[237] this author believes that a balance must be struck between the amount of destruc-

---

233. As early as 1949 Jessup envisaged this possibility:

It would seem that the only possible argument against the substitution of collective measures under the Security Council for individual measures by a single state would be the inability of the international organization to act with the speed requisite to preserve life.

JESSUP, *supra* note 169, at 169. *But see* Brownlie, *Gunmen, supra* note 192, at 145-46.

234. Reisman, *supra* note 4, at 178.

235. *See* Lillich, *Self-Help, supra* note 7, at 347 ff.; Moore, *The Control of Foreign Intervention in Internal Conflicts*, 9 VA. J. INT'L L. 205, 263-64 (1969) [hereinafter cited as Moore]; Nanda, *supra* note 131, at 475; Perez-Vera, *supra* note 139, at 416 ff. *See generally* Reisman, *supra* note 4; Thapa, *supra* note 188. *Compare* discussion and authorities in notes 87 ff. *supra* and accompanying text.

236. Reisman generally refers to an "overriding necessity" for intervention. Reisman, *supra* note 4, at 193. *Compare*, De Schutter, *supra* note 130, at 28-29, requiring a "breach . . . of a certain qualitative and quantitative gravity." *See also Proposed Resolution, supra* note 216, at 357-61.

237. Perez-Vera, *supra* note 139, at 418.

tion which almost inevitably will be caused by armed intervention, and the importance of the human rights sought to be protected. This weighing process tends to result in a restriction, in principle, of the permissibility of humanitarian intervention to those situations where there is a threat to, or deprivation of the *most fundamental* types of human rights, such as the right to life or the freedom from torture.[238]

b) Exceptionally large scale of the human rights deprivations: To the extent that unilateral resort to force for humanitarian motives is to be considered "an *exceptional* measure, available as a last resort to prevent irreparable injury,"[239] armed intervention should only be permissible "when a substantial deprivation of human values"[240] is involved. While "[j]ust counting heads . . . is not sufficient for decision-making purposes,"[241] the number of people affected by the human rights violations is not completely irrelevant. There ought to be a reverse correlation between the latter and the seriousness of the violated human rights:[242] the larger the number of people involved, the more readily will a deprivation of a lesser fundamental human right provide sufficient justification for intervening.

Analyzing each specific case in a cost-benefit fashion, it would be necessary, "using the principles of relativity and proportionality as guidelines,"[243] to balance the destruction intervention would cause and the size of the group affected by the violations, as well as the fundamental character of the threatened human rights. Additionally, the degree of potential persistency of

---

238. Moore requires a threat "to fundamental human rights, *particularly* a threat of widespread loss of human life." Moore, *supra* note 235, at 264 (emphasis added). *See also* Moore, in HUMANITARIAN INTERVENTION AND THE UNITED NATIONS 49 (R. Lillich ed. 1973); Lillich, *Self-Help*, *supra* note 7, at 348.

239. BOWETT, *supra* note 7, at 98 (emphasis added).

240. Lillich, *Self-Help*, *supra* note 7, at 348. Perez-Vera limits it to "des crimes spécialement révoltants, d'une cruauté extrême . . . ou bien des massacres de nature à blesser la conscience de l'humanité." Perez-Vera, *supra* note 139, at 418. Thapa refers to "a substantial threat to a large number of persons. . . ." Thapa, *supra* note 188, at 67. Reisman requires "a grave threat to minimum human rights." Reisman, *supra* note 4, at 187. *See also* Moore, *supra* note 235, at 264.

241. Lillich, *Self-Help*, *supra* note 7, at 348.

242. "[I]t is necessary to examine the type as well as the extent of human rights deprivation . . . ." *Id. See also* Claydon, in HUMANITARIAN INTERVENTION AND THE UNITED NATIONS 91-93 (R. Lillich ed. 1973).

243. Lillich, *Self-Help*, *supra* note 7, at 348.

The Use of Force in International Law

the situation and the chances of independent internal solution of the problem should be taken into consideration.[244]

c) Immediacy of the human rights violations: Being an extraordinary measure of last resort, humanitarian intervention would be justified only when "the substantial deprivation . . . has occurred or is threatened."[245] However, a problem of perception and appraisal arises. While the seriousness of the situation can by and large be assessed once the deprivations are taking place, whether a threatened violation actually turns into physical violence must necessarily remain a matter for speculation. This is particularly applicable if this potential development is in fact prevented by a foreign intervention allegedly justified by this danger.

However, since:

> [T]he main basis of humanitarian intervention is the protection of humanity, there cannot be a principle forcing the intervening party to wait until the destructive act has been committed. Such intervention being preventive rather than punitive, the existence of the *imminent danger* is sufficient.
> . . .[246]

It would be illogical and inconsistent with the purpose of the intervention to require "a state . . . [to] wait for an actual violation to occur before taking preventive action."[247] The test must be one of reasonableness: a good faith determination by the prospective intervenor that human rights violations are *in fact* imminently threatening, on the brink of evolving into actual mass deprivation.[248]

---

244. This might constitute an exceedingly difficult criterion to apply due to its highly contingent and subjective character. Nevertheless, this author submits that even in an extreme case of violation of the most fundamental human rights of a large group of people (such as in the case of an organized policy of genocide carried out by the local authorites), foreign intervention of a forceful nature would probably not be warranted if there is a reasonable prospect that the deprivations will end in the immediate future as a result of internal political or other processes. The preservation of values to be achieved by intervention must be weighed against the extent of the disruption of internal structures and domestic processes which will necessarily result from the foreign action. In such a case, this author would certainly oppose anything beyond preservation measures merely intended to allow the domestic process of resolution of the crisis to operate without the hardship and cost in human values it might otherwise have been accompanied with.

245. Lillich, *Self-Help, supra* note 7, at 348. *Compare,* Moore's reference to "[a]n *immediate* and extensive threat. . . ." Moore, *supra* note 235, at 264 (emphasis added).

246. Thapa, *supra* note 188, at 40 (emphasis added).

247. Lillich, *Self-Help, supra* note 7, at 348.

248. *Compare, Proposed Resolution, supra* note 216, at 361-62. Perez-Vera

2. *Characteristics Relating to the Motivation of the Intervening State: "relative" disinterestedness*—As one writer observes:

> The States are not generally responsive to the call of humanity at the risk of incurring blame for intervention, unless they are also motivated by other and more selfish considerations.[249]

Disinterest is indeed "a highly altruistic principle [and] as such . . . practicable only for individuals but not to an entity like a state."[250] If an opportunity is to be maintained for States to intervene in human rights situations without breaking the law, it seems surely "naive,"[251] to use Professor Lillich's terms, and unrealistic to require that "where the decision to intervene falls to a single state, it should be safeguarded by a requirement that the state be totally disinterested."[252] The presence, among the reasons of the intervenor, of some considerations of national interest should not be taken to necessarily "invalidate the resort to [force] if the overriding motive is the protection of human rights."[253]

---

further requires that the violation of human rights be "imputable à la puissance publique elle-même," and this "aussi bien par une action que par une omission." Perez-Vera, *supra* note 139, at 418. This author is compelled to disagree with this criterion, undoubtedly inspired by the traditional principles of State responsibility for injury to aliens, applied by analogy. It disregards the essentially *remedial* character of humanitarian intervention and introduces the notions of guilt regarding the State intervened in and of a right of punishment on the part of the intervening State. From a pragmatic point of view, it would seem to put an undue limitation on the protection of human rights by foreign intervention in situations where the deprivations are the result of, for instance, persistent public unrest which the local authorities are unable, not unwilling, to control, or of violence exerted by a portion of the population in rebellion against the *de jure* government. *Compare*, De Schutter, *supra* note 130, at 29. *See also* Farer, in HUMANITARIAN INTERVENTION AND THE UNITED NATIONS 66 (R. Lillich ed. 1973), referring to a possible distinction "between the case where the threat [to human rights] is the consequence of governmental action and the case where it is the result of a breakdown in government."

249. Thapa, *supra* note 188, at 14-15. *See also id.*, at 86-87. *Compare*, authorities in note 128 *supra* and accompanying text.

250. Thapa, *supra* note 188, at 83. *Compare*, Moore, in HUMANITARIAN INTERVENTION AND THE UNITED NATIONS, at 30 & 70 (R. Lillich ed. 1973).

251. Lillich, *Self-Help, supra* note 7, at 350.

252. Bogen, *supra* note 131, at 311. *See also* Perez-Vera, *supra* note 139, at 416.

253. Lillich, *Self-Help, supra* note 7, at 350. Thapa rejejcts the current relevance of the requirement of absolute disinterestedness, as included in the traditional doctrine of humanitarian intervention, on the basis that this criterion has

> [N]ot been able to play a convincing role. The [reason] mainly being that . . . the U.N., as a proper agency (having assimilated . . . [this

3. *Characteristics of the Intervention Itself.*

a) No unnecessary force:[254]   This criterion is in fact an application of the general principles of necessity and proportionality,[255] and has a double aspect.   For one thing, the intervening State should not only utilize the *modality* of coercion required for the achievement of the humanitarian objectives it seeks to attain.[256]   If it then appears that recourse to armed force is unavoidable, the intervenor should "employ only *the amount of troops reasonably necessary* to accomplish the objective,"[257] so as to reduce to a minimum the infringement upon the territorial integrity and political independence of the State intervened in.

b) No unnecessary affectation of the authority structures of the State intervened in: Closely related to the requirement of disinterestedness of the intervenor,[258] this criterion is again an application of the general principles referred to in the preceding paragraph.   To the extent that it does not flatly prohibit *any* intentional impact upon the domestic political processes, it clearly

---

condition] in its constitution) of intervention for the sake of humanity, has proven, at present, to be incapable of intervening as efficiently as the States are able to.
Thapa, *supra* note 188, at 14. *See also Proposed Resolution, supra* note 216, at 365-66. *Contra,* Gottlieb, *supra* note 189, at 416, requiring that "[g]enuine humanitarian intervention . . . must be . . . kept free from political objectives."

254. *See* Lillich, *Self-Help, supra* note 7, at 349-50; Moore, *supra* note 235, at 264; Nanda, *supra* note 131, at 475; Perez-Vera, *supra* note 139, at 420-21; Reisman, *supra* note 4, at 177; *Proposed Resolution, supra* note 216, at 367-68. *See also* Nanda, in HUMANITARIAN INTERVENTION AND THE UNITED NATIONS 78 (R. Lillich ed. 1973).

255. Nanda, *supra* note 131, at 478. *Compare,* Reisman, *supra* note 4, at 193, requiring "compliance with the international law of the use of force."

256. *Compare* authorities in notes 264 ff. *infra* and accompanying text.

257. Lillich, *Self-Help, supra* note 7, at 349-50 (emphasis added). This criterion is particularly important, both for the appraisal *a posteriori* of the legality of an actual intervention and for purposes of decision-making. In determining whether to intervene for the protection of human rights in another State, governments should take into consideration the amount of force which the safe achievement of this objective is likely to require, and balance out the inevitable destruction this will cause against the value of the objective to be attained by it. *Compare* Moore, *supra* note 235, at 264, referring to "a proportional use of force which does not threaten greater destruction of values than the human rights at stake." On the different aspects of the proportionality principle in this context, *see generally* the exchange between Profs. Franck, Weston, Nanda and Cardozo (Moderator), in HUMANITARIAN INTERVENTION AND THE UNITED NATIONS 8-9 (R. Lillich ed. 1973). *See also* Moore, *id.,* at 50; Farer, *id.,* at 7.

258. *See* authorities in notes 249 ff. *supra* and accompanying text. Nanda, *supra* note 131, at 475, refers broadly to a "specific limited purpose." *See also* Nanda, in HUMANITARIAN INTERVENTION AND THE UNITED NATIONS 78 (R. Lillich ed. 1973); *Proposed Resolution, supra* note 216, at 364-65.

reflects the fundamental value-choice that human rights protection justifies at least some degree of interference with the
political independence and sometimes even territorial integrity of
the State intervened in.[259]   At the same time, it purports to limit
the lawfulness of extensive alteration by the intervenor of the
internal authority structures of that State, to those situations where
overthrow of the government in power or even secession of a
part of the population appears to be the only available means
of putting an end to ongoing or threatened human rights violations of particular gravity.[260]

    c) No unnecessary duration of the operation: Based on the
same principles as the previous two criteria, the requirement of
limited duration,[261] should be considered a relative one[262] in that
removal of the intervening troops should be required only when the
objectives of the operation have been achieved[263]—provided they

---

    259. The importance of this fundamental value choice is highlighted by the
finding that "the most important abuses of human rights are those committed
by governments, and often by governments acting within their own territorial
domain." Falk, in HUMANITARIAN INTERVENTION AND THE UNITED NATIONS 27
(R. Lillich ed. 1973). In further support of this basic value choice, McDougal
and Reisman invoke the reference in article 1(2) of the Charter to "[r]espect
for the principle of equal rights and *self-determination of peoples* . . . ." (Emphasis added). This would be enhanced by necessarily authority-oriented humanitarian intervention. McDougal & Reisman, *supra* note 7, at 442. *But see*
Adamarola, *supra* note 232, at 80-81:

> It must be pointed out that the principle of self-determination has been
> accepted by the United Nations as a lever of action for the liberation
> of subject and dependent peoples of the world, and not as an instrument
> for the dismemberment or desintegration of states.

    260. *See generally* Farer, *Humanitarian Intervention, supra* note 197, at 153-
54; Franck & Rodley, *supra* note 7, at 283. *See also Proposed Resolution, supra*
note 216, at 367. *Compare*, Moore, who implicitly limiting the practical possibility of lawful humanitarian intervention to mere rescue operations of nationals
of the intervening State, or eventually of third States, clarifies his requirement
of "minimal effect on authority structures" as follows:

> If the protection of human rights requires the overthrow of authority
> structures, it would seem best to require United Nations authorization
> as a prerequisite for action. To allow unilateral action in such cases
> would be to permit all manner of self-serving claims for the overthrow
> of authority structures.

Moore, *supra* note 235, at 264. *But see* Moore, in HUMANITARIAN INTERVENTION
AND THE UNITED NATIONS 50 (R. Lillich ed. 1973). *Compare*, Remarks by
Louis Henkin, *supra* note 192, at 96.

    261. Nanda, *supra* note 131, at 475. *Compare*, Perez-Vera, *supra* note 139,
at 420.

    262. Lillich concludes merely that "[t]he longer the troops remain in an-
other country, the more their presence begins to look as [political] intervention."
Lillich, *Self-Help, supra* note 7, at 350.

    263. Moore formulates this requirement as follows: "[A] prompt disengage-
ment *consistent with the purpose of the action.*" Moore, *supra* note 235, at 264

264   CALIFORNIA WESTERN INTERNATIONAL LAW JOURNAL   Vol. 4

are at the same time lawful, realistic and necessary—or once there has been an effective take-over by the United Nations or another appropriate international organization.

B. Procedural Criteria

1. *Exhaustion of peaceful means of settlement.*[264]—In view of the United Nations' primary goal—conflict minimalization—and of the positive duty of its Members to seek a solution to international disputes by peaceful means,[265] recourse should be had in the first instance to non-coercive methods of settlement[266]—through bilateral or multilateral diplomatic contacts or resort to international organizations, including eventually non-governmental ones—unless there is clearly no time left for this type of procedures because of the imminence of the violations.

2. *Absence of any reasonable prospect of timely action by an international organization.*—Considering what Professor Sibert calls "the subsidiary character of humanitarian intervention,"[267] priority should always be given to the international organizations,[268] both universal and regional, as the best suited instruments to represent the inclusive interests of the world community. It seems indeed advisable that States should only be allowed to resort to force unilaterally for the protection of human rights,

---

(emphasis added). Lillich advances an equally relative and flexible criterion: withdrawal as soon as the mission is completed. Lillich, *Self-Help, supra* note 7, at 350. *Compare, Proposed Resolution, supra* note 216, at 366-67.

264. Nanda, *supra* note 131, at 475, refers to the "lack of any other recourse." *Compare,* Nanda, in HUMANITARIAN INTERVENTION AND THE UNITED NATIONS 78 (R. Lillich ed. 1973); Perez-Vera, *supra* note 139, at 419; Reisman, *supra* note 4, at 179. *See also* De Schutter, *supra* note 130, at 29-30, setting out a complete set of procedural steps to be taken by a prospective intervenor; *Proposed Resolution, supra* note 216, at 349-50 & 364-65.

265. U.N. CHARTER, art. 2, para. 3. *See also id.,* art. 1, para. 1, & art. 33.

266. *Compare, Proposed Resolution, supra* note 216, at 362-64.

267. 1 M. SIBERT, TRAITE DE DROIT INTERNATIONAL PUBLIC 353 (1951). *Compare* authority in note 234 *supra* and accompanying text.

268. "*Wherever practicable* any such intervention should be undertaken by or on behalf of the United Nations, or through the appropriate regional organization. . . ." JENKS, *supra* note 191, at 30 (emphasis added). *See also* Reisman, *supra* note 4, at 188; *Proposed Resolution, supra* note 216, at 357. *Compare,* Falk, in HUMANITARIAN INTERVENTION AND THE UNITED NATIONS 68-69 (R. Lillich ed. 1973); Moore, *id.,* at 99. This seems particularly advisable in situations where the solution of the human rights problem is likely to require fundamental alterations of the authority structures of the State intervened in. *See* authority in note 260 *supra. But see* De Schutter, *supra* note 130, at 31, who considers the United Nations the *only* agent likely to carry out a humanitarian intervention with sufficient guarantees of independence and disinterestedness.

where the inevitable delay, still inherent in international decision-making as a result of the present structure and composition of the United Nations and of other international organizations,[269] would prevent timely action,[270] or where it has become obvious that the likelihood of such a body taking significant measures to remedy the situation[271] has actually become illusory.[272]

    3. *Immediate full reporting and submission to the appropriate international organization.*—In order to ensure an acceptable degree of disinterest on behalf of the intervening State, and to reduce the opportunities for abusive invocation to a minimum, it is of fundamental importance that the intervenor's motives be submitted without delay to the appraisal of the regional or world community.[273] In an attempt to avoid repetition of the jurisdictional conflicts between the United Nations and regional organizations,[274] such as arose for example in the context of the 1965

---

    269. Thapa argues that:

    [T]he regional organizations such as OAS, OAU . . . , as miniature forms of collectivity, confront lesser problems than the universal collectivity of the United Nations, and could be helpful for maintaining regional peace and order. [T]he difficulty with this arrangement is that regional organizations do not cover all geographical regions of the world, and where they exist they do not fully represent the States within the region. Interblock hostilities have penetrated into the activities of these organizations; each organization is dominated by one or other rivals. Besides, the intra-regional rivalry among the members themselves poses some practical difficulties in launching a unified action.

Thapa, *supra* note 188, at 71 and 73. *Compare*, Frey-Wouters, in HUMANITARIAN INTERVENTION AND THE UNITED NATIONS 96 (R. Lillich ed. 1973). *See also* note 188 *supra*.

    270. Reisman, *supra* note 4, at 178 and 193.

    271. "Collectivity of regional or universal organizations has not, up till now, proven itself effective in taking over the task of humanitarian intervention." Thapa, *supra* note 188, at 15.

    272. Thapa concludes that:

    In absence of armed sanctions, it seems too optimistic to hope that the United Nations will ever be able to coerce the States to follow its pronouncements on human rights. As a result of the impotence of the United Nations, the only possible means of protecting the life of nationals as well as foreigners can be said to have been left in the hands of the States who have the might and means.

Id., at 68. *Compare*, Weston, in HUMANITARIAN INTERVENTION AND THE UNITED NATIONS 85-86 (R. Lillich ed. 1973).

    273. Reisman, *supra* note 4, at 188 and 193. *See also* Nanda, in HUMANITARIAN INTERVENTION AND THE UNITED NATIONS 78 (R. Lillich ed. 1973). *Compare*, Gottlieb, *supra* note 189, at 416, requiring *authorization* by "appropriate international instruments."

    274. *See generally* Moore, *The Role of Regional Arrangements in the Maintenance of World Order,* in 3 THE FUTURE OF THE INTERNATIONAL LEGAL ORDER 122 (C. Black & R. Falk eds. 1970) [hereinafter cited as Moore, *Regional Arrangements*].

intervention in the Dominican Republic, this author is inclined to limit the *obligation* of reporting and submission to the Security Council to the following five cases:

a) where no regional organization covers the area of the world where the intervention occurs, or has jurisdiction over this type of operation;

b) where the situation is not of a purely local nature, for instance where the intervenor and the subject of the intervention are not both members of the same regional organization;

c) where the regional organization, although competent, refuses to take jurisdiction over the case or fails, for whatever reason, to take a stand on the matter within reasonable time;

d) where the Security Council itself, or the General Assembly, sees fit to assume jurisdiction and requests information;

e) where any of the parties directly involved voluntarily refers the case to the Security Council or General Assembly. In all other instances, reporting and submission to the competent organs of the appropriate regional organization would be sufficient.[275]

This solution is supported by various provisions of the Charter,[276] and would have the advantage of retaining the "primary responsibility" of the Security Council in enforcement matters and situations affecting international peace and security. At the same time this would increase the chances to avoid, whenever possible, interblock rivalries by leaving the regional organizations in charge of purely local disputes, whenever the parties involved wish so and no overriding universal community interest is at stake.[277]

C. Preferential Criteria

1. Collective Action.—Even in the absence of action by the universal or regional *institutionalized* community, collective

---

275. *Compare*, Reisman, *supra* note 4, at 191-92. *Contra*, Moore, requiring "immediate full reporting to the Security Council *and* appropriate regional organizations." Moore, *supra* note 235, at 264 (Emphasis added). *See also* BROWNLIE, *supra* note 17, at 299; JENKS, *supra* note 191, at 30; *Proposed Resolution, supra* note 216, at 349-50, 352-53 & 364-65.

276. *Compare*, U.N. CHARTER, arts. 24, para. 1, 52, para. 4, 34 and 35 *with* arts. 52, paras. 1 & 3, and 53, para. 1. *See also id.*, art. 103.

277. On the potential advantages of a regional approach over a universal one, *see* Moore, in HUMANITARIAN INTERVENTION AND THE UNITED NATIONS 100 (R. Lillich ed. 1973). *See generally* Moore, *Regional Arrangements, supra* note 274.

operations should be preferred over individual measures.[278] While it is true that "intervention does not gain in legality . . . by being collective rather than individual,"[279] there is nevertheless, a presumption[280] that collective action is more likely to ensure the relative purity of intentions required from the intervenors.[281]

This criterion, however, is merely a statement of preference meaning that, before taking action, a prospective intervenor is expected to consult with other States and to attempt to obtain their support and cooperation for the intervention. The requirement of collectivity *cannot* be an absolute one,[282] for lack of widespread interest on the part of other States for the ongoing or threatened human rights deprivations should not leave the victims unprotected. Provided both the causative situation and the conduct of the intervenor meet the standard set out earlier a single State ought not, in principle, to be precluded from taking the necessary steps to remedy the offending situation.

2. Invitation by or consent of the State intervened in.— Technically, there is no intervention if the intervenor has been asked in by, or obtained the consent of, the *de jure* government of the State intervened in, provided at least the authorization or

---

278. Reisman, *supra* note 4, at 188. *See also* Weston, in HUMANITARIAN INTERVENTION AND THE UNITED NATIONS 88 (R. Lillich ed. 1973); *Proposed Resolution, supra* note 216, at 371-73. It has even been argued that the big powers should be barred from participation in humanitarian intervention so as to avoid cold war involvement and reduce the likelihood of abusive utilization of the doctrine. Franck, in HUMANITARIAN INTERVENTION AND THE UNITED NATIONS 33 (R. Lillich ed. 1973); Frey-Wouters, *id.*, at 52; Rogers, *id.*, at 71-72. It is arguable, however, that such a restriction would eliminate any possibility of humanitarian intervention to the extent that smaller nations would lack the necessary power and resources to carry out a humanitarian operation on a large scale such as might be required where the human rights deprivations cannot be remedied without fundamental alteration of the authority structures of the state intervened in.

280. *But see* Thapa, *supra* note 188, at 14, who observes: "[I]f we take a group or concert of States as a proper agency, the States even in this conjunction have never been disinterested with respect to other affairs of the State intervened." *Compare*, on collective decision-making in the United Nations: Friedmann, in HUMANITARIAN INTERVENTION AND THE UNITED NATIONS 56 (R. Lillich ed. 1973).

281. Thapa reasons that: "[B]y entrusting the power of decision to intervene to a group of States, the requirement may reduce, though not eliminate, the risk of an intervention which would primarily serve the aims of self-interest." Thapa, *supra* note 188, at 42.

282. Reisman, *supra* note 4, at 178-79 and 188. *See also* Moore, in HUMANITARIAN INTERVENTION AND THE UNITED NATIONS 49 (R. Lillich ed. 1973); Perez-Vera, *supra* note 139, at 416.

invitation is clear and unambiguous.[283]   However, the importance of this criterion should not be overrated,[284] for two reasons:

a) Every invitation cannot be considered valid.   Even express consent by an unquestionably authoritative government cannot always be retained as an automatic, fully conclusive test, since it is always possible that it was granted only under pressure.[285] Furthermore, in certain cases particularly where various factions are struggling for the power, and certainly in a clear civil strife situation with uncertain issue, the representative character of the *de jure* government may be questioned.[286]   This is even more applicable where the invitation has actually been issued by some *de facto* authority in rebellion against the "legal" government.

b) Absence of consent,

> [w]hen a considerable number of human beings . . . are in imminent danger of destruction or mulilation due to the existence of an unlawful element in the State, and especially when the alleged act has been committed deliberately by the government of the State intervened into,[287]

should not be taken to preclude the possibility of lawful humanitarian intervention, provided the other requirements of legality set out above have been fulfilled.   Indeed,

> [i]t seems certain that whether there is an express right under the terms of [a] treaty, or express consent of the State, they are simply among the evidence in support of an act of humanitarian intervention, and are not the essential prerequisite for such an act.[288]

---

283. *See, e.g.,* Brownlie, *Gunmen, supra* note 192, at 144; Lillich, *Self-Help, supra* note 7, at 349; Thapa, *supra* note 188, at 93-94. *See also* discussion and authorities in note 16 *supra.*

284. "[C]onsent of the State intervened is not the 'sine qua non' for . . . legitimacy [of humanitarian intervention] . . . ." Thapa, *supra* note 188, at 94. *See also* Lillich, *Self-Help, supra* note 7, at 349; Moore, *supra* note 235, at 264; Moore, in HUMANITARIAN INTERVENTION AND THE UNITED NATIONS 49-50 (R. Lillich ed. 1973); Nanda, *id.,* at 78; Perez-Vera, *supra* note 139, at 417; Reisman, *supra* note 4, at 187 n.88; *Proposed Resolution, supra* note 216, at 368-69.

285. *Compare,* Reisman, *supra* note 4, at 184.

286. *See* Thapa, *supra* note 188, at 100, *and* Reisman, *supra* note 4, at 184. *Compare,* Moore, *supra* note 235, at 348, who restricts the validity of an invitation by the constituted authorities to a pre-insurgency situation.

287. Thapa, *supra* note 188, at 94.

288. *Id.,* at 104. *Compare,* on treaty rights of intervention, Reisman, *supra* note 4, at 184-85.

VI.   CONCLUSION

In advocating recognition of a limited right of unilateral humanitarian intervention, this author is not unaware of the serious dangers this approach entails, particularly the risk of abusive invocation.[289] But, as an early proponent of humanitarian intervention pointed out almost a century ago: "It is a big mistake, in general, to stop short of recognition of an inherently just principle, [merely] because of the possibility of non-genuine invocation."[290]

As long as the world community appears unable or unwilling to promptly respond in a collective manner to those dramatic situations where the very nature and existence of man are threatened, individual initiatives by concerned States will have to be relied upon if a viable world is to be maintained.[291]   Even minimum world public order, as the primary goal of the present international legal system, encompasses more than the sole elimination of forceful interactions between States, and demands a certain amount of justice and respect for the human person, as explicitly referred to in the Preamble and in article 1(3) of the U.N. Charter. This implies, of course, a refusal to allot an absolute value to the mere avoidance of armed conflict as such, and a conviction that certain extreme situations justify and require a temporary departure from a non-violent world order to achieve a more permanent stabilization of the world structure.   As the Thomases put it:

---

289. De Schutter, *supra* note 130, at 26. This, coupled with the fear that in some future instance a theory permitting intervention for humanitarian purposes might be invoked against them, seems to be the main reason why so many States vehemently oppose this doctrine while at the same time, rather inconsistently, advocating the legality of assistance to *colonial* peoples. *See generally* Fonteyne, *supra* note 146, at 220 & nn.87-88.

290. Rolin-Jacquemyns, *supra* note 59, at 679. *Compare,* Fonteyne, *supra* note 146, at 220; Reisman, in HUMANITARIAN INTERVENTION AND THE UNITED NATIONS 24 (R. Lillich ed. 1973).

291. Perez-Vera notes that:

En fait, nous sommes en train d'assister à l'effacement progressif du rôle tenu par l'intervention d'humanité au sens classique, au fur et à mesure que la société internationale se développe dans le sens de sa propre organisation. . . . Mais seule la tendance est acquise; le but, c'est-à-dire la mise sur pied d'un véritable système de sécurité collective, fait encore figure d'idéal lointain; ce n'est qu'au jour de sa réalisation que l'intervention d'humanité, en tant que droit étatique, aura vecu. [E]n attendant cet ordre international nouveau, il reste indispensable de préserver-dans les limites que nous avons définies—l'intervention humanitaire. Dans l'étape de transition où nous sommes, elle apparaît comme le recours ultime là où les organisations internationales se révèlent impuissantes, et où les mécanismes conventionnels de contrôle ont échoué.

Perez-Vera, *supra* note 139, at 423-24.

270   California Western International Law Journal   Vol. 4

[T]here is deemed to exist a conflict between the defense of human rights and a consideration of international peace threatened by such intervention. Historical hindsight proves that in the long run the conflict is more apparent than real, for peace is more in danger from tyrannical contempt for human rights than from attempts to assert, through intervention, the sanctity of the human personality.[292]

---

292. Thomas & Thomas, *supra* note 132, at 374. *Compare* Lauterpacht, *supra* note 125, at 186; M. McDougal & Al., Studies in World Public Order 360-61 (1960).

[20]

Humanitarian Intervention: Legality, Justice and Legitimacy

by Terry D. Gill*

Abstract

This article explores the controversial topic of humanitarian intervention and the relationship between legal, political and ethical considerations in assessing the legality of intervention to prevent or halt major ongoing violation of human rights. The author's position recognizes the distinctness of all three sets of considerations, while at the same time stressing that ethical and political considerations should be taken into account as possible mitigating circumstances within the context of the legal assessment of humanitarian intervention.

---

*   Associate Professor of Public International Law, Utrecht University; Professor of Military Law, University of Amsterdam. This article first appeared in Dutch in the June 2001 edition of the Mɪʟɪᴛᴀɪʀ Rᴇᴄʜᴛᴇʟɪᴊᴋ Tɪᴊᴅsᴄʜʀɪғᴛ (Military Law Review). That article in turn was based on a lecture which was held on 24 November 2000 to the Military Law Association of the Netherlands in the Peace Palace. The present article was translated and slightly modified by the author in August 2004.

I. Introduction

The current humanitarian crisis in the Sudan has reawakened the discussion concerning the rights and wrongs of humanitarian intervention.[1] Some four to five years and two wars ago, this discussion was carried out intensively at the diplomatic level and in the pages of academic journals against the background of the NATO intervention in Kosovo.[2] The recurring nature of the discussion reflects not only the unfortunate reality that large scale violations of human rights form a systemic problem for which the international community has no instant solution. It also reflects the fact that humanitarian intervention is a highly complex subject which can, and to at least some extent must be approached in a way which takes account of political, ethical and legal considerations.

This is illustrated by the above-mentioned example of the intervention by NATO in Kosovo. The fact that it was carried out without a specific mandate from the UN Security Council was an important, but by no means the only consideration relating to the way the intervention was viewed and assessed by the international community. An analysis which only took account of whether or not a specific case of humanitarian intervention was carried out with a UN mandate would ignore important elements of the overall problem and would contain a large measure of artificiality.[3] On the other hand, it is impossible to ignore the legal dimension of any decision to utilize force, including in relation to humanitarian intervention, without potentially undermining the international system, risking the possibility of diplomatic isolation or friction and the loss of public support for a given military intervention. This in turn is illustrated by the example of the invasion and occupation of Iraq by the United States and a handful of its closest allies, which while not primarily based upon the doctrine of humanitarian intervention, does show the pitfalls of military intervention without a clear and generally accepted legal basis. It makes a great deal of difference whether a given military intervention has a clear legal basis, or is widely

---

1   *See e.g. "Sudan Can't Wait,"* THE ECONOMIST NEWSPAPER, 31 July–6 August 2004, pp. 32-33 and cover illustration.

2   *See inter alia* the Report issued by AMNESTY INTERNATIONAL, *Kosovo: After Tragedy Justice* (1999); Antonio Cassese, *Ex inuria ius oritur: Are We Moving Towards International Legitimization of Forcible Humanitarian Countermeasures in the World Community?*, 10 EUROPEAN JOURNAL OF INTERNATIONAL LAW 23 (1999); Christine M. Chinkin, *Kosovo: A "Good" or "Bad" War?*, 93 AMERICAN JOURNAL OF INTERNATIONAL LAW 84 (1999); Louis Henkin, *Kosovo and the Law of Humanitarian Intervention, ibidem,* at 824; PETER MALANCZUK, HUMANITARIAN INTERVENTION AND THE LEGITIMACY OF THE USE OF FORCE (1993); Bruno Simma, *NATO, the UN and the Use of Force,* 10 EUROPEAN JOURNAL OF INTERNATIONAL LAW 1 (1999); and (semi) official reports by *inter alia* the DANISH INSTITUTE OF INTERNATIONAL AFFAIRS, *Humanitarian Intervention: Legal and Political Aspects* (1999); NETHERLANDS MINISTRY OF FOREIGN AFFAIRS; Legal Advisory Committee on International Law and the Advisory Council on International Affairs (AIV)(CAVV), *Humanitarian Intervention* (April 2001), INDEPENDENT INTERNATIONAL COMMISSION ON KOSOVO: *The Kosovo Report* (2001).

3   This is completely clear from the sources referred to in the previous note. See additionally, Richard A. Falk, *Kosovo, World Order and the Future of International Law,* 93 AMERICAN JOURNAL OF INTERNATIONAL LAW 847 (1999), at 852-53.

perceived as being illegal, or perhaps is seen as falling somewhere in between these two extremes.

In order to provide an indication of the present legal status of humanitarian intervention, we will first attempt to provide a clear definition of what is meant by the term, and indicate its place within the contemporary legal framework regulating the use of force. This will be followed by a short historical excursion to examine the possible relevance of the natural law concept of "just war" (*bellum justum*) and of nineteenth century State practice to the current debate concerning the legality and acceptability of humanitarian intervention, since both of those precedents are often referred to in one way or another in the context of the current debate. Finally we will advance a set of criteria which take account of the political and ethical dimension of humanitarian intervention within a legal context. We will conclude by attempting to illustrate how political and ethical considerations, alongside legal ones, can function as mitigating or exonerating factors in relation to humanitarian intervention and its overall status within the contemporary legal system.

II. Humanitarian Intervention and Contemporary International Law

A. Definition of Humanitarian Intervention

There are few topics within public international law which are the subject of so much controversy and disagreement and for which there are so many conflicting definitions as humanitarian intervention.[4] Sometimes it is defined very broadly so as to include various forms of diplomatic activity and humanitarian assistance alongside different types of military activity, ranging from UN peacekeeping missions with a humanitarian objective to full-scale warfare (ostensibly) on behalf of an entire population, or a population group.[5] Other definitions limit it to military activity undertaken by the international community as a whole, by a regional organization or by an individual State or group of States in situations whereby fundamental human rights of a population or minority group are severely threatened.[6]

The classic definition of humanitarian intervention is even narrower in scope and only includes military activity by one or more States to put an

---

4   See in addition to the sources referred to in notes 2 and 3 *supra inter alia*, Ian Brownlie, *Humanitarian Intervention, in* LAW AND CIVIL WAR IN THE MODERN WORLD (John Norton Moore ed., 1974), at 217 *et seq.* and Richard B. Lillich, *Humanitarian Intervention: A Reply to Ian Brownlie and a Plea for Constructive Alternatives, ibidem*, at 229 *et seq.* for a "classical" polemic on the topic. A different primarily non-legal perspective and approach to the subject is given by OLIVER RAMSBOTHAM & TOM WOOD-HOUSE, HUMANITARIAN INTERVENTION IN CONTEMPORARY CONFLICT (1996).

5   This is the approach taken by RAMSBOTHAM & WOODHOUSE, *supra* note 4, who argue that the classic definition of humanitarian intervention is inadequate and instead propose a broad definition and concept of humanitarian intervention; see in this regard at 106-13 in particular.

6   This is the approach taken in *inter alia*, the Report by the LEGAL ADVISORY COMMITTEE TO THE NETHERLANDS MINISTRY OF FOREIGN AFFAIRS referred to in note 2 *supra*, at 6-7.

end to widespread and flagrant violations of fundamental human rights, in particular the right to life, without any form of authorization or consent from the government of the State where the intervention takes place.[7] It should be borne in mind that the choice of a particular definition has much more than mere semantic or academic significance. The definition chosen will inevitably have great importance for determining the existence and nature of a possible legal basis for such an intervention.

Only military activity falls within the scope of prohibition of the use of force,[8] while diplomatic pressure, other types of non-military sanctions and humanitarian assistance are governed by other rules and principles of international law. Even if one limits the definition to military activity, it is necessary to make a clear distinction between activity which has the consent of the government of the State where the military activity is conducted and situations where no such consent or authorization is given, or where it meets with active resistance. In the first type of situation, there is no question of intervention in a legal sense and no violation of sovereignty occurs,[9] while in the second there is clearly a situation of intervention, which will require some form of legal justification.

Another equally fundamental distinction is that between interventions which are carried out with a clear authorization by the Security Council; either to a (coalition of) State(s) under Chapter VII of the Charter, or to a regional organization or arrangement acting within the (implicit) authorization of the Security Council under Chapter VIII of the Charter; and interventions which are carried out without any such authorization, either by a State, or by a regional organization. Although a UN authorized military intervention which is carried out without the consent of the target State is clearly a form of "intervention," it is one which has a generally recognized legal basis and as such will possess a presumption of legality.[10]

---

7   This is the definition used by *inter alia* Wil D. Verwey, *Humanitarian Intervention, in* THE CURRENT LEGAL REGULATION OF THE USE OF FORCE 57 (Antonio Cassese ed., 1986), at 59. This definition is based in turn on the classic definition of intervention in a general sense which was described as "dictatorial interference" by L. Oppenheim. "Dictatorial Interference" in this context signifies forcible action against the will of the target State without any degree of authorization. *See* LASSA F. OPPENHEIM, INTERNATIONAL LAW (3rd ed., 1920), at 220.

8   Article 2(4) of the UN Charter contains the prohibition of the use of force under contemporary international law and provides that: "All Members shall refrain from the threat or use of force against the territorial integrity or political independence of any State, or in any other manner inconsistent with the Purposes of the United Nations."

9   See note 7 *supra*. The granting of consent by the State concerned not only removed the qualification as "intervention" from the action, but also provides it with a legal basis. See Article 29 of the Draft Articles on State Responsibility (Draft Articles ILC 1996), amended in 1998. Consent appears in Article 20 of the Final Version adopted by the ILC in 2001. *See* JAMES CRAWFORD, THE INTERNATIONAL LAW COMMISSION'S ARTICLES ON STATE RESPONSIBILITY: INTRODUCTION, TEXT AND COMMENTARIES (2002), at 163.

10   See *inter alia* Articles 1, 24, 39 and 42 UN Charter.

HUMANITARIAN INTERVENTION: LEGALITY, JUSTICE AND LEGITIMACY

The UN Charter provides the Security Council with far-reaching powers in the maintenance of international peace and security and a wide degree of discretion in the determination of whether a given situation constitutes a threat to or a breach of the peace. The practice of the Security Council since the end of the Cold War clearly shows that the Council is prepared to utilize its enforcement powers in response to humanitarian crises and serious violations of human rights, provided the political will to act is present and the interests of the major powers and regional groups within the UN coincide sufficiently to ensure that they will at least not actively oppose initiatives within the Council to provide authorization for military action.[11]

The non-intervention principle contained in Article 2(7) of the Charter does not apply to enforcement measures taken by the Council, or with the Council's authorization. Such intervention is often referred to as "collective humanitarian intervention" to distinguish it from situations in which no such authorization by the Security Council is forthcoming. Only in situations in which the Council is unwilling or unable to provide such authorization, is there a need to justify the military intervention on the basis of a separate legal doctrine of "humanitarian intervention."

A final distinction should be made to avoid confusion. A significant number of States and numerous authors take the position that military intervention which is aimed at protecting or evacuating the nationals of the intervening State has a basis in the right of self-defense. A related theory is that action undertaken by a State to rescue its nationals from a grave threat to their lives or physical safety has its basis in a customary right of "rescue of nationals" which is separate from, but related to the right of self-defense.[12] There is considerable controversy concerning the existence and scope of such a right, although on balance the arguments for accepting a limited right of protection of nationals within the scope of the right of self-defense seem to this author to be the most persuasive.[13] However, be that as it may, and irrespective of whether one agrees or not, there are good reasons to distinguish such a right from a broader right of humanitarian intervention in order to avoid confusion. Keeping such a distinction avoids

---

11   Examples of such UN mandated collective intervention include Somalia (SC Res. 794 (Dec. 3, 1992)), Rwanda (SC Res. 929 (June 22, 1994)) and Haiti (SC Res. 940 (July 31, 1994)). For a general analysis of the evolution of UN practice in this respect see *inter alia* THE NEW INTERVENTIONISM 1991-1994: UNITED NATIONS EXPERIENCE IN CAMBODIA, FORMER YUGOSLAVIA AND SOMALIA (James Mayall ed., 1996).

12   See in this respect Derek W. Bowett, *The Use of Force for the Protection of Nationals Abroad, in* THE CURRENT LEGAL REGULATION OF THE USE OF FORCE, *supra* note 7, at 39 *et seq.* who places protection of nationals within the context of the right of self-defense. In contrast, Natalino Ronzitti rejects this position and argues instead that there is a(n) (emerging) rule of customary law which provides for the possibility of forcible evacuation of nationals in RESCUING NATIONALS ABROAD THROUGH MILITARY COERCION AND INTERVENTION ON GROUNDS OF HUMANITY (1986).

13   In this respect, the views of the late Sir Humphrey Waldock still strike this author as the most persuasive on this topic over half a century since they were first published. *See* Humphrey Meredith Waldock, *The Control of the Use of Force by States in International Law,* 81 RECUEIL DES COURS DE LA ACADÉMIE DE DROIT INTERNATIONAL 455 (1952), at 467.

confusion as to what is meant by the term "humanitarian intervention" and further avoids the application of the concept of self-defense to situations where it would be wholly inapplicable, such as military intervention on behalf of a threatened population to protect it from depredations by its own government, or other groups within the State where the intervention takes place.

Consequently, the "classic" definition of humanitarian intervention is clearer and more precise than definitions which are broader in scope or can have other legal justifications, such as collective security or self-defense. As such, humanitarian intervention is defined for the purposes of this article as: *military activity by one or more States—irrespective of whether they are part of a military alliance or regional organization—aimed at putting an end to or protecting persons not of its (their) nationality who are subjected to serious violations of fundamental human rights, in particular the right to life, without the consent of the target State and without any form of authorization by the UN Security Council.*

a) The Legal Status of Humanitarian Intervention

The choice for the abovementioned classic definition of humanitarian intervention signifies that the legality of humanitarian intervention depends upon the content and scope of the prohibition of the use of force contained in Article 2(4) of the Charter—and the existence of a further exception to the prohibition alongside those explicitly named in the Charter; namely the maintenance or restoration of international peace and security through collective security measures taken under the authority of the UN Security Council and the right of Member States of the UN to individual and collective self-defense.

a.1) Humanitarian Intervention and Article 2(4) of the UN Charter

Most proponents of humanitarian intervention contend that the prohibition of the use of force is not incompatible with the concept of humanitarian intervention. According to this reasoning, humanitarian intervention is in accordance with one of the main objectives of the UN Charter—the promotion of respect for and observance of human rights, and as such, humanitarian interventions are said not to be directed against the territorial integrity or political independence of States, but simply aimed at protecting the inhabitants of States from abuses or breakdowns of State authority.[14]

---

14   This position is derived from a teleological interpretation of the Charter that postulates that the objectives contained in the Charter should be seen in relation to each other and that Article 2(4) only prohibits force directed against the political independence and territorial integrity of another State. *See e.g.* JULIUS STONE, AGGRESSION AND WORLD ORDER (1958), at 92; William M. Reisman, *Criteria for the Lawful Use of Force in International Law*, 10 YALE JOURNAL OF INTERNATIONAL LAW AND POLICY 279 (1985), and by the same author *Sovereignty and Human Rights in Contemporary International Law*, 84 AMERICAN JOURNAL OF INTERNATIONAL LAW 866 (1990) and Lillich, *supra* note 4, at 229.

HUMANITARIAN INTERVENTION: LEGALITY, JUSTICE AND LEGITIMACY

This teleological interpretation of the UN Charter (and of international law in a more general sense) is especially influential in the United States among the supporters of the "policy oriented approach" developed by Professors Mc Dougal, Lasswell and Reisman of Yale University.

This theoretical approach says—at the risk of a degree of oversimplification—that treaties and other rules of public international law should be interpreted in such a way as to promote democratic values and human dignity to the maximum extent as long as this does not entail the risk of a dangerous confrontation or war between nuclear powers, referred to as "minimum world order." According to this approach, the realization of the objectives of the UN Charter is dependent upon the extent which democracy, the liberal world economic order and human rights are strengthened.[15] As such, humanitarian intervention can be a necessary and legal response to large-scale violations of human rights—as long as it does not involve the risk of nuclear confrontation or all-out war between major powers. This was the reason why humanitarian intervention in the former Soviet bloc, or in the Peoples Republic of China was and is unfeasible, while it can be a possible and legal option in Haiti, Somalia or Kosovo. This theoretical approach to international law has considerable prestige within the United States and has had a certain influence upon US foreign policy. Since the United States is such a powerful and influential country it is impossible to ignore this school of opinion whatever one otherwise thinks of it in legal terms.

Notwithstanding the influence of this particular theoretical approach, this is by no means the most persuasive or widely accepted interpretation of the Charter, or of the prohibition of the use of force. The premise that force which is used for a benign purpose is legal so long as it does not entail a risk of nuclear confrontation, is not one which is easily reconcilable with the text and drafting of the Charter, or which commands much support in the wider international community.

An analysis of the text of Article 2(4) of the Charter within the context of the rest of the Charter, together with the drafting history of the Charter makes it clear that the prohibition of the use of force should be interpreted broadly. This conclusion is reinforced by important interpretative resolutions of the UN General Assembly and the *Corfu Channel* and *Nicaragua*[16] decisions of the International Court of Justice. It is also the position of the

---

15 See in addition to the sources cited in note 14 *supra* in particular MYRES S. MACDOUGAL & FLORENTINO P. FELICIANO, LAW AND MINIMUM WORLD PUBLIC ORDER (1961) which can be seen as laying the theoretical groundwork for this particular approach to international law in relation to the use of force.

16 In the *Corfu Channel* case, the ICJ implicitly rejected the contention that uses of force which were not aimed at permanently altering the political independence or territorial integrity of a State did not constitute a violation of Article 2(4) of the Charter or the prohibition of intervention (1949 ICJ REPORTS 3 (April 9, 1949), at 35). This was reinforced in its *Military and Paramilitary Activities in and Against Nicaragua* decision (1986 ICJ REPORTS 14 (June 27, 1986) at 109-110), where the Court rein-

clear majority of leading authorities on the use of force in international law including a large number of American publicists.[17]

According to this leading interpretation, Article 2(4) should be seen as prohibiting all uses or threats of force, except those which are specifically provided with a legal basis in the Charter. The exceptions named in the Charter are the maintenance or restoration of international peace and security within the context of the UN collective security system and the right of individual and collective self-defense. This means that other uses of force are in principle illegal, unless perhaps there is convincing evidence of emergence of a new customary rule which would provide a legal basis for a new exception.

a.2) Humanitarian Intervention as Customary Law

As stated previously, alongside the possibility that humanitarian intervention does not fall under the prohibition of the use of force, a second argument in favor of the legality of humanitarian intervention has often been advanced, in the form of an alleged customary basis for such a right.

This alleged customary rule of law is said to have its roots partly in the natural law theories of the founders of international law, as well as in the 19th century practice of the European Great Powers.[18] Moreover, this historical basis is said to have been further developed in the post-Charter era through the practice of a number of interventions by various States to put an end to large-scale human rights violations. Only those interventions without a UN Security Council authorization will be considered for the purpose of ascertaining whether humanitarian intervention is recognized a providing as an independent legal basis for the use of military force, at the inter-State level.

The interventions which are most often cited in this context in the period since 1945 include the Indian intervention in Bangladesh in 1971, the intervention by Tanzania to put an end to the regime of Idi Amin in Uganda in 1978-79, the intervention by Vietnam in Cambodia which overthrew the rule of Pol Pot and the *Khmer Rouge* in 1978-79 and the French intervention

---

forced the prohibition of armed intervention. Important interpretive resolutions of the UN General Assembly in this respect include the "Declaration on the Inadmissibility of Intervention," GA Res. 2131 (XX) (Dec. 21, 1965) and the "Declaration on Principles of International Law Concerning Friendly Relations and Cooperation Among States in accordance with the Charter of the United Nations," GA Res. 2625 (XXV) (Oct. 24, 1970).

17 *See inter alia* IAN BROWNLIE, INTERNATIONAL LAW AND THE USE OF FORCE BETWEEN STATES (1963); YORAM DINSTEIN, WAR AGGRESSION AND SELF-DEFENCE (2nd ed. 1994); LELAND M. GOODRICH, EDVARD HAMBRO & ANNE P. SIMONS, CHARTER OF THE UNITED NATIONS (3rd ed. 1969), Louis Henkin, *International Law: Politics, Values and Functions*, 216 RECUEIL DES COURS DE LA ACADÉMIE DE DROIT INTERNATIONAL 9 (1989-IV); OSCAR SCHACHTER, INTERNATIONAL LAW IN THEORY AND PRACTICE (1991) and Waldock, *supra* note 13. Some of these authors were or are among the most highly regarded publicists in international law in the United States.

18 See para. c) *infra* of this article.

HUMANITARIAN INTERVENTION: LEGALITY, JUSTICE AND LEGITIMACY

in the Central African Republic, which put an end to the rule of self pro-claimed emperor Jean Bedel Bokassa in 1979. More recent examples in-clude the military intervention by a number of the Western members of the Gulf War Coalition to protect the Kurdish population of Northern Iraq in 1991 and the aerial campaign by the members of NATO in Kosovo in 1999, aimed at ending human rights violations by Yugoslav Government against the ethnic Albanian population.[19]

We will turn to the significance of natural law concepts of "just war" (*bellum justum*) and 19th century State practice in relation to a customary right of humanitarian intervention in a subsequent part of this essay.[20] At present, we will concentrate on the question whether there is a customary right of humanitarian intervention under contemporary international law.

The requirements for the existence of a rule of customary law are well known and have been formulated in a number of decisions of the Interna-tional Court of Justice, as well as in the writings of numerous publicists. Es-sentially these are the existence of a reasonably widespread and consistent practice by a representative group of States over an indeterminate period of time, which is accompanied by the manifestation of a legal conviction that the practice reflects a legal right to do (or to abstain from doing) what-ever it is that the practice is concerned with.[21]

If we apply these criteria to the question of humanitarian intervention it is open to serious doubt whether there is sufficient evidence for the existence of a customary basis for humanitarian intervention, much less for a new ex-ception to the prohibition of the use of force contained in the UN Charter.

The interventions of India in Bangladesh, of Vietnam in Cambodia and of Tanzania in Uganda in the 1970's were primarily based upon the claims of self-defense and not upon an alleged right of humanitarian intervention.

---

19 These examples are the most recurring examples of State practice examined in the works cited in notes 2, 4 and 7 *supra*. Other examples which are sometimes mentioned include the Belgian inter-vention in the Congo (1964), the US intervention in the Dominican Republic (1965), the Franco-Belgian intervention in Zaire (1978) and the US interventions in Grenada (1983) and Panama (1988). These examples are less appropriate for a discussion of humanitarian intervention because they were primarily related to claims of protection of nationals and in the cases of the Dominican Republic and Panama various other motives aside from humanitarian concerns. See also note 13 and accompanying text *supra*. The reason for not including the interventions by the Nigerian led ECOMOG forces in West Africa is that these were subsequently authorized by the UN Security Council, thereby rendering them collective rather than unilateral interventions.

20 See para. c) *infra*.

21 The requirements for the (proof of the) existence of a rule of customary international law were stated by the ICJ in *inter alia*, the *North Sea Continental Shelf* case (1969 ICJ REPORTS 3 (Feb. 20, 1969), paras. 70-77), *Asylum* case (1950 ICJ REPORTS (Nov. 20, 1950) at 266 *et seq.*), *Military and Paramilitary Activities*, *supra* note 16, at 98 and by the arbitrator in the *Texaco* case (17 INTERNATIONAL LAW MA-TERIALS 3 (1978), paras. 80-89) in relation to the requirements of "representativeness" of the prac-tice in question. These requirements are also reproduced in virtually every textbook on the subject; *see inter alia* IAN BROWNLIE, PRINCIPLES OF PUBLIC INTERNATIONAL LAW (4th ed. 1990), at 4 *et seq.*; PETER MALANCZUK, AKEHURST'S MODERN INTRODUCTION TO INTERNATIONAL LAW (7th rev. ed. 1997), at 39 *et seq.* and MALCOM N. SHAW, INTERNATIONAL LAW (4th ed. 1997), at 56 *et seq.*

As such, they form dubious precedents for the existence of such a right. This becomes even clearer if we take the reaction of the international community into account. The intervention of Vietnam met with the almost universal condemnation of the international community, while that of India in Bangladesh was opposed by a significant number of States, although its outcome—the independence of Bangladesh—was ultimately accepted by the international community. Although the intervention of Tanzania in Uganda enjoyed a greater degree of understanding, at least initially, its value as a precedent in favor of a generally accepted right of humanitarian intervention is limited due to the reputation and degree of isolation of the overthrown dictator Idi Amin, and the fact that the Tanzanian supported administration of President Obote quickly earned an almost equally negative reputation in the area of respect for human rights as its predecessor. The French intervention against 'Emperor' Jean Bedel Bokassa was not so much condemned or supported as tolerated—a point which we will return to presently.[22]

The intervention by a number of Western States which formed the core of the Gulf War Coalition in Northern Iraq in the aftermath of the Gulf War of 1990-91, does not serve as a clear precedent of the existence of a right of humanitarian intervention. *'Operation Provide Comfort'* which was carried out by more than 13,000 troops under the leadership of the United States, the United Kingdom and France to protect hundreds of thousands of Iraqi Kurds, was largely justified on the basis of UN Security Council resolutions and was viewed by the most concerned States within the Council and in the region as a special case which was closely linked to the Gulf War and the role of the Council in that conflict.[23] Under the specific circumstances which prevailed in the immediate aftermath of the expulsion of Iraqi armed forces from Kuwait and the bloody suppression of a popular uprising against the Iraqi Government, the Council was willing, by a narrow majority, to condemn Iraqi repression of its Kurdish population; and States such as Russia, China, India and Iran, which are normally critical of humanitarian intervention, were willing to condone Western intervention in that specific case, but this cannot be inflated into an acceptance of a general right of humanitarian intervention.[24]

---

22   See para. d.3) *infra*. For a discussion and analysis of these and other examples of practice, *see inter alia* Fernando R. Tesón, Humanitarian Intervention: An Inquiry into Law and Morality (1988), at 175 *et seq.* and Schachter, *supra* note 17, at 123-25, and Verwey, *supra* note 7, at 60-66.

23   See S/PV. 2982 (April 5, 1991) in Iraq and Kuwait: The Hostilities and Their Aftermath (Marc Weller ed., 1993) at 123 *et seq.* for the debates in the UN Security Council relating to the repression of the Kurds in Northern Iraq by the Iraqi Government and the adoption of SC Res. 688 (April 5, 1991) in which the Iraqi repression was sharply condemned, but which did not expressly provide the Western Coalition States with a mandate to intervene militarily. *See also* Peter Malanczuk, *The Kurdish Crisis and Allied Intervention in the Aftermath of the Second Gulf War*, 2 European Journal of International Law 114 (1991).

24   *See* Malanczuk, *supra* note 2, at 17-18 and *supra* note 21, at 399-402.

HUMANITARIAN INTERVENTION: LEGALITY, JUSTICE AND LEGITIMACY

The fact that the Security Council was prepared to condemn the Iraqi Government's repression of its Kurdish population and that the international community showed a significant degree of understanding towards the Western intervention in Northern Iraq contributed to a shift in Security Council responses to humanitarian crises in subsequent situations, such as Somalia, Haiti and Bosnia, but this provides little support for the existence of a customary right of humanitarian intervention outside the context of the UN collective security system.[25]

At this point, we can conclude that there is insufficient evidence for the existence of a customary right of humanitarian intervention as defined earlier in this essay. The most frequently used examples were neither based upon, nor were they accepted as precedents for the existence or emergence of such a right. Although the example of *'Operation Provide Comfort'* is significant in the sense of indicating a partial shift in the attitude of the Security Council in relation to internal conflicts and humanitarian crises, it is too closely bound up with the Gulf Conflict to serve as a precedent for a general customary right of humanitarian intervention.

On the other hand, we can also conclude that in a number of situations, probably a growing number, the international community did not openly condemn, or if it did it often did not go beyond verbal condemnation of a number of interventions which were at least partly motivated by humanitarian considerations or which had favorable humanitarian consequences.

This was the case in relation to the Tanzanian intervention in Uganda, the French intervention in Central Africa and the Western intervention in Northern Iraq. It was also arguably the case—albeit to a lesser extent—in relation to the Indian intervention in Bangladesh, although it was definitely not the case in relation to the Vietnamese intervention in Cambodia. This was the state of the law at the outset of the Kosovo crisis of 1998-9; namely in some cases no open acceptance of a right of humanitarian intervention, but no open condemnation either, which can best be described as a form of tolerance or condonement, provided certain conditions were met. The significance of this will be examined subsequently in this essay.

c) Historical Antecedents for a Right of Humanitarian Intervention

As stated earlier, proponents of humanitarian intervention often point to the historical roots of the modern day concept in natural law theory relating to "just war" and in 19th century State practice as providing further support for the existence of its customary status. In this paragraph we will

---

25 Malanczuk, *supra* note 2, at 18. Malanczuk is careful, however, to distinguish between the question of SC Res. 688 as a precedent for determinations by the Council that human rights violations with transboundary effect can pose a threat to international peace and the question whether it can be treated as a Council mandate for the use of force, much less as a precedent for unilateral humanitarian intervention.

briefly examine the historical significance of these two traditions and the relation thereof to a modern right of humanitarian intervention.

c.1) The "Just War" Tradition and Humanitarian Intervention

The natural law doctrine of "just war" (*bellum justum*) is, or more accurately was, an amalgamation of various ethical and protolegal principles and attitudes which combined elements of ancient Greek and Roman philosophy of the Stoic tradition, Roman law and tradition relating to the conduct of war, medieval scholastic theology and renaissance humanism. These elements were worked out during the High Renaissance and Reformation into a reasonably coherent theory by the founders of modern international law, such as the Spaniards Francisco de Vitoria and Francisco Suarez, the Italian Alberico Gentili and the Dutchman Hugo de Groot (Grotius). Although this tradition combined a number of elements and divergent viewpoints on a variety of issues and extended over disparate historical periods, it did contain a number of core principles and a surprising degree of agreement regarding the conditions under which the use of force was justified.[26]

It is undeniable that within this tradition, one of the just causes for the waging of war as referred to in the writings of *inter alia* Vitoria, Gentili and Grotius, was on behalf of a population which was subjected to extreme tyranny, cruelty and "unnatural practices," such as human sacrifice, cannibalism and so forth. Another cause which was generally seen as providing an ethical-legal basis for war was on behalf of Christian subjects of a foreign (non-Christian) ruler who were subjected to systematic religious persecution. The condition or requirement of a "just cause" was one of the three basic core principles necessary for a "just war" within the *bellum justum* tradition and these references to humanitarian considerations for taking up arms can be seen as providing an ethical and historical basis for the modern day concept of humanitarian intervention to at least some extent, although they should not be exaggerated or taken out of context.[27]

---

26   *See inter alia* WILFRED L. LACROIX, WAR AND INTERNATIONAL ETHICS (1988); RICHARD TUCK, THE RIGHTS OF WAR AND PEACE (1999) and Terry D. Gill, *Just War Doctrine in Modern Context, in* REFLECTIONS ON PRINCIPLES AND PRACTICE OF INTERNATIONAL LAW (Terry D. Gill & Wybo P. Heere eds., 2000), at 17 *et seq.* The views of some of the major just war theorists can be found in the well known classics of international law series published under the auspices of the American Society of International Law in the *inter bellum* period with the participation of J.B. Scott as editor and annotator. For modern day proponents of just war theory see note 28 *infra.*

27   For the views of Vitoria see JAMES BROWN SCOTT, THE SPANISH ORIGIN OF INTERNATIONAL LAW (1934) which includes as Appendix B. a translation of Vitoria's work *De Jure Belli.* Scott comments on Vitoria's views regarding humanitarian intervention at 157 of his introduction. Grotius' views are to be found in *De Jure Belli ac Pacis Libri Tres*, CLASSICS OF INTERNATIONAL LAW SERIES (James Brown Scott ed.) at 582-84 of the translation. For Gentili's views on humanitarian intervention see his *De Jure Belli* in the CLASSICS OF INTERNATIONAL LAW SERIES published in 1933 with an introduction by C. Phillipson, vol. 1, at xvi. It is important to point out that Grotius and his predecessors Gentili and Vitoria limited this "just cause" of waging war for humanitarian purposes to cases of human sacrifice or other similar acts of extreme cruelty by a ruler against his people. For a modern

Modern day just war theorists, such as Walzer and Johnson have attempted to transform this theory into a more secular, modern and liberal system of ethics and have provided a worthwhile contribution to a moral philosophical perspective relating to the use of force.[28] However, its real importance in this author's view is in the historical significance and contribution of just war theory to the development of modern international law. Although it ceased to be the leading normative framework for the assessment of when force could be used from the early 18th century onwards, it can, to a significant extent, be seen as the historical antecedent of modern international law and continues to exert a certain influence today as part of Western perceptions of morality and ethics. We will return to its legal significance for the assessment of the use of force for humanitarian purposes in a contemporary context presently, after examining a second historical antecedent to modern day humanitarian intervention.

c.2) 19th Century Liberalism and State Practice in Relation to Humanitarian Intervention

At least as important as just war theory to modern day conceptions of humanitarian intervention, are the influence of 19th century liberalism and its influence upon the State practice of the major powers of the period between 1815 and 1914. In this period, which was characterized by a strongly positivistic conception of law that stood in sharp contrast to the natural law orientation of the "just war" tradition, States were in principle free to use force to further their interests and international law considered decisions relating to use of force and what constituted the national interest to be completely outside the scope of law.

However, alongside this strongly positivistic legal perspective, there was nevertheless a fairly influential liberal intellectual current of opinion which on the one hand tried to promote arbitration and other forms of dispute settlement as alternatives to war whenever possible and on the other hand supported military intervention and action as a means to suppress inhumane practices such as the slave trade and the suppression of the Christian subjects of the decaying Ottoman Empire.[29] This liberal current of opinion had a certain influence upon the policies of the Great Powers of the era, which often cited humanitarian considerations for the numerous interventions which were carried out in the Balkans, the Near East and the Carib-

---

perspective of Grotius' views see Raymond J. Vincent, *Grotius, Human Rights and Intervention, in* HUGO GROTIUS AND INTERNATIONAL RELATIONS (Hedley Bull ed., 1990), at 246-48. Needless to say Grotius' views and those of his predecessors on whose work he drew significantly, reflect the political, ethical and cultural values of their time and should not be taken out of their historical context.

28   Modern day theorists in the just war tradition include *inter alia* MICHAEL WALZER, JUST AND UNJUST WARS (1977, 2nd ed. 1992, 3rd ed. 2000), and JAMES TURNER JOHNSON, CAN MODERN WAR BE JUST? (1984).

29   *See* Malanczuk, *supra* note 21, at 20-21.

bean. Examples of such interventions include that of France, Great Britain and Russia in 1828 on behalf of the Greek insurgents, resulting in the independence of Greece from the Ottoman Empire in 1830; the French intervention in Lebanon of 1860 on behalf of its Maronite Christian population; the Russian intervention in Bulgaria in 1877-78 in support of Bulgarian resistance to Ottoman rule and the intervention in 1898 by the United States on behalf of the Cuban insurrection against Spanish rule. These interventions are often cited by proponents of humanitarian intervention as support for its customary status and can be seen as one of the historical antecedents of the present day concept of humanitarian intervention.[30]

c.3) Significance of Historical Antecedents from a Contemporary Perspective

The fact that humanitarian intervention is at least partially based upon the natural law tradition of "just war" of the Medieval and Renaissance eras and can also partially trace its roots to the practice of the 19th century Great Powers is of some significance in the discussion relating to humanitarian intervention in the contemporary era. Both supporters and opponents of humanitarian intervention make use of arguments relating to the relevance of these historical antecedents to support their own positions. The supporters refer to these historical antecedents both as evidence of the existence of an ethical underpinning for humanitarian intervention, as well as proof of its political acceptance and customary legal status in the period preceding the adoption of the UN Charter in 1945. According to this school of thought, the fact that such a right existed before 1945 can be seen as further evidence in favor of its continued existence. Moreover, the argument in favor of the customary status of humanitarian intervention is considerably strengthened if the 19th century practice is taken into account alongside the more recent examples of State practice which we examined earlier.[31]

The opponents of a right of humanitarian intervention argue to the contrary that the fact that humanitarian intervention was recognized within the natural law doctrine of *bellum justum* of a bygone era is irrelevant today within a wholly different historical and legal context. They also discount the legal significance of 19th century precedents in the contemporary legal order and point out that the 19th century interventions of the Great Powers were not primarily motivated by humanitarian considerations, but rather by considerations of power politics such as the desire to increase their re-

---

30   *See inter alia* Lillich, *supra* note 4, and Jean-Pierre Fonteyne, *The Customary International Law Doctrine of Humanitarian Intervention: Its Current Validity Under the UN Charter*, 4 CALIFORNIA WESTERN INTERNATIONAL LAW JOURNAL 203 (1974). The latter work undertakes an extensive analysis of pre-1914 State practice.

31   See the works cited in the previous note. See also note 22 and accompanying text *supra*.

spective shares of influence, while denying such an increase in power and prestige of their main rivals.[32]

In the opinion of this author, the significance of these historical factors depends upon the context in which they are viewed and the purpose for which they are used. From a legal perspective, that is to say, as proof for or against the existence of a right of humanitarian intervention under contemporary international law—they are of practically no significance. The fact that humanitarian intervention was recognized within the *bellum justum* tradition is neither evidence for, nor against the existence of such a right under contemporary international law. One should view "just war" doctrine as part of a normative tradition which preceded modern international law and which has played a significant role in the development of certain moral and ethical principles within Western philosophy. Since moral and ethical considerations play an important role in relation to considerations of justice, fairness and equity, "just war" tradition is of some significance within the debate concerning the ethical dimension of humanitarian intervention. However, this does not mean that the normative viewpoints of classical or modern writers within the "just war" tradition can be cited as proof of the existence of a rule of positive international law within the contemporary legal framework regulating the use of force. This is a question not of the morality of humanitarian intervention, but of its legality in the sense of a recognized rule of law which allows for or prohibits a certain course of action. The viewpoints of Grotius and his predecessors or successors within contemporary just war theory are of little importance in that context.

The same applies in a somewhat different sense to the importance of 19th century State practice within the contemporary legal context. The practice of the 19th century Great Powers demonstrates that where there is an influential liberal current of opinion, combined with a favorable distribution of power which enables States which are willing and able to undertake humanitarian interventions, it is possible to carry them out with a significant degree of public support and political acceptance. The fact that there may be certain parallels between the 19th century situation and the present is an indication that these factors are of importance for the realization of a favorable political climate in support of humanitarian interventions. This is a question of the legitimacy or political acceptability of such operations, not of their legality in relation to contemporary international law. There are several reasons for this.

Within the context of 19th century international law, humanitarian interventions were neither legal nor illegal. In a system in which States were free in a legal sense to use force to promote and secure national interests,

---

32   See *inter alia* Brownlie, *supra* note 4, at 224 *et seq.* and Malanczuk, *supra* note 2, at 7-10.

humanitarian considerations for the use of force were not so much a question of legal justification, as political and to some extent moral grounds for legitimizing the numerous interventions which were carried out in that era. Legal justifications were of little significance within a legal system that had practically no limitations upon the use of force.

Secondly, even if humanitarian intervention had some legal significance within the context of 19th century international law, this is of little or no legal significance today. We have already seen that the contemporary legal order is based upon a fundamentally different premise, than that which existed in the period between 1815 and 1914; namely the prohibition of the use of force in international relations. As a result, the 19th century State practice relating to humanitarian intervention cannot be cited as evidence of the existence of such a right in the contemporary legal order.

In conclusion, we can state that although the natural law tradition and the 19th century State practice of the European Powers have some relevance in relation to discussion concerning the moral and ethical dimension and the political legitimacy of humanitarian intervention, they have no real significance in relation to the question of the legality of such interventions under contemporary international law.[33]

d) Towards a (Legal) Framework for the Assessment of Humanitarian Intervention

We have previously concluded that humanitarian intervention which is carried out without some form of UN Security Council authorization cannot be legally justified in terms of either a teleological interpretation of the UN Charter, or on the basis of an established rule of customary law. We have also seen that while the historical antecedents of humanitarian intervention can be found in the natural law *bellum justum* tradition and in the 19th century State practice of the European Powers and that this may be of some significance in relation to its moral and political acceptability, it is of little or no legal significance. However, it is clear that while it is important not to blur the discussions between morality, political legitimacy and legality, it is equally unhelpful to conduct the discussion concerning humanitarian intervention without taking account of how the moral-ethical, political and legal dimensions of the question mutually influence each other and are of relevance in terms of the evaluation and assessment of such inter-

---

33   Writers who use a different framework for analysis than a legal one often arrive at a different conclusion. This is the case, for example, in the analysis of RAMSBOTHAM & WOODHOUSE, *supra* note 4, who combine moral, political and (quasi) legal elements in their "Framework Principles for Humanitarian Intervention" at 225-31. Although their analytical model is highly interesting, it is not the same thing as an analysis on the basis of positive legal criteria and makes little distinction between moral, political and legal considerations. It does include elements of the *bellum justum* tradition, but that belongs more to the realm of moral philosophy than it does to international law, at least from a modern perspective.

ventions. In this concluding paragraph, we will attempt to arrive at a framework for assessment of humanitarian intervention which take due account of political and moral considerations in relation to legal ones.

d.1) Exonerating and Mitigating Circumstances in International Law

The lack of a generally recognized legal basis for humanitarian intervention means that a possible diminution or exclusion of culpability for conducting a humanitarian intervention must be looked for in the grounds for excluding or mitigating the wrongfulness of any particular act which exists in general international law. In this context, it is important to distinguish between grounds which provide a total exculpation for what would otherwise be a wrongful act, and grounds which would reduce, but not totally remove the wrongfulness of a particular act. The former are generally referred to as exculpatory or exonerative circumstances, while the latter are usually referred to as mitigating circumstances. Grounds for exoneration or exculpation are also known as "circumstances precluding wrongfulness" within the context of the work of the International Law Commission (ILC) in relation to State Responsibility.[34]

The ILC has devoted considerable attention to the concept of circumstances precluding wrongfulness over the long period of time it has been engaged with the topic of State Responsibility. An examination of the (Draft) Articles on State Responsibility, together with the opinions of the Special Rapporteurs of the ILC engaged on the topic and of the State commentaries makes clear that none of the circumstances precluding wrongfulness identified by the ILC are applicable to the question of humanitarian intervention. Four of the six exculpatory grounds identified by the ILC have no relevance whatsoever to the topic of humanitarian intervention and need not concern us further.[35] The other two grounds which at least potentially could have some relevance are equally inapplicable to the ques-

---

34   The earlier versions of the (then) Draft Articles on State Responsibility can be found in the YEAR-
BOOK OF THE INTERNATIONAL LAW COMMISSION of 1996 (first reading) and 1998 (second reading).
For an overview of the history and reasons for a partial change of approach to this topic see
Crawford, *supra* note 9, who provides a clear account in his introductory chapter at 1 *et seq.* The final version of the articles (2001) is reproduced at 61 *et seq.* of the same work with supporting commentary. The distinction between grounds of exculpation and mitigating circumstances, is well
known in the majority of legal systems, both those which are (primarily) based upon the Anglo-American common law tradition and those which are (primarily) based upon the continental
European civil law tradition. As such, this distinction and the concept of mitigating circumstances
almost certainly qualifies as a general principle of law, which is one of the recognized "sources" of
international law enumerated in Article 38 of the ICJ Statute.

35   These four grounds are consent (Art. 20), *force majeure* (Art. 23), distress (Art. 24) and self-defense
(Art. 21). With respect to distress, the Special Rapporteur pointed out that this ground for precluding wrongfulness had no application to situations involving humanitarian intervention. See U.N.
Doc. A/AC.4/498/Add. 2., p. 23, para. 272. *See also* Crawford, *supra* note 9, at 174-77 where it is made
clear that "[d]istress may only be invoked as a circumstance precluding wrongfulness in cases
where a State agent has acted to save his or her life or where there exists a special relationship between the State organ or agent and the persons in danger" (at 177, para. 7). The irrelevance of the
other grounds named here to humanitarian intervention is self-evident.

tion of humanitarian intervention. The first of these, countermeasures in response to a prior illegal act, may never involve the use of force according to both the work of the ILC and numerous resolutions by both of the UN political organs, including the important interpretative Resolution 2625 of the General Assembly of 1970—which states categorically that "States have a duty to refrain from acts of reprisal involving the use of force."[36] This also applies to the other potential candidate termed "state of necessity" by the ILC. Not only is this because "necessity" is not necessarily premised upon the occurrence of a prior illegal act, which would hardly be credible in relation to military action to put an end to serious violations of fundamental human rights, but more importantly, because a "state of necessity" may never be invoked to transgress a rule of a peremptory character, which certainly includes Article 2(4) of the UN Charter.[37]

Since humanitarian intervention cannot be based on any of the recognized legal exceptions to the prohibition of the use of force and none of the hitherto recognized grounds for exculpation in the form of the ILC's circumstances precluding wrongfulness are applicable, this means that humanitarian intervention is illegal. The question of the degree of illegality of humanitarian intervention and the legal consequences of such an act, is in fact a reference to the concept of mitigating circumstances which have their basis in general principles of law, and which alongside treaty and custom are recognized as one of the primary sources of public international law.

The application of mitigating circumstances forms part of virtually every system of law. The application of mitigating circumstances—whether in the context of private law or criminal law—is seen as part of the legal process itself, although it necessarily involves the taking into account of extra-legal considerations. These include the factual circumstances relating to a particular act, the motivation of the parties and the moral and legal policy implications of the act, which in the context of national legal systems are generally applied within the framework of a formal legal trial. This is the task of either the judge, or in legal systems where juries are employed, the task of the judge and jury working in conjunction within their respective functions.

At the international level, the evaluation and application of both extra legal and legal factors which possibly can play a role in the mitigation of an illegal act take place in a wholly different context. Only rarely will this be even partially within the framework of formal legal proceedings before an inter-

---

36 See additionally GA Res. 2131 (XX) (Dec. 21, 1965) as well as GA Res. 2625 (XXV) (Oct. 24, 1970) which is quoted here.

37 See YEARBOOK OF THE INTERNATIONAL LAW COMMISSION (1980, vol. II Part I) at 14 *et seq.* See also REPORT by Special Rapporteur J. Crawford, U.N. Doc. A/CN.4/498/Add. 2, paras. 286-87 and the REPORT OF THE INTERNATIONAL LAW COMMISSION'S 51ST SESSION, 3 May—23 July 1999, U.N. Doc. A/54/10, at 185, paras. 384-87. *See also* Crawford, *supra* note 9, at 185, para. 21.

HUMANITARIAN INTERVENTION: LEGALITY, JUSTICE AND LEGITIMACY

national court or tribunal. One example where this did occur was within the context of the *Corfu Channel* case, where the International Court after determining the wrongfulness of the United Kingdom's conduct in sweeping mines from the territorial waters of Albania, went on to determine that Albania's conduct had contributed to the situation, that a declaratory judgment in favor of Albania's claim was sufficient satisfaction for its claims and that Albania was liable for the payment of damages to the United Kingdom for the loss of life and material damage the United Kingdom had suffered. In short, the Court took account of these factors as constituting mitigating circumstances in relation to the United Kingdom's culpability for its illegal action.[38] While this illustrates the recognition of mitigating factors at international law, it remains a lonely example of a Court decision where mitigating circumstances were applied. This is, of course, due to the wholly different role that international courts play within the international legal system as compared to their domestic counterparts.

In the decentralized international legal system, the evaluation and application of possible mitigating factors will normally take place within the informal structure of international relations, both at the level of institutionalized diplomacy in UN organs, as well as within the context of more traditional diplomacy. Within this process, the factual circumstances, the motivation of the parties, the way in which the act was conducted and justified and its wider political, legal and moral implications will all play a role in the way States react to it. When a State carries out a humanitarian intervention which takes account of these extra legal as well as legal factors, it is likely that the reaction of the international community will be one of a significant degree of acceptance or tolerance, without necessarily wishing to declare such acts legal in the abstract.[39] This is in fact the application of mitigating circumstances at the international level, and this is where the extra legal considerations of morality and political acceptability are relevant to the legal process.

To the extent a larger number of States openly welcome, or express understanding and tolerance for a particular intervention, it will enjoy a greater degree of legitimacy, especially if this includes States from more than one particular region or political alignment or cultural tradition and among these, the major powers are represented. Within this context, different considerations and factors will play a role including ones of a political, ethical and legal nature. If the three elements are reasonably balanced, there will be a greater likelihood that the intervention will be accepted or condoned.

---

38 *Corfu Channel* case, *supra* note 16, at 22-23 and 33-35.

39 This is in fact what happened in the majority of cases discussed earlier in this article. See note 19 *supra* and accompanying text. See also notes 2, 4 and 7 *supra* in which works by various authors are cited in relation to the discussion of the most pertinent examples of humanitarian intervention.

This in turn has a legal significance, in that it demonstrates a willingness to apply mitigating circumstances to an otherwise illegal act in terms of positive international law in such a way that the consequences of illegality and culpability are diminished—in some cases potentially to a merely formal reaffirmation of the transgressed norm, while refraining from attaching any practical consequences to the illegality of the act, in much the same way the International Court did in relation to the abovementioned *Corfu Channel* case. However, since international law largely functions outside the courtroom, the process of applying mitigating circumstances will likewise usually take place within the setting of international relations and diplomacy. This in turn is a product of the decentralized and largely non-hierarchical character of the international legal system itself. The fact that international law functions within a more overtly political environment than its domestic counterpart does not, however, deprive it of its juridical character.[40]

d.2) Criteria for the Evaluation of Humanitarian Intervention

Various authors and organizations which have treated the subject of humanitarian intervention have formulated criteria for the evaluation of humanitarian intervention which pose requirements that any such intervention should meet. Interestingly enough, these criteria and requirements display a large degree of similarity, irrespective of the perspective of the analyst and even irrespective of whether the analyst supports or opposes humanitarian intervention as a general proposition. These criteria can be summed up as follows:[41]

a) humanitarian intervention should only be undertaken in situations where serious and large scale violations of fundamental human rights, especially the right to life, are taking place or are clearly likely to take place in the immediate future;

b) humanitarian intervention by individual States or coalitions of States should only serve as an *ultimum remedium* in situations where other means of protection or pressure would clearly be inadequate and in which the UN Security Council is either unwilling or unable to act on the basis of the UN collective security system;

---

40   This is where a legal framework of reference differs essentially from one which takes a different approach. See notes 28 and 33 *supra*.

41   These criteria correspond closely to those put forward by *inter alia* Lillich, Fonteyne, Verwey, Ramsbotham & Woodhouse, the Netherlands Advisory Commission of International Law and the Danish Institute of International Affairs. *See e.g.* Verwey, *supra* note 7, at 74-75; Netherlands Advisory Commission (AIV/CAVV Report) *supra* note 2, at 30-34; RAMSBOTHAM & WOODHOUSE, *supra* note 4, at 225 *et seq.*

HUMANITARIAN INTERVENTION: LEGALITY, JUSTICE AND LEGITIMACY

c) the intervening State(s) should be relatively disinterested in the sense that they are not using humanitarian intervention as a pretext to realize other interests, or in any case humanitarian motives should play an important role in any decision to intervene;

d) the intervention should have a reasonable prospect of success;

e) the intervention should be carried out in conformity with the principles of necessity and proportionality, that is to say, sufficient force to bring an end to the violations, but no more than is necessary to achieve that end and no longer than the violations occur, or threaten to continue;

f) the intervention should moreover be proportionate in the sense that it does not pose a greater risk to regional stability, or to international peace and security in a wider context.

These criteria contain legal, political and ethical considerations to a greater or lesser degree. They are closely related and interdependent, but retain their distinctness nevertheless. The relationship between these elements is so close and so important, precisely because we are dealing with a form of action which is widely considered to be illegal in principle. This lack of *prima facie* legality both increases the importance of the political and ethical dimension of the question, while at the same time serving as a means of distinguishing between degrees of illegality, so as to prevent too wide a gulf appearing between what the law allows and what is considered to be morally imperative and politically acceptable.[42]

It is often contended that humanitarian intervention is open to abuse. Moreover, it has often been pointed out that there are few—if any—examples of disinterested humanitarian intervention which have not been undertaken to promote other interests. The fact that these criticisms contain large elements of truth is not a reason to conclude that mitigating factors may not be present where interventions significantly conform to the requirements laid down in the above stated criteria. Many legal rules are susceptible to abuse and many do not contain criteria for their assessment which are more precise than those which have been formulated for humanitarian intervention.

---

42 Thomas M. Franck, *What, Eat the Cabin Boy? Uses of Force that Are Illegal but Justifiable, in* RECOURSE TO FORCE (2002), at 174 *et seq.* Franck's very interesting and readable book appeared subsequent to the original publication of this article in Dutch in the MILITAIR RECHTELIJK TIJDSCHRIFT (vol. 94, June 2001). Although this author did not have the benefit of Prof. Franck's insight at the time this article first appeared, Prof. Franck makes the case for the necessity of a relationship between law and morality and the argument for recognition of mitigation in relation to humanitarian intervention more eloquently than any other work on the topic.

As regards the question of "purity" of motivation on the part of the intervening State(s), it would seem that a degree of realism is called for. However universal fundamental human rights such as the prevention of genocide may be, it is unrealistic to expect that States will be willing to undertake military intervention, with all the risks that such action entails, without regard to other interests alongside the protection of human rights. The fear of destabilization in the region concerned, the limitation of spill over effects in the form of refugee flows, ideological opposition towards the government of the target State or solidarity with an ally which is confronted with these problems will usually also play a role alongside humanitarian considerations. This is not a reason in itself to deem such interventions as "impure". As long as they meet the general criteria for the assessment of humanitarian intervention to a significant extent, there will be grounds for accepting the mitigation of responsibility. The examples from both 19th century and more recent State practice indicate that precisely those States which have the most interests in a particular region will be most likely to undertake a military intervention which aims to put an end to a serious violation of human rights.[43]

d.3) Application of Mitigating Criteria and their Legal Consequences

The question arises as to which (legal) consequences should be attached to a given humanitarian intervention on the basis of the above stated evaluation criteria. Closely related is the question as to which further requirements of a procedural nature can be posed upon States which undertake a humanitarian intervention, in order to enable a reasonably effective and objective evaluation and assessment of their conduct. It is reasonable that a State or group of States which undertake an action which is *prima facie* illegal, should be expected to provide a full explanation and motivation for its conduct if it expects mitigating factors to be taken into account. This is even the case where a State makes use of a recognized legal right, such as self-defense, so there should be no reason to expect less from a State which undertakes a humanitarian intervention.

As long as there is no generally recognized legal basis for humanitarian intervention, it seems clear that the burden of proof will rest upon the intervening State(s). This means at least that any State which undertakes a humanitarian intervention is under an obligation to provide as full an

---

43　E.g. France in the Lebanon in the 1860's where it had an historic interest, the United States in Cuba in 1898, India in Bangladesh, Tanzania in Uganda, etc. In contrast, there are very few, if any, examples of totally disinterested States intervening unilaterally on grounds of pure humanitarian concern, a point which has been emphasized repeatedly by opponents of humanitarian intervention. In point of fact, there are no more "pure" States than there are individuals in general which is why a dose of realism is called for in this respect.

HUMANITARIAN INTERVENTION: LEGALITY, JUSTICE AND LEGITIMACY

explanation of its conduct and motivation, as well as of its objectives in carrying out the operation, as is possible. Since the UN Security Council exercises primary responsibility in the maintenance of international peace and security, it is logical and reasonable to expect the intervening State(s) to provide such explanation and motivation to that body. Providing such an explanation and motivation is not necessarily the same thing as requesting an authorization. In situations where it is clear that an authorization is unlikely to be forthcoming, it is not so much a question of a symbolic attempt at obtaining an authorization, as providing an explanation to the competent international authority.

This would contribute to the avoidance of miscalculation and escalation and the limitation of damage to the international legal order and system of collective security. It would, moreover, confront the Council with the consequences of its own inaction. There are, roughly speaking, three situations which can result from such a course of action:

a) the Security Council decides after all to provide an authorization for the action, in which case it would obtain a legal basis and enjoy a much greater degree of political legitimacy;

b) the Security Council comes to a clear condemnation of the action and issues a cease and desist order. This would usually signify that the intervention did not possess either a basis for political legitimacy or for the application of mitigating considerations in a legal sense. In practice, such a condemnation would likely only occur in cases where a claim of humanitarian intervention was merely a pretext for aggression. It is improbable that a State or group of States which could plausibly demonstrate legitimizing factors would be confronted with a condemnation although there could be exceptions to this general proposition;

c) the Security Council is incapable of reaching either an authorization or a condemnation, in which case it will be up the wider international community to determine to what extent mitigating circumstances were present on the basis of the general criteria for evaluation.

To the extent a particular intervention meets the criteria, the legal situation would be one of an illegal act, but one to which no significant legal or political consequences were attached. This is the best description of what has actually transpired in a number of more or less recent examples of humanitarian intervention. The interventions of India in Bangladesh, of Tanzania in Uganda and of France in the Central African Republic were all treated as violations of the prohibition of the use of force to a greater or lesser extent, but ones to which no significant legal or political consequences were attached. The same applies to the intervention of the Coalition States in

Northern Iraq, the interventions of ECOWAS in West Africa preceding their subsequent endorsement by the Security Council and most recently the NATO intervention in Kosovo. None of these interventions singly or taken together have given rise to a generally accepted right of humanitarian intervention. On the other hand, these interventions have conformed by and large with the general criteria for the application of mitigating circumstances. In none of these cases were any lasting or significant legal or political consequences attached to these interventions; on the contrary the resulting situations were given a wide degree of acceptance.[44]

V. Conclusions

The question of humanitarian intervention possesses an ethical and political dimension alongside a legal one. In legal terms it seems clear that notwithstanding contentions to the contrary, there is as of yet no widely accepted legal basis for it, either in terms of Charter or customary international law. Nor does the fact that humanitarian intervention can at least partially base its intellectual and historical roots in the *bellum justum* tradition and in the 19th century practice of the European Great Powers change this, although these traditions are not without relevance in demonstrating the ethical and political dimension of humanitarian intervention.

Since humanitarian intervention does not have a generally recognized legal basis and none of the circumstances precluding wrongfulness worked out by the ILC over a long period apply, it follows that humanitarian intervention is illegal in principle.

On the other hand, illegality comes in various degrees and the consequences of an illegal act will vary and can be mitigated in international law as in any legal system. This is where a combination of legal and extra-legal factors play a role in assessing what the consequences of a given example of humanitarian intervention should be, on the basis of a set of generally recognized criteria which take account of the various elements involved. However, this exercise, though influenced by extra-legal considerations, nevertheless forms part of the legal process, even though this usually takes place within the context of international diplomacy rather than within the formal setting of court proceedings, due to the specific characteristics of the international legal system itself.

As such, and until the time is ripe for the recognition of a legal basis for humanitarian intervention, this seems to be a reasonable solution to a difficult problem. The fact that there are situations in which it is morally and politi-

---

44   See note 39 *supra* and accompanying text.

HUMANITARIAN INTERVENTION: LEGALITY, JUSTICE AND LEGITIMACY

cally unacceptable to stand by while large scale violations of fundamental human rights are taking place is no reason to deny the importance of legal considerations relating to the use of force, to pretend that the law already allows new exceptions to the prohibition of the use of force which the international community is not ready to accept, or still less to cast the prohibition aside. The first victim of such a course of action would almost certainly be the most fundamental of human rights itself—the right not to live under the perpetual threat of war.

[21]

The responsibility to protect

Spencer Zifcak

> The norm itself is good, we agree. But the problem is bad behaviour – and that
> is very difficult to control, when it gets down to it.
> Asian Permanent Representative to the UN

Since the UN Charter's regime for collective security was established immediately after the Second World War, there have been several significant changes to the global security environment. These, in turn, have created not just
political but also legal tensions for the framework then set in place. The
principal challenges to the regime are well known (Triggs, 2006, 558). States
have continued to use force unilaterally, justifying their decisions to act pre-
emptively or preventively upon a broad reading of the Charter provisions
governing individual and collective self-defence. Particularly after 11 September 2001, states have used force in violation of the territorial integrity of other
states believed to be harbouring terrorist organizations. And the claim has
been made, by developed nations in particular, that international law may
now recognize a right to engage in humanitarian intervention, even without
Security Council authorization, in order to prevent the commission of large-
scale genocide and crimes against humanity. It is with this third major development, particularly in its recent incarnation as the 'responsibility to protect',
that this chapter is concerned.

Humanitarian intervention is a relatively new development in international
law. The idea that nations may intervene in the internal affairs of others in
pursuit of humanitarian objectives is yet to establish any firm legal footing.
There is some recent evidence of state practice that may support a claim that
the doctrine has achieved international legal recognition (Chesterman, 2001,
53; Byers and Chesterman, 2003, 177; Gray, 2004, 31; Welsh, 2004, 176;
Wheeler, 2004, 29; Byers, 2005, 92; Stahn, 2007, 99). For example, it may be
said that India's intervention in East Pakistan in 1971, Tanzania's intervention in Uganda in 1979, Vietnam's invasion of Cambodia in 1978, and the
creation by Britain and France of a no-fly zone over Iraq in 1994, are practical examples of the progressive acceptance of such a doctrine in law and
political practice (Gordon, 1993, 520; Chesterman, 2001, 140; Roberts, 2004,
78; Weiss, 2007, 40). It is notable, however, that the interveners in these cases

made no claim that their actions were founded principally upon humanitarian considerations.

The Security Council itself has authorized military interventions for humanitarian purposes. It determined that the situation in Somalia in 1992 constituted a threat to international peace and security, and urged member states to pursue all necessary means to create a safe environment for humanitarian relief operations in the absence of Somalia's consent. It approved the use of force by NATO for humanitarian reasons in Bosnia in 1992. Together with the Organization of African Unity (OAU), the Security Council supported a regional peacekeeping exercise by the Economic Community of West African States (ECOWAS) in Liberia in 1990. And, all too late, it sent a French-led peacekeeping mission into Rwanda to reduce the prospect that the preceding genocide should be reignited. These latter interventions suggest, at the very least, that humanitarian intervention with Security Council authorization may have gained some tentative legal foothold.

A further step on the path to formal recognition was taken by the Security Council in 1999, when it issued a presidential statement on the protection of civilians in armed conflicts, and soon after approved two resolutions in relation to the matter.[1] The two resolutions consolidated the principle that where governments attacked their own citizens or denied them humanitarian relief, such action may in itself constitute a threat to international peace and security. In so doing, the Council opened the door to the possibility that it might take coercive action under Chapter VII of the Charter where large-scale loss of civilian lives was in prospect.[2] It was not, however, until the lead-up to the World Summit that the United Nations took seriously the task of conceptualizing and endorsing a more comprehensive doctrine of humanitarian intervention in response to genocide and other similar intra-state crimes.

Humanitarian intervention in international law

In legal terms, the *prima facie* position with respect to military interventions undertaken for humanitarian reasons appears to be as follows (see also Chesterman, 2001; Farer, 2003, 53; Franck, 2003, 204; Gray 2004, 31; Wheeler, 2004, 32; Molier, 2006, 37; Triggs, 2006, 598). Pursuant to Article 2 of the Charter:

> 2(4) All states [are to] refrain in their international relations from the threat or use of force against the territorial integrity and political independence of any state, or in any other manner inconsistent with the purpose of the United Nations.

This injunction against the use of force is reinforced by the terms of Article 2 (7), which declares: 'Nothing in the present Charter shall authorize the UN to intervene in matters which are essentially within the domestic jurisdiction of any state.' The principle of non-intervention, together with that of the sovereign equality of states, is designed to ensure that each state respects the prerogatives and entitlements of every other state.

As noted in the previous chapter, there are in the Charter only two exceptions to the Article 2(4) prohibition. First, Chapter VII of the Charter empowers the Security Council to authorize the use of force in response to threats and breaches of international peace and security. Pursuant to Article 39, therefore, the Security Council may make recommendations as to what measures, including the use of armed force, should be taken to address an identified threat to international peace and security or to any act of aggression. Secondly, in accordance with Article 51, member states of the United Nations may take measures, whether individually or collectively, in pursuit of their inherent right to self-defence should they be subject to armed attack. Such action in self-defence may continue until the Security Council itself has instituted whatever further measures are necessary to maintain international peace and security.

When laid down plainly in this way, it is apparent that the express terms of the Charter do not readily embrace humanitarian intervention. The principle of non-intervention stands steadfastly in its path. The NATO intervention in Kosovo, for example, neither was declared by the Security Council as a threat to international peace and security, nor could it be characterized as an exercise of a right to collective self-defence by NATO's membership. For that reason, it is generally accepted that, however well intentioned, the bombing of Serbia was, although perhaps legitimate, illegal (Independent International Commission on Kosovo, 2000).

Further, the UN Declaration on Friendly Relations of 1970 states the duty of non-intervention in similar and compelling fashion:

> No State or group of states has the right to intervene directly, or indirectly, for any reason whatsoever in the international external affairs of any other State. Consequently, armed intervention and all other forms of interference or attempted threats against the personality of the state or against its political, economic and cultural elements are in violation of international law.[3]

Of course, the Charter's provisions are capable of competing interpretations. These can occupy the full spectrum from the literal to the liberal. International lawyers have, for example, argued that, despite what appear to be the plain words of the Charter text, a doctrine of humanitarian intervention may be insinuated into its interstices (Chesterman, 2001, 47; Farer, 2003, 64; Holzgreve, 2003, 37). One argument that has been made is that Article 2(4) prohibits the use of force only against 'the territorial integrity or political independence of a state'. If, therefore, force is used in the pursuit of some other objective, particularly one that is consistent with the objects of the Charter, it may be permissible. A humanitarian intervention, properly conducted, may pose no long-term threat to either the territorial integrity or the political autonomy of a state. Its sole purpose may be said to be to prevent the further commission of atrocities pending the restoration of stability.

Such an interpretation faces great difficulty, however, because it creates the prospect of a damaging ambiguity in the Charter's interpretation. Even a brief look at the *travaux preparatoire*, as a means of resolving such an ambiguity, demonstrates clearly that such an adventurous interpretation of the qualification has little, if any, plausible foundation. Instead, the original aim of the non-intervention principle appears to have been to protect smaller states, and the words 'territorial integrity and political independence' were added as supplements to, not as detractions from, the general prohibition on the use of force (Triggs, 2006, 569).

Alternatively, it may be suggested that the use of force is permitted so long as it is not, in the terms of Article 2(4), 'in any other manner inconsistent with the purposes of the United Nations'. Clearly, if the objective of the intervention is to prevent gross violations of human rights, it cannot be said to be anything other than consistent with the Charter's fundamental purposes. This argument also runs into immediate problems, not the least of which is that even if the disputed intervention is aimed at protecting and preserving the human rights of the afflicted people of a nation, the prohibition on infringements upon territorial integrity and political independence still stands. The better position is simply to acknowledge that the achievement of one of the fundamental purposes of the Charter may naturally conflict with the attainment of another. The question is one of balance, not absolutes.

Third, perhaps, a right or obligation of humanitarian intervention may arise in consequence of its progressive acceptance as part of customary international law (Cassese, 1999, 791; Chesterman, 2001, 53; Stahn, 2007, 99). Such an approach reviews the relevant actions of the Security Council – and broader international responses to declared instances of humanitarian intervention – to ascertain the consistency of the rationales for the action; traces the emergence of identifiable patterns of international behaviour; and assesses their degrees of acceptance if and when certain conditions are met. On this basis, an informed decision may be made by international political institutions and courts as to whether such interventions are legal in accordance with the normative framework governing the use of force.

Here, however, there are significant methodological problems. The International Court of Justice, for example, has had only limited opportunity to develop the rules governing the use of force. Nations themselves are not often clear or straightforward about their motivations for acting, and mix legal justifications with political and security concerns in a way that makes the interpretation of state action an uncertain exercise. The UN's norm-creating bodies, in particular the Security Council and General Assembly, may not always be at one in their judgement of events, raising complex questions about the weight to be given to the opinions of each and the relative merits of both. And there may be considerable doubt as to when an apparently illegal action, taken by a state or group of states in response to a novel set of circumstances, should suggest that the governing international norm of behaviour should be revised. These are difficult matters not readily amenable to resolution.

Until recently, therefore, it has been difficult to demur from the conclusion of the British Foreign Office in 1986 that:

> The overwhelming majority of contemporary legal opinion comes down against the existence of a right to humanitarian intervention for three main reasons. First, the UN Charter and the corpus of modern international law do not seem specifically to incorporate such a right; secondly, state practice in the last two centuries, and especially since 1945, at best provides only a handful of genuine cases of humanitarian intervention; and finally, on prudential grounds, that the scope for abusing such a right argues strongly against its creation.[4]

This does not, however, preclude the foreseeable prospect that, through uniform and generally accepted country practice, an exception allowing states to intervene to tackle humanitarian crises may emerge. Thus, for example, it may at least tentatively be argued, in the light of events post-dating Foreign Office opinion, that the interventions in Kosovo and northern Iraq in particular, and developments in the Security Council and General Assembly in general, may already have traced the contours of an international legal norm permitting the use of force to prevent or overcome the commission of gross human rights violations. Kosovo and northern Iraq are significant instances because they are the first in which the nations engaging in the use of force have sought explicitly to rely on a doctrine of external intervention for a humanitarian purpose.

Clearly, the provision of just two examples of action so characterized is too uncertain a foundation at present for the unambiguous establishment of the norm. The actual evidence, in terms of both practice and *opinio juris*, that such an exception has emerged remains insufficient (Stromseth, 2003, 233; Gazzini, 2005, 176). Perhaps the most that can be said is that the Security Council has not categorically declared such cases unlawful. These two instances, when combined with others initiated for a similar humanitarian purpose and with explicit Security Council authorization, are sufficient to suggest only that a new norm may be in the process of crystallization. As Professor Gillian Triggs has summarized the matter:

> If it is accepted that legal norms should be applied to the facts in their social context and political reality, and it is believed that they should be, Article 2(4) can accommodate bona fide interventions that are both necessary and proportionate to the humanitarian objective. As further instances of asserted humanitarian interventions arise in the future, they will be accepted or rejected by the usual international processes. In this way a consensus may be built for applying the prohibition on the use of

force so as to countenance limited resort to humanitarian intervention (Triggs, 2006, 607).

It is within the framework of this still ambiguous legal and political circumstance that the following discussion of the United Nations' support for some limited acceptance of a doctrine permitting humanitarian intervention, or the engagement of a 'responsibility to protect', will be developed.

From 'humanitarian intervention' to the 'responsibility to protect'

Speaking in an address to the General Assembly in 1999, the Secretary-General challenged member states to resolve the apparent conflict between the principle of non-interference with state sovereignty, embodied in Article 2(4) of the Charter, and the responsibility of the international community to respond to massive human rights violations and ethnic cleansing. He posed what he described as a tragic dilemma (Annan, 1999, 39). Military intervention without Security Council authorization may erode the legal framework governing the use of force and undermine the Council's authority by setting potentially dangerous precedents. At the same time, however, the Council's failure to act in the face of horrific atrocities would betray the human rights principles that underpin the Charter and erode respect for the United Nations itself. In this, Kofi Annan was clearly mindful of the recent tragedies that had blighted the UN's peacekeeping record. The humanitarian crises in Somalia, Rwanda and Srebrenica had revealed a yawning gulf between the principles underlying the UN Charter and the grim reality of recent state practice.

In an attempt to resolve the political and legal dilemmas, the Secretary-General emphasized the need to ensure that the Security Council could rise to the occasion and agree on effective action to defend fundamental human rights. He argued that the core challenge to the Security Council in particular, and the UN in general, in the twenty-first century was: 'To forge unity behind the principle that massive and systematic violations of human rights – wherever they may take place – should not be allowed to stand.'[5]

The Secretary-General's call to action prompted the Canadian Government, in a singular initiative, to form an international panel of experts, the International Commission on Intervention and State Sovereignty (ICISS). It consulted widely with governments, non-governmental organizations, intergovernmental organizations, universities and think-tanks. On the basis of these extensive consultations, the Commission issued a final report, *The Responsibility to Protect* (International Commission on Intervention and State Sovereignty, 2001).

This report did three important things. First, it sought to reconceptualize forcible international action in defence of peoples at risk and, in so doing, to forge a new understanding of the necessary preconditions and actions that may be involved. The international community would no longer engage in 'humanitarian intervention' but would exercise its responsibility to protect.

Secondly, the new approach placed primary responsibility for taking action to prevent humanitarian catastrophes on the sovereign government of the nation in which it occurred. Only when that responsibility had not been exercised would the larger global community's parallel responsibility to intervene in the national and international interest be engaged. Thirdly, new operational rules of engagement were to be developed and refined to ensure that any such intervention had the maximum possible opportunity for success (Acharya, 2002, 373; Evans and Sahnoun, 2002, 99; Thakur, 2006, 250).

The Commission placed its weight behind the proposition that the responsibility to protect was in fact the reflection of a new, emerging norm of international behaviour:

> Based on our reading of state practice, Security Council precedent, established norms, guiding principles, and evolving customary international law, the Commission believes that the Charter's strong bias against military intervention is not to be regarded as absolute when decisive action is required on human protection grounds (International Commission on Intervention and State Sovereignty, 2001, 16).

Much as with the concept of 'sustainable development', which sought to overcome the oppositional relationship between exploitation and conservation, the responsibility to protect sought to forge a new unity between the values of state sovereignty on the one hand and intervention to prevent atrocities on the other. Sovereignty, therefore, was reconceptualized as entailing 'responsibility'. The responsibility to protect civilian populations from genocide and crimes against humanity was to be exercised first and primarily by the nation state concerned. Only when that responsibility had failed to be exercised would the international community step in as proxy.

This conceptual shift was significant. It made clear that it was the nation state that bore the principal responsibility for the safety and welfare of its citizens. It signified that the nation state is responsible not just to its population, but also to the international community, to ensure that its population is made secure. It implied that nation states are responsible in this sense, and may therefore be brought to account for their actions or omissions.

The ICISS developed its conceptual framework further by distinguishing between different classes of responsibility. So, for example, it placed great emphasis on the idea that the responsibility would best be exercised by prevention. This 'responsibility to prevent' spoke to the need to take every reasonable step to ensure that predicted humanitarian catastrophes would not occur. Preventive options such as aid and development assistance should therefore be the first to be used. Next, 'the responsibility to react' emphasized that in the exercise of its preventive role, the international community should always prefer non-forcible measures, such as diplomatic negotiations and economic sanctions, to instigating armed intervention. Once a crisis had been averted, whether militarily or otherwise, a 'responsibility to rebuild' would be engaged. In this, the international community would be involved in both peacekeeping and economic and social reconstruction.

The central thrust of the report, then, was upon the prevention of conflict through a range of non-military measures that may entail significantly larger transfers of wealth, expertise and opportunity from developed to developing countries. It entailed taking Third World development seriously (Byers, 2005, 111).

The High-Level Panel's endorsement

Three years after ICISS had reported, its recommendations received new and powerful endorsement from the Secretary-General's High-Level Panel.[6] The panel adopted the conceptual framework embodied in the idea of the responsibility to protect. It favoured the ICISS's conclusion that any such responsibility should be exercised only with the endorsement of the Security Council. And it incorporated, with some minor alterations, the cautionary principles that had been set down in the original report.

Addressing the relevant legal issues, the panel observed that the Charter reaffirms a fundamental faith in human rights, but does not do much to protect them. Article 2(7) prohibits intervention in matters which are essentially within the jurisdiction of any state. However, the panel asserted that the principle of non-intervention embodied in that Article could not be used to shield nations from the consequences of state-sponsored genocidal acts or other atrocities, such as large-scale ethnic cleansing or violations of international humanitarian law. These may be considered as threats to international peace and security under Article 24 and, as such, might properly provoke a response from the Security Council.

> We endorse the emerging norm that there is a collective international responsibility to protect, exercisable by the Security Council authorizing military intervention as a last resort, in the event of genocide and other large-scale killing, ethnic cleansing or serious violations of international humanitarian law which sovereign governments have proved powerless or unwilling to prevent.[7]

Responsibility to protect in World Summit negotiations

Taking his lead from the panel, the Secretary-General recommended that the World Leaders Summit embrace the responsibility to protect.[8] Under the general rubric of the 'rule of law', Kofi Annan urged that the principle be embraced by the General Assembly. Nevertheless, it was unclear whether the responsibility to protect would survive the exhaustive and exhausting negotiations that would occur in the months preceding the Summit. The principal line of objection was clear. Some states would argue strongly in favour of the international community's entitlement to intervene in the face of genocide, crimes against humanity and other mass atrocities committed by a state.

Others, however, would maintain that the Security Council was prohibited legally from authorizing coercive action against sovereign nations in relation to any matter that occurred within their borders. As the Permanent Representative of Algeria put the matter in an early discussion on the Secretary-General's report:

> ... interference can occur with the consent of the State concerned ... we do not deny that the United Nations has the right and duty to help suffering humanity. But we remain extremely sensitive to any undermining of our sovereignty, not only because sovereignty is our last defence against the rules of an unequal world, but because we are not taking part in the decision making process of the Security Council ... [9]

Generally speaking, the Western Europe and Others Group (WEOG) nations supported the inclusion of a resolution in favour of the responsibility to protect in the World Summit outcome document. The United States, however, had significant reservations. A powerful bloc in the Non-Aligned Movement (NAM) either opposed its inclusion or sought significant amendments to the basic principles that had been set down. African nations tended to support the principle. Latin American countries were less certain. Since it was hoped that the Summit outcome document would be adopted by consensus, it was inevitable that the pre-summit negotiations would result either in the rejection of the concept or in some form of compromise. In the end, the strength of the African Union position was a critical factor in ensuring that it stayed in. Even so, the resolution that was finally accepted was hedged with very significant qualifications. These emerged one by one as the negotiations progressed and as draft after draft of the Summit outcome document was presented and amended (Bellamy, 2006, 165).

Unsurprisingly, given its pivotal role in establishing the ICISS, Canada played a leading role in advocating for the adoption of a resolution encapsulating and underpinning support for the responsibility to protect. It expressed its strong support for the recommendations contained in the ICISS report and, subsequently, in the report of the High-Level Panel. Noting that the responsibility to protect embraced a parallel responsibility to rebuild, Canada shrewdly twinned its argument with one for the successful establishment of a new Peacebuilding Commission. The Commission, it argued, was an essential institutional foundation which would underpin the larger conception. The responsibility to protect, in turn, would in time be 'universally respected as a fundamental component of state sovereignty and independence. There can be no greater goal.'[10]

Outside North America, the most significant support for the adoption of the doctrine came from the nations of Europe. There was little or no dissent here that the nations of the world should recognize their collective responsibility to protect civilian populations who were the subject of genocide, war crimes, ethnic cleansing or crimes against humanity:

114   *The responsibility to protect*

> The EU believes that international agreement on the concept of respon-
> sibility to protect is long overdue. We cannot stand by as genocide ... or
> other gross violations of international humanitarian law and human
> rights are committed ... The Summit should, therefore, send a clear
> message that the international community has the responsibility to decide
> and to act case by case through a comprehensive range of measures,
> including collective action through the Security Council, and in extreme
> cases, and out of necessity, by use of force, authorized by the Security
> Council.[11]

Perhaps the most interesting aspect of the pre-summit discussions was the
strong support for the doctrine provided by the nations of Africa. In a sense,
this was not surprising. It has been in Africa – perhaps more than in any
other region of the world – that mass violations of human rights, of the kind
sought to be prevented here, had occurred. African nations had first-hand, or
near-hand, experience of the atrocities and consequent human suffering with
which the doctrine was concerned, and an intimate and devastating knowledge of the consequences of both state and international failure. Further, it
was no giant step for African countries to embrace the responsibility to protect on the global stage. Authorization for outside intervention to prevent the
commission of large-scale human rights abuse had already been incorporated
into Article 4(h) of the Constitutive Act of the African Union (Kioko, 2003,
807). In this context, the Tanzanian President had made the case plainly:

> We must now stop misusing the principles of sovereignty and non-inter-
> ference in the internal affairs of states to mark incidences of poor gov-
> ernance and unacceptable human rights abuses ... In the aftermath of the
> genocide in Rwanda, and in light of the massive influx of refugees in the
> Great Lakes Region, it is inevitable to conclude that the principle of non-
> intervention in the internal affairs of a state can no longer find unquali-
> fied, absolute legitimacy ... Governments must first be held responsible
> for the life and welfare of their people. But, there must also be common
> agreed rules and benchmarks that would trigger collective action through
> our regional organizations and the United Nations against governments
> that commit unacceptable human rights abuses.[12]

Such arguments, based as they are on the moral responsibility of the nations
of the world to prevent the large-scale destruction of their peoples, wherever
they may be, appear, at least in principle, difficult to refute. And yet, as fore-
shadowed earlier, there was and is a significant problem. That is, that the
United Nations, as the representative institution of the community of nations,
must necessarily act within the terms of its Charter. And Article 2(4) of the
Charter would appear to prohibit the international community's undermining
of the sovereignty of any nation. This is not a moral principle of a similar
order to that invoked when speaking of the responsibility to protect; it is,

nevertheless, a constitutional principle which is fundamental to the common understanding and working of the international order. Not unnaturally, therefore, it was upon this principle, and on the supporting terms of the Charter, that opponents of the responsibility to protect founded their principal arguments (Bannon, 2006, 1157).

India and Pakistan made lucid statements, warning their counterparts of the conceptual and practical dangers attendant upon an uncritical acceptance of the new doctrine. The Permanent Representative from India made clear his country's view that the terms of the Charter should be regarded as paramount. The framers of the Charter, he argued, never intended Article 51, permitting collective action mandated by the Security Council, to cover anything 'beyond its text'. The text was sufficient to cover any presently conceivable danger to peace. Where action was required to deal with situations of gross human rights abuse, it was not the text that stood in its path. Rather, the problem was in garnering the requisite political will to take such action. He warned against conferring legitimacy on a doctrine of humanitarian intervention or turning it into some new ideology of 'military humanism'.[13]

Pakistan, similarly, cautioned against the General Assembly adopting the doctrine of humanitarian intervention, upon which world opinion was very divided, under the semantic cloak of the responsibility to protect. Instead, the international community should focus its attention on the right to development. The global community's responsibility with respect to state failure and the consequent commission of human rights abuse must be principally preventive. Countries should be assisted before they collapse. The problems of such 'stressed states' could only be made worse by external interference and regional power plays. Pakistan's ambassador, Munir Akram, acknowledged that if a state had collapsed, international action may become necessary. But in such a case, he argued, care should be taken not to court the prospect that any such intervention might simply further the strategic interests of the intervening parties. In institutional terms, this would require the authorization of the Security Council or the General Assembly. And in any such case, it would be imperative to preserve the sovereignty, territorial integrity and unity of the state concerned.[14]

China, which had been joined by Russia, adopted a similarly cautious and conditional position. Focusing upon the complexity of causes that may bear upon state failure and the commission of large-scale abuses of civilian populations, the Chinese delegation urged the Assembly to focus on situations as they arose, on a case-by-case basis. It should eschew the adoption of general principles invoking some intangible and impractical notion of international intervention in the internal affairs of sovereign states:

> When confronting large-scale humanitarian crisis, it is appropriate for the international community to respond by easing and checking the crisis and to offer timely assistance. However, we must not fail to see that disturbances of a country often have complicated causes, and judgment

116 *The responsibility to protect*

should be made cautiously on whether a country is able or willing to protect its nationals. Acts of interference should not be taken wilfully. When it is decided to take necessary actions, it is essential for the international community to strictly abide by the UN Charter and the cardinal principles of equality of sovereignty and non-interference in other countries' internal affairs. The Security Council should act on realities, make clear evaluations and use, to the greatest extent, peaceful means within the UN framework. In adopting mandatory actions, it is even more important to act prudently on a case-by-case basis and avoid generalization.[15]

This cautionary and legally formal opposition was backed by the countries of the NAM, and was lent further support by several of the nations of the Middle East including Egypt, Syria and Iran. Egypt characterized the responsibility to protect as a licence for the strong to judge the weak. The adoption of the doctrine, it argued, would serve only to deepen suspicions among civilizations and cultures, rather than to overcome them.

In public, at least, there did not seem to be much room for compromise between these competing perspectives. Statements on the floor of the General Assembly took the form principally of a reassertion of existing, strongly held positions, rather than a concerted endeavour to address arguments from the other side. In this, Canada was the notable exception. While firmly maintaining its support for the doctrine, it sought also to mollify the concerns of others less sure of the altruistic motivations of its movers. In a thoughtful contribution to pre-summit discussion, the Canadian Permanent Representative, Allan Rock, sought to allay the fears of those for whom the issue of sovereignty was primary. Sovereignty, he argued, would be strengthened rather than weakened. This was because intervention by the international community was predicated upon a failure by a state to exercise the responsibilities inherent in the idea of sovereignty itself. When seen in this way, the protection of citizens and the primacy of sovereignty could be seen as mutually reinforcing rather than as antagonistic. The responsibility to protect was founded, he argued, on the idea of prevention. Thus, in all but the most extreme cases, the responsibility of states to protect and nurture their own populations would be assisted when grave situations threatened. The international community's responsibility would be to step forth to provide the material conditions and resources necessary to avoid state failure. Nevertheless, there may be situations in which the use of military force to achieve a cessation in genocide or other atrocities is the only course left. In such cases, the Ambassador argued, it was incumbent upon the international community to assume its protective duty. One could not deplore the failure in Rwanda and at one and the same time reject a proper framework of principle within which the conditions for, and terms of, international intervention could rationally be explicated and implemented. It was better in relation to the use of force, Canada argued, for the global community to be governed by a commonly understood and accepted framework of rules rather than to leave the exercise of military force at the absolute discretion of states motivated, as they are, principally by their strategic and political concerns.[16]

Under heavy pressure to adopt some form of the responsibility to protect formula, diplomatic representatives in New York haggled into the last week before the Summit to try to find the words that might permit a compromise text to go to the world's leaders for endorsement. After frenzied last-minute negotiations, the final text was concluded, although it was weaker and more qualified than that which had been proposed in the ICISS and High-Level Panel reports. Nevertheless, the very fact that the concept and principle had been agreed to at the World Summit represented a major success. The concluded wording was as follows:

138. Each individual State has the responsibility to protect its populations from genocide, war crimes, ethnic cleansing and crimes against humanity. This responsibility entails the prevention of such crimes, including their incitement, through appropriate and necessary means. We accept that responsibility and will act in accordance with it ...

139. The international community, through the United Nations, also has the responsibility to use appropriate diplomatic, humanitarian and other peaceful means, in accordance with Chapters VI and VII of the Charter, to help protect populations from genocide, war crimes, ethnic cleansing and crimes against humanity. In this context, we are prepared to take collective action, in a timely and decisive manner, through the Security Council, in accordance with the Charter, including Chapter VII, on a case-by-case basis and in cooperation with relevant regional organizations as appropriate, should peaceful means be inadequate ... We stress the need for the General Assembly to continue considerations of the responsibility to protect populations from genocide, war crimes, ethnic cleansing and crimes against humanity and its implications, bearing in mind the principles of the Charter and international law. We also intend to commit ourselves, as necessary and appropriate, to helping states build capacity to protect their populations from genocide, war crimes, ethnic cleansing and crimes against humanity and to assisting those which are under stress before crises and conflicts break out.[17]

This final formulation embraced the core principles which underlay the ICISS report. The doctrine had survived despite the concerted opposition of governments such as China, Russia, Cuba, Venezuela, India, Pakistan and Egypt. This, in turn, had been due in significant part to the support of key members states from the global South: Mexico, Chile, Argentina, and most importantly the African Union countries, among whom the most forceful advocates had been Rwanda and South Africa. These divisions in South ranks had prevented the doctrine from being characterized exclusively as part of a North agenda. Interestingly, the USA also issued a strong reservation to the effect that its adoption might create an unacceptable obligation under international

118   *The responsibility to protect*

law to intervene in specific and definable circumstances (see Groves, 2008). It had taken a lot of work, and the last-minute intervention of national leaders had been critical to seal the deal:

> As for R2P it was a minor miracle that we got this through. And that was achieved only because, in the end, there was political will at high levels to push it. If Paul Martin [Canadian PM] hadn't spoken with Singh [Indian PM] and others, this would not have happened. This kind of political push, from those without a particular axe to grind was crucial.[18]

The Summit resolution: an agreement to disagree?

Despite this success, a close look at the Summit resolution makes it plain that several of the doctrine's underlying principles will be heavily qualified in practice. In the process of negotiating the final text, victory went to those favouring the acceptance of the new norm. However, those opposing it, whether absolutely or conditionally, extracted very substantial concessions. The qualifications set in place were as follows.

- The crimes in relation to which a responsibility to protect may arise are limited to genocide, war crimes, ethnic cleansing and crimes against humanity. A suggestion from the US that an additional phrase 'or other major atrocities' be added to avoid further definitional argument was not adopted.
- The international community is enjoined in the first instance to exercise its responsibility by using all appropriate diplomatic, humanitarian and other peaceful means in accordance with the Charter. Collective action will be triggered only when such peaceful means are considered to have been inadequate. Such a general criterion will, naturally, leave a great deal of scope for argument as to whether and when the point of inadequacy has been reached.
- The international community, in its Summit embodiment, has indicated that it is 'prepared to take collective action'. Following from an American recommendation, the words 'we recognize our shared responsibility to take collective action' were removed. So, action on the responsibility to protect proceeds at the instigation of the member states but is not assumed to be an obligation arising from grievous circumstance. The term 'responsibility', insofar as it applies to the international community, is made referable only to the use of peaceful measures to halt a state's destruction of its peoples.
- Collective action by the international community must be authorized by the Security Council in accordance with the terms of Chapter VII of the Charter. The idea, referred to briefly by the High-Level Panel, that there may be certain circumstances in which intervention may be countenanced without such authorization did not make its way into the text. This leaves

open the question of what should happen, if anything, if the UN, for example as the result of a veto cast by one of the Security Council's permanent members, fails to fulfil its pledge.

- No criteria for intervention are specified. Instead, the international community, through the UN, will determine on a 'case-by-case' basis whether collective action to defend populations from criminal activities is required. This was a late insertion, at the behest of the US and the resolution's opponents, including China. It leaves open the prospect that the Security Council, as the representative institution of the international community, may make decisions to intervene in a manner more pragmatic than principled. And it opens the possibility that very considerable inconsistencies in practice may develop.
- The resolution includes a non-mandatory recommendation that regional organizations be consulted 'as appropriate' prior to collective action being taken through the relevant organs of the UN.
- Collective action under Chapter VII will be considered only where national authorities 'manifestly fail to protect their populations' from the relevant crimes. This is a standard considerably higher than that initially suggested. The original recommendation was that intervention may be countenanced where a state is demonstrated to be either 'unable or unwilling' to exercise its own responsibility to its peoples.
- The resolution stresses the need for the General Assembly to continue to consider the responsibility to protect, bearing in mind the principles of the Charter and international law. While desirable in principle, further discussion in the General Assembly, as post-summit statements by China make clear, raises the prospect that the operation of the new norm may be even further restricted as that discussion proceeds.
- Finally, a recommended qualification – that the permanent members of the Security Council should refrain from exercising the veto in cases of genocide, war crimes, ethnic cleansing and crimes against humanity – did not make its way into the final text.

There is no doubt that the formal recognition of the new doctrine of the responsibility to protect by the world's political leadership stands as one of the principal achievements of the UN reform process. However, as is plain from this analysis of the resolution's text, there remains ample room for argument as to its meaning and exercise. This remains a formidable hurdle for its practical application.

Another related difficulty which became clear was that, even shortly after the Summit, there were significant players who sought to deny that any agreement on the new norm's acceptance had ever really been concluded (see Saxer, 2008). There were a number of threads to this seeming retreat. Several interviewees suggested that their delegations had been pressed into agreement because for them to have stayed out would have destroyed the consensus necessary to ensure the World Summit succeeded in generating the final outcome document. For the sake of that overall consensus, they had been willing to endorse the new norm even though they did not support and would not adhere to it. Others pointed to the generality of the adopted text and questioned whether it could mean anything of significance unless elaborated further in discussion by the General Assembly:

> There was limited agreement on this at the Summit. It was agreed that the primary responsibility for the protection of people rests with sovereign states themselves. It is not for the international community to march in and protect people for them. The international community is engaged only if the state fails. And it was agreed further that R2P would go back to the GA for further discussion and refinement. But that has not happened. The problem is that there are all sorts of contradictions here with the principles of state sovereignty and non-intervention and so on. And we don't know what the parameters of the new doctrine are and are not talking about them. So, the issue is back in the freezer and is likely to be there for some considerable time.[19]

Others who still opposed the new norm were willing to concede that it had received some limited form of endorsement. At the same time, however, they were at pains to point out that, even so, its adoption signified nothing new. There were more than sufficient existing powers under the Charter and in associated treaties to permit the international community to take action upon genocide without pulling the new doctrine of responsibility to protect out of the drawer:

> You need to understand that the World Summit document did not create a radically new power. We already had the Genocide Convention. Genocide could already have been referred to the SC and the GA. With a stretch this may have allowed the referral of war crimes and crimes against humanity. So the problem was not the absence of law – the problem is the lack of political will. In Rwanda and Srebrenica, it was not the law at issue – it was the failure of the great powers to agree on any action. And then sanctions were imposed on victims and aggressors alike. Srebrenica was particularly shameful because there were UN troops and these withdrew knowing all the time that the victims would be taken. So, in 2005, member states did not do anything more than recognize their existing obligations under international law.[20]

Still others worried about the many qualifications and ambiguities that had remained or been deliberately situated in the resolution's text. Among this group of diplomats there were some who expressed doubts that the norm would ever be applied in practice because any debates with respect to it would become bogged down in endless discussions about terminology and interpretation. For that reason, the Security Council may have to look elsewhere for the authority to take action in cases of genocide and crimes against humanity. Other delegations took a quite different view. They expressed their fear that the resolution's lack of clarity would create the opportunity for more powerful states to impose an interpretation upon the new norm so that that it would favour their political and strategic interests.

Further, the whole issue became bound up with the institutional contestation between those who favoured the General Assembly's more active involvement in matters of international peace and security, and those in whose interests the Security Council's continuing domination of that subject matter was paramount. The clear view of delegations in the latter category was that once having achieved consensus on the existence of a responsibility to protect, it could only court trouble to reopen General Assembly discussion on the matter. Things should be left as they were – for fear of something worse:

> The summit made its statement, and the Security Council has adopted its own version. So, really, it's about as strong a statement of the norm as one could have hoped for. I suppose one could now try to move to some sort of elaboration or treaty. But I think this would take things backwards. Even if there could be agreement, which I doubt, a treaty would be opened for signature – and then there would be an endless wait. It remains, in the meantime, as an aspirational norm and, for the moment, that is just fine.[21]

Since the World Summit, the most significant development with respect to the responsibility to protect has been its recognition by the Security Council. In the context of a debate upon the protection of civilians in armed conflict, the Security Council approved Resolution 1674 dealing with all aspects of that question, including the promotion of economic growth, poverty eradication, national reconciliation, good governance, democracy, the rule of law and the protection of fundamental human rights.[22] This resolution reaffirmed 'the provisions of paragraphs 138 and 139 of the 2005 World Summit Outcome Document regarding the responsibility to protect populations from genocide, war crimes, ethnic cleansing and crimes against humanity'. Apart from the normative importance of this reaffirmation, the adoption of the resolution marked the first occasion upon which the Security Council acknowledged that its role may extend not just to the prevention of threats to international peace and security, but also to the cessation of mass atrocities taking place within state borders.

Here again, however, the Council's affirmation did not occur without significant reservations being expressed in other UN forums. In General Assembly debates concerning the protection of civilians in conflict that postdated the Security Council affirmation, for instance, China expressed its clear intention to limit the new norm's application to the maximum extent possible short of abandoning it altogether. Thus it emphasized that it was

122   *The responsibility to protect*

the primary responsibility of the government of a state to protect its civilians, and that the international community would have a role to play in supporting governments in this respect. In doing so, however, China repeated in the strongest of terms that no state had the right to infringe upon the sovereignty and territorial integrity of a state in the provision of any such assistance. The World Summit's text, therefore, should be given the narrowest possible reading:

> The World Summit Outcome last year gave an extensive and very cautious representation of the responsibility to protect populations from genocide ... and went on to request the General Assembly to continue to explore this concept. As many member states have expressed their concern and misgivings in that regard, we believe that it is not appropriate to expand, wilfully interpret or even abuse this concept. Resolution 1674 only reaffirmed in principle the relevant statement as contained in the Summit Outcome without any further elaboration. All sides should continue to abide by the relevant agreed elements of the Summit Outcome in interpreting or applying this concept. In that context, the Security Council cannot and should not take over the role of the General Assembly or make any prejudgment.[23]

The Russian Federation took a very similar position.

As in the debate prior to the Summit, both European and African states were prepared to re-commit to the doctrine. So, for instance, both Ghana and Tanzania proposed that member states had a moral duty to act to protect civilians, and not only in the face of genocide, war crimes, ethnic cleansing and crimes against humanity. They should, on this view, 'stop paying lip service to the concept of the responsibility to protect and have the political will to stand by their convictions'.

Soon after, without any further elaboration of the concept, the Security Council invoked the new norm for the first time – in relation to the situation in Darfur. In Resolution 1706, the Council resolved, among other things, to deploy a UN peacekeeping force in Darfur, and sought the consent of the Sudanese Government to do so. This peacekeeping force would replace the African Union force that had been in place until that time, but which had not been conspicuously successful in halting the genocide. In its preliminaries, the Resolution recalled Resolution 1674 and its reaffirmation of the terms of the World Summit Outcome in this respect. It reaffirmed the Council's strong commitment to the sovereignty, unity, independence and territorial integrity of Sudan, but made it clear that the nation's sovereignty would not be affected by the transition to a UN force devoted to the cause of peace. At the time of writing, the Sudanese Government has still refused to give the requisite permission. However, the invocation of the preceding resolutions concerning the responsibility to protect marked a further step, however small, in establishing its standing in international law.

Looking to the future

Considered in the context of the fraught and contested history of humanitarian interventions undertaken under the auspices of the UN, and those that proceeded in the absence of such authority, it can be counted as a remarkable achievement of the Summit that the relevant text, however qualified, obtained endorsement. In its reconceptualization of sovereignty as responsibility; its calibrated approach to the duty of states and the international community collectively in the protection of citizens; its recognition of the entitlement of the international community to intervene in situations of grave criminal activity perpetrated by states against their people; and in its embrace of corresponding duties to prevent and rebuild, the new doctrine can fairly be regarded as a significant addition to the normative framework of international law. It may not be, as the Secretary-General remarked in his speech to the World Summit, a 'revolution in international affairs', but the potential for it to be one is there. The endorsement of the norm so soon after the Secretary-General had been criticized severely for his advocacy of humanitarian intervention in 1999 is, in its turn, a testament to the work of the commissions that preceded the Summit, to the Secretary-General's own forceful advocacy, and to the last-minute interventions by influential national leaders. Indeed, as one commentator noted, paragraphs 138 and 139 may represent the World Summit's only major normative development (Chesterman, 2006, 14).

So, much may readily be acknowledged – although it will have become apparent from the preceding discussion that, despite the Summit's endorsement, there remain significant divisions between nations as to the appropriateness of the doctrine's adoption and its application in practice (Evans, 2008). Further, it would be an error to dismiss out of hand the arguments of those countries expressing continuing reservations. Despite the moral force attaching to the necessity and duty to protect civilians subject to grave breaches of human rights within state borders, the appeal these opponents have made to the UN Charter's principle of non-intervention deserves respect and a considered response. Those with reservations about the new doctrine's application need to be satisfied that the responsibility to protect will not emerge simply as code for the extension of the self-interest of its most powerful protagonists (Ayoob, 2002, 81; Thakur, 2004, 201). The Prime Minister of Malaysia encapsulated the principal problem in this respect as follows:

> We live in a time of uncertainty and change. New concepts and doctrines have been foisted on us, including such notions as 'humanitarian intervention', the 'responsibility to protect' and pre-emptive war, among others. All of these pose a challenge to traditional and universally accepted concepts enshrined in the UN Charter. We should strongly oppose any attempts at eroding them ... We should steadfastly uphold the fundamental principles regarding the sovereignty and inviolability of states.

124   *The responsibility to protect*

> The future of the developing countries, indeed, the entire world, lies
> best in an international order that is based on active multilateralism. It
> should not be domination by one country or group of countries. It should
> observe international law and norms. International relations should be
> based on a more equitable and just system that ensures a more prosper-
> ous, secure and peaceful world. It is therefore in our fundamental interest
> to work for an international system that guarantees equitable rights and
> benefits for all countries, not just a few.[24]

If one thing is evident since the World Summit, it is that, despite some
appalling candidates, no international crisis has yet been identified as one to
which the new doctrine should be applied. The situation in Darfur has been
riddled with too many political, logistical and interpretative difficulties
(Feinstein, 2007, 38; Piiparinen, 2007, 365). In Burma, neither the sickness
nor starvation consequent upon the cyclone persuaded either the Burmese
generals or the international community that intervention in support of
humanitarian operations should be embarked upon. In both instances, there
has been neither consent from within nor sufficient determination from without
to make military or humanitarian intervention a practical possibility.

Further, and in particular in the context of this discussion, the lack of
action may also have been attributable to the reality that much more needs to
be done to clarify the new norm's meaning, parameters and application. It is
for this reason that Ban Ki-moon decided early in 2008 that it was necessary
to appoint a high-level special adviser to work through the new norm's very
considerable conceptual and practical difficulties.

The first thing that needs to be done is to determine more precisely in what
situations the responsibility to protect should be applicable. Failing that,
almost anything, or effectively nothing, may happen:

> What is an R2P situation? If we don't nail that down we create an
> environment in which the spoilers will thrive. The whole idea will just be
> considered as an all-purpose excuse for the big guys to intervene here,
> there and everywhere. And, from the other side, we need to be insistent as
> to what this is really about. When you actually put the proposition to the
> big guys who are resistant, they duck and weave but when you say do we
> want another Rwanda or Srebrenica, no one disputes that something has
> to be done. And, on the other hand, we need to avoid silly statements
> about its extent, as when Lloyd Axworthy [former Canadian Foreign
> Minister] gave a speech asking 'shouldn't R2P apply to protect the
> human rights of the Inuit people from the effects of climate change?'[25]

Next, it is plain that a broader international consensus in favour of the
responsibility to protect in principle, and its application in practice, must be
attained. No nation objects to the idea of international action to protect
peoples from genocide, crimes against humanity, ethnic cleansing and other

gross and systematic abuses of human rights – in the abstract. It is the contestation in the particular case that obstructs. If greater international acceptance is to be achieved, one necessary precondition will be that, in principle and practice, the application of the doctrine must be seen to be fair. That, in turn, will require a more precise specification of the conditions under which intervention should be contemplated – and when it should not be contemplated. Those in the developing world with legitimate concerns about the potential misuse of the doctrine by nations possessing political power and military muscle need to be more or less satisfied that military intervention in the exercise of the responsibility to protect will be contemplated only in predefined and broadly acceptable circumstances.

It follows naturally that agreed criteria for action under the Charter should be considered and adopted (Charney, 1999, 834; Evans and Sahnoun, 2002, 99; Stromseth, 2003, 232; Evans, 2004, 60; Thakur, 2006, 260). As has previously been illustrated, however, this is an immensely difficult enterprise, and one that has been quite unsuccessful to date. There is likely to be disputation around any set of criteria. And even the development of any criteria at all will be opposed by nations that wish to proceed case-by-case so as to retain their political room to manoeuvre. Nevertheless, the successful negotiation of criteria seems essential to obtaining broader agreement on the doctrine's acceptance. To proceed case-by-case, without accepted guidelines, invites the prospect that disagreement will prosper in every case. And without at least some measure of consensus around the prerequisites for action, fears that the doctrine will be applied arbitrarily and in the interests of the dominant powers appear certain to stymie progress, perhaps indefinitely.

Both the ICISS and the High-Level Panel advanced a set of principles for intervention. The Commission proposed that certain cautionary principles should frame any relevant discussion. Having determined that international crimes are being committed and that military intervention should be contemplated, it recommended that the Security Council should consider four criteria.

- *The principle of right intention*, which involves an examination of the motivations for intervention and, more particularly, the desirability of ensuring that the primary objective should be the alleviation of human suffering.
- *The principle of last resort*, which requires consideration as to whether it may reasonably be concluded that all less invasive means of intervention have been tried and failed.
- *The principle of proportional means*, which requires that the intensity, scale and duration of any planned intervention should be the minimum necessary in order to achieve the purpose set down.
- *The principle of reasonable prospects*, which entails both an examination of the likelihood of success and a careful consideration of the possibility that the damage inflicted by any such success may outweigh the projected alleviation in human suffering to be achieved thereby.

126   *The responsibility to protect*

These principles, which are the product of detailed consideration by at least two major international inquiries, would be as good a place as any to begin.

Further discussion around process will also need to take place. Here, the critical question concerns authorization (Welsh, 2004, 177; Badescu, 2007, 52). The World Summit resolution makes it plain that only the Security Council possesses the standing and legitimacy to resolve upon military action. And yet the weaknesses of the Security Council as a deliberative and decision-making body in this regard are well known. In the absence of any reasonable alternative, however, it is likely that the existing consensus upon the Security Council's exclusive authority will remain in place. This fact will necessitate, at the very least, significant procedural reform as one precondition for the legitimate and effective exercise of its discretion. So, for example, in the negotiations that preceded the final draft of the World Summit resolution, consideration had been given to the ICISS recommendation that the P-5 should voluntarily relinquish their exercise of the veto when action was contemplated by the international community in response to a situation of genocide. A reconsideration and adoption of this recommendation, or something similar, would appear to have much to commend it.

Finally, for the responsibility to protect genuinely to take its place in the panoply of measures to secure peace and the observance of fundamental human rights, there are many logistical questions that need to be addressed and resolved (Hamilton, 2006, 289; Holt and Berkman, 2006, 179; Banda, 2007, 25; Evans, 2007; Feinstein, 2007; Weiss, 2007, chapter 5). So, for example, considerably greater thought will need to be given to how best to ensure responsibility to protect situations do not arise in the first place. This may require the development of better and more sophisticated early warning and monitoring systems. The next step in a calibrated set of responses may be the imposition of targeted sanctions. More work needs to be done in determining which sanctions – political, legal, economic or military – are likely to be most effective, and in what circumstances each kind might best be applied. Should sanctions fail to prevent grave human rights abuse, the deployment of peacekeeping forces, preferably with the consent of the government concerned, may be necessary. The new Peacebuilding Commission is well placed to take the initiative here. But even with its assistance, standing questions such as how quickly to assemble any such force, with what degree of military training and expertise, and with what specific mandate and instructions, remain to be resolved. Should military intervention be contemplated, it may first be appropriate to engage those deployable by existing regional organizations rather than endeavouring to assemble an international force. Memoranda of understanding between the Security Council and these regional organizations require development, together with clear and agreed terms of engagement. In both cases, plainly, it will be crucial to make sure the material capacity – military forces, equipment and money – required to ensure humanitarian missions are successful will be forthcoming. By whom this capacity may be provided, in what configurations and coalitions, with what lines of responsibility and within what kinds of timelines are all questions that need to be addressed now, if the world organization's commitment to implement the responsibility to protect is to move from norm to reality.

It is for these reasons, among others, that even the most ardent advocates of the responsibility to protect acknowledge that the full acceptance and implementation of the doctrine may still be still many years off:

> I think really that this is a ten year project. There is a great deal of thought that now has to be given to implementing this. What does the concept mean in more detail? What steps should be taken prior to military intervention? Forced intervention is only the measure of last resort. What are the resource implications? Who should buy in? How can a UN force be put together rapidly? Who will supply troops? A lot more work needs to be done in clarifying the respective roles of the Security Council and the relevant regional organizations who should also play a part. The [African Union] is in principle still well disposed but others are uncertain ... So, we need to think still harder about this, to flesh out the idea, let alone working to get the required political will.[26]

Beneath it all, it is the fundamental absence of political will that must be addressed. Perhaps all that can be said in this respect is that the in-principle acceptance of the international community's responsibility to protect was founded, in the end, upon its concern not to witness a reprise of the Rwandan, Bosnian or East Timorese genocides. In philosophical, psychological, legal and practical terms, this has represented a recognition, though not without reservation, that the world may no longer stand by as large numbers of its citizens, whether situated within or across national borders, are butchered or starved. Of course, as has been illustrated here, much remains to be done before the abstract principle can be translated into some practical reality. But, at least, the *prima facie* recognition by the international community that it does have a responsibility to protect its global citizens from genocide and other similar crimes constitutes one incremental step towards the fulfilment of that moral aim. To what extent the World Summit will have contributed to that quest remains to be determined.

200 **Notes**

1 UN Documents S/RES/1999/1265 and S/RES/2000/1296.
2 UN DocumentsA/55/305-S/RES/2000/809.
3 Declaration on Principles of International Law Concerning Friendly Relations and Co-operation among States in Accordance with the Charter of the United Nations of October 24, 1970, Article 1.
4 Policy Document No. 148; *British Year Book of International Law*, Vol. 57, 1986, p. 614.
5 Address by Kofi Annan to the 54th Session of the UN General Assembly, 20 September 1999, reprinted in Annan (1999), p. 39.
6 *A More Secure World: Our Shared Responsibility*, Report of the High-Level Panel on Threats, Challenges and Change, UN Document A/59/565, 2004.
7 *ibid.*
8 *In Larger Freedom: Towards Development, Security and Human Rights for All*, Report of the Secretary-General, UN Document A/59/2005, 2005, p. 35.
9 Abdallah Baali, Permanent Representative of Algeria, Statement to the Informal Thematic Consultations of the General Assembly to Discuss the Four Clusters Contained in the Secretary-General's Report 'In Larger Freedom', Cluster III: Freedom to Live in Dignity, 19 April 2005.
10 Allan Rock, Permanent Representative of Canada, Statement to the Informal Thematic Consultations of the General Assembly to Discuss the Four Clusters Contained in the Secretary-General's Report 'In Larger Freedom', Cluster III: Freedom to Live in Dignity, 20 April 2005.
11 Sir Emyr Jones Parry, Permanent Representative of the United Kingdom, Informal Meeting of the Plenary to Discuss the Revised Text of the Draft Outcome Document of the High Level Plenary Meeting of the General Assembly, Statement on behalf of the European Union, 28 July–2 August 2005.
12 President of Tanzania, Benjamin Mkapa, Address to the First Summit of the International Conference of the Great Lakes, Dar-es-Salaam, November 2004.
13 Nirupam Sen, Permanent Representative of India, Nations, Informal Thematic Consultations of the General Assembly to Discuss the Four Clusters Contained in the Secretary-General's Report, *In Larger Freedom*, Cluster III: Freedom to Live in Dignity, 20 April 2005.
14 Munir Akram, Permanent Representative of Pakistan, Informal Thematic Consultations of the General Assembly to Discuss the Four Clusters Contained in the Secretary-General's Report, *In Larger Freedom*, Cluster III: Freedom to Live in Dignity, 19 April 2005.
15 Xie Bohua, Counsellor, Diplomatic Mission of China, Informal Thematic Consultations of the General Assembly to Discuss the Four Clusters Contained in the Secretary-General's Report *In Larger Freedom*, Cluster III: Freedom to Live in Dignity, 20 April 2005.
16 Allan Rock, Permanent Representative of Canada, Informal Thematic Consultations of the General Assembly to Discuss the Four Clusters Contained in the Secretary-General's Report. *In Larger Freedom*, Cluster III: Freedom to Live in Dignity, 20 April 2005.
17 2005 World Summit Outcome, UN Doc. A/60/L.1.
18 Personal interview, WEOG foreign minister, September 2007.
19 Personal interview, African ambassador, May 2007.
20 Personal interview, Asian ambassador, April 2007.
21 Personal interview, WEOG ambassador, May 2007.
22 S/Res/1674.
23 Open Debate on the Protection of Civilians in Armed Conflict, Security Council, 4 December 2006, Statement of Mr Liu Zhenmin.
24 Prime Minister Datuk Seri Abdullah Ahmad Badawi, Speech at the Opening of the Ministerial Meeting of the Non-Aligned Movement Coordinating Bureau, 29 May 2006.
25 Personal interview, WEOG foreign minister, September 2007.
26 Personal interview, WEOG ambassador, May 2007.

References

Acharya, A. (2002). 'Redefining the Dilemmas of Humanitarian Intervention'. *Australian Journal of International Affairs* 56: 373.

Ayoob M. (2002). 'Humanitarian Intervention and State Sovereignty', *International Journal of Human Rights* 6(1): 81–102.

Badescu, C.G. (2007). 'Authorizing Humanitarian Intervention: Hard Choices in Saving Strangers', *Canadian Journal of Political Science* 40(1): 51–78.

Bannon A. L. (2006). 'The Responsibility to Protect. The U.N. World Summit and the Question of Unilateralism'. *The Yale Law Journal* 115: 1157–1165.

Bellamy A.J. (2006). Preventing Future Kosovos and Future Rwandas: The Responsibility to Protect after the 2005 World Summit

— (2006). 'Whither the Responsibility to Protect?'. *Ethics & International Affairs* 20(2):143–169.

Byers, M. (2002), *War Law*. London, Atlantic Books.

Byers, M. and S. Chesterman (2003). 'Changing the Rules about Rules: Unilateral Humanitarian Intervention and the Future of International Law'. *Humanitarian Intervention*. eds J.L. Holzgreve and R. Keohane. Cambridge, Cambridge University Press.

Charney, J. (1999). 'Anticipatory Humanitarian Intervention in Kosovo'. *American Journal of International Law* 93(4): 834–41.

Chesterman, S. (2001). *Just War or Just Peace?* Oxford, Oxford University Press.

— (2006). 'Reforming the United Nations: Kofi Annan's Legacy gets a Reality Check'. *Strategic Insights*, Australian Strategic Policy Institute.

Evans, G. (2004). 'When is it Right to Fight?' *Survival: Global Politics and Strategy* 46(3): 59–81.

— (2007) 'Preventing Mass Atrocities: Making the Responsibility to Protect a Reality'. United Nations University/International Crisis Group Conference on Prevention of Mass Atrocities: From Mandate to Realization. New York, 10 October 2007.

— (2008). 'The Responsibilty to Protect: An Idea Whose Time has Come…and Gone?' Lecture to David Davies Memorial Institute, University of Aberystwyth, 23 April 2008.

Evans, G. and M. Sahnoun (2002). 'The Responsibility to Protect'. *Foreign Affairs*, Council on Foreign Relations. 81: 99.

Farer, T. (2003). 'Humanitarian Intervention Before and After 9/11: Legality and Legitimacy'. *Humanitarian Intervention*. eds J.L. Holzgreve and R. Keohane. Cambridge, Cambridge University Press.

Feinstein, L. (2007). *Darfur and Beyond: What is Needed to Prevent Mass Atrocities*. Washington, DC, Council on Foreign Relations.

Gazzini, T. (2005). *The Changing Rules on the Use of Force in International Law*. Manchester, Manchester University Press.

Gordon, R. (1993). 'United Nations Intervention in Internal Conflicts: Iraq, Somalia, and Beyond'. *Michigan Journal of International Law* 15(2): 519–90.

Hamilton, R. (2006). 'The Responsibility to Protect: From Document to Doctrine – But What of Implementation?' *Harvard Human Rights Journal* 19: 289–97.

Holt, V. and T. Berkman (2006). *The Impossible Mandate? Military Preparedness, the Responsibility to Protect, and Modern Peace Operations*. Washington, DC, The Henry L.Stimson Center.

Holzgreve, J. (2003). 'The Humanitarian Intervention Debate'. *Humanitarian Intervention*. eds J.L. Holzgreve and R. Keohane. Cambridge, Cambridge University Press.

Kioko, B. (2003).'The Right of Intervention Under the African Union's Constitutive Act: Non-Interference to Non-Intervention'. *International Review of the Red Cross* 85(852): 807–25.

Molier, G. (2006). 'Humanitarian Intervention and the Responsibility to Protect after 9/11'. *Netherlands International Law Review* 53: 37-62.

Piiparinen, T. (2007). 'The Lessons of Darfur for the Future of Humanitarian Intervention'. *Global Governance* 13(3): 365–90.

Saxer, M. (2008). 'The Politics of Responsibility to Protect'. *Briefing Papers*. Berlin, Friedrich Ebert Stiftung.

Stahn, C. (2007). 'Responsibility to Protect: Political Rhetoric or Emerging Legal Norm?' *American Journal of International Law* 101(1): 99–120.

Stromseth, J. (2003). 'Rethinking Humanitarian Intervention: The Case for Incremental Change'. *Humanitarian Intervention*. eds J.L. Holzgreve and R. Keohane. Cambridge, Cambridge University Press.

Thakur, R. (2004). 'Developing Countries and the Intervention-Sovereignty Debate'. *The United Nations and Global Security*. R.M. Price and M.W. Zacher, eds. New York, PalgraveMacmillan.

— (2006). *The United Nations, Peace and Security*. Cambridge. Cambridge University Press.

Weiss, T. (2007). *Humanitarian Intervention: Ideas in Action*. Cambridge, Polity Press.

Welsh, J. (2004). 'Authorizing Humanitarian Intervention'. The United Nations and Global Security. R.M. Price and M.W. Zacher, eds. New York, Palgrave Macmillan.

— (2004). 'The Evolution of Humanitarian Intervention for Humanitarian Purposes in International Society'. *Humanitarian Intervention and International Relations*. J.M. Welsh, ed. Oxford, Oxford University Press.

Wheeler, N. (2004). 'The Humanitarian Responsibilities of Sovereignty; Explaining the Development of a New Norm of Military Intervention for Humanitarian Purposes in International Society'. *Humanitarian Intervention and International Relations*. J.M. Welsh, ed. Oxford, Oxford University Press.

[22]

The Responsibility to Protect Doctrine and Humanitarian Intervention: Too Many Ambiguities for a Working Doctrine

Carlo Focarelli*

Abstract

The question about possible remedies, including military intervention, to avoid or to put an end to massive violations of human rights committed by a state towards its own citizens or in situations where state authorities critically lack effectiveness has been extensively debated since the issuance in 2001 of the report of the International Commission on Intervention and State Sovereignty (ICISS) on the responsibility to protect. After a succinct and critical review of the ICISS' report and the subsequent international instruments dealing with the responsibility to protect, this contribution focuses on the positions adopted by states, especially over the last three years at the General Assembly and at the Security Council of the United Nations on humanitarian intervention as a 'corollary' of the responsibility to protect doctrine. It appears that humanitarian intervention aimed at implementing the responsibility to protect is not only feared as imperialistic by several weak states, but it also significantly fails to find an unconditioned support even amongst the most powerful states. Given its extreme and multifaceted ambiguity, which is discussed in the last section of this contribution, the innovative content of the purported 'emerging norm' on the responsibility to protect, as well as its prospect to emerge in the future, remain rather unclear.

Keywords: responsibility to protect; humanitarian intervention; gross violation of human rights; UN General Assembly; UN Security Council; failed states.

1. Introduction

The 'responsibility to protect' in international law has been widely debated over the last few years. As is well known, the discussion originated in the report issued in December 2001 by the International Commission on Intervention and State Sovereignty (ICISS), an initiative of the Canadian government.[1] The debate is about the possible remedies, including military intervention, to avoid or to put an end to massive violations of human rights committed by a state towards its own citizens or in situations where state authorities critically lack effectiveness. The report was born with a view to finding a positive solution – legally acceptable and compatible with state sovereignty – to the traditional problem of humanitarian intervention, and more precisely to the question posed by the then UN Secretary-General Kofi Annan, who asked 'if humanitarian intervention

* Professor of International Law, University of Perugia and LUISS University of Rome, Italy. E-mail: carlo.focarelli@alice.it

[1] The report is available at <http://www.iciss.ca/pdf/Commission-Report.pdf>.

is, indeed, an unacceptable assault on sovereignty, how should we respond to a Rwanda, to a Srebrenica – to gross and systematic violations of human rights that affect every precept of our common humanity?'.[2]

The doctrine of the responsibility to protect has now been extensively discussed both in legal doctrine and in international practice,[3] with positions that range from vibrant acceptance, through relative indifference as a mere political catchword, to rejection.[4] The opposition between advocates and critics is supposed to be encapsulated by the notion that responsibility to protect is the

---

[2] *We the Peoples: The Role of the United Nations in the 21st Century*, Millennium Report of the Secretary-General of the United Nations, September 2000, p. 48. Available at <http://www.un.org/millennium/sg/report/full.htm>. The Secretary-General's answer was that 'surely no legal principle – not even sovereignty – can ever shield crimes against humanity. Where such crimes occur and peaceful attempts to halt them have been exhausted, the Security Council has a moral duty to act on behalf of the international community. The fact that we cannot protect people everywhere is no reason for doing nothing when we can. Armed intervention must always remain the option of last resort, but in the face of mass murder it is an option that cannot be relinquished'.

[3] And extended to natural disasters, at which the report did make a hint (para. 4.20), see T. R. Saechao, 'Natural Disasters and the Responsibility to Protect: From Chaos to Clarity', (2007) 32 *Brooklyn Journal of Int. Law* 663–707; the doctrine has also provided an opportunity to justify – as a 'corollary', but going well beyond its original strictly humanitarian grounds – pre-emptive military operations against states being suspected of using weapons of mass destruction or of making it possible for terrorist groups to use such weapons, cf. M. F. Feinstein, A.-M. Slaughter, 'A Duty to Prevent', (2004) 83 *Foreign Affairs* 136–150.

[4] See, e.g. R. C. Thakur, 'Intervention, Sovereignty and the Responsibility to Protect', (2002) 33 *Security Dialogue* 323–340; J. I. Levitt, 'The Responsibility to Protect: A Beaver Without a Dam?', (2003) 25 *Michigan Journal of International Law* 153–177; R. C. Thakur, 'In Defense of the Responsibility to Protect', (2003) 7 *International Journal of Human Rights* 160–178; D. Warner, 'Responsibility to Protect and the Limits of Imagination', (2003) 7 *Int. Journal of Human Rights* 154–159; A. J. Bellamy, 'Responsibility to Protect or Trojan Horse? The Crisis in Darfur and Humanitarian Intervention after Iraq', (2005) 19 *Ethics & International Affairs* 31–53; T. G. Weiss, *Military–Civilian Interactions: Humanitarian Crises and the Responsibility to Protect* (2005); P. Williams and A. Bellamy, 'The Responsibility to Protect and the Crisis in Darfur', (2005) 36 *Security Dialogue* 27–47; M.-J. Zahar, 'Intervention, Prevention, and the "Responsibility to Protect"', (2005) 60 *International Journal* 723–734; G. Molier, 'Humanitarian Intervention and the Responsibility to Protect after 9/11', (2006) 53 *Netherlands Int. Law Review* 37–62; R. C. Thakur, *The United Nations, Peace and Security from Collective Security to the Responsibility to Protect* (2006); A. L. Bannon, 'The Responsibility to Protect: The U.N. World Summit and the Question of Unilateralism', (2006) 115 *The Yale Law Journal* 1157–1165; R. J. Hamilton, 'The Responsibility to Protect from Document to Doctrine – But What of Implementation?', (2006) 19 *Harvard Human Rights Journal* 289–297; P. Hilpold, 'The Duty to Protect and the Reform of the United Nations, a New Step in the Development of International Law?', (2006) 10 *Max Planck Yearbook of United Nations Law* 35–69; L. Boisson de Chazournes and L. Condorelli, 'De la 'Responsabilité de Protéger', ou d'une Nouvelle Parure pour une Notion déjà Bien Établie', (2006) *Revue Générale de Droit Internationale Public* 11–18; A. J. Bellamy, *Preventing Future Kosovos and Future Rwandas: The Responsibility to Protect after the 2005 World Summit* (2006); A. Bellamy, 'Whither the Responsibility to Protect?', (2006) 20 *Ethics & International Affairs* 143–169; C. Stahn, 'Responsibility

subject of an international 'emerging norm', meaning a norm situated in limbo halfway between existence and non-existence. Scholars rarely endeavour to check if, and to what extent, it is supported by states as a whole. On the other hand, the responsibility to protect doctrine was introduced precisely to overcome 'from outside' – for humanitarian purposes – the 'natural' aversion of states to limitations to their sovereignty. Any wait for states' consent to a limitation to their sovereignty while massacres occur without being able to intervene has clearly appeared morally unsatisfactory. In short, while the initiative was owed to one state, and welcomed by others, it hoped to encourage consensus amongst non-state entities, like NGOs, which could then exert a positive influence over reluctant states.[5]

But if this is true, then it is also true that without support from states as a whole, an 'emerging' norm can hardly 'emerge' and credibly be binding upon them. The issue recently arose at the UN General Assembly and at the UN Security Council, both in general terms and in respect of specific instances, where states have had the opportunity to express their positions thereupon. Furthermore, on 31 August 2007, the UN Secretary-General notified the President of the Security Council his intention to appoint a Special Adviser on the Responsibility to Protect,[6] obtaining a green light on 11 December 2007.[7] The responsibility to protect doctrine thus seems destined to keep attracting attention in the near future. The purpose of this paper is to evaluate it in the light of the attitudes taken by states at the United Nations, especially during the last three years.

2. The 2001 Report of the International Commission on Intervention and State Sovereignty (ICISS)

Before examining the positions of states, it is convenient to critically review the responsibility to protect doctrine, at least in its major points, as it was first formulated in the 2001 ICISS report and has subsequently evolved in other international instruments.

The ICISS report addresses the question of possible remedies to avoid massacres in civil wars, insurrections, acts of state repression and failed states by first

---

to Protect: Politic Rhetoric or Emerging Legal Norm?', (2007) 101 *American Journal of Int. Law* 99–120. M. Benzing, 'Sovereignty and the Responsibility to Protect in International Criminal Law', in D. König, P. T. Stoll, V. Röben, N. Metz-Lück (eds), *International Law Today: New Challenges and the Need for Reform*? (2008) 17–50.

[5] The responsibility to protect doctrine finds wide acceptance amongst NGOs; see <http://www.responsibilitytoprotect.org/index.php/civil_society_statements/293? theme = alt1>.

[6] UN doc. S/2007/721.

[7] <http://www.un.org/apps/news/story.asp?NewsID=25010&Cr=appoint&Cr1=>. On 21 February 2008 the Secretary-General announced the appointment of Mr Edward C. Luck as Special Adviser on the Responsibility to Protect (cf. <http://www.reformtheun.org/index.php?module=uploads&func=download&fileld=2828>).

and foremost changing the nominal label of the problem, namely by posing the question in terms of responsibility to protect rather than in terms of humanitarian intervention. To quote the Commission, 'the language of past debates arguing for or against a "right to intervene" by one state on the territory of another state is outdated and unhelpful' (para. 2.4). Clearly, the intention of the ICISS was to promote – and hence to do so as effectively as possible – a new international law regime capable of solving a no-longer evadable problem (para. 6.17). From this perspective, it is hardly surprising that the Commission was concerned with the 'look' of its product, though in its view the look corresponded to some substance.[8]

The report's central idea is that in today's globalised world, sovereignty as control, which is deemed to be typical of the so-called Westphalian system, must give way to sovereignty as responsibility, both external (towards other states) and internal (towards citizens) (para. 2.14), as a result of the dramatically growing impact of international norms on human rights and of the concept of human security. The opposition between control and responsibility is neither clear, nor does it appear coherent within the report. In fact, it could be objected that it is precisely thanks to control that states can be responsible. Furthermore, the report underscores in various points that sovereignty (as control) is still necessary *inter alia* to respect and ensure respect for human rights. For instance, the Commission pointed out that 'the key to the effective observance of human rights remains, as it always has been, national law and practice' (para. 2.20) and that 'sovereignty does still matter', since 'effective and legitimate states remain the best way to ensure that the benefits of internationalization of trade, investment, technology and communication will be equitably shared'. Significantly, the Commission was convinced that 'a cohesive and peaceful international system is far more likely to be achieved through the cooperation of effective states, confident of their place in the world, than in an environment of fragile, collapsed, fragmenting or generally chaotic state entities' (para. 1.34). Of course, the Commission also emphasised the need for sovereignty to be limited. But it may be contended that state sovereignty has always been limited in one way or another, the problem being to determine what different and new limits it has today rather than theoretically contrasting an old concept to another which is supposed to reach more consensus.[9] It may be added that even assuming that the distinction between control and responsibility is satisfactory, it still remains unclear why from sovereignty as responsibility certain practical consequences,

---

[8] According to the Commission, 'if people are prepared to look at all these issues from the new perspective that we propose, it may just make finding agreed answers that much easier' (para. 2.5). As states hardly let themselves mislead by words, it seems that the Commission intended to find answers more easily acceptable in the world at large outside states (for instance, in the world public opinion and in its representing entities), so as to indirectly force the most reluctant states to accept it as a response to their own peoples' pressure.

[9] On the question of the relationship between sovereignty and pursuance of global values, see C. Focarelli, 'Il Sistema degli Stati e il Governo dell'Umanità nel Diritto Internazionale Contemporaneo', (2007) 6 *Quaderni di Relazioni Internazionali* 42–53.

such as humanitarian intervention, should be inferred. In other words, even assuming that sovereignty is today better made sense of in terms of responsibility, it does not necessarily follow that humanitarian intervention is lawful, nor does it necessarily follow that – in the Commission's words – an 'emerging guiding principle' in favour of said intervention exists (para. 2.26). New general concepts may well better explain new realities, but it does not follow that they are able to generate *by themselves* new legal norms.

According to the Commission, while 'there is not yet a sufficiently strong basis to claim the emergence of a new principle of customary international law', the responsibility to protect is indeed the subject of an 'emerging guiding principle' (paras. 2.24 and 6.17) inasmuch as it is 'supported by a wide variety of legal sources', including 'fundamental natural law principles', the UN Charter's provisions on human rights, the numerous existing treaties on human rights and on international humanitarian law and the Statute of the International Criminal Court (para. 2.26). The Commission's conclusion is 'that there is a large and accumulating body of law and practice which supports the notion that, whatever form the exercise of that responsibility may properly take, members of the broad community of states do have a responsibility to protect both their own citizens and those of other states as well' (para. 2.27). Clearly, if no problem may arise in respect of existing treaty norms on human rights and international humanitarian law, the appeal to natural law can hardly go unnoticed and raise doubts. One cannot help but wonder whether natural law is in actual fact a source of international law and whether, if so, one can or even must from its principles necessarily or automatically draw a right (if not an obligation) of humanitarian intervention. In fact, natural law is not mentioned in Article 38 of the Statute of the International Court of Justice and all attempts aimed to introduce – in the works of the Committee of Jurists who drafted the Statute of the Permanent Court of International Justice – the principles of justice corresponding to 'la loi du juste et de l'injuste, telle qu'elle est gravée et tracée de façon ineffaçable au cœur des peuples civilisés' failed and the more objective formula 'general principles of law recognised by the civilised nations' was preferred, while decisions *ex aequo et bono* were made dependent on an *ad hoc* agreement between the parties.[10] On the other hand, while using humanitarian expressions from time to time, states do not seem to be inclined to accept natural law as a source of international law. It is true that natural law could be relied on precisely to 'moderate' states' exclusive role in the present-day world system, as held by those who invoke it,[11] but it is also true that, perhaps today even more than in the past, states are indispensable

---

[10] Permanent Court of International Justice, Advisory Committee of Jurists, *Procés-verbaux of the Proceedings of the Committee, June 16th–24th July 1920 with Annexes*, The Hague, 1920, p. 325. For the English version, whose text reads 'the conception of justice and injustice as undeniably written on the hearts of civilised people', see p. 324.

[11] A critique to the 'relativism' of current international law, as well as to the United Nations as a body dependent heavily on the behaviour of states which are detached from the natural moral law, was recently made by Pope Benedictus XVI in a speech on 1 December 2007, addressed to Catholic NGOs. Available at <http://

for ensuring respect of human rights. Attention should be paid to avoid identifying international norms which, without any state support, only exist on paper. Nor can it be overlooked that natural law, though it may reflect objectively universal values, is historically the result of western cultural and legal elaboration, representing the Euro-Christian subjective projection of what has been presumed as universal.[12] In addition, caution should be exercised when passing from natural law to humanitarian intervention. Natural law may provide for responsibility principles and standards towards citizens, yet it may not allow humanitarian intervention in case those standards should be transgressed. It is well known that the debate on the use of military force within the just war doctrine – which has its roots in the Euro-Christian theological thinking – has historically produced a variety of solutions in different authors and contexts. It is thus difficult to prefer in the abstract, i.e. as a mere and direct consequence of the *concept* of the responsibility to protect, one solution to another, unless the concept is aimed at promoting practical consequences that are not yet provided for by the existing law – though possibly 'inspired' by what is believed to be a natural law – but are hoped to emerge in the future for the benefit of humanity.

According to the Commission, the new concept of sovereignty, understood more as responsibility than as control, gives rise to three types of responsibility, or tasks or duties,[13] of both individual states and the international community as a whole: the responsibility to prevent, to react and to rebuild. Indeed, it is precisely within this broader framework that in the Commission's view, the problem of humanitarian intervention – which in any event remains at the heart of the report – justifies *inter alia* the linguistic sliding from the traditional 'right of intervention' to the new 'responsibility to protect' (para. 2.29). The duty to protect is in the first place vested with the state in whose territory the violation of human rights is occurring (paras. 3.1–3.43). It is only when this state proves unable or unwilling to discharge the duty to prevent that the international community's duty to react as a whole would set off. This duty should preferably be discharged by peaceful measures – ranging from early warning mechanisms through development assistance to economic sanctions – but can ultimately also take the form of military intervention. Finally, at the end of the conflict, the international community has the duty to rebuild a lasting peace and the political and institutional structure (in

---

www.vatican.va/holy_father/benedict_xvi/speeches/2007/december/documents/hf_ben-xvi_spe_20071201_ong_it.html>.

[12] Cf. L. Daston and M. Stolleis (eds.), *Natural Law and Laws of Nature in Early Modern Europe: Jurisprudence, Technology, Moral and Natural Philosophy* (2007).

[13] No doubt the report plays upon the ambiguity of the term 'responsibility' which can denote either a generic task, or a duty to deal with or take care of something or (more specifically) the consequences of a violation of a distinct primary obligation (presumably *erga omnes*), namely the obligation to respect fundamental human rights and international humanitarian law. This ambiguity extends to the question of whether the international community's reaction is the subject of a mere power or else of a veritable obligation, since a 'duty' to react leads one to think of both a legal obligation and a legal power which is only the legal counterpart of a moral duty.

respect of security, justice and reconciliation, as well as development) of either the state or the territory where the intervention has taken place (paras. 5.1–31).

As regards more specifically the responsibility to react – certainly the most sensitive issue in the report – humanitarian intervention, both concomitant and pre-emptive, is only admitted in 'extreme cases' when peaceful measures prove insufficient (para. 4.1) and in the face of violations of human rights which 'genuinely shock the conscience of mankind' (para. 4.13), provided that six requirements are met: just cause, right intention, legitimate authority, *extrema ratio*, proportionality and reasonable prospect of success (para. 4.16). It is almost commonplace to observe that these conditions reflect faithfully enough those elaborated upon by the Christian theological tradition of just war.[14] No one would doubt that these principles are perfectly reasonable, yet the question remains whether reasonableness is sufficient to conclude that one conduct is permitted under international law. Admittedly, the true problem is not about conditions in general terms, but rather on how those conditions are concretely interpreted. In other words, it may well be that in medieval Christian Europe the requirements for just war were operating in a social and cultural context so homogeneous to generate particular outcomes which were predictable and generally accepted.[15] Yet, today's world does not appear so homogeneous and the same principle may practically lead to very different outcomes. For example, the just cause requirement was interpreted by the Commission to the effect that humanitarian intervention is only permitted in two extremely grave hypotheses (large-scale killings, with genocidal intent or not, and ethnic cleansing) (para. 4.19), thereby excluding interventions aimed at reacting to other violations of human rights or at reinstalling a democratically elected government or at protecting one's own citizens abroad (paras. 4.24–27).[16] The point is that the general concept of just cause can equally lead to other solutions, more or less inclusive. The same holds true for intervention aimed at reinstalling democratically elected governments, which the report does not include within the responsibility to protect, in that it exceeds the right intention requirement (para. 4.33). On the other hand, if the concepts of just cause and right intention are too indeterminate and may lead to equally plausible but different solutions, the question arises of determining how one could better specify them, which transforms the problem from promotional into properly

---

[14] For an analysis of these conditions, see S. C. Neff, *War and the Law of Nations. A General History* (2005) 45–59.

[15] In fact, it is almost commonplace amongst historians of international law to observe that the realities of medieval war were poles apart from the just war theory, (cf. for instance, W. G. Grewe, *Epochen der Völkerrechtsgeschichte* (1984) 131–147, English translation: *The Epochs of International Law* (2000) 105–118.

[16] J. Levitt, *op. cit.*, fn. 4, p. 166, suggested that the report 'docs not go far enough', in that it does not include within the just cause threshold racial discrimination and massive violations of human rights (which he regards as peremptory norms) as well as interventions aimed at reinstalling democratically elected governments, although these hypotheses are covered by the African practice and, in particular, by the treaty establishing the African Union.

legal. The problem becomes how to determine *specific* rules that are generally accepted as such by their addressees rather than broad principles, a task which was clearly beyond the Commission's reach.

The report provides for a combination of 'authorities' for the implementation of the responsibility to protect. In the first place, it is the authorities of the state concerned that are supposed to act, in that they are 'best placed to take action to prevent problems' (para. 2.30), if need be with the assistance of the international community. In case they should be unwilling or unable, it will be for the international community to react. The report does not draw the line between the action of the state concerned and the action of the international community, nor does it explain what should be properly meant by international community.[17] It only says that the United Nations is 'unquestionably the principal institution for building, consolidating and using the authority of the international community' (para. 6.8) and that its authority 'is underpinned not by coercive power, but by its role as the applicator of legitimacy' (para. 6.9). In the Commission's view, it is essential for the Security Council to authorise interventions (para. 6.15) and its permanent members should refrain from using their veto unless their vital interests are at stake (para. 6.21). Of course, this recommendation can remain unheeded or can be listened to only depending on the interests of the day, not only because permanent members are not willing at all to renounce their veto right, but also because their view on the existence of the conditions allowing interventions can diverge.[18] On the other hand, the veto right at the Security Council, though generally viewed by public opinion as 'anti-democratic', is advocated even by the weakest states, in that it *guarantees* them by safeguarding a balance of power within the Council.[19] In case the Security Council should not act, according to the report it may be for the General Assembly to authorise the intervention pursuant to the procedure provided for by Resolution 377/V of 3 November 1950 (commonly known as *Uniting for Peace*), if for no other reason than conferring on the intervention 'a high degree of legitimacy'. However, the recourse to this procedure seems not only unlikely, as it requires (as the report recalls) a two-third majority, but also presumably illegitimate if reference is made to the provisions of the Charter and the objections raised in the past.[20] The report goes on providing for interventions by regional organisations under Chapter VIII of the Charter (para. 6.35). The hypothesis of intervention by coalitions of states or by individual states unilaterally is not expressly ruled out. The report confines itself to state that they 'do not – it would be an understatement to say – find wide favour', after having pointed out that they might offend against the right intention requirement (para. 4.34).

---

[17] On the meaning to be given to the concept of international community as a whole, see C. Focarelli, 'Customary Foundations of *Jus Gentium* in Francisco Suárez's Thought and the Concept of International Community in Contemporary International Law', (2006) 16 *Italian Yearbook of Int. Law* 41–56.

[18] As recently occurred with respect to Burma (cf. *infra*, fn. 103).

[19] See A. J. Bellamy, *op. cit.*, fn. 4, p. 4.

[20] See B. Conforti, *The Law and Practice of the United Nations* (2005) 225–226.

A final central point is the one concerning the very rationale of the responsibility to protect. One is led to take for granted that the rationale of the responsibility to protect is respect for human dignity as a supreme value, so important to even justify military interventions which would be otherwise not only unlawful, but amongst the most serious unlawful acts that states can commit. Yet, some points in the report – admittedly, in the face of many others underlying moral and strictly humanitarian reasons (para. 2.23) – let one suppose that the need for intervention depends upon international order and security, i.e. it is also political and strategic in character rather than moral, or than only moral. For example, at the outset of the chapter dealing with the responsibility to react through humanitarian interventions, the Commission pointed out that there exist exceptional circumstances 'in which the very interest that all states have in maintaining a *stable international order* require them to react' (para. 4.12).[21] The conferral itself of authority on the Security Council tends to frame the question in terms of global security if account is taken of the fact that the Council can act if it establishes the existence of a 'threat to international peace and security' under Article 39 of the Charter. No doubt massive violations of human rights may amount today to a threat to international peace or security, but the assessment thereof hardly enables the interpreter to distinguish humanitarian from political and strategic considerations. A certain weight is thus to be given to critics holding that humanitarian intervention implementing the responsibility to protect depends largely upon political and strategic interests of the intervening states (or in any event of those states sustaining it at the Security Council), i.e. of the strongest states. It is worth noting that the report does not really discuss the possible discrepancy between moral and political or strategic motivations. They generally remain mixed together, as occurs, for example, when the Commission points out that the exceptional circumstances justifying a humanitarian intervention 'must be cases of violence which so genuinely "shock the conscience of mankind", *or* which present such a *clear and present danger to international security*, that they require coercive military intervention' (para. 4.13). No doubt political and strategic considerations lend themselves easily to the objection that humanitarian interventions follow a double standard. On this point, the Commission remarked that 'the reality that interventions may not be able to be mounted in every case where there is a justification for doing so, is no reason for them not to be mounted in any case' (para. 4.42). However, as will be seen below, a number of states do not share this position.

3. The Other International Instruments Dealing with the Responsibility to Protect

As already hinted, the ICISS report has been known far and wide both in legal doctrine and in various international *fora*. We confine ourselves here to mention

---

[21] Cf. also para. 1.21.

some (not legally binding) documents which have placed it at the heart of the debate. We are referring to the report 'A More Secure World: Our Shared Responsibility' issued in 2004 by the High-Level Panel on Threats, Challenge and Change created by the UN Secretary-General,[22] to the report 'In Larger Freedom: Towards Development, Security and Human Rights for All' issued in 2005 by the Secretary-General himself[23] and to the 'World Summit Outcome' adopted on 24 October 2005, by the UN General Assembly.[24]

The High-Level Panel shared the view that the responsibility to protect is the subject of an 'emerging norm' (para. 203). Furthermore, the report confirms both the need for an authorisation from the UN Security Council (para. 202) and, although with some slight differences, the conditions to be met (para. 207).

The report 'In Larger Freedom' expressly refers to the part of the High-Level Panel's report where the responsibility to protect was described as the subject of an 'emerging norm'. The Secretary-General preferred to discuss it in the report's section dealing with 'freedom to live in dignity' rather than in that dealing with the use of force, thereby resuming the intention to shift attention from military intervention to the protection of human rights. Here again, provision is made that only the Security Council may declare the humanitarian emergence and authorise an intervention (para. 135). The conditions for intervening are also confirmed (para. 126), although the relevant hypotheses are mentioned far more broadly in terms of 'human rights and well-being of civilian populations' (para. 135).

Finally, the World Summit Outcome document no longer speaks of an 'emerging norm'. States confine themselves to affirm that in order to protect the people oppressed, they are 'prepared to take collective action... through the Security Council', but 'on a case-by-case basis' if peaceful measures prove insufficient and national authorities of the state where violations occur fail to protect the victims (para. 139). The conditions for intervention are not even resumed. Rather, the document insists on the specific hypotheses under which states are 'prepared' to react, i.e. genocide, war crimes, ethnic cleansing and crimes against humanity (paras. 138–139).

It should be noted that neither the High-Level Panel's report, nor the report 'In Larger Freedom', nor the World Summit Outcome document expressly rule out unilateral humanitarian interventions, although all of them presuppose a priority – which tends towards an exclusive competence – of the UN Security Council.[25]

---

[22] UN doc. A/59/565.

[23] UN doc. A/59/2005.

[24] UN doc. A/RES/60/1.

[25] For an accurate comparison between the three documents, see Stahn, *loc. cit.*, fn. 4 pp. 102–110.

4. The Position of States at the UN General Assembly

It is now possible to test the responsibility to protect doctrine against the data provided by states. We do not intend to resume the discussions on humanitarian intervention and the corresponding international practice – indeed, rather scarce and hardly conclusive – of the Cold War period, much less the nineteenth-century practice of European powers in the non-European world,[26] and even less the practice subsequent to the end of the cold war which culminated with the NATO bombardment of the Federal Republic of Yugoslavia (FRY) in 1999.[27] Rather, we intend to discuss the positions adopted by states on the very question of the responsibility to protect – or on this particular restyling of the traditional concept of humanitarian intervention – to determine which states are in favour and which are not, and for what reasons. This is not to imply that the position verbally expressed by states is sufficient for a general international law norm to be proved as existing (or not), yet the fact remains that state positions constitute *opinio juris ac necessitatis* which – faced with absent, scarce or dubious practice – let the interpreter reasonably presume what reaction the international community would concretely take should the problem arise in practice.

We are referring, first and foremost, to the wide debate which took place at the UN General Assembly in April 2005 on the occasion of the presentation of the UN Secretary-General's report 'In Larger Freedom', a debate whose results would merge a few months later into the (quite succinct) section of the World Summit Outcome document devoted to the responsibility to protect.[28]

From an overall reading of statements made by states, it may be summarily found that: (i) all states were perfectly mindful that the only problem – beyond labels and contrary to the efforts made by the ICISS to justify the new doctrine as something new from traditional concepts – is humanitarian intervention; (ii) a considerable number of states were strongly against humanitarian intervention implementing the responsibility to protect doctrine and some expressly opposed it even if intervention should be authorised by the Security Council; (iii) a certain number of states denied that the responsibility to protect rule is 'emerging', thus denying its existence in any sense, whether actual or potential; (iv) states supporting the responsibility to protect doctrine firmly believed that humanitarian intervention must be backed by the United Nations, thereby showing *a*

---

[26] See W. G. Grewe, *Epochen der Völkerrechtsgeschichte, op. cit.,* fn. 15, pp. 573–583, English translation: *The Epochs of International Law, op. cit.,* fn. 15, pp. 487–496.

[27] See more recently, V. A. Kartaskin, 'Humanitarian Intervention in the Globalizing World', (2005) 5 *Baltic Yearbook of Int. Law* (2005) 27–40; P. Valek, 'Is Unilateral Intervention Compatible with the U.N. Charter?', (2005) 26 *Michigan Journal of Int. Law* 1223–1255; R. Goodman, 'Humanitarian Intervention and Pretexts for War', (2006) 100 *American Journal of International Law* 107–141; R. Janse, 'The Legitimacy of Humanitarian Interventions', (2006) 19 *LJIL* 669–692; J. Zajadlo, 'Humanitarian Intervention Threat to International Order, Moral Imperative or Customary Norm "in Statu Nascendi"?', 27 *Polish Yearbook of Int. Law* (2006) 33–48.

[28] UN doc. A/59/PV.86-90.

contrario that no state seems apparently to accept unilateral humanitarian interventions, with the only possible (but also ambiguous) exception of the USA; (v) as a rule, states supporting the responsibility to protect converged on limiting humanitarian intervention to very few hypotheses, namely genocide, ethnic cleansing and crimes against humanity; (vi) no state supporting the responsibility to protect grounded its reasoning in natural law, whereas a certain number of states reiterated the 'emerging norm' formula, but without any qualification; (vii) states rarely distinguished between interventions in institutionally strong states and interventions in territories where authorities are not objectively in a position to ensure the protection of fundamental rights; however, when they did so, either they opposed interventions *also* or, in reverse, they admitted interventions *only* in the latter hypothesis.

A. *States Opposing the Responsibility to Protect Doctrine*

Amongst states that opposed humanitarian intervention implementing the responsibility to protect, a certain number underscored that the responsibility to protect concept is vague and requires more accuracy and further discussion in order to make clear what its difference from traditional humanitarian intervention is. According to Algeria, for instance, the responsibility to protect 'is extremely difficult to distinguish from the idea of humanitarian intervention which the countries of the South formally rejected in 1999',[29] whereas Egypt stated that 'the legal underpinnings of the theory remain unclear'.[30]

Several states, in particular those belonging to the Non-Aligned Movement (NAM), severely critiqued the responsibility to protect doctrine by both excluding that it is an emerging (still less an already existing) norm and by believing that the significant aspect amongst the three suggested by the ICISS (i.e. to prevent, to react and to rebuild) is the military one. In their view, the responsibility to protect doctrine is nothing other than a mere expedient of the great powers to impose their interests and values on the weakest states. They do not believe that the responsibility to protect, at least as it was then formulated, can operate in a sufficiently impartial way to protect human rights. At times these states emphasise the contradiction of the responsibility to protect doctrine by showing that, on the one hand, it is aimed at reducing sovereignty in the name of universal humanitarian considerations and, on the other hand, it expands sovereignty itself in an interventionist sense, thereby only limiting the sovereignty of the weakest states while extraordinarily reinforcing that of the strongest ones. No state doubts that as a rule populations should be protected from massive violations of human rights committed by their governments, nor do they exclude that the power to intervene (particularly in case of genocide, ethnic cleansing and crimes against humanity) can be seriously considered for further and constructive discussion designed to determine when it is admissible and consistent with sovereignty and

---

[29] UN doc. A/59/PV.86, p. 9.
[30] UN doc. A/59/PV.86, p. 13.

non-interference, i.e. with equal dignity of states and their peoples. However, they stressed that the responsibility to protect doctrine was formulated in a way that lets major powers discretionally decide whether and where to intervene. As the strongest states have a power, not an obligation to intervene, these states predicted that interventions will only be made by the strongest to further their interests and values. This would not be altered by the fact that interventions are subject to the UN Security Council's authorisation, since within such an organ power is in the hands of the strongest, at least negatively by virtue of their veto power. It is worth noting, that as a rule states opposing the responsibility to protect are also critical of any pre-emptive use of force – which is admitted, as noted earlier, by the ICISS report – and of any re-interpretation in this direction of Article 51 of the UN Charter. Finally, some critique the Security Council itself and its authorisation as an instrument capable of justifying interventions.

The notion that the responsibility to protect doctrine is devoid of any legal basis and favours the most powerful states against the weakest ones was advocated by Pakistan,[31] Algeria,[32] Egypt,[33] Colombia,[34] Vietnam,[35] Venezuela,[36] Iran,[37] Cuba,[38] Syria[39] and Tanzania.[40] Venezuela *also* opposed intervention in weak and failed states as a breach of the principle of self-determination of peoples.[41]

B. States Supporting the Responsibility to Protect Doctrine

States supporting the responsibility to protect underscored that the decision to militarily intervene only falls on the UN Security Council. Some of them pointed out that an authorisation may be issued by the Council exclusively as a last resort measure and before intervention. They also reiterated the conditions that any authorised intervention must meet. Amongst the violations of human rights that justify humanitarian intervention, a convergence existed on genocide, ethnic cleansing, war crimes and crimes against humanity.

Support for the responsibility to protect did not prevent states from refuting that it was endorsed by existing international law. Particularly clear on this point was the Russian Federation, which strongly denied that the responsibility to protect is provided for by international law. In its opinion, though the UN Secretary-General had characterised the responsibility to protect as a doctrine reflecting an

---

[31] UN doc. A/59/PV.86, p. 5.
[32] UN doc. A/59/PV.86, p. 9.
[33] UN doc. A/59/PV.86, p. 13.
[34] UN doc. A/59/PV.86, p. 15.
[35] UN doc. A/59/PV.89, p. 22.
[36] UN doc. A/59/PV.89, pp. 24–25.
[37] UN doc. A/59/PV.87, pp. 17–18.
[38] UN doc. A/59/PV.89, pp. 14–15.
[39] UN doc. A/59/PV.90, p. 19.
[40] UN doc. A/59/PV.90, p. 26.
[41] UN doc. A/59/PV.89, pp. 24–25.

emerging norm, '[s]trictly speaking, the establishment of an international norm presupposes that there is wide support within the international community for such a norm. However, that is not the case here'.[42]

The responsibility to protect was upheld by San Marino,[43] France,[44] Japan,[45] Australia,[46] Canada,[47] New Zealand,[48] Norway[49] and Liechtenstein.[50] Uganda stated that is was favourable to the responsibility to protect, provided that it would be formulated in greater detail.[51] Ukraine affirmed that 'such measures can be taken only as a last resort and under the explicit mandate of the Security Council'.[52] A bit vague was the position adopted by Indonesia, whereby 'although there are some moral justifications', the issue should be further discussed both politically and legally.[53]

Finally, the USA took a rather ambiguous stance, sharing 'in a more general and *moral* sense' the responsibility of the international community to act, and pointing out that this responsibility is different from that of the state concerned. First and foremost, the USA reiterated its position favourable to pre-emptive self-defence 'in appropriate circumstances', in line with its opinion on Article 51 of the UN Charter.[54] In respect of the responsibility to protect, the USA held that 'the Council may, and is fully empowered to, take action under the Charter, including enforcement action, if so required'. On the other hand, 'the Charter has never been interpreted as creating a legal obligation for Security Council members to support enforcement action in various cases involving serious breaches of international peace'. As a result, the US Government recognised the UN Security Council's competence under the Charter to authorise humanitarian interventions, but excluded any obligation to do so. In other words, the Security Council is viewed as absolutely free to act or not, and thus to act in one case but not in another. Individual states themselves are regarded as empowered, though not bound, to act: they are only 'prepared to take action', a formula which was eventually introduced (as was said earlier) in the World Summit Outcome document. Furthermore, according to the USA, the possibility to act even failing a UN Security Council's authorisation should not be ruled out in instances 'that involve

---

[42] UN doc. A/59/PV.87, p. 6.
[43] UN doc. A/59/PV.86, p. 24.
[44] UN doc. A/59/PV.87, p. 5.
[45] UN doc. A/59/PV.87, p. 29.
[46] UN doc. A/59/PV.88, p. 4.
[47] UN doc. A/59/PV.89, p. 27, as well as A/59/PV.96, p. 9.
[48] UN doc. A/59/PV.88, p. 4.
[49] UN doc. A/59/PV.88, p. 13.
[50] UN doc. A/59/PV.88, p. 19.
[51] UN doc. A/59/PV.88, p. 9.
[52] UN doc. A/59/PV.88, p. 22.
[53] UN doc. A/59/PV.88, p. 26.
[54] UN doc. A/59/PV.87, p. 23.

humanitarian catastrophes but for which is also a legitimate basis for states to act in self-defence', the latter viewed, as already seen, in pre-emptive terms.[55]

As regards the important question of whether intervention is admitted in failed states or territories where authorities are not sufficiently effective, a few states tended to answer in the affirmative only in these cases, such as South Korea[56] and Chile.[57] Other states, such as Bulgaria,[58] while accepting the responsibility to protect in general terms, stressed that intervention is *particularly* justified in such cases.

5. The Position of States at the UN Security Council

After its 'official' endorsement in the World Summit Outcome document, the UN Security Council itself has occasionally made reference to the responsibility to protect beginning with Resolution 1674 of 28 April 2006, on the protection of civilians in armed conflicts (para. 4).[59] The question of the applicability of the responsibility to protect doctrine to the protection of civilians was already discussed on 9 December 2005, on the occasion of a debate on a report of the Secretary-General on the matter.[60] On that occasion, several states supported the doctrine. It is true that the problem was specifically focused on the protection of civilians in armed conflicts, as the United Kingdom pointed out;[61] nonetheless, the general sense of the statements made by states let one reasonably suppose that the support was general in character. It is in fact perceivable that the responsibility to protect doctrine had been adopted a little before at the General Assembly, as is evidenced by the perfect agreement between supporting states on the four hypotheses permitting humanitarian intervention (genocide, war crimes, ethnic cleansing and crimes against humanity) which are laid down therein. However, this consensus is on the general principle, i.e. on the fact that there exists a primary responsibility of every state and a subsidiary responsibility of the international community (vested with the Security Council) in case a state is unable or unwilling to protect civilians in an armed conflict, while nothing is said on the specific consequences of this subsidiary responsibility and in particular on humanitarian intervention.

[55] See the letter of the US permanent representative J. Bolton of 30 August 2005, to the President of the UN General Assembly concerning changes to be made to para. 118 of the Outcome document draft on the responsibility to protect (available at <www.un.int/usa/reform-un-jrb-ltr-protect-8–05.pdf>). The United States' stance – generally favourable, but not less ambiguous – on the responsibility to protect doctrine can be read in (2006) 100 *American Journal of International Law* 463–464.

[56] UN doc. A/59/PV.87, p. 13.

[57] UN doc. A/59/PV.86, p. 20.

[58] UN doc. A/59/PV.89, p. 10.

[59] UN doc. S/RES/1674 (2006).

[60] UN doc. S/PV.5319 and S/PV.5319 (Resumption 1) for debates and S/2005/40 for the Secretary-General's report.

[61] UN doc. S/PV.5319 (Resumption 1), p. 9.

Support for the responsibility to protect was expressed by Argentina,[62] Benin,[63] Italy,[64] Germany,[65] Greece,[66] Japan,[67] Tanzania,[68] Switzerland,[69] Mexico,[70] Denmark,[71] Nepal,[72] France,[73] the United Kingdom,[74] Norway,[75] Slovakia,[76] Spain[77] and Rwanda.[78] Of interest, amongst favourable states, was the suggestion made by Peru[79] and Liechtenstein[80] that the veto right should not be exercised by the Security Council's permanent members. A critical stance was conversely taken by Brazil,[81] the Russian Federation,[82] China,[83] Algeria[84] and Egypt.[85] Rather lukewarm was the position adopted by the USA, whereby 'the primary responsibility for protecting civilians lies with States and their Governments and... international efforts should complement Government efforts rather than assume responsibility for them'. The USA posited that '[i]mproving the protection of civilians from the devastating effects of armed conflict depends largely not on what we say or do here, but on what Governments do to protect their own people and on how they allow others to assist'.[86]

Open debates subsequently took place at the Security Council on the question of the protection of civilians in armed conflicts. In these discussions too, a tendency in support of the responsibility to protect is detectable, but again states failed to take position on the very question of humanitarian intervention, such as in the open debate of 28 June 2006.[87] A widespread, but as much vague,

[62] UN doc. S/PV.5319, p. 9.
[63] UN doc. S/PV.5319, p. 11.
[64] UN doc. S/PV.5319, p. 12.
[65] UN doc. S/PV.5319, p. 20.
[66] UN doc. S/PV.5319, p. 22.
[67] UN doc. S/PV.5319, p. 23.
[68] UN doc. S/PV.5319, pp. 25–26.
[69] UN doc. S/PV.5319, p. 29.
[70] UN doc. S/PV.5319, p. 28.
[71] UN doc. S/PV.5319, p. 31.
[72] UN doc. S/PV.5319 (Resumption 1), pp. 4–5.
[73] UN doc. S/PV.5319 (Resumption 1), p. 7.
[74] UN doc. S/PV.5319 (Resumption 1), p. 9.
[75] UN doc. S/PV.5319 (Resumption 1), p. 10.
[76] UN doc. S/PV.5319 (Resumption 1), p. 13.
[77] UN doc. S/PV.5319 (Resumption 1), p. 17.
[78] UN doc. S/PV.5319 (Resumption 1), p. 19.
[79] UN doc. S/PV.5319, pp. 13–14.
[80] UN doc. S/PV.5319 (Resumption 1), p. 15.
[81] UN doc. S/PV.5319, p. 10.
[82] UN doc. S/PV.5319, p. 19.
[83] UN doc. S/PV.5319, p. 30.
[84] UN doc. S/PV.5319 (Resumption 1), p. 3.
[85] UN doc. S/PV.5319 (Resumption 1), p. 6.
[86] UN doc. S/PV.5319 (Resumption 1), p. 8.
[87] UN doc. S/PV.5476 for the favourable statements of the United Kingdom (pp. 6–7), Slovakia (p. 8), Ghana (p. 11), Tanzania (p. 13), Congo (p. 15), Argentina (p. 16), France (p. 20), Denmark (p. 21), Austria on behalf of the European Union (p. 22),

consensus can be noticed at the open debate of 22 June 2007,[88] where a particularly revealing statement was made by Mexico, whereby '[d]espite the consensus reached in 2005, we cannot deny that an atmosphere of mistrust prevails over that subject. While some States see in the new principle the mere continuance of interventionist policies aimed at destabilizing political regimes, others promote its application in a selective manner, limiting its scope to cases significant for their foreign policy interests'.[89] Again China opposed.[90] Qatar accepted the principle, but observed that 'we should be cautious though in dealing with this principle so as it would not to be exploited and abused'.[91] The USA stressed the primary responsibility of the conflicting parties,[92] and the Russian Federation reiterated both the Security Council's competence and the fact that it falls on the General Assembly to discuss the matter 'on the basis of the principles of the Charter and international law'.[93] Finally, in the open debate of 20 November 2007, besides numerous states supporting the responsibility to protect in general terms[94] and a few opposing it[95], certain states pronounced themselves specifically on humanitarian intervention and on the possibility to adopt measures under Chapter VII of the UN Charter. Against military intervention was

Liechtenstein (p. 26), Canada (p. 27) and Guatemala (p. 31). Slovenia suggested permanent members of the Security Council abstain from casting their veto (p. 24). China again took a critical stance (p. 10).

[88] UN doc. S/PV.5703 for the favourable statements of Panama (pp. 7–8), Peru (p. 8), Italy (pp. 10–11), Congo (p. 16), Slovakia (p. 17), the United Kingdom (p. 20), Ghana (pp. 20–21), Belgium (p. 24), Guatemala (p. 25), Japan (p. 26), Argentina (p. 27), Germania on behalf of the European Union (p. 30), Nigeria (p. 32), Canada (pp. 35–36), Liechtenstein (p. 35), Korea (pp. 36–37) and Rwanda (p. 37).

[89] UN doc. S/PV.5703, p. 28.

[90] UN doc. S/PV.5703, p. 17. China affirmed that 'no arbitrary intervention [should] be imposed on the government concerned over its objection' and that 'the Security Council should refrain from invoking the concept of the 'responsibility to protect'–still less should the concept be abused'. Colombia as well underlined the need that state sovereignty is safeguarded (p. 39).

[91] UN doc. S/PV.5703, pp. 11–12.

[92] UN doc. S/PV.5703, pp. 9–10.

[93] UN doc. S/PV.5703, p. 23.

[94] UN doc. S/PV.5781 for the statements of Belgium (p. 7), Panama (pp. 10–11), France (p. 13), South Africa (p. 15), Ghana (p. 17), Slovakia (p. 22), Peru (p. 24), Congo (p. 25), Iceland (p. 29), Portugal on behalf of the European Union (*ibidem*, Resumption, p. 2), Senegal (p. 8), Guatemala (p. 9), Nigeria (pp. 12–13), Australia (p. 13), Canada (p. 13), Liechtenstein (p. 16), Nepal (p. 18), Argentina (p. 19), Mexico (p. 20) and Colombia (p. 22).

[95] In particular, Qatar observed that '[w]hile the principle of the responsibility to protect reflects a noble human value, it is easily exploited and abused; this prompts us to be cautious in dealing with this principle. Our objectives must therefore not be politicised; they must transcend individual interests and reflect pure humanitarian motives' (in UN doc. S/PV.5781, p. 18). Cautious was also the attitude of Vietnam (*ibidem*, Resumption, p. 22).

China,[96] while a favourable position was taken by the United Kingdom.[97] Supportive of collective measures under Chapter VII of the UN Charter was New Zealand.[98] Angola made reference to the express provision of humanitarian intervention in the treaty establishing the African Union.[99] Finally, the Russian Federation, along with other states, significantly emphasised that the responsibility to protect should also apply to non-state actors and particularly to military security companies.[100]

The Security Council also dealt with the responsibility to protect in relation to the specific case of Sudan and Burma. In both cases, the responsibility to protect doctrine – intended in the sense of humanitarian intervention rather than in general terms – was not upheld. In respect of Sudan, though a UN High-Level Mission's report on the situation of human rights in Darfur recommended in March 2007 an intervention of the international community on the basis of the responsibility to protect doctrine, the Security Council confined itself in Resolution 1755 of 30 April 2007, to reaffirm the World Summit Outcome document's part devoted to the responsibility to protect.[101] In the subsequent Resolution 1769 of 31 July 2007, authorising the dispatch of a military force in Darfur (UNAMID) and the use of force for the protection of civilians, the Council, while recalling Resolution 1674, actually reaffirmed 'its strong commitment to the sovereignty, unity, independence and territorial integrity of Sudan' and expressed 'its determination to work with the Government of Sudan, in full respect of its sovereignty, to assist in tackling the various problems in Darfur'.[102] As for Burma, in a meeting on 12 January 2007, a draft resolution submitted by the USA and the United

---

[96] UN doc. S/PV.5781, p. 10. The Chinese delegate added that '[t]he Security Council should not become a forum for extrapolating this concept or engaging in other similar legislative activities, because that is a task for the whole membership of the United Nations. At present, this concept is not yet mature, and many Member States have considerable concerns about it'.

[97] UN doc. S/PV.5781, p. 11. The United Kingdom affirmed that 'in those exceptional cases in which states cannot or will not protect civilians from the gravest abuses of their human rights, the international community not only has a right to act, but a responsibility to do so. That action can come in a range of forms, from sanctions against those responsible to direct intervention to protect civilians and should always be proportionate and carefully chosen'.

[98] UN doc. S/PV.5781, pp. 30–31.

[99] UN doc. S/PV.5781 (Resumption), p. 5.

[100] UN doc. S/PV.5781, p. 8.

[101] UN doc. S/RES/1755 (2007) for the text of the resolution and UN doc. S/PV.5670 for the debate at the Security Council.

[102] UN doc. S/RES/1769 (2007) for the text of the resolution (which commends 'the agreement of Sudan that the Hybrid operation shall be deployed in Darfur, as detailed in the conclusions of the high-level AU/UN consultations with the Government of Sudan in Addis Ababa on 12 June 2007 and confirmed in full during the Council's meeting with the President of Sudan on 17 June in Khartoum') and UN doc. S/PV.5727 for the debate at the Security Council. It is worth noting, that in this debate no state expressly raised the question of the responsibility to protect. See A. De Waal, 'Darfur and the Failure of the Responsibility to Protect', (2007) 83 *International Affairs* 1039–1054.

Kingdom was not adopted on account of the veto cast by both China and the Russian Federation, which stated (together with other states) that there was no 'threat to international peace and security'.[103] On 11 October 2007, faced with the recent brutal repression of demonstrators against the Burmese regime, the Security Council limited itself to a presidential statement where the use of force in the country is deplored.[104]

6. Too Many Ambiguities for a Working Doctrine

The responsibility to protect doctrine, although it was first presented as a larger construction, is essentially focused on the question of humanitarian intervention. At least this is the way states have perceived it. It is thus explicable why states opposing humanitarian intervention in the past have simply reiterated their opposition. The change in language does not seem to have generated a substantially broader consensus, as the ICISS hoped, when, apart from general labels and ideas, the specific topic of humanitarian intervention is addressed. It has been convincingly suggested that a negative influence is to be ascribed to the war in Iraq in 2003,[105] as well as to the immediate advocacy of a 'duty to protect' against rogue states as a 'corollary' to the responsibility to protect, a corollary which was grounded, just as much ambiguously, in the vague need that global problems be solved through global remedies and that new problems need new rules.[106]

In fact, humanitarian intervention implementing the responsibility to protect is not only feared as imperialistic by several weak states, but it also significantly fails to find unconditioned support even amongst the most powerful states. The latter have clearly no intention to be bound – an obligation which inevitably follows from the need to avoid selective interventions – to militarily intervene in some remote place abroad exclusively for humanitarian motives. Economic and logistic costs add to military costs in order to re-establish an acceptable level of social life and post-war political institutions, while there are few certainties on results and length thereof. In addition, governments of democratic states are reluctant to intervene since (as experience attests to) military interventions, even when they are demanded by public opinion, do not attract votes in case of success while losing them in case of failure.[107] Telling is the 'moral' position – against any obligation to intervene of both the Security Council and individual states – taken

---

[103] The draft resolution obtained nine votes in favour, three votes against (China, Russian Federation and South Africa) and three abstentions (Congo, Indonesia and Qatar) (UN doc. S/2007/14). Objecting states underline that neighbour states of Burma had denied that there was a threat to regional peace and security and that the question was domestic beyond the competence of the Council (UN doc. S/PV.5619).

[104] UN doc. S/PRST/2007/37. It is to be noted that no recourse to the procedure provided for in the *Uniting for Peace* resolution has been made.

[105] See, for instance, Hamilton, *loc. cit.*, fn. 4, p. 293.

[106] See, *loc. cit.*, fn. 3.

[107] See Bellamy, *Preventing Future Kosovos and Future Rwandas, op. cit.*, fn. 4, p. 8.

by the USA, as well as the support given by the Russian Federation on the condition that the responsibility to protect remains under the authority of the Security Council. Clearly, the Russian Federation reserves its right to cast its veto – as it did, along with China, in respect of Burma – whenever it thinks that an intervention is not convenient. And it goes without saying that none of the Security Council's permanent members, although a number of suggestions in the opposite direction came from certain states and by the ICISS, is prepared to renounce its right of veto. It is equally significant that non-aligned states themselves, while opposing humanitarian intervention, are favourably disposed to the right of veto of the five permanent members as a *guarantee* against abuses of the great powers. In sum, some consensus on the principle does exist, but disagreement is still considerable on the specific question of a general legal regime allowing military intervention.

If it is true that humanitarian intervention keeps being resisted by several states, then it is also true that in general states agree on the notion that massive violations of human rights (in particular, genocide, ethnic cleansing, war crimes and crimes against humanity) must be firmly contested. Indeed, there are a number of remedies other than military intervention on which states converge, such as measures of political pressure, economic sanctions, as well as national and international criminal courts. Admittedly, these measures may easily prove inadequate, but they are the only ones gathering in principle states' support. As for military measures, states require guarantees of impartiality against abuse, given the seriousness of their consequences, or reserve to make a decision on a case-by-case basis, clearly depending on the interest at stake in each instance.

Nor can one bypass the opinion of objecting states in the name of the 'necessity' in a globalised world for rules that admit humanitarian intervention. In fact, no one would presumably doubt the *abstract* necessity of humanitarian intervention as an adequate measure to bring massacres to an end. It is on the *legal* admissibility of humanitarian intervention that consensus ceases to exist. Of course, it would be different if objecting states changed their mind through persuasion, so that one could fully take their view into account once this has become supportive of humanitarian intervention. It is precisely in this sense – concerned rather with the dynamic and norm-generating process of international law, as well as with the sphere of political communication – that the responsibility to protect doctrine seems to be more properly situated.

The foregoing analysis is confirmed by the extreme ambiguity surrounding the responsibility to protect. Firstly, the very notion of 'responsibility' is ambiguous. To suggest that today states are 'responsible' – in that they have international obligations, both negative and positive – towards their citizens is to identify exactly what *already* derives from existing international norms on human rights and from international humanitarian law; but to draw from this the admissibility of humanitarian intervention is arbitrary in the face of a considerable number of objecting states. Secondly, the responsibility to protect doctrine swings between power and obligation to intervene. This point is crucial because a mere power entails in practice a wide discretion (if not arbitrariness) for the great power states,

The Responsibility to Protect Doctrine and Humanitarian Intervention 211

which are the only states which can in fact intervene and, of course, the ones which will inevitably decide if and how to intervene according to their interests and values. Thirdly, the responsibility to protect doctrine does not conceptually distinguish, while it should, between human rights and international humanitarian law as prescribed by a treaty or by international customary law: in the first case, the admissibility of humanitarian intervention could in principle be drawn by way of interpretation – more precisely, by using interpretative criteria which are independent from state practice – within the subjective and objective scope of, for example, the Geneva Conventions of 1949 and the two additional Protocols of 1977;[108] whereas in the second case, general state practice and *opinio juris* are needed and are indeed lacking. Fourthly, the responsibility to protect doctrine fails to sufficiently clarify the role that should be accorded to the various 'authorities' called upon to decide the recourse to humanitarian intervention. It is apparent that the Security Council should be the main actor and that, in the event of veto, other entities could replace it, such as the General Assembly (on the basis of the 1950 Uniting for Peace resolution) or regional organisations. Nor is intervention by coalitions of the willing states or even by states unilaterally clearly ruled out.[109] In sum, in the event that it is precisely for the Security Council (or other international bodies) to prove unable or unwilling to fulfil its 'responsibility' on behalf of the international community, it remains unclear whether individual states are allowed to do so as a last resort. The risk is not to be overlooked – given the inherent altruistic nature of humanitarian intervention – that in one given instance, no able or willing state 'of last resort' will exist and the responsibility to protect will not be fulfilled by anyone. Nor has the doctrine of the responsibility to protect clearly specified the criteria for measuring a state's lack of capacity and unwillingness to protect its own citizens. Some states have in fact showed to fear the possible use of the responsibility to protect doctrine to justify military interventions aimed at suppressing – if need be, in certain states rather than in others – repressive measures against insurrectional or secessionist movements. Finally, the responsibility to protect doctrine fails adequately to distinguish interventions in institutionally strong states and interventions in failed states, although the ICISS did make a hint at the fact that in failed states intervention might have a stronger chance to be agreed upon (para. 4.22). Overall, states have generally avoided specifying how the responsibility to protect doctrine would apply to failed states. However, some of them have raised the risk that interventions are being directed against states which for some reason – including their being what in the past one would have said 'uncivilized' – do not

---

[108] See L. Boisson de Chazournes and L. Condorelli, *loc. cit.*, fn. 4, pp. 14–16.

[109] A. L. Bannon, 'The Responsibility to Protect', *loc. cit.*, fn. 4, p. 1162, remarked that unilateral intervention is admissible, subject to conditions laid dawn in the World Summit document of 2005, *inter alia* because 'in the absence of a functioning international institutions, one must look to the overriding purpose of the Summit agreement', an argument which in our view is hardly compatible with the positions taken by states on the specific issue of military intervention.

'reach' the standards of justice as well as of political and institutional efficiency of the strongest states or at least of states having a long institutional history.

Finally, if the admissibility of unilateral intervention seems to be ruled out, as the whole debate and states' opinions ultimately suggests, the question is, first, whether the Security Council is empowered under the Charter to authorise it and, second, whether its authorisation makes the intervention lawful (assuming evidently that it would be otherwise unlawful) under general international law. In fact, the General Assembly has no power to authorise military interventions and the power of regional organisations to do so depends again upon an authorisation given by the Security Council under Article 53. Having said that, the answer stemming from states' positions on the responsibility to protect doctrine seems to be positive to the effect that the Security Council is empowered (but not bound) to authorise the intervention, and that the intervention thus authorised is internationally lawful. Needless to say, the exclusion of any obligation to act – advocated time and again by various states – coupled with the extremely modest success of suggestions claiming an abstention from veto, does not avoid the major risk of humanitarian intervention, namely the risk that the Security Council proceeds on a case-by-case basis, inevitably depending on the interests of its members of the day and particularly of its five permanent members, thereby providing authorisations in one case and not in another as much (if not more) serious.

7. Conclusion

It is difficult to grasp the innovative content of the purported 'emerging norm' concerning the responsibility to protect as well as the prospect of it emerging in the future. While the need for intervention in the most serious humanitarian crises – 'according to law' rather than in the name of 'exceptional circumstances' beyond or above what positive law prescribes[110] – is undeniable, still humanitarian intervention is perceived (rightly or wrongly) more threatening than beneficial. It seems at the moment unlikely that the responsibility to protect may generate authorisations of the Security Council except perhaps for the hypothesis – on which a growing consensus exists, but still the opposition in principle of China – of extremely serious violations of human rights and of international humanitarian law against civilians *in an armed conflict*, assuming that the interests

---

[110] In a well-known speech on 5 March 2004, Sedgefield, the former UK Prime Minister T. Blair affirmed that '[i]t may well be that under international law as presently constituted, a regime can systematically brutalise and oppress its people and there is nothing anyone can do... This may be the law, but should it be?', thereby concluding that 'we do not accept in a community that others have a right to oppress and brutalise their people' (available at <http://www.number-10.gov.uk/output/Page5470.asp.>). This statement reflects the new stance taken by the United Kingdom supporting humanitarian intervention 'in exceptional circumstances', beginning with the statement made by the Legal Adviser to the Foreign Office, A. Aust on 2 December 1992, (cf. [1992] *British Yearbook of International Law*, p. 827) and recently resumed in relation to the responsibility to protect doctrine (*loc. cit.*, fn. 97).

of the five permanent members of the Security Council converge. Admittedly, no satisfactory answer has been given to the imperative 'no more Rwandas and Kosovos', i.e. to cases where it is precisely the Security Council which is unable or unwilling to protect. It is true that sometimes ambiguity can help reach a broader consensus, but in this case, given the stakes, it seems that it works rather the other way round.

Name Index